Battling the Plantation Mentality

The **John Hope Franklin** Series in

African American History and Culture

Waldo E. Martin Jr.

and Patricia Sullivan

editors

Battling the
Plantation Mentality

Memphis and the
Black Freedom Struggle

LAURIE B. GREEN

The University of North Carolina Press
Chapel Hill

© 2007 The University of North Carolina Press
All rights reserved
Manufactured in the United States of America
Designed and typeset in Arnhem and Rockwell
by Eric M. Brooks

This book was published with the assistance of a generous
University Co-operative Society Subvention Grant awarded by
The University of Texas at Austin and of the John Hope Franklin
Fund of the University of North Carolina Press.

The paper in this book meets the guidelines for permanence
and durability of the Committee on Production Guidelines for
Book Longevity of the Council on Library Resources.

Library of Congress Cataloging-in-Publication Data
Green, Laurie Boush.
Battling the plantation mentality: Memphis and the Black freedom
struggle / Laurie B. Green.
p. cm. — (The John Hope Franklin series in African American
history and culture)
Includes bibliographical references and index.
ISBN 978-0-8078-3106-9 (cloth: alk. paper)
ISBN 978-0-8078-5802-8 (pbk.: alk. paper)
1. African Americans — Civil rights — Tennessee — Memphis —
History — 20th century. 2. African Americans — Segregation —
Tennessee — Memphis — History — 20th century. 3. Civil rights
movements — Tennessee — Memphis — History — 20th century.
4. African Americans — Tennessee — Memphis — History — 20th
century. 5. Racism — Tennessee — Memphis — History — 20th
century. 6. Memphis (Tenn.) — Race relations — History — 20th
century. 7. Memphis (Tenn.) — History — 20th century. I. Title.
F444.M59N485 2007
323.1196'0730768190904—dc22 2006039792

cloth 11 10 09 08 07 5 4 3 2 1
paper 11 10 09 08 07 5 4 3 2 1

for Jim and Sarafina

Contents

Illustrations

Photographs

Maps

Abbreviations

AAA	Agricultural Adjustment Act
AFL	American Federation of Labor
AHF	American Heritage Foundation
AME	African Methodist Episcopal
ANP	Associated Negro Press
AVC	American Veterans Committee
BOP	Black Organizing Project
CIO	Congress of Industrial Organizations
CME	Colored Methodist Episcopal
COME	Citizens on the Move for Equality
CORE	Congress of Racial Equality
CWA	Civil Works Administration
DCC	Dedicated Citizens Committee
EEOC	Equal Employment Opportunity Commission
ERC	Emergency Relief Committee
FEPC	Fair Employment Practice Committee
FLSA	Fair Labor Standards Act
FTA	Food, Tobacco, Agricultural and Allied Workers of America
HUAC	House Un-American Activities Committee
ILA	International Longshoremen's Association
ILGWU	International Ladies' Garment Workers' Union
IWA	International Woodworkers of America
MCCR	Memphis Committee on Community Relations
MCIC	Memphis Commission on Interracial Co-operation
MCRC	Memphis Community Relations Committee
MOWM	March on Washington Movement
MSCIA	Memphis and Shelby County Improvement Association
MSR	Memphis Street Railway
MUL	Memphis Urban League
MWRO	Memphis Welfare Rights Organization
NAACP	National Association for the Advancement of Colored People
NIRA	National Industrial Recovery Act
NLRB	National Labor Relations Board

NMU	National Maritime Union
NWLB	National War Labor Board
NWRO	National Welfare Rights Organization
NYA	National Youth Administration
OEO	Office of Economic Opportunity
OPM	Office of Production Management
OWI	Office of War Information
RCNL	Regional Council of Negro Leadership
SCLC	Southern Christian Leadership Council
SISS	Senate Internal Security Subcommittee
SPD	Social Protection Division
STFU	Southern Tenant Farmers' Union
TSES	Tennessee State Employment Service
UA	United Artists
UAW	United Auto Workers
UCAPAWA-CIO	
	United Cannery, Agricultural, Packing and Allied Workers of America
UFWA	United Furniture Workers of America
USES	United States Employment Service
WPA	Works Progress Administration

Battling the Plantation Mentality

Introduction

Migration, Memory, and Freedom in the Urban Heart of the Delta

"The struggle was we didn't have a water fountain! No water fountain in 1965!" Sally Turner, a mother of twelve and retired worker who had labored at the Farber Brothers automobile accessories plant in Memphis from the 1960s to the 1980s, raised her voice to a shout when she responded during a 1995 oral history interview to a query about why she had risked her job to help organize a union in her shop. Seated in her living room, surrounded by family photographs of her twelve children, Turner recounted how she and other African American women workers had complained about the lack of drinking water in the sweltering, non-air-conditioned plant. The white manager had reacted, she exclaimed, by giving them "one of them country buckets I already done left in Mississippi! They goes out in this hardware store and buys a bucket and a dipper. A dipper! And brought it back there and had everybody dipping!" For Turner, the bucket and dipper purchased by the white male plant manager became emblematic of what she and other black Memphis workers perceived as their urban white employers' efforts to perpetuate in the city the plantation relations of the South's rural history, whether the relations of the sharecropping system of the recent past, which many had directly experienced, or those of master and slave, shared in the cultural memories of slavery. It represented *un*freedom.[1]

Sally Turner's story gets at the heart of what this book is about: struggles by the postplantation generation of African Americans in the urban South to articulate and achieve a new kind of freedom, freedom that would represent a genuine break from the daily humiliations they associated with the oppressive rural relations of race, class, and gender they had already abandoned. Her account presented this struggle in a Memphis factory by black women workers, many of them recent migrants from the Mississippi

Delta, as a dramatic confrontation with the plantation legacy, as if it had migrated with them, unwanted, to the city. In the context of the black freedom movement of the 1960s, their outrage at their boss's action tipped the scales toward union activism, despite the risks involved. The dynamic relation between migration, memory, and activism elaborated in Turner's story spurred working-class African Americans to challenge the urban attitudes and practices that they identified as barriers to freedom.

During oral history interviews three decades later, Turner and other working-class black Memphians invoked what to them were powerful symbols of unfreedom, such as the bucket and dipper, to denote what some speakers termed a "plantation mentality." The term captures both the perpetuation *and* mutability of racial ideology and practices in American culture. Most obviously, those who talked about the "plantation mentality" referred to white racist attitudes that promoted white domination and black subservience, which they construed as reminiscent of slavery and sharecropping. However, their critiques also included other African Americans. Sally Turner, for instance, recalled her frustration with coworkers whom she perceived as afraid to join the union because they feared losing their jobs. As a migrant from Mississippi, Turner compared these women to sharecroppers who felt bound to the plantation. "It was like they was glued in and they was afraid to step out of it," she asserted, "because they was thinking they didn't have anywhere else to turn to. . . . And so you were just kind of locked in." The "plantation mentality" thus referred simultaneously to racist attitudes among whites and perceived fear and dependency among other African Americans. Turner and others measured their own sense of self, especially their commitments to mobility, activism, and independent thought, against these negative perceptions. During the civil rights era, vernacular terms such as "plantation mentality" and "slave mentality" became central to critical thinking about everyday life and shaped the various struggles that together comprised the black freedom movement. They provided African Americans in southern cities with a language for talking about freedom and unfreedom — a language that encompassed but went beyond the constitutional parameters of equal rights generally associated with the modern civil rights movement.

The potency of these critiques became most publicly apparent during the 1968 Memphis sanitation workers' strike, when participants carried placards that read "I *Am* a Man" in boldfaced capital letters. The strike's famous slogan meant *freedom*, according to former sanitation worker Taylor Rogers, who had grown up in north Memphis yet shared cultural memories of the historical plantation experience of African Americans. "All we wanted was some decent working conditions, and a decent salary," Rogers asserted. "And be treated like men, not like boys. But I guess [Mayor Loeb] had that 'plantation mentality,' just wanted to keep us down. Whatever he said went."[2] Rogers's comment, articulated in gendered terms, denounced racist attitudes that degraded black men by categorizing them as if they were neither independent adults nor fully human. His statement also conveyed the sanitation workers' rejection of such views. By posing freedom as an opposite to the "plantation mentality," Rogers and others referred to both society and identity, to both equal rights and the envisaged self. Indeed, the very process of demanding change and respect — "being men," in Taylor's terms, or refusing to be "glued in," as Turner put it — represented an enactment of freedom.[3]

Significantly, the sanitation strike followed, rather than preceded, federal approval of the 1964 Civil Rights Act, which, together with the 1965 Voting Rights Act, has frequently been seen as marking the end of the civil rights movement. However, instead of quelling black working-class activism with its promise to end racist employment practices, the landmark legislation stimulated extensive protests by workers who seized upon its passage to demand changed racial attitudes and practices within plants. Perhaps more than any other single event of the years directly after the passage of the Civil Rights Act, the Memphis sanitation strike, which culminated in the tragic assassination of Dr. Martin Luther King Jr., publicly hammered home the fact that for working-class African Americans in southern cities, freedom remained an elusive goal.

Taking its cue from narratives such as those by Sally Turner and Taylor Rogers, this book explores how working-class African Americans thought about freedom, how they conceived of their own activism, and how these perceptions reflected their historically specific experiences in the changing postwar urban South. While recent years have seen a stunning outpouring of important new studies of local freedom struggles, written by scholars strongly committed to reinterpreting the civil rights movement by shifting attention to the participation of grassroots activists rather than nationally known leaders, or the interplay between the two, this book has somewhat different concerns. Although it builds on this preoccupation with the agency of local activists, it focuses more specifically on the understandings and articulations of freedom that both inspired and emanated from these local struggles.

The following analysis makes clear that for urban black southerners in the civil rights era, the process of claiming freedom was about simultaneously uprooting white racist thought and liberating black minds from forms of consciousness they identified with slavery and its long aftermath. It locates these struggles in specific urban moments in Memphis, many of which occurred outside the boundaries of what is generally recognized as the civil rights movement, in contexts as disparate as manufacturing plants and movie theaters. More broadly speaking, the book focuses on the consciousness, culture, and politics that inspired and shaped the black freedom movement, which in southern cities typically spilled beyond the better-known organized campaigns for desegregation and voting rights to various arenas of everyday life.[4]

The chapters that follow illuminate historically specific, complex, and contested understandings of freedom articulated during the modern civil rights movement, amidst the economic, cultural, and political upheaval that engulfed the urban South between the Second World War and the sanitation strike. Although studies abound of clashing interpretations of freedom after the abolition of slavery in the United States and the Caribbean in the nineteenth century, few works besides biographies and religious studies attempt such analysis for the twentieth-century civil rights movement, despite its common appellation among participants as the black freedom movement. Civil rights scholars frequently incorporate the word "freedom" into the titles of our works, yet its meaning a century after the end of slavery is still far from self-evident. We are familiar with the ideals articulated by Dr. Martin Luther King Jr., including his vision of the promised land in his famous final speech, delivered in Memphis on April 3, 1968, on the eve of his assassination, but we know much less about what freedom meant to black working-class Memphians who came out to Mason Temple on that stormy evening.[5] The paucity of analyses of the specific, complex meanings of freedom during the civil rights era makes it possible to equate freedom with the juridical and legislative achievements of the movement and to conclude that freedom was attained by these achievements. Such assumptions make it difficult to fathom the persistence of struggles over racial justice well into the post–civil rights era.

Black Memphians' vernacular use of terms like "plantation mentality" in oral histories I conducted in the mid-1990s profoundly influenced this project and is key to the analytic framework of the book as a whole, providing new insights into black experience, consciousness, and agency in the mid-twentieth century. Working-class African Americans struggled against white hegemony by asserting views of themselves that countered racist thought. In doing so, they acknowledged that such thought would be internalized unless it were explicitly and persistently challenged.[6]

Critiques of the "plantation mentality" and concomitant understandings of freedom articulated during the 1960s were deeply rooted in the social movements, structural changes, and cultural developments of the recent past, most notably the years during and after the Second World War. Even as they migrated away from the cotton fields to northern and southern cities, working-class African Americans compared and contrasted the racial parameters of city life to cultural memories of the plantation. These critiques thus emanated from the crucible of the historic plantation South but served as a means to assess contemporary urban culture in the cities that served as destinations for black migrants.

Indeed, although the term "plantation mentality" would likely not have been used until the 1960s, this book uses it as a framing concept for a narrative that begins on the eve of the Second World War and continues through the sanitation strike. In a sense, the chapters of the book establish a kind of genealogy of such language. In the decades before this particular emphasis on "mentality" arose, for example, black Memphis activists sometimes characterized contemporary urban power relations between whites and blacks as ones of master/slave, or in other terms that similarly invoked the past of slavery to assess the present and anticipate the future. They also seized upon contemporary political discourse about democracy, justice, equality, and freedom, making it their own by using it to express their own critiques and aspirations, building a kind of counter-hegemony.

In Memphis, the urban vortex of the Mississippi Delta cotton region and the focus of this study, the conflicting ideas of freedom that emerged during and after the Second World War accompanied momentous economic, social, and cultural restructuring. The crumbling of the sharecropping system, urban migration, and innovations in mass culture generated new sites of struggle and fresh possibilities for change as everything from labor markets and police violence to housing and popular entertainment became flashpoints for conflict. In these multiple contexts, African Americans in postwar Memphis demanded freedom by contesting racial ideologies and practices that they perceived as reminiscent of the master/slave relation, even though nearly a century had passed since emancipation.

Until the mid-1950s, black Memphians also faced one of the most formidable political machines of the era, the Democratic organization headed by Boss Edward Hull Crump. While a majority of African American leaders sought advancement for their communities via cooperation with the machine, others adopted a more defiant posture. Repeatedly throughout this period, therefore, working-class protest exposed tensions among blacks over issues of class, culture, and ideology, in addition to conflicts between the races.

Even as it became a site of internal struggle, Memphis also served as a crossroads of local, regional, national, and international cultures and politics. During the intervening years between the New Deal's restructuring of the cotton economy and the assassination of Dr. King during the sanitation strike three decades later, black activism reflected the city's persistent ties to the surrounding region, on the one hand, and to major national developments, on the other. Struggles in Memphis reverberated well beyond the city limits, as when the Crump machine received national attention for its control over local elections, intervention in labor conflicts, and censorship of Hollywood movies, or when black Memphis activists appealed to national civil rights officials for support. Likewise, both the international Cold War and anticolonial movements influenced local debates about Memphis's direction in the postwar era. This multifaceted political context assured that competing understandings of race and freedom that clashed with one another in Memphis were never the mere products of isolated conflicts but instead reflected this interaction between local, regional, national, and global concerns.

As the following chapters reveal, freedom was neither a static nor monolithic principle, despite its status as a founding American ideal. We know that President Franklin D. Roosevelt's "Four Freedoms" speech in 1941 made freedom into a keyword of U.S. political parlance during the Second World War, along with his far more frequent references to democracy. However, whereas Roosevelt spoke in general terms about human freedom as the basis for a "democratic way of life" that was the opposite of tyranny,[7] African Americans challenged the idea of fighting against the Axis powers abroad on behalf of world freedom and democracy without linking this fight to both self-determination for the peoples of color in the colonized world and genuine equality for blacks at home in the United States. The idea of freedom surfaced even more dramatically during the early Cold War, when U.S. anticommunist diplomacy hinged on guarantees of freedom promised by American democracy. Concomitantly, members of a new postwar generation of African American activists presented themselves as champions of black freedom and, especially after the student sit-ins erupted in 1960, demanded it immediately. By the end of the

1960s, black liberation and Black Power had gained more international and militant connotations than black freedom and won the adherence of young activists.

To put this differently, distinct understandings of freedom emerged out of specific historical struggles, several of which are traced in the pages that follow. Although the book considers areas of activism typically perceived as the core of the civil rights agenda, such as desegregation and voting rights, it also encompasses conflicts over labor, police brutality, politics, movies, radio, and other issues that helped shape understandings of freedom, issues without which it would be difficult to understand the intense popular support generated by the 1968 sanitation strike.

As the urban center of the tri-state Delta region that extends from southeast Arkansas to west Tennessee to northwest Mississippi, Memphis was crucial to the regional cotton and hardwood industries. In addition to its role in the grading, compressing, trading, storing, and transporting of cotton, Memphis by the dawn of the twentieth century had spawned manufacturing industries based on cotton by-products and hardwood such as cottonseed oil and furniture. Its ability to expand in these economic areas depended upon not only regional agricultural products but also a steady supply of workers from the surrounding area. Even as the city diversified its economy into new areas of manufacturing and attracted major corporations to establish production plants in the area, its reliance on a regular influx of migrants and a racially segmented low-wage labor force belied its ties to the rural Delta. Indeed, when African Americans poured out of Memphis for northern cities during the First World War and the Great Migration, the Chamber of Commerce took steps to enhance living conditions for blacks, asserting that "from an industrial viewpoint the negro labor is one of the best assets of this community."[8]

Memphis's position as an urban-rural crossroads also spurred its national and even international prominence as a distribution hub and an entertainment center. Its role first as a Mississippi River port and later as a major railroad depot meant that both goods and people moved in and out of the city on a daily basis. This development helps explain the rise of a small black middle class that did not rely upon local employers — including, for instance, Pullman porters — and a tiny but notable black business elite. Memphis also acquired a national reputation for its regionally based popular culture. Paradoxically, the sounds emanating from the nightclubs of Beale Street (black Memphis's "Main Street") and the churches that

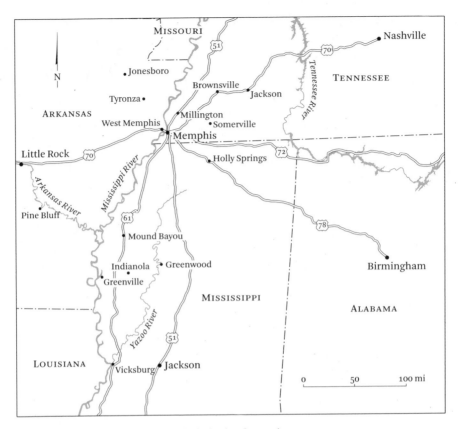

The Arkansas and Yazoo–Mississippi Delta Region

reigned in the rest of black Memphis together intertwined to make the city into a musical hub, first for jazz, blues, and gospel, and later for rhythm and blues and soul.[9]

Significantly, beginning during the New Deal era and continuing through the Second World War and the postwar period, boundaries distinguishing the urban and rural South became more porous. As the sharecropping system in the Delta started to collapse, white and black southerners sought nonagricultural livelihoods. Once wartime jobs became available, millions abandoned the rural South altogether.[10] Although a large portion of these migrants moved to the North, many headed to southern cities like Memphis, either to stay briefly before moving farther north, or to remain permanently. Still others literally traversed these urban/rural boundaries on a daily basis, either holding down Memphis jobs while residing in rural areas, or working as day laborers in cotton fields while inhabiting the city. Music, radio, religion, and politics also crossed this rural-urban divide.

While migrants had brought their sacred and secular music to Memphis in earlier times, new black radio stations and recording studios attracted many more to the city in the postwar era. Black radio also beamed urban music and talk radio back out to the small rural towns of the Delta, even to the people living in the shotgun shacks that still littered the countryside, who may have had battery-operated radios even before they had electricity. Just as significantly, roads such as Highway 61, running from Memphis down into the Delta, became two-way political thoroughfares, as rural activists sought support in the city and their urban counterparts not only lent assistance but also found inspiration in rural areas.

These dynamics helped destabilize the Democratic political machine of Boss Crump that loomed over city life and west Tennessee politics from the early twentieth century until Crump's death in 1954. Several spheres of everyday life transformed into political battlegrounds. At the end of the Second World War, for instance, police brutality against veterans and police sexual assaults of women sparked heated protest movements in neighborhoods heavily populated with black migrants. Simultaneously, popular culture became a major locus of controversy. The city's practice of censoring movies that did not adhere to southern racial conventions prompted widespread outcry both inside and outside of Memphis. Meanwhile, new media outlets, especially radio stations that converted to all black-oriented programming, provided new virtual public spheres, creating spaces for a cultural consumption by blacks that was grounded in a politics of pride, despite their Jim Crow origins. Together, these struggles addressed highly charged issues of racial identity and power that can be obscured when civil rights is approached from narrower perspectives.

However, ideological tensions among blacks and among whites made the trajectory of racial politics far from straightforward or obvious. Although freedom, in the broadest sense, had to do with ending white domination, it also represented a crucial struggle of culture, consciousness, and politics among different groups of African Americans, a point that needs to be more fully elaborated in civil rights histories. On the eve of the Second World War, for example, students at historically black LeMoyne College decried not only the Crump political machine but also its supposed opposition. During a spate of police harassment, Daniel Carter, president of a new college NAACP chapter, declared that "the Negro mass [was] in terror either of their jobs or their lives." Nevertheless, he complained in a letter to the NAACP's national office that "[t]he Negro press has accepted its gag; the white press attempts to soften things; the city N.A.A.C.P. chapter is lethargic." For these reasons, LeMoyne students had decided to organize their own NAACP branch, separate from the notoriously inactive city branch.[11] Over the next two decades, LeMoyne students and graduates would help establish a fresh basis for civil rights agitation. Furthermore, the "Negro mass" to which Carter referred rebelled on a number of fronts during the 1940s, pushing traditional black leaders to take political stances they might not have otherwise assumed.

This internal black struggle intersected with rifts among white Memphians. As historians Jane Dailey, Glenda Gilmore, and Bryant Simon have argued, scholars "stunned" by the power and magnitude of white supremacy in the Jim Crow era often "minimize the contingent nature of white supremacist ideas and regimes," thereby missing "the complexities of racism and power."[12] In the postwar era, sectors of Memphis society with clashing visions of postwar development pushed to enact their own agendas, bringing them into conflict with each other. Prominent white moderates seeking to undermine the Crump political machine and implement municipal reform, for example, publicized incidents of police brutality against black women and men as evidence of the Crump machine's corruption.[13] Such claims unintentionally reinforced black agitation for racial justice. This is not to say that the vast majority of whites retreated from Jim Crow but that the maelstrom of postwar politics created unexpected openings for change.

The process of transforming consciousness, culture, and politics, therefore, was far from linear and is difficult to chart, a point underscored by outside observers' antithetical descriptions of Memphis's black political scene in different periods. "I've never seen a community as together as Memphis!" exclaimed Dr. Martin Luther King Jr. during the 1968 sanitation strike, in a speech to 15,000 people at Mason Temple. No doubt this response to the unity and passion he observed is part of what drew him back to Memphis two more times before his assassination on April 4.[14] However, just one and a half decades earlier, NAACP southern regional coordinator Ruby Hurley bemoaned the state of the Memphis branch, writing to the central office that it was "dying slowly" because "conservative influence dominates the thinking and the little action that is taken." "I could actually cry about Memphis," she concluded.[15] What had happened in the interim between Hurley's and King's observations? The Memphis story is a not a narrative of a steady progression from an accommodationist "Uncle Tom" consciousness to a militant one; rather, the very meanings of these terms changed in various periods, and varying attitudes coexisted — and clashed — in each period. This book is really about the struggles that gave rise to those clashes and changing understandings.[16]

The following pages examine this dynamic from the ground up, not only among elites but also among working-class black Memphians. Path-breaking civil rights studies published since the mid-1990s have shifted historical attention from national politics and well-known leaders to local trenches where vital day-to-day freedom movements took place. John Dittmer's *Local People: The Struggle for Civil Rights in Mississippi* (1994) and Charles Payne's *I've Got the Light of Freedom: The Organizing Tradition and the Mississippi Freedom Struggle* (1995) were particularly influential in pressing for this changed orientation within civil rights scholarship. This investigation builds on these studies; however, it approaches political agency in this era from new vantage points. The book situates the racial agitation of the period, for instance, within the broader context of postwar modernity in southern cities characterized by paradoxical relations of urban and rural, tradition and progress.[17]

The book also reconsiders the contours of urban black struggles for racial justice during and after the war. "Agency," a concept frequently boiled down to mere resistance or activism by already constituted subjects with preconceived interests, refers here to struggles over not only external issues of rights but also internal, subjective problems of identity, both of which comprised understandings of freedom. In addition, agency is expanded to include social protest and critical thought about everyday life and activism itself, exemplified by Sally Turner and Taylor Rogers's commentaries.

To more deeply engage these problems, this analysis traverses historical and intellectual boundaries that generally separate spheres of life and scholarship from each other.[18] Taking off from studies that have explored the ramifications for civil rights of such aspects of postwar urban life as popular culture, labor organizing, housing, and municipal politics, the chapters in the book follow black urbanites, including recent migrants, as they crossed the boundaries of these different arenas and developed understandings of freedom that spilled beyond any unitary root cause. In doing so, the study draws jointly on social, political, cultural, and economic history, and on insights from literary criticism, media studies, musicology, and religious studies.[19]

In recent years, the politics of everyday life have increasingly come under scrutiny by historians and other scholars in an attempt to rethink the sources and contours of modern political movements by focusing not only on elites and public protests but also on daily encounters with race and power. Robin D. G. Kelley, a contributor to this discussion, has focused attention on "black working-class history from way, way below."

He encourages scholars to excavate aspects of resistance that precede and parallel organized political movements and illuminate the dynamics of power relations. Politics, in this conception, is not walled off from either everyday life or "the imaginary world of what is possible" but unfolds everywhere there are power struggles.[20]

Here, I am similarly concerned with dimensions of everyday life that typically appear outside the realm of politics and with groups Kelley would categorize as "way, way below." However, I build on these foundations by interrogating how specific experiences in the realm of the everyday become politicized, taking on symbolic meanings that influence organizing efforts. Why, for instance, did Sally Turner single out the "bucket and dipper" experience to explain why she helped organize a union in the 1960s? Why did she compare her coworkers in a Memphis factory to sharecroppers in Mississippi? And how did highly charged responses to everyday experience influence understandings of abstractions such as freedom? This book explores the ways in which participants in various concrete struggles made meaning out of these struggles, on the one hand, and freedom, on the other.

Although much of this work could be considered social history, it does not aim to be a straightforward social history of postwar Memphis but draws equally on cultural and political history. If social histories frequently take race and gender identities for granted, cultural studies often present these identities as imposed on the oppressed by dominant elite groups. Merging social, cultural, and political history allows me to show that race and gender were deeply embattled categories. Black working-class women, for instance, eschewed labor practices that cast them as natural servants, while city officials attempted to pigeonhole them as maids, cooks, or laundresses. Similarly, Hollywood's images of African Americans provoked fierce debate within Memphis and other southern cities. Disagreements over blackness and whiteness, manhood and womanhood, lay at the heart of struggles over freedom.

Throughout, the book explores the language used in specific historical contexts to discuss contemporary urban problems of freedom, power, and identity. Well before the term "plantation mentality" came into popular use, black political discourse compared urban racial domination to the "master and servant" relation emblematic of cotton culture. In 1943, for example, after Boss Crump strong-armed several African American leaders into canceling a public speech by renowned black labor and civil rights personality A. Philip Randolph, one courageous minister in Memphis, Reverend George A. Long of Beale Avenue Baptist Church, invited

Randolph back to town. "Christ, not Crump, is my Boss," Long publicly declared. Randolph, for his part, announced in his speech at Long's church that "Negroes do not want to be well-kept slaves. Like white people they, too, want to be free."[21] Long and Randolph had two intended audiences—Crump and his cronies, on one side, and black Memphians, on the other—that reflected their twin intentions. If one concern involved critiques of white domination, the other involved the perception that white domination could be internalized by African Americans and manifested in complicity. Similarly, during the 1945 protest against police sexual assaults, black public commentary blasted police brutality and castigated African American leaders for their "supine" attitudes.

These critiques of barriers to freedom were profoundly gendered, a quality that added to their resonance as African Americans fought against practices that enforced racial dependency and challenged perceived black submissiveness. Struggles against the "plantation mentality" turned battles over racial domination into conflicts over manhood and womanhood. During the sanitation strike, "being men" made freedom contingent upon addressing external problems of racial domination and internal issues of identity. Because invoking manhood rejected racial subservience, both men and women identified with "I *Am* a Man." But women also challenged specific identities assigned them by white society, rallying against being perceived as natural domestic servants or as sexually licentious. Black southerners articulated ideas of freedom that rejected racist gender identities while staking claims to new ones.[22]

Not intended as a seamless chronological narrative, the book is instead organized around a set of themes that illuminate how African Americans in Memphis from the postplantation generation struggled to imagine, articulate, and realize ideas of racial justice, equality, and freedom, from the eve of the Second World War through the 1968 sanitation strike. Rather than concentrating solely on what has been recognized as the civil rights movement, the following chapters address different cultural, political, and economic arenas that became sites of contestation over race, power, and identity. After an introductory chapter that discusses racial politics in Memphis on the eve of the Second World War, Chapters 2 through 5 explore in depth specific aspects of everyday life and political culture that influenced understandings of freedom: labor and black working-class struggle; community protest against police brutality and sexual assault; postwar racial politics, particularly surrounding the 1947–48

Freedom Train, a project of the American Heritage Foundation; and popular culture, especially motion pictures and black radio. Looking through the prism of this analysis of overlapping arenas of urban life in the Jim Crow South, the final three chapters, 6, 7, and 8, turn to the more well-known years of the black freedom movement, from the period surrounding the Supreme Court's 1954 school desegregation decision through the 1968 Memphis sanitation strike.

In 1925, Lt. George W. Lee, a Beale Street literary commentator, insurance executive, and Republican political leader, argued that in the aftermath of slavery, both the white man and the black man suffered from "mental reservations" that needed to "be banished from the seats of thought control."[23] Four decades later, black laborers made the slogan "I *Am* a Man" central to a mass movement against the "plantation mentality." As the chapters of this book show, the road in between these two expressions was a complex, nonlinear one, involving various dimensions of Memphis life.

At the core of the book are nearly sixty oral history interviews conducted for the most part between 1995 and 1997 with black Memphians who were involved with struggles for racial justice between the Second World War and the late 1960s, in addition to many months of archival research in Memphis, Washington, D.C., College Park, Atlanta, and elsewhere. These interviews greatly influenced my thinking about the protest movements and daily lives of African Americans in the urban South of this period. Given the book's interest in the impact of everyday life on both protest and critical thought, the interviews proved invaluable in probing areas that do not easily come to light in archival sources. The majority of these interviews were with working-class African Americans, and among that group there was a preponderance of migrants from the rural South. Moreover, well over half the interviews were with working-class women, whose struggles had particular salience in this period, in part because of their fierce challenges to racial, gendered images of black women as natural servants.

For sanitation strike supporters such as Sally Turner and Taylor Rogers, freedom necessitated but was not exhausted by constitutional rights protections. Rather, as their comments show, it extended to battles against commonplace experiences of humiliation that resulted from power relations of race, gender, and power, bound up in critiques of the "plantation mentality." These understandings of freedom are far from a merely academic matter; rather, they are of great importance for grappling with problems of race in the post–civil rights era, into the twenty-first century.

Memphis before World War II

1

Migrants, Mushroom Strikes, and the Reign of Terror

Susie Bryant opened her door on election day morning in 1940 to a man who had promised to help her get registered African Americans out to vote. "Miss Bryant, I ain't going to be able to vote with you," he confessed. "The boss says I got to vote the way he says." His statement dismayed but did not surprise her. After migrating to Memphis from Greenwood, Mississippi, in January 1936, Bryant had registered to vote, casting her ballot for the first time when she was in her thirties. In the early-twentieth-century Mississippi of her youth, she recalled, "it was right after slavery almost. People were still under that influence. They didn't turn them loose and turn around and treat them like they were citizens. They couldn't even vote." In Memphis, on the other hand, African Americans could vote so long as they paid the annual poll tax required by the Tennessee Constitution — or if Boss Edward H. Crump's Democratic political machine paid it for them.[1]

Bryant quickly learned, however, that voting rights for African Americans in Memphis were not as different from voting restrictions in Mississippi as they appeared. Many working-class black Memphians who cast ballots were pressured into supporting candidates endorsed by Crump, who paid their poll taxes. Going to the polls, elsewhere a marker of independent citizenship, thus denoted the opposite, servility, for these black Memphis voters. In fall 1940, when this moment at Bryant's doorway took place, politics in Memphis had become even more fraught, as the Crump machine launched an unabashed harassment campaign, dubbed the Memphis "reign of terror" by civil liberties proponents, aimed at repressing black Republicans, subduing labor activism, and exerting social control over incoming migrants.

For Bryant, urban migration represented another leg of a journey that her family had undertaken in the Yazoo-Mississippi Delta. Born in 1904 in Carroll County, Mississippi, Bryant moved "down in the Delta" into LeFlore County, just west of Carroll, with her paternal extended family, the Holmans, in 1913. The large family went first to work on a plantation outside of Morgan City, then to Swiftown, and finally to Greenwood. Moving to Memphis during the Great Depression represented the next logical step. "Times were so tough in Mississippi then," Bryant remembered. Her father had died and her oldest brother had moved to Memphis, leaving her mother unable to making a living from farmwork with her remaining children. Bryant recalled that her mother worked as a domestic servant in white households but received almost nothing for her labor: "She got I think fifty cents sometimes and clothes and things." Bryant herself was unable to farm or work as a domestic because she had become crippled as a child as a result of a leg injury for which she received inadequate medical care.

Moving, however, signified as much a quest for racial independence from white planters as a pursuit of economic stability for at least three generations of Holman family members who shared or inherited the memory of an incident in the 1910s. Bound by debt to the landowner for whom they had been farming, Bryant recalled, her uncles and grandfather tried to leave the farm in the middle of the night to go "up on the Dog" — a reference to the Yazoo and Delta Railroad, nicknamed the "Yellow Dog," or "Dog."[2] A white mob pursued and beat them, she recounted, ultimately forcing them back to the plantation. Although Bryant had not witnessed the beating, it had become part of shared family stories about Mississippi. Memories of her mother toiling as a servant and her older male kin being subjected to white violence when they attempted to exert economic independence, framed Bryant's lasting images of the Delta, along with her own inability to receive proper medical care as a six-year-old. Inherent in African Americans' decisions to leave the rural South were desires to alter the degrading identities assigned to them — and even violently reinforced — by a racist plantation culture.

Bryant also carried to Memphis a deep and abiding commitment to education for African American children that had emerged as a response to the racially and economically circumscribed conditions she and other youth confronted in rural Mississippi. African American children received drastically truncated educations because the segregated schools they attended were open only during months when they were not needed for fieldwork. Bryant's parents, she recalled, countered this situation by emphasizing the importance of education, devoting time to schoolwork at home. Bryant particularly valued the home-based education that they insisted upon since her leg injury kept her from attending school regularly. She also learned how to cook and nurse children during her time at home with her mother. In Memphis years later, Bryant became involved with community projects dedicated to black children. She established the Dunbar Elementary PTA and a nursery for children of working mothers and became a mainstay of her church's youth group.

Bryant's lifelong dedication to civic and community activism in Memphis reflected both continuities and discontinuities between rural and urban life in the Deep South. In Mississippi, as a member of the Willing Worker Society, a church-based mutual aid association in Greenwood, she had helped her mother prepare soup and deliver it to sick members of their community. In Memphis, however, Bryant extended her community service work to political organizing, a step that would have been prohibitively dangerous in Greenwood, a town that became a focal point for civil rights activism three decades later.[3] In the Orange Mound neighborhood in Memphis, one of the more established black neighborhoods, Bryant discovered that there was only "one little place over there somewhere on Lamar at a store" for black Memphians to vote. Dismayed, she joined black Republican leader Lt. George W. Lee's efforts to register voters, organize voter education schools, and pressure city officials to establish precincts in every black neighborhood.

Susie Bryant discovered an urban milieu in Memphis that opened new possibilities for African Americans yet perpetuated aspects of the degrading and oppressive culture she associated with the Mississippi Delta. On one hand, Memphis's economy offered opportunities to escape the racism inherent in the social and labor relations of the plantation. Moreover, migrants found in the variegated social terrain of Memphis a mobility and anonymity that contrasted with the personal power structures of rural life. On the other hand, the rural Delta's "influence of slavery" reverberated in Memphis, according to Bryant. As in Mississippi, African Americans in Memphis had to go around to the back of restaurants to be served. "You went to that hole," Bryant recalled, "where they could hand you a sandwich through if there wasn't a back door. And you couldn't drink water out of the fountain. You better not!" Private employers, likewise, required women domestic servants to enter their homes through the back door. In addition, when Bryant moved to Memphis with her mother, one of her own children, and two of her sister's children, they lived with her brother in what she called a "shanty" — little better than a shack on a rural plantation. Migrants thus encountered racial practices that appeared to re-create, albeit in specifically urban forms, aspects of plantation culture. Nevertheless, many young migrants arrived in the city with little commitment to the status quo and determined to alter their lives.[4]

At the same time, however, African American political leadership that had been in place in Memphis since the First World War, comprised largely of businessmen, professionals, and ministers, seriously fractured during the late 1930s under a variety of pressures that included severe intimidation and harassment by the Crump machine. For many black leaders, the uneasy coexistence they had managed to work out with the Crump machine now unraveled, forcing them to either increase their fidelity to the machine or pay the consequences. Confronted by the Crump machine's 1940 "reign of terror," only a handful chose open defiance.

Outside critics assessed Memphis in 1940 as a place where the Crump machine reigned supreme. As black political scientist Ralph Bunche put it, "Edward H. Crump, or 'Mistuh' Crump[,] as he is popularly known, is the boss of all things political in Memphis and Shelby County." Bunche and other outside observers expressed concern that ordinary African Americans had been intimidated into silence and black political and business leaders had chosen cooperation over confrontation with the machine. Those who did seek to ameliorate working and social conditions were accused of being subversives and faced reprisals. Bunche, an astute political observer, assessed the consequences for black Memphians as dire: "Beaten into submission by police nightsticks and guns, the Negroes of Memphis are in a terrible predicament."[5]

Reexamined from a fresh vantage point, this situation appears far more complex than Bunche's observations would suggest. Despite the Crump machine's strenuous efforts to dominate economic, social, and political life, central to which was the assertion of racial control, multidimensional struggles over racial authority and identity emerged within this crucible of the urban South, poised between Depression and war. They challenged the domination of the Crump machine and the leadership of black elites, whether the challenge took the form of a CIO-backed labor movement, a youth branch of the NAACP organized at historically black LeMoyne College, or defiant stances taken by a small number of black ministers. Beneath these overt protests, however, lay the daily struggles of recent migrants such as Susie Bryant to reorganize their own lives in Memphis. These travails led many migrants into new terrain, from the political work conducted by Bryant to the "mushroom strikes" that sprouted in sweatshop manufacturing shops even before the CIO formally visited these workplaces. Together, these efforts prompted repression by the Crump machine and anticipated the persistent clashes over race and democracy that would arise during and after the Second World War.

Memphis's Roots in the Plantation Economy

Memphis's historic symbiotic relationship with the broader Mississippi Delta region bound it to far-flung national and world markets. Its position as a key river port along the Mississippi River made it an excellent site from which to ship the region's cotton as early as the 1830s and 1840s. The city's role as the linchpin of the Delta cotton economy greatly expanded after the Civil War, leading cotton factors and merchants to open the Memphis Cotton Exchange in 1873, and for Memphis to capture from New Orleans the honor of being the world's "Largest Spot Cotton Market" (where cotton was traded on the spot, rather than through a futures market). By the turn of the twentieth century, Memphis had also become the hub of a burgeoning hardwood industry that was transforming the Mississippi Delta's native forests into immense profits for lumber companies, most northern-based. As the center of an extraction-based industry that included over 500 mills within a 100-mile radius and produced a billion feet of lumber annually, Memphis had become a world leader in hardwood markets. The large lumbering operations that cleared timber fed the area's development as a plantation region, as lumber companies sold off immense tracts of cleared land to local, northern, and foreign investors.[6]

These roots in the cotton and hardwood industries attached Memphis's fate to that of the surrounding agricultural region. Regional hardwood and cotton by-products spawned the city's homegrown manufacturing companies, including such spectacularly successful corporations as the Plough Chemical Company, which in 1971 became part of Schering-Plough, Inc., a world leader in pharmaceuticals, and the E. L. Bruce Company, a major producer of hardwood flooring, along with firms such as the Memphis Furniture Manufacturing Company and the Buckeye Cotton Oil Company, owned by Procter & Gamble. As a transportation, distribution, and manufacturing hub, the city brought cotton and lumber in from the surrounding region and shipped raw goods and processed products out. The Memphis Chamber of Commerce's efforts to diversify the economy only amplified the city's ties to the rural Delta. When Fisher Body Corporation, a General Motors subsidiary, was looking for a site to build automobile frames in 1923, it gravitated to the city because of the availability of hardwood, out of which auto bodies were constructed. Firestone Tire and Rubber Company opened a plant in 1937, taking advantage of the city's access to cotton, used in tire fabric, along with raw rubber shipped to Memphis by barge up the Mississippi.[7]

Even Memphis's municipal services and housing reflected its rural influence. Although the city began addressing urban squalor by building sewer lines, draining waste-filled bayous, and improving neighborhoods in the early twentieth century, most black families continued to live in slums comprised of ramshackle structures that city officials referred to as "Negro housing." As late as 1941, a federal survey reported that "Negro slums are usually shacks and tenements that were never properly equipped with sanitary requisities [sic] in the first place. They were built for negroes by those who knew that negroes could never afford anything better than the worst." Such conditions fed racial stereotypes, as whites identified poor African Americans with this squalor. Likewise, as the city tackled public health, blacks were cast as bearers of tuberculosis, syphilis, and other communicable diseases. Memphis's notoriety for violent crime and murder also became a race issue, with daily newspapers limiting coverage of African Americans to crimes they allegedly committed. Even municipal corruption became insidiously associated with race, as blame shifted from those who bought votes to those whose votes were bought.[8]

Despite the fact that hundreds of black Memphians worked as teachers, postal workers, and railroad porters, or owned cafés, beauty salons, and barber shops, the vast majority toiled as servants and unskilled laborers. In the 1930s, few black women found openings outside private domestic service or public service establishments, such as commercial laundries, hospitals, and restaurants. Men had more options, but most worked as unskilled laborers in cotton compress plants, lumber mills, manufacturing plants, construction sites, railroad yards, on river boats and wharves, or in personal service. Job opportunities for black men had narrowed during the 1920s, as white trade unionists pushed skilled black workers out of several professions. In addition, city officials used vagrancy laws to force blacks to the countryside at cotton harvest time until the 1930s, when public agencies systematized the process of supplying this labor.[9]

Beale Street, the hub of Memphis's urban black culture, offered a sharp contrast to these restrictive labor practices, attracting both local residents and rural visitors to its commercial and cultural venues. Lt. George Lee, who served as one of the few black officers during World War I before becoming a political leader, insurance executive, and author of Beale Street: Where the Blues Began (1934), marveled at how "the cooks, maids, houseboys and factory hands" took over the famous avenue on Saturday nights. Beale offered public spaces where they could claim identities far differ-

Housing for African Americans in north Memphis, Tennessee, December 1940.
(John Vachon photo, for Farm Security Administration, courtesy of Library of Congress Prints & Photographs Division)

ent from the subservient ones they likely acted out at work. "The working people are on parade; going nowhere in particular, just out strolling, just glad of a chance to dress up and expose themselves on the avenue after working hard all the week," Lee observed. On Beale, black Memphians attended movies, caroused in cafés, and danced to live music, celebrating it as a space free of the racial tension of Main Street, just a turn of the corner away.[10]

The Crump machine, meanwhile, increasingly dominated Memphis's public life during the 1920s and 1930s. Originally from a planter-mercantile family in Holly Springs, Mississippi, Edward Hull Crump migrated to Memphis in 1894 and eventually created a business empire that extended from plantations to insurance underwriting. Elected as mayor on a good-government platform in 1909, Crump served in that office only until 1916, when the Tennessee legislature ousted him for violating the state's prohibition law through cultivating lucrative ties to illegal alcohol establishments. During the late 1920s and 1930s, however, he consolidated a powerful political machine and ultimately gained more personal power, relative to the city's size, than had any other political machine boss of the time.[11] Crump touted what contemporaries euphemistically referred to as "racial harmony" — a goal intended to augment, not diminish, white domination. His organization became adept at "buying" black votes, collecting payments from illicit saloons and gambling dens to use for poll taxes, and distributing registration receipts to blacks who were transported to polling places. Crump drew into his circle a select group of black leaders who delivered votes and advocated racial cooperation, in return for patronage positions and the construction of segregated institutions such as public schools. Crump, however, also ruled with an iron fist, assisted by a notoriously brutal police force.[12]

From Migration to Mushroom Strikes: Responses to the New Deal

During the New Deal, Memphis became the site of impassioned, multifaceted debates over the implications of federal programs that affected southern agriculture and industry. To grasp the parameters of this turmoil, one must peer over the conceptual barrier that typically separates the rural and urban South and consider how federal agriculture, industry, and relief programs, and conflict over them, intertwined.

Agricultural recovery programs raised burning questions about the future of farm laborers in southern agriculture, especially African Americans. The 1933 Agricultural Adjustment Act (AAA) bolstered the plunging prices of cotton and other farm commodities by paying growers to reduce acreage under cultivation, thus limiting output. Although, theoretically, landowners should have passed on a portion of their payments to their tenant farmers, loopholes in the legislation and large growers' domination of local oversight boards made it possible for many planters to avoid this step.[13] Some evicted their tenants and either replaced them with day laborers, whom they paid cash wages only for the weeks they were needed, or let the land lie fallow.

The upheaval that resulted from New Deal agricultural recovery programs made the Delta cotton region an embattled terrain. Most famously, black and white tenant farmers, assisted by white socialists H. L. Mitchell and Clay East, organized the Southern Tenant Farmers Union (STFU) in Tyronza, Arkansas, in 1934, to protest evictions and demand higher wages for cotton pickers. Although black participation reflected a longer history of rural activism, extending back to the aftermath of the First World War, this coalescence of blacks and whites in Arkansas was nothing short of incendiary. Strikes of cotton pickers to raise wages were met with fierce reprisals in 1935, 1936, and 1937, including night riding, beatings, torching of homes, and breaking up of meetings, and a few large growers also began transporting Mexican workers to their farms from south Texas to avoid wage hikes. After the STFU moved its headquarters to Memphis in an effort to avoid this violence, the city became a key site for this rural movement.[14]

In response to protests by the STFU, the Department of Agriculture made changes in its 1938 agricultural legislation, which Congress passed after the Supreme Court invalidated the 1933 Agricultural Adjustment Act. The new bill mandated payments to tenants "in the proportion that they share in the principal crop"; however, this requirement unintentionally made the most stable farmers the most vulnerable to eviction. By putting cash in the hands of planters eager to intensify production per acre, federal intervention also spurred mechanization, contributing to a restructuring of the cotton economy that would take place over the next three decades and ultimately displace thousands of sharecroppers. Growers first mechanized plowing and seeding, while chopping and harvesting remained labor intensive. This unevenness in the mechanization process made growers dependent on day laborers in the spring and fall, when literally thousands of African Americans were transported to the fields from Memphis.[15]

As was the case with Susie Bryant, an important response to Depression and New Deal upheaval was migration. Migrants chose to move for a variety of reasons. Tumbling cotton prices had made it even harder to survive during the 1930s. In addition to raising their own crops, many sharecroppers had to "work out," that is, pick cotton, work as maids, labor in lumber mills, or build levees. Those who had been evicted now had to choose between day labor, finding another tenant situation, and migration. However, the decision to move to Memphis usually began with economic concerns but rarely ended there. In addition to Susie Bryant's story, the oral histories of two African American women who migrated to Memphis as young adults in 1941, as the U.S. defense industry was on the rise, illustrate the complex racial and gendered reasons behind African Americans' decision to move.

Naomi Jones migrated to the city at age eighteen from Canton, Mississippi, north of Jackson. In Canton, she chopped and picked her own family's cotton, in addition to "chopping out" for white families for seventy-five cents a day. Jones concluded that she wanted more than this endless cycle of field labor for her father and for white households. But the racist structure of public education in Mississippi, which helped keep young African Americans from advancing beyond farm labor, also became an important impetus for her decision to migrate. One of Jones's first memories of racism was white youth passing by in a yellow school bus hurling objects out the windows at her and her siblings trudging to their own schools. Jones also remembered vividly her father's response to her desire to attend college: she would have to earn her keep by doing laundry for white students. "I just got tired," she asserted. "I was going to Memphis and get me a job."[16]

Jones "expected things to be a whole lot different" in Memphis. Instead, like Susie Bryant a few years earlier, she encountered the same "whites only" signs. "In some instances," she felt, Memphis was more segregated than Mississippi, "because this was a bigger city. You would have to use the side door, back door, next door for a restroom. You couldn't drink out of the same fountain." Jones found that as a black woman, the only job she could get was as a domestic servant in a private home. Ironically, she had never been forced to do such work in Mississippi, although her mother and oldest sisters had. Her duties now included shopping for her employer's daughter in stores that would not let her try on hats or clothes without special permission from her white employer. When Jones finally secured a job at a furniture factory that began to hire black women in 1946, she left with four hours notice.[17]

Artherene Chalmers also moved to Memphis in 1941, at age twenty-four, from Mt. Pleasant, Mississippi. As with many young women disenchanted with sharecropping, Chalmers's critiques of farming indicated the significance of gender in her choice to leave. She, rather than her husband, Percy, initiated the decision to migrate, asserting her own authority in the process. "You told me you were going to take me out [of Mississippi] when I got married to you," she told him. "And you didn't. . . . I'm going to get out of here myself." Her husband conceded, even agreeing to go to Memphis first to find a job while she took care of their three children. Chalmers hated farming, work that she associated with male authority and, paradoxically, reversed gender roles. As the oldest child in a sharecropping family that never saw money at year's end, Chalmers resented her father making her miss school to work in the fields. Because her brothers were younger, she "had to plow, chop, and everything like a boy. I was the boy." Chalmers also recalls gendered ramifications of the Depression. While her father picked cotton "out," in addition to working his own fields, her mother "washed and ironed for Miss Annie Davis."[18]

Moving to Memphis did not erase the gendered meanings of race and class culture in the Deep South. Chalmers never obtained work outside domestic service — ironically working "like a girl" only after moving to the city.

She saw little difference in the racist attitudes of her employers from those of the women for whom her mother had worked in Mississippi. Moreover, getting to work now involved the trial of riding segregated buses. Nevertheless, in contrast to the Delta, Memphis offered a more modern, urban milieu: "First thing I noticed was the lamp lights," she recalls. "I got to see the lights! And then it was a lot of places you could ... take the children.... They didn't have anywhere in Mississippi to go. Nothing."[19]

Despite the New Deal programs and, later, defense industry contracts that opened up thousands of jobs, most African American migrant women toiled as maids, cooks, or laundry workers. Women who sought relief or public works jobs in the 1930s complained about racial designations that funneled them into domestic service. Ralph Bunche reported that many women "tell bitterly of their experience in having been cut off [from relief] and sent to do work for some white person at three or four dollars per week." The Memphis NAACP received complaints from women obtaining groceries from the Civil Works Administration (CWA) who reported that they had been sent to work as maids for local CWA administrators' friends. The local programs of the National Youth Administration (NYA) and Works Progress Administration (WPA) became, in part, opportunities for white directors to train black women to be, in their eyes, model servants. "I sometimes say a good servant is almost as great a blessing as a good husband," declared Mrs. Thomas Coppedge, director of the Tennessee WPA's women's and professional projects, at WPA "commencement exercises," where trainees served a gala luncheon.[20] Even the Community Welfare League, a National Urban League affiliate directed by black business executives, set up a domestic worker training program in 1937. In an effort to place trainees, project director Lucien Searcy guaranteed that any worker who proved unreliable would be blacklisted.[21]

Black men who tried to use New Deal programs as an entrée into jobs in the skilled trades confronted similar barriers. Since skilled trades work had long signified independent manhood, such obstructions sent a message to black male workers that their place lay in labor and service positions. Community Welfare League secretary Nebraska Jones helped form the Independent Craftsmen Association in 1939 to help black workers gain acceptance into all-white building trades unions affiliated with the American Federation of Labor (AFL), since membership was needed to qualify for public works jobs. The association won small gains, including a nondiscrimination clause on a federally funded slum clearance project and jobs as "carpenters' helpers" on a public housing project. Black carpenters also formed their own union and had some luck in procuring jobs for members. However, the Independent Craftsmen Association collapsed after the police commissioner accused Nebraska Jones of being a Communist, convincing Community Welfare League directors that continuing the association would be "inimical to the interests of Negro workers particularly—and to labor generally." As Jones put it, "The red scare that was raised against us pretty nearly dispersed our group."[22]

Instead of being welcomed into urban jobs, many black migrants to Memphis faced pressure to return to the cotton fields as seasonal laborers. Local, state, and federal relief and employment services officials eyed African Americans on relief and public works rolls as potential field laborers. Given the restructuring of the cotton economy, Memphis in the late 1930s literally became the linchpin in efforts to maintain a steady supply of day laborers during the chopping and harvesting seasons. The mayor's office, the Tennessee State Employment Service (TSES), and the United States Employment Service (USES) jointly oversaw the transportation of laborers across the Mississippi River to Arkansas. A TSES administrator, after witnessing one morning's roundup near the Harahan Bridge together with U.S. Agriculture Department observers in the 1940s, reported that "all parties were greatly impressed with the unusual spectacle that does not exist in any other city in the country—some 15,000 workers leaving within a short space of time every morning to pick cotton."[23]

Planters requesting cotton pickers generally sought only African American laborers, reinforcing a vicious cycle of racial ideology that cast blacks as best suited to such labor. Their insistence upon black workers affected the distribution of relief in Memphis, since officials balanced relief and public works programs against planters' needs for laborers. In late 1940, after over 10,000 black workers had been sent to the fields, city welfare director Aubrey B. Clapp closed relief rolls in an effort to fill further requests for labor. In doing so, he rejected concerns expressed by WPA district supervisor Hal Peel that many cotton pickers were in dire need of relief, since inclement weather had kept them off work for several days.[24] Peel himself, however, also manipulated WPA rolls at cotton harvest time. "We have always made it a policy to encourage our workers to accept private employment whether it is seasonal employment or not," he wrote Congressman Clifford Davis, "and this has made it very convenient for the farmers and other employers because we have a reservoir of workers into which they can dip at any time."[25]

The relationship between work relief and cotton generated protest, however. In 1937, national WPA assistant director Aubrey Williams, a southern liberal and New Deal official, responded to queries during a con-

Black workers getting on trucks in Memphis for a
day's work hoeing cotton in Arkansas, June 1937.
*(Dorothea Lange photo, for Farm Security Administration,
courtesy of Library of Congress Prints & Photographs Division)*

vention of the Southern Tenant Farmers' Union, held in Memphis. Williams told STFU delegates that the WPA did not compel workers to pick
cotton for planters who used force to keep them in their employ; however,
he acknowledged, it did remove workers from its rolls at harvest time. And
Memphis's mayor Watkins Overton responded to planter complaints that
city relief programs served as a refuge for migrants trying to elude cotton
picking by assuring them that the city cut back on relief when workers
were needed in the fields.[26]

Conflicts also developed over the racial contours of federal industrial
recovery and labor relations programs. The 1933 National Industrial Recovery Act (NIRA), through boards comprised of business, labor, and
consumer leaders, set industrywide "codes of fair competition" that set
minimum wages and maximum hours. Its Section 7(a), which sanctioned
workers' rights to form unions, triggered organizing and strikes by thousands of southern workers. Following the Supreme Court's rejection of the
NIRA as unconstitutional in 1935, the new National Labor Relations Act

(also called the Wagner Act) further stimulated such struggles by ensuring employees' rights to organize unions and choose their own representatives and by creating the National Labor Relations Board (NLRB). Three years later, the Fair Labor Standards Act (FLSA) established national minimum wage and maximum hour requirements. The FLSA excluded from its provisions agricultural and domestic workers, along with a variety of other service workers, thereby exempting employers of a majority of African Americans in the South. Nevertheless, the NIRA, the Wagner Act, and the FLSA inspired thousands of southern workers to fight for better wages and shorter working hours.[27]

The Wagner Act's support for unions also helped spark the formation of the Congress of Industrial Organizations (CIO). Black workers, largely excluded from AFL unions, became central to CIO organizing nationwide. The first CIO forays into Memphis, however, involved white women clothing workers targeted by the International Ladies' Garment Workers' Union (ILGWU) and the white male auto workers at Ford Motor Company and Fisher Body who captured the attention of the United Auto Workers (UAW).

In March 1937, the ILGWU launched its first strike of garment workers at the Tri-State Dress Company, touted as the city's first CIO strike. During the same week, much to the surprise of observers who had anticipated the Tri-State strike, over 1,300 workers, a majority of whom were African American, initiated walkouts in six other manufacturing plants and mills. Startled by this outbreak of strikes outside the aegis of any union, journalists quickly began referring to them as mushroom strikes. The first such strike occurred at the E. L. Bruce Company, one of the South's largest lumber firms, only one day after fifty white women at Tri-State walked off their jobs. "The unorganized walkout was a colorful scene to labor reporters, who have seldom seen any but carefully planned strikes," commented a local reporter. When an incredulous journalist asked, "Where is the boss of this strike?," an African American man "in worn overalls" responded, "We haven't a boss." When asked "What's the name of your union?" several men chimed in, "We haven't got a union." Workers had walked out after management agreed to only half the five-cents-an-hour raise they demanded. However, a day after the walkout, they accepted the lower rate and returned to work, unable to win support from the AFL-affiliated Memphis Trades and Labor Council, whose president chastised them for the unauthorized strike.[28]

The E. L. Bruce walkout nevertheless inspired further mushroom strikes, some biracial, suggesting that even though black workers were, as a rule, paid less than whites, workers of both races at these plants shared concerns about wages, hours, and working conditions, and that possibilities for biracial organizing existed at this juncture. In the next week, walkouts took place all over the city: 400 black and white barrel makers at Chickasaw Wood Products; 450 black and white workers at Memphis Furniture Manufacturing Company; 142 men at the Hartwell Brothers wood handle plant; 42 black women charcoal packers at the Forest Products Chemical Company; and over 100 black women at the Memphis Pecan and Walnut Company. In early April, 70 women, a majority of them African American, staged a "sit-down" mushroom strike at the Newsum-Warren Laundry, remaining in the plant and awaiting news of negotiations by "reclining on tables and in laundry baskets." Several months later, black cotton compress workers walked out after a foreman struck one of them. Meanwhile, white ILGWU members launched strikes at the Nona-Lee and Kuhn Manufacturing companies, and black members of the International Longshoremen's Association (ILA) organized several stoppages.[29]

The mushroom strikes followed similar courses, illustrating that workers had formulated modes of action in the absence of formal union structures and organizers. At Chickasaw Wood Products, a major barrel company with plants in other southern cities and worldwide orders, workers gathered outside the plant after walking off their jobs and elected a biracial seven-man delegation. Memphis Furniture workers held what the press described as a "miniature community election meeting" in a nearby field. Strikers at Hartwell Brothers, an old Memphis firm now under Chicago ownership, likewise selected delegates after walking off their jobs. The adoption of similar tactics in each strike created temporary union organizations.[30]

In general, however, striking workers won only tiny wage increments and remained extremely vulnerable. Black women workers, the lowest paid and least secure, faced especially ominous threats. Forest Products Chemical Company managers warned the women charcoal workers that the plant would be closed if they did not return to work, while the Memphis Pecan and Walnut Company threatened to "distribute out work to charitable organizations" if the women refused to end their strike. Memphis Furniture workers had already lost their Carpenter and Joiners Union local a year earlier after union advocates were discharged from their jobs. Even where there were tiny wage victories, pay scales that allocated different rates to blacks and whites remained in place, with strikers at this point incorporating racial differentials into their demands.[31]

On the docks, African American workers' efforts to define their own form of unionism became a central feature of labor activism. Between 1937 and 1939, black ILA members resisted pressure by the Memphis Trades and Labor Council to place their local under its direction. Such conflicts came to a head during coordinated strikes by black ILA members and white members of the CIO-affiliated International Boatmen's Association, in concert with strikes in other ports. ILA leader Tom Watkins refused the intervention of council president Lev Loring, including efforts to end the strike, thus raising the specter of a full-fledged biracial union movement. In May 1939, police officers arrested and attempted to kill Watkins. His remarkable escape by leaping into the river made it possible for him to tell the story to FBI agents, fellow unionists, and community members before fleeing Memphis for St. Louis. Nevertheless, Loring took control of the direction of the ILA local with Watkins's departure.[32]

Conflicts with the Crump Machine

These labor struggles and related problems exasperated existing tensions among white Memphis elites and among blacks, as well as between the races, when it came to relations with the Crump machine. For Mayor Watkins Overton and Crump officials, maintaining low wages and keeping the CIO out of major industrial plants appeared vital to attracting new industrial concerns at a time when the CIO was rocking northern cities with sit-down strikes.[33] On the other hand, Edward Meeman, editor of the *Memphis Press-Scimitar*, one of two daily newspapers in town, threw his support behind federal wage and hours policies and, like President Roosevelt, perceived unionization as a stabilizing factor in industry. The newspaper ran a series of critical exposés of southern municipalities that had welcomed sweatshop industries, thereby providing jobs but also lower standards for local workers.[34] Meeman stopped short of endorsing CIO sit-down strikes but celebrated the Wagner Act as a promise of a more stable business climate. A 1937 *Press-Scimitar* editorial applauded Roosevelt's labor policies, arguing that they would "take the place of the costly anarchy that has reigned in management-labor relations for so many years."[35]

These rifts among white elites deepened when CIO organizers appeared in Memphis to sign up white workers at Ford and Fisher Body in September 1937. Mayor Overton blasted them as "imported CIO agitators, Communists and highly paid professional organizers." "They will not be tolerated," he declared. "Their tools are violence, threats, sitdown strikes, destruction. They demand the American workers to submit or starve. They seek strife and conflict." Public Safety commissioner Clifford Davis added ominously that he was familiar with UAW organizer Norman Smith and would "take care of that situation very soon."[36] The brutal beatings two days later of Smith and Charles Phillips, a former Ford worker, prompted widespread outcry. The *Press-Scimitar* denounced Overton's statement as a violation of the Constitution, and the Memphis Ministerial Association declared its support for workers' rights to form unions.[37] Nationally, organizations such as the American Civil Liberties Union, the Non-Partisan League, the National Committee for People's Rights, the UAW, and the CIO demanded an investigation by the U.S. Justice Department. Norman Smith testified before the LaFollette Senate Committee on Civil Liberties.[38]

Just three days after the Smith and Phillips beatings, the CIO's presence in the city deepened when the STFU formally affiliated with the labor confederation. At the STFU convention, 400 delegates representing thousands of members, over 80 percent of whom were black, and the rest Anglo, Mexican, or Indian, voted to merge with the United Cannery, Agricultural, Packing and Allied Workers of America (UCAPAWA-CIO). This multiracial labor movement gave "the city fathers a slight headache," stated one attendee gleefully in a letter to Thurgood Marshall at the NAACP. Prentice Thomas, a recent Fisk University graduate working with the union, described the convention to Marshall as "the most colorful thing that I have ever witnessed." Noting the green, white, and red union banners, he speculated that the "red might or might not have had a significance." Slogans on the walls included: "All power to the Southern Tenant Farmers' Union"; "To the disinherited belongs the future"; "End peonage in the South"; and "The land is the common heritage of the people." "[T]o say that a social change is taking place in the south," Thomas concluded, "is putting the case very mildly." Another letter from Thomas asserted that disputes between Crump and his rivals in the Tennessee statehouse in Nashville made this period an auspicious one in which to make demands on behalf of black workers, but he warned that the NAACP was not prepared for such a struggle.[39]

As labor concerns grew more pressing, the problems of race, power, and identity at the core of such struggles were also addressed in other realms of everyday life. Memphis's racial geography literally changed as a result of city officials' use of federal slum clearance and public housing funds to redesign public space. A WPA study of Memphis's housing situation made clear the dire need for new homes, particularly for black Memphians, 77 percent of whom lived in shacks that inspectors deemed substandard and lacking indoor plumbing. The opening of the city's first public housing projects, Lauderdale Courts (1938) and Lamar Terrace (1940), designated for whites, and Dixie Homes (1938), William H. Foote Homes (1940), and LeMoyne Gardens (1941) for blacks turned so-called gray zones (mixed neighborhoods) into racially segregated areas. Families who moved into these projects were offered a striking improvement on previous living situations. However, when the city cleared "blighted" areas, in some cases they razed black middle-class housing, destroying stable black neighborhoods.[40]

Blatant police harassment and brutality, used by the Crump machine to enforce white domination and labor compliance, evoked more public criticism than perhaps any other issue in the late 1930s. Utillus Phillips, a railroad postal worker who headed the Memphis NAACP beginning in 1939, wrote to U.S. Attorney General Frank Murphy that the police assault on ILA leader Tom Watkins was one of "numerous violations of the basic civil rights and liberties of Memphis citizens; aided and abetted by the city administration and the police force." Another writer told Murphy that three blacks had been "murder[ed] in cold blood ⁚ . . in the last eighteen months," and referred to the "murderous assaults and manhandling of innocent people; all for intimidation." National Committee for People's Rights investigator Laurent Frantz, who was sent to Memphis after the Smith and Phillips beatings, gave an account in his 1938 report, *People's Rights in Memphis*, of shooting incidents that occurred within a two-week period. In one, Sergeant A. O. Clark shot and killed mail carrier George Books after receiving a complaint from a white woman that "he had been annoying her." Clark was "exonerated by his superiors." Indeed, most brutality incidents ended with the police officer's exoneration and the victim's criminalization. Patrolman Roy Faught, for instance, was commended for his investigation of a robbery of a ham, cigars, and a radio from Kilpatrick Drug Store, during which he spotted two men along the railroad tracks and opened fire, killing one and wounding the other. By 1939, police violence in Memphis had attracted national attention from organizations like the Southern Conference for Human Welfare, the Southern Negro Youth Congress, and the NAACP.[41] Within the city, Crump's white moderate critics, such as *Press-Scimitar* editor Meeman, denounced police violence, not as racial liberals, but as opponents of the machine's abuse of power and obstruction of democracy. All told, in 1937 the *Press-Scimitar* reported the murder of two black men, seven shooting incidents in which black suspects were wounded, three of them critically, and six other instances of brutality against blacks.[42]

African American protest against police violence fueled the Crump machine's efforts to undermine independent black politics. During the 1938 election campaigns, prominent black Republican leader Robert Church Jr. urged voters to show their disapproval of police brutality by refusing to support Crump's gubernatorial candidate, Walter Chandler. As Ralph Bunche later described it, "Many Negroes stayed away from the polls and 'Mistuh' Crump did not pile up his usual huge majority in Shelby County."[43] In response, city officials cracked down on Church, whose major local and national stature in the Republican Party had earlier protected him. Having previously exempted him from paying taxes on his many real estate properties, now they insisted he pay up immediately. In 1939, while Church was out of town, city officials confiscated his properties and auctioned them off, a display no doubt intended not only for Church but for other African Americans as well. After Church relocated to Chicago, his mansion was torched, purportedly as part of a practice exercise for the fire department.[44]

Historical Tensions over Race and Politics in the Jim Crow Era

For black Memphians, tensions over how to respond to the Crump machine's combination of benevolence, police brutality, and enforcement of segregation had become a major political fault line among African Americans during the Jim Crow era. As early as 1905, outrage over a new state streetcar segregation law prompted conflicting responses. The influential Rev. Thomas O. Fuller entreated African Americans to respect the law and promote "the most peaceable conditions and the most perfect harmony and cooperation between the races that can be secured." Most black Memphians protested with their feet by avoiding the streetcars and walking, but Fuller's appeals resulted in thwarting the kind of formal boycott that took place in Nashville and Chattanooga. In contrast to Fuller's position, other prominent African Americans in the city demanded the statute's repeal. When Mary Morrison defied the law, for instance, black attorneys pursued the case all the way to the state supreme court, albeit unsuccessfully. Black women's organizations, among the most outspoken critics of the new law, established the City Federation of Women's Clubs to coordinate their work.[45]

Differences among prominent black Memphians, many with national reputations as business or religious leaders, deepened during the World War I era. Reverend Fuller, founder of the Inter-Racial League (an all-black organization) and the Industrial Settlement Home, and Rev. Sutton E. Griggs, organizer of the Public Welfare League, a National Urban League affiliate, won support from the Memphis Chamber of Commerce for their social welfare programs but came under fire from black contemporaries locally and nationally. Griggs, ironically, remains well known as a militant race novelist, based on works such as *The Hindered Hand*, a critique of Thomas Dixon's racist tract *The Leopard's Spot: A Romance of the White Man's Burden, 1865–1900* (1902). Far less discussed by literary scholars, however, is the fact that by 1913, when he moved to Memphis to pastor the Tabernacle Baptist Church, Griggs had radically altered his outlook, becoming an outspoken supporter of Booker T. Washington's conservative ideology of racial cooperation. Having become disillusioned by the weak sales of his books—which he believed showed the black masses' lack of potential for protest—and skeptical about white society's willingness to change, he sought a "mode of cooperation that could be followed in spite of the many unsettled and puzzling questions."[46] Griggs developed a social engineering uplift theory aimed at forging a "class of Negroes" that would secure white respect. Urging blacks to emulate whites, he elaborated an ideology of "social efficiency" that promoted "self-renunciation" on behalf of collective advancement. Black critics denounced Griggs for blaming racial subordination on black "social inefficiency" while presenting white southerners as their benefactors.[47]

Thomas O. Fuller likewise came of age in time to see reversals of many important gains of Reconstruction. A minister and Baptist school principal in North Carolina in the 1890s, Fuller was elected to the state senate in 1898. The last African American to win office in that body before disfranchisement ended black representation, he vowed, "I shall DEMAND nothing, but shall gently and earnestly PLEAD for a continuance of the sympathetic and friendly relations which have been the proud boast of us all."[48] Fuller moved to Memphis to pastor First Baptist Church in 1900, just eight years after the departure of journalist Ida B. Wells, following her scathing editorials denouncing the lynching of black men, including three close friends who had owned the People's Grocery in Memphis. After becoming principal of Howe Institute, he retained the religious and academic curriculum but added courses that prepared girls for household service and boys for skilled trades. A believer in both racial cooperation and race pride, Fuller later published a pictorial history of African Americans and tracts such as *Bridging the Racial Chasms: A Brief Survey of Inter-Racial Attitudes and Relations* (1937). In a 1922 column in the *Commercial Appeal* discussing the Great Migration, he assured white readers that "the negro . . . loves the south and its people." Because "the south need[s] strong, steady, dependable and efficient labor," he suggested, whites should address the social welfare problems that were convincing blacks to look for a "railroad ticket" to the North.[49]

Griggs and Fuller, like most black leaders in this period, espoused the idea that independent economic achievement formed the cornerstone of black advancement; however, other Memphis businessmen and professionals perceived it as a springboard for direct challenges to white supremacy. With the National Negro Business League's encouragement, entrepreneurs, including real estate magnate Robert Church Sr., Memphis's first black millionaire, established the Solvent Savings Bank and Trust in 1906, and funeral directors H. Wayman Wilkerson and J. Jay Scott founded the Fraternal Savings Bank four years later. Bert Roddy opened Roddy's Citizen Cooperative Stores, an independent grocery chain. Dr. Joseph E. Walker, founder of the Universal Life Insurance Company, along with Merah Stuart and Lt. George Lee, ranked among the South's leading black insurance executives. In 1916, a group led by the elder Church's son Robert R. Church Jr. — whose home would later by razed by the city — founded the Lincoln Republican League, drawing hundreds of participants to its meetings. The league challenged white domination of the Republican Party by registering thousands of African Americans, whose votes earned Church a seat at Republican conventions and, under Republican president Warren Harding, control over west Tennessee federal appointments. The league became a national organization and called for black voting rights, inclusion of blacks in labor unions, rights of black soldiers, antilynching legislation, and equal participation for women.[50]

This protest spirit also led prominent black Memphians in 1917 to found a branch of the NAACP, headed by Bert Roddy, which recruited over 1,000 members by 1919. Memphis became a base for NAACP investigations of racial violence in the Delta, and local members assisted groups starting NAACP branches.[51] Pursuing issues that concerned working-class blacks, the branch complained about police brutality, wartime vagrancy laws, and "Work or Fight" orders, especially after black women were placed in wartime laborer jobs considered men's jobs. The NAACP also became involved when black railroad switchmen, members of the Association of Colored Railway Trainmen, tried to prevent the white trainmen's union from having them fired. After a period of low activity and plunging membership in the early 1920s, the branch was reorganized in 1923 by Mrs. Wayman Wilkerson and other prominent women activists.[52]

Working-class African Americans' northern migration provoked conflict among black leaders. From 1916 through the 1920s, black Memphians rejected southern life and purchased railroad tickets to go north, even as other black southerners moved from farms and small towns into Memphis. Like Fuller, Griggs insisted that the destiny of "the race" lay in the South and assisted white employers in efforts to keep black laborers there. In contrast, Memphis NAACP president Bert Roddy declared that "every man, white or black, should determine where he should live."[53]

At the same time, a resurgence of the Ku Klux Klan in the early 1920s forced Memphians to take positions on another challenge to existing relations of race, religion, and class. Between 1921 and 1923, local Klan membership soared to an estimated 10,000, as audiences responded to invective against blacks, Catholics, Jews, and foreigners. The strongest Klan support came from lower-middle-class white neighborhoods bordering black communities. Many white business and political leaders, including Crump, perceived the Klan as a threat to economic stability and growth. As a means to prevent a Klan victory in the 1923 municipal elections, Crump backed incumbent Mayor Rowlett Paine, who had no affiliation with his machine. Paine's campaign promises to African Americans also won black support, helping him clinch the election.[54]

The 1927 mayoral election, however, illuminated the potential and the limitations of black political power. Disgusted with Mayor Paine's reneging on his campaign promises, and embittered over his choice to locate an incinerator in close proximity to Booker T. Washington High School and LaRose Grammar School, black leaders opposed his reelection. Twenty-five prominent African Americans, including women's club leaders Laura Jackson and Annie Brown, issued a call for a convention in June 1927 at Beale Avenue Baptist Church. Convention participants founded the West Tennessee Civic and Political League, headed by Lt. George Lee, and established chapters in every heavily black ward, more than tripling black voter registration from 3,500 to 11,000. The league endorsed Watkins Overton, a member of one of Memphis's founding families, who was also backed by Crump. In response, Paine resorted to virulent race-baiting against Overton, prompting the latter to declare that he was "opposed to Negro police, Negro firemen and general admission to the white parks." The league maintained its endorsement but, in doing so, not only compromised its principles but helped Crump consolidate power.[55]

This pressure forced into the open long-brewing tensions among African American leaders, exposing different political philosophies regarding black advancement in the age of Jim Crow. Sutton Griggs publicly blasted the West Tennessee Civic and Political League, declaring that it was "laying the foundation of a race riot." Griggs and Lee sparred at a National Negro Insurance Association meeting after Griggs urged the body to lecture at churches against black criminal behavior. Lee leaped to the floor to deride the proposal as "repulsive," charging that it would convey to African Americans that they were from an inferior, criminal race. Instead, Lee argued, the association should be targeting injustices by white society that led to black homicides.[56]

For Lee, who was attuned to broader black intellectual debates of the 1920s, these disputes were central to contemporary conflicts over how to address the so-called Negro Problem. Writing for the black journal *The Messenger* in 1925, Lee asserted that whites in west Tennessee "do not use shot gun methods to make the Negro docile and servile workmen" but "control the Negro's thought and progress" more insidiously, "by elevating and holding up as examples . . . the so-called best Negro Leaders." "This is a new day that calls for a new deal," he concluded. The "white man with mental reservations that made his father master — the Negro with mental reservations, that made his father the slave, must be banished from the seats of thought control." This perception of the ongoing hold of "mental reservations," rooted in the master/slave relation, shaped Lee's ideas. In the *Baltimore Afro-American*, Lee railed against "Apostles of peace at any price," who promoted "compromise in our racial adjustment programs," making promises about the "other world" while failing to critique "the hell of the world in which we now live." He called for "aggressive and two-fisted" leaders "that will contend, contend, contend."[57]

However, Lee also declared that African Americans faced a second leadership problem: the need "to force consciousness down the throat of the Negro," a perspective not wholly unlike Griggs's.[58] The advancement of the race, Lee argued, had been slowed by "the Negro's unwillingness to accept and follow qualified and talented leaders." Lee publicly disagreed with renowned black historian Carter G. Woodson, who, in Lee's view, had "missed the mark by crediting the uneducated Negro with progress for the race." Lee's dispute with Woodson revolved around W. E. B. Du Bois's concept of a "talented tenth" of educated African Americans who would achieve progress and lead the masses. Whereas Woodson was critiquing members of the "talented tenth" for increasing their distance from the masses, Lee blamed the masses for not following their leaders.[59]

Robert Church, Lt. Lee, and other members of Memphis's African American civic-business elite ultimately lost political ground during the Depression and the New Deal era. The collapse of the city's black-owned business economy increased the political gap between Memphis's black leaders and working-class African Americans. Even before the onset of the Great Depression, the demise of the Fraternal and Solvent Savings Bank (created by the merger of the Solvent and Fraternal Savings banks) in 1927 left the angry black depositors who had placed their meager savings in the bank wary of these "race men" and their calls to "buy black."[60] As business elites lost credibility, working-class African Americans began finding new organized outlets through which to protest inequality. Moreover, black popular enthusiasm for the Republican Party was dampened as early as 1928 by Herbert Hoover's coldness to the "black-and-tans," Church's faction, in favor of the "lily-whites" in his party. Roosevelt's apparent concern for ordinary Americans fueled black support for the Democrats in the 1930s, at least in national elections. With the ascension of a Democrat to the White House, Robert Church and the black-and-tan Republicans lost control of federal patronage positions. Even Church's move to show some black electoral muscle in the 1938 elections by opposing police brutality belied growing weakness in his faction. This loss of influence left Church and his cohort vulnerable to attack by the Crump machine.[61]

The Memphis "Reign of Terror"

The multifaceted conflicts brewing during the 1930s exploded in the fall of 1940, in a months-long racial and political crisis that national civil liberties and civil rights organizations referred to as the Memphis "reign of terror." Although media attention at the time focused on the Crump machine's harassment of African American Republican leaders, working-class black Memphians were equally concerned with police abuse of ordinary citizens, especially recent migrants, and efforts to crush the CIO. The "reign of terror" was neither singular in objective nor monocausal in origin but represented a complicated reaction to the upheaval of the New Deal. In addition to inspiring fear, the 1940 police harassment campaign spurred other responses, including new voices of opposition that would grow in significance during the war.

Just days before the 1940 national elections, Public Safety commissioner Joseph Boyle ordered police surveillance and customer searches at Dr. J. B. Martin's South Memphis Drug Company and Elmer Atkinson's Beale Street establishment, which included a café, taxi stand, and pool hall. This harassment continued for six weeks, after which police maintained a regular watch outside the two sites. Martin and Atkinson's businesses served as social and political hubs for African Americans, with Martin's drug store, which doubled as a U.S. postal substation, representing a particularly prominent symbol of achievement. Martin, the leading black Republican in the wake of Church's departure, served as chairman of the local black Republican committee. In this position, he led the campaign for presidential candidate Wendell Willkie, who had publicly denounced machine bosses who supported Roosevelt, including Crump, by likening them to Hitler. Owner of the Memphis Red Sox, a pillar of Negro League

Baseball, and president of the American Negro Baseball Association, Martin until now had been on cordial terms with the Crump machine, as evidenced by his patronage position as a bail bondsman.[62]

Boyle declared this harassment part of his clean-up campaign aimed at driving out gambling, prostitution, and drinking establishments and accused Martin and Atkinson of being "dope peddlers," although he failed to provide evidence. A year before the 1939 repeal of state prohibition, Crump had begun to shut down the red-light district, anticipating that legalizing alcohol would eliminate a lucrative source of funds. A Senate investigation had also brought considerable negative attention to the Crump organization's reliance on payments from the "underworld." Despite Boyle's claims to the contrary, Martin declared that Boyle's actions were political and that harassment had begun when Martin failed to comply with an order to cancel a Willkie rally on October 28. He also reported being pressured to resign from the Willkie campaign and shut down its headquarters. Similarly, Nashville civil rights attorney Z. Alexander Looby, arguing for Atkinson in a lawsuit, insisted that he had committed no "unlawful acts." Instead, he argued, Atkinson's affiliation "with a political party opposite to that of [Boyle and the police officers]" motivated police to disrupt and eventually destroy his business.[63]

In a public statement sent to the *Memphis Commercial Appeal*, a daily newspaper, Boyle identified Martin as an advocate of "social equality" who sought to undermine "friendly relations" between the races by fomenting black hatred of whites. "Dr. J. B. Martin and his wife went out to Barnum & Bailey Circus," he declared, "and being of light color bought tickets and sat in the seats reserved for white people. He gloated over this social equality." Beyond attacking Martin, Boyle also derided nonsubservient attitudes among "a young element of the negroes," arguing that this "element" had "become insolent, reaching a point where their restraint is necessary." "This is a white man's country," he declared, ordering any African American who disagreed to "move on." Mayor Walter Chandler declared publicly that "the commission is wholeheartedly behind Joe Boyle," while Public Service commissioner Robert Fredericks announced that the Willkie campaign would have to remove a banner spanning Beale Street that read "Our Own Joe Louis Is for Willkie," because it constituted a public figure making a political endorsement.[64]

Boyle's police harassment campaign not only targeted election-related activity and African American leaders. In mid-November, Boyle announced intentions to clear the city of "undesirables" and launched a series of raids on cafés and saloons on Beale Street and in other black neighborhoods.

The raids netted scores of black men accused of carrying knives and being "suspicious persons," with sixty-five arrested the first night. To Collins George, NAACP adviser at LeMoyne College, these raids were designed to intimidate: "Police enter any Negro café or pool-room at any time, force the patrons to raise their hands, then proceed to paw over them, male and female, searching for God-knows-what!" They also used "vulgar and abusive language" and arrested anyone who talked back. In addition, "any Negro on the street at any time, day or night, is liable to search and insult and in many, many cases physical injury."[65]

Boyle accused individuals arrested in these raids of idleness, insolence, and vagrancy, asserting that "every honest colored man and woman in Memphis would be glad to see [those arrested] do some honest work or be driven out." In early October, city officials had begun complaining about the low turnout for the cotton harvest. The *Commercial Appeal* declared that it was time "to scan the relief lists and for the police to check on the consistent nonworkers," urging officials to visit locales "notorious as places for consistent idling." In December, Boyle made clear that the city would be a hostile place for black migrants who did not want to do agricultural labor, declaring that those hoping to find jobs in the defense industry should return to the fields, "for there isn't enough work for the unskilled labor in Memphis." Migrants, therefore, were depicted as pariahs unless they surrendered to the farm labor roundup.[66]

Simultaneously, city officials attempted to maintain control of labor activism at Firestone, where the workforce included substantial numbers of African Americans supportive of the CIO. Earlier in 1940, efforts by white United Rubber Workers organizer George Bass and others to establish a CIO beachhead at Firestone had been met with violence, with Bass mobbed by white workers. The AFL rubber workers union, endorsed by the Crump machine, initiated a parallel union drive, winning support from white workers through race-baiting tactics. The AFL emerged victorious from elections held in late December, with votes split along racial lines, 1,008 for the AFL and 805 for the CIO. Red-baiting had also become central to the Firestone struggle. A couple of weeks before the vote, in a speech in Nashville, Texas congressman Martin Dies, head of the House Special Committee on Un-American Activities, warned that subversives, including CIO leaders, were trying to drum up black support by fomenting racial hatred. Besides adding to the animosity at Firestone, Dies's statement bolstered the "reign of terror" by encouraging city officials and even the *Commercial Appeal* to justify the police crackdown as necessary to thwart race warfare and Communism.[67]

From outside the city, national civil rights and civil liberties organizations urged President Roosevelt and the U.S. Justice Department to intervene in the "terror" in Memphis. The Southern Conference for Human Welfare warned Roosevelt that the Memphis administration was "seeking to establish 'an efficient dictatorship' which could be used as a pattern to undermine democracy in other parts of the United States, especially in the South." The Southern Negro Youth Congress, the American Civil Liberties Union, the National Federation for Constitutional Liberties, and the NAACP also contacted federal authorities. Attorney General Robert Jackson finally sent Special Assistant Col. Amos Woodcock to Memphis in early January 1941 to investigate their allegations against the Crump organization; however, Woodcock talked to only a few individuals, including Boyle, and concluded that he could not prosecute the case in federal courts.[68]

In Memphis, some whites publicly opposed Boyle's tactics.[69] The Memphis Commission on Interracial Co-operation (MCIC), organized earlier in 1940 and affiliated with the much older Atlanta-based CIC, charged the police department with creating a "state of tension and fear unprecedented in the recent history of our city" through indiscriminate searches of black citizens, including children. The MCIC called upon the mayor to have any individuals guilty of crimes so charged, and to cease all harassment. In a vituperative response, Boyle declared that white MCIC members must be unaware of the type of black men with whom they were consorting, including newspaper editors associated with the MCIC who opposed white supremacy. Only after the MCIC announced plans for a mass interracial meeting, keynoted by national CIC leader Will Alexander, did Chandler and Boyle agree to meet with white MCIC representatives, but they insisted on excluding black members.[70]

Efforts by Crump's white opponents to have the state's poll tax abolished added to these tensions. These moderates steered clear of the racial significance of the proposal, instead focusing on issues of corruption and elitism evoked by the poll tax. Edward Meeman and the *Press-Scimitar*, for example, called for extension of full constitutional liberties to all the state's adults, 73 percent of whom had not voted in 1940. In early 1941, however, repeal bills were crushed in both chambers of the state legislature, with Crump henchmen arriving in Nashville shortly before the votes took place to engineer the Democrats' efforts to halt the bills.[71]

Crisis of Black Leadership

The "reign of terror" created a more immediate crisis for Memphis's black leaders, forcing them to redefine their relations to the Crump machine, on the one hand, and their constituencies, on the other. Just prior to the election, but after the "reign of terror" had begun, Mayor Chandler tested the loyalty of an array of black ministers and enlisted their help in ensuring that their constituencies voted the straight Democratic ticket in the November 5th election. Assisted by black Democrats, he had letters hand delivered to prominent African American ministers, attaching a list of the Memphis City Commission's projects benefiting black Memphians. Responses to Chandler's letter clarified who could be counted on to remain loyal while isolating those who articulated independence. Their statements illuminate changed understandings of the obligations of black leadership, a decade and a half after Lt. Lee and Sutton Griggs sparred over this issue.

At least nine ministers replied to the mayor's letter. Although their words no doubt were guarded, much can be gleaned from their letters to Chandler. Most expressed their fidelity to the Crump machine while also asserting their authority in relation to their congregations. Rev. J. H. Johnson, pastor of two Baptist churches in south Memphis, assured Chandler that he would help ensure the city administration's success, since to do otherwise would be self-defeating: "I think I would be an ingrate, to turn against the one who has meant so much to me, as far as my lively-hood [sic] and existence is concerned [sic]." Rev. W. C. Paine, pastor at Smother's Chapel Methodist Church in north Memphis, declared that he was urging church members to vote "the straight Democratic Ticket."[72] These ministers sharply distanced themselves from the black leaders under attack. Johnson asserted that to "[t]hose who are trying to stir racial hatred," he would "say as Jesus 'forgive them for they know not what they do.'" Rev. W. H. Winston, pastor of the Seventh Day Adventist church, stated that he stood "ready one-hundred per cent to carry out your sincere desire and instructions along the line of better feelings between the races." Rev. Arthur W. Womack and Rev. W. A. Johnson, ministers at Colored Methodist Episcopal churches with more elite memberships, assured Chandler of their congregations' loyalty, "in every sense of the word."[73]

Through their letters and other kinds of responses to Crump, key community leaders who were allied with the machine revealed the ambiguities of their positions, wedged between their constituencies and the machine. Blair Hunt, T. O. Fuller, and Dr. J. E. Walker, all close Crump allies, visited his office in an unsuccessful effort to convince him to end harassment of Martin and Atkinson. Hunt, pastor at the prestigious Mississippi Boulevard Christian Church and principal of Booker T. Washington High School, exclaimed in his written response to Mayor Chandler's letter, "Mr. Crump is almost a human idol to us" and asserted that black Memphians "do not condone crime" and "appreciate the clean-up efforts of Mr. Boyle." However, he stated that many African Americans were "thinking that the time was inopportune to police the two places." Dr. Walker's colleague at Universal Life, Merah S. Stuart, similarly restated his loyalty but expressed concern about the targeting of black businesses that had become treasured symbols of black advancement.[74] Reverend Fuller, on the other hand, not only proclaimed his sympathy with the administration but publicly declared himself an opponent of any "fifth columnist" and an enemy of idleness, a response to Boyle's statements about "vagrants" in Memphis. "Work," he declared, "is the answer to subversive propaganda." Fuller announced plans for a "Children's Loyalty Demonstration," which would include "patriotic songs and recitations" and instructions for saluting the flag.[75]

Lt. Lee, a leading Republican and colleague of Robert Church, had to choose between protesting the attacks on Church, Martin, and Atkinson and strengthening his ties with Crump. Opting for the latter, he engineered a display of allegiance to the machine at the annual Blues Bowl festival and football game between champion black high school teams in Memphis and Mississippi, at which "father of the blues" W. C. Handy played his famous "Memphis Blues." Lee invited Mayor Chandler as keynote speaker and Crump as honored guest and staged a parade at which black city employees of different city departments provided corporeal evidence of the machine's support for black Memphians. Yet Lee's own speech called for an end to "blind prejudice," declaring that only then would the world recognize the immortality of Handy's works, which would "live when the embattlements constructed by Mr. Hitler shall have crumbled to dust."[76]

In contrast to such ambivalence among these prominent Crump allies, Rev. George A. Long, minister at Beale Avenue Baptist Church, reasserted his autonomy in his response to Chandler's letter. Expressing gratitude for municipal benefits designed for African Americans, he nevertheless declared, "We should [not] be unman[n]ed because of these kindnesses." Manhood, in his view, was staked to black citizenship rights: "You do not want to deprive the Colored citizens . . . of the rights of citizens because of what has been done and what you plan to do for them in Memphis and Shelby County," Long declared. "I have spoken out for what I think is right," he insisted, "forgetting [sic] not that there was and is an unseen Judge, to whom I must give an account." When Boyle later named Long as one of a few "discontented colored preachers" who "object to white supremacy," Long wrote the Commercial Appeal, insisting, "[I will] continue as I have and leave the results in the hands of God."[77]

In addition to Reverend Long's public voice of dissent, another expression of protest emerged among students at LeMoyne College, who, frustrated with the quiescence of the adult Memphis NAACP branch, organized a NAACP youth council in response to the "reign of terror." In October, before the police harassment campaign began, NAACP membership secretary Daisy Lampkin's visit to Memphis prompted over seventy students to join. Support soared as the "reign of terror" began and spread to black neighborhoods, convincing students to apply for a charter in November. "A unity of Negro spirit arose from this occurrence," wrote president Daniel Dean Carter for the NAACP youth newsletter, noting that over 200 students had joined the council, supported by faculty advisers Collins George and Marguerite Bicknell, a white civil rights activist.[78] Students lodged complaints with Chandler, Boyle, and Crump, asserting that police had violated the Bill of Rights and the Fourteenth Amendment and denouncing Boyle's assertion of white supremacy. In letters to federal postal officials, they accused police of interfering with Martin's postal substation. Students also collected affidavits from victims of police brutality for the National Federation for Constitutional Liberties and the NAACP.[79]

The LeMoyne activists argued that the Crump machine's goal was not so much to punish Martin and Atkinson as to assert authority over the city's black working-class population. Daniel Carter wrote NAACP special counsel Thurgood Marshall in January 1941 that although "individual persecution of Negroes" seemed to have abated, "the Negro mass has been terrorized to the extent that the police have had recently to deny a wide-spread rumor that Mr. Boyle had forbidden Negroes to wear high waisted pants and long coats." Carter referred to the "zoot suit" style popular among urban working-class black and Mexican American youth that had become emblematic of the rebellious, hipster persona.[80] Confirming this allegation, Collins George related an incident in which police stopped and beat a carful of students returning home from a nightclub. "The crux" of the "reign of terror" was not the violation of Martin's rights, George asserted, but the "hundreds of Negroes searched, insulted, and arrested for nothing at all during this period when Dr. Martin . . . was receiving all the publicity." In the face of this muscular assertion of white power, youth council members cast themselves as champions of ordinary black citizens, who, in Carter's words, were "in terror either of their jobs or their lives." Carter contrasted their group's efforts to Martin and Atkinson's flight, the adult NAACP's "lethargy," and the black press's retreat, while George described the council as a "large, growing working and militant group." As the

Black youths jitterbugging in a Memphis juke joint, November 1939.
*(Marion Post Wolcott photo, for Farm Security Administration,
courtesy of Library of Congress Prints & Photographs Division)*

United States edged toward war, however, the draft interrupted this activism, sending most black male students and faculty into the military.[81]

As these individuals and groups attempted to reconfigure the bounds of leadership, other struggles unfolded in a different register. Many working-class black Memphians, both longtime residents and newcomers, found ways, in addition to labor militancy, to display their opposition less formally. In south Memphis, indignant patrons of Martin's drug store responded to the police campaign by swelling its business. Police reacted by shifting from "patting pockets" to more intrusive searches, requiring adult customers to remove certain garments and shoes and searching children buying candy and ice cream to humiliate their parents and elders who could not protect them from these violations. Many patrons at the drug store and Atkinson's café refused to be searched or loudly complained about police treatment, which led to their arrest. Before being arrested, one man loudly announced, "[I'm] not going to stand for it anymore."[82]

Such individuals transformed the conflict between the Crump machine and Republican leaders into a face-off between black residents and the police. When police began riding city buses and arresting riders for not obeying Jim Crow laws, they were likewise met with resistance. Collins George recounted one incident in which police arrested a black man sitting in the last row for refusing to give up his seat to a white passenger, and then arrested a woman seated nearby after she exclaimed, "Lord what are we coming to!" Such occurrences suggested that the Memphis "terror" had impelled many to find public ways to express their dissatisfaction. The Crump machine's tactics created a climate not only of fear and compliance but also of assertiveness and resistance.[83]

Many migrants pressured to return to the farm refused to succumb despite their dire economic circumstances. As the defense industry pulled migrants to Memphis, city officials began pressing for changes in federal rules that would enable them to force relief applicants to accept jobs outside the county in which they resided. Administrators concerned with a shortage of cotton laborers sought to lure migrants back to the farm but found that black families spurned their offers, with women playing particularly assertive roles. Fifty percent of black relief applicants stated that they would accept only WPA work, the *Commercial Appeal* announced. According to a reporter, when one family with ten children was offered a farm job in Tunica, Mississippi, that provided a house, food, a pig, and some chickens, the wife, who was born and raised on a farm, rolled her eyes and declared, "[I] would rather starve than return to farm life." Officials argued that individuals like her were lazy and would end up permanent "reliefers."[84]

During the war, persistent struggles over these issues would take on new life. In a variety of labor conflicts, involving not only union organizing but also individual complaints filed with the mayor's office or the president's wartime Fair Employment Practice Committee (FEPC), working-class black Memphians, many of them recent arrivals from the rural plantation region, further challenged racial constructions that cast them as laborers and servants. Moreover, other areas of conflict that had emerged in the 1930s also broadened, from police brutality to movie censorship to public health crusades. The clashes over race and rights were not limited to one arena but encompassed myriad dimensions of urban life.

Where Would the Negro Women Apply for Work?

2

Wartime Clashes over Labor,
Gender, and Racial Justice

In a letter to Franklin Roosevelt, Altha Sims described a visit to the Memphis U.S. Employment Service (USES) office, where she was "coldly refused by a lady" who informed her that "there was not defense work for Negro woman." Written in July 1942, a year after the president, under pressure from African Americans, issued an executive order banning racial discrimination in war production industries and creating the FEPC, the letter asked him to confirm this information and explain "why there is no work for" black women, since the news "was hard to beleave coming from local authority." Sims wondered why black women would be barred from doing their "part to help win the war," even though her two grown sons would shortly be called to military service, leaving her with three children to support.[1]

In September, with her case still unresolved by the FEPC, Sims indignantly penned a second letter that exemplifies African American women's frustration with their seeming invisibility in the wartime economy. This time she wrote to Mayor Chandler, protesting being rejected when she responded to newspaper advertisements for defense workers, including one that proclaimed, "So Mother Can Do War Work," and another that called for black and white laborers. "I want a Job but I dont [want] no cook Job," Sims insisted, reporting that she had been informed there was "no Job for [her] but a skilet an pan." "Where would the Negro woman apply for work?" she asked. "I am verry anchous to no." Chandler's response would not have pleased her: "I know of no positions for unskilled colored women other than domestic work," he wrote, "and I imagine that is why [the welfare director] told you that he could not give you a place."[2]

Letters like the ones Sims sent to Roosevelt and Chandler provide a window into how working-class blacks in the urban South perceived their wartime struggles over labor and racial justice. Some of these stories have fallen through the cracks of histories of race and labor during the Second World War because they involve protests from outside unions. But these are the stories that fueled indignation among African Americans over black women's exclusion from the "Rosie the Riveter" wartime industrial defense jobs open to white women, and their restriction to private work as maids or to its public equivalent in government hospitals, military supply depots, and industrial laundries.[3] Black men were more likely to find employment in the defense industry, but their exclusion from most skilled positions elicited equally bitter responses.

Men and women's encounters with discrimination, despite the national emergency, paralleled concerns over segregation in the armed forces. Black workers seized on wartime discourse about democracy to demand the elimination of racist practices that prevented them from fulfilling American ideals of citizenship. What may previously have appeared as individual struggles that had little to do with vital matters of democracy and national unity now took on far different significance. With racial tension mounting in southern cities like Memphis, nationally prominent black leaders and the black press demanded "Double V"—victory over fascism abroad and racism at home. They insisted that world democracy could only be achieved if it were based on genuine freedom for African Americans and for people of color in colonized nations.

As these local struggles show, wartime clashes over race and labor in the urban South involved more than demanding that employers comply with the president's executive order against racial discrimination; they also involved redefining the social meaning of black and white manhood and womanhood. In the eyes of many black workers, exclusionary policies and racist job classifications perpetuated degrading racist views of blacks as servile and dependent. While women like Altha Sims refused to be pigeonholed as cooks and maids, men like Clarence Smith, a porter and floor sweeper at Firestone who wanted to work as a riveter, argued that they were as skilled, efficient, and intelligent as whites, as eager to advance, and as essential to the war effort. "What I really want is what a great portions of my race want," Smith wrote to the War Manpower Administration, "a chance to do something to help win this war and peace to come to every nation, to also win recognition in this our country, as citizens, human, and a important spoke in the wheel of progress."[4]

The unprecedented level of federal intervention in matters of labor had contradictory ramifications for wartime daily life. The federal government assumed oversight of major aspects of employment, from the assessment of labor needs to mediation in disputes between unions and employers. In the South, however, local USES officials and city administrators frequently worked closely with employers to perpetuate racist hiring practices. Conversely, the presence of FEPC investigators and War Labor Board mediators on the labor scene spurred many workers to protest racist practices and to view individual predicaments in light of greater issues of justice.

During the war, migrants flocked to urban centers across the South to work in the defense industry. White workers typically found it easier to locate skilled or semiskilled jobs in mass production factories than did African Americans. In Memphis, however, this imbalance was exasperated by the city's practice of shuttling African Americans across the Mississippi River for the cotton harvest. Black workers who did find jobs in the city toiled as unskilled laborers in mass production plants, or in cotton compresses, cottonseed oil mills, hardwood processing plants, laundries, or private domestic service.

To protest job discrimination, thousands of black Memphis workers joined unions, appealed for help from the FEPC and other federal officials, or sought assistance from black community leaders. However, the racial parameters of these struggles made them complex, since many black union members were at odds with white union leaders who impeded efforts to eliminate racist job classifications. Class tensions also surfaced among black Memphians. Most dramatically, Boss Crump's success in pressuring black leaders to cancel a mass labor rally featuring national labor and civil rights leader A. Philip Randolph, who was a well-known leader of the movement for desegregating the defense industry and the military, provoked a storm of controversy. Jumping into the fray, Randolph denounced black advocates of "racial harmony" as "well-kept slaves" and stressed that freedom, like justice, was unattainable without struggle. Public dramas such as the one involving Randolph called into question conciliatory attitudes toward segregation and the Crump machine.[5]

Few black laborers emerged victorious from wartime struggles to eliminate discrimination. However, their responses to racist wartime labor practices established a palpable climate of dissent that dovetailed with critical national and international debates about the future of democracy and freedom, not only abroad in the fight against fascism, but at home, in the struggle over racial justice.

Workers at a Memphis cotton compress moving a
bale that was just compressed, November 1939.

*(Marion Post Wolcott photo, for Farm Security Administration,
courtesy of Library of Congress Prints & Photographs Division)*

Memphis Defense Contractors
and Fair Employment Practice

A broad range of Memphis industries won government defense contracts
during the Second World War, prompting unprecedented employment
levels and a major expansion of mass production industries in the city. Between September 1942 and September 1943, the number of employees in
selected nonagricultural industries soared from 27,269 to 48,857, nearly
doubling.[6] Ford began manufacturing airplane engines; Fisher Body, a
General Motors subsidiary, transformed into an aircraft subassembly
plant; Firestone produced rubber rafts, army vehicle tires, and gas masks;
and Continental Can began turning out shell cases. Kimberly-Clark and
Quaker Oats opened new plants in Memphis during the war with lucrative
defense contracts. Manufacturing plants based on regional products also
boomed, as facilities such as Procter & Gamble's Buckeye cottonseed oil
plants, Plough, Inc., and National Fireworks began filling defense orders.
Newly built army and navy supply depots, Kennedy General Hospital, and
other military installations also became major wartime employers.[7]

As an "interstate labor market," the city absorbed thousands of workers from the area. The fact that white migrants could obtain defense jobs with relative ease made it more attractive for them to move to the city on a permanent basis.[8] African Americans had different experiences. "Paradoxically, a large number of Negroes who have moved into Memphis from the farms," the USES reported, "work in seasonal employment on the farms in the tri-state area within a 50-mile radius of Memphis." Among those black migrants who found jobs in Memphis plants, most wound up in unskilled labor or service jobs.[9]

Dissatisfaction among black workers helped fuel a massive unionization wave. Beginning in mid-1941, thousands of workers at lumber mills and woodworking plants, cotton compresses and cottonseed oil mills, joined CIO unions such as the UCAPAWA, and the International Woodworkers of America (IWA), the United Furniture Workers of America (UFWA), and the National Maritime Union (NMU). Simultaneously, employees in mass production plants also won union recognition, often for the first time. Between fall 1941 and spring 1942, workers at Ford and Fisher Body voted to join the UAW-CIO. At Firestone, a vote in April 1942 reversed the December 1940 vote in which the white majority had opted for the AFL over the CIO. All told, over 20,000 Memphis workers joined CIO unions between 1941 and 1945. The AFL, competing with the CIO, began reaching out to more workers, stepping outside its base among white skilled craftsmen to organize workplaces such as laundry–dry cleaning plants.[10]

In response to black workers' protests and under massive pressure from the March on Washington Movement (MOWM), President Roosevelt issued Executive Order 8802, which banned racial discrimination in the defense industry, on June 25, 1941, even before the United States officially entered the war. The MOWM, led by A. Philip Randolph and other civil rights leaders, had threatened to bring 10,000 African Americans—later increased to 100,000—to the nation's capitol on July 1, 1941, if Roosevelt failed to desegregate the defense industry and military. The executive order did not address segregation in the military and, in establishing the FEPC, created more of a scaffolding for vetting complaints than an agency that could mandate compliance. Nevertheless, defense contractors now had to sign a nondiscrimination provision and could be investigated by the FEPC.[11]

Noncompliance, however, remained rampant in Memphis and elsewhere. Most mass production plants that hired African American men confined them to unskilled and semiskilled jobs. In Memphis, major defense contractors hired thousands of white women yet nearly universally refused to hire black women. The number of white women in the industrial sector had nearly doubled by the midpoint of the war, rising from 16.6 percent of manufacturing jobs in September 1942 to 31.3 percent one year later. During this same year, white women employed at Firestone alone rose from 18.9 percent to 33.8 percent of the workforce or an increase of 5,752 workers.[12] Later in the war, Firestone opened a small number of jobs to black women but placed them in work wholly distinct from production jobs assigned to white women. Black women at Firestone toiled outdoors in a field sorting tires or indoors sweeping the plant, cleaning machines and restrooms, or throwing rubber in trays, according to worker Evelyn Bates. Elsewhere, the majority of black women continued to labor in service positions as maids and cooks, or in laundries, dry cleaners, hotels, and restaurants. Only in the low-wage, labor-intensive manufacturing sectors, such as cotton processing and woodworking, where African Americans made up a sizable portion, if not the majority, of the employees, did black women enter the workforce in more significant numbers, to replace black men entering the armed forces.[13]

During a May 1942 visit to Memphis, FEPC field examiner John Beecher and Office of Production Management (OPM) investigator Cy Record documented egregious violations of the president's executive order.[14] At Firestone, black men comprised about a quarter of the workforce in 1942, but few held production jobs. The company planned to employ white women to produce gas masks; however, personnel manager Cliff Reynolds flatly stated that he could not hire black women to work in the same plant with white men or white women, adding that, in any case, the plant had no toilet or bathing facilities for black women.[15] Similarly, Fisher Aircraft had hired 700 white women as riveters and expected to employ more but had no plans to hire black women. In addition, after the company's conversion from auto body production, management had failed to rehire 166 (15 percent) of its black workers, including many with long service records, claiming that they were too old or could not be trained for complicated jobs. Workers, however, insisted that many of those laid off had histories of union support. While touring the plant, Beecher and Record observed black men doing jobs they believed were as complex as those performed by white women riveters, but for lower pay at lesser classifications.[16]

Ordnance plants in the area hired only a few African Americans. Chickasaw Ordnance Works in Millington, operated by DuPont, produced gunpowder under government contract. The plant employed a labor force of 3,000, only 45 of whom were African Americans, working in janitorial, laundry, or garage positions. At National Fireworks Company in Cordova, which produced ammunition, the workforce of 629 included 16 blacks, who worked as porters and maids. Chickasaw expected to begin employing white women, while National Fireworks anticipated expanding its white female workforce from one-half to two-thirds of the total. Neither plant had plans to hire more African Americans. OPM investigator Record described National Fireworks's policies as the "most brazen and bare-faced violations of contract provision and national policy" he had seen and characterized Chickasaw's practices as a "gross and systematic discrimination on account of race." After visiting the plants, he wondered whether "Tennessee [was] still a part of the United States and subject to the national policy as outlined by the President."[17]

At National Fireworks, a Massachusetts-based company, General Manager E. H. Luce claimed that when the plant operated in Memphis, before moving to Cordova, it employed only African Americans, including women, but his new policy reflected the concerns of the Cordova Civic Club, an organization of businessmen-landowners who insisted that the company not "disturb the Negro supply of farm labor." Luce invoked a panoply of racial stereotypes to further explain his policy. "He is under the impression that Negroes of the area are largely infected with venereal diseases," Beecher reported, "and says that persons who have had such diseases are very allergic to the high explosive tetryl which is used in loading shells. He says, however, that he considered the use of Negroes as operators of tetryl because this is very laborious work which Negroes can perform better than whites on account of the fact that they can stand hot weather better. This plan was dropped, however, when the company's attorney advised against it, since white women were employed in the same room, and some sort of sexual outbreak might be feared."[18] Luce presented himself as a victim of circumstances rather than a violator of the president's orders, forced to exclude blacks by local leaders who used these supposed physiological differences between the races to claim blacks as field hands.

The Crump Machine and the USES

The "flagrant examples" of discrimination the FEPC examiners encountered in Memphis roughly mirrored those they found throughout the Deep South; however, in Memphis, the direct intervention by public officials on behalf of employers was more extreme than in other cities, and it frequently took the form of intimidation.[19] Officials also influenced appointees to local offices of such powerful federal agencies as the USES.

The 1940 "reign of terror" and events leading up to it had taken their toll on black leaders, according to John Beecher and Cy Record. During their May 1942 trip, they learned that organizations such as the Community Welfare League would not be sending representatives to regional FEPC hearings in Birmingham in July, due to concerns about the "intimidation and terrorism practiced by the Crump machine." Beecher and Record reported that L. J. Searcy, executive secretary of the Community Welfare League, and Louis Swingler, editor of the *Memphis World*, felt they were "in no position to act because of the positions they hold and because of the real possibility of actual physical violence to their persons if they made the effort." Memories of how police officials had crushed the league's efforts to help black skilled workers in 1939 still concerned Searcy.[20] FEPC officials determined that the CIO offered the strongest force against racial injustice. However, they felt that because the CIO had limitations on what it could accomplish, even a small number of outspoken black leaders, willing to risk the consequences, could make an enormous difference. Significantly, they did not comment on the NAACP. The membership of the local branch rose during the war, with a campaign in spring 1943 netting 1,541 new members; however, not until the end of the war did the organization play a major role in working-class leadership when its involvement in police brutality struggles attracted thousands more working-class members.[21]

Officials representing Crump's Memphis and Shelby County Democratic machine pressured corporate employers who were not indigenous to the region to adhere to local employment practices. In June 1943, for example, Mayor Chandler sent welfare administrator Aubrey Clapp to chat with local Ford manager M. C. Boone about the labor force Ford planned to hire upon completion of its conversion to defense production. Ford planned to pay its new employees, including white women, at the highest wage scale of any Memphis plant. Clapp reported that he had "discussed the negro women situation thoroughly" and learned that "we have nothing to fear from this source of anticipated trouble." Boone had confided that "pressure has been brought to bear to put negro women to work but that under no circumstances or conditions would it be sanctioned or allowed."[22] Ford's Memphis approach differed from its practice in Dearborn, Michigan, where the company hired black women, although even there it placed them in the least desirable jobs.

Crump allies in Washington also intervened with wartime federal labor mediators. Senator Kenneth McKellar and Congressman Clifford Davis, for instance, contacted U.S. Department of Conciliation director John Steelman on behalf of Memphis Furniture, which produced bomb racks, army beds, and lockers during the war and employed a majority black and female workforce. After the company refused for months to negotiate a contract with Local 282 of the UFWA and a federal mediator was assigned to the case, the company protested the mediator's apparent support for Local 282's request for union security through "maintenance of membership" and dues checkoff clauses in the union's contract. In a letter to Steelman, McKellar described Memphis Furniture as "one of the oldest concerns in Memphis," arguing that its owners were "high class, honorable men" whom he hoped would not be "black-jacked in this situation." Steelman assured him that the mediator was impartial and that union security was, as a rule, supported by the War Labor Board; ultimately, however, the union agreed to drop its request in exchange for a wage increase of four cents an hour.[23]

Similarly, in November 1943, Mayor Chandler attempted to stall an "adverse ruling" by the U.S. Conciliation Service involving complaints of discriminatory job classifications at Fisher Aircraft. Upon request from Chamber of Commerce president Phil Pidgeon, Chandler sought Congressman Davis's assistance. In a letter to Davis suggesting how to approach the issue, he warned that federal officials might not understand the South's problems. "Naturally, if wage differentials which have existed in the South because of the superior mental ability of the white worker are to be destroyed, I fear for the negro's welfare here," Chandler wrote. "He has kept his job because he has not competed with the white worker in character of work or rate of pay, and, when work is not so plentiful as it is now, he will be laid off indefinitely and become a charge on the public." "It is to the interest of the negro that some differential should exist," he concluded. "His rate of pay has increased very steadily in the last four or five years, and the present rate of progress should not be stepped up lest it destroy the negro's own advancement, and cause him to lose the gains that he has made. We must not let war extremities destroy our peace-time economy."[24] Chandler both presented white officials as guardians of African Americans and justified dual wage rates based on the presumed natural superiority of whites. He hoped it would take "a long time to decide this highly dangerous question." Davis did, in fact, speak to Steelman, reporting back that the latter had "shudder[ed] to think of the difficulties which we approach in connection with negro labor standards in the South." He believed that the case had been buried "on the bottom of a very heavy stack of pending matters," although that this was the case cannot be verified. Not until 1945 did the UAW win an agreement on Fisher job classifications.[25]

Because the USES handled work orders for defense contractors, the agency constituted another formidable force in wartime employment. FEPC examiners, called upon to scrutinize another federal agency, reported that southern USES offices engaged in discriminatory employment practices and that personnel refused to cooperate with investigations. In Tennessee, the USES's discriminatory practices were particularly egregious. Elsewhere in the South, with the exception of Jacksonville, Florida, USES managers divided their offices into "white" and "colored" areas with separate entrances. In Memphis, Nashville, Knoxville, and Chattanooga, however, the USES established black and white offices in entirely separate locations. Black job applicants in Memphis went to a location on South Second in the Beale Street area but were barred from entering an office on Union Avenue, in the downtown business district. By establishing different addresses, the local USES could separate work orders intended for whites from those slated for African Americans without using explicitly racist language in its on-site job listings or in advertisements. The result of this strategy differed little from the outcome of newspaper advertisements from private employers that explicitly advertised for "whites" or "colored." These practices assigned racial meaning to people, jobs, and urban geography itself.[26]

A complaint sent to the FEPC by George Townsel Sr., a tradesman skilled in drafting, tool designing, and metal machine operations, indicates that as late as November 1945, the USES was still infuriating black applicants by maintaining job descriptions for skilled workers at its Union Street office while advertising only for "common labor job[s]" at the South Second Street office. When Townsel refused to accept a laborer job, he found that his unemployment benefits were terminated. "[T]he law of the constitution of the United States give the commissioner of the state the rights [to s]ay a common labor job are suitable for you," he wrote, "and you have no right to say it is not suitable for you regardless of what your skill trade are, or how high you skilled trade are here." Townsel called upon the FEPC to investigate this troubling interpretation of states' rights.[27]

Black applicants also complained about USES staff. In 1942, directors of the Community Welfare League, Dr. J. E. Walker, M. S. Stuart, and M. W. Bonner, all successful insurance executives, protested the derogatory treatment of applicants, which, in the case of Louis Harold Twigg, whom they described as "a highly respected, well-educated young colored man who was born and reared in Memphis," had led to police brutality. Twigg had been beaten by police and arrested on orders of John Guinozzo, USES manager, after he complained to Guinozzo that he had been addressed "in an abrupt and humiliating manner." The men asserted that "harmonious relations" would best be served by replacing Guinozzo with a black manager. A year later, Benjamin Bell, the executive secretary of the Memphis Urban League (MUL), which emerged out of the Community

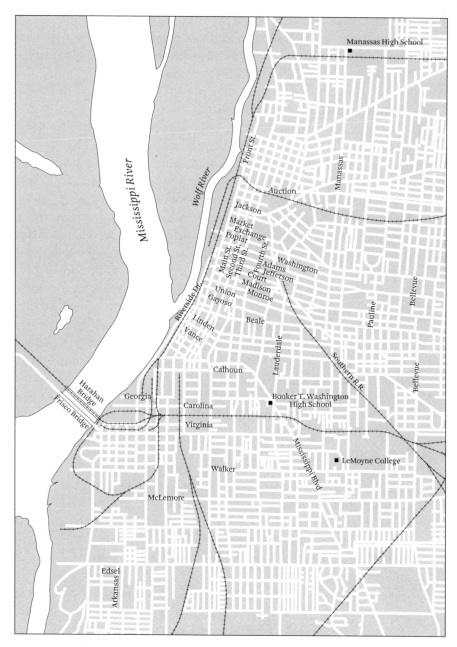

Downtown and Beale Street Area of Memphis

Welfare League, complained that the office was still under Guinozzo's supervision and "staffed for the most part with interviewers and Placement Secretaries who from their reactions are more prejudiced than some of the industrialists."[28]

Maids and Laundry Workers

As Altha Sims's letters showed, black women's exclusion from industrial defense jobs associated with popular images of "Rosie the Riveters" became a crucial focal point for dissent during the war. Many women tenaciously strived to locate jobs outside private households. And those who did find work outside households in the city's laundry and dry cleaning facilities, where African American women had labored in large numbers since the late nineteenth century, battled racist job classifications that slated black women for certain kinds of work and white women for others.

As black women strived to escape domestic service during the war, some white Memphians feared a genuine servant uprising. Congressman Clifford Davis reported to Mayor Chandler in 1942 that he had heard rumors about "Eleanor Clubs," alleged organizations of domestic workers, named after the First Lady, that purportedly urged black women to refuse to work in white women's kitchens. However, Davis declared that he had found no concrete evidence of organizing by black maids. "I really believe that a few citizens have so thoroughly worked themselves up over their antipathy to Mrs. Roosevelt, and the loss of cooks," Davis observed, "that they have been honestly mislead [sic] and are possibly responsible for the rumors."[29] The rumors persisted, however. In 1945, a white citizen wrote to the *Memphis World*, a black newspaper, condemning purported clubs scheming "to disappoint white women regarding maid service" and "Sidewalk Clubs" aimed at humiliating white women by forcing them off sidewalks. The potential "loss of cooks," he argued, threatened white women, southern traditions, and God's plan of determining people's natural places based on color.[30]

Letters to President Roosevelt and federal officials offer evidence of how African American women themselves perceived domestic service. Mrs. Ella Rose Dotson, who lived a few blocks from Altha Sims on Vance Avenue, first wrote President Roosevelt in October 1942, seeking help in getting a defense job. She continued to write to him for the next year and a half before she finally received a referral to a small Memphis plant. In a letter to the president in January 1943, she described visiting the USES offices, armed with a letter from the War Manpower Commission instructing her to apply for work with the agency. The letter was sent to her after she requested some kind of document from Roosevelt or a top federal official that would help her get a job. Dotson first went to the South Second Street location and then to the one on Union. At Union, she reported, she was sent back to South Second, but upon returning there, she wrote, "they didn't give me any work, only said they could give me white lady day work in their homes which they have alway gave me that but that is not defence work to help my country."[31] Dotson's letters prompted an FEPC investigation of local USES operations, which concluded that the agency did not provide duplicate copies of work orders that arrived in the "white" office on Union to the "colored" office on South Second, as required by federal guidelines.[32]

In her letters to the president, Dotson focused on her desire to work at Fisher Aircraft, Anderson Tulley Mill, or another plant, rather than clean private homes for five dollars a week, an amount so low she could not afford to buy a defense bond. Indeed, all her letters underscored her dedication to the war effort. "I have people who are sheading [sic] their blood for our country and god knows I should help," she wrote in January 1943, telling the president she had heard his radio address that morning and hoped God would care for him "until we are all safe again in our world of freedmen."[33] Yet Dotson's "world of freedmen" differed from that of USES and even some FEPC officials: In early 1944, Dotson received a referral for work outside private household service, but she turned it down. The job as a charwoman—the equivalent of a maid, but in a mill—would have required her to relocate to Knoxville, Tennessee. When FEPC regional official A. Bruce Hunt admonished her for not taking this job and reminded her that she was only qualified as a maid, Dotson wrote back describing the emotional pain his message had caused her: "Mr. Hunt, you will find me to state the truth about things of it hurt me, because it is the only way in life." Eventually, she was referred to a job in a small Memphis plant, likely as a result of her persistence. While federal officials considering Dotson's case suggested that black women who had been maids could only be maids in the future, Dotson and other women adamantly rejected this logic.[34]

It is not clear whether Memphis women who wrote such letters knew each other, but many resided within a few blocks of each other in south Memphis near Booker T. Washington High School, or in north Memphis near Manassas High School. Their shared language and interpretations of their experiences suggest that black working-class women traded stories about their job-hunting plights and together distilled their meanings. Mrs. Susie Brister, for instance, a neighbor of Dotson and Altha Sims, told Roosevelt she had a son registered for the draft yet had been barred from all jobs but private household work. "They have built a fence around the jobs here against Colored people, and if it's any way you can tear it down and let me into the work I would appreciate it," she wrote.[35] Margaret Jackson, another neighbor, objected to newspaper advertisements for war workers that turned out to apply only to white women. After being turned down from Firestone and Fisher in 1942, she wrote to Roosevelt, describing herself as "very bitter and disappointed this morning" after "a long hot tramp of trying to get work." "Our men have to go an fight as well as the white," she wrote. "I cannot understand why our men should fight for a country that starves their womenfolks. Any decent job the whites get them."[36] Angry at being excluded from a decent wage and the call to help defend democracy, some women seized upon formal complaint channels. A few won concessions. More commonly, women's informal conversations contributed to a climate of resistance inspired by the bitterness and disappointment evoked by their job searches.

Simultaneously, civilian laundries and those attached to military hospitals became sites of heated racial struggles. Jobs at these facilities combined the service tasks of domestic work with the arduousness of sweatshop labor and the management style of field gangs. However, such positions removed women from the personal oversight of individual white employers, and even the worst institutional pay rate was higher than the roughly five dollars a week that domestic workers made. Wartime federal oversight appeared to extend at least the possibility of new leverage to laundry workers, who had been exempted from minimum wage and maximum hour requirements established by the Fair Labor Standards Act (1938).[37]

Laundry workers at Kennedy General Hospital, which opened in late 1942 under the Army Service Forces Fourth Service Command, organized a protest against the discriminatory wage and classification system. Because two women employees later brought their concerns to the FEPC, we have available to us rich details of this struggle.[38] In December 1943, Gertrude Carter and Katie Hall, who worked as a team checking ironing presses and keeping track of finished items, circulated a petition requesting wage increases to other black employees, thirty-five of whom signed it. In response, the laundry manager, Albert Hattendorf Jr., called the black employees to his office and demanded to know who had initiated the petition, at which point several workers insisted they knew nothing about it. In contrast, Carter, while not confessing, declared that if Hattendorf wanted to know who wrote the petition, he could compare the handwriting to the signatures. Shortly thereafter, he called a meeting of all laundry employees, black and white, at which he pledged to secure a raise for them, and in April 1944, Mrs. Carter learned from white coworkers that they had received a pay increase. Meanwhile, the two women continued to be classified as press operators on flat piece work (ironing items such as sheets) — a job typically assigned to black women — for which they were paid a wage of 41 cents per hour, five cents less than what white women were paid for performing the same duties but with higher classifications. Indeed, FEPC examiner John Hope later confirmed that not a single job classification was shared by both black and white employees.

At a meeting in May of the black employees, Hattendorf declared they would get no raise. According to Thelma Mitchell, as well as other employees later interviewed by FEPC examiner John Hope, Hattendorf declared that they "weren't going to get a raise there and if they didn't like it they could get out." He also threatened to "get German prisoners for ten cents an hour" to replace them. Hattendorf concluded by calling for any employees who still felt dissatisfied to see him in his office. After Carter and Hall did so, they were fired. In their complaints to the FEPC, the women expressed ire at Hattendorf's demeaning treatment of black employees. Hall, for example, reported that black women were required to ask higher ranked white employees for permission to use the restrooms. Carter accused Hattendorf of using Kennedy employees as personal servants in his own home to prepare for evening parties.

Hope's investigation suggested that Hattendorf and Mr. Thorpe, the plant supervisor, valued Carter and Hall as efficient, conscientious employees who helped the laundry run smoothly, but since the women had asked for wage increases, they categorized them as, in Thorpe's words, "uppish niggers" who were hard to handle. As Hope put it, "The attitude of both Mr. Thorpe and Capt. Hattendorf toward the petition for a wage increase . . . was one of deep resentment that these workers should engage in direct concerted action to attain an objective." He added that since no union was involved, their attitude "reflects a Southern pattern with regard to Negro workers." All black workers received a raise from forty-one to fifty cents per hour after Carter and Hall were terminated, making it likely that the two women lost their jobs simply because they challenged Hattendorf's control.

Outside military facilities, many of the city's 3,000 laundry workers joined the Laundry Workers International Union, Local 263, an AFL affiliate, and struck during the war, in concert with organizing by laundry workers in other southern cities. The black and white women and men who labored in Memphis's largest laundries endured steamy, hot conditions, slippery floors, and unsanitary workrooms without chairs, drinking fountains, or adequate restrooms. Black women laundry workers, who generally ran the presses, received the lowest wages, averaging from twenty to twenty-eight cents an hour during the war. Those paid on a piecework basis pressed up to 500 shirts a day to earn the higher rates. In 1943, however, the federal government designated commercial laundry business as an essential war industry because it provided services to military camps. The designation increased the likelihood of government intervention in its labor disputes.[39]

Among African American women in the South, commercial laundries had long been a target of unionization and a site of racial contestation. Beginning in the late nineteenth century, such establishments began to replace the work of independent black laundresses; however, they became more prevalent during the early twentieth century.[40] During the First World War, a confrontation erupted in Little Rock, Arkansas, 200 miles west of Memphis, between the employees and managers of commercial laundries that served military bases, requiring extensive intervention by National War Labor Board officials.[41] Such conflicts took on racial parameters when African American women complained that they were paid less and treated worse than white women in comparable jobs. In New York, a major breakthrough occurred in the 1930s when tens of thousands of African American, Caribbean, and Puerto Rican laundry workers joined the United Laundry Workers, which became part of the Amalgamated Clothing Workers of America (CIO).[42] During the Second World War, thousands of women laundry workers in the South, most African American, joined unions.

In Memphis between 1941 and 1945, workers struck for union recognition at Crescent Laundry, Model Laundry-Cleaners, and Kraus Cleaners, each of which employed hundreds of workers. Even at Loeb's Laundry, the family business of Henry Loeb, who later gained notoriety as mayor during the 1968 sanitation strike, some 200 employees walked off their jobs in 1945, for the first time since the plant's opening in 1887. In some cases, white male drivers and black women seamstresses and pressers walked off their jobs together. At Kraus, for example, twenty-three drivers, members of the Teamsters and Chauffeurs Union, along with 183 black women members of the Laundry Workers International Union, struck for union recognition in July 1943. The National Labor Relations Board responded to these laundry strikes by ruling that service industries not involved with interstate commerce fell outside its jurisdiction; therefore, the Department of Labor's U.S. Conciliation Service stepped in to help avert or settle strikes and oversee union elections.[43]

In Memphis and other southern cities, such struggles took on significance that reached beyond plant walls. In poor, working-class black neighborhoods, the plight of workers who engaged in these struggles became well-known in their communities, symbolic of larger issues of racial injustice. In Miami, for example, when the Laundry Workers International Union threatened to trigger a general laundry strike in 1942, leaders warned that it would spread to the "general Negro population, who are acquainted with the situation" and experienced similar working conditions.[44] Similarly, in Atlanta, when 1,400 laundry workers struck for over a month in fall 1943, they held daily mass meetings at the Wheat Street Baptist Church and won support from the NAACP and the Interdenominational Ministerial Alliance.[45]

In Memphis, as in Atlanta, organizing by workers in several of the city's fourteen major laundries grabbed headlines in the black press, which reported in far more detail than did the white daily newspapers about the issues that had particularly embittered workers. Although the laundry strikes primarily addressed union recognition, wages, and working hours, participants also spoke out about other problems on the job, in an unusual public airing of complaints. Women interviewed by the *Memphis World* criticized Loeb's Laundry's practice of keeping them in the dark about weekly earnings until they received their pay envelopes. They also denounced the restriction of "vacation time" to Christmas and Independence Day. Perhaps most indicative of women laundry workers' complaints was a Kraus worker's comment during a mass meeting at Labor Temple that she "resented the fact that Kraus officials practiced the habit of searching their pocketbooks, as if they were suspects." Workers responded to her statement by pledging their "hundred percent" support for the union.[46]

Tensions over the portrayal of the woman laundry worker resonated beyond the immediate workforce, suggesting that the laundry worker had become iconic for working-class black women more generally.[47] In October 1942, the Memphis Negro Chamber of Commerce and its affiliate, the Housewives League, sent a vehement letter of protest, signed by hundreds of black Memphians, to owners of the White Rose Laundry. They charged that White Rose's new "mechanical sign" on Linden Avenue, picturing "a Negro washer-woman" washing a pair of underwear was "a complete effrontery to Negro people, in its subtle although effective ridicule of the race." The petitioners, who understood that "most colored people have to work hard for a living," felt that "the many servile tasks that they have to perform should [not] be held up in ridicule and be made a public laughing stock on the highways and streets."[48]

So embedded in American popular culture had the "washer-woman" image become that not only the laundry owners but even the petitioners accepted its use to display meaning, yet they disagreed about its message. The laundry owners, responding to a letter from Mayor Chandler, argued that the sign "represented the kindly old negro mammy who is loved by people of both races such as the one featured by Aunt Jemima." The petitioners, in contrast, perceived the image as mocking the laundry worker by sexualizing her. They insisted that White Rose should have instead presented "a symbol of the hundreds of thousands of poor Negro mothers—who, with a prayer in their humble hearts and a song on their lips, toiled long hours daily, to help support their families, to educate their children—and to make of them worthy and respectable citizens of a great country." Their letter demanded that the "washer-woman" image be stripped of its sexualization and made respectable. Yet their romanticized version of the laundry worker did not necessarily fit the actual workers at White Rose and elsewhere who not only were faithful American mothers but also demanded union representation, higher wages, and respect.[49]

An editorial cartoon in the *Memphis World*, drawn by black artist Charles Alston for distribution to the black press by the Office of War Information (OWI) and published shortly after laundry work was declared essential to the war effort, offered a portrait of the laundry worker and other black women workers that inverted the "mammy" image. Captioned "They also serve!," it shows four black women labeled "laundry worker," "railroad worker," "farm worker," and "other essential civilian workers." The laundry worker, a slim, neatly dressed young woman with a resolute expression on her face, strides toward the viewer beside her counterparts. An American flag forms the backdrop of the cartoon. The illustration forged a new image of the laundry worker—still iconic, yet altered—who could take her place beside other American defense workers essential to national purposes.[50]

Outside these competing representations, real laundry workers rejected their sexualization by white employers, which could have serious consequences.[51] Black women had long struggled to protect themselves from sexual abuse by white male employers. Previously, women had few options besides quitting their jobs when threatened by sexual assault or unwanted sexual advances; however, in the wartime context some attempted—not necessarily successfully—to retain their jobs by requesting government assistance. In 1945, as the war finally ended, Veteran's Hospital laundry workers protested to the FEPC that they had been fired because they refused to concede to their white male supervisor's demands for sex. By summer 1945, however, the FEPC's funding had been slashed

"THEY ALSO SERVE!"   No. II

"They Also Serve!" published in *Memphis World*, August 6, 1943.
*(Charles Henry Alston cartoon, for Office of War Information,
National Archives photo no. 208-COM-129)*

and its future as a permanent, postwar agency was already in jeopardy; thus no agency official ever investigated this case through a trip to Memphis, leaving it permanently unresolved. For several months, however, the case provoked extensive correspondence and heated debate over whether or not the women had actually suffered from racial injustice.[52]

Gertrude Carter, a leader in the laundry worker protest at Kennedy General Hospital a year earlier, again played a key role at the Veteran's Hospital, where she had received a new civil service appointment in January 1945. By late spring, she, Mrs. Dovie McManius, and Mrs. Mammie Holloway had been dismissed, ostensibly for poor ratings on their jobs. All three asserted in letters to the FEPC that they had always received excellent ratings in the past and that the real reason for their being fired had been their unwillingness to "date" — i.e., have sexual relations with — laundry supervisor Albert Miller. Dovie McManius wrote that her ratings had plunged from "Very Good" or "Excellent" to "Just Fair" after Miller was hired and she refused his advances. The women accused Miller of establishing a favoritism system in which black women who had sex with him evaluated other black employees. Mammie Holloway added that when she reported Miller's demands to the plant manager, Dr. H. C. Dodge, he had discharged her. Writing to the FEPC on May 23, she pleaded with officials to help her retain her job, since she supported her children. Carter also begged the FEPC for immediate intervention, even telegraphing the regional office for help when she received notice to not return to work. She detailed Miller's harassment, including one instance in which he asked her how much she "would charge him for a date" and another in which he laid down a blanket in the laundry dressing room and "got angry because [she] would not go in there with him."

For the three women, writing to the FEPC made sense because they perceived this abuse as racial injustice. Holloway and McManius stated that Miller assessed the white women's work himself in order to make "sure they get what is due them," but he didn't "care enough about the colored people's work to try to take care of [the ratings]." While not caring about the black women, Miller demanded sexual favors of them. He tried to justify these requests by presenting himself as "a Northern man" who "like[d] colored women," rather than a southern supervisor threatening his employees with dismissal if they refused to "date him." Carter recalled telling him that she "was afraid. . . . [Y]ou know they don't mixed in the South," thus trying to shield herself through reference to southern antimiscegenation laws. To the women, Miller's appeals for sexual favors meshed with his "not caring" about them as black women.

Federal officials had sharply divergent perspectives on the case. G. H. Sweet, personnel director at the Veterans Administration in Washington, simply informed the FEPC that the "allegations" were "without foundation," since the women were poor workers and fired for this reason. O. E. Myers, director of the Fifth U.S. Civil Service Region, declared that the cases "do not constitute racial discrimination." FEPC regional director Witherspoon Dodge shot back that Miller's behavior might not technically fit the government's definition of racial discrimination but some government agency must be able to "afford job protection for decent people of all races against the personally immoral and socially economic depredations" in the case. Dodge, a southern white Congregational minister who had been a CIO organizer, was unable to initiate an investigation before the FEPC closed.

Even Dodge's thinking did not entirely mirror that of the women complainants. McManius, Holloway, and Carter's comments drew no distinction between sexual abuse and racial discrimination. Paralleling the White Rose incident, laundry workers struggled with the consequences of the sexualized washerwoman image in real life. They presented themselves as hard-working government employees with years of work experience, as dedicated Americans, and as mothers responsible for supporting their families. Unlike the White Rose petitioners, they portrayed themselves as far from helpless, attaching images of respectability to their cause.

Race, Riveting, and Manhood

Paralleling these conflicts over the roles of maids and laundry workers, heated battles took place over black men's exclusion from skilled jobs. Employers and public officials worked strenuously to maintain distinctions between white and black men's work, even in plants that hired white women to fill skilled production positions considered white men's work. Men bitter over these issues talked with other workers, wrote letters, filled out federal complaint forms, demanded action by union representatives, and initiated wildcat strikes that overrode union authority. They strongly rejected language that assigned dependence and lack of aptitude to black men while categorizing white men as independent workers capable of advancement.

Construction work, a locus of conflict before the war, continued to generate controversy, especially around the building of Kennedy General Hospital, a multimillion-dollar project at Park and Getwell Streets in east Memphis. Henke Construction Company, with a workforce of 1,888, employed 886 black workers, none of whom were carpenters. A concerned black minister, Rev. George Bell, alerted Dr. Robert Weaver, director of the Negro Manpower Service in Washington, that white migrants were finding work as skilled tradesmen but black carpenters were being referred out of state for jobs. Shortly thereafter, members of the black United Brotherhood of Carpenters and Joiners of America Local 1896 began lodging FEPC complaints after submitting applications and being turned down.[53] "There seems to be so many reasons for Negro carpenters not being able to get on Defense Jobs in this section," wrote Robert F. Jones, a carpenter and the local's business agent. "Sometimes we are told it will cause a Race Riot, or there is no place for Negro carpenters to live in a white settlement, or that there is plenty of other work Negroes can do besides carpenter work." In a complaint against Lee Construction, he reported that the personnel manager had told him he "did not like Negroes." "He says Negroes are not qualified, and not dependable," asserted Jones. Lee hired several black carpenters following the FEPC investigation, reinforcing the view that the federal complaint process could provide some relief, however small.[54]

In industrial plants, black workers took particular offense at being barred from riveting positions, which were emblematic of America's effort to build planes and ships for the Allies. James Smith, a riveting training graduate, complained to the War Manpower Commission in 1943 that Fisher Aircraft had "the notices of the president's 8802 FEPC sticking on the wall, but it don't mean a thing as far as the hiring is concern its just some more paper on the wall." He was "told by the employment head they did not have any jobs like that open for colored but I saw him hire a white man right there for the same kind of work." Smith placed his concerns as an individual within the larger context of the war. "We have a war on, and that goes double with me," he wrote, in words that echoed the language of the *Pittsburgh Courier*'s popular "Double V" campaign for victory against fascism abroad and racism at home. "We have a war to win with General MacArther [sic] pleading for airpower, and Lord Halifax said in a speach here they needed more airpower. So in my estimation every rivit counts. And to have an all out war effort we don't have any room for discrimination in the war plants."[55]

Various black Fisher Aircraft employees filed grievances with their union, UAW-CIO Local 988, or complained to the FEPC that, despite having been trained as riveters, they were placed in unskilled classifications and paid as common laborers. "During my employ at Fishers," stated Lawrence B. Matlock in October 1943, "many whites have been employed as riveters with nothing more than the training experience in a government sponsored school as I had," yet no blacks had ever been hired in such positions. Both Matlock and James L. Jackson had been hired as file-burr men and classified as common laborers. However, after three additional workers, assisted by Benjamin Bell, executive secretary of the Memphis Urban League, filed similar complaints, all five men received upgrades to semiskilled positions as bench assemblers — jobs that included riveting.[56]

However, the problems at Fisher Aircraft did not end there. Even as Mayor Chandler and U.S. congressman Clifford Davis collaborated to stave off an "adverse ruling" by the U.S. Conciliation Service regarding UAW charges about discriminatory job classifications at Fisher Aircraft, workers there continued to press their complaints. In mid-March 1944, forty-four African American men signed a petition to Local 988 stating that they had been unfairly classified as bench assemblers even though they were performing skilled tasks, such as "Drilling, Riveting, Dimpling, Counter-

Sink, Spotfacing and assembling." Frustrated with the lack of response by Local 988 leaders, several of these men met in April with FEPC examiner John Hope and Benjamin Bell, continuing the meeting the next day at the home of Lawrence Matlock, now a union district committeeman. Matlock had worked as a clerk and first sergeant in the Civilian Conservation Corps and as an adult education instructor and insurance agent prior to his job at Fisher. At the meeting with Hope, the men explained that as bench assemblers they made sixty-nine cents per hour while white women recently hired to conduct the same tasks made eighty-nine cents per hour as "Sub-Assemblers." They protested their subordination to white men and to the white women hired to fill in for them, a situation that doubly excluded them from categories of skill and manhood. It was more palatable for employers to hire white women to temporarily fill in for white men than to hire black men who staked claims to manhood on a permanent basis.[57]

A few months after this meeting, black male heat treat operators at Fisher filed FEPC complaints after they were relieved of the technical aspects of their jobs and reclassified at a lower level, with their sole task restricted to placing products in the ovens. Osie A. King complained that although he had been working in this job for nearly three years, his foreman had informed him that "the white man with him would relieve me of all tabulating and chart reading." King and others believed Fisher management wanted to ensure that whites were in this position before it was upgraded to a skilled status.[58] As with the bench assemblers, the men felt that the local UAW-CIO leadership had not responded to their grievances. Workers pursued an alternative complaint mechanism with the support of emerging in-house leaders such as Matlock, black community leaders such as Bell, and the FEPC.[59]

African American workers at Procter & Gamble's Buckeye Cotton Oil Company plants in Memphis diverged from union leaders on the job classification issue, although in this case the union had the reputation of being militant and antiracist, with Communists among its leaders. The UCAPAWA Local 19 represented workers in over twenty different low-wage Memphis plants, including cotton compresses, cottonseed oil plants, and other concerns, many with majority black labor forces. Local 19's Buckeye members, who in October 1941 chose UCAPAWA over a company union with mostly white members, comprised one of the union's largest workforces.[60]

Procter & Gamble's Buckeye Memphis facilities were among the region's most important suppliers of cottonseed oil and cotton linters. The

Hollywood plant, a cottonseed crushing mill, employed 250 workers, 90 percent of whom were African Americans, all male. The Jackson Avenue plant included a soybean expeller mill and a pulp mill and maintained a workforce that ranged from 750 to 950 workers, 70 percent of them African Americans. The company hired as many as fifty women toward the end of the war. Roughly half of the Jackson Avenue plant's output of cotton linters, a fiber removed from cottonseeds, went to defense plants run by the army or DuPont for the production of gunpowder used in explosives.[61]

Even the most straightforward problems at Buckeye, such as wage rates, reflected racial and regional tensions. A report prepared for the National War Labor Board (NWLB) by Arthur Weimer, dean of Indiana University's School of Business, concluded that rates at Buckeye compared favorably to those at similar Memphis plants; but he did not measure them against manufacturing wages nationally. Furthermore, the union argued, Weimer had not addressed the discrepancy between wages paid at Procter & Gamble's northern and southern plants. In addition, John Green, a mediator representing the employees' position in an NWLB hearing in June 1942, argued that a dual-wage system was an "untenable practice" that could not be "condoned by the fact that it is the custom in the area." Indeed, the annual incomes of black workers at Buckeye were so low, the mediators' report stated, that "they are unable to purchase sufficient food and other necessities without falling into debt. Consequently, an increasing number of men are being garnished every pay day." Arguing that reducing these "racial differentials" would be "a step in the direction of a greater national unity," he supported a wage increase that would be formulated to decrease these differentials. Company officials justified current wages by claiming that Procter & Gamble had the most modern cottonseed crushing technology in the region, where workers were employed year-round, not just during the cotton harvest. The company, they argued, already paid wages that were among the highest in comparable plants in the area.[62]

Union officials had a different impression of Procter & Gamble's impact on local and regional labor relations. At the NWLB hearing, they argued that the company had bribed workers to implement a company union, a strategy it used in other parts of the country. Buckeye had also colluded with the Crump machine, which had sent plainclothes policemen to the homes of black workers "to obtain admissions from them that the CIO advocated racial equality." Buckeye had attempted to provoke white workers into opposing UCAPAWA Local 19, headed by black radical unionist John Mack Dyson, a worker in Buckeye's Hollywood plant, by branding it as "just a nigger union." Procter & Gamble clearly contributed to local and regional tensions by drawing on local racial practices and implementing measures it carried out elsewhere in the country, such as the company union.[63]

Black Buckeye employees repeatedly filed union grievances and FEPC complaints protesting discriminatory job classifications and the dual-wage system, which together resulted in low pay and fed stereotypes of black men as unskilled and servile. Men who assembled and disassembled machines and did general repair work vehemently protested their classification as mechanics' helpers while white workers performing the same tasks were considered "apprentices" or "learners." Several complained that, even after working at Buckeye for years, they had never advanced past "helper." Eldridge Westbrooks, who was hired at the Jackson Avenue plant in 1925, was still classified as a "millwrights' helper," although he did "everything a millwright does." Harry Owens, an employee at the Hollywood plant since 1922, still worked as a mechanics' helper for fifty cents per hour while white apprentices earned over ten cents more an hour. In April 1944, at a meeting held by FEPC examiner John Hope just before he met with Fisher employees, Edward Johnson, a mechanics' helper and president of the Jackson Avenue unit of the union, related an extreme case of discrimination. "Mr. Johnson states that Mr. Will Anderson, as a mechanic's helper, carried tools for Mr. W. F. Bowld 20 years ago when he was a mechanic," Hope reported. "Mr. Bowld is now President of the Buckeye Cotton Oil Company and has recently been appointed as vice president of Procter and Gamble Company. Mr. Anderson still receives the common labor wage rate of 50¢ per hour, and is now engaged in handling chemicals and keeping records of this." Johnson's account exemplifies the kind of racial subordination that all black workers experienced.[64]

Black Buckeye workers demanding changed job classifications encountered resistance from top white Memphis CIO officials like William Copeland, regional CIO director. At the end of 1944, during a NWLB hearing about contract renewal, black committeemen refused, over Copeland's objections, to concede to a company offer to grant a four cents an hour raise in exchange for a pledge that the union would not reopen the job classification issue for the duration of the contract. "The race issue is very much alive within this plant," noted Conciliation Service commissioner W. M. Whorton. "The negro committeemen were not concerned with wages. . . . They have claimed that in the question of classification the negro has been discriminated against." Whorton commented that "the white CIO representatives made every effort to get the committee to agree to the wage increase offered and not reopen either question for the duration."[65]

Buckeye plant managers' claims that they placed white workers in higher job classifications because they were more intelligent, or worked more efficiently, particularly irked black workers. Lucius Jones and Charles Burton complained that once the company installed expeller machinery, black men were informed that they were going to be replaced by "men with more intelligence." In May 1942, management assigned white workers to these jobs, paying them ninety to ninety-five cents per hour. Several months later, black workers returned to these positions, at 60.6 cents per hour. Likewise, in a 1943 case arbitrated by the Regional War Labor Board, the union reported that black wash tank operators had been replaced by white workers after being told they were not working efficiently. These white workers received sixty-four cents per hour, while black workers conducting similar tasks as bleach tub operators made 53.5 cents per hour. Individuals who were removed from the wash tank jobs insisted that they had taught the whites how to operate the tanks properly. The arbiter's decision, May 28, 1943, ruled against the union's demand that the bleach tank operators be paid at the higher rate.[66] In response to the decision, on June 7, 1943, sixteen workers at the Jackson Avenue plant walked off their jobs in an unauthorized wildcat strike. Only after union officials and Whorton pledged to seek a review by the Regional War Labor Board did strikers agree to return to work. However, on June 22, the board ruled not to reconsider the arbitration decision.[67]

African American workers at both Buckeye plants threatened repeatedly to strike and conducted several unauthorized walkouts. Indeed, Commissioner Whorton described workers at the Jackson Avenue plant as having a "smoldering desire to strike."[68] Strike threats and actual walkouts demonstrate workers' resistance to wartime no-strike pledges made by many unions, including UCAPAWA. Black workers' wildcats against racist job classifications temporarily pitted strike participants against union leaders and officials, who pressured workers to return to work. In September 1942, less than a year after the union election at Buckeye, a one-hour wildcat at the Jackson Avenue plant prompted disciplinary actions by Local 19's executive committee against Edward Johnson and a coworker.

These tensions dramatically resurfaced in 1944, making headlines in the black press, after union members, led by Edward Johnson, conducted an unofficial strike vote. Opposing perceptions of patriotism, racial justice, and labor unity emerged as this conflict unfolded. Shortly after the March 17 vote, Edward Johnson wrote directly to President Roosevelt, informing him that workers had "voted unanimously for a strike Ballot effective thirty (30) days from said date." He reminded Roosevelt that the plant had won two army and navy "E" Awards for its excellent production, and warned that "unrest is steadily growing" among the workers because their wages were not keeping up with the cost of living. UCAPAWA Local 19 business agent Reuel Stanfield, the *Memphis World* reported, urged workers to drop their plans, declaring that "an unauthorized strike there by the union members, a large percentage of whom are colored, would be a strike against the government and not against the company, and would do more harm than good to the workers themselves." Stanfield counseled them to await an NWLB decision on wages. Privately, Local 19 officials branded Johnson as a "trouble maker." At this point, Johnson and other workers also held meetings with John Hope about the job classification issue. In September, in response to the company's transfer of Edward Johnson off his regular job, nearly 900 workers at the Jackson Avenue plant, both black and white, walked off their jobs for five days, in the most disruptive wildcat of the war. Only with pressure from labor and mediation officials and a promise from the company that it would reconsider a wage increase did participants vote to return to their jobs.[69]

Black carpenters, Fisher Aircraft employees, and Buckeye cottonseed oil workers all engaged in wartime struggles that targeted not only wages but underlying job classification systems that sorted out workers according to purported inherent differences between blacks and whites. At the core of these struggles were beliefs about masculinity, since skill itself denoted independence, intelligence, and at least a minimum amount of power to control one's own labor. At both Fisher, a modern mass production plant, and Buckeye, a cotton-based manufacturing facility, black workers staked claims to identities different from those imposed upon them by humiliating job classifications, with some becoming indigenous leaders. Even as members of antiracist CIO unions with radical leaders, they encountered barriers to their pursuit of racial justice and forged different understandings of labor and American freedom.

Crump's "Well-Kept Slaves"

A series of highly public confrontations beginning in late 1943, including verbal sparring between A. Philip Randolph and Boss Crump, thrust issues of labor, power, and freedom into the limelight. These events dramatically illuminated problems being addressed on a daily basis by working-class black Memphians. They also placed a number of black leaders on the spot with both the Crump machine, on the one hand, and working-class black Memphians, on the other. In 1943, the local chapter of the Brotherhood of Sleeping Car Porters made plans for a "mammoth labor rally" on November 7 featuring Randolph, touting it as the "most widely-heralded [meeting] ever scheduled by Negro labor groups in Memphis." During his trip to Memphis, Randolph also planned to address a Brotherhood of Sleeping Car Porters banquet and the STFU's annual convention. Randolph had first gained prominence as coeditor with Chandler Owen of *The Messenger*, founded in 1917 as the "only radical Negro journal in America." In 1925, he became president of the newly established Brotherhood of Sleeping Car Porters, organized to address the railway brotherhoods' exclusion of blacks. After the union affiliated with the AFL in 1929, Randolph continued to pressure the AFL to accord equal rights to black workers. Randolph's national visibility greatly increased with his leadership of the March on Washington Movement.[70]

The day before the scheduled 1943 rally, the Crump machine pressured African American community leaders into canceling the event, provoking a storm of controversy. As the *Memphis World* reported, "Approximately twenty Negro leaders received orders direct from the Sheriff's office to be present at a meeting Saturday afternoon at three o'clock. No indication as to the purpose of the meeting was given until their arrival." The newspaper asserted that "virtually behind jail bars these men were impressed with the fact that should Mr. Randolph speak in Memphis it would likely be the signal for a race riot." Sheriff Perry, Attorney General Will Gerber, police commissioner Joe Boyle, Shelby County commissioner E. W. Hale, and Shelby County attorney Charles Crabtree addressed the group, with Boyle announcing that he had a list of whom to seize should a riot erupt. Brotherhood of Sleeping Car Porters local president H. F. Patton and other leaders present, including Lt. George W. Lee and Booker T. Washington High School principal Blair T. Hunt, agreed to cancel the rally. In response to criticism after the so-called jailhouse meeting, Hunt stated in the *Memphis World* that he had intended to "promote the larger good for all concerned."[71]

Randolph delivered his speech to the STFU convention anyway. Situating the Memphis conflict in the context of national and global questions about the meaning of democracy, he assailed Crump, declaring that the "fascists are represented not only by Mussolini, Hitler, and Hirohito, but by local politicians." "Labor's mouth has been muzzled in France, Italy, and Germany," he continued. "It was attempted in Memphis by the political machine, but it must not and will not succeed." Randolph argued that the "one answer to fascism in Memphis" would be a "public meeting of white[s] and Negroes exercising the right of assembly and expression." After leaving Memphis, Randolph continued to make headlines for his statements about home-front fascism, and March on Washington Movement leaders sent protest letters to Mayor Chandler.[72]

Meanwhile, AFL president William Green, under pressure from Randolph and eager to wrest votes from the CIO, ignited further controversy by directing southern AFL representative George L. Googe and local AFL organizers to arrange a return trip to Memphis for Randolph. Memphis Trades and Labor Council president and Crump friend Lev Loring reacted by attacking Randolph as "a demagogue of front rank" whose appearance would not be "good for this section of the country" or "beneficial to the relationship between the races." In turn, black AFL organizer Cornelius Maiden denounced Loring, despite his AFL affiliation, and Green issued a rebuttal reproduced in the advertisement for the mass meeting. AFL leaders also pilloried efforts to block the meeting by two black Memphians, former school principal T. J. Johnson and businessman G. L. Young, who visited William Green in Washington. Benjamin Bell joined Maiden in rallying support from AFL locals, and Rev. George Long offered Beale Avenue Baptist Church as a meeting site. As the day of the event approached, Lt. George Lee, in a letter to Republican leader Robert Church, now living outside Memphis, warned that "Randolph will be here Friday and this town is hot as a . . . stove and newspapers are fanning the flames. Anything is liable to happen."[73]

Randolph's speech, on March 31, 1944, which drew over 1,000 black and white participants, hammered home the idea that fascism was a problem not just abroad but at home as well, a theme central to his message since the start of the March on Washington Movement. Randolph castigated Crump for undermining freedom, declaring that Mr. Crump "out-Hitlers Hitler." Significantly, he also challenged black leaders. As the *Memphis World* reported, he "scor[ed] local Negro leaders and berat[ed] the circumstances and personalities which stood in the way of his delivering an address here last November." Randolph ridiculed the language of "racial harmony," including Crump's claims that blacks were content. "Pointing to the establishment of schools and playgrounds by the city for Negro citizens is no proper justification for denying them or anybody else freedom of speech," Randolph declared. "Negroes do not want to be well-kept slaves. Like white people they, too, want to be free." By comparing Crump's paternalism and black complacency with slavery, he threw down the gauntlet not only for Crump but also for black Memphis leaders, whom he posed as obstructions to, rather than vehicles for, genuine freedom.[74]

Randolph's statements in Memphis expanded upon his arguments in national debates about America's participation in the war and the challenges facing African Americans. As early as September 1942, Randolph contributed to a special "Victory" supplement in the *Chicago Defender*, in which white and black leaders and scholars, ranging from President Roosevelt and General Douglas MacArthur to W. E. B. Du Bois and Langston Hughes, addressed top issues they saw at stake in the war. Randolph's statement, titled "Freedom on Two Fronts," demanded that blacks "call for freedom now." It anchored the challenge of freedom and democracy in both "the problem of the Negro" in the United States and the problem of people of color under colonial rule, particularly in India.[75]

Randolph elaborated on this international perspective on freedom in 1943, first in a column reprinted in the *Memphis World* and then in a rejoinder to critics of the March on Washington Movement, published in the *Defender*. In these writings, he further underscored the need for African Americans to reconsider their own role in defining and winning freedom. Randolph proclaimed that "Negroes are at the crossroads," arguing that the "decisive challenge" faced by the "darker races" internationally was assuming responsibility for their own freedom. "Freedom is never given; it is won," he insisted. "Justice is never granted, it is exacted. It is written in the stars that the darker races will never be free until they make themselves free." To do so required a "well-developed philosophy of thought and struggle," the lack of which had led some black leaders to endorse Jim Crow policies. Segregation must be a primary target, he concluded, as the "main pillar" of racial oppression.[76] Randolph's words reverberated in the Memphis context, in his critiques of both Crump and local black leaders. He also articulated what some black Memphis workers had been expressing, whether in comments linking their protests to the global war against fascism, or in their complaints about labor contracts that conceded to segregated job classifications.

Crump's rebuttal reasserted his view that city officials played the role of benefactor to black Memphians, who remained dependent on them. "Randolph scoffs at what has been done for the Negroes in Memphis and Shelby County in the way of schools, parks, playgrounds, swimming-pools, health facilities and housing," he fumed. "I would hate to think that he voices the sentiment of the colored citizens of this community in his belittling the many things that have been done for them, notwithstanding the fact they only pay 5 per cent of the taxes." City police had protected the black community from itself, he announced, "cleaning up Beale Street dives that were harboring criminals with pistols and longbladed knives." Crump accused Reverend Long of "spreading race hatred," asserting that if a riot erupted, "the blood of his race is on his altar in the House of

God." He also declared that Memphis would be "better off without . . . the preacher who gave permission to hold that meeting in his church."[77]

Although Randolph's speech received "wide acclaim by his hearers, white and colored," according to the *Memphis World*, outside Beale Avenue Church it elicited conflicting responses. Several preachers dissociated themselves from Randolph and reaffirmed their allegiance to Crump: "Did the speech delivered by Randolph in which he lambasted and vilified E. H. Crump represent the attitude of the colored people of Memphis? We say NO."[78] A *Memphis World* editorial struck an ambivalent note, insisting that it "deplor[ed] the action of Memphis leaders in bringing about a cancellation of Mr. Randolph's appearance" yet did not support his March on Washington Movement. The paper asked for "the matter to be forgotten" and for "the best elements of responsible citizens [to] continue their efforts for harmony and democracy for all."[79]

Reverend Long, for his part, greeted Crump's warning with the declaration that "Christ, not Crump, is my Boss." Printed in the *Memphis Press-Scimitar*, Long's response reinforced Randolph's own themes. "The issue raised by Mr. E. H. Crump in Memphis is the issue around the world — Freedom," he argued. "Thousands of my group are dying around the world for that freedom. If they can take it there, I can take it here, although I must take it unarmed, but the pity of it is that men should have to die there for what is denied here."[80] In fact, Long hosted several labor gatherings at his church, including public meetings of both the STFU and the UCAPAWA.[81]

Concomitantly, conflicts within the MUL, successor to the Community Welfare League, drew further attention to differences among blacks over labor and politics in early 1944, when the MUL fired Executive Secretary Benjamin Bell because of his involvement in Memphis labor struggles. Hired in May 1943 following the death of Lucien J. Searcy, Bell, a Chicagoan, had received a master's degree in social work from Atlanta University and worked as a social worker, journalist, and researcher, including for Gunnar Myrdal's study on blacks in America. By fall 1943, MUL officers had become anxious about his high profile, prompting an investigation by the Urban League's southern regional office.[82] The final straw for the MUL came in January 1944, with Bell's publication of an article in the *Chicago Defender* about Memphis labor problems. "Memphis has leviathan plans for the post-war period," Bell asserted, yet "no information has been divulged bearing on employment opportunities for the Negro worker." Bell also attacked police brutality and other problems black Memphians faced.[83] A week later, the *Defender*'s front page declared, "Crump Wrath May Oust Urban League Leader in Memphis." The article decried the

Crump machine's threat to pull all Community Chest funding from the MUL if Bell continued as executive secretary. It also assailed MUL directors who were most intent on removing Bell, including Dr. J. E. Walker, M. W. Bonner, and Blair T. Hunt, referring to them as representatives of the "local Negro appeasement bloc which believes in the 'see no evil, hear no evil, speak no evil' approach to race relations."[84]

Ultimately the MUL replaced Bell with Rev. James A. McDaniel, minister of Bethel Presbyterian Church and a member of the Negro Chamber of Commerce. Whereas Bell, after he was fired, began to work formally with the AFL's laundry workers union, McDaniel, as the new MUL executive secretary, helped the USES advertise for African Americans to work as common laborers and domestic workers. "No one can afford to dissipate his or her energies in idleness," he declared in a typical announcement, emphasizing black workers' need to obtain jobs. Yet even McDaniel assured John Hope that he would refer complainants to the FEPC and stressed that USES policies were "definitely dangerous, both for the present and the post-war world when Negroes return in search of jobs."[85]

Other Memphis leaders eschewed any note of protest, urging black workers to develop workplace efficiency in Memphis plants and in the cotton fields. Dr. J. E. Walker, who headed the black Democratic organization in Shelby County and the Universal Negro Life Insurance Company, issued radio announcements that encouraged African American men to take jobs in the cotton compresses and named the cotton economy "one of the pillars of the economic life of Memphis." The Memphis Junior Negro Chamber of Commerce posted placards in streetcars instructing blacks to develop good work habits, to "pay no attention to rumors," and to do their part in the war effort. And the Colored Methodist Center sponsored a "Workers Clinic" that emphasized that to be a good "Christian, citizen, family member," one must learn how to do a full day's good work.[86]

These clashing perspectives on black labor, racial identities, and urban politics all existed prior to A. Philip Randolph's visits to Memphis and E. H. Crump's public posturing against the New York-based labor and civil rights leader. Yet this confrontation stirred various black community leaders to take a public position on these issues. Nevertheless, the incendiary words on both sides that surrounded Randolph's Memphis speeches would have had little significance outside the unique context of the wartime urban South. Daily confrontations provoked by African American male and female workers over the meaning of the war itself and racial justice prompted these leaders to vie for particular standpoints on labor and their relation to the Crump machine.

Thousands of black migrants who arrived in Memphis found it difficult to avoid seasonal work in the region's cotton fields and discovered that they were considered field hands even after permanently relocating to the city. At the same time, both newcomers and established residents who succeeded in locating work in Memphis were subject to racist labor distinctions that cast them as dependent and servile, preventing them from advancing beyond domestic work or unskilled labor. By excluding blacks from skilled industrial production jobs at a time when Roosevelt had recast the American economy as an "Arsenal of Democracy," such practices placed them outside the markers of American progress and democracy.

African Americans living in Memphis during the war seized upon new openings created by the wartime context itself. In particular, they took advantage of contradictory state interventions in their efforts to combat discrimination and alter powerful racial perceptions. Competing aims of federal agencies such as the USES and the FEPC, for example, enlivened debate about racial justice and created openings for protest. For thousands of workers, the first order of protest was unionization. Many facing severe barriers in employment and wages also sought out other routes, whether that meant filing government complaints or pressing community leaders for help.

Black women struggled with the anachronistic image of "mammy," the happy-go-lucky household servant in white households, ascribed to them. In the context of the "Arsenal of Democracy," women like Altha Sims, Ella Rose Dotson, Susie Brister, and Margaret Jackson rejected their role as servant. As white women entered nonfarm paid labor in record numbers during the war, purported racial differences might have collapsed had they labored side by side with black women. But city officials and employers shored up these boundaries through racist hiring practices. Black women working in industrial laundries and similar sites also protested classifications and wage scales that distinguished them from their white women coworkers. In non-military workplaces, women joined unions in massive numbers, while those laboring in non-union military facilities formed self-styled groups that complained about job discrimination to their employers and the federal government. These women also protested their sexualization, which added to perceptions of black women as outside the category of normal womanhood and made them vulnerable to sexual abuse by employers. While individuals who initiated the White Rose Laundry protest sought to substitute the existing image with that of a desexualized, ennobled war worker and mother, laundry workers cast themselves as activists on behalf of a changed American democracy that would eradicate racial injustice.

Black male workers in mass production factories such as Fisher Aircraft and cotton-based manufacturing plants such as Buckeye battled over racist job classifications and the dual-wage system. They rejected being cast as dependent, subordinate, and inferior to white men. Some of the most energetic protests were against black men's exclusion from skilled jobs that were being assigned to white women. At the same time, black men drew on a notion of agency missing from the racialized persona of the dependent laborer. As Clarence Smith stated in his effort to get a job as a riveter rather than continue as a porter and floor sweeper, he wanted "to . . . win recognition in this our country, as citizens, human, and a important spoke in the wheel of progress." Benjamin Bell drew attention to this issue when he demanded to know why black workers were absent in discussions of postwar Memphis.

These wartime struggles did not reverse racist practices, although by the end of the war, African Americans had been hired into many jobs from which they had previously been excluded, largely due to the pragmatic need for more defense workers. Nevertheless, blacks' protests helped establish a climate of dissent that continued into the postwar period, both locally and nationally. Public dramas such as those involving A. Philip Randolph, Rev. George Long, and Benjamin Bell, in which issues of agency, power, and identity were writ large, contributed to this atmosphere of resistance. The Crump machine had suppressed the "mammoth labor rally" featuring Randolph just months after race riots occurred in several American cities. On the heels of these riots, Randolph aroused ire with his declaration that "racial harmony" was based on sustaining "well-kept slaves" within a segregated world. The concept of "racial harmony," an ideological accompaniment to plans for Memphis's progress, represented the opposite of Randolph's view of having to win freedom rather than having it handed over. Most importantly, it countered the kind of subjectivity being seized by many working-class African Americans.

Moral Outrage

3 Postwar Protest against Police Violence
and Sexual Assault

At 1:30 A.M., August 3, 1945, two young African American women awaited a bus at the corner of Poplar and Cleveland in midtown Memphis. According to their sworn statements, made later before a white attorney retained by the NAACP, Alice Wright and Annie Mae Williams had just finished their shifts as dishwasher and cook at Fred's Café and were headed home to the working-class Binghampton neighborhood, a few miles east of their workplace.[1] Daughters of domestic workers, the young women lived with their mothers and various siblings and their children next door to each other on Broad Avenue, near the Paradise Grill and the Early Grove Baptist Church, where Wright's family attended church.[2] Both Wright, seventeen, and Williams, twenty, had young sons, with Wright the mother of a fourteen-month-old and Williams the mother of a three-year-old. Annie was a recent migrant; she had moved to Memphis with her mother and son from Fayette County, in west Tennessee, in December 1944, after separating from her husband.

Wright and Williams stated that two white policemen, later identified as J. W. Torrey and B. J. Lewis, pulled up beside them in a squad car and accused them of loitering. Implying that they were prostitutes, the men said they had seen them at the corner an hour and a half earlier. When the young women insisted they had just left their jobs at Fred's, the policemen accused them of working without health cards, which Tennessee required of food service workers to verify that they did not have syphilis. Wright and Williams assured them that their health cards, in accordance with state law, were kept at their workplaces. Instead of checking for the health cards at the café, the officers ordered them inside the squad car and drove north on Cleveland, then east on Jackson Avenue. "I thought you didn't pick up girls that were working," Williams said. "[W]e had to get this month's number somehow, just as well start with you two," an officer responded. "We are going to fill this car up with girls." However, they continued to drive in a direction away from the police station, and made no effort to detain other women.

Along the way, the women stated, the men vulgarly taunted them. "What are you sitting so close together for? You can't f--k one another," one asked. And, "You all ever been f----d?" Williams remembered repeatedly crying out, "Lord have mercy!" until one of the officers responded, "That damn prayer won't get you nowhere." She also recalled one man ordering her to empty the change purse she was clutching, then demanding to know why she had a slip from the ear, nose, and throat clinic, insinuating that she had syphilis. In tears, Williams ripped up the clinic slip and threw the pieces on the seat; later they were recovered and used as evidence in court. Amid the harassment, she remembered, one of the men remarked to the other that she "might be telling the truth."

The circuitous, hour-long drive ended at a secluded, wooded site only a mile southeast of the women's homes, off Union Avenue Extended. One of the men remarked, "Ain't a S.B. out here. I thought [it] would be full," in a reference to similar acts by other policemen. According to Wright and Williams, during the next several minutes, Torrey raped Williams while Lewis forced Wright to perform fellatio, threatening to blackjack her when she tried to resist him. The women's statements detailed their attackers' use of physical and psychological coercion, emphasizing that they had not willingly submitted to the men. After the attack, Lewis warned Wright that if she told anyone what had happened, he would "put in a claim and it will fall on [you]," referring to charging her with either prostitution or health card violations.

Williams recounted that, during the attack, she pleaded with Torrey to leave her alone. She told him that in Somerville, her home town, the sheriff and deputies would "put colored girls in jail if they are out with white men," and asked him to put her in jail rather than rape her. "This ain't no Somerville," he retorted, as if Somerville were merely backward and his sexual assault of a black woman were sanctioned in the city. After raping her, Torrey complained that her fear had spoiled his pleasure. She responded that she was afraid of policemen.

In their own affidavits, Viola Wright, Alice's mother, and Hazel Byrd Smith, Annie Mae's mother, recalled their daughters returning home in tears at 3:00 A.M. Friday, after being dropped off by the policemen. Despite the policemen's warnings about not talking to anyone, the mothers reported, their daughters poured out the story. The four women and

Alice's sister stayed up for the rest of the night discussing what to do. In this initial kernel of protest, the mothers — who described themselves as domestic workers supporting large families, one separated from her husband and the other a widow — considered how to safeguard their daughters from further harm at the hands of the police, the very men who should have safeguarded them as they awaited the bus.

At 8:00 A.M., instead of going to their jobs, the mothers went to Fred's Café to tell the white owner, William Frederick Dudzick, that their daughters were quitting, a step that would at least take them off the street at night. "Mr. Fred," as they called him, urged them to report the assaults at the police station and offered to accompany them. This intervention unintentionally triggered the initial stages of a police cover-up. At the station, according to the affidavits, Police Chief Carroll Seabrook announced that he would detain the daughters until the next day, Saturday, proceeding as if they, not the policemen, had broken the law. After jailing Wright and Williams overnight, Seabrook delayed their release until Monday, barring the mothers access to their daughters.

By Monday, police investigators had recovered evidence corroborating the young women's account, including the ripped up clinic slip and a handkerchief soiled and cast aside by Torrey. At this point, Public Safety Commissioner Joe Boyle, Seabrook's superior, quietly fired the two patrolmen, but they were not arrested and Boyle made no public statement about the case.[3] Seabrook, meanwhile, had accumulated evidence that could be used to undermine the young women's credibility. For example, he had arranged for a line-up so they could identify their attackers. According to the young women's later statements, however, he threatened to send them to the penal farm if they selected the wrong men. So intimidated, the women picked out Torrey and Lewis but did not positively identify them.

Seabrook had also subjected both women to blood tests for venereal disease, under the guise that the young women had been detained for working without health cards.[4] He declared that Wright was disease-free but that Williams was in the early, contagious stage of syphilis. On the basis of this report, Seabrook announced that he would quarantine Williams for eleven days at the West Tennessee Medical Center, to "keep little children from getting [syphilis]." He released Wright, who in any case could not file rape charges against Lewis because the state defined rape as forced sexual penetration, which allegedly had not occurred. Seabrook ordered her mother to "take Alice on home and don't talk." Outraged, the mothers chose to defy what the press later termed Seabrook's "gag orders."

Memphis, 1940s

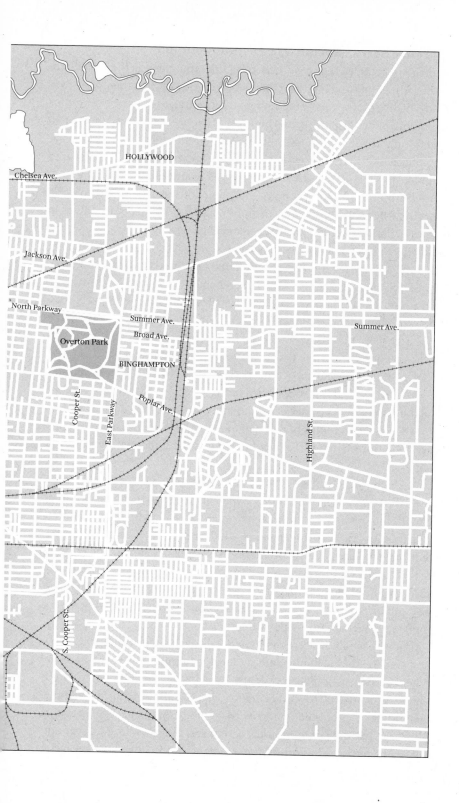

HOLLYWOOD

Chelsea Ave.

Jackson Ave.

North Parkway

Summer Ave.

Broad Ave.

Overton Park

BINGHAMPTON

Cooper St.

East Parkway

Poplar Ave.

Summer Ave.

Highland St.

S. Cooper St.

Police Sexual Assault and Postwar Politics

This 1945 police rape case, occurring the same week as the U.S. bombing of Hiroshima and Nagasaki that ended World War II, ignited a postwar racial justice movement by inflaming public outrage against the notorious Memphis police department. The *Press-Scimitar*, the first newspaper to publish an account of the assaults, presented the story as one "so revolting that it shocked even veteran newspapermen." The black newspaper the *Memphis World* described the attacks as "wantonly and bestially committed criminal assaults on two young, poor, and defenseless Negro working girls." By condemning the corruption and legal injustices involved in the case, both statements transposed racial images that typically assigned bestiality to black men and sexual aggression to black women. By late August, the *Memphis World* had declared that "Memphis citizens have been aroused as never before over the charges made by the girls."[5] This comment referred primarily to the city's African American civic, religious, and civil rights organizations; however, it also encompassed white moderates. The assault was by no means the first incident of police brutality in the recent past, nor the first instance of police abuse of black women, nor even the sole occurrence that week. However, the widespread publicity given to the legal injustices in this case, the combustive racial climate, and the assault's occurrence at this juncture between war and peace, when African Americans reinvigorated demands for racial justice, together produced widespread outcry that would have major ramifications for postwar politics.[6]

The moral outrage this case provoked among black Memphians involved its familiarity as much as its atypicality. Swedish sociologist Gunnar Myrdal's famous 1944 work, *An American Dilemma*, based on local studies by African American sociologists, concluded that police brutality had become one of the paramount problems in the urban South. As the ranks of the NAACP and other groups swelled during the war, scholars have shown, extralegal racial violence by police officers, the most visible symbols of white public authority, at a time when Americans were trumpeting the triumph of democracy, fueled postwar protest.[7]

Although scholarly accounts have noted the outrage prompted by police brutality, they seldom examine black communities' particularly vehement responses to police violence involving sexual assaults. In Montgomery, Alabama, in 1949, and Panama City, Florida, in 1950, for example, black residents protested incidents that closely resembled the Memphis police rape case.[8] Such community responses, in turn, fueled further outrage against other instances of police violence, especially those involving racial issues of sexuality and gender. Protest against police brutality thus placed race, manhood, womanhood, and sexuality at the center of postwar political strife.[9]

In Memphis, police sexual assaults of black women galvanized not only African Americans but also diverse sectors of the city against police lawlessness, mobilizing a language of justice that had significant purchase directly after the war. Such language became freighted with sharply conflicting meanings, however. Statements by the *Press-Scimitar* and editor Edward Meeman reflected efforts by southern moderates and veterans' groups to oust corrupt political machines after the war. Crump officials combated this challenge by staking out their own claims to justice, ultimately facilitating, for example, the arrest and prosecution of the two police officers who assaulted Wright and Williams.[10] Such actions aimed at shoring up, not breaking up, their civic authority in Memphis, including their control over what they portrayed as a dependent black population.

In addition to these conflicts among white elites, political tensions among black Memphians that had surfaced during the 1943 Randolph episode now reappeared, spurred by the black press. In response to accusations that they had become overly submissive toward the Crump machine and hence incapable of safeguarding African American women, young people, and veterans, civic and religious leaders defended their manhood by asserting themselves as the rightful protectors of the black community.[11] These leaders vigorously demanded the police officers' prosecution and called upon the city to hire black policemen.

Within working-class black neighborhoods, protest against police violence and sexual assault bore further meaning. While male leaders emphasized black women's dependency and vulnerability, black women carved out a political space in which they considered themselves as both victims and their own protectors. Viola Wright and Hazel Byrd Smith, for instance, presented themselves as mothers with rights to secure their working daughters' safety. Black Memphians had complained about police racial violence for decades, and many migrants, like Annie Mae Williams, were familiar with police harassment before moving to Memphis. Now, amid the political turmoil following the war, the women's courage to speak out pushed concerns about police sexual violence from the margins to the center of public consideration about racial justice.[12]

Historically, slave states had not acknowledged the forced sexual relations between black women and white slaveholders as sexual assault or rape; however, freedwomen's change in status converted such acts into illegal violence. As extralegal racial violence, especially lynching, rose during and after Reconstruction, it became coupled with overtly sexualized representations of both black men and women, particularly representations of black men as bestial rapists of white women. The perception of black females as sexual aggressors largely excluded African American women from consideration as victims and undermined legal protections they might have been accorded. The public reiteration of such images had serious consequences for daily realities, within and beyond the plantation South.[13] As Robin Kelley points out, although lynching became less common and public attention to police brutality intensified in the mid-twentieth century, the sexual and gender parameters of racial violence persisted.[14]

During the Second World War, expanded police intervention in various aspects of social life multiplied the circumstances in which patrolmen interacted with urban residents. Campaigns aimed at halting vice and eradicating syphilis, for example, augmented the regulation of working-class women and heightened perceptions of migrant and African American women as dangers to the population.[15] Although such programs targeted both black and white working-class women, arrests of young white women migrants addressed conditions presumed to be temporary and curable. Detentions of African American women, in contrast, reflected racial perceptions of them as inherently threatening and overly sexualized. Wartime antivice and syphilis programs thus became bound up with ideas of natural racial difference among white and black women. Many black Memphians perceived this increased police regulation of and access to women's bodies as a license for police sexual abuse. Urban migrants already familiar with police brutality from experiences with rural sheriffs and deputies also balked at this intensified police intervention.

In general, postwar protest against police violence provoked discussion about black and white womanhood, manhood, and sexuality as part of a broader reconsideration of the politics of racial justice. Protesters of the 1945 police rapes denounced narratives that cast the young women as prostitutes, not café workers; syphilitic rather than healthy; threats to children, not mothers; sexual aggressors not victims. Black leaders' political emphasis on the hiring of black policemen partially eclipsed these issues by the end of the decade. Additionally, the legal dramas that unfolded following the police brutality of the mid-1940s reinforced the personal risks involved with bringing the perpetrators of racial violence to trial. The sentiments stirred by the 1945 police rape case and other incidents persisted well into the postwar years.

Police Violence and Wartime Racial Control

A constant influx of migrants and servicemen, including shore patrol and military police, exacerbated racial tensions during the war. Memphis's Grand Central Station served as a major hub for servicemen traveling between military bases, bringing throngs of sailors and soldiers into the downtown area on a regular basis. Military hospitals in the city and the location of a Naval Air Station just north of Memphis in Millington, Tennessee, likewise added to the numbers of servicemen in the area. Public officials interpreted wartime overcrowding as a powder keg for racial conflict, especially in the wake of the 1943 Detroit race riot. They responded by enforcing segregation in public areas, for example excluding white naval personnel from Beale Street and black naval personnel from Main.[16]

Migrants from the surrounding rural region who sought a lengthier sojourn in Memphis confronted severe overcrowding. In 1942, a Board of Census survey reported in Memphis a housing vacancy rate of only 3/10 of one percent. Since most new housing built during the war was designated for rental or sale to white defense workers this figure obscured an even more severe housing crisis for African Americans. Even when the city secured federal approval for housing construction, contractors were reluctant to submit bids for "Negro housing"—which sold or rented for less and was built out of inferior materials. The return of veterans at the end of the war made conditions even more dire.[17]

African American newcomers to the city frequently "doubled up" with family members, most of whom were already living in substandard housing, especially in neighborhoods such as Binghampton, the Chelsea Avenue area, and sections of north and south Memphis. In 1942, Memphis Housing Authority director J. A. Fowler cautioned that as a result of black migrants moving into such housing with relatives, "maintaining health standards for negro [war] workers is a recognized impossibility. The absentee records of negro employees in local war production due to illness is becoming an alarming problem."[18] Spurred not by natural population growth but by segregation and a racist approach to housing, "doubling up" placed extreme burdens on both households and neighborhoods.

The aggressive presence of white policemen in these urban spaces became a source of constant concern for black residents. Acts of violence against individuals accrued public significance when witnesses protested police behavior, accounts appeared in the black press, or stories circulated informally within communities. In a 1942 letter to Mayor Chandler, P. L. Harden, the district commander of the Colored Posts of the American Legion in Tennessee, assured him that rumors about a planned uprising among blacks were false but warned that the police department provoked more bitterness than any other aspect of city life. Just off Beale Street on Fourth Avenue, he wrote, he had recently observed an officer "strike a Colored man, cursed him, and abused him. . . . Some others stopped to see what it was all about, and was driven away." In black neighborhoods, he declared, white officers "come right into our homes, search them, and many times abuse the occupants, using profane language etc." "In making arrests," he stated, "the prisoner is abused, and in jail prior to his trial, forced to give confessions, which in many instances are not true." Others echoed his perception that policemen ignored "our laws and procedure" in their dealings with African Americans.[19]

Police brutality had provoked concern across the region during the war, even in the small towns that dotted the rural South and contributed migrants to cities such as Memphis. In local farming crossroads, the police had become notorious for kicking or beating blacks they perceived as too uppity, and even shooting and killing crime suspects. From Warren, Arkansas, in the Arkansas Delta, to Oakdale, Louisiana, in Allen Parish, local residents sought assistance from the NAACP and other local organizations to help quell police violence. In one of the most infamous incidents, the police chief in Batesville, South Carolina, dragged returning black veteran Isaac Woodward off a bus and beat him in 1946, permanently blinding him.[20]

Many urban migrants, therefore, already considered police brutality a significant problem before moving to cities such as Memphis and New Orleans, where worries about encounters with policemen became daily concerns. Lovie Mae Griffin, who, like Annie Mae Williams, migrated to Memphis during the war from Fayette County, Tennessee, recalls that in the small town of Moscow, the sheriff was "ready to kick and beat whether you caused anything to do or not." At least one of her uncles left Fayette County after being beaten by the police and accused of drunkenness. Moving to the city during the war at age fifteen, she found that police harassment had become a feature of everyday life in certain sectors of the city. The city, in contrast to Moscow, offered openings for protest, however; Griffin, for example, remembers attending church meetings on police brutality.[21]

Observers of police violence noted in particular assaults on northern blacks who passed through Memphis during the war. Some incidents involved black women whose behavior did not conform to acceptable local norms. In March 1943, for example, the *Memphis World* reported that police officers had beaten and arrested Lorraine Guilford Brown, saxophonist in an "all-girl orchestra" visiting from New York, after she failed to address them as "sir."[22] A majority of these beatings involved black soldiers whom police perceived as threatening to the southern racial order. Sergeants Walter Frazier and Clifton Robinson, patients at Kennedy Hospital, filed complaints about a 1944 brutality incident in which, according to their affidavits, two patrolmen accosted them on Beale Street. Announcing that they wanted to "learn this smart northerner how to act," the officers blackjacked and kicked Frazier, smashing his glasses, but spared Robinson, declaring that as a southerner, he had learned how to conduct himself. The mayor later forwarded a police report to the commanding officer at Kennedy, denying wrongdoing and accusing Frazier of smashing his own glasses while drunk.[23] In another 1944 case, *Memphis World* columnist Nat D. Williams reported that shore patrol officers had beaten a black soldier who was waiting in line with his luggage in Grand Central Station. The assault spurred women bystanders, both black and white, to attempt to intervene. "[M]y God!" Williams exclaimed. "What is Democracy?"[24]

Police presence in outlying working-class neighborhoods with large concentrations of African Americans was of particular concern for young people. Lovie Mae Griffin remembers that patrolmen harassed her and her siblings and cousins in their neighborhood. "They would come and mess with you in order for you to say something and this was their excuse," she recalled. "They didn't mind hitting a person with the sticks that was on their sides when they get out of those cars and come across in front of you and start harassing you . . . knowing that you might say something. And this was what they was expecting. This gave them an excuse to hit you." Although policemen usually beat young men, Griffin recalls, they occasionally hit young women who spoke out in defense of their male companions.[25] Nevertheless, she remembers young people becoming bolder about asserting themselves in public; for example, instead of stepping into the street to allow whites to pass, they sometimes locked arms and stayed on the sidewalk.

Griffin also recalled the flip side of police violence: white paternalism, which protected its recipients in many ways but reinforced images of blacks as dependents. When she and other family members were harassed by police, she recalled, her mother's employment as a maid by a prominent white family became an important resource. Griffin learned that mentioning the family's name kept police from further harassing her. An incident involving Griffin's father was resolved by the employer's direct intervention. Griffin's father, who did yard labor for his wife's boss in addition to working at Firestone, was arrested on the employer's grounds by police who claimed, as she put it, that he "looked like somebody that did something." The employer demanded that the police release her father, unharmed, and desist from any further such actions on his property. White Memphis employers frequently resented police meddling with their employees and generally considered patrolmen as low-class whites.[26]

In addition to police brutality on commercial and residential neighborhood streets, altercations that culminated in police violence frequently erupted on city buses and streetcars. Memphis activist Benjamin Bell complained in the *Chicago Defender* that "many instances of inhumane treatment and police brutality emanate from street car and bus incidents." In addition, he declared, "not in any instance has an officer or transportation operator been reprimanded for manhandling a Negro soldier or sailor."[27] Public transportation brought whites and blacks into close proximity on a regular basis and might have served as a kind of social leveler had it not been for racial segregation and police enforcement. However, the local streetcar segregation code provoked persistent disputes. The code stipulated white seating from front to back and black seating from back to front but designated no fixed dividing line, in order to remain flexible for the varying needs of different routes. Drivers frequently called for police intervention when black riders ignored requests to relinquish their seats to white passengers, or when fights broke out between black and white riders.[28]

Women riders expressed the most persistent ire over bus segregation. In general, working-class women relied heavily on public transportation to get to work or to travel downtown. White women's complaints made it clear that they resented being crowded together with African Americans, whom they described as disrespectful to them and threatening to public health. A 1942 letter from a group of white working women to Mayor Chandler, for example, complained that black riders "make you wait till they all get on; and they take up all the seats on the car and you [stand] up; and as they pass you they RUB & STOMP all over you with that deasese [sic] that nearly every negro has" — likely a reference to syphilis. They also demanded that Chandler address their concerns about black men, whom they saw as a threat to white women with so many white men entering the army. Chandler, in a note to Boss Crump the same year, asserted, "Hardly a day passes that white women do not call me about negroes' jostling them on the street car" and warned that white reaction to "the growing insolence of the negroes" might provoke race trouble.[29] The following year, a city survey of racial conditions on bus and streetcar lines took note of African American women's complaints about having to stand while whites sat, or other indignities that differentiated them from white women.[30]

African American women also worried about their vulnerability on public transportation at late hours. Evelyn Bates, for instance, began work as a cook for Boss Crump's daughter, a job that required working until 2:00 A.M. on nights when her employer threw parties. Bates quit the job because she had to get home on her own on these late evenings. She never returned to domestic service, instead working at a cafeteria, a dry cleaner, and a mattress manufacturer before becoming one of the first black women employees at Firestone in 1944. Other young women took jobs in restaurants, hotels, and other establishments that required nighttime hours, either because they found no other jobs available, refused to work as maids, or needed to take care of small children during daytime hours. Their reliance upon public transportation stirred anxieties about harassment and assaults.[31]

Vice, Venereal Disease, and Regulation of Black Women's Bodies

In general, police sexual assaults represented white men wielding extreme authority that took advantage of black women's vulnerability, especially in public spaces. In 1950, the local NAACP protested a case in Panama City in which a policeman sexually assaulted a young black woman after ordering her into his car, claiming that he needed to question her about a fight between two black men. In Montgomery in 1949, two police officers picked up a young woman ostensibly for public drunkenness before taking her to a secluded spot and raping her.[32]

Wartime campaigns against vice and syphilis intensified this authority. Although these campaigns made all working-class young women in public spaces vulnerable to police harassment, racist representations of African American women as promiscuous, immoral, and even syphilitic made them especially subject to harassment. In Memphis, the intersection of these sexualized representations of black women and wartime antivice and antisyphilis campaigns became the basis for a pattern of abuse.

During the late 1930s, Memphis had developed a multipronged venereal disease control program, in response to national concerns and federal initiatives aimed at eradicating syphilis. In May 1938, Roosevelt signed into law the National Venereal Disease Control Act, allocating funding for treatment facilities.[33] Aided by this funding, Memphis health officials established the Memphis-Shelby County Venereal Disease Control Project in February 1939. In its first two years, the program expanded its syphilis treatment clinics from a single one at the public hospital to clinics in north and south Memphis, Beale Avenue Park Auditorium (specifically for blacks), the police station, Collierville, the penal farm, and one mobile unit. The program treated 12,587 patients for syphilis, developed plans for gonorrhea control, enlisted doctors and employers in its crusade, and presented educational programs to parent-teacher groups and civic clubs.[34] The police department forced women detained for prostitution or "disorderly conduct" to be tested for syphilis, and judges had the option of quarantining infected women instead of fining them. At the state level, Tennessee required tests for all individuals employed in retail food processing establishments and, after mid-1941, for all marriage license applicants.[35]

Nationally, as men were drafted into the armed forces, public officials raised concerns about syphilitic civilian women who might "prey on soldiers and sailors," as an Atlanta police official put it. The May Act, signed by Roosevelt in 1941, expanded federal powers to police civilian life in regions surrounding military bases, as part of a national effort to eradicate prostitution and keep alcohol away from designated "moral zones." With the United States' entry into the war, Federal Security Agency chief Paul McNutt established the Social Protection Division (SPD), to assist the Justice Department in its efforts to quell vice. If city governments failed to crack down on prostitution and venereal disease, the federal government was authorized to intercede. Nationally, thousands of women underwent mandatory venereal disease examinations and forced treatment under detention in jails and Civilian Conservation Corps camps, and over 700 U.S. cities shut down their red-light districts. This number included Memphis, although there, efforts to eradicate vice had begun in the 1930s, when Crump, assisted by Commissioner Boyle, had decided to "clean up" the city, in part to quiet charges of corruption. In the early 1940s, the city assisted army and navy programs that combated venereal disease among servicemen. "As they prepare to fight for us, we must defend them against the dangers of syphilis and gonorrhea," wrote one business leader on behalf of the American Social Hygiene Association. Such schemes presented servicemen as the prey of unscrupulous and diseased women.[36]

Concerns about an incursion of women who might be bearers of syphilis escalated in June 1942, when twenty-seven middle Tennessee counties passed local May Acts to "protect soldiers against venereal disease," raising the specter of increased migration to Memphis by infected young women.[37] Memphis police officers were instructed to keep "all strange women under close scrutiny." At the end of the year, the police department reported that among 56 white women arrested in the first two weeks of December alone, half were infected with syphilis. The arrests of 133 African American women in November had shown an equal rate of infection.[38]

Although antivice crusades in southern cities involved both white and African American women, southern black communities charged that such programs targeted black women. African Americans in Atlanta accused police of limiting arrests to black women who were with black servicemen.[39] In Memphis, pressure from African Americans led the Venereal Disease Department director, Lt. Col. A. F. Brand, to defend his office against critiques that police officers were singling out black women for harassment. In June 1945, Brand attempted to dispel the "confusion" prompted by black citizens' charge that the police were using local law to "pick up women not having health cards" and quarantining women requiring treatment for venereal disease in the city's penal farm. The police department, he claimed, arrested women only for "violation of some law." Brand explained that the state issued cards to ensure that food service workers were syphilis-free and that city health clinics issued them "for the information of employers of domestic help." Women needing treatment were attended by visiting nurses and quarantined only when they failed to cooperate — at the West Tennessee Medical Center, not the penal farm.[40] To Brand, neither rationale involved racial bias. However, according to local strictures, most maids and a large number of food service workers in Memphis were black women. Health card requirements thus reinforced white perceptions of syphilis as a disease spread by African Americans, especially women. Myrdal's *American Dilemma* noted that publicity about syphilis had led many northern white women to stop hiring black domestic workers or to require that they obtain health cards. Southern white women continued to employ black women as maids, but now many of them required that their employees have health cards.[41]

These racial stereotypes also influenced the perspectives of prominent black Memphians who supported wartime anti–venereal disease programs for African Americans. The *Memphis World*, in late August 1945, trumpeted a film program on venereal disease prevention at LeMoyne Gardens, a new public housing project for blacks. Its endorsement declared that the program would offer black sailors "the maximum in protection from the temptations and lure of greedy individuals" — i.e., black women.[42]

Following Wright's and Williams's assaults, residents of one of the city's poorest black neighborhoods exposed the ties between antivice and syphilis campaigns and police abuse. Wright's, Williams's, and their mothers' accounts detailed how the racist perceptions that were bound up in these campaigns could produce serious consequences for black women. By telling their stories to the media, to the NAACP, to their ministers, and to the court, they exposed these criminal methods to public scrutiny.

Gender and the Racial Politics
of Postwar Political Leadership

Less than a week after the August 1945 assaults, with Williams still quarantined, the two mothers spoke with a *Press-Scimitar* reporter who had learned about the case. The *Press-Scimitar* seized on the story as the latest evidence of the Crump machine's unbridled corruption. "Officials are trying to cloak in silence a crime committed by two uniformed officers," the article began, describing the details as "revolting" enough to "shock" even "veteran newspapermen." The account presented the mothers as concerned parents of large families, and reported that they had been "permitted to see [their] daughter[s] for only a few minutes from Friday until the following Monday." One was quoted as saying that Seabrook had ordered her to "take [her] daughter, go home, and keep [her] mouth shut." This stark contrast between the corrupt, powerful officials and beleaguered, vulnerable mothers added fuel to *Press-Scimitar* editor Edward Meeman and other white moderates' criticism of the Crump machine. The racial identities of the officials and mothers served to underscore the women's vulnerability. As did moderates elsewhere in the South who promoted good government and economic modernization as twin goals at the end of World War II, those in Memphis eschewed racial violence, viewing it as a form of extremism that impeded the South's development.[43]

The story accrued multiple meanings as it appeared in other contexts. In the pages of the black press, public criticism of black leaders that had been developing since the beginning of the war became integral to the story. The first sign of an unusual response to this particular instance of police assault appeared on the front page of the August 10 issue of the *Memphis World*, in a letter to the editor. Writing under the name Edward Smith, the commentator blasted what he characterized as "an apparently totally demoralized, disorganized, program-less, fearful, 'back gate' talking, 'front-page' whispering, bewildered, and supine Negro leadership." He held black leaders responsible for not doing more to address "police brutality, police rapine and coercion of defenseless Negro women and girls, police intimidation of Negro soldiers and defense workers . . . [and] police coercion of an entire segment of the local population under the convenient cloak of venereal disease eradication." Smith's sharply worded critique of black leaders who, in his view, failed to protect the black population, echoed A. Philip Randolph's declaration that black Memphians did not wish to be "well-kept slaves." However, Smith even more pointedly singled out black elites for what he characterized as their dependence on the Crump machine.

The author presented his concerns in the context of international and national political debate about the postwar world, calling for a Memphis version of the international conference that had launched the United Nations, held in San Francisco in Spring 1945, as the war in Europe was concluding. Such a conference, he declared, could "chart a current as well as a post-war program for the civic welfare of the Negroes of Memphis." Racial injustice and failed democracy, from Smith's perspective, resulted from a lack of vision and leadership.[44]

This front-page critique of local elites and community leaders in the *Memphis World* helped spur more public outrage. Five days later a front-page editorial placed next to a reprint of the *Press-Scimitar* exposé exhorted "self-respecting" black readers and sympathetic whites to demand the arrest and prosecution of the police officers who had raped two young African American women and the hiring of black policemen. "The whole city has had about two weeks now," it declared, "to quiver, shake heads, bemoan, deplore, wax indignant, express disgust, and otherwise castigate a system" in which such an assault could take place; nonetheless, it asserted, a "creeping moral paralysis" prevailed.[45]

Together, the letter to the editor and the editorial insisted upon more politically muscular leaders who would boldly assist the young women and demand that justice be served. As public outcry snowballed over the next few weeks, the church-based Deacons and Trustees Union issued a statement regarding the rape case, declaring that "to make Memphis safe, the Deacons and Trustees Union faces this challenge like men." Several ministers alliances and civic and welfare organizations also condemned the attacks. Calling the rapes a "bestial outrage," they condemned the policemen and assigned the role of moral protector to themselves. Critiques of black leaders for not "being men" persisted, however. A year later, during a labor conference featuring A. Philip Randolph at the Beale Avenue Baptist Church, Reverend Long received "enthusiastic applause" when he proclaimed to Randolph, "You are a man . . . in a man's position, and perform a man-sized job. I wish to heaven we had just a few men like you in Memphis."[46]

Significantly, the Early Grove Baptist Church in the Binghampton neighborhood, located down the street from Wright and Williams's homes, helped raise money to assist in the prosecution of the case. In addition to the fact that the Wrights attended Early Grove, pastor A. J. Campbell was a member of the NAACP and would later correspond about the case directly with NAACP officials in New York, including Thurgood Marshall. Between 1945 and 1948, Binghampton residents grew increasingly vocal about frequent police brutality in their neighborhood.[47]

The local NAACP, largely inactive from the time of the "reign of terror" until the end of the war, now established itself as the locus of efforts to help the young women and push for the prosecution of the police officers. Although the LeMoyne College branch had been hard hit by the draft of most of its male students, membership in the main branch had risen sharply from 400 in 1939 to 1,500 in 1943, even though, to the dismay of those in the national office, the branch continued to offer little in the way of actual programs apart from its annual membership campaign. From 1943 to 1946, membership further soared to 3,600, reflecting an increasingly working-class base of support.[48] In the *Memphis World* on August 21, the NAACP branch announced that it would serve as a local coordinator for individuals seeking to "donate funds to the prosecution of the case." The funds, the article announced, would be used for legal expenses and to assist "the distitute [sic] mother of eight children, who is the mother of one of the outraged girls."[49] The branch hired a white attorney, who launched an investigation that included obtaining affidavits from the two young women and their mothers.

Prior to the Memphis NAACP's announcement, the expectation that local groups would not mount a protest prompted a series of urgent communications among prominent activists in Memphis, Nashville, and New York. Their letters suggest that a series of complaints about similar assaults of black women had reached the attention of top civil rights leaders. Even before the story first broke in the newspaper, H. L. Mitchell, white cofounder of the Southern Tenant Farmers' Union, headquartered in Memphis, forwarded a confidential report obtained from a concerned *Press-Scimitar* reporter to black sociologist Charles S. Johnson at Fisk University in Nashville. Mitchell asked Johnson to help ensure that action was taken in the case but intimated that it would be dangerous for his own name to be attached to it.[50]

The report, which Johnson immediately sent to NAACP headquarters in New York, linked the incident to other recent police attacks on young black women in Memphis. In addition to the assaults on the two Binghampton girls, asserted the report, the fifteen-year-old daughter of a black shoe repair shop owner named Pipes had also been "picked up the same night and held in the city jail for 48 hours." Even though the girl was not assaulted, the report stated, the "Pipes family are members of the Catholic Church and many of the leading Catholic citizens of the city are aroused about this case"—an indication of the protective role Catholic leaders often played toward African American church members. The report also claimed that a "number of other young Negro girls have been assaulted by policemen in Memphis but have been fearful to bring their complaints into the open." In all these incidents, "the girls [were] stopped by police on the pretex [*sic*] of investigating whether or not they [had] a health card." Given the concerns of both white and black Memphians about such incidents, the report gauged that the attorney general for Shelby County might prosecute the policemen if pressure were brought to bear on him.[51]

From New York, NAACP officials concerned about the Memphis branch's immobility pressured local branch leaders to respond. Roy Wilkins urged branch president Utillus Phillips, a railroad postal worker who had headed the local NAACP since 1939, to "make an effort to get justice," despite the climate of terror in Memphis. Special Counsel Thurgood Marshall exhorted Phillips as well. "There has been too much of this type of discriminatory action by policemen in the South," he wrote, "and it is our job to break it down." In the meantime, A. Philip Randolph, whose offices were also in New York, learned of the incident. An outspoken opponent of Crump since the two men's clash in fall 1943, and still concerned about black leadership in the city, Randolph called upon U.S. Attorney General Tom Clark to investigate "police lawlessness" in Memphis.[52]

Black Women's Sexuality on Trial

The combination of local and national pressure, including the threat of a federal probe, led Will Gerber, the attorney general for Shelby County and one of Crump's closest allies, to publicly call for justice in the case in early September.[53] This step allowed the Crump machine to demonstrate its authority. With white moderates and African Americans together demanding the prosecution of the police officers, the Crump machine positioned itself as the body that would uphold the law and secure racial harmony. City leaders had worried throughout the war about growing resistance among African Americans and possible white reactions. They now seized upon the case to demonstrate their commitment to justice — if not "social equality" — even if this meant clamping down on corruption and violence perpetrated by their own police officers.

Although Commissioner Boyle had dismissed Torrey and Lewis from the police force, the two remained outside police custody and were not charged for over three weeks. During the first week of September, a grand jury indicted Torrey for rape, a capital offense that bore the death penalty in Tennessee. Lewis was indicted for aiding and abetting a capital offense, since his actions fell outside the state's strict definition of rape.[54]

The same week, Gerber declared that he would "personally prosecute" the ex-policemen, placing the Crump machine at the forefront of those calling for law and order. In a statement reported in the black press, Gerber also denounced contributors to the NAACP's legal fund and criticism that his office had not acted immediately, and he announced that he would take over the case. Rev. Dwight Kyle, a young African Methodist Episcopal (AME) minister new to Memphis and now NAACP Executive Committee chairman, took the bold step of publicly defending the organization's decision to hire an attorney to investigate the case.[55]

Gerber's effort to demonstrate the machine's commitment to justice extended to the trial. In November 1945, spectators jammed into the Shelby County Criminal Court chamber to witness the trial, packing both sides of the segregated courtroom, with African Americans spilling out into the corridor. The trial, the black press claimed, was the first any could remember in which "a Southern law enforcement agency had apprehended and brought up for trial two Southern white men accused of violating the honor and person of Negro women."[56] In a dramatic display, Gerber asked fifty prospective white male jurors whether they could "give a Negro justice in a case involving a white man," rejecting each man as he responded negatively.[57] The trial halted at this point, after defense attorney Harry Scruggs fell ill. When the trial reconvened in January, with jurors finally sworn in, Gerber called witnesses, some from the police department, who corroborated Wright and Williams's stories and undermined Torrey and Lewis's argument that the case was one of "mistaken identity." In his closing arguments, Gerber appealed to the jury to avoid hinging the case on "the color question," asking each juror to employ "reason, justice and common sense" and to reach a conclusion "as a family man, citizen, and officer of the State."[58]

The white men on the jury may have believed they were following Gerber's instructions. However, their interpretations of "reason, justice and common sense" were influenced by the narrative constructed by the defense attorneys, based partly on the syphilis tests Police Chief Seabrook had ordered directly after the assaults. During their cross-examination of Williams and Wright, the defense attorneys employed language that conjured up derogatory, sexualized images of black women. Attorney Weinstein referred to Alice Wright as "the mother of the bastard baby" and to Annie Mae Williams as "the syphillectice [sic] stiff."[59] Defense attorney Scruggs replaced Wright and Williams's narrative with his own version of that happened: "Now isn't the truth of this matter that you . . . went to town on a whoopee party and that your mothers upbraided you for getting home so late and you two made up this 'cock and bull' story?"[60]

Given the state's definition of rape, the outcome of this kind of trial usually hinged on whether or not the woman had been forced. The chastity of the woman typically played an important role in this determination, with judges and defense attorneys frequently suggesting that unchastity implied consent. Representations of black women as naturally promiscuous made it especially unlikely that white jurors would read the evidence as proof of rape. In this case, Weinstein and Scruggs's use of language that linked the young women to unmarried motherhood and syphilis overrode evidence of the policemen's guilt.[61]

On January 24, in under an hour of deliberations, the jury reached a not-guilty verdict, despite evidence and testimony that disproved the defense's claim that the men had been mistakenly identified. The sole juror who held out briefly for a ten-year sentence later explained he believed the policemen had lied but concluded that "because of the character of the girls, force was not necessary for the accomplishment of their purpose."[62] The jurors thus reinforced racist stereotypes the women sought to dispel. The jurors' response to Gerber's presumably race-neutral terms—"reason, justice and common sense" and "family man, citizen, and officer of the State"—illuminates the extent to which they interpreted foundational constructs of American democracy in racial, gendered terms.[63]

Weinstein and Scruggs's courtroom drama provoked different responses from African American spectators, who understood these terms differently from the white jurors, and were emboldened during the trial. When Weinstein accused Wright and Williams of bringing charges only because of organized pressure, his reference to the NAACP as the "League for the Protection of Colored People" prompted several African American spectators to nudge each other and giggle. One of them was Benjamin Bell, whose outspokenness had resulted in his dismissal as executive secretary of the Memphis Urban League two years earlier. In response to the pokes and giggles, Weinstein dramatically berated the spectators. The judge sent the jury from the room and further reproached them, singling out Bell for particularly harsh criticism.[64] However, these African American spectators had most likely *not* lost control of their emotions but used their laughter as a political commentary on the proceedings. This behavior made them into participants instead of spectators, transforming the trial into a rare public referendum on racial justice and the courtroom into an unlikely public sphere in which the politics of race could be contested by ordinary black Memphians, albeit under circumscribed conditions.

Racial Justice and Postwar Protest

That protest refused to die with Torrey and Lewis's acquittals in late January 1946 suggests that the police rape case had tapped deeply rooted sentiments about racial justice. At the national level, NAACP special counsel Thurgood Marshall proclaimed that a victory had been achieved by bringing the case to trial and that, despite the outcome, it would serve as a warning to southern police officers.[65] Locally, however, outrage at the acquittals persisted, especially within black working-class neighborhoods and among college students.

Outside Binghampton, the acquittals stirred anger among black Memphians who had little or no contact with individuals or organizations directly involved in the case. Sixty years later, Jeraldine Sanderlin, who was a teenager living in south Memphis, a more economically stable neighborhood than Binghampton, when the trial took place, vividly recalled the details of the case. She admired Williams for having the presence of mind to leave the torn-up card in the car as evidence and was upset that Williams, only a few years older than she, had been disrespected in court. The young women's testimony "did not mean anything," she asserted. "The judge, the jury, no one believed them. . . . It just did not happen then, taking a black person's word over a white's." Sanderlin also recalled her parents insisting that she and her sisters be off the streets before dark; and she remembered her relief that they did not require her to take a job. The trial thus became an allegory about dangerous urban spaces, class differences, and legal injustice.[66]

In Binghampton, anger at the acquittals worried community leaders. Rev. A. J. Campbell at Early Grove Baptist Church wrote to Thurgood Marshall to request assistance and caution him about criticism of the NAACP. "Unless something is done through this organization [the NAACP]," he asserted, "it will be a hard matter to influence members to join again." Writing this letter, he intimated, could bring trouble upon him from the authorities. "[B]ut I am staking my life for Justice," he declared. Replying for Marshall, Assistant Special Counsel Marian Wynn Perry encouraged Campbell to contact Nashville civil rights attorney Z. Alexander Looby.[67]

Despite Campbell's worries, NAACP meetings attracted notable crowds in the months directly following the acquittals. NAACP assistant field organizer Donald Jones, visiting Memphis to bolster the annual membership drive in March 1946, commented on this attendance in a letter to Ella Baker, NAACP director of branches. "I'm told the monthly meetings have been overflowing," stated Jones, "and the Branch has gone to bat in one or two recent cases — rather timidly, but astounding for Memphis — and the public is beginning to rally." Baker skeptically responded that she hoped he would "do [his] part to get blood, even out of the turnips." The NAACP continued to attract new members through the late 1940s, before lapsing back into timidity and losing members at the end of the decade.[68]

The February 1946 police riot in Columbia, Tennessee, further spurred black Memphians' interest in the NAACP. In Columbia, two hundred miles east of Memphis, a fight between a black and a white veteran led the former to flee for his life. It also precipitated a police riot in which local police and state highway patrolmen rampaged through "Mink Slide," the black business district, as African American men mounted an armed defense. In Memphis, 500 blacks showed up at Centenary Church for an NAACP meeting featuring Maurice Weaver, the white Tennessee attorney first on the scene to investigate the riot for the NAACP.[69]

At LeMoyne College, reactions to the police rape acquittals intertwined with efforts to renew campus activism as veterans returned to campus.[70] In a January 31 article titled "Speak Up!," the *Private Chatterer*, a college newsletter, decried the acquittals in the face of overwhelming evidence of the policemen's guilt and called upon LeMoyne students to speak out on southern justice. Issued during the war by women students, the *Private Chatterer*, edited by Miss Elsie Van Ness, had published letters and poems from LeMoynites in the armed forces, including many denouncing discrimination in the military. The "Speak Up!" article reappeared in the *LeMoyne Democrat*, newly revived in February as the *Chatterer* began wrapping up operations.[71]

These expanding concerns over legal justice continued to spotlight racial issues of sexuality and gender. The *Private Chatterer* emphasized this larger point in the "Speak Up!" article when it paired the case of Fred Jackson, a sixteen-year-old black youth accused of raping a white mother, killing her infant sons, and setting her house on fire, together with its commentary on the police acquittals: "An all white jury freed the two men who all but said — 'Yeah, we done it! But what are you gonna do 'bout it?'" The *Chatterer* pointed out that Jackson had mental deficiencies that made him an unlikely criminal but an easy mark and questioned whether he would receive just consideration.[72]

Regardless of such concerns, Attorney General Will Gerber pronounced the crime "the most heinous ever committed in this country" and quickly secured indictments and demanded the death penalty, despite crucial unresolved issues. During the trial, the public defender appointed to assist Jackson sided with the prosecution and also recommended the death sentence, leaving the sixteen-year-old to defend himself. The jury found

Jackson guilty of first-degree murder in just minutes and sentenced him to death, ignoring that he was a minor.[73]

In February 1946, following Jackson's trial, his parents, Young and Mary Jackson, assisted by the *Memphis World*, established a legal defense fund that enabled them to hire a private investigator and defense attorneys J. C. Rutschman Jr. and Grover McCormick. Although Jackson's father had initially cooperated with the prosecution, after the trial both parents insisted that their son was incapable of such a crime.[74] The Jacksons won support for their son from an array of Memphians, including whites who petitioned the governor to stay the execution. They argued that Fred, with a child's mental capacity, could not have orchestrated the crime, and that the real murderers had used him to cover up their own guilt — a view supported by the private investigator. Some of the Crump machine's staunchest African American allies likewise challenged the conviction, suggesting that Jackson's confession had been forced by the police and that the trial had ignored the youth's mental capacity. The depth of black support for Jackson could be seen at a mass fund-raising meeting at Mason Temple in April 1947. According to the *Memphis World*, after the youth's execution in August 1947, at age seventeen, thousands of black Memphians visited the T. H. Hayes funeral home to view Jackson's body and show their dismay.[75]

As with the police rape case, Jackson's mother played a central role in efforts to protect and defend the young man. Most notably, Mary Jackson personally visited Tennessee governor Jim McCord to plead for a stay of her son's execution, following the state supreme court's failure to overturn Jackson's conviction and the U.S. Supreme Court's refusal to hear the case. Other black women also helped support Jackson. The members of the Ladies' Willing Workers Club, for example, each contributed five dollars to the Fred Jackson Defense Fund.[76] Jackson's supporters viewed him as a victim and a dependent who needed protection from a racist legal system. In contrast, Gerber, the jury, and even the public defender cast Jackson as a bestial rapist and murderer. Although this case represented the flip side of the police rape incident, in both instances, black supporters, including women, claimed roles as protectors while fighting racist narratives that cast their daughters and sons as threats to society.

An incident the same month as the Jackson execution, involving the police beating of a visibly pregnant young domestic worker, further illustrates the heated struggle over protection and vulnerability, race and sexual identity that had become central to these local urban postwar conflicts over justice and democracy. The beating of Adelaide Hudson at her apartment in Foote Homes, a public housing project in south Memphis, took place nearly two years to the day after the 1945 police rapes. Originally from rural west Tennessee, Hudson had migrated to Memphis as a young-ster and later lived in Detroit before returning to Memphis. In early August 1947, two officers burst into her home in pursuit of her teenaged nephew—one of five children of a deceased sister in Hudson's custody—after a pellet from his BB gun grazed a young girl. One of the officers became incensed when Hudson failed to address them as "sir." "I don't know where in the [hell] you come from, but you are in Tennessee now. . . . N[igger]s should know how to talk to white people," he shouted at one point, according to witnesses quoted in the *Memphis World*. The witnesses stated that the of-ficer then dragged Hudson outside to a tree and beat her in front of neigh-bors and relatives using the butt end of the BB gun. Finally, the policemen arrested Hudson, taking her away in their squad car. Although she had to be hospitalized because of a threatened miscarriage and broken rib, a city judge found her guilty of disorderly conduct.[77]

The outcry provoked by this incident emphasized Adelaide Hudson's vulnerability to the extreme imbalance of power that characterized ac-tions by the Memphis police toward African Americans. Witnesses quoted by the *World* asserted that Hudson's neighbors had "cried out in horror at what was happening and begged the officer to stop beating the expect-ant mother." Their descriptions emphasized both her pregnancy and her slight stature; moreover, they depicted the policemen's violent actions as sexual in nature, noting that she had been scantily clad when the officers had burst into her home on a hot summer Sunday afternoon.[78]

The Memphis NAACP responded by establishing a legal defense fund. The branch retained Robert Tillman, the attorney who had investigated the police rape case, to appeal her conviction and sue the patrolmen for damages. In September, the NAACP issued a call for support through the churches and reported that contributions had been flowing in on a daily basis. The organization's appeal presented Hudson's case as emblematic of a universal need for "justice to all human beings regardless of race." Over the next several years, Utillus Phillips cited responses to the Hudson beating and the police rape case as highlights of the branch's work during his tenure as local NAACP president.[79]

The Politics of Police Brutality

In 1948, a group of prominent African Americans, including *Memphis World* editor Lewis O. Swingler, moved the demand for the hiring of black police officers to the front and center of public discussion about racial jus-tice and democracy in Memphis. Police brutality became emblematic of an array of issues folded into the larger problem of "southern justice," as the *Private Chatterer* had put it. Outcry against police brutality contributed to the highly charged racial politics that made the 1948 elections hotly contested locally and nationally, most famously with the withdrawal of the southern Dixiecrats from the Democratic Party in response to Truman's civil rights platform.

The hiring of African American police officers became a key reform issue in dozens of southern cities and towns in the years directly following the Second World War. By fall 1948, fifty-one southern locales had appointed at least a token number of black officers. In Atlanta, for example, the city agreed to hire black policemen after vigorous pressure from local organizations. Such prominent residents as Rev. Martin Luther King Sr., pastor of Ebenezer Baptist Church, and Dr. Benjamin E. Mays, president of Morehouse College, promoted the measure, with Mays arguing that it would promote "goodwill among the races" and was the democratic and morally right step to take.[80]

In Memphis, intensive publicity about a series of police brutality incidents in 1948 included editorials and statements by local leaders demanding the appointment of black policemen. In May, the *Memphis World* began printing gruesome photographs of brutality victims on its front page, starting with the shocking image of Eli Blaine, a Firestone retail employee, with his face swollen nearly beyond recognition and a white bandage wrapped around his head following the removal of one eye and damage to the other. Blaine had gone to the police station to report that officers who had entered his home in the Beale area during a party and searched the guests had stolen money from him. The same officers had then assaulted him in front of their superiors, smashing his glasses and damaging his eyes. They continued to blackjack and hit him with a pistol butt while transporting him to the hospital, later claiming Blaine had fallen from the moving car. The police chief fired both men, and they were indicted. Ultimately, however, the jury found one officer guilty but fined him only fifty-one dollars and found the other not guilty.[81] Several weeks after the Blaine picture appeared, the *Memphis World* printed a photograph of Mrs. Viola Moore, eyes still swollen shut after two weeks of hospitalization. A domestic worker and wife of an Illinois Central Railroad employee, Moore had been beaten by police officers who arrested her at the Jefferson Market, after they were called in to resolve an altercation regarding her bill. After her release from the hospital, a city judge fined her seventy-eight dollars.[82]

A citizen's committee of influential African American men, ranging from the director of the Memphis Urban League to members of the Junior

Negro Chamber of Congress, lobbied for the appointment of black police officers. While underscoring that such a step would reduce racial police violence, they also argued that black policemen would be more effective in suppressing crime in black neighborhoods. Most notably, they declared that such appointments would mark a recognition of African American men's historic and honorable service to the nation, thereby making black manhood central to the discussion. Memphis Urban League director Rev. James McDaniel, for example, declared in a published statement that black men had proven themselves in "every war in American history." He called upon the mayor to hire a "high type of Negro" — "men with good character, men with college degrees, and veterans" — who could ameliorate black crime. McDaniel's statement echoed appeals made in other southern cities, such as Atlanta and Birmingham, that similarly articulated a desire to recognize men with such profiles as protectors and authorities in their communities.[83]

With Mayor James Pleasants adamantly opposed to appointing black officers, police brutality became central to both black civic clubs' and white municipal reformers' efforts to register and rally voters. This political activity mattered to the August primary elections — more important in statewide races than the November ballot because of the dominance of the Democratic Party — more than Pleasants anticipated. As we shall see in Chapter 4, alliances between white moderates and black leaders helped deal the Crump machine its first electoral blow since the 1910s, helping to send Estes Kefauver to the Senate and Gordon Browning to the governorship. As the *Memphis World* celebrated the defeat of incumbent Senator Tom Stewart, a civil rights opponent, and Governor Jim McCord, who had refused to stay the execution of Fred Jackson, its commentary linked results at the polls to black voters' memories of the Torrey and Lewis acquittals, the Jackson execution, and the Columbia riot.[84] Moreover, AME minister Dwight Kyle, who as chairman of the NAACP Executive Committee had helped spearhead the 1945 fight to prosecute Torrey and Lewis, ran as the first black candidate to run for Congress from Memphis since the early twentieth century.[85]

However, outcry over police violence crested after the August 5 Democratic primary, with protest against the police slaying of James Mosby, a twenty-three-year-old veteran and sanitation worker in Binghampton. Policemen called to Mosby's home during a domestic fight between him and his wife shot the young man to death, an action they alleged was justified because Mosby assaulted them. A flurry of petitions from such organizations as the Memphis NAACP, several ministerial alliances, and the Memphis CIO placed the issue within the context of postwar leadership and democracy.[86] The AME Ministers Council, one of the most outspoken African American organizations of the 1940s, denounced the "unbridled brutality" of the police against the "colored citizens of the city," calling it a "constant shame" in "democratic America." Police brutality, it declared, was "anti-Christian, anti-democratic, anti-humanitarian and against the best interest of the community—and not conducive for the building of a community of goodwill." The council positioned itself, not the city machine, at the helm of racial justice and as the guardian of the black community.[87]

In Binghampton, a complex set of issues came to the fore. Furious over the Mosby shooting, the second police killing in their neighborhood since the start of 1948, four days later, community members held a "mammoth mass meeting" at First Baptist Church, at which neighborhood residents and ministers from the AME church, the Colored Methodist Episcopal (CME) church, and the Baptist church formed the East Memphis Citizens Club. In addition to men, women and young people played key roles in the organization; women, for instance, served on the Resolutions Committee. At a forum held at Avery Chapel AME Church, pastored by Dwight Kyle, speakers representing the club included two young women, along with male students from both LeMoyne College and Booker T. Washington High School. Such organizations as the Modernette Social Club, headed by Mrs. Lillie Branscomb, also collected funds for Mosby's widow.[88]

A petition to the mayor from the East Memphis Citizens Club, signed by just under 1,500 residents, championed Mosby's manly honor while denouncing the police actions and calling for the appointment of black officers. The statement challenged the police depiction of Mosby as a rabid beast who had to be shot because he supposedly assaulted an officer and bit his arm. The petition defended Mosby as "a young World War II veteran who served his country as a soldier both in the States and Overseas"; a "father of two infant children, and an employee of the City"; and the son of "property owners in Binghampton, and devout Church communicants." In contrast to these depictions of Mosby, the petitioners called the police savages. They did not address the domestic conflict, which observers agreed had concluded by the time police entered the scene; unfortunately, Mosby's killing had underscored the danger of bringing an incident of domestic conflict to the attention of the police, a conclusion that increased black women's vulnerability to domestic abuse.[89]

Significantly, the Binghampton petition did address ongoing sexual racial violence against young African American women by policemen. Reminding the mayor of the 1945 police rapes of "two Binghampton girls," the petition asserted that policemen had continued to "molest . . . our young girls and women, making indecent approaches." The statement argued that "fears of reprisals on the part of many of these Binghampton residents" had kept individuals from reporting these crimes. The Torrey and Lewis acquittals coupled with the treatment of Wright and Williams in court had likely contributed to this reluctance. Discussed among families, neighbors, coworkers, and church members without being publicly prosecuted, these continuing incidents shaped postwar understandings about racial injustice.[90]

From one angle, this intensive protest activity led to a victory for African Americans and white moderates. In September, Public Safety Commissioner Joe Boyle announced his intention to hire African American police officers following the November elections. The assignment of black patrolmen to one of the most notorious police departments in the South, for the first time since 1919, prompted celebrations. "Beale Street was unusually crowded last Saturday night," crowed the *Memphis World*. "The answer wasn't hard to seek. For the first time in the memories of thousands of colored and white Memphians, Negro police officers were patrolling the Beale Street 'beat' . . . the street where the blues began, and where, according to tradition, 'business never closes until somebody gets killed.'"[91]

However, from another perspective this victory left unresolved issues that had been addressed by community residents in the years directly following the war. Boyle, for example, declared that despite his concession he had no intention of supporting "social equality." "Not only thinking Memphians, but the people who come in here from out in West Tennessee and in our neighboring states of Arkansas and Mississippi will not have it," he declared. Boyle refused to allow the new officers to arrest whites, made them patrol without weapons, and required them to report to a police substation in the Beale area instead of the main police station. While appointing black police officers may have been perceived by black Memphians as elevating them to a status of manhood equal to that of white officers, these measures re-racialized them.[92]

Even as these first black policemen sought to assert themselves as the protectors of their community, they sometimes found their authority disrespected by black Memphians on Beale Street. Wendell Robinson, an early appointee, believed blacks were more likely to fight with them than with white officers. In part, these problems stemmed from the policemen's attempts to enforce public morality. "So that the decent black woman could

Wendell L. Robinson and Ernest C. Withers, shortly after
their appointments as Memphis police officers in 1948.
(© *Ernest Withers, courtesy of Panopticon Gallery*)

come down there, we wanted to cut out the profanity," asserted Captain
R. J. Turner thirty-five years later. "The white officers didn't care if people
cussed or fought."[93] While black Memphians took pride in the new appointments, black policing also exposed tensions among African Americans, even as the officers—who consistently faced efforts by the white police hierarchy to emasculate them—sought to both stop crime and protect
women.

The appointment of black officers did not resolve the struggles over
race, sexuality, and gender that had surfaced so powerfully in the wake of
the 1945 rapes. The consequences of cultural representations of black men
and women were all too obvious. Because the police rape case had hinged
on images of black women as promiscuous and syphilitic, it ultimately left
Wright and Williams's attackers on the streets rather than behind bars,
while bestial images of black men had contributed to Fred Jackson's execution and James Mosby's slaying.

Just as men such as the nine new police officers assumed public roles as protectors of their communities, African American women had also seized on the spaces opened up by postwar life to assert themselves as activists and guardians. The postwar political climate in southern cities, including both black dissent and white challenges to entrenched machines, offered previously unavailable possibilities for protest to longtime residents, wartime migrants, and returning veterans intent on securing racial justice. Opposition to police racial violence, especially against those perceived as the most vulnerable, became a means of demanding an altered, postwar American democracy.

Nevertheless, the competing agendas under the umbrella of police brutality protest led to victories in some instances and failures in others. African American leaders in southern cities won the appointment of black police officers to previously all-white forces. And in Memphis, ferment against police violence had an impact on the formal political process in the 1948 elections. In neighborhoods such as Binghampton, however, this victory failed to resolve persistent, daily incidents of police violence or to address the contested images of black and white sexuality and gender that undergirded them. The costs of protesting these highly charged images could be severe, as seen by the slurs against Wright and Williams in court and the "fear of reprisals" that persisted three years later. In addition, even though the local NAACP's activism against police violence in the mid-1940s brought it thousands of new members, on a national level this issue did not become central to the postwar agenda. Not surprisingly, however, throughout the next decade, Binghampton would become one of the most important sources of working-class agitation over civil rights and labor issues, with community groups consistently adding their own meanings to otherwise formal demands.

Night Train, Freedom Train

4 Black Youth and Racial Politics
in the Early Cold War

"Returning to Memphis from a small town in northern Alabama recently, I found myself humming and reflecting on Roy Acuff's classic invitation: 'Take that night train to Memphis / Take that night train to Memphis / I'll be waiting at the station,'" wrote LeMoyne College student Charles E. Lincoln for the *LeMoyne Democrat*, a campus newspaper, in February 1946. He contrasted Acuff's country music lyrics about a much-anticipated romantic rendezvous to his own sentiments aboard a segregated Memphis-bound train. "Irresistibly," he wrote, "I was being rushed through the night back to the world cotton market, back to Beale Street, back to the terrors of the Memphis police brutality, the far-reaching, all seeing Cerberus of the Crump machine and the unpleasant daily contact with the little Crumplets." Torn about his own choice to return to the city, Lincoln — better known as C. Eric Lincoln, who would become a leading scholar of religion and African American culture in subsequent years — noted that as a World War II veteran, he could have attended a northern university on the GI Bill. Despite his misgivings, he viewed LeMoyne as an intellectual "oasis," where "[f]or a few hours each day one can feel that he is man among men, that life holds a future, and education a promise."[1]

Two years after Lincoln's poem appeared in a LeMoyne paper, another train ride placed the city at the heart of local and national controversy over the meaning of freedom in postwar America. Scheduled to visit Memphis in January 1948, the much-heralded Freedom Train, sponsored by the American Heritage Foundation (AHF), altered its itinerary to avoid Memphis after Mayor James Pleasants Jr. declared that he refused to concede to the foundation's desegregation policy for visitors to the train. Originally proposed by the U.S. Justice Department at the commencement of the Cold War, the Freedom Train surpassed any previous project in the nation's history to promote allegiance to American democracy. The exhibit, installed on a high-speed modern streamliner, showcased original historical documents hailed as milestones of American democracy, usually held at the National Archives and other institutions. Freighted with this precious cargo, the train visited all forty-eight states, traveling over 37,000 miles to 322 cities and towns between September 1947 and January 1949.[2] Greeted at each stop by thousands of enthusiasts, it kicked off community "rededication" celebrations at which local citizens pledged their commitment to American democracy.

Paradoxically, the AHF's goal to unify American citizens behind a presumably shared history based on democracy ignited conflict over the postwar meaning of freedom, especially in the South. The train's journey from town to town and state to state united Americans but at the same time divided them by becoming a lightning rod for local tensions about race. Even the historical documents became part of the struggle, as various groups disputed their representativeness of American democracy and their original and contemporary meanings. For example, hundreds of individuals from around the country sent letters to Memphis newspapers and the mayor to articulate their own opinions about the Crump machine's refusal to adhere to the AHF's desegregation policy, imbuing the local dispute with national significance. Memphis residents also weighed in, suggesting that the train's bypassing Memphis had prompted many citizens to view themselves, the city, and the idea of freedom in new light.

At LeMoyne College, the Freedom Train conflict spurred returning veterans and newly entering students to forge identities as members of a new generation of activists who would fight for freedom for African Americans. Even as the Crump machine defiantly espoused a view of freedom as the absence of Yankee tyranny, students pursued their own understandings of this ideal. In the immediate aftermath of the war, a majority of LeMoyne students joined the college chapter of the NAACP. As the Freedom Train controversy erupted in fall 1967, college NAACP members published the premier issue of their newsletter, *The Beacon*, in which they declared that it was their role to "lead the way in the fight for freedom."[3] They contrasted themselves as students to the "man on the street" who lacked educational opportunities. They also distinguished themselves from older black leaders, including those at the helm of the Memphis NAACP. The following January, two Greyhound buses filled with LeMoyne College students and faculty left Memphis bound for Jackson, Tennessee, ninety miles away, to tour the traveling Freedom Train exhibit under nonsegregated conditions.

As young African American activists sought to build on the momentum from the war by insisting on the eradication of racial injustice, the Truman administration attempted to lash this same momentum to its effort to present the United States as the leader of the "free world." While bearing powerful connotations related to the recently ended World War, the idea of freedom connected blacks with the historical legacy of slavery and emancipation. It also reached back to the Declaration of Independence's "life, liberty and the pursuit of happiness," bound to the idea that "all men were created equal" — however different the founding fathers' eighteenth-century understandings of equality may have been from post–World War II perceptions. During and after the Second World War, the concept of freedom began to take on new and often conflicting meanings.

The Freedom Train's initiators, who included Truman administration officials, New York advertisers, and Hollywood executives, initially attempted to bypass the knotty problems of race and place in order to promote national unity. In their planning, the nation's citizens remained generic and U.S. social geography was undifferentiated. Once the Freedom Train had begun its actual journey, speeding inexorably toward the South, however, the language of freedom it engaged began taking on powerful racial meanings. In the Deep South cities of Birmingham and Memphis, the American Heritage Foundation's policy mandating desegregated viewing, quietly set two months before the train's departure, provoked sharp conflicts.

Most immediately, the Freedom Train controversy had ramifications for the 1948 elections in Memphis, that rippled up to the state and national levels. Crump and Pleasants denounced not only the American Heritage Foundation but also President Truman's apparent support for civil rights. Their outcry turned out to be a rehearsal for their advocacy of the States' Rights Democratic Party, or Dixiecrats, who broke away from the Democratic Party in 1948 and ran their own presidential and vice presidential candidates. Conversely, Crump and Pleasants's position on the Freedom Train, perceived as extremist by their opponents, fueled opposition to the machine-backed candidates in the 1948 U.S. Senate and gubernatorial races.

C. Eric Lincoln's poetic depiction of LeMoyne as an oasis where a student could be a "man among men," distinct from those he derided as the "little Crumplets," anticipated the further politicization of LeMoyne students in the years immediately following the penning of his article in 1946. This politicization intersected with the Freedom Train controversy and the 1948 elections. For these emerging postwar activists and intellectuals, "freedom" took on complex meanings that drew together cultural memories of slavery and contemporary analyses of postwar politics. These modern, multilayered understandings were always hard-fought, as an array of contenders weighed in on the significance of American freedom in the postwar world.

Building an American Heritage

Many months before the Freedom Train sped across the Mason-Dixon line into the South, its planners crafted a message they hoped would unite American citizens around the idea of a common heritage of freedom. The train's official journey began six months after Truman's March 1947 "Truman Doctrine" speech conceptually launched the Cold War by dividing the world into two opposing "ways of life": one "distinguished by free institutions," the other by totalitarian ones; one governed by "the will of the majority," the other governed by "the will of the minority." This timing ensured that the Freedom Train would be perceived as a weapon in the global struggle between dictatorship and democracy.

Even as the Freedom Train promoters honed their plans, however, participants in another kind of public event pursued a different concept of freedom. In April 1947, young black and white members of the Congress of Racial Equality (CORE) launched what they called a "Journey of Reconciliation," a precursor to the 1961 "Freedom Rides," in which they defied Jim Crow transportation laws during a two-week ride on buses through the Upper South, in an attempt to enforce the Supreme Court's 1946 *Morgan v. Virginia* decision that outlawed segregation in interstate public transportation. Because the Journey of Reconciliation was well covered in the black press, by the time plans for the Freedom Train became public knowledge, black southerners had already been confronted by stories about another kind of freedom mission into the South, this one aimed at breaking down Jim Crow.[4]

When planning for the Freedom Train had commenced in early 1946, not only global political crises but also domestic ones consumed the United States as workers staged the most massive strike wave since the walkouts of 1919 at the conclusion of World War I. In addition, rising racial violence, including postwar riots such as the one in Columbia, Tennessee, and a series of lynchings, threatened to reproduce the "red summer" of race riots that followed World War I and to jeopardize the United States' projected image as a world democratic leader.[5] The advertising executives, Hollywood producers, and U.S. Justice Department officials who initiated the Freedom Train endeavored to eliminate these cleavages and bolster Americans' dedication to the nation. "More than ever before," declared the American Heritage Foundation, "we must work at freedom to make freedom work."[6]

The Freedom Train project emerged from two parallel tracks of postwar political initiatives, one within the Truman administration, the other among advertising executives.[7] In April 1946, Justice Department officials floated the idea of a traveling exhibition showcasing historical documents that illustrated America's democratic legacy. Initially proposed by William Coblenz, assistant director of public information after he toured a National Archives exhibition of Nazi documents, the proposed "Bill of Rights Exhibit" would contrast Nazi and American history while bringing historical materials to ordinary Americans. Championed by Attorney General Tom C. Clark, the concept also won the endorsement of Truman, who considered it a propitious time to launch a citizenship project to enlist Americans in the battle against communist "subversion." As Justice Department officials began working with National Archives personnel, Clark secured support from business and media executives, including Paramount Pictures president Barney Balaban, who had previously helped promote the war effort.[8]

In the meantime, advertising executives had independently begun formulating plans for a similar project. The Advertising Council, an outgrowth of the War Advertising Council that had collaborated with the Roosevelt administration, had reorganized after the war. In 1946, Thomas D'Arcy Brophy, Advertising Council director and president of advertisement agency Kenyon and Eckhardt, Inc., worked with other council members on a campaign organized around the theme of "Our American Heritage," which would, as with the Justice Department project, encourage loyalty to American institutions.[9]

These parallel tracks merged on December 10, 1946, when Advertising Council executives joined business leaders, media representatives, and government officials at a meeting sponsored by Clark and the Justice Department to move forward with plans for the traveling exhibition and accompanying patriotic celebrations. In February 1947, this coalition incorporated the AHF. In addition to promoting the traveling exhibit, the AHF also encouraged localities to hold "Rededication Weeks" to coincide with the train's visit. Its publicity included a film, a musical recording, Captain Marvel comics, publications of documents and commentaries on America's heritage, and an enormous mass media blitz complete with newspaper, radio, and television coverage.[10]

In early 1947, however, this gigantic promotional project for American democracy had still not yet taken on the rubric of "Freedom" that would ultimately shape its public presentation. In January, project organizers changed the exhibition's name from the "Bill of Rights" to the "Liberty Train," and decided to focus exclusively on American democracy instead of contrasting it with Nazism. Anticommunism, rather than the war against fascism, now became central to the project's message. However, the name changed again following the president's March 12 "Truman Doctrine" speech urging Congress to allocate funds to assist Greece and Turkey in suppressing the threat of communism posed by civil rebellions. Seizing on language from Franklin Roosevelt's 1941 "Four Freedoms" speech, which rallied Americans to support U.S. involvement in the Second World War, Truman made frequent references to "free peoples," "free institutions," and "freedom." His uncoupling of "freedom" from the fight against fascism and repositioning it at the heart of the Cold War convinced AHF directors to retitle the exhibit a second time by changing its name to "Freedom Train."[11]

The Truman administration presented the project to the public at a White House conference, May 22, that drew together 175 business, media, and civic leaders. In a letter published in the conference program, the president argued that there was a "need today for a dramatic reminder to our people of the American heritage which they enjoy" and declared it his "fervent hope" that "the rights and privileges guaranteed to every American citizen by our system of government may be shared by freedom loving people throughout the world." The AHF added its own sense of urgency regarding the purported threat of communism at home. "Subversive forces in various guises," it asserted, "seek to undermine the form and spirit of American government." A "national program of rededication to [America's] ideals and institutions," it continued, would "immunize" Americans against such forces.[12]

The AHF, however, avoided staking freedom to the Truman administration's concurrent display of support for civil rights, which aimed in part at quelling both domestic and international criticism of racial violence and discrimination in the United States. Apart from one sentence decrying "[d]emagogues and bigots" for their "disruptive game of setting one group of Americans against another," the AHF statement made no mention of race or civil rights.[13] Truman, meanwhile, had issued Executive Order 9808, establishing a President's Committee on Civil Rights in December 1946—the same month in which Clark assembled the coalition to oversee the Freedom Train project. On June 29, 1947, Truman became the first president to publicly address the NAACP when he delivered a speech at the Lincoln Memorial to 10,000 attendees of the NAACP's annual convention, a talk heard nationwide via radio broadcast.[14] In contrast, the AHF Board of Trustees included no African Americans, despite the Justice Department's advice to the contrary. NAACP executive secretary Walter White and National Urban League director Lester Granger were the only two African Americans among the attendees at the much-ballyhooed May White House conference. And the AHF, which had veto power over documents chosen by National Archives personnel, approved several documents about the end of slavery but overrode requests from Walter White and others to include several more recent documents, such as Roosevelt's 1941 Executive Order banning discrimination in the defense industry.[15]

The AHF's efforts to keep "freedom" safe from contemporary racial conflict produced ambiguous results. On July 9, for example, the Executive Committee of the AHF Board of Trustees responded to pressure from civil rights advocates by privately resolving that "no segregation of any individual or groups of any kind on the basis of race or religion [will] be allowed at any exhibition of the Freedom Train held anywhere." However, to the frustration of NAACP officials such as Walter White, who were privy to certain information about the project, AHF chairman Winthrop Aldrich did not make the resolution public until September 29, two weeks after the Freedom Train send-off in Philadelphia, on the 160th anniversary of the signing of the Constitution.[16]

The Freedom Train's designers conceived of the streamliner itself as a moving emblem of America's past, present, and future. Christened "The Spirit of 1776," with a locomotive painted with flashes of red, white and blue, the train became a symbol of both patriotism and modernity while bearing its historical freight of encased documents. Stock press releases and newsreels composed by AHF advertisers and producers linked this history to the postwar future, projecting it to the public via assorted mass media.

However, the exhibition, as a display that visited its viewers in their home towns, simultaneously promoted and undermined its message of national unification. Leading black journalists and others generally hailed the project, but they challenged the AHF's prepackaged messages of freedom and history. The *Pittsburgh Courier* ran a column by J. A. Rogers, titled "The Negro's Part in the Freedom Train," that conveyed his own version of U.S. history, including illustrations of African Americans' roles in the Revolution. The *Chicago Defender*, in a pointed twist of Truman's words, questioned whether the documents would expose "the traditional white supremacy way of life" in the United States or sweep it under the rug.[17]

Celebrated author Langston Hughes, recognized as one of the most elo-

The Freedom Train, 1947.
(Photograph by "Red" Heppner, Metropolitan Photo Service, National Archives photo no. 200[5]-AHF-110-2)

quent black writers in the United States since the 1920s Harlem Renaissance, penned an impassioned critique in a poem that appeared in the *New Republic* the week of the train's send-off. Hughes's poem bound the Freedom Train's significance to African Americans' historical quest for equality: "I read in the papers about the Freedom Train. / I heard on the radio about the Freedom Train. / I seen folks talkin' about the Freedom Train. / Lord, I been a-waitin' for the Freedom Train!" Presenting freedom as an ideal, not a reality, for black Americans, Hughes continued: "Down South in Dixie, only Train I see's / Got a Jim Crow car set aside for me. / I hope there ain't no Jim Crow on the Freedom Train. / No back door entrance to the Freedom Train, / No signs FOR COLORED on the Freedom Train, / No WHITE FOLKS ONLY on the Freedom Train." The poem addressed lynching, employment, and voting and reminded readers of African Americans who sacrificed their lives during the Second World War. Transforming the meaning of the Freedom Train from a historical exhibition to a force in contemporary struggles for racial equality, Hughes exhorted readers to "Get on board our Freedom Train!" with "our" taking on fresh significance.[18]

Paul Robeson's performances and recording of Hughes's "Freedom Train" ensured that the poem's travels paralleled those of the exhibition. Blues master W. C. Handy also expanded the poem's reach by marketing sheet music for "Checkin' on the Freedom Train," Hughes's poem set to music by Sammy Heyword. These renditions of Hughes's poem about freedom's meanings in postwar America differed from the AHF's official "Freedom Train" song, a snappy Irving Berlin composition recorded by Bing Crosby and the Andrews Sisters, that compared the train to Paul Revere's ride for liberty and applauded Americans' rights to vote and voice their opinions.[19]

Widely circulated critiques like Hughes's poem convinced the AHF to publicly announce its policy for desegregated viewing for the first time in the last week of September. As the train threaded its way through New England and down toward Washington, D.C., southern officials and local welcome committees deliberated about the terms of its visits to their cities.[20] Most southern officials would eventually assent to the AHF's policy, or work out a compromise acceptable to the AHF. Nevertheless, tensions mounted in the weeks leading up to the Freedom Train's first swing through the South, scheduled to include stops in nearly fifty cities and towns beginning December 1, 1947.

Midway between the Freedom Train's departure and its crossover into the South, a major development in civil rights further complicated this planning. The release on October 29, 1947, of *To Secure These Rights*, by the President's Committee on Civil Rights, created a major media splash. Over the next few months, literally hundreds of thousands of copies of the report in pamphlet form or in serials published by black newspapers made their way into homes around the country. Truman himself asserted that the report would become "an American charter of human freedom in our time."[21] Shortly after these remarks, U.S. Attorney General Tom Clark followed through on one of the report's recommendations by filing an amicus curiae brief on behalf of the plaintiff in *Shelley v. Kraemer*, a civil rights case before the Supreme Court that concerned restrictive housing covenants that prohibited homeowners from selling their houses to racial and religious minorities. The Justice Department's use of amicus curiae to intervene in civil rights cases would be repeated, most famously in *Brown v. Board of Education*.[22] Thus as southern city officials weighed whether to countenance the Freedom Train's visit, the release of *To Secure These*

Rights, followed by Truman's accolades and Clark's unprecedented legal step, entered their deliberations. In Memphis, Mayor Pleasants blasted the report's proposals for desegregation, declaring, "Such ideas go to the very teeth of our way of life."[23]

The Freedom Train, White Memphians, and Thought Control

By the time the Freedom Train crossed the Mason-Dixon line on December 1, local responses to the President's Committee on Civil Rights report, nearly coinciding with the AHF's statement about desegregated viewing, brought race and rights to the forefront of national consideration of the project. Mayor Pleasants's announcement in Memphis that the city and county commissions had decided to have whites view the exhibition for one-half of the train's day-long stay, and blacks the other half, prompted a quick, sharp response from the AHF. On November 17, Executive Vice President Louis Novins issued a statement declaring that he was canceling the train's Memphis visit because the proposed arrangement directly violated "not only the letter but the spirit" of the foundation's resolution against segregation. In a rejoinder issued the next day, Pleasants declared that if he adhered to the AHF's policy, the "jostling and pushing that must result" from thousands of white and black citizens attempting to view the train would surely provoke "race trouble." All "thinking people, both white and colored," he argued, would agree that the commissioners' plan would prevent such trouble.[24]

Hundreds of letters deluged the mayor's office and the local newspapers as word of the controversy spread nationwide. Among the roughly 300 letters, cards, and telephone messages that supported the mayor's position, slightly over 40 percent came from outside the city, with a majority of those from neighboring Mississippi, Arkansas, and west Tennessee. Others came from more distant southern states; from southerners living in the North or West; or, in a few cases, from native northerners. Such communications congratulated Pleasants for standing up to a Yankee effort to force the mixing of the races, hailing him as "strong-" or "stout-minded" and expressing the wish that the South had more men willing to defend the southern way of life.[25]

Many writers linked the AHF to communism, giving the anticommunism that was sweeping the country a local southern stamp. Oscar Bledsoe III, owner of a 3,600-acre Mississippi plantation and director of the Staple Cotton Cooperative Association, asked: "Can the Yankee make himself as obnoxious to the South as the Russian Communist? We have been forced to live with the Yankee. I cast my vote for him as he continually disparages his neighbor; both are guilty of trying to force their ideologies on others." A St. Louis lawyer discussed the attorney general's amicus curiae brief in *Shelley v. Kraemer*, likening such federal intervention to a "surrender to subversive and un-American philosophies." Some writers added anti-Semitism to this ideological mix. "I notice a Russian Jew, Louis Novins, in charge of the freedom train refuses to allow the people of your city to see the train unless they hob nob with negroes," wrote a New Yorker, adding that the "Communist Jews here are trying to force social equality between negroes and whites." In such missives, the oft-used word "freedom," whether counterposed to Yankee federalism or Russian communism, denoted southern liberty from external tyranny, that is, the AHF's imposition of racial integration.[26]

Nearly half of the roughly ninety letters to the mayor that opposed his position came from writers in the North and West, who accused Pleasants of violating American principles of democracy and equality. "We understand our Declaration of Independence is among the famous historical documents on exhibit in this 'Freedom Train,'" wrote two women from Olympia, Washington. "Quoting from this document we find this: — 'We hold these truths to be self evident: That all men are created equal, that they are endowed by their Creator with certain unalienable rights; that among these are life, liberty and the pursuit of happiness.'" These women and many others associated this founding statement with Christian principles of brotherhood, suggesting that even as increasing numbers of Americans linked freedom to secular concepts of rights, they continued to understand them in relation to religious precepts.[27]

Some of the most strongly worded comments came from southerners eager to distinguish themselves from Memphis's city leaders. "Compared to you and your kind, Mayor, Hitler was a ten carrot angel," wrote a white ex-Mississippian who now lived in California. A group of eighth graders from Hubert, Arkansas, called upon the mayor to practice democracy and expressed regret that they would not be taking the trip to Memphis to view the train, since it would bypass the city. Several writers contrasted Pleasants to Atlanta's Mayor Hartsfield, who had announced that there would be no segregation of viewers who visited the Freedom Train in Atlanta.[28]

Memphis's daily newspapers, the morning *Commercial Appeal* and the evening *Press-Scimitar*, both Scripps-Howard publications, criticized the mayor's decision. The *Press-Scimitar*, under the editorship of Edward J. Meeman, made the issue of the Freedom Train central to its postwar crusade for good government and published a steady stream of letters to the editor.[29] Its editorials hammered away not so much at segregation on the Freedom Train but at the machine's deprivation of liberty to potential exhibition viewers. "Memphians Have Right To See Freedom Train," declared a headline after the AHF announced that the Freedom Train would not be stopping in Memphis. Quoting a local resident, the article insisted that city officials had "no right to insist on segregation — depriving thousands of the privilege of seeing the Freedom Train." Witnessing the Freedom Train, it asserted, was a national "civic exercise," like "voting and paying taxes." The newspaper presented segregation on the train as a nonissue, reminding readers that black and white Memphians rode the same buses, visited the same grocery stores, and had even visited the same train displays, including the new "City of New Orleans" and "City of Memphis" streamliners.[30]

The *Press-Scimitar* presented city officials as out of sync with not only the nation but also the rest of the South. Staff writer Richard Wallace declared that "Memphis officials seemed as lonely today as a Yankee corporal beside a Rebel camp fire during the years 1861–65." Following this striking image of Memphis as an outsider to the South, the article cited positions taken by mayors in Richmond, Montgomery, Atlanta, New Orleans, and elsewhere. Suggesting that Memphis officials might pose a security threat, the *Press-Scimitar* charged that their position would strengthen the Communist Party's reported effort to sabotage the Freedom Train's success.[31]

Together, liberal organizations formed the Committee to Bring the Freedom Train to Memphis. The Memphis chapter of the American Veterans Committee (AVC), a biracial organization of World War II veterans, called for "veterans' groups, churches, civic clubs, business organizations, labor unions, student and educational associations" to pressure city officials to uphold democracy by altering their policy on the Freedom Train. Local chapters of the League of Women Voters and the Americans for Democratic Action issued statements supporting the train's visit as part of a broader liberal, anticommunist political perspective.[32]

Overall, white Memphis citizens remained deeply divided. Some irately condemned Pleasants's proposal as a violation of the principles undergirding Americans' participation in the Second World War. "I went to war with the negro and all the other races that go to make up this great country," wrote a Memphis veteran. "I sailed the seas on the same transports with them. I was on the front lines with them. I went to hospitals with them. I stood in chow lines with them — and I certainly wouldn't mind seeing what we were fighting for with them."[33] Other writers railed about black bodies on public transportation, using these racist complaints to bolster their opposition to integrated viewing of the Freedom Train.[34] T. R. French, a west Tennessee planter and descendent of a Declaration of Independence signer, derided the Freedom Train as the work of "conniving politicians" hoping "to break down our southern tradition of racial separation." French blasted liberals such as Florida senator Claude Pepper and Tennessee congressman Estes Kefauver, referring to them as "Stalin's friends," who flouted southern ideology.[35]

The Freedom Train episode also sparked conflict within the white Memphis Ministers Alliance. A majority first voted for and then rescinded a resolution criticizing the mayor. It included a quote from Paul: "God has made of one blood all nations of men that dwell on the face of the earth." When it became clear that the organization would not take a stance against the mayor's position, Rev. Malcolm MacMillan, pastor of Holy Trinity Episcopal Church, excoriated his fellow members. "One reason the church has so little respect is that when it comes to moral issues we give in to the expedient thing," he declared. "And this is a moral issue. God has proclaimed all men as brothers." In contrast, Rev. E. E. McNatt of First Pentecostal Church of Memphis argued, "The sooner some of these racial agitators learn that our good colored Southern people are proud enough of their race to take pride in and enjoy segregation, the better off we will all be."[36]

Likewise, the Freedom Train exposed fault lines among labor leaders. The editor of the Memphis AFL *Labor Review*, Tom Simmons, a self-described "dyed-in-the-wool Southerner," demanded to know why the train should stop in Memphis, where "THERE'S NO FREEDOM?"[37] His query prompted debate at a meeting of the AFL-affiliated Memphis Trades and Labor Council, where a majority tabled a motion to formally criticize the city's position, proposed by International Typographical Union representative Robert Tillman and seconded by James T. Walker, a black member of the Coopers International Union. The Memphis CIO Council, in contrast, unanimously approved a resolution condemning the mayor's action, which they saw as indicative of an "increasing trend in the city and county administrations to exercise measures of regulation over the thinking as well as the actions of the people of this city and county."[38]

This concern with the machine's control of thought and action became more acute for many residents following a radio broadcast by the mayor, November 23. Pleasants threw the first stone when he declared that he had deliberately bypassed the newspapers in order to bring the truth to the public. In a speech broadcast over seven radio stations, he argued that only by upholding segregation laws had Memphis been able to experience "less trouble between the races than in any other American City." Given the "large negro population in Memphis and Shelby," he claimed, it was necessary to have "constant supervision" to avoid racial conflict. Placing blacks and whites together on the Freedom Train, he declared, "would surely lead to trouble and perhaps bloodshed, which we are ever alert to prevent." He insisted, moreover, that "every thinking negro agrees with our position," a revision of his November 18 statement that all "thinking people, colored and white," agreed with him.[39]

Pleasants's speech triggered a fresh round of criticism among white Memphians. In a front-page editorial, the *Press-Scimitar* declared that it would cease its efforts to bring the Freedom Train to Memphis. "In the light of the speech which [Pleasants] delivered—which was so reckless as to mention the possibility of 'bloodshed,'" the editorial declared, "we do not believe that the Freedom Train can be shown here with that assurance of order and good feeling which would have been a matter of course if this city had legitimate and responsible government." AVC leaders took to the airwaves to state that the AVC was also "withdrawing its request that the Freedom Train come to Memphis." However, they declared that the "Freedom Train has actually come to Memphis already insofar as its ideals are concerned." The train had already left its mark on the city, they argued, by provoking a renewed interest in America's founding principles.[40]

Pleasants's speech placed the issue of "thought control" at the center of debate about freedom. His supporters perceived the AHF as a Yankee organization attempting to enforce racial mixing and control their thinking. His white opponents resented the implication that they were incapable of making their own judgments about whether to visit the Freedom Train under integrated conditions. The Freedom Train had become a catalyst for debate among white Memphians about race and postwar democracy.[41]

"Checkin' on the Freedom Train"

The absurdity of Pleasants's declaration in his radio address that "every thinking negro agree[d]" with him was not lost on black listeners. A letter to the *Press-Scimitar* from Theo Bond, a planter from Madison, Arkansas, just west of Memphis, declared, "I don't know what the Mayor's idea of a thinking negro is, nor to whom he points or who the said thinking negroes are, but I do know that I have a reputation among men of affairs in my own community for which I do not apologize." Bond attacked the mayor's position as "an obstacle on the floor of the assembly room of the United Nations conference," declaring that such a "juggernaut" would advance the Russians' cause to obstruct freedom.[42]

Apart from Bond's letter and a handful of others, the *Press-Scimitar* mostly published the viewpoints of white readers; however, African Americans expressed opposition to Pleasants's stance regarding the Freedom Train through other venues, including the black press. The theme of thought control also surfaced in commentaries in the *Memphis World*. In his regular feature, "Down on Beale Ave.," high school history teacher, emcee, and journalist Nat D. Williams reported being inundated with telephone calls about the Freedom Train. His November 21 column appeared under the headline, "Beale St. Speaks of Trains," a twist on Langston Hughes's famous poem, "The Negro Speaks of Rivers," which invokes black historical and cultural knowledge. "Whole flocks" of "God's Chillun," Williams claimed, had demanded to know his thoughts about the Freedom Train. Williams suggested that if he answered their question directly, he would find himself minus a paycheck. Instead, he canvassed "Beale Streeters" and found they scoffed at the idea that blacks boarding the train together with whites would incite violence, since they already rode in elevators, on buses, and — as servants — in cars with whites. One interviewee proposed that Memphians head to Jackson, Mississippi, to view the train, adding that white folks especially should make the trip, since "Us cullud folks already have a notion of what's on the train," suggesting that African Americans were more familiar than whites with the importance of freedom.[43]

A more overt critique, in a *Memphis World* editorial titled "Checkin' on the Freedom Train" — a reference to Hughes's recent poem that had appeared in the *New Republic* in September — warned that city officials might pressure black leaders to endorse Pleasants's position. It declared that no "Negro would of his will and accord accept any other position regarding the Freedom Train except that laid down by the American Heritage Foundation." Nonetheless, it cautioned, some individuals who owed their jobs to the administration might feel obliged to support its stance. Alluding to Pleasants's claim about "thinking negroes," the editorial asserted that any leader who capitulated to such pressure would "find himself as far out of line with the more advanced thinking of the people on racial matters as our representatives of the City and County Governments." A second editorial scored anyone opposing interracial viewing as a proponent of "the philosophy of Fascism of which we already have too much in the Deep South." An accompanying cartoon captioned "State's Rights at Any Cost," depicting a giant bird, "Jim Crow," cawing at the passing Freedom Train, mocked those who defended their allegiance to segregation by claiming it was a matter of states' rights.[44]

Perhaps the harshest criticism came from the AME Ministers' Council in a press release sent to the mayor and the *Memphis World*. Signed by Rev.

A. L. Gilmore, chairman; F. D. Coleman Sr., secretary; and Rev. E. Coleman Jr., treasurer, on behalf of twenty-seven named council members, the release charged that the mayor "sounded more like Hitler than an American; here where people of both races work together and are proud of their ability to give and take and live in peace." The ministers denounced the mayor's address as "the most unusual, the most ruggedly ignorant statement ever profounded [sic] over a radio station to a peace loving people." "It was devoid of social vision or social conscience," they declared. "It was undramatically un-American, paganistic and anti-Christian." The ministers thus characterized Pleasants's abandonment of American and Christian principles as a result of not thinking.[45] The mayor, in turn, blasted their message as "arrogant and impertinent," accusing them of signing a statement dictated by "some low-down white man or some imported negro," suggesting they were incapable of formulating a critique on their own. Privately, the mayor's office gathered information on each member, his congregation, and his church. The list included members who ranged from pastors of small wood-frame churches to Rev. Dwight Kyle, pastor of the brick Avery Chapel AME Church, with a congregation of 2,000.[46]

Whether or not their silence about the mayor's position was a result of the Memphis World's warning to black leaders, none of those who typically supported the machine publicly defended his stance. Some, however, found less direct ways to publicly indicate their ongoing support for the machine. In early December, Blair T. Hunt, principal of Booker T. Washington High School, convened a meeting at Crump's behest to discuss the use of funds raised during an annual Crump-sponsored benefit football game to raise funds for blind African Americans. The group unanimously passed a resolution of appreciation for Crump's concern, on behalf of black Memphians as a whole.[47]

As Memphians battled over the canceled Freedom Train visit, the streamliner entered the Upper South and headed down the eastern seaboard from Virginia to Florida, and then up through Alabama and Georgia before trekking west through Tennessee. Conflicting reports on local receptions to the train's visit became central to the debate. The Press-Scimitar described crowds in Roanoke, Richmond, Raleigh, Greensboro, and elsewhere as huge but orderly and excerpted interviews with whites pleased at having viewed the exhibit alongside blacks.[48] The mayor's office, meanwhile, sent out undercover observers to report on over twenty southern Freedom Train stops between early December and mid-January. The investigators agreed that there had been no incidents of violence but reported that white observers with whom they had spoken resented the

Exhibit-goers entering the Freedom Train on
desegregated basis in Columbus, Georgia, in fall 1947.
*(*Ledger Enquirer *Photo, National Archives photo,* RG 200-AHF,
Box 1, M-26 *Columbus, Ga. 58)*

presence of African Americans. They also noted that a few cities in South
Carolina and Georgia had segregated the waiting queues and allowed viewers from only one line at a time to enter — an arrangement similar to the
proposed Birmingham plan that the AHF had shot down.[49]

The black press reported on local racial struggles over the train's visit.
The *Memphis World*, for example, published a report by Mrs. Rosa L. Parks,
secretary of the Montgomery NAACP and soon to become famous for her
role in the Montgomery bus boycott. Parks detailed actions initiated by
branch president E. D. Nixon when he discovered that the city's Freedom
Train committee had no black members. In response to stonewalling by
Mayor John Goodwyn, Nixon requested that the AHF cancel its Montgomery stop and called for support from NAACP executive secretary Walter

White. In response to pressure from the NAACP and the AHF, Montgomery city officials appointed black co-leaders to each planning subcommittee and Goodwyn announced that racial segregation "would not be any issue" during the visit.[50]

The *Memphis World* also published a report from Emory O. Jackson, Birmingham NAACP executive secretary, president of the Alabama state NAACP conference, and editor of the *Birmingham World*, on opposition to public safety commissioner Eugene "Bull" Connors's plan for black and white residents to form separate lines and enter the train in groups of twenty, with one group leaving before the other entered. Rev. James L. Ware from Trinity Baptist Church headed a committee of representatives from local black organizations, including women's groups, churches, business associations, fraternities, and the NAACP, that pressured Connors to alter the plan. When he proved intransigent, they threatened to boycott the train's visit if the AHF did not cancel the Birmingham stop. With added pressure from Walter White in New York, the AHF canceled the Birmingham visit, leaving Memphis and Birmingham as the only two locales deemed inhospitable to the Freedom Train.[51]

LeMoyne NAACP and the "Fight for Freedom"

Although the Memphis NAACP did not publicly protest the city's stance on the Freedom Train, the LeMoyne College branch called on students to distinguish themselves as a new generation of leaders in the black struggle for freedom. On January 6, the day before Memphis's originally scheduled Freedom Train date, two Greyhound bus loads of LeMoyne College students and faculty joined hundreds of other black Memphians who traveled to Jackson, Tennessee, nearly ninety miles northeast of the city, to visit the train there. The trip became a kind of reverse migration, from city to outlying town. It also signified a different kind of migration, a figurative journey from the stifling confines of Crump-dominated thought to a nationwide dialogue centered on freedom. The train then sped past Memphis en route to integrated audiences in Arkansas later in January.

Reporting on the Jackson Freedom Train pilgrimage became nearly as important as the actual visit. Ophelia Watson, a LeMoyne sophomore and NAACP member, glowingly described her trip in an article for the *Memphis World*. "Every American citizen whether young or old, white or black," she asserted, "should have been given the opportunity to visit the 'Freedom Train.'" Another *Memphis World* article reported that blacks had outnumbered whites five to one, adding that the first two people to board the train were black Memphians who had arrived in the city at 4:00 A.M. In an ar-

Desegregated waiting line for Freedom Train
in Pine Bluff, Arkansas, January 21, 1948.
(Adamsfotos, National Archives photo, RG 200-AHF, Box 1,
M-28 Non Segregation Group–Pine Bluff, Ark. 59)

ticle titled "A Glance At Freedom," which appeared in the *LeMoyne Democrat*, a student vividly depicted huge lines of people waiting for hours in blustery weather to board the train yet described his experience of viewing the documents as "soul-stirring" and "dramatic." Crump's undercover observer argued that the size of the crowd had been exaggerated by the press, yet even he noted the large number of black Memphians arriving in Jackson via train, bus, and automobile and commented that blacks were often in the majority.[52]

LeMoyne students directly attacked the mayor's position. In "Not Yet, Freedom," published in the *Democrat*, the writer declared, "When the citizens, as a whole, demand the overthrow of a dictator and gestapo type of government, freedom reigns, and would make way for the Freedom Train." A few months later, the college NAACP publication, *The Beacon*, lampooned the mayor in an article titled "Segregation Streamlined." The writer, education director Luther Ward, imagined a world in which blacks and whites were truly separate, with every public facility maintaining two offices; blacks and whites ordered not to get sick at the same time; and death itself restricted to separate hours.[53]

LeMoyne students' interest in the idea of freedom, however, neither began nor ended with the Freedom Train dispute, although the conflict brought new dimensions to the subject. Students' poems published in the *Democrat* had addressed the problem of freedom for African Americans both before and after the war. The contradictory feelings of weariness and expectation conveyed in first-year student Odessa Johnson's poem "I Am a Negro," which appeared shortly after the formation of the college NAACP and just before the United States entered the war, are representative of those of other students:

I am a Negro, but I can feel,
Though my hands are bars of steel.
My back still bears a heavy load,
The world says, "Wait!—stand still in the cold.
Must I wait and wait and wait some more,
Wondering how far is freedom's shore?

I've smiled when my heart was burning within;
I've said yes, when no! It should have been.
A chance in America is all I ask.
I stand of freedom's brink at last;
I've fought my way through a weary fire,
All for my race;—I could not tire.
Keep faith in me! I shall stand fast.

Johnson's poem portrays freedom as not only equal opportunity for jobs but recognition of emotions shared by African Americans, who endured despite their experiences of degradation.[54]

More poems appeared in the *Democrat* after the war, half a decade later, but these conveyed less a sense of patience than a sense of urgency. In a terse, unsigned poem, "An American Pattern of Freedom and Justice in Black and White," published May 30, 1947, amid outcry over police brutality, a student issued a biting critique of the legal justice system that inevitably placed whites' interests over blacks'. Another piece by Harry

Lemmons, printed in fall 1946, questioned America's commitment to democracy when blacks still were not granted even the basic "Four Freedoms" outlined by Roosevelt: freedom of worship, freedom from fear, freedom of speech, and freedom from want. In these postwar writings, the young authors critiqued American society for uncoupling freedom from racial equality and positioned themselves as advocates of a different kind of freedom.[55]

The inaugural issue of *The Beacon*, launched by the college NAACP the week that the Freedom Train controversy erupted, also demanded that students become leaders in the "fight for freedom." The newspaper outlined work the college NAACP had undertaken since reorganizing in 1946, from securing the dismissal of streetcar drivers who harassed black riders to lobbying downtown businesses to treat black customers as they did white patrons.[56] After a wartime suspension of activities beginning in late 1942, the LeMoyne NAACP had reconvened in early 1946, amidst public clamor over the police rape trial, the Fred Jackson case, and the race riot in Columbia, Tennessee. Two-thirds of the LeMoyne student body joined the branch over the following year, many of them returning veterans.[57] From the outset, the college branch sought to forge a new kind of youth leadership. NAACP field secretary Donald Jones, visiting Memphis to assist the citywide NAACP membership drive, underscored "the importance of youth leadership in the permanent eradication of the 'Uncle Toms' of the race." Echoing C. Eric Lincoln's February 1946 commentary in the *LeMoyne Democrat* contrasting LeMoynites to Memphis's black "Crumplets," another student writer complained about black leaders in a *Democrat* article a few weeks later. Mentioning one minister in particular who "thinks this city is the 'most wonderful city he has ever seen,'" he demanded, "Is the man blind or is he just oozing 'soft-soap?'" The article urged LeMoyne students to think of themselves as part of the "intelligentsia" and to challenge "prejudice and bigotry with sound, common sense and logic" rather than cooperating with the machine's racial paternalism.[58]

LeMoyne NAACP members thus sharply distinguished themselves from Memphis's established black leaders. Charles Tisdale, then college NAACP vice president and columnist for the *Democrat*—and later a journalist and eventually editor of the *Jackson Advocate*, Mississippi's most important black newspaper—criticized Memphis's Negro Junior Chamber of Congress for rewarding established leaders as outstanding role models in race relations, rather than younger men. In addition, college NAACP president Bernard Cotton complained to NAACP regional secretary Ruby

Hurley about what he interpreted as the national office's slighting of the college branch. "[O]ur chapter here at the college is not composed wholly of inexperienced Youth," he wrote. "This is a college chapter true enough, but veterans of World War II are taking the lead in most organizations which mean something to our race and our country. The conclusions we reach on problems aren't ones determined by 'wild' irresponsible non-mature minds." Cotton described the college branch as a "Vatican City (a city within a city)." He and Tisdale portrayed LeMoyne students as repre-sentatives of a new generation of leaders.[59]

The college branch's activities reflected this concern with building a new cohort of race leaders. The *Beacon* announced in November 1947 that the branch's "major contribution toward the training of Negro Youth for leadership" would be to establish NAACP youth councils in all high schools for black students. "As an American Youth who must soon assume responsibility for leadership," the statement further asserted, "you must begin now to plan our part in building a new world order out of the present day chaos." This goal dovetailed with the central Memphis NAACP's decision to sponsor its first city youth council, with Annie Bell Milligan as director. Six months later, however, the LeMoyne NAACP reported that the city administration had threatened to instantly dismiss the principal of any school in which NAACP activities were discovered. This move placed high school organizing on hold until the 1950s.[60]

LeMoyne activists' focus on black youth also took the organization in a different direction from the postwar national preoccupation with "juvenile delinquency." In March 1947, the Negro Division of the Memphis Youth Service Council sponsored a "mammoth program" at Mason Temple and Booker T. Washington High School, involving institutions such as the Boy Scouts (Seminole Division), the YMCA and YWCA, and churches from every denomination. Following a kick-off parade, the conference featured several speakers, including Memphis insurance executive Dr. J. E. Walker and Tuskegee Institute president Dr. Frederick Patterson, who analyzed and proposed remedies for juvenile delinquency, with some emphasizing evangelization as the antidote. Organizers invited Mayor Sylvanus Polk, former mayor Walter Chandler, and other Crump officials, whose attendance lent the imprimatur of the city administration. Olympic track star Jesse Owens also came to Memphis to deliver a series of lectures on health and hygiene, venereal disease, and juvenile delinquency in March 1947, and a year later the AME church's state Youth Congress sponsored a program on juvenile delinquency at the New Tyler AME Church in Binghampton. At LeMoyne, the *Democrat* reported on these programs targeting juvenile delinquency but kept its primary focus on racial justice and youth leadership.[61]

As aspiring young leaders in the "fight for freedom," LeMoyne activists positioned themselves in the context of national and global postwar issues. They participated in two national student organizations founded in the early postwar period, the National Students Association and Students for Democratic Action, which brought them into contact with white and black student activists from other colleges. Some LeMoyne students also joined the American Veterans Committee, a biracial organization of World War II veterans that pursued a more liberal agenda than the Veterans of Foreign Wars. Like many Americans at the end of the Second World War, student activists emphasized the need for "one world"; however, they framed their mission in terms of both international peace and racial equality in the United States. The LeMoyne NAACP, for example, applauded President Truman's stated support for civil rights but criticized his Truman Doctrine speech for "rallying to the military" and "driving the world into spheres of influence." At another point, the student newspaper hailed the Nuremberg Trials while demanding to know why the United States could not bring a halt to lynching.[62]

By anchoring their understanding of "one world" in issues of "human relations"—a term that in postwar parlance usually meant race relations—LeMoyne students distinguished their viewpoints from those articulated by leading white Memphis moderates, who connected "one world" to international peace. Business and professional leaders such as hardware wholesaler Edmund Orgill, newspaper editor Edward Meeman, and attorney Lucius Burch together organized a chapter of the Federal Union, which promoted Clarence Streit's idea of a system of cooperation among various western democracies against Communism and militarism. Orgill lectured on these ideas to an array of different audiences in Memphis, including LeMoyne students.[63]

Because of this emphasis on "human relations" both at home and abroad, a group of faculty and students at LeMoyne began meeting with professors and students at Southwestern, a private white liberal arts college in Memphis (now Rhodes College). Together they organized the Memphis Community Relations Committee (MCRC) during the fall 1947 semester, at the same time the Freedom Train conflict was taking place. Beginning informally with about a dozen black and a dozen white members, the group launched a series of public meetings in early 1948.[64]

The meetings generally attracted over a hundred participants, mostly from LeMoyne and Southwestern, with each program held at a different site, including the LeMoyne and Southwestern campuses, the black and white branches of the Y, the CIO hall, and various churches. At the MCRC's first public meeting, February 12, guest speaker Dr. Ina Brown, visiting from Nashville's Scarritt College, lectured on world human relations. Brown argued that race has been used by social scientists as a category of study but should not be treated as a matter of genetic superiority and inferiority, since humans have more in common than not. Later that semester, Dr. J. L. Ferguson, visiting from Belmont Methodist Church in Nashville, spoke on religion and "human relations," and Dr. Clarence E. Glick, from Tulane, gave a lecture titled "Practical Applications of Sociology in Improving Human Relations." The following fall, Dr. Haridas T. Muzumdar, an associate of Mahatma Gandhi, addressed human relations from a global standpoint, taking Gandhism as the jumping-off point for his lecture.[65] Other talks during the 1948–49 school year featured Edmund Orgill speaking on the proposed "Union of the Western Democracies"; Dr. Everett Hughes, from the University of Chicago, on the integration of the new worker in industry; Herman Long, from the race relations department of the American Missionary Association, on housing and minorities; and Dr. Neil Bruce, a visiting professor at Southwestern, on the British labor government and colonial policy.[66]

LeMoyne students' conception of themselves as "fighters for freedom" and black intellectuals, however, did not jibe with certain presentations. Rev. David Sprunt, a Southwestern religious studies professor, for example, declared at the meeting about industrial work that two problems keeping blacks out of equal jobs were their lack of education and "reticence to assume responsibility." Along similar lines, Dr. Neil Bruce, an Oxford University graduate, argued that Britain considered colonial Africa unprepared for independence, due to high illiteracy rates and the inability of all but a few to assume "the responsibility of total self-government." Bruce also declared that a premature shift to independence would pave the road for a Communist take-over. Elsewhere, LeMoyne students decried such claims about Africans' and African Americans' presumed unpreparedness for independence and full citizenship rights. Journalist Charles Tisdale, in a 1948 article in the *Democrat*, for instance, lambasted *Memphis World* writer Nat D. Williams for suggesting that blacks were not "ready for Democracy."[67] LeMoyne students' participation in the MCRC's interracial forums, therefore, exposed them to local, national, and international discussions about postwar politics, race, and democracy; however, as writers and leaders of their own organizations, they were pursuing distinct ideas of freedom based on independent thought and action.

The 1948 Elections: Remembering the Freedom Train

The Freedom Train conflict reverberated in the 1948 election campaigns. As a lightning rod for public debate about race and democracy in local, national, and global contexts, it helped transform the primary and general elections in Memphis into groundbreaking events.[68] Although only a relatively small number of black Memphians had traveled to Jackson, Tennessee, to see the Freedom Train, thousands more, including residents of working-class black neighborhoods, registered protest votes in 1948 against the Crump machine's domination and *its* conception of freedom.

LeMoyne students distinguished themselves not only by attending political rallies and encouraging students to vote but also by weighing in on proposed federal civil rights legislation and potential judicial decisions favoring civil rights. Following Truman's historic speech to Congress on civil rights, February 2, 1948, for instance, the *Democrat* declared that students had lost "round one" with the Freedom Train issue but now had an opportunity to redeem themselves by lobbying congressmen to support a civil rights bill. A few months later, a majority of male respondents to a campus NAACP poll expressed support for A. Philip Randolph's call for "passive resistance" against draft registration if Congress passed the Universal Military Training Act without desegregating the armed forces.[69] Students also closely followed higher education desegregation lawsuits, especially *Sipuel v. Board of Regents of the University of Oklahoma*, decided in 1948, in which the Supreme Court ordered Oklahoma to provide Ada Lois Sipuel with an education in law equal to that provided white students by the university's law school. Moreover, LeMoyne activists organized a protest against black educators who agreed to a proposal by southern state education officials to create regional black professional schools, which would allow them to skirt the Court's requirement in *Sipuel* that each state provide education to African American students equal to what it provided for white students. Regional schools would have allowed states to avoid the costs of providing "separate but equal" facilities for blacks.[70]

Just days before the Freedom Train fracas exploded in November 1947, a group of LeMoyne students attended a rally in St. Louis for Henry A. Wallace, who was later officially nominated as presidential candidate on the third-party Progressive ticket.[71] Wallace's speaking tour, like the Freedom Train, bypassed Memphis because the candidate refused to appear before racially segregated audiences. The rally featured Paul Robeson performing his Negro spirituals. Those who made the trip to St. Louis returned just in time to hear about the cancellation of the Memphis Freedom Train visit.

The *Democrat*, commenting on both the Freedom Train and on Wallace's tour, suggested sarcastically that Wallace's upcoming desegregated rally at Wheat Street Baptist Church in Atlanta should prove interesting to Mayor Pleasants, since the Ku Klux Klan had threatened violent reprisals.[72]

As LeMoyne students promoted civil rights, Crump swung strongly in the opposite direction following Truman's civil rights speech. "I would be willing to go to jail and stay there the balance of my life rather than abide by [civil rights]," he fumed in typical hyperbole. "In [Truman's] scheming, cold-blooded effort to outdo Henry Wallace and Governor Dewey of New York for the Negro vote, he has endeavored to reduce the South to a country of crawling cowards," he declared. Crump's willingness to rupture his fidelity to the Democratic Party and, by summer 1948, join the Dixiecrats, signaled the extent to which civil rights had created a political fault line.[73]

However, as the August 1948 primaries approached, the U.S. Senate and Tennessee gubernatorial races commanded as much if not more public attention than the presidential election. Leading white moderates and liberals, including Meeman, Orgill, Burch, and others, endorsed Congressman Estes Kefauver for Senate, in defiance of Crump's opposition to Kefauver. Their support helped make Crump's domination of local and state politics the central issue in the Senate race. Crump threw his support behind Judge John Mitchell, rather than incumbent Thomas Stewart, who had crossed Crump on some votes. The machine boss publicly blasted Kefauver, in part because of his vote against the 1947 Taft-Hartley Act, which reined in the power of unions, and his support for anti–poll tax legislation. Accusing Kefauver of voting like a Communist, Crump compared Kefauver to a "pet coon" who "turns its head" while it "puts its foot in an open drawer," hoping to "deceive any onlookers as to where his foot is and what it is into." Kefauver, in response to this red-baiting, wore a coonskin cap during an event at Memphis's famous Peabody Hotel, retorting, "I may be a coon, but I'm not Mr. Crump's pet coon."[74]

Kefauver's open challenge to Crump won him the support of white municipal reformers, African Americans, labor organizations, progressive women's groups, and others.[75] This same coalition backed former governor and Crump opponent Gordon Browning for governor, over the incumbent Jim McCord. The impact of the biracial coalition could be seen in events such as the Voters' School at the black Vance Avenue YWCA, sponsored by the League of Women Voters. The two-evening event targeted black voters but featured speeches by C. Arthur Bruce, the white president of LeMoyne's Board of Trustees, and Lucius Burch.[76]

Kefauver's mixed record left African Americans ambivalent; although he favored ending the poll tax, he opposed antilynching and fair employment practice legislation. However, his opponents had staked out extremist positions on civil rights. Stewart announced he would "fight [Truman's] civil rights bill as long as there is a drop of blood left in my body," and McCord pitched himself as an avid states' rights advocate. Kefauver's declared war on the Crump machine and opposition to the poll tax thus elevated him in the eyes of many African Americans, as did the candidate's announcement that he would call in poll watchers to prevent election fraud. Dr. J. E. Walker, founder of the Universal Life Insurance Company and the Tri-State Bank, had cooperated with Crump in the 1930s, but now, as head of the black Democratic Club, he championed the Kefauver-Browning ticket, as did Urban League executive secretary Rev. J. A. McDaniel, businessman Taylor C. D. Hayes, and other black leaders.[77] Some black Memphians who openly supported Kefauver and Browning faced reprisals. Minerva Johnican, later a civil rights activist and elected official, recalls helping her father and "Reverend Mac" (McDaniel), who lived next door, pass out handbills in 1948. Two weeks later, her father was fired from his job as a maintenance man at a public housing project — a job doled out by the Crump machine to those who exhibited loyalty.[78]

Despite such acts of intimidation, the Tennessee Democratic primary, on August 5, delivered Boss Crump the first electoral defeats of his career. A majority of Shelby County voters still backed Crump's candidates, but the margin of victory was a fraction of what it had been previously, sending enough Kefauver and Browning votes to statewide totals to clinch their victories.[79]

African American voters placed three predominantly black wards in the Kefauver and Browning columns, while twenty-one predominantly white wards also went for these candidates. Although the *Press-Scimitar* attributed the victories to the work of a small group of white men, the *Memphis World*'s headline crowed, "Negro Voters Join with Liberal Whites to Lift 'Iron Curtain' as Browning, Kefauver Win Posts." Its story, echoing A. Philip Randolph's comments in 1943, compared the Crump machine to Russian totalitarians, and placed black voters on the side of freedom. The article declared that Crump had come into power with black support and was going out "on the rising tide of the Negro voters' protest." It counted the Crump machine's incendiary opposition to the Freedom Train as one of several major postwar developments that had been seared in the memories of black voters, along with the Columbia race riot; the Fred Jackson case and McCord's refusal to stay his execution; the rising tide of police brutality, including the assaults on the young Binghampton women; and the mayor's refusal to appoint black officers. Significantly, the *Memphis World* also reprinted in its entirety an editorial from the black press in St. Louis that attributed Crump's "downfall" to his Freedom Train stance.[80]

The surge in black activism that took place in the three months between the primaries and the general elections underscored the extent to which the elections had energized ordinary black Memphians and unsettled Crump and Pleasants. When two police officers gunned down veteran James Mosby in his yard in the Binghampton neighborhood just days after the primary, black residents surpassed all previous efforts to protest police assaults in their neighborhood: the newly formed East Memphis Citizens' Club sent a petition with 1,500 signatures to the mayor's office, demanding the appointment of black officers. On September 9, Public Safety Commissioner Joe Boyle announced that he would hire several black policemen on a trial basis, following the November election.

In another reflection of black activism during the 1948 election season, Rev. Dwight Kyle, pastor of Avery Chapel AME Church and an NAACP board member, ran for Congress in the Tenth District on the Progressive Party ticket. Kyle had been involved with black labor struggles during the war and then spoke out forcefully to demand the apprehension of the police rapists of the young Binghampton women. His opponent, incumbent Clifford Davis, had run uncontested on the machine ticket since 1938. As the first African American congressional candidate in the district since 1918, when Republican Wayman Wilkerson ran for Congress, Kyle lost the election but still managed to garner over 3,500 votes after openly declaring that he was "for total equality for the Negro" and that he "favor[ed] complete integration of the Negro into American life as a citizen and an individual." Shortly after the election, however, Kyle was transferred to Atlanta.[81]

The most significant black activism came in the form of renewed efforts to register black residents in time to vote in the November elections. Activists zeroed in on the working-class neighborhoods that had established the strongest civic clubs, spawned the most vibrant labor organizing, and raised the loudest outcry over police violence. Many black labor activists had expanded their organizing to civil rights and voter registration after the war. Indeed, the final Kefauver-Browning rallies before the November elections took place at Manassas High School, drawing on the Klondyke, New Chelsea, New Chicago, Hyde Park, Hollywood, and Douglas neighborhoods; and at the Early Grove Baptist Church in Binghampton.[82]

The city administration's harsh suppression of these rallies indicated the extent to which it sought to contain and control black political activism. As black Memphians turned out for these events at community institutions, those who attended downtown open-air rallies encountered harassment not unlike the kind they had endured during the 1940 Memphis "reign of terror." On the one hand, city officials made a show of agreeing not to enforce segregation at a Wallace rally in Bellevue Park, in south Memphis, in September. On the other hand, policemen, apparently acting on orders from superiors, forcibly ejected African Americans from rallies held downtown in Court Square on behalf of Kefauver-Browning and Republican presidential candidate Thomas Dewey.[83] Given that the August Democratic primaries had been the key races for Crump, the machine's crackdown signaled an effort to restore the race relations of 1940. Firestone worker and shop steward Lonnie Jones reported that club-wielding patrolmen had chased him and between sixty and seventy other black Memphians from a Kefauver-Browning rally. In response, Jones defiantly declared in a statement printed in the black press that he had voted for Browning and Kefauver in the primary and would vote for them again in November, "if I can speak and get to the polls."[84]

A few days later, a similar crackdown prompted more strong statements. This time, policemen ordered prominent AME and CME ministers out of Court Square, where they were attending a Republican rally for presidential candidate Thomas Dewey. Although nationally the majority of African American voters had converted to the Democratic Party during the Roosevelt years, in Memphis many black voters still identified themselves as Republicans, signaling their independence from the Crump machine. Rev. A. D. Brown, pastor of New Tyler AME Church and president of the AME Ministers' Council, and Rev. Dewitt T. Alcorn, a CME minister and president of the Negro Chamber of Commerce, refused to comply, demanding to know whether they had "the right of free speech and free assembly in a park." "We're not slaves," they declared, thereby staking the problem of freedom to racial equality in the present and to the memory of slavery in the past, and revisiting a theme that had become influential in Memphis politics.[85]

Inside and outside the city, the Memphis Freedom Train controversy became a crucible for debate about historical and contemporary meanings of freedom in the aftermath of the Second World War, as the United States headed into another kind of global conflict—the Cold War. The American Heritage Foundation had not intended for the Freedom Train to take on the role of liberator in the South; rather, it had sought a means of rallying American citizens around the unifying ideal of democracy and against subversives. As the train journeyed from one southern locale to another, however, the exhibit became a lightning rod for racial conflict. It also prompted the articulation of clashing understandings of freedom. For white southern moderates who opposed the Crump machine, its stance against desegregated viewing of the exhibit symbolized the kind of antidemocratic tyranny that had been addressed by the Declaration of Independence. In contrast, those who championed the machine's position against the AHF portrayed freedom as the ability to pursue the "southern way of life" without Yankee interference.

For many African American voters who cast their ballots against the machine-backed candidates in 1948, Crump had become emblematic of racial barriers to freedom that had persisted for over eight decades since emancipation. Crump also represented paternalistic efforts to control black thought and activism. Within neighborhoods such as Binghampton, where the elections became interwoven with the most concerted police brutality protests of the 1940s, few likely visited the Freedom Train in Jackson on a workday. However, the confluence of protest against racist police violence and reaction to the mayor's notorious refusal to accept the Freedom Train on desegregated terms, led them to politicize their concerns about their communities.

At LeMoyne, the fact that the uproar over the Freedom Train intersected with students' efforts to carve out identities for themselves as leaders in the "fight for freedom" encouraged them to conceive of this battle in unique ways. Throughout the late 1940s, they cast their own demands for rights in international terms, in the context not only of the Cold War but also of contemporaneous anticolonial movements. Concomitantly, they considered themselves actors in both local and national struggles as part of their endeavor to distinguish themselves generationally and politically from current black leaders in Memphis.

Our Mental Liberties

5
Banned Movies, Black-Appeal Radio, and the Struggle for a New Public Sphere

In late September 1949, the LeMoyne NAACP ran a story in the *Beacon* that excoriated the Memphis Board of Censors for its "mental processes."[1] The board's notorious chairman, Lloyd T. Binford, according to the article, had once again exhibited his capricious logic by banning the Metro-Goldwyn-Mayer motion picture *Lost Boundaries*, about a light-complexioned African American doctor who "passes" as white in order to avoid racial discrimination that would have prevented him from practicing. The *Beacon* writer predicted the board would next ban 20th Century Fox's new release *Pinky*, about an African American nurse who had similarly opted to "pass" and was engaged to a white doctor. "We will not see [*Pinky*] unless we move into the FREE STATES and out of slavery territory," the article predicted. The writer's anachronistic statement, which rhetorically linked a debate over motion pictures to the slavery era, established Memphis as a place that stood outside of progress and freedom. "We speak, of course, in respect to our mental liberties," the author added, acknowledging the historical distinction but identifying independence of mind as a missing element in both contexts. The writer referred not to thought control in general, but to the literal evisceration of screen images of African Americans in roles outside those of household servant or menial laborer. Bitter as the author was, it would have come as little surprise in 1949 that the Memphis Board of Censors had banned a motion picture featuring a white actor (Mel Ferrer) playing a black character performing a so-called white role — in this case a doctor.

The same year this commentary appeared in the *Beacon*, radio station WDIA-Memphis converted its entire format from classical and country to black-appeal programming, becoming the first radio station in the United States to fully devote itself to African American listeners. This changeover had begun one week before the 1948 national elections, when the ironic laughter of Nat D. Williams spilling out from radios marked the debut of his new show, *Tan Town Jamboree*. Williams, a well-known journalist, high school history teacher, and emcee of the Palace Theater's renowned "Midnight Rambles" variety show, boasted in the *Memphis World* that the show featured "the only Negro 'disk jockey' in Memphis and points North, South, East, and West, within a radius of several hundred miles of this town." Overwhelming listener response to Nat D.'s show and subsequent pilot programs convinced the station's white owners to commit themselves fully to a black-oriented format.[2] Thus while the board of censors came under attack for attempting to impose on the silver screen a racial imaginary harking back to slavery, African Americans in and around Memphis seized upon black-appeal radio as a new public sphere where on-air personalities crafted by talented black DJs contributed to a very different imaginary of black identities.

In Memphis, site of one of the most notorious censorship boards in the nation, and home to the first all-black-oriented radio station, mass culture became a locus of racial struggle during the 1940s, energized by the wartime and postwar conflicts discussed in earlier chapters. Even as black Memphians criticized the racist stereotypes that undergirded their problems with job classifications, for example, they also contended with motion pictures in which black characters outside of "traditional" work roles had been spliced out of the films, leaving the stock, happy-go-lucky servant characters that moviegoers knew well. The postwar groundswell of black political mobilization in 1948, seen in outrage over police brutality and the Freedom Train cancellation, along with anti-Crump votes, was also culturally manifested in the embrace of black-oriented radio. In part, these responses to forms of entertainment involved concerns about equal rights; many young blacks, for example, resented being excluded from most first-run movie theaters or sent to the "buzzard's roost" in those that admitted them. However, the postwar consumption of mass culture, especially movies and radio — although in different ways — became crucial to contestation over racial images themselves, which loomed larger-than-life as a result of specific media technologies. Going to the movies or listening to network radio could be simultaneously entertaining and humiliating, while tuning in to black-oriented radio programming could produce laughter and pride.[3]

Most importantly, contemporary viewers and listeners on all sides believed that the visual and sound images of mass culture mattered in everyday life because they had extraordinary powers to shape popular thought.

While Crump officials, for example, declared that interracial movie scenes could incite rioting, many African Americans argued that demeaning portrayals of blacks perpetuated both racial discrimination by whites and a lack of self-respect among blacks. Historical scholarship on film, radio, and race has traced national efforts by a variety of parties, including the NAACP, the National Urban League, black artists and intellectuals, Roosevelt officials, and some industry insiders, to promote liberal racial messages about cultural pluralism in Hollywood movies and over network radio during and after the Second World War. Local dynamics in the urban South, including censorship, all but blocked these efforts. Moviegoers in cities such as Memphis, Atlanta, and Birmingham not only went to segregated movie theaters but also missed certain "message movies" and never saw deleted scenes featuring black stars. Conflict over racial representation and social control emerged differently in these locales than they did nationally, although throughout the 1940s what happened in southern cities influenced broader national debates about race and mass culture, just as they had with the Freedom Train.[4]

One need not assume a direct, causal relationship between postwar struggles over race in mass culture and the civil rights protests of the 1960s. It is clear, however, that some of the most explicit and intense postwar debates about racial identities addressed cultural portrayals of black people. Black Memphians resented their exclusion from or segregation within movie theaters, despite newsreels with messages about America's triumph over fascism, and they were painfully aware of how seldom black actors could be seen or heard in movies or radio shows. Yet their postwar concerns about race and freedom—what the LeMoyne *Beacon* referred to as "mental liberties"—would not have been fully resolved by the integration of movie theaters, movie casts, or radio studios. Black Memphis moviegoers and radio listeners also had complex reactions to the specific attributes assigned to black characters, whether that was subservience or criminality, docility or lasciviousness. These responses anticipated critiques of denigrating racial images and claims to black pride articulated during the later activism of the freedom movement, including the 1968 sanitation workers' strike.

Although Beale Street had long been a cultural crossroads for black music and entertainment, the particular technologies of movies and radio drew critical attention to media representations and their possible real-life consequences. However, neither motion pictures nor radio was isolated from other forms of leisure and entertainment. WDIA's first DJ, Nat D. Williams, for instance, emceed at the Palace Theater's celebrated musical variety shows, which were in turn broadcast by a local radio station, well before Williams pioneered on WDIA. Conversely, WDIA became a promoter of rhythm and blues (R & B) and gospel music. In a more contentious example, even after the censors cut entertainers such as Lena Horne, Cab Calloway, and Louis Armstrong from movies, their fans still followed them on the radio, in the black press, and in live performances on Beale Street. Debates over movies and radio related to black culture more generally, yet specific developments in film and radio in the 1940s opened up new opportunities for expression and debate.[5]

As struggles over race, gender, class, and sexuality unfolded in workplaces and neighborhoods, other conflicts addressed the racial imaginary in mass culture. At the same time that stereotypical characters of mainstream movies and network radio came under attack, black DJs' humorous, smart, and savvy constructions of black manhood and womanhood helped establish WDIA as a new black public sphere that reached from Beale Street to the rural Delta, bridging both geographic and social divides. Through the medium of black-appeal radio, issues of race and politics could be explored through an array of different programming, from R & B to religious shows, and from news analysis to public service announcements. Although circumscribed by Jim Crow, black radio encouraged listeners to seize the "mental liberties" that the Memphis censors sought to ban.

Historical Memory and the
Racial Geography of Moviegoing

Moviegoing featured centrally in the lives of black Memphians, especially young people, in the years following the Second World War. Viewers sat in the darkness, focused on the big brightly lit screen before them, removed from their everyday lives, and became part of a fantasy escape world. At the same time, however, attending movie theaters meant confronting both the segregated terrain of entertainment in the urban South, as well as the stereotypical racial characters of Hollywood motion pictures.

Rodie Veazy and Mary Lou McNeal each regularly attended movies in this period. Veazy migrated from Mississippi to Memphis with her family in 1945, at age five, and remembers spending Saturday afternoons on Beale Street. While her mother went to a black-owned café, she and her brothers watched motion pictures. "That's all we had to do in those days," she asserts, adding that there were no parks for black children. McNeal recalls attending movies on Friday nights with her husband. While she loved Humphrey Bogart films, he liked westerns — "shoot 'em up movies," as McNeal called them. They usually patronized Beale Street theaters but also went to one on Main, "where blacks was upstairs and the whites was downstairs."[6]

Memphis had over forty movie theaters by the late 1940s, yet only about ten admitted African Americans, under varying conditions. In Memphis and other southern cities, African Americans thus contended with at least three kinds of motion picture venues, attendance at each differently circumscribed by race. Downtown on Main Street, the Warner and Malco theaters admitted both African Americans and whites to first-run Hollywood movies. However, management sent African Americans around the side of the building to enter via an alley and climb several flights of stairs to sit in an upper balcony, dubbed "the pigeon's roost." Recalling the Malco, Naomi Jones, who migrated to the city as a young adult, remembers feeling that in some ways Memphis was more segregated than life in rural Mississippi; paradoxically, one had the opportunity to go to the movies in the city but had to contend with segregation there.[7]

Visits to these Main Street movie theaters thus produced shared cultural memories in which pleasure and resentment coalesced. Imogene Watkins Wilson, a journalist, remembers feeling so angry and humiliated in these theaters that upon graduating from high school she vowed never to return to them. In some cases, they became sites of impromptu confrontations. George Holloway, a labor activist, recalls that "blacks would be laughing at the film and having a lot of fun, and someone would call the police. The policemen might ask someone why they were laughing, and hit them and make them leave, or arrest them." Some youth, Holloway recalls, "protested it at that time, but to no avail. You'd just get a fine to pay and a mark on your record." Scholar Gloria Wade-Gayles describes the resentment of young people who climbed the stairs to the "pigeon's roost" at the Malco, only to be forced to sit on benches, in the cold, right outside the projection room. Emboldened by the anonymity of the dark, they occasionally harassed white moviegoers by dropping popcorn on heads below them, instead of passively disappearing into the dark. Such provocations may not have been formal protests, but they produced formative historical memories of racial circumscription and self-assertion, bound up with the pleasure of movies.[8]

Spontaneous, youthful "acting out" at movies provoked reactions by whites and fueled tensions among African Americans. In September 1944, for example, police received complaints from whites at the Malco that blacks seated above them had been "throwing small rocks, peanuts, light bulbs and other objects down on the[m]." When neither the ushers nor the police could identify the culprits, Malco's management ejected all black patrons from the theater after returning their admission fees, and denied entrance to those waiting for the next show. The *Memphis World* did not applaud these young rebels. Rather, its story about this incident empathized with "prominent Negro Memphians" who had been forced to leave the Malco and who reportedly expressed "disgust" with these "hoodlums."[9]

The entertainment landscape changed when black Memphians turned the corner from Main onto Beale, traversing the symbolic space between "downtown" and the heart of black Memphis. Although the Daisy, the New Daisy, and the Palace theaters catered specifically to African Americans, allowing them to sit anywhere, these moviegoing experiences could also elicit both pleasure and bitterness. On occasion, they showed movies independently produced for black audiences. For the most part, they offered Hollywood films, but instead of showing first-run motion pictures, they used reels that had already made the rounds of white theaters and had been damaged by overuse or even cut and spliced to accommodate censorship requirements. Gloria Wade-Gayles recalls that theaters on Beale were "accepted only for Saturday matinees with friends. On serious dates, we went downtown."[10] The Beale Street venues, however, also hosted celebrated black entertainers, in addition to movies. The Palace, for instance, drew hundreds of spectators Tuesday evenings for "Amateur Night," where performers competed for prizes and hoped to be cheered rather than booed off stage. As a center of Memphis's black entertainment world, the Palace produced contradictory cultural experiences.[11]

Many African American moviegoers, however, never left their own neighborhoods, instead attending local theaters catering specifically to black people, such as the Ace, the Harlem, and the Georgia in south Memphis, the Savoy in north Memphis, and the Esquire in Orange Mound. Reflecting the great popularity of movies in the 1940s, children were among the regular attendees at weekend shows. Lanetha Jewel Branch, a Memphis schoolteacher, remembers children going to the Ace at Mississippi and Walker, since they would have needed adult accompaniment to venture down to Beale Street. These theaters typically offered a weekly or semiweekly double feature, in addition to a short from All American Negro Newsreel, focusing on news about African Americans generally left out of mainstream newsreels. The fare usually included "race" movies featuring all-black casts, produced outside Hollywood by filmmakers such as Oscar Micheaux and Ted Toddy, and ranging from comedies starring Mantan Moreland to musicals featuring saxophonist Louis Jordan. Although such productions were on the wane by the late forties, they still played on a daily basis in southern neighborhood movie houses. Westerns, featuring such white stars as John Wayne and Gary Cooper, may have been the next most popular movie genre in such theaters.[12]

Well before 1960s civil rights campaigns targeted segregation at downtown movie theaters and other public facilities, this racial regulation of space, combined with the specific motion picture fare, produced complicated responses. Sitting in the darkness, removed from everyday lives, and watching one of the ubiquitous Westerns shown in all kinds of theaters during the 1940s, black male audience members could root for the leading white male characters and identify with the actors' display of rugged independent masculinity. They might also feel bitter about their own exclusion from such representations. Or they might experience both sentiments at once. Women, too, might have contradictory responses to these movies, especially to the white female characters who became the object of the men's attention. Historical memories rooted in these reactions became part of the perspectives that would shape the freedom movement.

Although movies primarily entertained, overwhelming the senses with the darkness of the theater, the larger-than-life screen, and the fast-moving images, in some circumstances they spurred critical commentaries about race, representation, and identity. Rather than numbing the senses, as was often assumed, Hollywood motion pictures simultaneously attracted and repelled black viewers, wedging open spaces for critical thought. Official measures such as censorship intensified this process, producing more outright conflicts that, in many cases, took on national proportions.

Race and Movie Censorship
before the Second World War

Nationally, anxieties about the social impact of motion pictures reached a feverish pitch at the end of the First World War, when a majority of state legislatures and numerous municipalities considered establishing censorship boards to eliminate indecent, immoral, and violent images from the screen. The U.S. Supreme Court, in *Mutual Film Corp. v. Ohio* (1915), provided legal ground for such boards by refusing to extend to movie producers, distributors, and exhibitors the same free speech and due process guarantees that constitutionally protected the press. Hollywood executives attempted to stem the tide of support for state and municipal censorship by instating a process of self-censorship in the film industry. In 1922 they created the Motion Picture Producers and Distributors of America (dubbed the Hayes Office, after its director, former postmaster general Will Hayes), and in 1930, the Motion Picture Production Code.[13]

Memphis's establishment of a three-member censorship board in 1921 reflected this national drive toward censorship. The Memphis City Commission's resolution made it "unlawful for any person, firm or corporation to exhibit any immoral, lewd or lascivious picture, or any immoral, lewd or lascivious act, performance, representation, play or pantomime, within the limits of the City of Memphis." However, while much of its language duplicated that of other censorship statutes, Memphis's resolution provided for control over multiple forms of popular culture, in addition to movies, assigning extraordinary license to the local board.[14] Moreover, it expanded that control following a 1929 Tennessee Supreme Court decision upholding Memphis's censorship of Cecil de Mille's movie *King of Kings*, which traced the life and crucifixion of Christ. The film, declared board chairman Lloyd Binford, was "one of the worst travesties of the Bible [he had] ever seen." The city commission amended its 1921 act to state that the censors' decisions were "final and subject to review only for illegality or want of jurisdiction" and that the board had the right to require exhibitors to submit advance information of all films to be shown in the city.[15]

The Memphis commissioners' 1921 resolution made no mention of race, which would have made it more vulnerable to legal challenges; nevertheless, race became integral to the board's very conception of its mission. As early as 1914, the first foray into motion picture regulation, by an early Memphis censorship board established to monitor vaudeville productions, had banned *Uncle Tom's Cabin*, claiming it might stir racial violence. It also barred the stage production of *The Leopard Spots*, by Ku Klux Klan apologist Thomas Dixon, after receiving complaints from African Americans.[16] In 1927, under the expanded powers of the new board created in 1921, the censors went so far as to ban dance contests they ruled were a "demoralizing influence" upon Memphis youth. Included in the ban was the "black bottom," a popular African American jazz dance involving circular gyrations of the torso that preceded modern tap.[17]

During the 1930s, as the Crump machine increased its racial and political control and reached the height of its power, the censorship board targeted one of the most important African American heroes of the twentieth century, heavyweight champion Joe Louis. In 1936, the board barred Loew's State Theater, which catered exclusively to whites, from exhibiting a fight film of the match between Louis and German heavyweight champion Max Schmeling. The ruling reprimanded Loew's for publicizing the show without the board's prior consent, expanding on its right to advance screening of films. It also invoked a 1912 federal ban on the interstate transportation of prizefight films, originally established out of concern that the film of the 1910 Jack Johnson–Jim Jeffries fight might spark race riots, as the actual fight did. In 1936, Louis lost to Schmeling, but not before audiences witnessed twelve rounds of a black man and white man pummeling each other as equals.[18]

While the 1936 fight film decision pertained to a theater serving white patrons only and referred to a decision involving the threat of white racial violence, African Americans demonstrated their own agency, privately and publicly, when it came to Joe Louis. In and outside the city, African Americans celebrated Louis as an emblem of black masculinity, identifying with his open, if controlled, aggression and independence — qualities that could be projected in prizefights but needed to be masked in real life in the South. Even if Louis's fight films were banned in Memphis, African American fans seized upon opportunities to listen to Louis's fights via radio, which had an immediacy unavailable in motion pictures or the press. In radio broadcasts, the announcer made it possible for the listener to actively imagine Louis's jabs as they were happening and, in 1938, his knockout of Schmeling in the first round.[19] The late *Chicago Defender* journalist Vernon Jarrett recalled during a 1998 speech that many families in his hometown of Paris, Tennessee, northeast of Memphis, purchased radios — and later returned them — to hear Louis's 1938 rematch with Schmeling. Amy Jones, who grew up in Bihalia, Mississippi, recalls that her family had no electricity but listened to Louis's fights via battery-operated radio. When Louis lost in 1936, her father became so angry he "had to leave home" for awhile to cool off. His identification with Louis's competitive, aggressive masculinity, in other words, overflowed the bounds of what was acceptable in his everyday life on a Mississippi plantation. Although such responses remained hidden from the eyes of the local white censors, they might be reflected at some other moment in aspects of daily life other than leisure time.[20]

Beyond the board of censors's banning of the Joe Louis fight film, different groups of Memphians clearly perceived racial implications in the control of motion pictures. In the early 1930s, the Memphis NAACP publicly protested the negative representations of African Americans in D. W. Griffith's *Birth of a Nation*. As part of an effort to publicize the work of the recently revived local branch, the group launched a boycott of the Warner Brothers Theater to protest its screening of the film. Indeed, at the time of the film's initial release in 1915, the NAACP had picketed theaters showing the movie across the country, criticizing its depiction of black southerners as content under slavery but too uncivilized and ignorant and of black men as too lustful of white women to be trusted with political power after slavery's end.[21]

Meanwhile, Memphis Board of Censors's chairman Lloyd T. Binford, a Mississippi-raised retired insurance executive who controlled censorship decisions from 1928 until 1955, increasingly captured national headlines for his decisions to bar movies that exhibited black independence or assertiveness or any criticism of southern race and class relations. Indeed, Binford promoted a perspective on race that differed little from that of *Birth of a Nation*. Born in 1869 and reared on a plantation, he boasted that his father had been a colonel in the Confederate army and, as state senator after the Civil War, had sponsored Mississippi's "Separate Car Law."[22]

In early 1942, just after Pearl Harbor and the U.S. entry into the Second World War, Binford barred Lillian Hellman's *The Little Foxes* (1941), set in a southern town at the turn of the twentieth century. African Americans played only servants, but their characters were far from docile, expressing open disdain for Regina Giddens (Bette Davis) and her brothers, whose greedy desire to buy a new cotton mill leads them to "borrow" the savings of Regina's husband, a terminally ill banker who has refused to back their plan because it would exploit cheap labor. Before he dies — at the hands of Regina, who refuses to administer his medicine — he kindles a friendship with his daughter's beau, a journalist who believes that poor whites and blacks alike will fall prey to the "foxes" if these New South industrialists have their way.[23] The release of *The Little Foxes* came only months after the fall 1940 Memphis "reign of terror" and a burst of CIO labor activism. Binford, who would be frequently painted as a maverick by the national media, issued such censorship rulings with full support from the Crump machine as part of a broader effort to maintain social control at a time of enormous instability.

Motion Pictures and the Struggle to "Liberate Our Own Minds"

As African Americans pressed for a "Double Victory" against fascism abroad and racial injustice at home during the Second World War, struggles over racial representations in movies intensified. Few would have suggested that altering racial representations in the movies would eliminate discrimination, yet many black moviegoers believed on-screen racial stereotypes had real-life consequences. In national news, NAACP executive secretary Walter White, a strong advocate for change in Hollywood movies, characterized the challenge to eliminate racial stereotypes as revolving around the need to "liberate our own minds." In October 1943, the *Memphis World* reported on a speech by White to the Writers Congress in Los Angeles during his trip to speak to studio executives. On-screen images had more power than any other medium to influence public perceptions of minority groups, he asserted. "If we liberate our own minds of half-truths and misconceptions and use our media to build a world free of racial and religious hatred, a world free of vicious and fictitious notions of the superiority of one race over another, a world free of imperialism and colonialism," he declared, "we can then help immeasurably to insure a durable peace."[24] White thus attached his efforts to change racial images in movies to the wartime goal of advancing democracy, at home and abroad, and to racial equality. His admonition to "liberate our own minds" pertained largely to whites, who were persistently exposed to racist images of blacks.

In Memphis, the Crump machine also worried about the power of motion picture images to influence public perceptions of race. Unlike White, however, Memphis officials did not seek to liberate minds from racist beliefs; they sought to control them by censoring images of blacks outside subservient roles. Beginning in 1943, the year the Crump machine canceled A. Philip Randolph's mass meeting, city officials declared war on any Hollywood representations of African Americans that deviated from the stock images of blacks as happy-go-lucky servants. Board of censors chairman Lloyd Binford, along with members of the city commission, attempted to eliminate all hints of "social equality" from the gaze of white moviegoers in order to avoid racial trouble.

The wartime conflict over on-screen racial representations in Memphis exploded in 1943, when race riots in Detroit and other cities coincided with the release of two Hollywood hit musicals with all-black casts, *Cabin in the Sky* and *Stormy Weather*. These films, among the first by major studios to feature star-studded all-black casts, resulted from pressure from the Office of War Information and the NAACP to diversify black roles.[25] *Cabin*, produced by Metro-Goldwyn-Mayer and starring Ethel Waters, Eddie Anderson and Lena Horne, with cameo appearances by Louis Armstrong and Duke Ellington, revolves around a religious working-class woman's efforts to save her husband from the devil, who tempts him with gambling and seduction. *Stormy Weather*, 20th Century Fox's version of the all-black musical, featured Lena Horne and Bill Robinson—who play up-and-coming song and dance stars who fall in love but encounter problems balancing careers and marriage—along with unforgettable performances by Fats Waller, Cab Calloway, the Nicholas Brothers, and others. Regardless of these stellar performances, the releases of the two motion pictures worried Memphis officials. Even before the outbreak of major race riots in June 1943, jittery about hate strikes erupting among white defense workers in Mobile, Alabama, Beaumont, Texas, and other southern cities, they worried that such confrontations might spread to Memphis if whites were permitted to view these all-black-cast films. In late May, as *Cabin in the Sky* was set to open at the Loew's State Theater, Commissioner of Public Service Robert Fredericks sent a memo to Mayor Chandler, along with a *Press-Scimitar* advertisement that superimposed a provocative picture of actress Lena Horne above jitterbugging dancers and musicians. Fredericks cautioned that it might be unwise to allow a movie billed as "an all star negro show" to open at all-white theaters.[26]

With the eruption of the Detroit riot just a few weeks later, followed by the "zoot suit" riot in Los Angeles, in which white sailors attacked Mexican American youth, some commentators speculated about possible links between the opening of these all-black-cast movies and racial enmity. *Cabin in the Sky* had already been released, but an Associated Negro Press (ANP) article reported on rumors that 20th Century Fox might cancel the release of *Stormy Weather* and that other studios might stop production on all-black musicals that were in planning or production. Studio heads worried, the story also noted, that media coverage of the Detroit riot had fanned the flames of white racial animosity, which would keep white audiences from wanting to see these pictures.[27]

In Memphis, Commissioner Fredericks's concern about whites viewing an "all star negro show" rapidly translated into a new censorship policy following the riots. The 1921 municipal code already provided for the banning of "immoral, lewd or lascivious" motion pictures and other entertainment. Now, the board adopted explicitly racial restrictions regarding what could and could not be shown to white audiences. From this vantage point, on-screen images of African Americans transgressing "traditional" racial boundaries could provoke white racial violence off screen:

> WHEREAS, serious public disorders and race riots have occurred in other sections of the country in areas where white and colored troops are stationed by reason of the exhibition of moving pictures with all negro casts or with casts of negro actors performing in roles not depicting the ordinary roles played by negro citizens; and
>
> WHEREAS, large numbers of white and colored troops and seamen are now stationed in the City of Memphis and the necessity of preserving the public peace from outbreaks of violence due to racial prejudices now exist[s].

NOW, THEREFORE, BE IT RESOLVED, that hereafter no moving picture shall be exhibited at any moving picture theater catering to white or to white and colored audiences in which an all negro cast appears or in which roles are depicted by negro actors or actresses not ordinarily performed by members of the colored race in real life.[28]

Yet, of course, not all African Americans worked as maids and butlers in real life, making censorship into a kind of wishful thinking. Ironically, when faced with films of Joe Louis's prizefights, Memphis censors sought to remove this glaring evidence that real life did not necessarily conform to on-screen representations of it.

While Memphis officials concentrated on blocking future all-black-cast Hollywood musicals from white audiences, many black spectators had their own critical responses to these new films. Black Memphians thronged to *Cabin in the Sky* in late May and early June 1943, before the riots. However, after seeing the movie, many objected to its representations of African Americans, assessing them not as incendiary but reactionary. Despite *Cabin in the Sky*'s outstanding musical numbers and its star-studded cast, *Memphis World* columnist Nat D. Williams denounced the film. The movie, he argued, relied on stock racial characters, with Waters playing a "praying fanatic" and Anderson portraying "the usual 'coon-jine prediliction [sic] to dice shooting." "[T]here is the usual and out-worn 'Heben' stuff," he declared, "and everybody and anybody 'breaks out' easily and expertly into the gyrations of the ubiquitous Jitterbug.'" Williams also claimed that he was not alone in his opinion. "Two-thirds of the thinking persons" who saw *Cabin* were "disappointed and very vocally so," he declared. By characterizing himself and other black moviegoers as "thinking persons," he established a crucial distinction between African Americans as critical spectators and as fictional characters created by white screen writers and producers. He also implied that some black moviegoers, in his estimation, needed a more critical standpoint.[29] Many of the same theater patrons who disliked *Cabin in the Sky* loved *Stormy Weather*, seeing its characters as less stereotypical than those presented in *Cabin*. Indeed, although most of the film is set in Harlem and California, part of it takes place on Beale Street. Due to delays by the board of censors, actual Beale Streeters could not see the film until several months after its summer 1943 release by 20th Century Fox.[30]

The 1943 resolution seemed to target whites only, but it also had consequences for African Americans. Unstated in the resolution but apparent to black observers was the reality that the new mandate trickled down to black moviegoers who attended first-run pictures in segregated downtown theaters or saw beat-up versions of the films months later in theaters on Beale. Henceforth, African Americans would miss the same Hollywood movies that were kept from the view of white audiences. Conversely, independent black-cast films shown in neighborhood theaters were barred from white view.[31]

In many cases, black Memphians attending motion pictures downtown or on Beale would now see evidence of splicing where favorite black performers should be, producing a sense of loss or lack — or even, for some, anger. After allowing *Stormy Weather* to play uncut, albeit many months late, in July 1944, board of censors chairman Lloyd Binford ordered the deletion of Lena Horne from *Broadway Rhythm* and Cab Calloway from *Sensations of 1945*. He also excised Eddie Anderson from *Sailor Takes a Wife* (1946) and Louis Armstrong from *Pillow to Post* (1945); in the latter case, viewers saw a nightclub marquee with Armstrong's name but not his performance. In response to censorship, some producers protected their investments by structuring films in such a way that their overall integrity would be preserved if scenes with black actors were cut.[32]

The fact that Binford appeared to take particular umbrage at Lena Horne placed him in direct opposition to many black Memphians, especially women, for whom Horne had become a favorite star. Not incidentally, Horne had gained a national reputation as a black female actress who refused to play domestic servant roles. Even after deleting her from *Broadway Rhythms* in 1944, Binford then cut her from *Ziegfield Follies* (1946) and *Words and Music* (1948), boasting to Mayor Chandler in a letter that he had "deleted Lena Horne in all pictures since *Stormy Weather*."[33] In a public statement, he declared that if Horne were not going to play traditional black roles, there were plenty of white women to be used instead. For black female spectators regularly exposed to Hollywood movies in which white women played objects of men's desire while black women played their servants, Horne's films offered the chance to see different possibilities. For some, Binford's actions spurred critical thinking about the roles of black and white women in film. Meanwhile, black Memphians could still see Horne's early "race films," *Bronze Venus* and *Boogie Woogie Dream*, at black neighborhood theaters or hear her on network radio, which could not be as easily censored as movies. Nat D. Williams acknowledged her popularity in 1947 when he urged *Memphis World* readers to create fan clubs for Lena Horne and others who avoided stereotypical roles, as a way to influence Hollywood casting decisions.[34]

Cab Calloway's fans likewise found ways not only to continue to enjoy him as an entertainer but also to publicly demonstrate their enthusiasm. When Calloway visited Memphis for a show at Beale Avenue auditorium in 1947, black businesses and organizations took out a full-page newspaper advertisement welcoming the "Hi-De-Ho King." In conjunction with Calloway's visit, moviegoers attended showings of *Hi-De-Ho* (1935) at one of six different theaters catering to black audiences or saw *Stormy Weather* at the Harlem or Georgia theaters.[35]

These conflicts over Horne's and Calloway's scenes sparked national outcry in 1944, which in turn influenced the struggle in Memphis itself. An ANP story published by the *Memphis World* blasted Binford for launching a new kind of "southern jim crow," while another article denounced the "censor's shears and the censor's blue pencil" as descendants of the "rope, faggot, tar and feathers" of earlier times.[36] These stories framed Binford's actions in a broader, historical context, presenting the elimination of movie representations of African Americans outside servant roles as a new form of segregation and even linking it to the horror of lynching. This latter argument turned inside out censors' claims that on-screen representations of blacks could incite white racial violence, transforming the censors' own actions into a kind of symbolic white violence. The *Memphis World* also reported on a statement, endorsed by 500 performers at an emergency meeting in New York, that castigated writers for presenting blacks as "happy-go-lucky, lazy illiterates, clowns, cowards, superstitious, ghost ridden, liquor drinking, chicken-stealing, watermelon-eating, jazz-crazed Aunt Jemimas or Uncle Toms who at their worst are villains and at their best slavish admirers of their white 'superiors.'" Similarly, media experts at an Institute for Education by Radio conference protested broadcasts that represented African Americans as "slow-moving" and "lazy" servants.[37]

Despite this criticism, Binford barred several major films in 1945, including *Brewster's Millions* (1945), the re-release of *Imitation of Life* (1934), and Jean Renoir's *The Southerner* (1945). These rulings aroused particular ire because of their intersection with the end of the Second World War and national discourse about postwar democracy. Binford's banning of *The Southerner*, a decision supported by other Crump officials, addressed the film's depiction of poor white southerners and, more importantly, the cotton economy's reliance on farm tenancy.[38] The rulings on *Brewster's Millions* and *Imitation of Life*, on the other hand, involved important battles regarding representations of blacks.

Binford's banning of the 1945 re-release of *Imitation of Life* (1934), like his actions against Lena Horne's films, addressed film representations of

African American women. This time, ironically, the central black female character, Delilah (Louise Beavers), is a self-sacrificing, devoted mammy character who never wavers in her loyalty to the white "Miss Bea" (Claudette Colbert), even after the two women begin a successful pancake flour company that turns Bea into a well-known socialite, entrepreneur, and object of male desire. The film culminates with Delilah's death from heartbreak after her daughter Peola (Fredi Washington), despite years of her mother's devotion and sacrifice, leaves home to pass as white, never to see her mother again. Delilah is a tragic character, quite unlike the typical happy-go-lucky servant of the screen, and her daughter Peola displays such intense, fraught emotions that the viewer is unlikely to come away without considering the formidable impact of race on this beautiful young woman. Black feminist scholar bell hooks has written of her own reactions to Peola as an adolescent: "I will always remember that image. I remembered how we cried for her, for our unrealized desiring selves. She was tragic because there was no place in the cinema for her, no loving pictures." In 1945 Memphis, Binford banned the film because, he asserted, Peola's and Delilah's characters showed too much unhappiness about the lives of African Americans.[39]

Binford's censorship of the popular comedy *Brewster's Millions* prompted the fiercest outcry of perhaps any of his censorship decisions. An update of earlier film renditions of the Winchell Smith/Byron Ongley play, the 1945 version cast Brewster (Dennis O'Keefe) as a World War II veteran who learns he could inherit eight million dollars — if he can spend a million dollars before his birthday, two months away. Binford objected to Eddie Anderson's portrayal of Brewster's valet, Jackson, a character akin to his "Rochester" on *The Jack Benny Show*. Although Anderson played a servant, Binford felt he was not subservient enough. "Rochester (Eddie Anderson), has much too familiar a way about him," he declared, "and the picture presents too much social equality and racial mixture." Again, he claimed that violence might be sparked by this Hollywood intrusion into southern life: "We don't have any trouble with racial problems here and we don't intend to encourage any by permitting movies like this one to be shown."[40] The *New York Times*, *Time* magazine, and other media immediately condemned Binford's statement, and author Lillian Smith issued a statement accusing Binford of fueling racial discord, not maintaining peace.[41]

Similar to Memphis public response to the police rape cases in August 1945, the widespread condemnation of the *Brewster's Millions* ruling exposed the deep indignation aroused by its timing at the end of the war. Binford's ruling became emblematic of the larger struggle over white domination. Binford's insinuation that black movie characters not only had to be servants but needed to display dependence, ignorance, and other servile qualities, fueled anger among many who might not generally have publicly addressed conflicts over movies. The censor himself acknowledged the scope of public response to his decision in a letter to the mayor, asserting that he had been pilloried in the press and in Hollywood publications. He had received over 300 letters, both critical and supportive, with most favoring his action. Locally, he had been inundated with telephone calls and comments on the street, which he summed up as largely supportive.

Many of Binford's critics were young African American men and women in the armed forces, employed in the war industry, or students at LeMoyne. They indicate the depth of this generation's sentiments about racial representations in the mass media, in juxtaposition to the principles of democracy articulated in national wartime discourse. Nearly all of the twenty-one critical letters Binford received, by his own accounting, came from black soldiers who asked, "What are we fighting for?" At LeMoyne College, the *Private Chatterer*, published by young women, lampooned the ruling in an issue that included poems and letters about racial discrimination in the military.[42] And a Memphis migrant to the California defense industry wrote to the *Memphis World* expressing her humiliation after reading an article in the *Los Angeles Sentinel*, a black newspaper, that ridiculed Memphis for banning *Brewster's Millions*. War workers, she declared, "regardless of race, color or creed . . . sweat here in smoke and heat, toiling toward a better future for ALL the people."[43]

The *Memphis World* added to this ferment by publishing front-page articles about black servicemen's responses to racial stereotypes in movies, which likewise affixed the issue of representations in the mass media to wartime principles of democracy. An ANP story printed after Binford's decision reported that troops in the Pacific, including some whites, had criticized racial stereotypes in a Merry Melody cartoon, *Sunday Go to Meeting*, and that black GIs in Europe had resented *Syncopation* (1942), a movie about jazz that hinged on a white romance.[44] The *World* also published an open letter from Private Charles W. Brown Jr. and forty-three black marines stationed "Somewhere in the South Pacific." Brown described hostility from local people whose views about African Americans came from Hollywood, pointing to transnational consequences of racial stereotypes portrayed in American films. He declared that they had "fought this menace by every means, with our hands and minds"—a remarkable statement that made this struggle over movies a parallel to the fight against the threat of fascism. He called upon black performers to "discontinue accepting roles or parts that they took in the past" so that "we can then raise our heads and fight our handicaps without being ashamed."[45] This letter, like the one from the California war worker, emphasized personal feelings of shame. In such commentaries, ideas akin to Walter White's comment about "liberat[ing] our own minds" pertained as much to the self as to the gaze of white viewers.

In another way, this concern about "our own minds" surfaced in differences among African Americans about appropriate movie fare. In 1945, Blair T. Hunt, principal of Booker T. Washington High School and an important interlocutor between the Crump machine and black Memphis, accepted the position of assistant censor, making him responsible for advising the board on movies shown to black audiences. In one of Hunt's first actions, he helped stop the Ace Theater's showing of *A Woman Is a Fool*, a "race movie" starring blues singer Ida Cox, declaring that it was "vulgar and unfit to be shown to juvenile or even adult audiences." Black female blues singers like Cox, who were famous for songs like "One Hour Mama," had long evoked criticism from middle-class African Americans who perceived their overt sexuality as playing into racial stereotypes they sought to escape. Conflicts over on-screen racial stereotypes thus involved multiple power relations and perceptions about racial identities.[46]

"Mental Liberties": Movie Censorship after the War

The fight over motion picture censorship, race, and democracy shifted in the climate of the emerging Cold War. Nationally, censorship rulings in Memphis, Atlanta, and other southern cities accrued fresh political significance, even receiving attention in Congress. Hollywood producers and distributors and their attorneys began to take southern censorship boards — starting with the one in Memphis — to court, demanding protection of their constitutional rights to free speech and due process of law. In Memphis, white moderates increasingly spoke out against Binford and the Crump machine's violations of their own civil liberties and basic American democratic principles. Generally, their complaints about the lack of civil liberties concerned their individual rights as citizens, but occasionally they addressed the racial issues invoked by censorship.

Within a month of Truman's famous March 1947 speech that framed the Cold War as a struggle between two ways of life, one democratic, the other totalitarian, Binford banned a total of six movies. By far the most controversial decision pertained to David O. Selznick's film *Duel in the Sun*, which Selznick had hoped would live up to the standard set by his earlier epic,

Gone with the Wind. *Duel in the Sun* portrayed a post–Civil War confrontation between a crusty, powerful Texas rancher, Senator Jackson McCanles, and the encroaching railroad, backed by the U.S. cavalry. The overlay of a second drama about the rancher's sons, Lewt and Jesse (Gregory Peck and Joseph Cotton), and their competing sentiments for Pearl Chavez (Jennifer Jones), a young woman staying on the ranch, raised censors' hackles because of images of interracial lust, miscegenation, violence, and religious hypocrisy. Nearly every censor ultimately approved the film with minor deletions, with the exception of Binford, who banned it in its entirety, calling it "the most repellant movie I have seen this year."[47]

Binford's ruling became even more politicized when Mississippi congressman John Rankin denounced *Duel in the Sun* on the floor of the U.S. House of Representatives, calling it "filthy, debasing and insulting to the moral instincts of decent humanity." Rankin, notorious for his open advocacy of white supremacy and attack on civil rights as a communist plot, had written to Binford a day earlier to praise him for "rendering one of the greatest services of any person I know in either public or private life." He also thanked him for aiding his cause in the House by sending him a letter and other materials that had provided the basis for his speech. Selznick, meanwhile, wired all congressmen in southern California, where the film debuted, thanking those who had defended him and asking others, including Richard Nixon, to oppose Rankin.[48]

While many Memphians supported Binford's ruling, hundreds of white and black residents defied it by attending *Duel in the Sun* in West Memphis, Arkansas, when it opened in October 1947. A letter to the *Commercial Appeal* from a white reader who made the trip across the Mississippi River to West Memphis and liked the film castigated Binford for "depriv[ing] fellow Memphians and Shelby Countians of the opportunity to see this." Black Memphians could not see the film for a few weeks longer, in accordance with practices by which new movies opened first at whites-only theaters. The *Memphis World* urged its readers to attend one of the showings of *Duel* at the Harlem Theatre in West Memphis. In addition to printing large advertisements that hailed it as "Banned in Memphis by the Censor Board," the newspaper ran an accompanying story reporting that whites had "left Memphis by the hundreds to see the picture." It also let readers know that the film featured African American actress Butterfly McQueen, well-known for her role of Prissy in *Gone with the Wind*, now in the role of Vashti. The story exhorted African Americans to "pack the Harlem Theatre . . . every night in view of the racial attitude that has been assumed by Mr. Binford relative to pictures in recent years." Crossing the river to see the film thus became not just a question of entertainment but an organized act of protest against the Crump machine.[49]

Duel in the Sun was not without its own racial complexities and problems. Although it may have been groundbreaking for depicting interracial sexuality, all three of the central female characters, Pearl, Vashti, and Senator McCanles's wife, Laura Bell (Lillian Gish), were built from racial stereotypes. Vashti, the sole black character in the movie, differed little from the vacuous servant played by McQueen in *Gone with the Wind*, and was the only female character that did not figure as an object of male desire. Pearl, the daughter of a Mexican-origin man and an Indian prostitute, exudes a sensuality she seems unable to control and that ultimately tears the McCanles family apart. Laura Bell, in contrast, is also the only really sympathetic character, a deeply devout, angelic white woman who is the object of both her husband's and Pearl's father's desires. For black Memphians who crossed the river to see the movie, trumping Binford did not resolve the troubling issues of racial representation raised by the movie.[50]

Another Binford ruling in September 1947 drew particularly heated national publicity, partly because of its occurrence just two weeks after the Freedom Train send-off from Philadelphia. This time, he barred the showing of *Curley*, a comedy about schoolchildren. Produced by *Our Gang* originator Hal Roach, *Curley* drew on premises and conventions similar to those in the earlier movies, such as the inclusion of black children among its "little rascals." Binford declared he was "unable to approve [the] '*Curley*' picture with the little Negroes" because "the south does not permit Negroes in white schools nor recognize social equality between the races, even in children."[51] The baldness of this statement drew condemnation not only from Roach, the film's producer, but also from Eric Johnston, head of the Motion Pictures Association of America. Readers of the *Memphis World* learned about Roach's and Johnston's reactions from a front-page ANP story headlined "Memphis Ban on Film First Challenge to 'Freedom Train'" and datelined Philadelphia.[52] As with *Duel in the Sun*, however, opposing Binford's ruling was not necessarily the same as embracing the movie, since the *Our Gang* movies, while including a black child among its "little rascals," relied on racial caricatures, typified by the Buckwheat and Farina characters.

Binford simultaneously drew heat locally and nationally for preventing the traveling Broadway production of Rogers and Hammerstein's celebrated musical, *Annie Get Your Gun*, starring Mary Martin, from coming to Memphis, after he learned that the cast included three black men who appeared in scenes with white women. Although the show's black characters were hardly unusual—they included a porter, a waiter, and a conductor (none of whom appear in the 1950 movie version)—Binford objected to dance numbers in which they shared the stage with white women. His decision, reported in the *New York Times*, triggered objections by progressive white southerners. Harold Austin, president of the interracial Methodist Student Movement of North Carolina, for example, characterized the decision as "far from an ethical and Christian act" in a letter to Binford. Locally, a letter from a white *Commercial Appeal* reader lambasted Binford for not understanding the biblical notion that God made all people "of one blood," and another reproached him for trying to "chop the role of the Negro in life down to the size he wants it to be regardless of the fact that we have fought, bled and died a good many times for equality of opportunity for all." Perhaps because it involved live actors in a Broadway production rather than a motion picture, this decision prompted especially indignant responses.[53]

Amid this turmoil over Memphis's censorship rulings, Hal Roach Studios and United Artists (UA) took the *Curley* case to court. In a petition for a writ of certiorari, attorneys argued that Binford's decision violated the First Amendment's guarantee of free speech, the Fourteenth Amendment's protections against the deprivation "of life, liberty or property, without due process of law," and the Tennessee Constitution. *Curley*, they contended, did not violate any precepts of Memphis's 1921 statute against "immoral, lewd, or lascivious" productions. The decision had therefore been capricious, they asserted, based on the film's portrayal of black and white children together. Because the decisions of the Memphis Board of Censors were not subject to judicial review, the censors had deprived citizens of entertainment and inflicted "irreparable injury" upon the producer, distributor, and exhibitors without due process. Finally, they addressed the issue of censorship in general, arguing that movies were "one of the greatest of all instrumentalities for the dissemination of information" and should "be provided the same protection of free speech accorded to any other medium." In 1948, however, a circuit court judge disagreed that the ruling had been capricious and dismissed the case on the basis of a technicality. Because the board's decisions applied only to local exhibitors, not out-of-state producers or distributors, he asserted, the letter from Binford barring the film was only "advisory." In 1949, the state supreme court seemed to nod in UA's favor by declaring that there were no legal grounds for censorship based solely on issues of "race or color"; however, the justices declared that the UA's business did not constitute interstate commerce, nor did the distributor qualify as a local business operator. In 1950, the U.S.

Supreme Court declined to hear the case, allowing the Tennessee decision to stand.[54]

The *Curley* case was one of several efforts by the film industry to overturn the Supreme Court's 1915 ruling that motion pictures were not covered by First Amendment guarantees protecting the press. Most involved southern censors and racial message movies, such as Atlanta's censorship of *Lost Boundaries*. Unlike the school desegregation cases under review by the Supreme Court, however, these cases addressed the constitutional rights of producers, distributors, exhibitors, and viewers, not the impact of censorship decisions on African Americans. When the Supreme Court finally accepted a movie censorship case for review in 1952, it chose a challenge to New York City's ban of *The Miracle*, a Federico Fellini film attacked as sacriligious, rather than a ban on a film involving racial issues.[55]

Black Memphians' responses to Binford's 1949 censorship of *Lost Boundaries*, a movie aimed at exposing racial discrimination, made clear that at issue was not civil liberties alone but also the freedom to envision racial identities not circumscribed by the narrow confines of the Jim Crow South, on-screen and in real life. In the LeMoyne *Beacon*, a writer declared that Binford's censorship of the film infringed upon "mental liberties." The writer, who had seen *Lost Boundaries* in West Memphis, praised the film for "point[ing] out many thought provoking things to many people, unaware of the problems faced by members of the group concerned in THE PROBLEM." By invoking W. E. B. Du Bois's searing question in *Souls of Black Folk* (1903) — "How does it feel to be a problem?" — the author tied the constitutional issue of free speech to both on-screen racial representation and off-screen racial identity. Even in *Lost Boundaries* and *Pinky*, about African American professionals who chose to "pass" — and could pass — blacks received implicit messages that unless they looked white, they could be only servants, swindlers, or Jezebels. Censorship, paradoxically, prompted black Memphians to develop a more critical perspective toward the issues of race, gender, and sexuality that were raised but not resolved by the images and missing images on the motion picture screen.[56]

"Talking to the People No One Wanted to Talk To": Black Radio

In a 1995 interview, Martha Jean "the Queen" Steinberg, a popular WDIA-Memphis DJ during the 1950s, commented on the importance of black DJs in an era when, in her view, Memphis lacked black leaders. "If you got a popular DJ in a city, that DJ was the mayor of the city," she declared. "We were talking to the people that no one wanted to talk to. Everybody was talking about, but no one would talk to. And it was like — they're over there, those Negroes over there, you know, are 'nigras.'" Steinberg added that DJs "were able to get by because no one paid us attention because they didn't believe that anything was going to happen."[57]

Steinberg's comments help get at the significance of radio oriented to African American listeners during the postwar period, prior to the sit-in movement and other public protests of the civil rights era. Radio broadcasting reached into households throughout Memphis and the Delta. DJs seemed to speak personally to their listeners, as their voices beamed directly into people's everyday lives. While movies' visual racial caricatures, and even their missing images, could alternately spark amusement and rage on the part of viewers, the medium of radio and, in particular, stations oriented to black listeners, worked differently, cultivating race pride and, at times, critical political standpoints at the same time as they entertained.

When WDIA began broadcasting Nat D. Williams's *Tan Town Jamboree* in October 1948, hundreds of black listeners telephoned the station to express their enthusiasm, convincing the station's white owners to add additional black-oriented shows. They were added so rapidly that by mid-1949 the station had become the first station nationally to commit entirely to black-oriented programming. WDIA won an astounding portion of the listening market. An early-1950s Hooper ratings survey found that 69.6 percent of African American households in Memphis tuned to WDIA daily. By 1954, when the station upgraded from 250 to 50,000 watts, its broadcasting blanketed the Delta, and WDIA announced that it reached 115 counties in Tennessee, Mississippi, Arkansas, and Missouri, twenty-four hours a day.[58]

As a product of the Jim Crow urban South and the brainchild of two white southerners with no inclination toward racial equality, WDIA's transition to all-black programming may not have appeared to jeopardize the status quo. All the DJs, including Nat D. Williams, were emcees, educators, and entertainers whose established reputations made them seem familiar, not threatening. However, WDIA proved subtly subversive of white supremacy in the years before Memphis's public civil rights protests, weakening segregation even as it nurtured a black world of mass culture. Black-oriented radio opened up a new public sphere in which DJs and listeners experimented with racial identities as individuals, as black Memphians, and as members of an even broader black listening audience. In the racially and politically circumscribed context of postwar Memphis, WDIA offered a precious space for artistic expression, group interaction, and political commentary.[59]

Radio encouraged listeners to conjure up visual images based on aural impressions. WDIA's DJs grabbed listeners' attention with on-air person-alities that, of necessity, deviated sharply from the racial caricatures of earlier network radio.[60] In doing so, they established an imagined commu-nity of listeners that reached far beyond the actual bounds of any physical cultural space, bridging both geographical and social divides.[61] WDIA's in-novative programming, from rhythm and blues and gospel shows to news talk shows, homemaker advice programs, and listener call-ins, helped nurture a politics of pride and a critical exploration of black identities.

Ironically, as scholar Mark Newman has shown, WDIA's reliance on advertisers' sponsorship contributed to the station's cultivation of race pride. Many advertisers withdrew their business when the station switched to black-appeal programming, but this trend reversed when black listen-ers proved extremely responsive to WDIA DJs' personally stamped sales pitches. In contrast to previous advertising that either ignored blacks for fear that whites would shun commodities stamped as "Negro products" or attempted to sell them second-rate products, these DJs treated black listeners respectfully. *Sponsor* magazine, an industry publication, warned against "talking down" to African American listeners, arguing that they would become great consumers if they felt that purchasing the "good things in life and articles of better quality" would allow them to achieve equality with whites. While soliciting consumers, therefore, WDIA's man-agement, despite its disinterest in racial equality as a principle, broadcast ads that implied the opposite.[62]

WDIA owners John Pepper and Bert Ferguson initially converted WDIA to black-appeal programming as a way to avoid bankruptcy, not to address racial discrimination. The rise of television in the late 1940s and early 1950s eroded the strength of national network radio broadcasting. Local stations frequently responded to this shift by developing a "narrowcast-ing" approach that targeted specific communities. This strategy especially benefited new stations with weak signals, which proliferated in the decade after the war despite the soaring popularity of television.[63] Pepper and Ferguson faced the need for innovative approaches soon after purchasing WDIA, a 250-watt outlet competing with five other Memphis stations, in 1947. By 1948, it was clear that neither country nor classical programming was attracting new audiences.[64]

Since all shows required sponsorship by advertisers, Pepper and Fergu-son sought not just a group of listeners, but consumers, and saw a pos-sibility in Memphis's African American population, swelled by the arrival of wartime and postwar migrants intent on becoming wage earners. Both

Pepper and Ferguson had limited experience with programming involving black culture but had encountered Nat D. Williams through the broadcast of the "Midnight Rambles," over WHBQ, where Ferguson had worked. The two men were not enamored of African Americans, Williams claimed, but they were innovative businessmen who "love[d] progress" and had identified the "Negro market" as "one of the most neglected markets in the Mid-South."[65]

African American audiences in various cities had already demonstrated their enthusiasm for black-oriented broadcasting. In Chicago, WGES's Al Benson, originally from Jackson, Mississippi, was voted the city's favorite DJ in 1948, based on his appeal to working-class African Americans, especially southern migrants. The same year, Chicago's Daddy-O Daylie (Holmes Bailey) and Austin's Doctor Hep Cat (Lavada Durst) began radio careers, immediately winning audiences with their hip rhyming and signifying styles. KFFA in Helena, Arkansas, launched its famous "King Biscuit Flour Hour," featuring blues man Sonny Boy Williamson in 1941, the year that *Cab Calloway's Quizzical*, showcasing black entertainers and live audiences, became a hit on New York's WOR. Black Memphians already tuned in to local broadcasts of gospel quartets, religious services, variety shows, and other programs, although Joe Louis's fights continued to top the charts of network radio broadcasts.[66]

Even after making the decision to experiment with a black-oriented music program, Ferguson and Pepper worried about being shut down by Crump. "The atmosphere was such," Ferguson recalls, "with Crump running everything . . . we could see him saying: 'Look, we don't want any nigger radio station in town.'" Williams received hate calls after his first broadcast.[67] A warning signal had come earlier in 1948, when Public Safety Commissioner Joe Boyle ordered the destruction of 400 records after he ferreted out all copies of three recordings he termed "rotten, indecent and vulgar," including Julia Lee's "King Size Papa." Policemen had seized records from jukeboxes in black-owned cafés and removed them from record stores. Boyle likened his order to Binford's censorship of offensive movies. He also expressed disgust for what he called "the indecent and vulgar radio programs that are coming in over the air" but acknowledged that he was "powerless to stop" what was coming in over the airwaves. Taking the warning, Williams played rhythm and blues on WDIA but talked and laughed over "vulgar" lyrics.[68]

From Martha Jean "the Queen" to "Hot Rod" Hulbert

From the start, DJs were the linchpins in the station's ability to rivet the attention of their audiences. Listeners' feelings of connection to WDIA's on-air personalities encouraged them to tune in at regular times to regularly scheduled shows. In part, as Nat D. Williams pointed out to his *Memphis World* readers after his *Tan Town Jamboree* premiered, listeners loved the show because its "jump tunes, blues, and jive" made it fun. But what really made the show stand out, he said, was "the fact that a Negro disk jockey has been employed . . . in the face of local traditions which ordinarily exclude your folks from such spots."[69] A black DJ on the air in the mid-South represented a major breakthrough in radio. As the station added more shows, a bond developed between on-air personalities and listeners, a phenomenon specific to the postwar era.

Black Memphians who listened to WDIA in its first decade recall their favorite on-air personalities. Joan Lee Nelson, later a civil rights activist, adored Willa Monroe, the Tan Town Homemaker, as a youngster. Eddie May Garner recalls Theo "Bless My Bones" Wade, a folksy, entertaining gospel DJ who also managed the Spirit of Memphis Quartet. She similarly recalls Rufus Thomas, who had danced, sung, and performed comedy with traveling troupes before becoming host of Amateur Night, in place of Nat D. Williams. Thomas's *Hoot'n'Holler* show placed him in a perfect spot from which to promote first R & B and then soul recordings by other artists, even as he began to record his own. Naomi Jones names Ford Nelson, A. C. "Moohah" Williams, and B. B. King, along with Nat D. and Rufus Thomas as her favorites. Ford Nelson, one of WDIA's renowned gospel DJs, had a subdued, sophisticated style. A. C. Williams, a high school biology teacher at Manassas, started the famed *Teen Town Singers* show in June 1949, bringing to the air the voices of such talented students as future soul stars Isaac Hayes and Carla Thomas. After moving to Memphis from Indianola, Mississippi, and winning acclaim at Amateur Night, B. B. King convinced WDIA managers to give him a fifteen-minute spot promoting Peptikon, a patent medicine elixir, and then he was made DJ of the *Sepia Swing Club* in late 1950.[70]

Hiring these DJs was part of WDIA's strategy to attract a target audience. As mass media scholar Susan Douglas has shown, DJs became crucial to postwar radio "narrowcasting" as a result of station managers' searches for new means of building listener loyalty. These postwar DJs brought far more personal style to their radio personae than had earlier announcers. DJs used inflections, signature phrases, nonlinguistic sounds, and musical excerpts to establish on-air personalities. For listeners, the repetition

WDIA disc jockeys, 1955, on occasion of Rufus Thomas's fifth anniversary at the station. Seated, from left: Martha Jean Steinberg, Gerry Brown, Robert Thomas; standing, from left: J. B. Brooks, engineer, Willa Monroe, Nat D. Williams, Rufus Thomas, A. C. Williams, Ford Nelson, and Theo Wade. *(Courtesy WDIA)*

of such devices allowed them to develop a sense of familiarity with DJs, as if they knew them personally. Radio not only encouraged listeners to imagine the person behind the voice, it also allowed them to imagine the DJ was talking directly to them, a perception enhanced by DJs' frequent use of a linguistic style that incorporated an I-you mode of communication. As Douglas puts this, the technology of radio required DJs to develop a "monologue that had to sound like a dialogue."[71]

WDIA DJs did not create on-air personalities from scratch, however, since all had previously worked as educators or in the entertainment industry. On radio, they transformed their former roles into new on-air personalities through sound.[72] At WDIA, Williams created a new radio voice that built upon and transformed his earlier roles as teacher, journalist, and emcee. On his early morning *Tan Town Coffee Club*, aimed at working-class adults, for example, Nat D. drew on the casual style he used in his newspaper columns, speaking directly, and humorously, to his sleepy listeners: "Arise, Jackson, and peck on the rock; it's six-thirty by this man's clock," he began. "That's right, ladies, it's time to jump into those corsets.

You too, Jackson, get out of that bed, you know where to head—that's enough said!" After hooking his listeners' attention, he played music and commented on various topics.[73]

Nat D. and other DJs also brought a lively sense of humor to WDIA. Historian Lawrence Levine argues that humor allowed African Americans to play with the absurdities, hypocrisies, and double standards of racism. Participants could release suppressed emotions and "assert the invincibility of their own persona against the world, and . . . accomplish all of this, as Freud put it, 'without quitting the ground of mental sanity.'" Indeed, Nat D. Williams claimed that the laughter that spilled out over the airwaves at the start of his very first broadcast hid the fact that his anxiety had made him forget what he planned to say. "I broke out in a raucous laugh because I was laughin' myself out of the picture," Williams confessed. "When you see me laughin'," he added, "I'm laughin' just to keep from cryin'."[74] His laughter became the *Tan Town Jamboree*'s trademark opening. Shared humor and laughter also fostered a sense of community by distinguishing participants from those outside the "circle of laughter."[75] Finally, humor allowed DJs in the Jim Crow South to mask their messages from most whites while conveying them to black listeners. Martha Jean "the Queen" Steinberg, a radio star at WDIA in the 1950s and later in Detroit, commented on the significance of humor for black DJs: "We were considered clowns, we were considered ignorant, we were considered jokes, but if we hadn't been laughing, we couldn't have gotten our point across." She and other DJs were "bright people, independent thinkers, philosophers," she declared, "but we had to act like clowns to get our point across and not upset anything or let anybody know we were upsetting anything." "Acting like clowns," as Steinberg put it, incorporated enough of a racial stereotype to get blacks on the air, but they were able to at least partially undermine that stereotype with the messages they conveyed.[76]

Women DJs' relations to their audiences illuminate the subtle ways in which WDIA encouraged listeners to consider new gendered, racial identities and to challenge existing racial representations. Women DJs became stars at WDIA, as hosts of homemaker and advice programs and gospel and R & B shows. Although most DJs in postwar black-oriented radio were men, and historians of radio in this period concentrate largely on male radio personalities, radio personnel at the time were keenly aware that much of their audience was female. Eddie O'Jay, a celebrated black DJ during the 1950s and 1960s, first in Milwaukee, then Cleveland, and then Buffalo, goes so far as to assert that "radio was designed to be appealing to the woman." He explained in an interview that while men worked at jobs where radio was prohibited, women housekeepers generally had the radio on, whether they took care of their own homes or worked as maids in white women's homes. Men on the air modulated their voices to appeal to women, and black-oriented stations began hiring women to host their own shows.[77]

WDIA's first attempt to design such a show came with it's initiation of *Tan Town Homemakers*, hosted by Willa Monroe, starting in August 1949. In this same period, stations in Birmingham, New Orleans, Atlanta, Nashville, and elsewhere created similar homemaker programs hosted by black women. Significantly, WDIA's decision to launch the show resulted from listener requests, in response to a 1949 promotional brochure. Monroe, a friend of Nat D. Williams, had appeared as a guest on his show before being asked to host *Tan Town Homemakers* weekday mornings at 9:00. A well-known socialite, Monroe lived in a mansion purchased for her by Robert Wright, a successful bandleader and nightclub owner. Martha Jean Steinberg described Monroe, for whom she frequently substituted after the latter became ill, as "a diva." "She was sharp, she had furs, and she had this guy and they were high livers," Steinberg commented. "And she believed in all of the nice things a lady should have, the caviar and the jaguar and all that kind of stuff. She was really, really, really a character."[78]

Tan Town Homemakers targeted middle-class housewives, but Monroe won listeners well beyond that category, including domestic workers cleaning other women's homes. Hooper ratings showed that a sensational 40 percent of the Memphis listening audience tuned in to Monroe's show on weekday mornings. Joan Lee Nelson, one of several Lee sisters who became civil rights activists, calls WDIA her "first socialization [and] culturalization" and remembers listening to Willa Monroe. Monroe played music by singers such as Sarah Vaughan, Eartha Kitt, and Dinah Washington; distributed recipes and advice; circulated society news; and interviewed prominent African American women. The show thus combined images of middle-class domesticity with positive images of black women. Outside the studio Monroe held advice sessions for listeners and promoted community activism. In 1950, for example, she organized a "tag day," or garage sale, benefit for the NAACP, using the profits to purchase memberships for black youth.[79] Through not only advice but also example, Monroe encouraged independence and self-respect among black women, not unlike middle-class African American women's clubs did.

Monroe's show was so successful that WDIA also hired other women. Gerry Brown, an English teacher who was a colleague of Williams and the winner of a station contest, came to WDIA as DJ of a weeknight rhythm and

Willa Monroe (right) interviewing Marion Anderson for WDIA
at the Memphis train station, early 1950s. Beside Anderson are
(left to right) M. M. Watson and Madame McCleave.
(© *Ernest C. Withers, courtesy of Panopticon Gallery*)

blues show called *Nite Spot*, and Carlotta Stewart Watson as "Aunt Carrie"
gave advice on *Spotlight*. Star McKinney, a Cotton Makers' Jubilee beauty
queen, became both "society editor" and co-host with Robert "Honeyboy"
Thomas of a popular Saturday morning romantic music program, *Boy
Meets Girl*.[80]

Martha Jean "the Queen" Steinberg, however, became WDIA's most
successful female DJ and, ultimately, one of the best-known women radio
personalities nationally, with a career that took her from WDIA to WCHB-
Inkster/Detroit and then to WJLB-Detroit. Born and raised in Memphis as
Martha Jean Jones, she married trumpeter Luther Steinberg and developed
a reputation as a producer of fashion shows by black women before going
to WDIA. Hired to co-host a Sunday evening show with Nat D., she took
over Gerry Brown's *Nite Spot* show when Brown left the station, hosted a

hot R & B new releases show, *Premium Stuff*, and did the *Tan Town Homemakers* after Monroe's health faltered.[81]

A major promoter of both black music and civil rights, Steinberg was also one of a group of black female DJs in this era who dedicated themselves to elevating and inspiring black women. "I saw a need where women, especially black women, had such a need to be lifted up because we worked so hard and done so much," she asserted in an interview. "Any man, anybody who wanted a black woman, he could come and take her, do whatever he wanted to do and she was not appreciated by anybody. She was always a second best woman." When Steinberg said she wanted to "talk to the people that no one wanted to talk to," she had women in particular in mind.

Steinberg's on-air radio personalities reflected this determination to inspire women listeners. On her evening music shows, "the Queen" adopted a sexy, smart persona and introduced the latest R & B recordings at a time when most black women on radio were hosting gospel or homemaker shows. Expressive black female sexuality, she showed, could be a strength, rather than a problem, and earn respect. Of her daytime shows, however, she said, "I'd just come on and talk to the women about political issues and try to tell . . . the people in Mississippi, that we didn't have to take all that racial discrimination. You got to be educated." She had not only urban but also rural black women in mind. In an interview, she recounted a trip she had made to a fashion show in Mississippi, where the women "had on cotton stockings, bandanas, snuff in their mouth and a potbellied stove." They had made her feel, she recalled, that black women "needed to realize that we had a worth and a value." By making black women listeners the insiders not the outsiders — the people she spoke to, not about — she encouraged self-respect and confidence about making changes.[82]

Meanwhile, Steinberg struggled to retain control over her own radio persona by insisting upon an on-air name that commanded respect. "If you were black [and on radio], you could not just use your name," she recalled. "You had to have a nickname to go along with it. Aunt Jane or somebody. I say: Look, you can forget Aunt Jane with me, honey." First called "Princess Premium Stuff," after the title of her show, she changed her on-air name to Martha Jean "the Queen" after Robert "Honeymoon" Garner, a DJ and the station's first engineer, came up with this rhyming, royal alternative. African American women DJs at other white-owned, black-oriented stations also battled over this naming issue. Hattie Leeper, at WBIV in Charlotte, was known as "Chattie Hattie" but insisted upon using "good diction" and acting with dignity to combat this clownish image. The "OK" radio chain assigned franchise names and personalities to black DJs. Novella Smith on KYOK-Houston, called "Dizzy Lizzy," rebelled by signing off after the news with her real name. And at WGOK in Mobile, Irene Weaver Johnson disliked being called "Miss Mandy" and being pushed to adhere to a certain sound, as if she were uneducated and uncouth. Despite their renown as DJs, these women struggled to assert their own names and original styles.[83]

Steinberg was not the only WDIA DJ to make urban-rural relations central to her broadcasting outlook. Maurice Hulbert Jr., better known as "Hot Rod" Hulbert, grew up in a Beale Street entertainment family, yet as a DJ he became acutely aware of radio's rural audiences. His brief WDIA career, from spring 1949 to fall 1950, when he moved to a more lucrative position at Baltimore's WITH, illustrates how black-oriented radio linked Memphians to the rural Delta. Hulbert's father, Maurice Sr., was one of the most well-known personalities in the Beale Street entertainment world as a performer, the founder of the first black dancing school, and a nightclub owner. Inducted into show business at an early age, Maurice Jr. was a well-known dancer and the host of musical shows, and he produced the annual talent show at Booker T. Washington High School. Hulbert's versatile background translated into multiple radio personae crafted to complement specific musical styles and to cultivate certain audiences. In spring 1949, Hulbert launched the *Sepia Swing Club*, an early-afternoon program, as "Hot Rod Hulbert." He soon added two morning shows, hosting *Delta Melodies*, an early-morning gospel program, as Maurice Hulbert Jr., and *Sweet Talking Time*, a show featuring romantic crooners aimed at women, as "Maurice the Mood Man."[84]

Hulbert consciously packed his *Sepia Swing Club* with emblems of the jet age and contemporary black culture, drawing urban and rural listeners alike. Each show began at 2:00 P.M. with sounds of a jet engine revving up and Hulbert, as a "high-octane" radio pilot, calling out the names of all Memphis's black neighborhoods—Binghampton, Orange Mound, New Chicago, etc. In addition to listeners in these neighborhoods, he recalled, he also lured "a great audience of people who had their radios in the cotton fields listening to me." In the imaginary Hulbert constructed, these workers "blasted off" with him on a fantasy rocket into a modern urban world far removed from the cotton fields yet connected to them through black music's Delta roots. Listeners could be on the plantation and yet conceive of themselves as the inhabitants of another place. Hulbert's rural fans influenced him as much as he influenced his fans. "They would invite me up there . . . and they'd load my car up with vegetables, fruit, watermelon, meats and everything," Hulbert recalled. "It was fantastic. That's what I strived for, a great mutual affection with my audience." Through radio, Hulbert hitched black identities to modernity, linking listeners, whether they were on the plantation or in the city, to the rocket age and cutting edge of postwar music.[85]

Race, Radio, and Religion

WDIA's gospel and religious shows became at least as important as pop music shows when it came to building race pride and encouraging listeners to see themselves as part of the WDIA family. Given the significance of religion to African American culture in and around Memphis, it was not surprising that an early WDIA listener-preference test placed gospel and spiritual music at the top. Since gospel quartets had performed over area radio stations for two decades, WDIA seized on this format by scheduling daily fifteen-minute slots for the famed Spirit of Memphis, the Southern Wonders, and the all-female Songbirds of the South. Religious listeners could soon spend most of Sunday with WDIA, even "going to church" a second time by tuning in to services at East Trigg Missionary Baptist Church, from which WDIA broadcast the *Gospel Treasure Hour* with well-known minister Dr. W. Herbert Brewster.[86]

Because radio unhinged both gospel and secular music from their physical foundations in churches and nightclubs, WDIA created ambiguity where many listeners presumed boundaries. Like many others of his generation, Nat D. Williams, born on Beale Street in 1909, recalled "catch[ing] the devil" from his grandmother when he sang the blues. Years later, his minister nearly expelled him from church when he sang the "Beale Street Blues" at Amateur Night. Although neither Williams's grandmother nor his minister succeeded in their efforts to enforce the boundaries between the sacred and the profane, radio made that task even more difficult. Since both "God's music" and the "devil's music" emanated from the same source — WDIA — listeners could enjoy *Saturday Night Fish Fry* at 4:00 P.M. and stay tuned in for the *Hallelujah Jubilee* at 7:00 P.M.[87]

These complex relations and conflicts between religious and secular radio programming surfaced in the actual lives of certain WDIA DJs. Dwight "Gatemouth" Moore, WDIA's first gospel DJ, apparently went through a religious conversion when he halted his career as a blues singer and became a radio preacher. Moore grew up in north Memphis before winning national acclaim as a blues singer during the Second World War. On stage in Chicago in 1949, he suddenly found himself mute, he recounted, until he began to sing the gospel song "Shine on Me." Moore began preaching as a protégé of the radio minister Rev. Clarence Cobb, at the Church of Deliver-

Gospel on the air from East Trigg Missionary Baptist Church, ca. 1952.
Rev. W. Herbert Brewster is standing in rear, and Queen C. Anderson is
standing in the foreground, third from right, in profile.
(© Ernest C. Withers, courtesy of Panopticon Gallery)

ance. On a visit to Memphis to preach at Reverend Brewster's church in
1949, he agreed, at the behest of Nat D., to come to WDIA. His daily show,
Light of the World, made him one of the station's most popular DJs, with
his habitual "I'm grateful, I'm grateful" becoming a common Memphis expression. In making the transition from blues to religion, Moore remained·
a performer, albeit with a different message.[88]

In contrast, Ford Nelson, who came to WDIA as B. B. King's keyboardist
and initially hosted an R & B show, simply slid into his on-air gospel role
after the station manager, impressed by Nelson's resonant voice, decided
to cultivate him as a gospel DJ. He took over Maurice Hulbert Jr.'s gospel show after Hulbert left for Baltimore in late 1950 and piloted his immensely popular *Highway to Heaven* program shortly thereafter. Both Ford
Nelson and Brother Theo "Bless My Bones" Wade traveled throughout the
mid-South with the area's best gospel quartets.[89]

Parents who were concerned about gospel musicians performing R & B
tunes on the radio attempted to reinforce the perceived boundary between
the two genres. "Cousin" Eugene Walton, a gospel DJ on KWEM (West
Memphis) and a quartet singer, observed in an interview that, in his estimate, Memphis's black radio audience would not tolerate mixing gospel

and R & B. Gospel quartet singer George Rooks expressed such a view when he criticized "crossover" musicians, declaring, "If you gonna serve God, then serve God. If you gonna serve the Devil, then just put it all over in that category."[90] Many parents sought to control what their children listened to on the radio. Everlena Yarbrough comments that during her youth in Mississippi, "you just couldn't go over and click on the radio like children do now. If an adult put the radio on, you could hear it then." Joan Lee Nelson recalls listening to the radio with her brothers and sisters "until the blues would come on and my Mama would turn it off." Her mother, a religious woman who sang in her church choir, made her feel they might be, in Nelson's words, "honky-tonked . . . bluesified . . . like a mojo working on you" if they listened to R & B. WDIA acknowledged these concerns, going so far as to split its annual "Goodwill Revue" event into separate R & B and gospel shows, so that audience members could attend one venue without being exposed to the other.[91]

WDIA listeners who wanted to hear only the station's religious programs were able to steer clear of its secular ones, but others were happy to listen to both, as was the case with teens, who did so on the sly. Ford Nelson, for example, recalls that the kids would "slip and listen to [the blues]" when they had a chance. But WDIA's pragmatic approach to black-oriented radio intensified the growing overlap between postwar secular and religious music. That convergence would be manifested in the emergence of soul music, as young artists influenced by both R & B and gospel began to secularize gospel music, and others whose musical careers started in church crossed over into popular music. A direct correlation cannot be made between the rise of black-oriented radio and the rise of soul, but WDIA no doubt nudged artists toward the convergence of gospel and R & B in soul music. With the founding of Stax Records, Memphis would become a recording center of soul, based on the city's earlier roots in blues, R & B, and gospel. Even earlier, however, WDIA's appeal to audiences dedicated to both gospel and blues nurtured a wider community identity.[92]

On-Air Community and Politics

Some of WDIA's most innovative shows involved not only entertainment but also news and public service programming, whose historic roots lay, in part, in the black press. Unlike WDIA's music shows, these programs were aimed explicitly at education, information, politics, and community. Nat D. Williams became the prime motivator in developing programming that brought historical features of the black press to the mass medium of radio, while also creating new kinds of shows. Programs such as *Brown*

America Speaks, a news commentary show that tackled local, national, and international issues of interest to African Americans, reached more people than did the *Memphis World* or, after its founding in 1951, the *Tri-State Defender*. News commentary and community service programs promoted spontaneous conversations among listeners and spun connective threads among listeners in Memphis and the Delta.

WDIA debuted *Good Neighbors*, a show that spotlighted black Memphians who made significant contributions to the black community, only a month after *Tan Town Jamboree* premiered. Nat D. underscored the significance of the half-hour Sunday evening show in the *Memphis World*, referring to it as "the first Negro News-cast in the history of Memphis and the Mid-South." He had been considering such a show, he informed readers, because he wanted to "give to the Negro American some of that long-needed favorable publicity and advertising which he has needed for so long." Williams also acknowledged a second goal — to attract both black and white listeners — which grew out of his observation that racial prejudice resulted from "the fact that so many Americans don't know the first fundamental thing about each other." Most whites did not see blacks as human beings, he declared, while blacks could not believe that whites could be Christians. *Good Neighbor* would "'bridge' this gap of intergroup 'illiteracy.'"[93]

Brown America Speaks, a Sunday afternoon news commentary program initiated in September 1949, more directly addressed Williams's political and educational objectives by creating one of the first radio forums in the nation in which African Americans discussed issues of concern to the black community.[94] In 1950, the show won WDIA its first award from the Institute for Education by Radio and Television at Ohio State University — the same institute that in 1944 had issued a statement critiquing racial stereotypes in movies and on network radio. Although WDIA avoided addressing controversial issues, *Brown America Speaks* occasionally broached such topics as police brutality, segregation, and discriminatory wages. As a guest host on *Brown America Speaks*, Maurice Hulbert discovered the limits of the station's willingness to challenge the status quo, however, after he read a poem calling for racial justice: "We helped fell your lumber, we breast-fed your babies, cooked your food. Ruling powers of this country, won't you give us justice now?" he queried. "We helped you build your railroads, we helped you fight your wars. Ruling powers of this nation, won't you give us justice now?" After a firestorm of criticism from white listeners, Ferguson and Pepper pulled Hulbert off the show. By the mid-1950s, however, Williams was able to host a panel discussion on *Brown v.*

Board of Education and to invite Dr. Martin Luther King Jr. to be a guest on the show.[95]

Brown America Speaks inspired other news programs that became crucial sources of information and political analysis. In 1953, KWEM launched its daily *Negro in the News* show, broadcast from the newsroom of the *Tri-State Defender*, which had begun publication in Memphis two years earlier.[96] For those who did not receive a newspaper, these shows became their primary news source. Naomi Jones remembers that radio was her family's link from Mississippi to other parts of the world. These newscasts deeply influenced perceptions about racial justice. Joan Lee Nelson recalls first hearing about the 1955 lynching of Emmett Till on WDIA, making her begin to question "the whys and the wherefores" of segregation, at age nine. In her large family, she remembers, "We'd just sit around the radio and talk about what we'd heard." Similarly, Everlena Yarbrough remembers hearing at her home in Marion, Arkansas, in the early 1960s news reports about civil rights protests in Memphis. The reports impelled her to take a bus to Memphis to join the protests.[97]

Perhaps the most unexpected source of political dialogue was WDIA's public service programs. WDIA management primarily created these shows to help solidify relations with listeners by encouraging them to identify with the station as the heart of a larger community. Its *Goodwill Announcement* show broadcast requests for assistance in finding missing persons and stray farm animals, news of upcoming church and social events, charity appeals, and employment notices.[98] Such programs quickly took on new importance, however. During a bitter, eight-month strike at Memphis Furniture, begun in January 1949 (discussed in more detail in Chapter 6), strikers broadcast appeals for solidarity. Although the strike, involving over 700 workers, the majority black women, began shortly after WDIA began its crossover to black-oriented programming, strike organizers with the UFWA already perceived the station as a means of reaching potential supporters. Workers Rebecca McKinley, Daisy Quiller, and Laura Sanders, accompanied by two union representatives, used this radio spot to talk personally about miserable wages and conditions, including a lack of bathroom privacy. Their direct appeal for support was significant in light of the uphill battle they faced. In addition to eliciting aggressive strike-breaking tactics by the police, the company trucked in cotton pickers from Arkansas as strike breakers and used red-baiting strategies against UFWA leaders who had refused to sign affidavits swearing that they were not communists, in accordance with the 1947 Taft-Hartley Act recently passed by Congress. Initially, the Memphis CIO, the NAACP, and the Urban League backed the strike, but as their support eroded, strikers used WDIA to appeal directly to black Memphians facing similar working conditions.[99]

Although ultimately the Memphis Furniture strikers lost, they initiated a new mode of soliciting support for labor and civil rights struggles. Two decades later, similar radio appeals would be made during the 1968 Memphis sanitation workers strike. Minerva Johnican remembers hearing an appeal for help over WDIA while driving home from work, which convinced her to change directions and head to a mass meeting at Clayborn Temple. The announcement changed her life by convincing her to join the support committee, a step that set her future political career in motion. Whether in 1949 or 1968, black radio encouraged real community identification with not only the station and its DJs but the imagined community around it.[100]

Nevertheless, WDIA community outreach programs also illustrate the paradoxes of black-appeal radio, poised between the forces of "separate-but-equal" racial ideology and the black freedom movement. These contradictions surfaced in the major charity events sponsored by WDIA. Beginning in 1949, the station staged an annual Goodwill Revue, which by the mid-1950s attracted 6,000 people and was held at Ellis Auditorium. Initially the Revue featured the station's own DJs as emcees and local gospel and R & B talent, but then record companies began sending their biggest names to perform in return for the great publicity. Receipts from the Revue allowed the station to fund major charity projects, including buses for disabled African American children, college scholarships, youth clubs, a juvenile home, and Little League uniforms and equipment. WDIA later established the Starlight Revue, which raised funds for institutions such as the Goodwill Home for black children. By 1956, the two shows generated annually over $20,000.[101]

Reflecting the Jim Crow context out of which WDIA emerged, however, both the Goodwill Revue and the Starlight Revue remained racially segregated events into the 1960s, and the charities they funded did not fundamentally differ from the Jim Crow projects carried out by the Crump machine. WDIA, for example, helped fund a facility for handicapped black youth — a project long promoted by Crump as part of a plan for a separate black hospital to supplement the existing public hospital. By the time the student sit-ins of the freedom movement began in 1960, this contradiction between WDIA's Jim Crow foundations and its projection of black pride had become glaring to movement participants, resulting in an NAACP boycott of the Starlight Revue and other segregated WDIA events until the station changed its policy.[102]

WDIA's *Workers Wanted* employment announcement program con-

WDIA-sponsored Little Leaguers in Memphis, 1960s, with, from right, Big Joe Turner, Muddy Waters, Howlin' Wolf, and B. B. King.

(© Ernest C. Withers, courtesy of Panopticon Gallery)

tained similar ironies. Although the station sought to win listener loyalty by providing an important community service, most announcements came from the Tennessee Department of Employment or the Tri-State Farm Labor Office, who were advertising for cooks, maids, laborers, and agricultural workers, and specifically targeting African Americans. WDIA's community service programs thus circulated contradictory messages about black identities.[103]

In some ways, WDIA DJs' dual identities as on-air personalities and ordinary black Memphians placed them at the heart of these paradoxes of postwar black-oriented radio in Memphis. In an interview, Rufus Thomas was blunt about such conditions, comparing them to his earlier experiences at nightclubs, where black performers "had to come in through the kitchen and never inter-fraternize" with white patrons. At WDIA, he found that black DJs controlled the microphone but white men ran the control boards. "I don't know what people . . . thought at this time — that we couldn't get our things together with twisting knobs," Thomas commented satirically. He also spent as little time as possible at the studio because "for a long time there was only one bathroom" on the floor, which was for whites. Furthermore, he found WDIA's pay too meager for him to give up his full-time factory job. Thomas's daily schedule thus dramatically illustrated the gap between his off- and on-air identities, as working-class black Memphian and as performer. Each afternoon, he raced home when his shift at American Finishing Company textile mill ended at 2:30, in order to clean up and make it to WDIA for his 3:00 show.[104]

WDIA DJs inhabited the segregated world of postwar Memphis, even as they created worlds of their own on the radio. In Thomas's case, his wife, Lorene, participated in civil rights protests and served as the NAACP local branch secretary, while Rufus and their daughter, Carla, became leading recording artists of soul music. Even as DJs themselves became important advocates for desegregation in Memphis, they helped construct a black public sphere as a kind of free space where identities need not be defined by the parameters of Crump's Memphis.

Listener-to-listener appeals, part of WDIA's strategy of encouraging identification with the station, paralleled other innovations of black-appeal radio that ultimately made it subversive to the same social conditions that had given rise to it. WDIA put together an amazing line-up of gifted entertainers and educators to serve as Memphis's first African American DJs, who encouraged race pride and critical thought while forging new directions for popular culture. It created formats on and off the air that encouraged bonds between jockeys and listeners and among audience members across the entire region. The station's advertising policy also formally encouraged race pride by shunning traditional stereotyping and demeaning approaches to African American consumers and instead appealing to them on the basis of respect.

The advent of WDIA and the struggle over racial representations in motion pictures encouraged black Memphians to formulate and articulate the critical ideas about gendered, racialized identities that would later capture national attention with the sanitation strikers' "I *Am* a Man" slogan. Even earlier, they helped shape movement participants' responses to the insulting, degrading racial images that undergirded many practices they had come to despise, whether in workplaces, on buses, in movie theaters, or in schools. Ironically, harsh restrictions on moviegoing, including the humiliating terms of segregation and the censorship of movies themselves, spurred in many black Memphians a more critical relation to racial representations in the mass media and their parallels in everyday life. Such critical perceptions were further influenced by broader postwar concerns about the future of racial equality and democracy in Memphis. As the debate raged over stereotyping, segregation, and censorship of Hollywood movies, black-appeal radio opened a small but significant space in which gendered racial identities and power relations could be explored through humor, music, political discussion, and even community announcements.

Rejecting Mammy

6 \\\ The Urban-Rural Road in the Era of *Brown v. Board of Education*

In April 1955, just before the Supreme Court ruled on how to implement its momentous decision in *Brown v. Board of Education*, declaring that desegregation of public schools should proceed at "all deliberate speed," the eyes of many black Memphians turned briefly in a different direction, to the case of the "Patio 6." The appellation referred to a group of six black employees of Joel's Patio, a downtown Memphis café serving southern-style food. The workers, all but one of them women, were offended by their bosses' new mode of attracting customers: seating an elderly black woman, Mrs. Savannah Keyes, outside the café, with a bandana around her head and ringing a bell. Behind Mrs. Keyes, a "mammy" rag doll sat in the window. According to Mrs. Marie Taylor, who approached the two white women employers on behalf of the group, they told her: "Look, if you all don't like it, get your clothes and get out." The workers chose to leave, at which point the employers locked the door and called the police, who arrested the workers. Mrs. Taylor later reported at a community meeting that one arresting officer had become verbally abusive: "He threatened to 'knock my brains out' if he ever caught me on the street." Jailed and charged with disorderly conduct and disturbing the peace, the employees were eventually found guilty and fined in city court. Not unusual in their content, these events nevertheless sparked an extraordinary response: the formation of the Memphis Citizens Committee for the Promotion of Justice by ministers and other community leaders, in order to defend these "heroes in a common place," as one AME minister put it.[1]

The same week that this community meeting took place, another group of black Memphians drove to Mound Bayou, Mississippi, for the annual meeting of the Regional Council of Negro Leadership (RCNL) and a speech by black U.S. congressman Charles Diggs Jr. They joined an astounding

13,000 African Americans from across the Delta, including, according to the black press, "tenants, sharecroppers, day laborers as well as farm owners, and a cross-section of the professional group." This crowd had turned out in defiance of threats from the white Citizens' Councils, formed in reaction to the 1954 Supreme Court decision. A week later, the "gangland style" murder of one of the meeting's speakers, Rev. George W. Lee, a black Baptist minister and leading Mississippi voting rights activist, drew black Memphians back to the Delta for his funeral. After the lynching three months later in nearby Tallahatchie County of fourteen-year-old Emmett Till, who was visiting from Chicago, the *Tri-State Defender*, a new black newspaper in Memphis, characterized race relations in the Delta as a "racial equation" of "master and servant and rigidly enforced."[2]

Indeed, black activism in Memphis in the years surrounding the Supreme Court's momentous decision emerged in the context of a powerful urban-rural matrix that focused attention on such wrenching reminders of the plantation regime as Mrs. Keyes's presence outside of Joel's Patio. Local understandings of freedom were shaped in profound ways both by this interchange between plantation and city and by the Supreme Court's redefinition of equal rights. During the 1950s, the one-way, rural-to-urban migration turned into two-way exchanges of activism and ideas. At the same time, black Memphians perceived what the black press referred to as a "racial equation" of "master and slave" as a description of not only rural but also city life, leading many to strike out against urban practices that were symbolic of the plantation. For the "Patio 6" workers, the "mammy" stereotype simultaneously evoked shame and anger. Protesting it bound them to the historical struggle for freedom.

In Memphis in the early 1950s, the race-baiting and red-baiting that defined the domestic Cold War in the South nearly crushed black-majority labor unions and put a damper on NAACP activism. Given this reactionary social context, marked by such dramas as Senator James Eastland's public anticommunist hearings in Memphis and the bombing of a home in which a black family was sleeping, one might conclude that the militant activism of the wartime and postwar years was obliterated. Rather than disappearing, hard-pressed struggles by working-class black Memphians went in new directions. Local organizing, for example, proliferated in Memphis's neighborhoods, building on the police brutality protests of the mid-1940s. Energized by two major developments—Tennessee's elimination of the poll tax in 1951 and the death of Boss E. H. Crump in 1954—many black Memphians joined neighborhood civic clubs, registered to vote, and campaigned for black political candidates. Even as the labor movement fractured over anticommunism and race, many black workers, including newly hired women in small manufacturing plants, struggled to organize and maintain unions. These efforts intersected with the desegregation lawsuits and campaigns that followed *Brown v. Board of Education*, led by young activists who transformed the Memphis NAACP from a nearly moribund organization into a vigorous one.

The intersections of rural and urban, local and national, and of historical memory and the present, shaped perspectives on equality, rights, and freedom. Given this multidimensional context, claims to racial democracy in the era of *Brown* posited constitutional rights as part of a broader challenge to the "master and servant" relation in the modern urban context. Yet the promise of this decade, signaled by the Supreme Court decision, also fueled frustration among many black Memphians when it translated into little real change in everyday lives.

Labor, Civil Rights, and the Cold War

When Cold War anticommunism arrived in Memphis, it came from both indigenous sources and in the person of Senator James O. Eastland, a Mississippi Delta planter who also sat on the Senate Internal Security Subcommittee (SISS), the Senate counterpart of the House Un-American Activities Committee (HUAC). An outspoken founding member of the Dixiecrat Party in 1948, Eastland had also become a sympathizer of Senator Joseph McCarthy. Eastland's role at the cutting edge of anticommunism helped ensure that red-baiting and race-baiting would be contiguous in the South. Most notorious for his role in initiating the white Citizens' Council movement in Mississippi in 1954, Eastland had earlier launched anticommunist hearings in the South aimed at crushing militant labor and racial democracy movements. As if to underscore his source of political power, Eastland in October 1951 came to the Memphis hearings directly from his plantation in Ruleville, Mississippi, and returned to Ruleville, not Washington, at the end of the hearings. The Senate subcommittee hearings pitted local white conservative Memphis CIO officials against an activist union comprised largely of black, low-wage workers, some of them former sharecroppers from Eastland's home state. The hearings also deepened existing gulfs between black elites and workers by relying on the testimony of a "friendly" African American witness.[3]

Four years before Eastland's visit, by passing the Taft-Hartley Act over both President Truman's veto and strenuous opposition by organized labor, the Republican-controlled Congress severely restricted rights of labor unions that had been accorded through the 1935 Wagner Act. One key measure required union officials to sign affidavits swearing they were not members of the Communist Party; if they refused to do so they would lose their right to participate in NLRB elections. This new requirement wreaked havoc within the CIO as a whole, triggering purges of radical-led unions whose leaders refused to sign Taft-Hartley affidavits. It also fueled existing ideological conflicts over leadership and direction, framing them in terms of anticommunism.

Even before Eastland's dramatic arrival in October 1951, white conservative leaders of the Memphis Industrial Union Council (CIO) used red-baiting to challenge labor militancy in black-majority unions. In 1949, W. A. (Red) Copeland, regional director of the CIO, and Earl Crowder, president of the state CIO Council and a member of the steelworkers' union, targeted the NMU and two unions with predominantly low-wage black members, Local 19 of the Food, Tobacco, Agricultural and Allied Workers of America (FTA, previously named the United Cannery, Agricultural, Packing and Allied Workers of America) and Local 282 of the UFWA. UFWA international representative Gene Day believed that this harassment reflected Memphis CIO leaders' anger over an FTA committee's protest against segregated restrooms in the council office, reportedly the only CIO office in the South with such a policy. Another Memphis-based UFWA international representative argued that Crowder and Copeland aimed "toward a white-washing of the discriminatory nature of the segregated toilets, and to substitute a campaign to rid the CIO of communism." The council demanded that FTA Local 19 and UFWA Local 282 comply with an anticommunist resolution, and in October 1949 it refused to seat radical NMU delegate "Red" Davis at a meeting, later applauding his expulsion from the NMU itself.[4]

These efforts by conservative white labor leaders to reassert control over the Memphis labor movement had serious consequences for the hard-fought 1949 strike at Memphis Furniture. In January, over 700 workers, a majority of them black women, voted to strike when Memphis Furniture refused to sign a contract with Local 282. Strike participants like Melvina Rebecca McKinley had become frustrated with low wages, dangerous machinery, and practices they considered insulting. "You didn't get your check [at work]," she recalled. "You had to stand around on a cold Saturday morning and wait for them to hand your check out the window." Women were especially bothered by their lack of privacy when using the toilets assigned to black women. The strike initially won support, even as Memphis Furniture management and city policemen cracked down brutally. In addition to bringing in truckloads of white and black strikebreakers from the city and the cotton fields, they supplied some with billy clubs produced at the plant to use against workers. Policemen visited workers' homes and interrogated them at the plant in the middle of the night. Rather than stepping up their support, Copeland and the Memphis Industrial Union Council eventually withdrew it completely and further undermined solidarity by denouncing union leaders as communists. The council accused Local 282 of using local money to send members to Communist meetings — which turned out to be a reference to McKinley and James White's attendance at Civil Rights Congress and National Negro Congress meetings in New York and Chicago to win strike support. These actions coincided with intense factional fighting within the UFWA at the national level over whether its leaders would sign Taft-Hartley affidavits or be purged from the CIO.[5]

Pressure from the Memphis Industrial Union Council persisted after the strike collapsed and disrupted Local 282's internal racial dynamics. For example, UFWA president Morris Pizer placed Local 282's African American president, Rudolph Johnson, under investigation for communism in 1951, after Memphis CIO officials complained about him. Johnson, like FTA members, had protested the segregated restrooms in the CIO hall, this time in the form of a letter to national CIO officials that provoked a fractious debate at the 1950 CIO convention and enraged officials back in Memphis. Earlier, UFWA representative Gene Day had praised Johnson for his strong organizing work, especially at U.S. Bedding. LeRoy Clark, the African American UFWA international representative assigned to investigate Johnson in 1951, reported that Johnson was not a communist. According to Clark's wife, Alzada, who became a member of Local 282 in this same period, Johnson "was just a young black guy who was ahead of his time, doing just what we wound up doing, complaining about the working conditions of black folks." Nevertheless, Johnson was defeated in the next election. LeRoy Clark stayed in town to build Local 282's membership until local CIO officials also complained about his positions on racial issues. The UFWA replaced Clark with Doyle Dorsey, a white international representative more acceptable to Memphis CIO leaders. In this climate, conflicts over race easily became masked as tension over anticommunism.[6]

Memphis CIO leaders also cracked down on Local 19, trying to erode the union's strong base of support among low-wage black workers. Copeland even backed "raids" on Local 19 shops, in which rival unions mounted organizing campaigns and competed in NLRB elections as a way to "steal" membership. In August 1949, for example, Gene Day of Local 282 reported that the United Packinghouse Workers of America were trying to take over FTA cottonseed oil shops, leaving workers "really confused." At Buckeye and Federal Compress, two mainstays of Local 19, attempts to decertify or raid the union failed to convince the majority of workers to abandon it.[7]

Senator James Eastland's SISS hearings, October 25–26, 1951, intensified this pressure on labor and racial justice movements in Memphis. In a public statement, Eastland declared that Local 19 (now in the Distributing, Processing and Office Workers Union of America, following an FTA merger) was not a genuine labor union but a "Communist organization that is designed to overthrow the Government of the United States and promote the interests of the Soviet Union." Putting the 1,100 members of Local 19, 95 percent of whom were African Americans, on the spot, his investigators first demanded and then illegally seized Local 19's membership lists in a raid on the union office. Eastland subpoenaed as witnesses W. A. Copeland and Earl Crowder from the Memphis CIO; Lee Lashley, president of Local 19; Local 19 business agent Ed McCrea; and Memphis Urban League executive secretary Rev. James McDaniel. Open to the public and covered heavily in the local press, the hearings became a major spectacle.[8]

Most obviously, Senator Eastland used the hearings to root out Communists and discredit militant labor unions; however, his public histrionics also aimed at putting African Americans in their "places." Clark Porteous, a reporter for the *Memphis Press-Scimitar*, noted in a story on the hearings that Eastland repeatedly addressed Lee Lashley, Local 19 president and Quaker Oats employee, as "Boy": "Boy, tell the truth"; "Boy, what have you got to hide?" He alternated between speaking "kindly" and threatening "imprisonment for contempt" if Lashley failed to name communists. In general, Eastland painted black union members as dupes of white Communist Party members. For example, he called to the witness stand a "mystery witness," Paul Crouch, who identified himself as having been a high-ranking party member between 1925 and 1942 and described a party strategy of trying to foment revolution in the South by provoking blacks to stir up racial strife. Unsuccessful at winning African American members in Tennessee, Crouch declared, the party was attempting to organize them into communist-led unions, where they could "be fed propaganda until they [would] join the party."[9]

And finally, in one of the most insidious aspects of the hearings, Eastland also subpoenaed Rev. James McDaniel, who several years earlier had replaced Benjamin Bell as executive secretary of the Memphis Urban League. McDaniel willingly complied, indicating that he had already warned black members against staying in Local 19: "I felt [Local 19] was a dangerous communistic organization and I sought to enlighten members of my race to these dangers." McDaniel's statement portrayed members of Local 19 as under the sway of communism and out of step with the majority of black Memphians. Although he articulated his views in terms of anticommunism, McDaniel's words echoed those of black leaders who publicly warned against race and labor militancy and encouraged cooperative relations with the Crump machine.[10] Eastland's SISS hearings prompted Local 19's disaffiliation from the Distributing, Processing and Office Workers Union and reaffiliation with the more conservative Retail, Wholesale, and Department Store Union. Local 19 also returned to the fold of the Memphis Industrial Union Council and lost members.[11]

This Cold War repression affected more than the labor movement. The Memphis NAACP, which had gained considerable membership and militancy in the mid-1940s, became a shadow of its former self. In March 1952, Ruby Hurley, southeast regional secretary of the NAACP, wrote to the organization's headquarters in New York, describing what she perceived as the slow death of the Memphis branch, due to its "conservative influence" and "little action." Hurley described a tense meeting in which members of the branch executive committee defended their support for a "separate but equal" public hospital facility planned by the Crump machine, despite the national organization's policy opposing segregation. She contrasted the Memphis branch to the NAACP in Indianola, Mississippi, in the heart of the Delta, where young veterans of the Second World War had begun to register voters, hold public meetings, and reach out to sharecroppers. "*The difference between Indianola and Memphis was an inspiration*," she emphasized. A year later, after another trip to Memphis following the bombing of a black family's newly purchased home by whites in the neighborhood, Hurley confided to the NAACP's director of branches, Gloster Current, that she "could actually cry about Memphis, because the community is ripe for dynamic NAACP leadership." These words turned out to be amazingly prescient; by the end of the decade, the NAACP's executive secretary, Roy Wilkins, was touting the Memphis NAACP as "the biggest Branch in the South." Hurley's criticism of Memphis and enthusiasm for Indianola contradicted the traditional assessments of the rural South as an unchanging backwater; from her perspective in 1952, it was Memphis that appeared stagnant. Her comments indicated the impact of deeply entrenched attitudes born out of decades of Crump machine oppression and the current repressive context of the Cold War.[12]

In the 1950s, ideological tensions in the NAACP came to a head over desegregation. At the meeting in 1952 that Hurley described, Memphis leaders, ranging from NAACP branch president Utillus Phillips, a railroad postal worker, to Dr. Hollis Price, president of LeMoyne College, expressed disapproval of the national organization's position on segregation because it backed them into a corner in local politics. "Further criticism of NAACP policy in opposition to segregation was made in strong terms," Hurley reported of the meeting, because those present felt that hospital facilities for African Americans were too badly needed for them to reject Crump's plan. Moreover, since the proposed black hospital would be in close proximity to the existing public hospital, they argued that it represented a "step toward future integration." Opposing the proposal, they felt, "would mean the death of [the] NAACP in Memphis." It is unlikely that these NAACP leaders personally opposed desegregation; indeed, in June 1952, they invited Harold Flowers, an attorney from Pine Bluffs, Arkansas, a leader in efforts to desegregate schools there, to speak at a mass meeting. For the time being, however, they chose a path to the betterment of the community within the bounds established by the Crump machine.[13]

During and after the war, this kind of approach had come under fire from individuals ranging from A. Philip Randolph in New York to young NAACP members at LeMoyne College. Racial turmoil over employment discrimination and police brutality during the 1940s had generated an explicit, public critique of local black leaders, especially ministers and business leaders, deemed overly loyal to the Crump machine. NAACP leaders like Utillus Phillips were not Crump allies but were not exempt from criticism during crises such as the 1940 "reign of terror." When the local NAACP championed protest against police brutality between 1945 and 1948, veterans and other working-class young men and women flooded its membership rolls. However, from an apex of 3,540 in 1948, membership plunged to a mere 731 in 1952, as the branch retreated from an aggressive agenda in the Cold War context. By the time Utillus Phillips retired as the branch president in 1953 after fourteen years of service, desire for fresh civil rights leadership had become widespread.[14]

From Memphis to the Delta and Back

The young, college-educated men (and eventually women) who assumed leadership of the Memphis NAACP after Phillips's retirement considered themselves representatives of a new generation whose political outlooks differed from those of their elders. Many of the attorneys and other professionals who played key roles in reshaping the branch had left Memphis during or after college to receive advanced degrees or serve in the military and returned in the late 1940s and early 1950s. Accountant Jesse Turner, who became chairman of the NAACP Executive Board in the 1950s, for example, first joined the NAACP at LeMoyne College and sought out the organization again after suffering humiliating racism in the army, attending graduate school at the University of Chicago, and returning to Memphis. Several young attorneys, first Benjamin Hooks and James F. Estes, and then H. T. Lockard, Ben F. Jones, and A. W. Willis, followed by Russell Sugarmon, began working with the branch in this period, creating an energetic legal team where before there had been only one African American attorney, A. A. Latting.[15]

Lockard became president of the local NAACP in January 1955, in the wake of *Brown v. Board*, following a brief term by Rev. Van Malone, who had served earlier as NAACP branch president in Jackson, Tennessee.[16] Raised in rural west Tennessee, Lockard had become one of the first members of the LeMoyne NAACP after moving to Memphis for college in the early 1940s. After a four-year stint in the armed forces and law school in St. Louis, he returned to Memphis in 1951. Lockard concluded that racial conditions there were worse than anywhere he had been, and he stayed only because of his conviction that the situation needed to change. Part of the problem was the NAACP. The branch, in his view, was run by "a bunch of courageous old men" who were doing "absolutely nothing." "People were so conditioned until anything that was suggested just didn't take on," he asserted. In a letter to the NAACP office in New York after his election, Lockard described the branch as "one of the most lethargic [*sic*] in the whole U.S." and asked for advice on "stimulating some interest on the part of our 'silk stocking group.'" He reported nevertheless that he had been "swamped with telephone calls as well as many words of encouragement."[17]

Lockard and other young civil rights activists returning to the city thus brought with them a keen sense of urgency about racial democracy in the United States and abroad, as well as in Memphis itself. They reached out to national civil rights leaders, to black communities in Memphis, and to the burgeoning rural struggle just outside the city.

Two events on the eve of *Brown* illuminate the dramatic influence that the proximity of Memphis to the Delta would have on these urban activists' responses to the Supreme Court decision and their efforts to reorganize the local NAACP. First, eager to attract a large audience to the Memphis NAACP's membership campaign kickoff in April 1954, Reverend Malone and the other branch leaders invited Dr. T. R. M. Howard, president of the RCNL in the Mississippi Delta, to address the meeting. Second, a month later, just ten days before the *Brown* decision, black attorneys, journalists, and community leaders traveled down two-lane Highway 61 to Mound Bayou, Mississippi, to join over 6,000 African Americans from across the

Delta for the RCNL's third annual meeting, where NAACP special counsel Thurgood Marshall was the keynote speaker. Before the meeting, Marshall met with several attorneys, most of them from Memphis, to discuss what initiatives the NAACP should pursue to implement the Supreme Court decision, which he expected any day. Two years after Hurley's letter contrasting Memphis and Indianola, thirty-five miles south of Memphis in Mound Bayou, important bonds had begun to form between rural and urban activists, and between local and national civil rights leaders, that would influence all of them.[18]

Marshall's speech roused an enthusiastic audience. The crowd erupted in "thunderous applause," the black press reported, when he traced the current struggle back to the days of the infamous Black Codes after the Civil War and denounced Mississippi's current "peanut head politicians" who sought to perpetuate segregation. The audience also exploded in applause when he declared, "We are on a great crusade for freedom and we won't be satisfied in Mississippi or anywhere else in this nation until the shame of segregation and discrimination have been wiped from the records." Overwhelmed, Marshall exclaimed, "This is an unbelievable crowd!" "You couldn't get such a crowd in New York to meet and talk on integration," he declared. "Only in the South is this possible, because here is where the fight is. The weak ones have moved on to Detroit and Chicago while the real ones have remained to fight." Marshall's stunning comment, like Hurley's observation about Indianola, rejected stereotypes of rural black southerners as passive, even fearful. Marshall's meeting with attorneys Benjamin Hooks, H. T. Lockard, A. A. Latting, James F. Estes, and A. W. Willis from Memphis, the well-known Nashville civil rights lawyer Z. Alexander Looby, and attorneys from Mississippi and Arkansas, took place in this context, with Marshall and the others energized by this resounding reception in the heart of the rural Delta.[19]

As was clear from the invitation by the Memphis NAACP to Dr. Howard a month earlier, the RCNL had already become an inspiration for city activists seeking new models of independent black politics. In late 1951, the Memphis *Tri-State Defender* had hailed the formation of a new "Negro Delta Council." The newspaper, a *Chicago Defender* affiliate founded earlier that year, promised to be more outspoken than the older *Memphis World*, and, accordingly, it described the RCNL's founding meeting on December 28, 1951, as a "historic milestone" that would lead to "first-class citizenship."[20]

Dr. Howard, the chief surgeon at the Friendship Clinic in Mound Bayou, an innovative planter, and the owner of the Magnolia Mutual Insurance

Company, also held positions in Memphis as vice president of the Tri-State Bank and board member of the Universal Life Insurance Company, linking him to a network of business leaders, professionals, and civil rights advocates. Howard first established the Negro Delta Council as a counterpart to the all-white Delta Council, an economic and political organization of white Mississippi planters. By May 1952, Howard had changed the name to Regional Council of Negro Leadership and challenged the Delta Council's intention to maintain white economic power. Assisted by young activists like Medgar Evers, Amzie Moore, and Aaron Henry, all veterans of the Second World War and NAACP members, the RCNL held spectacular annual meetings featuring nationally recognized speakers.[21]

Howard explicitly situated the RCNL's mission in relation to driving postwar issues, from urban migration to the Cold War. In his prospectus for the first annual meeting in May 1952, he noted that the state had "lost more people during the last ten years than any other state in the Union," with African Americans constituting 350,000 of the 455,000 who had left. He attributed this exodus to poor schooling for black children, inadequate living conditions, and "the lack of democracy and the insecurity of life for Negroes," a reference to the lack of voting rights for black Mississippians and the state's history of racial violence. Declaring that he had no interest in Communism and had "not lost faith in our American democracy," he nevertheless warned that "the cause of Jesus and the cause of Democracy is shuddering throughout the world today because of the inequality of Democracy in regards to Negro rights here in Mississippi."[22]

Unlike the NAACP, which focused largely on desegregation in this period, Howard was interested in building independent black political and economic power in the Delta. His ideas took on a new cast when merged with the plan for a mass-based organization of not only professionals but also sharecroppers challenging white domination. The prospectus rejected solutions based upon political dependence, in which "white men can go behind closed doors and work out all the Negro's problems and bring them to him on a platter." The RCNL would not "'Uncle Tom' and come in the back to the [Delta] Council table," he declared. The only vehicle to first-class citizenship would be an independent, mass organization uniting representatives from diverse Delta institutions. Howard rhetorically constructed the RCNL as the region's first militant organization. He argued that "since the days of American slavery," African Americans had been complacent about "*separate but in no case equal facilities*," leaving the solution up to "the drawn lash of the Supreme Court." The point of Howard's hyperbole was that black Mississippians themselves had to secure change. He condemned the lack of public restrooms for African Americans, the disproportionate number of blacks at the notorious Parchman Penitentiary, and the absence of blacks on juries. He also addressed the "shame, reproach and disgrace" visited upon black women, who could not "carry an account in the name of Miss or Mrs.," were harassed and raped by white men, and lacked protection by black men. "First-class citizenship," therefore, involved a collective agency in which African Americans claimed rather than received citizenship rights. Challenging "separate but in no case equal" meant quashing racist practices that demeaned black manhood and womanhood.[23]

Howard also connected the empowerment of disfranchised rural Mississippians to national agendas. The RCNL conducted press conferences, invited journalists to meetings, and attracted major figures to annual mass gatherings. The organization's initial mass meeting in May 1952, for instance, drew 7,000 participants to a speech by Representative William L. Dawson, the first black congressman to appear in Mississippi in six decades, and to a performance by renowned gospel singer Mahalia Jackson. The *Tri-State Defender* referred to Howard as "a modern 'Moses,'" marveling at the RCNL's militant endorsement of voting rights, "right on Highway 61."[24]

In the aftermath of the *Brown v. Board of Education* decision in May 1954, Memphis activists' relationship to the Delta encouraged them to see themselves as participants in an outright war over the future of white domination. With the formation of the white Citizens' Council movement in Indianola in July 1954, black Delta activists faced a virulent backlash. The RCNL announced its determination to combat the Citizens' Councils' "economic war," in which targeted voter registration activists found themselves unable to obtain credit from local banks or seeds and supplies from merchants. When 2,000 RCNL delegates met in Mound Bayou in late September 1954 to discuss how to fight this repression, they looked to Memphis for support. In January 1955, a war chest of $1 million was established at Tri-State Bank by bank president Dr. J. E. Walker, NAACP executive secretary Roy Wilkins, and RCNL leaders. The fund, to be built by donors from around the country, would support those affected by the "credit freeze."

The *Tri-State Defender* spurred support by publishing weekly reports about individuals targeted by the Citizens' Councils and contributions to the war chest. Such articles portrayed Memphis as central to the struggle over the future of American democracy. "Those citizens and organizations who are depositing funds in the Tri-State Bank of Memphis for the use of the embattled and economically squeezed Negroes of Mississippi," stated one editorial, "are fighting a frontline battle for the protection of American principles of fair-play and democracy." The newspaper put this crisis of democracy into Cold War terms, arguing that the threat to the American Constitution posed by the Citizens' Council movement was as grave as "the Communist threat to engulf the world and destroy all the best ideals for which this nation stands."[25]

The conflict between the two organizations escalated in spring 1955, when the highest attendance to date at an RCNL meeting was followed closely by the first murder of an individual targeted by the Citizens' Councils. In late April, Memphians joined 13,000 others at the fourth annual meeting of the RCNL, where Congressman Charles Diggs Jr. spoke. In a show of defiance against the Citizens' Councils, attendance at the mass meeting nearly doubled in size from the 1954 meeting, at which Marshall had spoken. Two weeks later, Memphis activists returned to Mississippi for the funeral of Rev. George W. Lee, an RCNL and NAACP leader who was gunned down in Belzoni, Mississippi, because of his voter registration work.[26]

The Delta movement now captured national headlines. *Ebony* magazine, published in Chicago, proclaimed that "a new militant Negro" was emerging in the South, describing him in gendered terms as "a fearless, fighting man who openly campaigns for his civil rights, who refuses to migrate to the North in search of justice and dignity, and is determined to stay in his own backyard and fight." When Emmett Till was lynched in August 1955, just days after the article appeared, Dr. Howard's home became a base for black reporters. The *Tri-State Defender* played a key role in locating witnesses and covering the story. Dr. Howard addressed protest rallies in Los Angeles, at Madison Square Garden in New York, and elsewhere, in each speech situating the Till lynching in the context of the deadly violence after *Brown*.[27]

Back in Mound Bayou, it became clear that not all African American leaders in the Delta were responding in the same way to pressure from the Citizens' Councils. In December 1955, the mayor of Mound Bayou, I. E. Edwards, previously an attendee at RCNL rallies, announced that he was considering an ordinance that would bar "race agitators" from convening meetings in the town. Edwards declared that anyone with "a chip on their shoulders" should "carry it elsewhere."[28]

This ideological conflict came to a head in Memphis when some 20,000 delegates from around the country gathered in September 1955 for the National Baptist Convention. In Mississippi, where the legislature was threatening to shut down all public schools in order to avoid desegregating them after *Brown*, some black leaders had called for cooperation rather than opposition, at a time when NAACP and RCNL members were risking their lives for black empowerment. Delegates shouted down Rev. H. H. Humes of Mississippi for over thirty minutes, calling him a "traitor" and an "Uncle Tom" and denouncing Humes's recent proposal for a voluntary public school segregation plan as a response to *Brown*. Atlanta minister Dr. William H. Borders declared that Humes's comments "were detrimental to all the convention stands for, and that, in a way, Humes had contributed to deaths of three Negroes in his state." These opposing images of the new "fighting man," as the *Ebony* article put it, and the "Uncle Tom" signaled a changing political context, in which demanding freedom involved challenges to both white supremacy and black compromise.[29]

In this highly charged atmosphere, the *Tri-State Defender* lambasted the "racial equation" in the Delta, categorizing it as "one of master and servant and rigidly enforced." Others pointed to parallel relations in the city. In May 1955, at a mass meeting held in Memphis just after Reverend Lee was murdered, Dr. Howard reportedly "served notice on the people of Memphis that they themselves are sitting idly by wearing a smug look as regards the situation in Mississippi when in downtown Memphis there exists many of the same conditions which the Negroes in Mississippi have risen up to buck." "Smugness," or complacency, in such views, represented an internal barrier to the struggle to "buck" the "master and servant" equation. This relationship between Memphis activists, the rural Delta, and national civil rights politics shaped Memphians' perceptions about their place in the larger struggle, adding urgency to convictions that "first-class citizenship" would not be served on a platter from the Supreme Court.[30]

Energized by this shared perspective, Memphis NAACP attorneys, fresh from their meeting with Marshall and eager to find some means of implementing *Brown* in Memphis, assisted several young African Americans, two recently returned from active duty in Korea, to apply for admission at Memphis State College in late May 1954. Because *Brown* had not addressed higher education, Marshall and the NAACP now hoped to win a ruling that would extend earlier Supreme Court decisions that had stopped short of overturning "separate but equal." These attorneys and other activists also saw the case as part of a larger strategy to resuscitate the Memphis NAACP and connect black Memphians to national civil rights struggles.

Most significantly for college students in Tennessee, in 1951 a federal district judge had ruled in *Gray v. University of Tennessee* that African American students who were refused admission to the university's graduate school and college of law solely on the basis of race had been denied their constitutional rights under the Fourteenth Amendment's equal protection clause. In *Gray*, the judge had not struck down the state's segregated education requirement but found that the state had failed to provide equal facilities for the black students, in accordance with U.S. Supreme Court's decisions in *State of Missouri ex rel. Gaines v. Canada* (1938) and *Sipuel v. Oklahoma State Board of Regents* (1948), both cases involving law school admissions. The judge also cited the Court's 1950 decisions in *Sweatt v. Painter* and *McLaurin v. Oklahoma*. In these cases the Court ruled that separate facilities provided for black students by the University of Texas Law School and University of Oklahoma School of Education were inadequate, in part because of intangibles, such as black students' inability to benefit from the "rich traditions and prestige" that enhanced their white peers' education. By the time that *Gray v. University of Tennessee* reached the U.S. Supreme Court in early 1952, the Court ruled the appeal moot because the University of Tennessee had decided to admit the students in the year since the lower court's ruling. However, neither *Gray* nor any of these earlier decisions had struck down in the realm of higher education the principle of "separate but equal" upheld in *Plessy v. Ferguson* (1896).[31]

By assisting the applicants to Memphis State, the NAACP hoped to procure a ruling that explicitly extended the logic of *Brown* to publicly funded colleges. One year later, directly after *Brown* II in 1955, James F. Estes, who was in charge of legal redress for the local branch, along with H. T. Lockard, Benjamin Hooks, and A. W. Willis, responded to Memphis State's refusal to admit the students by filing suit against the Tennessee Board of Education in federal district court. The state board, meanwhile, issued a plan for "gradual desegregation" that stretched out graduate school and college desegregation over several years. However, they did not address secondary schools and stipulated that the plan would not be implemented until the courts struck down the segregation mandate contained in the Tennessee Constitution. In federal district court in October, Judge Marion Boyd found school segregation in Tennessee unconstitutional but accepted the state's plan. Local NAACP leaders celebrated this decision as a victory, contrasting it to developments in Mississippi, yet warned that the victory was only partial. Not until 1959, after the U.S. Court of Appeals for the Sixth Circuit intervened, did black students enter Memphis State.[32]

In the meantime, the new NAACP leaders secured enthusiastic mass support for the Memphis State case, in part by making connections between the rural struggle and their own. A week after Howard's speech in

May 1955 inveighing against "smugness," the local NAACP established a fund to support the Memphis State suit. The branch asked local ministers to adopt July 3 as "NAACP Day" and appeal for contributions. In addition, branch members voted to collect donations from black workers at businesses and factories and to establish a committee of 100 women to canvas homes, to be headed by Mrs. B. F. McCleave, Miss Rosa Brown Bracy, and Mrs. Gold S. Young. The NAACP women's division quickly increased the number of canvassers to 500, indicating the extent to which women had already established important networks through civic clubs, women's organizations, and churches — despite their lack of representation on the NAACP's board. The black press added to the momentum by publishing donors' names and the amount of money they contributed (mostly one to five dollars), showing that every contribution was important. To climax this drive, the NAACP again asked Harold Flowers, the civil rights attorney from Pine Bluff, Arkansas — where "White America, Inc.," a home-grown citizens' council, had been formed — to speak at a mass meeting.[33]

The issue of school desegregation linked black city residents to the rural cotton region. African Americans in Memphis cared deeply about the conditions of education for black youth. Recent migrants from rural Mississippi, Arkansas, and west Tennessee, especially women, often identified achieving a better education for themselves and their children as the primary motive for moving to Memphis. For many of these migrants, the memory of white schoolchildren passing them by on bright yellow school buses as they trudged to inferior segregated schools was emblematic of the racial inequality they continued to experience in Memphis. For Memphis residents who attended city schools, the allocation of textbooks already used by white students for a few years to black schools had likewise become symbolic of racial prejudice.

The political impact of Memphis's relationship to the surrounding region was made apparent in a different way when Tennessee legislators from the plantation counties near Memphis sought a means of obstructing *Brown*. In December 1954, Tennessee senator-elect Charles A. Stainback of Fayette County proposed "pupil assignment" legislation that would empower local school boards to control student placement, allowing them to use a host of reasons besides race to keep black students from attending school with whites. Similar to legislation passed in North Carolina, it would give localities the tools to thwart desegregation but enable the state to avoid directly violating *Brown*. The sponsors of a comparable bill in the Tennessee House were from Fayette, Haywood, and Tipton counties, also in west Tennessee. Both houses passed the bill in March 1955, but Governor Frank Clement vetoed the legislation, an acknowledgment of the assistance he had received from black voters in the election in which he defeated incumbent governor Gordon Browning, who had denounced *Brown* and vowed to uphold white supremacy. No liberal, Clement deemed the legislation unnecessary, since the Tennessee Constitution mandated segregated schools. By 1957, his position had changed from advocacy of restraint to open obstruction. That year, he signed a pupil assignment law and other segregation bills and supported a manifesto of protest against *Brown*. By 1957, therefore, representatives of the plantation counties near Memphis were setting the agenda for the state.[34]

In Memphis, the *Tri-State Defender* denounced the legislation as indicative of racial practices and ideologies associated with the cotton economy. An editorial invoked the historical memory of Elbert Williams, who was lynched in 1940 after organizing an NAACP branch and a voter registration drive in Haywood County and whose killers were never arrested, even after the NAACP submitted a list of suspects to the FBI. The editorial also reported that at the public hearings for Stainback's proposed legislation, the senator and his colleagues had "denounced Negroes as ignorant, diseased, unclean, dangerous and both unfit and unable to compete with whites." The "leading citizens" of Haywood and Fayette counties, it continued, "depend on the availability of Negroes as a cheap, unprotected and terrorized labor supply." The Stainback bill, in this view, was an attempt to retain a plantation-like regime dependent upon subjugated black labor, denial of citizenship, violence, and racist ideology.[35]

African American organizations in Memphis, including the Bluff City and Shelby County Council of Civic Clubs, the Memphis NAACP, the Masons and Elks fraternal orders, and representatives of the PTA and state principals' association, sent resolutions protesting the bill to Nashville. In doing so, they pitted themselves against what the *Tri-State Defender* cast as "notorious Dixiecrat strong holds . . . where the Negro residents, although a majority, have long been denied citizenship rights, including the right to vote." James T. Walker, president of the Bluff City and Shelby County Council of Civic Clubs, a coalition of African American civic groups, declared that the bill hit "'below the belt' of the thousands of Negro citizens who have been loyal to the state of Tennessee." Together, these statements challenged the extension of planter domination to the entire state while drawing attention to the lack of citizenship rights for blacks living in the counties represented by the sponsors of this bill.[36]

Civic Clubs and Civil Rights at the Grass Roots

As seen in the fight over the Stainback bill, black Memphis civic clubs ranked among the most outspoken advocates of *Brown v. Board of Education*, helping to forge a network of local activists that could be called upon in the Memphis State lawsuit. Most of these civic clubs emerged in the late 1940s and early 1950s. In 1952 the Bluff City and Shelby County Council of Civic Clubs was established as a counterpart to the all-white Memphis and Shelby County Council of Civic Clubs.[37] Civic clubs in black neighborhoods often began with demands for improvements such as paved streets, curbs, sidewalks, and gutters. Participants interpreted such improvements not so much in terms of individual property rights as in collective racial terms, that is, in what distinguished black from white neighborhoods. Such acts became stepping stones to more overtly political ones, from registering voters to campaigning for African American candidates. Dependent upon neither citywide black leaders nor ministers, these civic clubs involved large numbers of working-class people, both men and women, boys and girls.

Many workers who had joined labor unions during the 1940s sought ways to alter race and class relations in other realms of their lives. Workers who labored in the same plants and lived in the same neighborhoods might also belong to the same civic clubs. Evelyn Bates, who began working at Firestone during the war, for instance, joined the Fortieth Ward Civic Club, in which black Firestone union activist Matthew Davis was a prominent member. Bates, Davis, and other black Firestone workers lived in the New Chicago section of north Memphis just east of the plant, extending their concerns about segregated union meetings and racist working conditions to their neighborhood organization.

Members of the Fortieth Ward club initially pressured officials for street paving, curbs, gutters, streetlights, and street markers, which they viewed as issues of not only beautification but also racial equality. In 1949, the club submitted a petition to the commissioner of public works signed by 500 residents protesting the city's policy of picking up garbage in front of homes in "Negro sections" but picking it up at the backs of white homes. Some residents stopped dragging their garbage around to their front yards, protesting that it led to infestations of flies and created eyesores.[38]

The Fortieth Ward club also expanded its horizons to voter registration and politics, although Matthew Davis recalls initially encountering pessimism and fear when he began urging members to move in this direction. Civic clubs, from this perspective, helped working-class African Americans build confidence to challenge the Crump regime. Voter registration, which became particularly important after the state legislature's lifting of the poll tax in 1951, became a springboard for further political education and activism. The Fortieth Ward club hosted banquets to which, according to Davis, they "invited some of the top speakers out," including attorney Benjamin Hooks, who had helped the group write its charter. "And then we just started moving on out and doing things," he remembers. For example, they demanded that the city change their polling place, which Davis describes as little more than a "hole down in the ground" that had been a whiskey still.[39]

Civic club activism linked concerns about home, family, schools, and community to collective political action and involved large numbers of women. In many cases, women's involvement in civic clubs built upon their existing ties to one another, with an older generation of women often serving as role models. Alma Morris joined the Klondyke Civic Club located in north Memphis just east of Davis's New Chicago neighborhood, at the encouragement of Marie Fort, a longtime activist and dance troupe director. After working on providing clothing to needy families and, in conjunction with the PTA, preventing school truancy, Morris joined the Shelby County Democratic Club and the NAACP while pursuing a career as a barber. Similarly, Lillie Kirklon helped organize the Tate Avenue Community Club in the area south of Beale near Booker T. Washington High School, at the urging of Lena Letcher, a neighbor already involved with civic club activism. At their meetings, Kirklon and other women members discussed voting and decided to register, later attending political rallies and urging other neighbors to register. Civic club activism also brought members into contact with neighborhood groups throughout the city, building broader networks. In 1953, for example, when members of the Klondyke Civic Club hosted a talent show to raise money for scholarships, they received assistance from the North Memphis Civic Club, the Belmont Park Civic Club, the Hyde Park Civic Club, the Hollywood Civic Club, and the Fifth Ward Civic Club. Rufus Thomas from WDIA served as the emcee, and Matthew Davis was a judge.[40]

Black civic clubs and their white counterparts wound up on opposite sides of conflicts over housing and urban space, some of the most volatile racial issues of the late 1940s and early 1950s. Complex struggles over housing led to the further spatial and cultural consolidation of residential segregation, rather than its dissipation, as both white and black Memphians, including veterans with support from the GI Bill, sought to purchase new homes, locate rentals, or improve current properties. African Americans, who represented 37.3 percent (147,141) of Memphis's population in 1950, occupied 65 percent, or 30,957 of the 47,343 Memphis dwelling units deemed substandard by the 1950 U.S. Housing Census, and most majority-black neighborhoods lacked basic improvements such as paved streets, curbs, and gutters.[41] Black demands for new housing, as with city services, challenged existing residential segregation patterns and the public allocation of funds.

The location of public housing projects funded through Truman's 1949 Housing Act, and proposals for new subdivisions, sparked heated racial conflicts in which civic clubs played central roles.[42] In 1952, African Americans in the Eleventh Ward Civic Club protested the Memphis Housing Authority's designation of the Railroad Avenue area in south Memphis for slum clearance and urban renewal. Club members argued that housing there was neither substandard nor symptomatic of "blight," a word used by housing officials to indicate inner city decay. On some blocks, formerly white-owned mansions were now occupied by African Americans who had renovated them, and many residents believed this plan was intended to consolidate segregation.[43] When developers proposed plans for new subdivisions for African Americans, white civic clubs fought back, protesting to the city and issuing threats of violence. In 1949, the white East of Highland Improvement Club pressured the city to drop plans for the Graham Gardens subdivision, and the following year over 500 white residents attended a meeting of the Union Villa Civic Club to protest plans for Chelsea Gardens, a proposed housing development for blacks. And in November 1952, hundreds of white residents at a meeting of the A. B. Hill Civic Club threatened to riot if African Americans purchased homes in their south Memphis neighborhood.[44]

These disputes involved more than local issues. Members of these civic clubs were also reacting to the Supreme Court's 1948 decision in *Shelley v. Kraemer*, which ruled that restrictive covenants barring home owners from selling to certain groups on the basis of race or religion were unenforceable. In "gray" areas in south Memphis, where whites and blacks had long occupied adjoining blocks, white residents tried to prevent black Memphians from purchasing white-owned homes that previously had been covered by restrictive covenants. On Easter Sunday 1953, an angry mob of white residents of the Fordhurst subdivision, near Riverside Park and the Ford plant, tried to intimidate a black family from viewing a home that was for sale on Waldorf Street. A month later, local white residents attempted to prevent the family of Rev. Charles F. Williams, grand master of the Tennessee Masons, from moving into a home Williams had purchased on the corner of Edsel and Arkansas streets. While Edsel had been previously all-white, the Arkansas block was occupied by African Americans. A trio of white neighbors paid a visit to Mrs. Williams on May 14, as she was fixing up the house, and tried to persuade her to drop plans to move her family in. After they failed to convince her, the white Riverside Civic Club filed for an injunction to uphold their restrictive covenant. Two years later, A. A. Latting, the NAACP attorney representing Williams, along with attorneys Benjamin Hooks, H. T. Lockard, and Ben F. Jones, won a chancery court ruling that invalidated restrictive covenants in Memphis.[45]

These housing conflicts in south Memphis culminated on June 29, 1953, with the bombing of a home at 430 Olive Street, recently purchased by African Americans, drawing the Bluff City Council, the NAACP, and other city-wide organizations into this battle over race and urban space. The house, purchased by brother and sister Wrenn Williams and Annie Eggleston, was dynamited while the adults and Williams's two children were asleep. During the two months prior to the bombing, crowds had been massing in the neighborhood and white residents had threatened black families who had moved into the area. In one instance, when a new black home owner failed to open his door to a group of whites, a woman participant had warned ominously, "You'd better come on out now before you find yourself hanging high as the sky." Despite knowledge of these actions, police took no steps to intervene. Following the bombing, Mayor Tobey and Police Commissioner Claude Armour condemned the violence and Tobey called for a halt of home sales in the area while he met with the interested parties. Yet no arrests were made until late August, when a white female real estate agent was sprayed with a garden hose as she showed a home to a prospective African American buyer. The sprayer, an elderly white woman, had joined a crowd of about twenty people who had gathered to intimidate the agent.[46]

Protests over the Olive Street bombing plunged the Bluff City Council and other organizations into conflict with the Crump administration over a central civil rights issue, residential segregation. After the bombing, a delegation of African American leaders met with Mayor Tobey, who was considered more moderate than his predecessors. Ten days later, leaders of the Bluff City Council, the Negro Chamber of Commerce, the NAACP, ministerial alliances, and fraternal organizations issued a joint statement that prompted a second meeting with the mayor. The statement denounced mob violence, criticized the police department, and called for an end to "artificial restraints" preventing the expansion of black home ownership beyond existing boundaries. It reminded the mayor about African Americans' military service and argued that combating racism was the only way to guard against Communism taking root in the United States. In this view, white vigilantism was responsible for advancing Communism. In addition, Ruby Hurley helped the Memphis NAACP write a statement charging that "some members of the police force who have similar prejudices as contained by the perpetrators of the bombing [may] fail to exert themselves sufficiently to bring the culprits to justice."[47]

These housing conflicts also provoked sharp tensions among African Americans over how to approach segregation and racial violence. In addition to Hurley's inveighing against the "conservative influence" of the local NAACP, the *Tri-State Defender* excoriated the Housing Committee of the Memphis Urban League for its statement after the bombing. "'As the needs for housing for white people are satisfied,'" the editorial quoted from the statement, "'the transfer of certain housing areas to Negro occupancy is a normal and healthy development. And is the pattern of growth of American cities.'" Objecting to the phrase "normal and healthy development," the editorial declared that only the "nefarious institutions of segregation and discrimination" could explain why African Americans had to wait for the housing needs of white citizens to be satisfied before they could move into housing vacated by whites. "Spokesmen for minorities," it continued, had to "be careful lest they lend aid and support to the inevitable opposition, which is notoriously quick to grasp at every opportunity to point and say, 'See here . . . this proves that these people are satisfied with the way things are going.'"[48] Black leadership had to remain independent from the opposition by committing to "the struggle for equitable racial adjustment" and not conciliation with white supremacy, the *Defender* argued.

The Bluff City and Shelby County Council of Civic Clubs became more outspoken on civil rights issues at a time when NAACP activism in Memphis had waned. In 1952, the organization submitted to city officials a survey of the city's segregated recreational and cultural facilities. African Americans, it showed, were excluded from recreational facilities, including all but a few public parks, or restricted to usage on particular days, as with the Overton Park Zoo, which blacks could visit only on Thursdays, "maid's day off." The council denounced the use of African Americans' tax dollars for facilities from which they were excluded.[49]

The civic club council also protested mistreatment of African Americans on the Memphis Street Railway (MSR). At the beginning of January 1954, after special MSR officers harassed black passengers with abusive language and ordered seated African Americans to relinquish their seats to standing whites, council president James T. Walker, secretary Willia McWilliams, and other members proposed a car pool boycott of the bus

Entrance to the Overton Park Zoo, 1950s, at a time when African
Americans were allowed to visit the zoo only one day each week.
(© Ernest C. Withers, courtesy of Panopticon Gallery)

system, similar to what had been done in Baton Rouge in 1953 and nearly
two years before the Montgomery bus boycott. The council scheduled a
mass meeting to consider a boycott, while attorneys Hooks, Lockard, and
Jones explored the legal parameters of the case. Then, on January 2, an
MSR driver aimed a revolver at an African American woman when she and
nearby white passengers complained that he would not allow her to exit
from the front door. Passengers nearby — both black and white — shouted
at the driver until he put away the gun. Civic club leaders demanded that
the MSR discharge the offending employees, institute a courtesy policy,
and hire black drivers. They succeeded in winning a reprimand of the two
officers and the dismissal of the driver, which deflated plans for the boycott, although the MSR president refused to hire blacks in positions other
than laborers.[50]

Civic clubs also became the backbone of the voter registration movement, reflecting the enormous impact of the repeal of the Tennessee poll
tax in 1951. Registering to vote no longer involved payments; moreover,
one could now acquire permanent registration, rather than having to re-
register annually. Eradicating the poll tax, an issue over which the Ten-

nessee legislature and courts had wrangled for over a decade, created an opening for working-class African Americans to exercise citizenship rights without being beholden to Crump. The vast majority had not registered under the conditions established by the machine. In 1951, Universal Life Insurance executive Dr. J. E. Walker, the Democrat who had spearheaded the 1948 campaign of African Americans for Kefauver, and Republican leader Lt. George W. Lee formed the Non-Partisan Voters' League to increase registration. By the time of the elections a few months later, black voter registration had tripled from 7,000 to 22,000, reaching one-fifth of the total city electorate of 106,000. Civic club and church members, especially women, lobbied neighbors to register, competing for prizes for the most registered voters, and brought neighbors to mass voter rallies.[51]

In June 1952, the success of a massive "citizenship rally" sponsored by the Non-Partisan Voters' League at Booker T. Washington High School hinged on the promotional efforts and participation of WDIA radio personalities. During the preceding week, DJs conducted voter registration at various sites, in addition to promoting the campaign on the air. At the rally itself, an "Oscar" award was given to the DJ who brought the most listeners to the rally. As the word got out, lines outside the registrar's office at the courthouse grew; on some days, African Americans stood in queues that stretched down the block.[52]

Civic clubs also campaigned in 1951 for Dr. J. E. Walker for the school board. The bank president was the first African American to run for a major city office in thirty years. Walker and his campaign manager, young civil rights attorney Benjamin Hooks, promoted voter registration and education and denounced race-baiting tactics by machine candidates. Walker lost nonetheless, winning 7,433 votes, compared to the average 21,000 votes each successful white candidate won, partly because only one-third of registered African American voters came to the polls. However, the election spurred future campaigns by showing that black candidates might possibly win if more African Americans registered to vote and stuck together.[53]

The *Brown* decision impelled the civic club council to assert its independence from city officials. In December 1955, a resolution by James T. Walker on behalf of the civic club council challenged statements by city officials that African Americans did not desire changes in the status quo. "Negro leaders and the masses" supported integration, he declared, despite the fact that white city leaders had "stated on various occasions that the masses of Negroes and their leaders do not want integration." "What leaders they refer to is not clear," the resolution continued. "This organization desires to let it be known to all and sundry, that its leaders and constituents are pledged to oppose all forms of discrimination based upon race or color." This public rejection of claims about the purported satisfaction of black Memphians attacked the racial paternalism that, like coercion, characterized Memphis's machine politics. The statement hailed *Brown* as the greatest development since the Emancipation Proclamation. The freedom it invoked by this comparison addressed both civil rights and the decision's impact on black Memphians' ideas of what was possible.[54]

The council's commitment to ending racial discrimination became especially significant to the complicated political terrain after *Brown*. Unlike in Mississippi or rural west Tennessee, city officials avoided open antagonism to *Brown* directly after the decision. The president of the Memphis Board of Education, Milton Bowers, immediately declared that the city would remain within the law, suggesting that it might even comply with the Supreme Court if it were so ordered. For the coming school year, 1954–55, however, there would be no changes in city schools, according to Superintendent Ernest Ball, since the Tennessee Constitution still required segregation and the Court had not yet ruled on implementing *Brown*. Over the next year, even after the death of Boss Crump in October 1954, the board proceeded in a style typical of the machine, soliciting black support by trumpeting various building projects to enhance and expand "Negro schools." The Shelby County Board of Education, which administered schools outside the city limit in the areas directly abutting Memphis, underscored its support of the status quo without making any incendiary comments, announcing that, as usual, black schools would close for six weeks during cotton picking season.[55]

White moderates, including business leaders and professionals in the Civic Research Council (CRC), pursuing municipal reform cast themselves as critical of racial "extremism" on both sides.[56] CRC member and business leader Edmund Orgill declared his support for the city's plan to "work out its problem within the law" and publicly criticized U.S. Representative Pat Sutton, Senator Estes Kefauver's opponent in the 1954 Democratic primary, for his proposal to introduce a constitutional amendment obstructing *Brown*. The *Commercial Appeal* likewise greeted *Brown* by counseling "calmness, reason, and . . . cooperation," while the *Press-Scimitar* characterized America's support for democratic principles of "equal opportunity" as key to winning the Cold War.[57]

The deaths of Boss Crump in October 1954 and Mayor Frank Tobey the following September presented CRC reformers with a chance to win municipal elections and restructure city government in 1955. Although

Tobey had been more moderate than his predecessor, Watkins Overton, he favored continuing the commission form of government on which the Crump machine had been based. When Tobey died suddenly and Overton announced he would run in his place, the CRC decided to support Edmund Orgill for mayor.[58]

For black voters, the *Brown* decision, the elimination of the poll tax, and the death of Boss Crump appeared to offer an unprecedented opportunity. "For the first time in many years," the black press declared, "the voters of Memphis will go to the polls without the shadow of implied or real 'boss' machinations." Civic clubs pulled out all the stops to increase black voter registration. Two hundred ministers, at a meeting held at Mason Temple, headquarters of the Church of God in Christ, formed the nonpartisan Ministers and Citizens League. In an effort to convince church members to register, they hired women to supervise door-knocking campaigns in all the black-majority wards of the city. Meanwhile, the Veterans Voters Movement, composed of veterans of the Second World War and the Korean War and headed by James F. Estes of the NAACP, a veteran himself, launched a drive to register 10,000 voters, in which 2,000 veterans would drive five registrants each to the courthouse. As a result of these combined efforts, the number of blacks registered to vote increased to over 40,000 by the time of the fall 1955 elections.[59]

Despite this unified voter registration campaign, African Americans did not agree about which mayoral candidate to support, for neither candidate could be expected to genuinely support their interests. Orgill, they argued, had no record of supporting black rights beyond his backing of the new "Negro hospital," Collins Chapel Memorial. Overton's critics perceived him as wishing to perpetuate machine politics. Ultimately, a majority supported Orgill, swinging the election in his favor, although Overton won support in wards with a significant black middle-class presence, such as Orange Mound. The opportunity for implementing *Brown* would not last long, however; by 1957, Orgill had retreated from even minor steps toward desegregation and declared his loyalty to southern tradition. His political waffling resulted in such a drastic loss of support from black voters that he withdrew from the 1959 mayoral race, leaving the path clear for Henry Loeb, an avowed white supremacist.[60]

Even if not all black Memphians agreed on which mayoral candidate to support in 1955, they were strongly united on two other points. First, since neither mayoral candidate, however reasonable he sounded, could be counted on to promote *Brown*, black voters solidly supported an African American candidate for the school board. Dr. Walker and Lt. Lee favored

Black Memphians registering to vote in March 1959.
(Memphis Commercial Appeal *photograph, courtesy of*
Special Collections, University of Memphis)

the selection of Rev. Roy Love, pastor of Mt. Nebo Baptist Church and president of the local Baptist Ministers Alliance, as a way to reach churchgoing voters. Without white support, Love lost. However, with 20,082 votes, Love won nearly three times the number of votes Dr. Walker won in 1951, and he garnered nearly as many votes as the four winning candidates did. Half of black registered voters turned out for the elections, as opposed to one-third a few years earlier.[61]

Black Memphis voters also expressed overwhelming concern with police brutality. "Here in Memphis, as in many Southern cities," the *Tri-State Defender* asserted, "Negroes have long endured a callous, disrespectful, and sometimes brutal expression of an administration's racial policies through the police." Black Memphians perceived the city commission system as conducive to police abuse, since commissioners had little accountability to the electorate. At a banquet held by the Non-Partisan Voters'

League, a minister related a story about a father who had been arrested while rushing his son to the hospital, and later fined. Only the officers' confidence that they would be backed up by "the top brass" could explain this "disregard for the Negro," the minister declared. At other meetings, black citizens queried candidates about their plans for stopping police brutality. As black voters decided which issues were most important to them at this critical juncture, they placed equal emphasis on police brutality and school desegregation, connecting the latter to other features of urban life that had became emblematic of white domination.[62]

Racial Justice, Politics, and Labor

In this period following *Brown*, black workers attempted to place their own stamp on the political terrain by bringing urban problems of labor, gender, and racial justice into the realm of politics. Significantly, even as most black leaders endorsed the candidacy of Henry Loeb in his 1955 bid for commissioner of public works — over a decade before Loeb as mayor became infamous for his determination to crush the sanitation workers' strike of 1968 — a group of women who attended a political rally cautioned against support for Loeb because of the "business policies of the Loeb Laundry-Cleaners establishment," as the press obliquely reported it. Indeed, at the end of the Second World War, workers at Loeb's Laundry had struck against poor conditions, especially a piecework system that made them work on the presses at a dangerous speed, in a hot, unhealthy environment. Loeb, if elected, would have authority over the city's sanitation department, where hundreds of low-paid African American men worked. The women's prescient critiques failed to deter African American political leaders' endorsement of Loeb, allowing him to sail into office with considerable black support, although he lost that backing in 1959, when he campaigned for mayor on an openly segregationist platform — and won.[63]

The impromptu protest by the "Patio 6" at Joel's café in April 1955 captured more attention than did the laundry workers' political commentary. Both the walkout and the media coverage that followed the employees' arrests placed "mammy," a gendered symbol of the plantation that had become a stock image of American advertising and mass culture, at the center of black public attention.[64] In addition to rousing indignation over the use of an elderly black woman as a living advertisement for southern food, the "Patio 6" case also sparked a protest movement against racial injustice in the courtroom, after press coverage of the arrests attracted people to witness the trial. A. A. Latting, who defended two of the employees, strategically requested the highest fine for his clients so that it would meet the minimum required for an appeal. Later that week, AME and Baptist minis-ters convened a meeting to hear reports of the initial incident and the trial from Mrs. Marie Taylor, one of the "Patio 6," and from Rev. W. L. Powell, presiding elder of the South Memphis District of the AME church. Powell argued that the judge had made the proceedings "purely a racial matter" and that his fellow ministers had the responsibility to speak out on behalf of these "heroes in a common place." Those in attendance organized the Memphis Citizens Committee for the Promotion of Justice, led by funeral home director T. C. D. Hayes and Baptist leader Dr. S. A. Owen, and hired attorneys Latting and Hooks to pursue the appeals.[65]

The "Patio 6" episode reflected concerns that energized other labor struggles, which persisted despite the harsh political climate of the 1950s. Workers sought to transform their unions into bodies that would fight for *both* economic gains and racial justice. In 1955, African American mem-bers of Local 282, many of them women, pressured the furniture workers union to replace their white international representative, Doyle Dorsey, who they accused of siding with the company on union matters and ex-cluding black workers from negotiations. However, Local 282 continued to place white organizers in Memphis whom workers considered similar to Dorsey until the early 1960s, when LeRoy Clark, Dorsey's predecessor, was reassigned to Memphis.[66]

Given the barriers they faced, it is significant that African American workers continued to organize at all during the 1950s. Despite plant clo-sures that caused significant membership losses and severe repression, membership in Local 282 more than doubled between 1950 and 1955, rising from 245 to 591 members. Part of this growth came from in-plant organizing in already organized plants. Many new members were black women, due in part to the decision of local manufacturers to expand rather than fire their female workforces after the war. Between 1950 and 1955, Local 282 also won a half dozen victories in new elections, although it launched organizing campaigns in roughly twenty plants, suggesting both widespread interest and continuing intimidation.[67]

Repeatedly, Local 282 organizers used the term "fear" to describe pre-vailing sentiments among black workers at Memphis Furniture and else-where in the years following the 1949 Memphis Furniture strike and the 1951 Eastland hearings. Notably, however, their reports also revealed per-sistent determination. As early as October 1949, even as organizer Gene Day reported that workers at Memphis Furniture were "scared to death, and will hardly talk about the union," he noted that many had indicated that "if an election is held that they will vote for the union." Two and a half years later, Doyle Dorsey described the workers' "company fear" and the continuing presence of scabs at Memphis Furniture but reported that he had managed to set up a shop committee among upholsterers. In March 1955, Edward Wertz, Dorsey's replacement, reported that "just plain fear" had scared off two employees from joining the shop committee. As Memphis Furniture workers tried to reorganize, they faced a fierce antiunion campaign, ranging from dismissals of union activists to flyers claiming that Memphis Furniture, not Local 282's "greedy organizers," was on the side of "colored women and men." In September 1953, workers voted 334 to 313 for the union — only to have the results thrown out on a technicality by the NLRB. In February 1955, fear persisted, according to Wertz, but Local 282 won a new election, by a vote of 387 to 299, and signed a contract five months later.[68]

For the men and women involved in these labor struggles, fear and resolve were not mutually exclusive; workers grappled with both sentiments, not only at NLRB election time but daily. In many cases they lost out. Some workers found resources to persevere, though, in civic clubs and church groups. They also found support among veterans of earlier struggles who brought their hard-won knowledge to new campaigns. Melvina Rebecca McKinley and Eddie May Garner, were two such veterans. McKinley, a key unionist at Memphis Furniture in 1949, began working at the Ivers and Pond piano factory in 1950 and became a union member there. In the 1940s, Eddie May Garner was a union member at Buckeye and then at E. L. Bruce flooring. She lost her job at E. L. Bruce after speaking up at a meeting of the International Woodworkers of America, and she attributes her firing to reactions to her as a black woman. Garner helped bring Local 282 to the Davis Chair Company as a worker there in 1953, before moving in 1956 to the piano factory, where she became a leading union activist. As with Memphis Furniture earlier, union members at the piano factory — part of the Aeolian Corporation, based in New York — became crucial to Local 282 as a whole due to the determination of black workers there, who comprised the majority of employees and perceived their problems in terms of both class and race. Workers at the piano factory took pride in their work; however, according to Garner, "the supervisor would curse [workers] like they was a bunch of dogs or something." As a steward, Garner also dealt with racial tensions among workers. In 1958, white workers at the factory attempted to form their own union rather than participate in Local 282, a black-majority local; however, the international ultimately maintained its constitutional ban on segregated locals.[69]

The conditions that black workers protested were similar to those that had been publicly addressed during the 1949 Memphis Furniture strike. Alzada Clark, an employee at Memphis Sales, joined Local 282 with the image still fresh in her mind of trucks carrying strikebreakers to Memphis Furniture during the 1949 strike. At Memphis Sales, where she helped organize the union, she recalled, "We couldn't go to the bathroom [when we wanted], and if we went to the bathroom, you were clocked. . . . The wages for what we were doing was not suitable. We were making dinette chair bottoms and backs and the men were assembling them into chairs. We were unhappy about the way we were being treated and the kind of money that we were earning."[70]

All three women went on to become civil rights activists in the 1960s, suggesting links of continuity between these different time periods and different dimensions of struggle. Their activism in this fraught Cold War context, also illuminates the difficult, complex process in which black worker-activists engaged as they contended with multiple problems: managers who treated them "like dogs"; racial tensions among workers; and frustration with union leaders. As with other rural and urban movements in this period, this process was also characterized by daily wrestling with fear of reprisals and humiliation and anger at demeaning racial practices.[71]

Workers also took part in strenuous voter registration and education campaigns within labor unions in the 1950s. Local 282 organizer Doyle Dorsey reported in April 1952, for example, that voter registration had been taking place among members of the furniture workers union: "Considerable interest is being aroused at the present time in getting our people registered or qualified to vote in the coming elections. A good job of it has been done to date," he noted, "but forty percent of them have not yet registered." Dorsey attributed this hard work to both local "civic interests" and the CIO educational program.[72] Labor organizing among black workers thus spilled over into other kinds of activism aimed at racial justice.

It was in black working-class neighborhoods like New Chicago and Binghampton where these workers' energies especially propelled other kinds of organizing. Indeed, the Binghampton Civic League issued one of the most pointed challenges to segregation of this period. The league had emerged out of the same neighborhood that had been the locus of protest against police brutality in the 1940s. In 1956, league president O. Z. Evers, a postal employee who had lived previously in Chicago, filed a bus desegregation suit against the city after he refused to move to the back of a bus and was ejected from it. Two years later, the league petitioned the city commission for complete desegregation of the zoo, fairgrounds, public parks, and recreational facilities. "For four years now, the Negro has adopted a 'wait-

and-see' attitude towards integration in public recreational facilities here in Memphis," the letter began. In 1959, the club demanded to know why African Americans were excluded from employment in city government and called for an immediate correction of this situation. The same year, municipal sanitation workers living in this neighborhood approached O. Z. Evers for help in organizing a union.[73]

Bettye Coe Donahue's family exemplifies the multifaceted approaches to the struggle for freedom many working-class African Americans took in the 1950s. Donahue's mother, an employee at the piano factory and member of Local 282, went on strike. Her father and uncle, Lint and Clarence Coe, both dedicated union activists at Firestone, spearheaded NAACP membership drives and led voter registration campaigns. Both her parents joined the Klondyke Civic Club, with her father becoming a club officer. After the 1954 *Brown* decision, Clarence Coe and other black union activists initiated a desegregation suit against Firestone, charging the company with maintaining segregated seniority lists, pay scales, water fountains, and restrooms.[74]

Although it has rarely been appreciated, working-class black Memphians, both men and women, frequently recent migrants from the outlying cotton region, organized in multiple, creative ways during the 1950s and established new terrains of struggle. As NAACP members, civic club leaders, and labor activists, they seized on *Brown* to challenge segregation in various spheres of urban life. These working-class migrants and veterans of the Second World War posed a formidable challenge to Memphis's racial structures, suggesting that urbanization did not end but rather politicized desires for changed conditions of life and labor.

The urban-rural matrix of the postwar era had powerful implications for the struggles surrounding *Brown v. Board of Education*. It ensured that protesters approached school desegregation not narrowly but as part of a complex set of problems revolving around rights, power, and identity, problems that the black press had summed up as a "racial equation" based on "master and servant." In practical terms, urban activists' engagement with rural struggles made it impossible to separate their own responses to *Brown* from the dramatic conflicts over white domination that surfaced in the rural Delta areas of Mississippi, Arkansas, and west Tennessee. The increasing presence of working-class migrants from these same areas made problems of police brutality and labor especially potent and symbolic. Those who protested against police brutality or became union activists also joined civic clubs and the NAACP. Therefore, demands for desegregation were energized by these other struggles.

American democracy took on highly charged meanings in the rhetoric of the Cold War era. One of the most powerful articulations of democracy during these years came from the Supreme Court when it reinterpreted the Fourteenth Amendment to end the notion of "separate but equal" put forth in *Plessy v. Ferguson* and establish desegregation as the basis for racial equality in modern life. Even as individuals and organizations hailed *Brown* as the greatest development since the Emancipation Proclamation—as did the Bluff City and Shelby County Council of Civic Clubs—and seized upon it to press for desegregation in public schools, buses, parks, and libraries, they also attempted to push forward on deeply rooted problems and issues that the Court did not—and perhaps could not—address. For African American activists in the urban South, who saw themselves as part of a new generation, the 1950s was also a period of starts and restarts, of working through fear and struggling to ground their activism in a new understanding of their role rather than in old patterns they associated with the past and with the "master-servant" equation.

We Were Making History

7 Students, Sharecroppers, and Sanitation Workers in the Memphis Freedom Movement

"Applause literally rocked Mason Temple," exclaimed the *Tri-State Defender* in a report on a "Freedom Rally" for the Volunteer Ticket, July 31, 1959, that drew 5,000 black Memphians to hear Dr. Martin Luther King Jr., gospel singer Mahalia Jackson, and local speakers. "Thunderous applause" repeatedly interrupted black Memphis political candidates Russell Sugarmon, Benjamin Hooks, Rev. Roy Love, Rev. Henry Bunton, and others. The crowd roared as speakers ripped into "Uncle Toms," declaring, as one speaker did, "Let this night be the burial of uncle toms of all shapes, forms and fashions!" "We're going to fight till hell freezes over and then skate across on the ice," yelled Lt. George Lee to deafening cheers. Placard-waving youth demonstrated for Russell Sugarmon, whose campaign for commissioner of public works had been vigorously opposed by white Memphians. In his speech, Dr. King declared that he "had never seen such enthusiasm at a meeting of Negroes." "I am delighted beyond power of word to see such magnificent unity," King cried, urging listeners to "[w]alk together children, for we just want to be free!" "Something [is] going to take place that never took place before," he predicted.[1]

A scene not from 1968 but 1959, only seven years after NAACP official Ruby Hurley despaired about the "conservative influence [that] dominates the thinking" among black Memphis leaders, this rally accompanied a vigorous effort to register voters and elect black officials to the all-white city government. The number of African Americans registered to vote in the August election had soared to an unprecedented 55,000, out of a total of 186,000 registered voters in Memphis. Besides Sugarmon's hard-fought race, Benjamin Hooks sought a juvenile court judgeship, and ministers Roy Love and Henry Bunton were campaigning for the school board. Elihue Stanback, an officer in the Binghampton Civic League, was running independently for city tax assessor. O. Z. Evers, president of the league, would have been running for city commissioner had he not been forced to drop out of the race under threat of being fired from his job at the post office.[2]

Panicked that racial bloc voting might usher an African American into the city commission in 1959, Shelby County representatives had convinced the state legislature to alter the process by which Memphis city commissioners were elected. Until now, the top four vote-getters won positions for nondesignated seats, which might have allowed African Americans voting as a bloc to elect a black candidate. After the changes, each post was voted on separately, ensuring that whites would likely win every post, since white voters were in the majority. However, when six white men announced their candidacy for commissioner of public works, to replace mayoral candidate Henry Loeb, it became evident that if whites split their votes, a black candidate might very well win. As the *Tri-State Defender* put it, "The word is out across the country that, for the first time in modern history, Negroes have a good chance of being elected to local offices. Negro voters are having a love affair with history."[3]

Three weeks after the rally, on August 20, 64 percent of Memphis's registered black voters turned out to the polls, with many in heavily African American wards lining up before 7:00 A.M. or casting ballots as late as 10:00 P.M. Sugarmon and Hooks won 94 percent of the black vote, with Love and Bunton close behind. Voter turnout among white Memphians reached the even higher rate of 73 percent, however, making the overall turnout the largest ever in Memphis. Aided by the last-minute withdrawal from the race by four of the six white candidates for commissioner of public works, leaving one clear leader, white voters avoided splitting their votes and defeated Sugarmon. The black candidates for other offices were also defeated. And Edmund Orgill's withdrawal from the mayoral race shortly before the election helped usher Henry Loeb, an avowed segregationist, into the mayor's office.[4]

This shutout of African Americans from elected office despite their strenuous efforts in the political process illuminated the formidable challenges faced by black Memphians. In rural plantation areas, where blacks formed the vast majority of agricultural laborers and, hence, of the population itself, white elites nearly totally excluded blacks from voting. In contrast, skyrocketing voter registration in Memphis made it seem as if democracy were flourishing. The election defeats despite the large black turnout made clear, as perhaps no other political event had since the 1940 "reign of terror," that racial justice would not come without a larger struggle. Nearly a decade of work to register black Memphians culminated in 1959, therefore, with a contradictory lesson about the strengths and limitations of political participation, and the meanings of freedom.

Concomitantly, other issues that had captured the attention of black Memphians since the end of the Second World War again came to a fore. Shortly after the 1959 elections, a renewed protest against police brutality; labor organizing by African American sanitation workers; and a gathering storm of opposition to the city's intransigence on desegregation all influenced perceptions of racial injustice. Moreover, the eruption of a voting rights movement among sharecroppers and tenant farmers in southwestern Tennessee served as a dramatic reminder of the historic and contemporary roots of the freedom struggle in the southern cotton economy.

With the heady emergence of the student sit-in movement and its emphasis on "Freedom Now!" young activists became exhilarated by their own role in what some referred to as "making history." In the process of gaining a new sense of self, they extended their demands for freedom to racial divisions in popular culture and religion that characterized Jim Crow urban society. While black Memphians in the late 1940s had seized on black-oriented radio as a new public sphere of self-expression, community building, and pride, for example, now demonstrators criticized black radio stations for sponsoring segregated community events. Many young people wished to transform popular culture itself, as seen with the rise of Stax Records and southern soul music. Other young activists challenged racist practices and ideologies in churches and in religion more generally. "Freedom" began to mean not so much achieving a separate public sphere within Jim Crow but breaking down the barriers that kept it separate and transforming popular culture itself. Here, however, activists experienced not only the exhilaration of "making history" but persistent obstacles as well.

Memphis's Political Terrain after *Brown*

Memphis's political terrain following *Brown v. Board of Education* produced openings for protest, on the one hand, and barriers to change, on the other. In 1955, white moderate business leader Edmund Orgill's election as mayor was secured with the support of African American voters, after Orgill greeted the school desegregation decision with a statement about respecting the Supreme Court's mandate. By the end of the decade, however, the moderate center of white politics had nearly dropped out of the picture, and African Americans articulated a more independent, black-oriented politics.

Upon first taking office, Orgill made a few token gestures to the black electorate that triggered a white backlash. In early 1956, for example, Orgill nominated Dr. J. E. Walker, whom he had endorsed for school board in 1951, to be the first African American on the board of directors of John Gaston Hospital, a public facility that served a majority-black clientele. Such a step would have created few ripples before 1954 but now sparked a flurry of hate mail, phone calls, and other harassment, convincing Orgill to drop the nomination.[5] He also rapidly distanced himself from his earlier position on *Brown*, which if not welcoming of desegregation was at least critical of those who declared their intention to defy the Court's mandate. When queried by a member of the pro-segregation Tennessee Federation of Constitutional Government during a packed city commission meeting in 1957, Orgill claimed that he had "never advocated or desired integration." In a comment that not only echoed but embraced Crump's legacy, he asserted that Memphis had always had "remarkably good race relations" because of "the wisdom of our political leaders." And in declaring his candidacy for governor in 1958, he insisted that as a born-and-bred Tennessean he had never favored integration and would "never do so" as governor. However, his assertion that he would use all legal means to prevent desegregation but would not "refuse to use his influence to prevent violence" in the case of court-ordered integration sealed his fate. He was defeated in the election.[6]

By the time of the 1959 mayoral race, Orgill's assurances that he supported the status quo in Memphis and the South had also alienated black voters, who had supported him in the 1958 gubernatorial race. Orgill and the city commission had stalled all attempts at desegregation of schools and buses, libraries, and public parks by tying them up in the courts. The *Tri-State Defender* greeted his announcement of his candidacy in 1959 with a front-page editorial headlined "Just What Do You Mean, Mayor?" that pilloried his statement that Memphis had "the best relations of any southern city." Interpreting his words as an endorsement for continued segregation, the editorial advised the mayor to "closet himself in his study and pore over some law volumes, the Constitution of the United States and the Holy Bible." Orgill withdrew from the race in early July, six weeks before the election, because of illness, leaving the field open to Henry Loeb. The Dedicated Citizens Committee (DCC), formed to support Orgill's candidacy and chaired by chemical manufacturer Stanley Buckman, shifted its attention to the Stop Sugarmon effort and city reform.[7]

Unlike black Memphians, who perceived municipal reform and ending white supremacy as aspects of the same struggle, Orgill and his colleagues separated the issues. White Memphis moderates organized two distinct groups in the late 1950s, one to address race relations and the other to concentrate on municipal restructuring. The Memphis Committee on Community Relations (MCCR) was founded in 1958 at the suggestion of attorney Lucius Burch in order to respond to rising racial "suspicion and tension" in Memphis and the "increasing wave of bombings, violence, threats, and demonstrations" elsewhere in the region, most notably in Little Rock, only 200 miles to the west. Burch argued that "extremists of both races" were dominating public discourse and proposed a biracial committee of "responsible and respected white and negro citizens to furnish a moderate leadership." The MCCR, comprised of white business and civic leaders and a few NAACP representatives, was intent not on desegregation but avoiding civil strife and initially confined itself to studying the situation. Only after the sit-in movement erupted in 1960 did the MCCR advocate steps such as desegregating buses and the zoo—which would likely have been accomplished by court order anyway. Not until a year and a half later did the group propose desegregating Main Street, and it was not until early 1962 that merchants actually implemented the changes. Even then, MCCR members Frank Ahlgren and Edward Meeman, editors of the *Commercial Appeal* and *Press-Scimitar*, respectively, kept most news about sit-ins and desegregation out of the headlines, giving the impression that race relations were nothing but amicable.[8]

White political reformers who had been involved in the DCC also formed the Citizens' Association of Memphis and Shelby County (CA). Intended to address government reform not race, the group nevertheless found that it could not avoid the issue. Acknowledging the strong, united black turnout in the 1959 elections—regardless of the ultimate results—CA members debated whether to include a plank in its platform that explicitly vowed to "maintain community patterns of segregation by all legal means," which had been a tenet of the DCC's program. While some insisted that potential white members would be alienated if this statement about segregation were removed, others, such as Judson McKellar, nephew of Crump crony Senator Kenneth McKellar, argued that while he personally did not support integration, he felt that inclusion of the plank would unnecessarily alienate a group with which they would clearly have to work in the future—that is, black voters. Only 10 members out of 120 voted to include the point, leaving the platform silent on the issue.[9]

Unlike white reformers, black Memphians perceived desegregation and political goals as inseparable. With lawsuits pending on desegregating Memphis State and city buses, the NAACP, civic clubs, and various individuals pursued other cases as well. In 1958, O. Z. Evers and the Binghampton Civic League petitioned the city commission for complete desegregation, "herein and forthwith," of the zoo, fairgrounds, public parks, and recreational facilities. H. T. Lockard likewise filed a lawsuit calling for the desegregation of public facilities after Mrs. Tarlease Mathews and Miss Annie Williams were evicted from the Overton Park Zoo for visiting on a whites-only day. And Jesse Turner, chairman of the NAACP Executive Committee, initiated a case against the library after he was barred from the facilities at the main branch. In 1959, the Binghampton club petitioned the mayor, demanding to know why African Americans were excluded from city jobs, outside of the sanitation department. "With thousands of Negro children graduating from high schools and colleges in Memphis yearly," the club argued, "it would be a paradoxical statement to say they are not qualified or that they do not want better city jobs."[10]

African American activists also attempted to remake the political terrain. When black attorney S. A. Wilbun ran for the state legislature in 1958, black political leaders urged "single shot voting," in which African Americans would vote only for Wilbun, thereby avoiding boosting the totals of any other candidates. Wilbun lost, but seeing the possibilities of racial bloc voting convinced Russell Sugarmon, A. W. Willis, and Dr. J. E. Walker to reorganize the old Crump-allied Shelby County Democratic Club. Civic club members, including Alma Morris, Marie Fort, and Matthew Davis, expanded their activism by joining this explicitly political organization. With Russell Sugarmon as executive director and Walker as general chairman (replaced by his son A. Maceo Walker upon his death shortly after the club's reorganization), the club established committees in every precinct with black voters, and in 1960 it helped establish the statewide Tennessee Voters' Council.[11]

Based on this groundwork, the bipartisan "Volunteer Ticket" united black Democrats and Republicans to register and mobilize black voters on a scale unprecedented since the days of the Lincoln League in the 1910s, with hundreds of volunteers emphasizing voter education. Secretaries from the Universal Life Insurance Company, for example, typed up sample ballots so that volunteers could instruct voters on how to mark them. The group's massive July 31 rally at which Dr. King and Mahalia Jackson appeared alongside local political leaders added to the mounting enthusiasm among black voters. Nevertheless, as determination grew among African Americans, calls for white racial unity by Memphis civic leaders also intensified, especially in the race for public works commissioner. Following his defeat on August 20, Russell Sugarmon acknowledged the success — and

Supporters of the Volunteer Ticket welcome Dr. Martin Luther King Jr.,
1959. They are carrying signs for Memphis political candidates Russell
Sugarmon and Benjamin Hooks, in addition to King.
(© Ernest C. Withers, courtesy of Panopticon Gallery)

the failure—of racial bloc voting with his comment: "We won everything
but the election."[12]

Police Brutality, Sanitation Workers, and Desegregation

As black Memphians regrouped in the wake of the August 1959 elections, two movements drove politics more deeply into everyday lives of
working-class blacks. First, African Americans renewed their protest
against police brutality. Second, city sanitation workers began organizing
in protest of the city's treatment of its all-black corps of garbage collectors.
Initiated largely in the Klondyke and New Chicago neighborhoods of north
Memphis and the Binghampton area of east Memphis these two struggles
captured citywide attention.

During the second half of 1959, civic clubs in north Memphis vigorously
protested police brutality after a spate of incidents that many believed
represented reactions against social and political assertiveness among

working-class African Americans. In September, the Bluff City and Shelby County Council of Civic Clubs convened a meeting at which they heard testimony from victims of police abuse. New Chicago resident Robert Vessell, age thirty-four, his head still in bandages, testified that police beat him after he queried them about arrests they were making at the New Chicago Grill. Twenty-five-year-old Waddell Jones reported that he had been assaulted just prior to the August elections, when officers interceding in a dispute in the Klondyke neighborhood spotted a leaflet for the Volunteer Ticket sticking out of his pocket. They also arrested four of his family members. On behalf of the 20,000 black Memphians the council claimed to represent, attendees at the meeting launched a new campaign against police brutality, beginning by sending a letter to Police Commissioner Claude Armour requesting help in preventing violence.[13]

By the time of the council's October meeting, at least two more brutality incidents had occurred, including a shooting death and the beating of a man lying unconscious after a seizure. Members were outraged over Armour's unsatisfactory response to their letter and discussed how to proceed. Previous council president and labor leader James T. Walker cast police brutality in racial terms. "What they've done to these Negroes, they wouldn't dare to do in a white neighborhood," he insisted. "The policeman is a servant of the public, and was never designed to be a tormentor." The council resolved to meet with Armour personally. Current council president Rev. James Gladney led a delegation, including Klondyke Civic Club president Howard Jackson, New Chicago Civic Club president Matthew Davis, and attorneys Russell Sugarmon and S. A. Wilbun to Armour's office. At a Memphis NAACP meeting a week later, Jackson and Davis announced that Armour's response to the delegation had been insulting. Davis had taken particular umbrage at Armour's use of the terms "boy" or "buddy" to refer to black men. Russell Sugarmon reported to the NAACP Executive Board that Armour apparently "approved of conduct of police."[14]

Incidents of police violence continued to capture public attention. In one of several stories in the black press, a badly hurt Waddell Jones, who, along with his sister, still had a suit pending for his beating before the elections, reported that policemen dragged him to a lot behind a supermarket and commenced to pummel him while calling him an "NAACP nigger." The officers took him to John Gaston Hospital before jailing him, but then they confiscated the medicine he had been given.[15]

In Binghampton, meanwhile, municipal sanitation workers began organizing a union, bringing to the fore not only labor and racial justice issues but political ones as well, since their boss was the new commissioner of public works, William Farris. Historians generally have not recognized that Memphis sanitation workers began organizing nearly a decade before the 1968 strike.[16] Their organizing coincided with the student sit-in movement that erupted in 1960. Many workers were migrants from rural southwest Tennessee and veterans of the Second World War, who had been angered when they returned to Memphis from the armed forces to face jobs with appallingly racist working conditions.[17]

The late 1950s presented an especially challenging convergence of economic and political exigencies, especially for African Americans. The economic recession of the late 1950s had forced many black men to seek jobs at the Public Works Department after being laid off from better-paid and less demeaning ones. Taylor Rogers had lost his job at the Army Depot and felt forced to "take anything [he] could." T. O. Jones, who became a key organizer of the sanitation workers' union, had previously worked at a West Coast shipyard. Robert Beasley had been employed at the airport, while Joe Warren had worked at Firestone. Some, like Jones and Warren, had been union members on their old jobs. Meanwhile, Mayor Loeb was elected on a white supremacist platform, which was particularly worrisome for sanitation workers, since he had previously been commissioner of public works.[18]

The sanitation workers protested deeply rooted racist practices endemic to the sanitation department. Workers had to deal with "biased foremen who will lay men off for several days for little or no cause," declared O. Z. Evers, president of the Binghampton Civic League, from whom workers solicited assistance in organizing. Evers, in his public statement on their behalf, also charged that the workers had inadequate protection from leaky tubs of garbage and inclement weather and were at the bottom of the "payroll totem poll," making as little as ninety-four cents per hour at a time when Chattanooga sanitation workers earned $1.60 an hour and those in Chicago made $2.90. As a spokesman for the workers, Evers called for a $1.65 hourly wage minimum, demanding, "How in the world can a man with a family live on anything less?" He also reported that workers had been informed that their vacation time would be cut.[19]

With Evers's help, the sanitation workers secured the support of Teamsters Local 984, which commenced a formal organizing drive in early 1960. A series of spirited meetings and rallies held in churches in the Binghampton neighborhood between February and June 1960 involved hundreds of workers. At a kick-off rally at the Rock of Ages Church in Binghampton in early March, for instance, 200 workers and their wives—many of them workers in similar service jobs themselves—cheered Evers and union leaders. Within weeks, the number attending mass meetings had nearly tripled, despite Commissioner Farris's warning that if they attempted to unionize, the city would dismantle the sanitation department and contract out the work to a private company.[20]

When Farris refused to negotiate, two-thirds of the 1,200 workers voted to authorize a walkout. This decision was especially significant because sanitation workers, like other municipal employees, were excluded from the 1935 National Labor Relations Act, which accorded other workers the right to form unions. In addition, Tennessee state law prohibited municipal workers from striking. Commissioner Farris warned that the Loeb administration would brook no challenge to its policies and threatened to fire all the workers if they formed a union. Ultimately the sanitation workers' strike plans came to an end when the Teamsters Union precipitously dropped its support under pressure from the city. Nevertheless, the sanitation workers had succeeded in creating a context in which problems of racial justice, labor, and politics all coalesced.[21]

The effort to break down city and state intransigence on desegregation also gathered momentum. Local civil rights attorneys, with the assistance of Constance Baker Motley from the NAACP legal team in New York, won a court order from the Sixth Circuit Court of Appeals in the Memphis State case. As a result, eight African American students entered Memphis State in September 1959 after a five-year legal battle. The following month, as a result of complaints to the U.S. attorney general by the Binghampton Civic League, Greyhound Bus Lines agreed to remove the "white" and "colored" signs from its interstate waiting rooms. The Memphis NAACP also pursued the desegregation of grand juries, which remained all white, despite the inclusion of black names in the pool.[22]

Public pressure for desegregation intensified when the national auto show, an annual fund-raiser for St. Jude Hospital, opened at the Ellis Auditorium in early January 1960. Outraged at the exclusion of African Americans from the show for the first time, over 300 black Memphians convened at Penecostal Temple, January 15, cheering speakers who denounced the city's exclusion of blacks from this event at the auditorium, a public space. The group issued a formal resolution calling for the desegregation of "parks, schools, playgrounds, museums, libraries, airport and train restaurants, bus terminals, and any other cultural, educational, or recreational facilities." Participants established the Memphis and Shelby County Improvement Association (MSCIA), electing Benjamin Hooks as chairman. The group called for a boycott of Memphis auto dealers and held regular meetings about racial justice issues throughout the winter of 1960.[23]

Meanwhile, student protests against segregation elsewhere in the South added to mounting tensions in Memphis. Just after the New Year, students and ministers in Nashville, about 200 miles northeast of Memphis, launched a direct-action desegregation campaign that targeted restaurants in downtown department stores. Led by Rev. James Lawson of the Nashville Christian Leadership Council (an affiliate of the Southern Christian Leadership Council), the group of twelve included students from Fisk University, a visiting attorney from Ghana, and clergymen. A month later, on February 1, a student sit-in at a Woolworth's lunch counter in Greensboro, North Carolina, triggered a chain of similar actions in other cities, first in North Carolina and then across the South.

At the NAACP's Southeast Regional Conference, held in Memphis on February 18–21, participants in meetings of the Youth Committee, including delegations from Memphis, resolved to initiate sit-ins in every locale in the South where the NAACP had a branch. "The Negro youth have just about lost patience with their adults," declared regional organizer Ruby Hurley at a mass meeting of over 600 people at Metropolitan Baptist Church, adjacent to LeMoyne College, during the conference. Referring to the sit-ins, Hurley warned presciently that the youth would take over the movement if the adults did not show more leadership.[24]

The West Tennessee Sharecroppers' Movement

Black Memphians' understandings of freedom in this period emerged out of concrete urban struggles, but their experiences were not isolated from an immensely significant rural voting rights movement among sharecroppers and tenant farmers in southwest Tennessee's Fayette and Haywood counties. Memphis activists became important supporters of the movement, whether as legal advisers, donors of food and clothing, or coordinators of nationwide support. The rural voting rights movement also took on particular significance for Memphis because thousands of African Americans had migrated to the city from southwest Tennessee since the war and many still had families and friends there. This rural-urban relationship also rippled out beyond Memphis as northern civil rights activists in Chicago, Cincinnati, and elsewhere became avid supporters of the sharecroppers' movement, establishing a mode of thinking about the freedom movement that would influence its future.[25]

In Fayette County, the third poorest county in the United States, African Americans made up roughly three-quarters of the population of 28,500, with the vast majority working as sharecroppers or tenant farmers. In neighboring Haywood County, just to the north, African Americans comprised a little less than two-thirds of the population, with a somewhat larger proportion owning their own land. Outside of a handful of individuals, African Americans had been barred from registering in either county since the end of Reconstruction. Many residents recalled the lynching in 1940 of Elbert Williams, after he had tried to register voters. This memory had also been kept alive throughout the 1950s by the annual NAACP Tennessee State Conferences, where black disfranchisement and the "reign of terror" in west Tennessee were repeatedly cited as key problems.[26]

When residents of the two counties renewed voter registration efforts in 1958, their proximity to Memphis became crucial. For Minnie Jameson, WDIA's radio coverage about voter registration drives made her wonder, "with Negroes being the majority in Fayette County, why they never voted." News about attorney James F. Estes's campaign to register veterans prompted Mt. Zion Church in Fayette County to invite him as a guest speaker in 1958. With Estes's help, fourteen men from the church, twelve of them veterans, registered to vote and a group in Haywood County formed a voters' league. In November, however, threats of economic reprisals kept all but one registrant in Fayette County from voting, leading Estes to file complaints with the state election commission on their behalf.[27]

Encouraged by Estes's work, the family of Rev. Burton Dodson retained Estes's services in April 1959 to represent the minister in his murder trial. Dodson, a CME minister in his mid-seventies, had been a fugitive since 1940, when he fled a Ku Klux Klan mob that had surrounded his house. Arrested in East St. Louis, Illinois, where he had been living under a pseudonym, Dodson was charged with killing a deputy sheriff during the melee, despite evidence that the sheriff had been shot by a Klansman in crossfire. As Dodson's attorney, Estes became the first African American to appear in the Fayette County courthouse as counsel rather than as the accused. "Farmers in the area postponed Spring plowing to witness the drama," the *Tri-State Defender* reported. Crowded around the perimeter of the segregated courtroom, they observed Estes asking prospective white male jurors whether they were members of a white Citizens' Council, whether blacks should vote, and whether blacks were equal to whites. All but one assured Estes that they had no quarrel with blacks voting. The irony of such assurances did not escape black onlookers. Once the trial commenced, Estes interrogated a series of white witnesses, forcing them to reveal information that contradicted their own statements. Dodson was exonerated through this cross-examination but was convicted nevertheless of second-degree murder and sentenced to twenty years in prison, a term later commuted to ten years.[28]

The trial had an important impact on black people who attended. Fayette County farmer Square Mormon claimed that the trial served as "the first thing that really give me and lots more people an ideal." That ideal encompassed both people's own agency and the quest for freedom: "[T]he main thing [was] that people need to stand on their foot and as a man, that truth could be found and justice could be found somewhere." Mormon felt that Estes's courtroom role had helped people overcome their fear that "something would happen to them if they'd stand up." Despite Dodson's conviction, his trial motivated local African Americans to transform their earlier efforts to register voters into a full-scale voting rights movement.[29]

Mormon and others in Fayette County launched an all-out voter registration campaign after the trial, coordinating work among civic clubs and sponsoring mass rallies to encourage people to register. In spring 1959, hundreds of African Americans lined up at the courthouse on the one day of the month when registration was scheduled, with over 500 registering in April and May. When officials obstructed further registration, Estes filed complaints with the federal Civil Rights Commission. After those who had managed to register were barred from voting in the August primary, local residents chartered the Fayette County Civic and Welfare League and Estes filed suit against the local Democratic Party. In late January 1960, Estes and the four leaders of this new organization, including John McFerren and Harpman Jameson, drove to Washington, D.C., to participate in a Volunteer Civil Rights Commission. There, they joined African Americans from elsewhere in the South who, in an effort to win new civil rights legislation, testified about being blocked from voting. The group also spoke with John Doar at the Justice Department, who promised indictments in the 1959 suit against the local Democratic Party.[30]

Energized by the trip to Washington, the Fayette County Civic and Welfare League organized a campaign to register 1,000 more voters in early 1960, but they faced severe repression. Banks withheld loans to farmers for spring furnishings, local merchants refused to sell to anyone on their blacklist, and health clinics denied service to families of those who had registered. John McFerren, who hastily established a general store for blacklisted farmers, was boycotted by oil distributors, thereby cutting farmers off from fuel for farm machinery. Although the league won their suit against the local Democratic Party in federal court in April 1960, local officials continued to interfere with registration by temporarily closing the registrar's office, turning up the courthouse heat on sweltering days, and threatening potential registrants with the specter of "Hatchie Bottom" — a reference to the site where Elbert Williams was lynched for organizing a

A young woman in Fayette County, Tennessee,
with a voter registration card in hand, 1960.
(© Ernest C. Withers, courtesy of Panopticon Gallery)

registration drive. Planters also began evicting families. Over 1,200 African Americans managed to vote in the 1960 national elections; however, some 400 sharecropper and tenant farm families were forced off the land. In mid-December, eighty families moved into Freedom Village, a tent encampment on land owned by black farmer Shepard Towles.[31]

The Memphis NAACP revisited the role local activists had played with the RCNL a half-decade earlier. In July 1960 members delivered food and clothing to families who had been denied credit. The organization established a relief fund, served as a clearinghouse for material and financial support sent from around the country, and helped residents of Fayette County charter their own NAACP branch. In December 1960, with hun-

A "Tent City" family living on Shepard Towles's land in
Fayette County, Tennessee, in 1960, after having been evicted
from their home during the voter registration movement.
(© Ernest C. Withers, courtesy of Panopticon Gallery)

dreds of families facing homelessness and destitution, Estes, Lt. George
Lee, and other activists held a yuletide program featuring Mahalia Jackson
to raise money and lift the spirits of evicted families.[32]

These rural-urban bonds took on national parameters as public attention turned to Fayette and Haywood counties, even as the student sit-in
movement exploded across the South. In June 1960, the Southern Conference Educational Fund called upon major oil companies to prevent local
distributors from boycotting black farmers, and a month later, the NAACP
asked its branches to boycott oil companies whose dealers refused to de-

liver oil to McFerren and other black retailers and requested that they send aid to activists in the area. Dr. King and the Southern Christian Leadership Council (SCLC) made a financial contribution. And northern chapters of CORE made Fayette and Haywood counties a major focus between mid-1960 and mid-1961, in addition to picketing local branches of stores targeted by the student sit-ins, such as Woolworth's. CORE representative Richard Haley lived in Fayette County for several months, working as a liaison between local residents and their out-of-state supporters.[33]

The support work by CORE members Sterling Stuckey and James Foreman in Chicago illustrates how influential these North-South, urban-rural relations became to activists seeking to expand the freedom movement in 1960, well before most histories assume. The Emergency Relief Committee (ERC) begun by Stuckey and Foreman as a CORE subcommittee became an independent umbrella organization for Chicago church, community and youth groups, some formed specifically to support the Tennessee movement. In December 1960, the ERC organized a "trucklift" that brought food, clothing, medical supplies, and building materials to Freedom Village. The ERC also arranged exchange visits, with Chicago activists traveling to Tennessee and Fayette and Haywood county activists going to northern cities for public meetings and fund-raisers. Testimony by southwest Tennessee residents was recorded for "They Chose Freedom," a record album that generated relief funds and built solidarity.[34]

These new relationships between activists influenced participants' understandings of freedom. A brochure produced by Operation Freedom, a Cincinnati group similar to the ERC, declared that "asserting freedom" had taken on distinct meanings in different settings, whether it was the lunch counters in Montgomery, Little Rock, and North Carolina or Freedom Village in southwest Tennessee. Rather than being fixed to any one struggle, the freedom movement, according to this view, was larger than any single movement and had to be won in multiple contexts. The brochure quoted an evicted Fayette County tenant farmer insisting that, despite their suffering, local residents "won't run away" and referring to the loan he had received as a "freedom loan." Freedom thus also meant developing the conviction to stand one's ground in the face of repression. And, finally, it also conveyed the significance of participating in this unique urban-rural relationship.[35]

The unfolding drama in Fayette and Haywood counties accrued national and international significance, becoming a "litmus test for American democracy," as the black press put it. Commentators referred to Fayette County as "Little Africa," drawing parallels to the drama unfolding in the Congo, which won independence in July 1960 only to have its leader, Patrice Lumumba, assassinated in January 1961. While editorials blasted European and American arguments that Africans were not prepared for self-government, they also insisted that it was time for African Americans in southwest Tennessee to achieve full citizenship rights.[36]

The Student Sit-in Movement:
Freedom, Identity, and History

As this dramatic confrontation unfolded in west Tennessee, black college students in Memphis initiated a sit-in movement aimed at the immediate desegregation of all public facilities. Adult activists in the NAACP, civic clubs, and other organizations, frustrated themselves by years of deliberate evasion of the *Brown* mandate by white city officials, became their greatest champions. As spontaneous as the sit-ins seemed, they emerged from years of activism addressing an interrelated set of rural and urban racial problems. While the civic clubs, NAACP, and newer political and civil rights organizations such as the MSCIA had steadily demanded change from white city officials, the student sit-ins sought to destroy segregation — now.

The student sit-in movement marked both a continuity and a rupture with earlier efforts to achieve civil rights. Although many Memphis students had worked as youth with neighborhood civic clubs and the NAACP, participating in the new movement made many feel that they were making history, bringing about a new world that could not wait on the timetable of white city politicians. Their changed sense of self became central to their understandings of freedom. Although it is important to understand that the sit-in movement's demand of "Freedom Now" had deep roots in the community, political, and labor organizing that preceded it, to overemphasize the continuity of the movement with these earlier forms would obscure newer dimensions of activism and thought.[37]

College students in Memphis responded to the Greensboro sit-ins by discussing how to launch their own sit-in movement. On Friday, March 18, 1960, two female and five male students from Owen Junior College seized the initiative by traveling downtown and entering McLellan's variety store on Main Street. Owen, a historically black junior college, conceived in 1947 by the Tennessee Baptist Missionary and Educational Convention and named for Rev. Samuel A. Owen, a leading black Baptist minister in Memphis and founder of the school, first opened for classes in September 1954, just a few months after *Brown v. Board*. Well before Owen merged with LeMoyne to form LeMoyne-Owen College in 1968, students at the two schools collaborated on ending racial segregation in Memphis. The seven Owen students quietly took seats at the "whites only" lunch counter, fanning out to position themselves between white customers already seated there. Several squad cars of policemen rushed to the scene, and the store manager closed the store, after which the students departed without being arrested, although George Hardin, a photographer for the *Tri-State Defender*, was briefly detained.[38]

This action precipitated impassioned responses among other college students determined to take up the call, leading many of them to assume responsibilities that previously would have seemed impossible. Early Saturday morning, students from Owen and LeMoyne met to consider further action. As momentum grew, LeMoyne College president Hollis Price attempted to dissuade the students from mounting further protests, threatening any students who took illegal action with expulsion. However, according to Evander Ford, later president of the Student Movement Organization at LeMoyne, student Elmer Moore's response helped convince others to proceed. "'Yes, you're right, we understand, but we're going,'" Moore declared. "And he was one of the quiet guys around school," Ford added. "And when he said that, I think that made a lot of folks who had reservations decide that they would go ahead." Marion Barry (a future mayor of Washington, D.C.), originally from Memphis but currently attending Fisk and recently released from jail following a Nashville sit-in, also participated in these discussions. Ultimately, the students decided to proceed, with thirty-six young women and men from LeMoyne and Owen opting to sit in.[39]

Significantly, the LeMoyne and Owen students chose to first concentrate on desegregating the public library, unlike in other cities where initial attention went to lunch counters at Woolworth's and other five-and-dime stores. For Memphis youth, years of opposition to the city's use of tax revenues for public institutions that denied full access to African Americans had oriented them to thinking about racial injustice in overtly political terms. As college students, they were also painfully aware of the city's exclusion of African Americans from all public libraries other than the small "colored" branch on Vance and, due to a recent change, the reference room of the downtown Cossitt Library. Directly after this Saturday morning meeting, the students caught the bus to either the Cossitt or the main library. They entered at around noon, and quietly took seats at tables or approached the desk to request library materials. Within the hour, they and five editors and photographers from the *Tri-State Defender* and the *Memphis World* had been arrested.[40]

Although the action of Owen College students the preceding day had served as a catalyst, this Saturday event captured the imagination of black Memphians, as word of the sit-ins spread. Saturday afternoon, with the students in jail, the NAACP Executive Committee issued a statement indicating their support and called for a meeting at Mt. Olive Cathedral that evening. Despite the short notice, eighty local ministers, the parents of the arrested students, and students from LeMoyne and Owen attended the evening meeting.[41]

In their first responses to this new form of protest and the initiative taken by college students, participants at the meeting did not all agree about what to do next. NAACP leaders proposed a prayer march on city hall, but the motion was eventually tabled after some ministers argued that such a demonstration would bring "Commissioner Armour and all his gang down on us." Participants also tabled a motion to boycott the upcoming Shriner's Circus, a segregated event, after some cautioned that many community members had already purchased tickets. In contrast to these cautionary notes, a LeMoyne student at the meeting declared passionately that this first action would be followed by others.[42]

Despite these different perspectives, participants at the Mt. Olive Cathedral meeting united behind the students with a mixture of religious and political support. After the meeting, parents, students, ministers, and NAACP and civic club leaders drove to the city police station, where the students, represented by law partners Russell Sugarmon and A. W. Willis, were being arraigned. Supporters later filled the street outside the criminal court building, where the students and journalists were held until being released on bail. As the students descended the courthouse steps, some as late as 1:30 A.M. Sunday morning, they were greeted with cheers and choruses of "Onward Christian Soldiers." Evander Ford recalls feeling confident that the civic clubs, with which he had worked, would back them. He describes the spirit he encountered upon release from jail: "It just gathered momentum all through the night. And that morning, when we got out, there were people all around the area, all around the jailhouse, just singing hymns and giving us total support. . . . And from that moment on, from that day on, it was just lightning fire."[43]

This community enthusiasm snowballed, especially at church on Sunday, after ministers urged their members to attend the students' trials. On Monday morning, over 2,000 supporters gathered outside the city court—many hundreds having lined up well before 8:00 A.M. After being denied entrance, they moved to Mt. Olive Cathedral for a mass meeting, at which $3,000 was raised for a student defense fund. In court, meanwhile,

Judge Beverly Boushe repeatedly characterized the students as members of a "mob." Deeming the issue of racial discrimination irrelevant to the proceedings, he fined each student twenty-six dollars for disorderly conduct. The following morning, Russell Sugarmon announced that defense attorneys would file an appeal, and undeterred by the previous day's events, twenty-three students sat in at the Cossitt Library and the Brooks Memorial Art Gallery.[44]

These events spurred weekly mass meetings at churches, drawing hundreds, sometimes thousands of students and community supporters, and student meetings at LeMoyne and Owen. Russell Sugarmon, one of the attorneys defending the arrested students, described one of these early student meetings when he appeared at 1962 hearings of the U.S. Civil Rights Commission taking place in Memphis: "There were some several hundred students present, and I think that the big problem was not getting students to participate; the big problem was one of selecting those who would go there. There seemed to have been a religious fervor at that period."[45]

A similar ferment prevailed at the general mass meetings among older African Americans. "It was like being in a revival," recalls Johnnie Rodgers Turner, then a junior at LeMoyne and a participant in the movement. "You got so much support and you got thousands of people, whole lives and generations of injustices, and I guess they said it's too late for me. And here they see these young people have put their lives on the line." At a mass meeting of 2,000 held at Mt. Olive Cathedral the night after the trials — only twelve hours after the morning meeting — the students and the ten attorneys who had represented them received cheers and a standing ovation when they filed dramatically into the church. Participants approved a proposal by the Interdenominational Ministers' Alliance for a "Stay Away from Downtown Days" campaign, in which supporters would boycott downtown stores and theaters on Mondays and Thursdays. Contributions for a "freedom fund" to pay for the legal defense of students arrested in the initial and subsequent sit-ins poured in from individuals, civic clubs, unions, church groups, and other organizations. Members of a bridge club, for instance, informed the NAACP that they had voted to forego their annual dance and donate $100 to the defense fund instead.[46]

The sit-ins had a major impact on the Memphis NAACP. The branch had been steadily growing and expanding its scope before the sit-ins; now, however, the organization grew exponentially. Two weeks after the sit-ins began, NAACP membership chairwoman Maxine Smith reported that she had received 2,600 new memberships in this short period. By July, mem-

NAACP attorneys and city officials at the sit-in demonstrators' arraignment. From left: Ben Jones, James F. Estes, A. W. Willis, Russell Sugarmon, Benjamin Hooks, Odell Horton, Patrolman Martin, Lt. Tim McCarver, Detective Tony Lowell, and Art Shay, deputy city attorney.

(© Ernest C. Withers, courtesy of Panopticon Gallery)

bership had swelled to nearly 6,000, making the Memphis branch the largest in the South. Attorneys associated with the NAACP defended students in court; members of the labor committee, headed by International Harvester activist George Holloway, worked to secure employment and financial assistance for students fired from their jobs; and the branch coordinated daily picketing.[47]

Students initiated waves of protests throughout the spring, shifting their focus to downtown lunch counters in mid-May. On Main Street, they experienced far more white resistance than they had at the libraries, art museum, and other public institutions. At the first downtown sit-in, for example, policemen stood by without intervening as four white men dragged two male students out of Woolworth's and others taunted two young women still at the lunch counter. At a sit-in at Walgreen's, a crowd of 200 cheered when students were arrested.[48]

Despite white resistance, high school students plunged into the movement when their summer recess began. These teenagers helped transform the sit-in into a daily activity by sitting in at Main Street lunch counters and elsewhere throughout the summer. High school student Elaine Lee Turner, for example, participated every day with four of her sisters, including the eldest, Ernestine Lee, a student leader at LeMoyne. "We would get up in the morning and get dressed as though we were going to school," Turner remembers. "And go down to the NAACP office where we congregated. And then we would go downtown and disburse to our assigned locations and sit in at whatever was segregated."[49]

In May, adult NAACP leaders, starting with three women, Maxine Smith, head of the Membership Committee, Ann Willis, head of the Entertainment Committee, and Eloise Flowers, secretary of the Labor and Industry Committee, began picketing on Main Street. And in August, several ministers and business leaders began riding city buses seated up front and picketing on Main Street. The protests, punctuated by mass meetings, boycotts, and marches, continued through the rest of 1960 and most of 1961, until downtown businesses began to desegregate.[50]

College and high school student protesters brought a spirit of urgency to the movement that transformed previous approaches to civil rights. Older activists who had come of age during and after the Second World War had rejected their predecessors' avoidance of conflict with the Crump machine. Led by talented, energetic young attorneys and other professionals, the NAACP of the late 1950s focused largely on legal strategies. Since the NAACP had a policy of nonpartisanship, these individuals created separate organizations to pursue political strategies. These NAACP leaders greeted the sit-ins enthusiastically, immediately jumping on board to help them succeed.[51] Nevertheless, they continued to pursue negotiations, assenting to a two-week cooling-off period in the hope of wringing concessions from the city commission. At least one member of the executive board proposed informing the students that "one time at the Library was sufficient for a suit, and another visit is not necessary." The students, for their part, agreed to suspend their sit-ins, but they immediately resumed them in early April, when the commissioners rejected their demands. "When it became obvious that the City Commission intended to do nothing at all about ending segregation in tax-supported facilities, we felt we were completely justified in resuming our protests," one student commented at the time. "We are committed to a goal. Jail will certainly not stop us from continuing the fight." Having discarded an approach that counted upon change coming from white officials and judges, the students chose to rely on their own direct actions.[52]

William Edwin Jones and his daughter Renee Andrewnetta
during a protest march on Main Street, August 1961.
(© *Ernest C. Withers, courtesy of Panopticon Gallery*)

These youth had come of age since the *Brown* decision and the Emmett
Till lynching and saw themselves, not city officials or the courts, as central
actors in effecting racial justice. When city officials agreed to integrate the
library and the Memphis Street Railway company finally announced that
black bus riders could sit where they chose, students did not end protests
but shifted to other targets, believing that only constant pressure would
win further change. In recalling her participation in the movement, Elaine
Lee Turner declared, "There was no way we would just stop and say that
maybe they're going to change everything else. . . . Just because they desegregated the buses, then they're going to desegregate everything else?

No." Turner recalls that this stance sometimes created friction with older NAACP activists, even though students appreciated and counted on their involvement. "We thought that we needed to put more force into things, and they were older," she commented. "We were young and energetic and ready to be involved in protesting everything that we thought needed to be protested. And of course they were doing most of the negotiations. [S]ometimes we might not have agreed . . . about times to stop the protests and talk." In contrast to NAACP branches in other cities, where the organization remained wedded to legal strategies or had been crippled by the backlash against it, it played a central role in the Memphis movement. However, at times relations between the students and their elders became strained. In December 1960, NAACP activist Dr. Vasco Smith reported to the NAACP Executive Board that some students had been "uncooperative and some times even disrespectful to their elders" and that Rev. James Nabrit would be visiting the campuses. At a meeting of the Student Movement Organization at LeMoyne in December, where students, including Olly Neal, Ernestine Lee, Grace Austin, and Ernest Withers Jr., discussed the movement, Reverend Nabrit urged the group to coordinate their activities with the citywide Freedom Committee to avoid problems such as more people than necessary turning out to a demonstration, as was the case at a recent rally.[53]

During the first year of the sit-in movement, the MCCR, concerned primarily with minimizing conflict, convinced city officials to desegregate the zoo, the library, and the city buses. Not until mid-1961, however, did members decide to help negotiate desegregation agreements with merchants on Main Street, and only in early 1962 did this desegregation take place. When restaurants and movie theaters did desegregate, it happened with a minimum of publicity, by arrangement with the editors of the *Commercial Appeal* and the *Press-Scimitar*, thus obscuring the enormous impact of the sit-in movement. In 1963, after reading Dr. King's "Letter from a Birmingham Jail," MCCR leader Lucius Burch sent copies to his colleagues along with a cover letter calling for a more active approach to civil rights. Burch, however, remained in the minority. In 1967, NAACP activist Dr. Vasco Smith submitted his resignation, accusing the MCCR of functioning "as a fire department" and arguing that unlike the MCCR, he was "more proficient at building fires than . . . at putting them out."[54]

Students in the sit-in movement developed a new sensibility about their individual and collective relations to ongoing history. In this dialectic of experience and thought, protesters found that underlying feelings of fear, intimidation, and powerlessness receded. Ernestine Hill Carpenter, an early sit-in participant, recalls her decision to keep protesting even after being painfully struck on the leg by a policeman's baton and despite her parents' fears for her safety. Mass meetings at which thousands cheered the students bolstered her determination. At the same time, the belief that their actions made a difference, that the "white powers [were] about to crumble," made Carpenter feel that "there was no way to compare fear with the need for this to happen." Evander Ford, who was prevented from graduating from LeMoyne because of his leading role in the movement, believed that momentum built despite the threat of reprisals because "there was a feeling that you had to be a part of this history-making event. We were making history and they knew that something had to be done." African Americans finally had a chance to influence the direction of American society, whereas previously they had lacked the power to do so.[55]

Johnnie Rodgers Turner emphasizes that the movement represented "a moment whose time had come," transforming years of frustration and isolated resistance into organized mass protest. "There was a revolution going on and we wanted to be a part of that," she declares. In her historical memories of the "psychological scars" of Jim Crow, riding the bus features prominently. Because of segregation, youth encountered whites neither at school nor at home but on the bus. Many associated public transportation with humiliating experiences, as well as individual acts of resistance. Even spontaneous moments in which youth subversively defied drivers' orders left few illusions that they had altered the structures of racial power. When the sit-in movement erupted, Johnnie Rodgers Turner recalls, "I was so glad . . . I didn't know what to do! It was like [with] all this pent-up frustration and anger, I now had a chance." This sense that her activism might make a difference overcame the daunting prospect of an arrest record — no small decision for a scholarship student who was the first in her large, financially strapped family to attend college.[56]

Young black participants in the protest movement experienced a heightened awareness of the spatial contours of the city. Elaine Lee Turner describes what it meant to turn the corner from Beale Street onto Main on her way to sit in at segregated lunch counters. "Beale Street was a street where black people congregated, and you could go in any building, any business, and you were treated like a first-class citizen," she explains. "You were at home on Beale Street. . . . And when you turned that corner, going on Main Street, then you had just a whole different atmosphere. . . . When you went to Main Street, you had to be on guard." Joan Lee Nelson, Elaine's younger sister, recalls being separated from her sisters during her first sit-in and joining a group that entered the Downtowner Motor Inn on Union

Street across from the famous Peabody Hotel. In her recollection, African Americans never went onto Union unless they worked there. The Lee sisters and others turned these corners on a daily basis during the summer of 1960. By confronting their sense of intimidation, they sought to transform this segregated terrain of downtown into "home."[57]

In the process of fighting for integration, students and other participants in the freedom movement also developed a politicized understanding of pride that differed sharply from the meaning of pride as an attitude of self-respect within a Jim Crow world.[58] Johnnie Rodgers Turner's account of her changed sense of pride suggests that she saw herself through new eyes after discovering what the freedom movement had meant to her mother. "[T]he proudest day in my memory . . . was the day that it was declared that black people could sit on the bus," she asserted. "My mother worked out in east Memphis and I remember . . . [she] said that morning, . . . 'I'm going to cut this article out of the paper and today, when I go to work, I'm going to ride on the front of the bus.' That's my mother's only statement about the civil rights movement. Now you tell me that's not a powerful statement," she exclaimed. "All her hopes, all her dreams and all her aspirations were tied up in me. . . . That made everything, the chances that I had taken, even going against her wishes, it made me know that I had made the right decision."[59] This politicized sense of self-respect made "freedom" into not just a goal of altering the segregated, material realities of Memphis but a changed perception of oneself, which also altered the relations of these young people to older family members.

Cultural Dilemmas: Religion, Radio, and Soul

As these college and high school students became deeply involved with the sit-in movement, they also questioned Jim Crow in cultural realms of their everyday lives, extending beyond the problem of segregated public facilities. Their new insights illuminated what it might mean to redefine and reshape secular and religious culture in a post–Jim Crow world. During the summer of 1960, students and many older activists began challenging segregated cultural institutions that had long served as important sources of race pride. These efforts coincided with new developments in popular music and radio and the burgeoning "youth market," especially with the start of Stax Records, located a few blocks from LeMoyne. Stax's famous "Memphis sound" emanated from recording sessions that combined young black and white musicians. Concomitantly, a group of their peers at LeMoyne initiated what became known as "kneel-ins," aimed at transforming southern white churches into integrated sites of religious worship. While the "soul" sounds coming from radios and record players seemed to hold out the promise of a new age, the church protests raised troubling, complex issues about faith and law in a still racially bifurcated society—about whether white and black "souls" could be "saved" together.

Two months after the sit-ins began, the 24th Annual Cotton Makers' Jubilee opened in Memphis, capturing the attention of student protesters, in addition to the many thousands of black and white Memphians who regularly attended the event. Founded by Dr. R. Q. and Mrs. Ethel Venson, the jubilee had since 1936 offered black Memphians an alternative to the annual Cotton Carnival, a gala of parties, parades, and cotton industry events that featured the crowning of a white carnival king and queen. White business leaders and city officials had begun the carnival in 1931 at the height of the Depression, organizing it around mythic historical reenactments of plantation life in order to spur interest in the cotton economy. African Americans' participation was limited to the few who played the slaves, mules, and horses—who literally pulled the floats in the parade. The Cotton Makers' Jubilee, on the other hand, showcased local talent, especially among youth, by featuring the city's renowned black high school marching bands. The jubilee also included a dance festival on Beale Street, at which a new dance was introduced annually and performed until the wee hours of the night. The event drew thousands each year, many of them white.[60]

In 1960, the jubilee became the target of protests by college students and by the NAACP, for whom this segregated celebration of southern cotton culture had become intolerable. Their protests brought them into direct conflict with event promoters, including Nat D. Williams, who typically emceed the jubilee. Students picketed daily with signs reading "What has King Cotton Done for the Negro?" and "Why Spend Your Money at a Segregated Second-Rate Carnival?" and a student spokesman blasted the affair for paying "tribute to the system that undergirded the entire slavery period." In truth, he argued, it was "another segregated institution just like the library, zoo and other facilities here and just like lunch counters." Thousands of black Memphians attended anyway, prompting the *Tri-State Defender* to demand to know why the students were "darlings" when they began the sit-ins but were mere "goats" when they asked for unity in opposing the jubilee. The festival went on as usual, but the following month organizers of the Tri-State Fair, the black counterpart of the Mid-South Fair, announced that they would cancel the event. Controversy over the Cotton Makers' Jubilee, however, persisted into 1961, when the NAACP protested the school board's practice of granting black pupils a holiday to attend the event. Newly appointed executive secretary Maxine Smith re-leased a statement accusing African American sponsors of the jubilee of being "so inculcated with the southern white man's doctrine of segrega-tion and discrimination, that they are willing to go against the tidal wave of Freedom that is sweeping over the entire nation in order to maintain their little island of decaying segregation."[61]

In an especially significant turnaround, freedom movement partici-pants also extended their campaign against segregation to WDIA's Star-light Revue, the summer counterpart to its renowned Goodwill Revue in December. Both events raised money to assist needy African American children and had become integral to WDIA's image as the radio station of the black community, despite its white ownership by the Sonderling chain. The revues brought some of the hottest black entertainers in the country to Memphis, many paid for by record producers, who perceived the promotional value in having them participate. Divided into two separate, back-to-back gospel and popular music shows, the 1960 Starlight Revue featured such revered gospel groups as the Caravans, the Gospelaires, and the Dixie Nightingales; and such popular stars as R & B balladeer Brook Benton, blues singer Wynonie Harris, and the vocal group the Coasters. Just as importantly, the 1960 event for the first time opened its doors to whites, who were seated in a separate section of Crump Stadium.[62]

Given the concurrence of the Starlight Revue and ongoing protests against segregation, controversy erupted over how to define black cultural pride in this changing context. Was WDIA, by holding a segregated event that nevertheless presented such a tremendous line-up of black perform-ers, advancing community pride or collective humiliation? Nat D. Wil-liams, in his weekly "Dark Shadows" column in the *Tri-State Defender*, came down on one side of this question, hailing the admission of whites for the first time as a major step forward. He also pointed to the long list of contributions the station had made to black Memphians, especially children, through its charity events. The NAACP, speaking on behalf of the Memphis branch, the LeMoyne College branch, and the Memphis NAACP Youth Council, came down on the other side, arguing that staging a seg-regated show at a time when students across the South were being jailed for demanding desegregation represented a lack of respect for "the Ne-gro's drive for freedom." "WDIA's presentation of this racially segregated show," the statement asserted, "becomes more humiliating to the Negro in his march toward first-class citizenship when one realizes the position to which WDIA has risen in the Negro's advertising market." And yet, even for those who opposed WDIA management's and Nat D. Williams's stance, the issue was not clear-cut, since most of them had strong allegiances to the station and its pioneering DJs.[63]

Many thousands of black Memphians voted with their feet on July 1, resulting in a record-breaking crowd of 11,000 at the Starlight Revue, including white fans. As they poured into the stadium, they brushed past student pickets carrying signs with messages such as "WDIA — 50,000 Watts of Segregation." As the summer wore on and sit-ins continued, criticism of such events intensified, however. At a meeting in August, NAACP members, representatives of the Interdenominational Ministers' Alliance and others expressed fiery opposition to WDIA's announcement that it would sponsor a Family Fair to replace the Tri-State Fair canceled earlier in the year. WDIA quickly canceled its plans. Moreover, shortly before the December Goodwill Revue, WDIA station manager David James announced that for the first time, it would be held on a nonsegregated basis, with "mixed seating" throughout Ellis Auditorium. He also listed an impressive line-up of performers for the event, including, for the R & B show, Little Junior Parker, Bobby Bland, Bo Diddley, the Five Royales, and Carla Thomas, Memphis's newest teenage star.[64]

In addition to marking a turning point in the struggle against segregation, David James's announcement hinted at groundbreaking changes taking place in Memphis music itself, which was blurring racial and cultural boundaries that supposedly distinguished black from white music and sacred from secular. Although most performers at the Goodwill Revue had national reputations, the inclusion of eighteen-year-old Carla Thomas on the Goodwill Revue roster acknowledged the impact teenagers were having on Memphis music. Carla Thomas, daughter of WDIA DJ and entertainer Rufus Thomas and NAACP secretary Lorene Thomas, graduated from Hamilton High School in May 1960. She had also been a member of the Teen-Town Singers, led by WDIA radio personality and former high school teacher A. C. Williams, which brought together talented students from all of Memphis's black high schools. The group performed weekly on WDIA, with a repertoire that ranged from gospel to rhythm and blues, and from classical to jazz, in a departure from programs that never crossed the line separating sacred from secular music. Carla Thomas's appearance at the integrated 1960 Goodwill Revue marked her debut solo performance. She had recorded "Cause I Love You," a duet with Rufus Thomas in August 1960, and then "Gee Whiz," her first hit on her own. The success of these singles, recorded by Stax (then Satellite), influenced the direction Stax's white owners, brother and sister Jim Stewart and Estelle Axton, would take the studio. Stax, one of many independent recording studios launched in the South in this period (Hi Records was around the corner), began with country music but would soon be recording such black artists as Otis Redding, Sam and Dave, Eddie Floyd, and Booker T. and the MGs, and later the Staple Singers, the Bar-Kays, and Isaac Hayes, another graduate of the Teen-Town Singers. Stax became identified with the "Memphis sound," known for impassioned expressiveness, rooted in gospel and R & B. Black performers became the stars, yet the sound resulted from joint efforts by black and white songwriters and musicians.[65]

Stax's close ties to the surrounding community and to black and white Memphis teenagers stamped it with a unique character. Located in south Memphis, in a neighborhood rapidly changing from a majority white to solidly black area, Stax was not far from the sites of racial violence over housing that took place in the early 1950s. Situated at the corner of College and McLemore in the old Capitol Theater building, which had fallen into disuse as neighborhood movie theaters closed down in the 1950s, Stax was a few blocks from LeMoyne and midway between Booker T. Washington and Hamilton high schools. Black teenagers from the neighborhood, such as Booker T. Jones (future leader of Booker T. and the MGs), and David Porter (soon a principal Stax writer, along with Isaac Hayes and Steve Cropper), began hanging out at the record store at the studio. Simultaneously, a group of recent white graduates of Messick High School, such as Donald "Duck" Dunn and Steve Cropper, also began spending time at the studio. The Messick graduates originally came to Stax as members of a band reorganized as the Mar-Keys, that included co-owner Estelle Axton's son Packy. Stax's recording sessions and song writing soon reflected an unprecedented interchange among young blacks and whites, as peers. By 1962, the interracial band Booker T. and the MGs had become a staple of Stax recording sessions.[66]

Black radio became integral to the musical and racial dynamics that characterized Stax. Despite Memphis's racial segregation, the African American and white youth who spent time working or flipping through records at Stax had already been listening to much of the same music. In part, they had been exposed to the same black musicians, who played to both white and black audiences, at segregated clubs and dances, albeit with different inflections.[67] Black and white teens also tuned in to the same radio stations, including black-oriented WDIA and WLOK, or to Dewey Phillips's renowned "Red, Hot and Blue" show on WHBQ.

WLOK, in particular, developed a special relationship to black Memphis youth, on the one hand, and to Stax, on the other. Members of the generation sitting in at downtown lunch counters associated WDIA with their parents' generation, and they devoted much of their own listening time to WLOK. Purchased in 1956 by the OK Group, which owned several black-oriented stations in the South, WLOK had originated as WCBR, an independent black-oriented station begun in 1954 on Beale Street. WLOK eventually hired such talented black radio personalities as Dick "Cane" Cole, Joan E. W. Golden, Al Bell, Bill Terrill, Bill Adkins, and Melvin Jones. A typical part of the unique relationship that developed between black-oriented radio, independent record companies, and youth listeners was someone from Stax rushing over to WLOK with a just-recorded test in hand to see how WLOK's young audiences would react to it.[68]

Conversely, WLOK DJ (and later Stax executive) Al Bell spent hours at the Stax record store checking out what latest releases were most popular among the teens there, and he also helped "break" new recordings by playing them repeatedly on his show. Bell, who had started on KOKY in Little Rock while in high school — entertaining black and white teens even as the 1957 schools crisis unfolded — and worked with Dr. King and the SCLC before coming to WLOK, became a role model in Memphis. He began his radio career in Memphis by refusing to broadcast under the OK Group's trademark name "Hunky Dory," insisting he "was Al Bell." Likewise, Joan E. W. Golden refused to become "Dizzy Lizzy," instead naming herself the "Golden Girl." WLOK's radio personalities, who appeared regularly at dances, community events, and civil rights marches, became heroes to black youth.[69]

Neither Stax nor WLOK brought about racial justice in Memphis. Indeed, WLOK, after relocating from Beale Street to Second Street at Talbot in the late 1950s, placed its white management and sales personnel in one half of the building and its black DJs in the other, with each half having its own entrance. And in 1968, the NAACP picketed WLOK for its racist hiring practices, which excluded blacks from management positions. Outside Stax and WLOK, struggles over desegregation, police brutality, and black political power persisted. Nevertheless, the early efforts of Stax and WLOK personnel to reach out to black and white youth held out possibilities for a post–Jim Crow popular culture that nourished black pride in a context based on mutual respect.[70]

Meanwhile, committed student participants in the freedom movement who were also jazz enthusiasts broke through other barriers. A jazz concert with the Larry Muhoberac and Onzie Horne orchestras, organized by WREC announcer Fred Cook and sponsored by the student council at LeMoyne College, became the first public jazz event in the city to include black and white groups on the same stage. This concert took place only after the white musicians union conceded to pressure from Fred Cook to allow its members to participate. The LeMoyne *Magician* (edited by many of the same student activists who participated in the freedom movement) also proudly announced that Muhoberac would be playing modern jazz, rather than the older standards.[71]

Parallel efforts to achieve an integrated, egalitarian religious culture, however, had quite different results. Participating in the freedom movement led many students to confront churches that excluded African Americans. In general, students' understandings of themselves as historical actors in a struggle for liberation had been influenced by their upbringing in black churches. Even for activists who had ceased regular church attendance, the movement's religious symbolism encouraged them to see themselves as participants in politicized, biblical narratives of deliverance and salvation. Throngs of supporters, for example, greeted the LeMoyne and Owen students being released from jail on March 19 with rousing choruses of "Onward Christian Soldiers," as students inside sang spirituals such as "Swing Low, Sweet Chariot," imbuing these hymns with fresh political meanings. Two nights later, the mass meeting at Mt. Olive Cathedral opened with a reading of First Corinthians, chapter 13, followed by the proposal of the "Stay Away From Downtown" campaign. This biblical emphasis on charity, rather than individual worldly pleasure, also took on new significance.[72]

Historically, many black southerners had perceived white churches as promoters of racial injustice in the name of Christ. Dr. Martin Luther King Jr., for his part, frequently observed that 11:00 A.M. Sunday was the most segregated hour in America. In August 1960, college and high school student protesters began to act on these critiques by holding "kneel-ins" at churches of various denominations, including Immaculate Conception, St. Peter's, Bellevue Baptist, Idlewild Presbyterian, and First Assembly of God. Apart from the Christian Science First Church, each one turned the students away or had them arrested, and students reported to the NAACP that members at Bellevue Baptist used profanity against them.[73]

This conflict over segregation and religion culminated on August 30, 1960, when fourteen black college and high school students attended a religious youth rally in a public park, sponsored by the all-white Assembly of God Church. Advertised as a public event, with no mention of race, and held at the band shell in Overton Park (where six years earlier Elvis Presley had debuted after his first record release with Sun Studio), the rally presented an opportunity to challenge segregation of public facilities and exclusionary religious practices. Evander Ford, who selected the event as a focus, recalled that the white Assembly of God and the black Church of God in Christ, to which his grandparents belonged, had common historic roots in a multiracial religious revival in the early twentieth century.[74]

The black students' participation in the revival sparked strong reactions. When they arrived at the revival, ushers informed them that they would have to sit in the back. They instead mingled with the crowd, sitting singly or in pairs. As they sat down, several white youth angrily got up and the revival leader, Reverend Scruggs, called the police. The students took part in the proceedings, even making contributions to the collection plate, before being arrested.[75] Charged with disorderly conduct, loitering, and violating a city ordinance, the students were also accused of disturbing a religious assembly in violation of a Tennessee statute that mirrored the First Amendment's guarantee of freedom of religion — a felony. During the arraignments, Judge Beverly Boushe characterized the sit-in as "a new low in political chicanery."[76]

In Boushe's courtroom, filled with freedom movement activists, attorneys for the prosecution and defense battled over competing constitutional claims, pitting First Amendment rights of freedom of religious assembly (as expressed in the Tennessee Constitution) against Fourteenth Amendment guarantees of equal protection. Yet neither side kept religion and rights in separate compartments, instead making religion central to arguments about secular law. The two sides, however, ascribed strikingly different meanings to Christianity and constitutional rights.[77]

While the pro-segregation attorneys referred only generally to religion, the defense referred specifically to scripture to justify an antisegregation interpretation of constitutional rights. The prosecutors and Judge Boushe insisted that religious freedom was protected by the Bill of Rights and sanctioned directly by God. As one attorney argued, the Ambassadors for Christ from the Assembly of God churches had "not only a Constitutionally given right" but "a God given right . . . [to] conduct religious services without interference or disturbance from anyone." Such statements cast the students as essentially immoral. The prosecuting attorneys also presented the students' actions as a danger to America. "[I]f we do not have religious freedom we fall and we become an Iron Curtain country because we become a Godless state," one of the attorneys argued, "and this great country of ours goes down the drain." It was the jury's responsibility, as Christians and Americans, to see justice served. Such arguments made no reference to race but mobilized highly charged religious and political language on behalf of white supremacy.[78]

In contrast, Benjamin Hooks, both a minister and an attorney, articulated a religious logic central to black Protestantism. He criticized the revival for promoting a "salvation of souls" that "exclud[ed] certain persons." Hooks asked the jury to examine their religious convictions before judging the students: "[I]f you believe in a Supreme Being, you will have to wrestle with your conscious [*sic*] as you come to a conclusion in this case." He recounted the story of the Good Samaritan, interpreting the commandment to "Love . . . thy neighbor as thyself" as proof of the righteousness of racial justice. Hooks argued that universal fellowship was "the supreme test of our Christianity and our Government."[79]

Hooks's message would no doubt have resonated with the freedom movement activists in the courtroom. His appeal to religious belief as a basis for racial justice and democracy reinforced linkages between race, rights, and religion that had originally motivated the students to challenge segregation in church. Johnnie Rodgers Turner, a participant, felt that the "Youth for Christ" seemed to care little for saving their souls. Ernestine Hill (Carpenter), also a participant, contrasted white politicians' campaign visits to black churches to prosecutors' aphorisms about religious freedom. Most importantly, the use of religious and political language to defend segregated churches violated core worldviews about equality and justice shared by these student activists.[80]

In the end, Hooks's arguments failed to win over any members of the all-white, male jury, who delivered felony convictions—the only ones of the Memphis freedom movement—to all the defendants. These felony convictions were never reversed despite a series of appeals, although the governor commuted their sentences to time served in 1965. Having approached the sit-in as another test of the Fourteenth Amendment's equal protection mandate, the students and their attorneys were forced to confront disturbing appeals to religion and morality.

Neither monolithic nor static, freedom took on multilayered, historical meanings in Memphis at the end of the 1950s and beginning of the 1960s. In 1959, speakers at the Freedom Rally for the Volunteer Ticket had staked freedom to "burying Uncle Toms"—that is, to rejecting political dependence on white elites and instead emphasizing a subjectivity based on independent black activism. Two weeks later, African American voters were forced to confront the stark limitations of their own agency in the urban South. During the sit-ins that began in 1960, college and high school students sought to confront these limitations.

As young black Memphians poured their energies into achieving desegregation, they acted within a multifaceted context that encompassed protests against police brutality, labor organizing among Memphis's poorest workers, and a struggle for political voice. Beyond the bounds of the city, the movement of sharecroppers and tenant farmers for political rights in Fayette and Haywood counties and contemporaneous struggles for liberation from colonialism in Africa also influenced black political thought in Memphis.

At the same time, freedom also denoted a new sense of agency, evident even in the poetry that began appearing in the *Magician* in this period. "In History there are places for all men to stand, / Hark! Stand Back! Make way for the Black Man," concluded a poem titled "The New Negro," penned in 1961 by student Thurmond Lee Snyder.[81] Here, claiming black manhood and making history became fused into one, as the poem challenged a concept of history that excluded black men. In the early 1960s, young activists also explicitly challenged those prominent African Americans whom they perceived as wed to the idea that power and pride could be achieved within the limits of Jim Crow culture. By protesting the Cotton Makers' Jubilee, for example, students challenged the organizers, critiquing them for being reluctant to let go of a political and cultural economy based on the cotton economy and black subjection. In contrast, they embraced new venues for cultural expression that they perceived as committed to a post–Jim Crow culture—whether at Stax, on WLOK, or in modern jazz. In doing so, they viewed themselves as members of a new, freedom-oriented generation.

Yet the predominance of desegregation as a goal in 1960 could also blur these larger ramifications of the movement, making "freedom" seem like the equivalent of the Fourteenth Amendment's provision for equal protection. That the movement had deeper implications became more apparent as students and other activists turned their attention to realms of everyday life. Ironically, freedom movement activists faced further challenges once many of their initial demands for desegregation were finally won. Struggles rooted in the postwar urban experience, such as ending police brutality and winning economic rights, would again become priorities in the aftermath of Congress's passage of the 1964 Civil Rights Act.

Battling the Plantation Mentality

8 From the Civil Rights Act to the Sanitation Strike

Eight and a half years after a spirited rally of 5,000 African American voters in 1959 prompted Dr. Martin Luther King Jr. to spontaneously predict that "Something is going to happen," King once again stood before a huge crowd of Memphians. This time, on March 18, 1968, 15,000 people crammed into the same cavernous Mason Temple to hear King and demonstrate their support for striking city sanitation workers. A few weeks prior to King's speech, reactions to Memphis policemen's use of mace against participants in a march by sanitation workers and supporters, including black clergymen, had transformed what had begun as a labor struggle for union recognition into a mass movement for economic justice, racial equality, and respect. King's appearance at Mason Temple publicly marked this crucial coalescence of labor, politics, and the black freedom movement.[1]

King had interrupted his planning meetings for the upcoming nationwide Poor People's Campaign to fly to Memphis to support the strike. Inspired by the enthusiastic crowd that rocked Mason Temple, which, to King, seemed to crystallize the impassioned spirit of the earlier southern black freedom movement and to anticipate the struggle for economic justice addressed by the Poor People's Campaign, King departed from his planned speech. To the surprise of his colleagues in the SCLC, he proposed a "general work stoppage in the city of Memphis" and promised to return to lead a march. "If you let that day come, not a Negro in this city will go to any job downtown," he declared. "And no Negro in domestic service will go to anybody's house, anybody's kitchen. And black students will not go to anybody's school, and black teachers, and they will hear you then. The city of Memphis will not be able to function that day."[2]

King's call for a general strike of black workers, issued two weeks before his tragic assassination at the Lorraine Motel during a return visit to Memphis, bore witness to the fact that four years *after* President Lyndon Johnson signed the 1964 Civil Rights Act into law, working-class African Americans in the South perceived genuine freedom as an unfulfilled promise. Black activism had broadened, not abated. The sanitation strike, although it has often been portrayed as erupting out of the blue in an otherwise placid city, represented the most visible and symbolically resonant labor struggle amidst a groundswell of activism among working-class black Memphians. The audience King addressed on March 18 included workers in occupations ranging from furniture manufacturing to television assembly, and welfare recipients who identified with the fact that the sanitation workers' low wages qualified them for food stamps.[3]

The language of freedom that emerged in this post-1964 milieu had roots deep in Memphis's past while also articulating fresh understandings. In this sense, the sanitation workers' slogan, "I *Am* a Man," which suddenly appeared in bold capital letters on hundreds of placards borne by strikers during a mass march midway through the 1968 movement, became a touchstone for myriad struggles for racial equality, economic justice, and dignity that emerged in the late 1960s. Its claim to manhood and freedom, as an assault on what many had begun to refer to as a "plantation mentality," resonated with thousands more urban working-class African Americans than just the standard-bearers themselves. Working-class African Americans who identified with the freedom movement desired a break from the plantation regime they associated with an earlier time and place but still saw reflected in everyday racial practices in the city. Grounded in memory, migration, and critical thought, their attack on the "plantation mentality" denounced not only whites who acted like plantation bosses but also blacks who appeared fearful of breaking free of their white supervisors. With the words "I *Am* a Man" the strikers and their supporters rejected both kinds of "plantation mentality" and claimed a vigorous political agency that made "manhood" central to being *free*. This gendered language of freedom referred to both internal problems of self-identity and external relations of power.

While "I *Am* a Man" resonated with Black Power's muscular rhetoric of masculinity, such language took on distinct meanings in the context of the sanitation strike and other working-class movements of this period. Most notably, not only men but also black working-class women identified with the slogan as a claim to freedom. For those involved with their own labor struggles in laundries and manufacturing plants, the slogan protested supervisors' paternalism and their desire to "drive you, that you hadn't worked enough," as one laundry worker put it in an 1995 interview.[4] Women's interpretations of "I *Am* a Man" however, also indicated a dimension of "freedom" involving understandings of womanhood and the household. In challenging paternalism, they embraced activism for racial and economic justice. Rather than aspiring to an ideal of womanhood in which they relinquished their roles of activist and wage-earner to male heads of household, they presented themselves as equals in both roles.

The sanitation strike, in fact, drew together several strands of organizing, protest, and thought, reflecting an accumulation of black working-class Memphians' concerns in the postwar period, ranging from discriminatory labor practices to police brutality, and from civil rights to political power. These deeply rooted struggles surfaced, however, in an altered context that encompassed the War on Poverty, economic restructuring, and the Vietnam War. They intersected with the rise of Black Power and with more explicitly political soul music that, through the venue of black radio, reached broad listening audiences. Memphis, moreover, had become a crossroads for the civil rights movement, with activists traveling into and out of the city enroute to rural movement areas in the Deep South, thus linking city residents to many more struggles than their own.

Across the South, in the period following the passage of the 1964 Civil Rights Act and 1965 Voting Rights Act, civil rights activists sought to reorient themselves. The riot in the Watts section of Los Angeles in summer 1965 influenced this redirection of the movement. In all the major civil rights organizations, participants focused far more attention on problems of poverty, housing, unemployment, police brutality, and other problems of racial injustice than they had in the past. In Memphis, the accomplishments of the sit-in movement and accompanying lawsuits did not resolve the problem of racial equality; most glaringly, Memphis schools still remained segregated at mid-decade. However, the hard-won achievements of the movement fueled protest regarding other urban issues that now became pivotal to redefining the freedom movement.

In the aftermath of the 1964 Civil Rights Act, civil rights leaders worried that black Memphians—indeed, African Americans across the South—might become complacent, assuming that victory had been won. Instead, the period between the 1964 legislation and the 1968 sanitation strike witnessed a plethora of black working-class struggles that suggested that participants, while seeing this legislation and the 1965 Voting Rights Act as milestones, had been energized by the freedom movement earlier in the decade and now looked to their own activism to bring about more extensive change in their everyday lives. In the altered environment of the mid-1960s, black Memphians reshaped organizing efforts and rearticulated understandings of freedom as an unfulfilled promise, inextricable from labor justice and racial and gender equality.

The Freedom Movement and
the Myth of "Racial Harmony"

The sanitation strike burst the belief, shared by most white Memphians, that the city had succeeded in eluding the racial conflict that had convulsed other southern cities in the decade following *Brown v. Board of Education*. The perception of Memphis as a place of racial harmony—a view promoted since the early years of the Crump machine's domination in the city—had been reinforced during the early 1960s by the downplaying of civil rights in the media. In fact, a contemporary Southern Regional Council commentator observed that demonstrations were "larger and more disruptive than many realized—owing to the policy of the Memphis press of minimizing publicity. Some say that Memphis had more sit-ins than any other city." In addition, although police brutality proceeded apace in Memphis during the 1960s, and many participants in the sit-ins of the early freedom movement met with derogatory treatment, few civil rights activists encountered actual police violence in Memphis, according to statements by attorney Russell Sugarmon at 1962 hearings of the U.S. Commission on Civil Rights. Distinguishing the city from movement locales such as Birmingham and Selma, this relative police restraint allowed the city to bypass the national headlines and federal intervention that occurred elsewhere before 1968. Nevertheless, the contrast between the intensity of the movement and the myth of the city's racial harmony caught thousands of white Memphians by surprise in 1968, contributing to the perception that the sanitation strike was provoked by outsiders.[5]

Only the persistent pressure of sit-ins, marches, and pickets and the intervention of federal courts had convinced public officials and private business owners to concede to desegregation demands. After six months of protest, the MCCR worked with officials to negotiate the desegregation of public libraries in September 1960 and the Overton Park Zoo a month later. After another year of pickets and sit-ins, the MCCR finally initiated talks with downtown merchants. In February 1962, after a delay for the holiday shopping season, ten retailers, including department stores such as Goldsmith's and Lowenstein's, and five-and-dimes such as Walgreen's and Woolworth's, desegregated restaurants, lunch counters and, in most cases, restrooms. This move prompted a protest rally by over 700 members and sympathizers of a newly formed Memphis white Citizens' Council, who heard Mississippi governor Ross Barnett exhort them to "save Memphis from the race mixers." It would take another year to desegregate Memphis's movie theaters. Even after the Civil Rights Act required desegregation of public accommodations, many restaurants and other establishments complied only after being picketed by civil rights activists.[6]

As Memphis's major retailers inched toward desegregation, several legal cases wound their way through federal courts. In *Turner v. City of Memphis*, argued by NAACP legal defense attorney Constance Baker Motley, the U.S. Supreme Court in March 1962 ordered the desegregation of Dobbs House at the Memphis Municipal Airport and of all restaurants at interstate and intrastate transportation facilities. The decision came on the heels of an incident involving Dobbs House's ejection of Carl Rowan, U.S. assistant secretary of state for public affairs. The same month, a federal appeals court ruled that the Memphis public school admission of thirteen black children to previously all-white schools in 1961 did not constitute desegregation and ordered the city to design a new plan. And in May 1963, in *Watson v. City of Memphis*, argued by Motley, the U.S. Supreme Court ordered the immediate desegregation of all public parks and other recreation facilities. The Memphis City Commission and Park Commission complied, but in a burst of defiance they mandated the closure of city pools.[7]

Persistent struggles to achieve full desegregation drew white college students into the freedom movement. In January 1964, students at Southwestern, a private liberal arts college in Memphis (now Rhodes), organized a campus march to coincide with a visit by U.S. Senator Herbert Walters and Governor Frank Clements. Students carried signs demanding that Walters vote in favor of the Civil Rights Act, then under debate in Congress. Three months later, a group of black and white students picketed the Normal Tea Room near Memphis State, facing police arrests and angry crowds of white students. The Intercollegiate NAACP, comprised of students from Southwestern, Memphis State, LeMoyne, and Owen colleges, grabbed even more headlines in 1964 for its controversial crusade to desegregate Second Presbyterian, a prominent, 1,400-seat church. These confrontations provoked debate within the denomination as a whole, since the church was the planned site for the following year's annual meeting. By this time, churches that had been objects of protest in 1960 had desegregated.[8]

At the same time, black Memphians intensified efforts to gain political power. In the November 1964 elections, strenuous precinct-by-precinct efforts by the Shelby County Democratic Club resulted in a massive black voter turnout — over 70,000 out of 80,559 registered — that placed attorney A. W. Willis in the Tennessee legislature and H. T. Lockard on the Shelby

County Court, the first African Americans to win election to these offices since Reconstruction. Black Memphians also provided the votes needed for Shelby County to go for President Johnson over conservative senator Barry Goldwater, who had voted against the Civil Rights Act.[9] Locally, the growing significance of the black vote led Memphis's Program of Progress committee, charged with writing a new charter for the municipal government, to forge a compromise in which a portion of the seats in the new city council would be voted on by district, rather than at-large, making it feasible for a black candidate to win. However, it was obvious that the remaining at-large seats would be out of range of black candidates, thereby limiting black representation on the council. The 1967 transition to a mayor/council structure broke up the old Crump city commission form by separating the executive from the legislative branch. However, because black voters split their votes between A. W. Willis and incumbent Mayor Ingram, the first mayor elected under this new system was Henry Loeb, an advocate of segregation and ex-boss of the sanitation workers, who had also been mayor at the beginning of the decade.[10]

Locally and nationally, although civil rights leaders worried that the 1964 Civil Rights Act might defuse the movement, protest over issues outside of the core problem of desegregation expanded the freedom movement in both its goals and constituencies. For example, although school desegregation remained at nearly a standstill, high school students marched in protest of double sessions, implemented by the board of education to address gross overcrowding in black schools, while all-white schools continued to be under-enrolled. Several hundred students also picketed the school board president's downtown real estate office. These demonstrations indicated growing ferment among high school students, who in 1968 thronged to support marches for striking sanitation workers and in 1969 boycotted schools to demand desegregation.[11]

Police brutality, which culminated during the sanitation strike in an incident involving police use of mace and billy clubs, also prompted protest. At LeMoyne College in 1967, the police beating of sociology major Clinton Jamerson prompted over 250 students to join a protest march from the NAACP office to city hall. In this case, Jamerson had been beaten by a black police officer, assisted by white policemen, after being arrested in a crowded coffee shop at 1:00 A.M. Whereas 1940s protests had called for black policemen, 1960s protests more directly challenged the Memphis Police Department's goals, standards, and training methods. Repeated complaints of police violence also led the Memphis NAACP to demand responses from city officials. Significantly, many incidents of police abuse involved reactions to African American men who insisted upon respect; in April 1964, for example, a police officer drew his gun after a postal service employee insisted that he not be addressed as "boy."[12]

As the Vietnam War escalated, black Memphians also raised complaints about all-white draft boards. After the NAACP sent letters to President Johnson, the Selective Service, and the governor of Tennessee in 1966, one African American was appointed to each of the six draft boards in Memphis—a step the NAACP deemed "only token in light of the fact that Negroes comprise approximately 40% of the population of Memphis and Shelby County, and that fifty-one percent of the Shelby County casualties in the Vietnam War are Negroes." Meanwhile, Rev. James Lawson Jr., minister of Centenary Methodist Church, a pacifist and member of the SCLC who in 1965 visited Vietnam with the Fellowship of Reconciliation, helped organize antiwar rallies in Memphis and in other southern cities.[13]

These developments and growing black youth unemployment helped fuel the rise of Black Power organizations. Indeed, local activists participated in the June 1966 March Against Fear, from Memphis to Jackson, Mississippi, during which the first shouts of "Black Power!" burst forth.[14] In 1967, black college students and recent graduates organized the Black Organizing Project (BOP) and began recruiting teenagers in their neighborhoods. BOP organizers Coby Smith, a Manassas High School graduate and one of the first blacks to attend Southwestern, and Charles Cabbage, a graduate of Carver High and Morehouse College and a Student Non-Violent Coordinating Committee (SNCC) activist, worked with a south Memphis antipoverty agency in this same period. The two formed a group within BOP, the Invaders (named after a television show), to serve as a more radical security wing. Their emphasis on masculinity and self-defense as central tenets of black liberation did not preclude young women from identifying with them. BOP also included the Black Student Union at LeMoyne, the Afro-American Brotherhood at Owen, and the Black Student Association at Memphis State. Probably no more than 100 youth joined these groups; however, their militant, in-your-face language and style had an impact on more than just these members.[15]

Never monolithic, Black Power's emphasis on liberation rather than equal rights; on self-determination instead of reliance on whites; on pride as a replacement for degradation, resonated in many aspects of politics and culture, especially the soul music emanating from black radio stations. A decade earlier, in the period of *Brown v. Board*, it would have been highly unlikely for the R & B played by WDIA to contain an overt political message; resistance in R & B music was more likely to be expressed indirectly through such means as masculine sexual bravado that parodied and reversed stereotypes of black men. In contrast, much soul music heard by WLOK and WDIA listeners in the mid- to late-1960s showed that the freedom movement had opened up a cultural space for more explicitly political themes. Overwhelming responses to such recordings as Aretha Franklin's "Respect" (1967), her version of an Otis Redding song, and James Brown's "Say It Loud, I'm Black and Proud" (1968), suggested that the music and lyrics of soul struck powerful chords with listeners. The artists themselves, meanwhile, concentrated increasingly on messages that made pride and respect central to the idea of black liberation. Working-class black struggles in Memphis and other cities emerged in this cultural context, drawing on a similar language of black pride, manhood, and womanhood yet imbued with distinct meanings.[16]

Labor Protest and the Civil Rights Act

African American workers' efforts to achieve racial justice surged in the mid-1960s. During the 1950s, black workers had struggled to organize and maintain labor unions, despite a hostile climate that included union-busting and red-baiting. By 1960, service employees such as hotel maids and the sanitation workers had begun to organize. Over the next several years, such organizing, along with formal complaints to the federal government, skyrocketed. In addition, growing concerns about deepening black unemployment fueled condemnations of racial discrimination that continued to exclude African Americans from many jobs and training programs, even after passage of the Civil Rights Act.[17]

The relationship between race, labor, and freedom in 1960s Memphis is a complex one. Deborah Brown Carter, in her study of Memphis furniture workers, argues that the freedom movement infused a nearly moribund Memphis labor movement with fresh militancy in the 1960s because it "provided an ideology and symbols around which black workers coalesced."[18] This important point can also be analyzed from the reverse perspective, showing how black workers imbued such "ideology and symbols" with fresh significance that expanded concepts of rights and freedom within labor and antipoverty struggles. Black labor militancy ultimately rejuvenated the Memphis freedom movement, which by the mid-1960s had become less focused and energetic.

Workers with incomes below the poverty line in sweatshop manufacturing industries initiated an unprecedented number of organizing campaigns and strikes during the mid-1960s. Membership in UFWA Local 282, for example, swelled from 797 in 1960 to 1,726 in 1970. In contrast to the five strikes the local sponsored in the two decades after its founding in 1943, it struck seven times between 1964 and 1968 alone and seventeen times between 1968 and 1980. The local also conducted forty-eight organizing campaigns between 1963 and 1975. In 1960, rank-and-file workers successfully pressured the union to replace the local's white leadership and to assign international representative LeRoy Clark, an African American, to Local 282. Eddie May Garner, a shop steward at the piano factory, also recalls that workers pressured the union to become more militant by mounting repeated wildcat strikes over such galling conditions as oppressive heat in the plant.[19]

Women like Garner had become central to such efforts. In part, this reflected changing hiring policies in Memphis's traditional hardwood and oil extraction industries, which employed increasing numbers of black women in the postwar era. Comments by African American women who worked in Memphis manufacturing plants and laundries help explain why they became avid labor activists. In many cases, their organizing drives preceded the sanitation strike, establishing a larger historic context out of which the strike emerged. These women's narratives reveal gendered aspects of freedom that may be hidden by the slogan "I *Am* a Man."[20]

Comments by Sally Turner, a migrant from rural Mississippi, show how historical memories of the plantation resonated within women's labor activism.[21] Turner first moved from rural Mississippi to Memphis in 1955, at age nineteen. In the early 1960s she commuted daily between Coldwater, Mississippi, and the city, before later relocating permanently to Memphis. She began working at Farber Brothers, an auto accessories manufacturing plant, in 1962. Her boss, she recalled, provided few fans in the stifling summer heat and workers believed that he paid them in cash so he could short their pay, which he calculated on a piecework basis, or postponed payday altogether for the same reason. "You know, those women worked it hard, very, very hard," Turner asserted. "And then on Friday, when we got paid, they just wouldn't give you all of your money." After leaving sharecropping, she was infuriated to get to Farber Brothers and find that "they start the same thing." The last straw before she and other black women employees began to organize a union, Turner declared, was their plant manager's purchase of a bucket and a dipper in response to their complaints that there was no water fountain in the wretchedly hot plant. Being pressured to use what they construed as an emblem of an older plantation regime led Turner and her coworkers to similarly interpret other labor practices as symbols of the rural South they had struggled to leave behind.

Just as significantly, the segregation of black and white employees made it very difficult for women to develop solidarity. She recalled that the plant manager assigned only white women to make slipcovers in a separate area of the plant that was "up the hill." With white and black women laboring in the same plants in the mid-1960s, potentially performing the same work, such divisions of jobs served as markers of racial difference. They also influenced labor organizing, Turner recalled: "[W]hen we got organized, we didn't have many whites that was for the union, because they was already getting benefits anyway." She and others sought better pay and working conditions while also striving to end racial practices that differentiated between black and white women.

Turner's critiques were not reserved for whites alone; she also targeted black coworkers who feared that joining the union would cost them their jobs. She compared them to sharecroppers afraid of the consequences of leaving their situations. Because Turner's concerns about submissiveness and emotional strength stemmed from her confrontations with sharecropping, they addressed not only white domination but black male household authority. As a young bride, she recalled, she learned that her husband had signed a sharecropping contract for the coming year, against her wishes. She responded by leaving on foot in broad daylight, suitcases in hand, in an act of defiance against both the sharecropping system and her husband. In contrast, her husband "slipped away at night" when he left for Memphis, an indication to her that he was the less courageous one. Turner's labor activism was thus shaped by historical memories not only of white domination but also of different responses to it, especially her own assertion of autonomy.

Hazel McGhee's account of organizing with Laundry Workers International Local 218 further illuminates these intersections of labor and household, race and gender. McGhee, originally from Tallahatchie County, Mississippi, began organizing at Metro Uniform in 1965 and participated in a seven-month strike that directly preceded her husband's walkout with the sanitation workers. Little attention has been paid to the fact that, in addition to supporting their husbands' strike, some of the sanitation workers' wives were themselves union activists. McGhee's story underscores the significance of women's activism in the period just before the sanitation strike, contributing to the volatile atmosphere out of which the strike emerged.[22]

McGhee recalled feeling that her bosses "wanted to . . . drive you, that you hadn't worked enough." In addition, "They talked to you . . . like you was their child. You don't talk to adults like you're talking to a child," she insisted. "And you ask them to do things, don't tell them you got to do nothing." Her comment about being "driven" suggests that she likened her contemporary urban workplace to slavery. Her emphasis on being treated like a child also suggests that this paternalism in the workplace could, like slavery, be represented as a domestic hierarchy instead of impersonal labor relations.

To McGhee, then, the slogan "I *Am* a Man" meant "don't let nobody push you around." "Stand up and be a man," as she put it, applied to women: "[I]f you can be a man, I can be a woman. If you're strong, I can be strong." McGhee's interpretation also pertained to her own household. She remembers telling her husband when his strike began, "'If I could stay out several months, I'm sure you can stay out.'" "I would not have liked it," she told me, "after I had done been out seven months and two weeks, and he done went out and stayed a couple of days, that would make me feel like that he wasn't like the slogan, *a man*." For women, the slogan encouraged them to assert their own courage, claim equality rather than subservience, and even challenge men.

McGhee also blasted management practices that created distinctions between black and white women. White women used the restroom in the office, she recalls, but black women had to use "a little one-stool thing over here on Wright Street" that was "stopped up and nasty." Although in other workplaces white working women also complained about infringement of their "bathroom rights," in this racially divided context, black women perceived such practices as privileging white women.

An interview with Naomi Jones, a Hungerford Furniture worker, shows how issues of respect and sexuality motivated African American women's labor activism. In 1967 women workers at Hungerford complained to the Equal Employment Opportunity Commission (EEOC) that they were being sexually harassed by white male supervisors and coworkers. "Back then," Jones asserted, "white men, they could say anything to a black woman, and she should fall for it or take it." Jones criticized women who "fell for it." On the other hand, Jones admired a woman who complained to the plant owner after being molested by a white male worker. Jones remembers this issue also influenced workers' support for Local 282. Union representation, they hoped, would provide protection from such abuse.[23]

Jones's comments suggest that freedom, to her, involved a collective redefinition of black womanhood, grounded in religious ideas emanating from the freedom movement. Before the movement, she reflected, "[W]e had thought that God made you [whites] different from me. . . . And I was not supposed to be equal. I was supposed to be your servant. . . . I was not supposed to be as free." Jones herself had in fact rejected domestic service and searched for a factory job as a young woman. Nevertheless, she identified the period before the freedom movement as one in which it was presumed that black women would work as maids for white women. In contrast, she described the 1960s as a time when many blacks began believing that "we had as much right because God made all of us." "He didn't say, let's make white and let's make black," she declared. "He said, let's make *man*. And I felt like . . . He meant for all of us to enjoy the freedom that He had made for us." In Jones's view, Dr. King's and other black freedom movement leaders' emphasis on universal "manhood" encouraged black women activists to target racial practices that cast them as subordinate to white women.[24]

Freedom, from this religio-political perspective, was both a goal and the process of reaching that goal, a point especially taken to heart by working-class women who began seeing themselves as agents of freedom. For Ida Leachman, a garment worker in the 1960s and later president of Local 282, attaining freedom required her to overcome her fear through participation in the movement. As with many black Baptist activists, Leachman's idea of freedom wove the Old Testament's story of deliverance together with the New Testament's vision of personal salvation, making freedom simultaneously collective and individual, political and personal. Salvation, moreover, was for the present, not just for the afterlife. Leachman envisioned the labor-freedom movement as a Manichaean struggle between good and evil, in which she positioned herself as an agent on the side of good. She and Jones and other activists thus replaced racist images of black women with identities based on collective protest. Freedom, as a counterpoint to the "plantation mentality," resided in that revised sense of self, in addition to equal rights.[25]

In the period just before the sanitation strike, a wide array of workers addressed the complex relation between rights and freedom not only through union organizing but also by pressuring the federal government to protect their rights to equal employment, as accorded by the landmark Civil Rights Act of 1964. Their appeals reveal concerns spilling beyond constitutional rights, extending to problems of identity that reverberate with Turner's, McGhee's, Jones's, and Leachman's views. They also help explain why the sanitation strike was fervently supported. The sanitation workers inhabited the same communities and addressed similar issues in a familiar language.

Ironically, the equal employment rights guaranteed by the 1964 Civil Rights Act did not quell but spurred new battles. This groundbreaking legislation prohibited discrimination in several key areas that had been addressed by the civil rights movement, including public accommodations, federally assisted programs, schooling, voting, and employment. The legislation's Title VII, a major achievement of the Johnson administration, ended two decades of congressional opposition to a permanent fair employment practice program like the one established on the eve of the Second World War by President Roosevelt, under pressure from the March on Washington Movement. Title VII banned discrimination by employers, labor unions, and employment agencies with regard to "race, color, religion, sex, or national origin," and established the EEOC to handle complaints and secure compliance. Wary of employer resistance, Congress delayed implementation of Title VII for one year, until July 1965.[26]

Despite this sweeping legislation, few working-class African Americans in Memphis perceived themselves as passive recipients of these federally protected rights, since they encountered widespread noncompliance by Memphis employers. Workers swamped the EEOC with complaints. In Memphis, most first approached the local NAACP, whose staff helped them complete affidavits and then forwarded their complaints to the regional office. Workers had filed complaints with the NAACP about local employers for years, but after passage of the Civil Rights Act, the volume of complaints shot up, with many workers not even waiting until Title VII formally went into effect to visit the NAACP. Between July 1965, when it became effective, and May 1967, the Memphis NAACP processed over 400 complaints by individuals and groups against local manufacturing firms, major corporations, and unions.[27]

Workers' most vehement and persistent complaints involved employer refusals to hire or promote African Americans outside service positions. Kennedy Veteran's Hospital workers, for example, reported that "all Negroes are assigned to housekeeping, laundry or dietetics and have extreme difficulty getting out," while whites hired in housekeeping transferred out within thirty days. At Kroger Baking, porters in the sanitation department found it nearly impossible to be promoted into production, a problem they attributed not only to the company but also to the American Bakery and Confectionery Workers Union.[28]

In their affidavits, complainants posited different identities for themselves. Men reminded the EEOC that they had other skills, decades of seniority, or had trained the white men who became their supervisors. Complaints about conditions at Kennedy Veterans Hospital, for example, named men who were qualified painters and heavy or light equipment operators yet were confined to work in housekeeping or similar areas. They thereby staked claims to independent manhood—generally associated in American culture with skilled work—while rejecting the dependency linked to domestic work. Women complained that jobs like clerical work and nursing were reserved for white women alone. Even black women who secured jobs typically assigned to white women in Memphis sometimes found they were forced to adopt markers of racial servitude; a black nurse, for example, complained she was fired by Mustin Nursing Home for refusing "to wear a green uniform as is customary for Negro maids to wear."[29]

Workers' complaints extended beyond job classifications and promotions to problems that fell into the category of "intangibles"—forms of discrimination that could not be measured in objective terms but had a significant impact on workers, nonetheless.[30] In a letter to the Veterans Administration, Memphis NAACP executive secretary Maxine Smith reported that Kennedy Hospital workers complained that white supervisors demanded deferential behavior from them. "[N]o Negro who asserts himself or conducts himself in a manner contrary to what personnel employers and administrators feel is consistent with 'Negro behavior' has any chance for consideration," Smith stated. "Intangibles" also included other kinds of racist behavior by supervisors. Humko Oil workers in the Salad Oil Division, for example, refused to work overtime after being subjected to abusive language from their foremen. When the workers were fired, they filed a grievance. Some of these same men had worked as laborers for thirty years without promotion. Elsewhere, workers complained that supervisors refused to use titles of respect, with men especially riled at being called "boy." These "intangibles" spilled beyond traditional bounds of both labor disputes and discrimination suits.[31]

In Memphis, pressure mounted as cases backed up at the EEOC and employers continued or even intensified daily forms of discrimination and humiliation. At Kroger Baking, some fifteen African American workers, led by James Holmes, a shop steward and Memphis NAACP Executive Board member, filed ten grievances from 1965 to 1967, most of them protesting their exclusion from production jobs. They also criticized the union for upholding a contract that calculated seniority on a departmental rather than a plantwide basis, locking African Americans into sanitation work with no contractual grounds for transferring out. By 1967, despite EEOC rulings, Kroger had made no attempt to remedy the situation. Meanwhile, white foremen threatened to shut down the plant if African Americans were promoted. In December, management fired Holmes, charging him with initiating a wildcat strike.[32]

As the intensifying frustration at Kroger shows, the Civil Rights Act's promise of rights invigorated preexisting forms of black working-class agency, but it also revealed the limitations of equal rights as a government-conceived project. Title VII may have provided a vehicle for workers to formally articulate what they perceived as untenable, and to explicitly link labor concerns to civil rights, but by soliciting complaints that then became tied up in a federal bureaucracy, the legislation unintentionally prompted black workers to pursue other forms of protest. Workers' affidavits may not have elicited concrete results but they did express underlying understandings of racial justice, in which "intangibles" of power and identity became central to appeals for rights.

"Memphis on the Move": RCA and Black Workers

This pressure from black workers for profound changes in the tangibles and intangibles of Memphis workplaces affected not only traditional low-wage service and manufacturing sectors but also the largest and most modern industrial plants in the area, and ultimately exposed fundamentally different understandings of progress pursued by city officials, employers, and working-class black Memphians. RCA's announcement in late 1965 that it would open a huge, ultramodern television assembly facility in Memphis illuminates the conflicting "investments" in the future that collided in the city in the mid-1960s. Just before Christmas, jubilant RCA representatives, Memphis Chamber of Commerce leaders, and Tennessee governor Frank Clement jointly announced the projected opening of the new plant in spring 1966. Hailed as a boon to the city, acquired through the untiring efforts of city and state boosters, RCA's plans symbolized "Memphis on the move" and a sign of its success in avoiding the highly publicized racial turmoil that had engulfed first Little Rock, to the west, and then Birmingham, to the southeast, as well as an antidote to the city's economic worries.[33]

Although G.E., International Harvester, Kimberly-Clark, and Borg-Warner all opened new production plants in Memphis after the Second World War, the closure of the Ford Motor Company assembly plant in the late 1950s had dealt a blow to the city's economy. The press now anticipated that the RCA plant would become the area's largest employer, hiring up to 8,000 workers (twice the number at Firestone), and its most modern facility, which would even include air-conditioning. Workers would be paid $2.25 per hour, the highest hourly wage in the area, and would be covered by a national union contract. Articles in the local press traced RCA's role in the spectacular rise of the color television industry, hitching Memphis to modernity, in contrast to its enduring association with cotton culture. Drawn to the city by local officials eager to supply the company with tax breaks, infrastructure, and other perks; by a ready supply of rural labor without union experience; and by apparent racial calm, RCA planned to move much of its production from Bloomington, Indiana, to Memphis.[34]

The fact that RCA's arrival in Memphis coincided with the implementation of the Civil Rights Act's prohibition of employment discrimination provoked conflict from the start. Shortly after announcing they would open a Memphis plant, RCA officials declared that the company "makes no distinction between hiring whites and Negroes." That statement, the promised pay rate, and RCA's expressed interest in hiring a workforce that would be two-thirds female prompted women (white and black) and African Americans (women and men) in Memphis and surrounding rural counties to flood the state employment office with applications even before the official hiring process began. However, black applicants began complaining to the NAACP that the company wasn't hiring blacks in all job categories, placing most on the assembly line, and that there were no African Americans working in the personnel office. The organization's labor and industry committee responded by establishing a special committee to talk with RCA and state officials. RCA quickly got its first hint that Memphis workers were not as docile as they had expected. Indeed, even assumptions that workers from rural west Tennessee would be ignorant of unions proved misleading; many commuted daily from counties where active civil rights struggles were taking place. RCA officials were likely aware of neither this rural legacy nor the rising dissatisfaction of black workers in the city.[35]

African American women applicants also had to contend with racially gendered images of the ideal RCA worker that bore little resemblance to their own lives. Following RCA's announcement that it desired a two-thirds female workforce, the local newspapers reported that RCA sought housewives, whose "nimble fingers" suited them to repetitive intricate work that was compared to crocheting and embroidery. Another set of media images presented RCA as a sexy, modern workplace for attractive young white women. After visiting RCA's plant in Bloomington, Indiana, one journalist reported glowingly, "You can admire the work of an endless line of electronic age blonds, brunets and redheads as they reach into bins for parts with which to assemble television sets." This image of "electronic age" female workers left black women — not to mention white women who did not fit this ideal — outside the public vision of progress, even though RCA would eventually hire thousands of black women in Memphis.[36]

At first, RCA drew accolades for its dazzling atmosphere, technological wizardry, and glamorous workforce, and workers seemed to validate management's approach, even opting for the union that RCA preferred, the IUE, rather than the International Brotherhood of Electrical Workers, which represented RCA's militant Bloomington workers.[37] However, a wildcat strike that halted production for four days in March 1967 presented a different message. Defying the no-strike agreement in their labor contract, RCA workers denounced foremen who demanded production levels above quotas in the contract, making it impossible to keep up with the assembly line unless they skipped sets. Paralleling protests by women workers elsewhere in Memphis, women strikers vented their greatest fury at foremen who refused bathroom use "on company time" or forced them to sign up to use the restroom. The press reported that picketers sang a new freedom song, "We want our bathroom rights," an indication of the freedom movement's impact on labor struggle. Women jeered IUE officials who sought to end the strike and ridiculed RCA's offers of time-and-motion studies to determine whether current quotas were inhumane. Protests over bathroom rights by black women in local sweatshop manufacturing plants rarely drew headlines; now, however, RCA's sexy image boomeranged when both white and black women employees charged that RCA was hostile to their intimate needs.[38]

By 1968, black workers' and the NAACP's initial call for equal employment opportunity at RCA had given way to workers' ardent participation in the sanitation strike. In a reflection of heightened militancy among black workers, union elections held in late 1968 resulted in a larger proportion of black officers, who addressed the "intangibles" of racial injustice, in addition to contractual workplace issues such as hourly wages and benefits. RCA workers also threw their support behind other labor struggles, such as the 1969 strike at the Hunter Fan plant, where black women had begun working only after the Civil Rights Act. RCA's expectations of a quiescent workforce that would advance the corporation's standing in the electronics industry did not pan out. By the close of 1970, RCA had shut down its facility and shipped production to Taiwan.[39]

"We Kept on Marching and Singing": Memphis Welfare Rights

Paralleling ferment among black workers in the mid- to late 1960s were the campaigns of women who were among the most impoverished and vulnerable working-class African Americans in Memphis. Welfare recipients, public housing residents, and others in the city's poorest neighborhoods initiated antipoverty organizations to end the harsh and even punitive social policies aimed at poor blacks, and especially women. The freedom movement, on the one hand, and the federal programs linked to

Memphis RCA workers returning to work, July 1967, after a month's layoff due to a shortage of parts that resulted from strikes at other RCA plants. *(Press-Scimitar staff photo, courtesy of Special Collections, University of Memphis)*

President Lyndon Johnson's Great Society initiative, on the other, fueled these deeply rooted struggles.

In his first State of the Union address in January 1964, President Johnson announced that his administration "today, here and now, declares unconditional war on poverty in America." The reform package unfurled over the next months addressed not so much the structural, economic origins of poverty but the lack of resources that kept the poor from climbing the economic ladder. It included such programs as Medicaid and Medicare, Head Start, Legal Services, Food Stamps, and VISTA (Volunteers in Service to America). The Economic Opportunity Act, the linchpin of Johnson's War on Poverty, established the Office of Economic Opportunity (OEO) to oversee job training, educational assistance, and other programs aimed at providing the poor with the "bootstraps" with which individuals could pull themselves up and out of poverty. Much of the OEO's budget went to the Community Action Program, which provided grants to local agencies that would, in turn, mobilize the poor to help themselves, based on the nebulously stated principle of "maximum feasible participation" by local community residents.[40]

Because Memphis's black service workers earned salaries so low that they lived below the poverty level, the line between federal civil rights mandates and antipoverty bills blurred. Complaints by maids, janitors, cooks, kitchen helpers, and orderlies in public hospitals, schools, and parks led the NAACP to pressure city officials about their salaries. Many service employees, including the sanitation workers and others employed by the city, earned wages low enough to qualify them for food stamps. Paradoxically, therefore, at the same time that Memphis mayor William Ingram established a Community Action Committee (CAC) to direct the local War on Poverty, city departments continued to relegate African Americans to service positions with wages that placed them below the poverty level.[41]

As in many cities that received antipoverty funds, clashes erupted over how to define the program's ambiguous goal of "maximum feasible participation," reflecting struggles over race, politics, and power addressed by the larger black freedom movement.[42] In late summer 1965, following complaints from community advocates, including the NAACP, that the mayor and city commissioners were attempting to control the CAC by preventing existing community organizations to elect their own representatives, the OEO announced it would freeze funds for Memphis's antipoverty program until city officials produced a plan in compliance with OEO guidelines. In response, Mayor Ingram pulled Rev. James Lawson and NAACP attorney A. W. Willis off the CAC, and threatened to appoint a representative of the white Citizens' Council to the committee to balance the NAACP's influence. The NAACP responded by organizing weekly Saturday marches to protest what it considered the mayor and city commission's obstruction of the War on Poverty. Only in January 1966 did the city commission draft a plan that the OEO would approve. The plan allowed thirty-six participating organizations to elect their own representatives to the new CAC, although final approval by the commission would be required. Washington Butler Jr., a black Tennessee OEO employee who had earlier served as a consultant in Memphis, was appointed executive director of the War on Poverty Committee, which would implement the program.[43]

In Memphis's predominantly black neighborhoods, residents seized on the War on Poverty to expand on their ongoing efforts to improve housing and local neighborhood environments and to raise incomes. Their projects attracted an array of participants, who together constituted a new kind of urban freedom movement. Experienced civil rights activists, members of Black Power organizations, college students, VISTA volunteers, and Legal Services workers (many of them white) joined neighborhood activists, a majority of whom were black women.

South Memphis, in particular, became a locus for grassroots antipoverty organizing. Since the racial housing conflicts of the early 1950s, this part of the city had become nearly solidly African American. Sections of the neighborhood, especially in and around LeMoyne Gardens, a public housing project near LeMoyne College, included many families living in poverty due to inadequate wages or insufficient public assistance. Organizing in this area predated the federal War on Poverty, extending back to 1958, when, with support from the Department of Health, Education, and Welfare, LeMoyne College formed a study group on local poverty. With additional funding from the YMCA, the YWCA, and the board of education, the group assisted individuals and families in need of jobs, medical attention, adult education, and other services. The organization became affiliated with the federal antipoverty program in 1965 and incorporated as the Memphis Area Project–South (MAP-South). Headed by Rev. James Lawson Jr., pastor of Centenary Methodist Church and well-known for his pacifist and civil rights activism in Nashville, before he moved to Memphis, and with the SCLC, MAP-South addressed problems of unemployment, job training, and supplemental food distribution; organized Summer Youth programs; and coordinated efforts of block clubs, public housing resident associations, and other groups, with funding from the OEO and the newly created Department of Housing and Urban Development. MAP-South's growing membership reflected its neighborhood roots and the energizing impact of the freedom movement. At a general meeting of the Citizens' Association, MAP-South's general membership body, held at Booker T. Washington High School in April 1967, it was reported that membership had topped 800.[44]

Dedicated to community empowerment, MAP-South structured the organization such that only its Citizens' Association could nominate and elect members of the governing policy committee, which included representatives from all neighborhood groups. The policy committee was comprised of community leaders, most of them women, and ministers such as Rev. Samuel A. Owen and Rev. Harold Middlebrook, along with Lawson. MAP-South director Autry Parker, appointed in January 1967, hired a staff of seventy-five men and women, comprised of fifty-nine neighborhood aides and sixteen college students, in addition to VISTA volunteers. By September of that year, seventy-five block clubs and public housing tenant associations were holding weekly meetings to address such issues as landlord neglect of housing and the treatment of African Americans by housing and welfare officials. MAP-South also organized a Summer Youth Project that placed teens in creative arts programs. Stax Records, located in south Memphis, ran one of the internship programs for teenagers.[45]

Significantly, MAP-South also focused on what it termed "consciousness" by confronting derogatory stereotypes of poor people and encouraging respect, self-esteem, and activism. An article in the *MAP-South Newsletter*, titled "Myth of Welfare Chiselers," hammered away at the stereotype of the typical welfare recipient: a healthy but lazy man who refused to work (like the "vagrant" of earlier decades). It showed that the vast majority of welfare recipients were over sixty-five or under eighteen, suffering from severe disabilities, or caring for children without other support. It also demanded a change of attitude among welfare administrators: "People, through no fault of their own who are forced to live on welfare should be treated with the respect due any citizen and should not be looked upon as morally inferior by those who have more money."[46]

With support from MAP-South, women welfare recipients living in public housing began discussing these issues of respect, as well as problems involving benefits. According to Willie Pearl Butler (then Ellis), the group began when thirteen public housing residents at LeMoyne Gardens, assisted by MAP-South staff member Bob Newell, a young white activist from the North, began meeting to discuss their concerns about housing and welfare. Butler, who in the 1960s was a charismatic young woman in her twenties, became a driving force behind the formation of the Memphis Welfare Rights Organization (MWRO) along with welfare and tenants' rights activist Frances Hale. The group drew up a list of demands that included funding for college, training for jobs that paid decent wages, child care, transportation money, and training for social workers on what Butler called "how to deal with humans." Butler presented the list to George Latham, director of Memphis's welfare department.[47]

As the group launched protests and organized more formally, it attacked the contempt members believed was accorded to them in language that invoked images of servitude. In May 1968, the *Press-Scimitar* reported that a group of ten women welfare rights activists paid a visit to William H. Roberts, assistant director of the Shelby County welfare department, to complain about the new Work Incentive Program (WIN) that, beginning July 1, would require welfare recipients to work or attend job training or lose their public assistance. The women termed the program "forced work" and declared that they did not want training as cooks or nurses' aides but rather jobs that would allow them to become self-sufficient, without welfare.[48]

Following this protest, the group gained momentum, expanding its base and formalizing its meetings. A speaker at the MAP-South Citizen's Association meeting in June 1968 announced that "mothers on welfare" would be meeting on a weekly basis at the Bethlehem Center, a Catholic community center near LeMoyne Gardens. In November, 130 women, joined by activists with SNCC and BOP marched to the state office building for an angry face-off with George Latham, at which they demanded winter clothing and raincoats for their children, from special needs funds they had learned were available to the welfare department but not being dispersed.[49]

The struggle for welfare rights quickly became the most vibrant antipoverty movement in the city, with members working on not just a single issue but, as participant Juanita Miller Thornton put it, "every little pea and pod in Memphis." The women organized themselves as the Memphis Welfare Rights Organization (MWRO) affiliated with the National Welfare Rights Organization (NWRO), officially founded in August 1967 following a series of nationwide demonstrations the previous summer. Frances Hale, who had initiated a rent strike at LeMoyne Gardens, became the MWRO's first president, with Willie Pearl Butler serving as vice president until she later took over as president. A core group of about thirty women regularly attended weekly meetings, but public protests attracted many more, including welfare mothers, civil rights activists, ministers, college students, and Black Power advocates. The MWRO picketed downtown department stores that refused to issue credit cards to welfare recipients and challenged violations of state welfare policy wherein the city shorted or denied them benefits. Helped by Legal Services attorneys, the organization won reforms to such policies as those that prohibited welfare recipients to regularly drive or own a car, to own a house valued at over $6,000, to receive aid before establishing Tennessee residency for one year, or to have a man living in the house. Members also helped women in north Memphis create a second chapter there and assisted women forming their own groups in Tennessee towns such as Dyersburg and Murfreesboro.[50]

Welfare rights activists began viewing their individual experiences in light of broader social issues and their relationships with other women throughout the country. Together with the NWRO, they challenged national welfare legislation proposed by the Nixon administration. Memphis activists attended national conventions and assisted in campaigns in other cities that took them out of the area for the first times in their lives. Ann Wilson Harper recalls taking part in a national caravan to Baton Rouge to help local activists form a welfare rights organization there. To

Welfare rights demonstrators march past the state
office building in downtown Memphis, November 1968.
(© *Ernest C. Withers, courtesy of Panopticon Gallery*)

Harper, meeting women from other cities made her realize that "we're not
the only ones."[51]

As with labor organizing, the black freedom movement encouraged
women activists in welfare rights to understand their individual experiences in the context of a larger pattern of racial and gender discrimination and poverty in the South. Willie Pearl Butler, who grew up in Walls,
Mississippi, recalls becoming angry about racial prejudice when fourteen-
year-old Emmett Till was lynched in 1955, when she was thirteen, and
wishing in 1961 that she could join the Freedom Rides but deciding not
to because she had an infant to care for. When she moved to Memphis in
1962, she worked on voter registration and, on her own, sat in at restaurants that were still segregated. Butler labored in private households, laundries, a hotel, and a nursing home before ending up on welfare in 1966

after her six-year-old son suffered a serious accident. As an outspoken person already, Butler went all the way to the mayor's office when a white woman housing authority official refused to help her locate a ground-floor apartment suitable for her disabled son. Butler began fighting for welfare rights, she asserts, after meeting a woman with a handicapped child who had been forced to live in an upstairs apartment even after he grew too heavy for her to lift. Because her social worker also refused to arrange for physical therapy, his legs had atrophied into the shape of his chair. In the context of the freedom movement, Butler interpreted this story not as one of personal misfortune, but as one reflecting the "built-in prejudice system" of the welfare department, which "worked one way for white folks and another way for black folks."[52]

Ann Wilson Harper, originally from rural west Tennessee, believed it was the civil rights movement, including the speeches of Dr. Martin Luther King Jr., that motivated women welfare rights activists to demand not only larger public assistance grants but also respect. She recalled the disrespect of white social workers, "like when people hadn't been to call us Mr. and Mrs., and by them just calling you plain Ann Harper." She felt she was mistreated both as an African American and as a woman. "[W]hen you're a woman you get less attention than . . . a man," she asserted. "And they always cite women, especially on welfare, as lazy or unworthy. And we're not that. I'm not any of those things. There are some lazy women on welfare. And there are some lazy rich people, white people, and everything. But you just cannot characterize black females by that." Harper recalled a white social worker who wiped off Harper's front doorknob with a handkerchief before entering her home and then pointed at each of her children, demanding, "Who is his daddy?" (In fact, they all had the same father.) As with Butler, welfare rights and the larger freedom movement gave Harper the confidence to see that such indignities represented more than personal problems. Openly discussing these humiliating experiences together emboldened activists to protest publicly, where previously they had felt ashamed about being welfare recipients. When they protested social workers' failure to use titles of respect and picketed downtown department stores that denied them credit, Harper recalls, white passers by "would look at you and say you're lazy and no good." "It was just downright disgusting," she declared. "But I remember we kept on marching and we kept on singing."[53]

Because they viewed welfare rights as part of the larger struggle of the black freedom movement, neither Butler nor Harper nor other activists focused on a solitary issue; rather, they extended their concerns to public housing, legal services, food programs, assistance to children with disabilities, and other problems. Juanita Miller Thornton, who was born in Memphis in 1942 and lived on Beale Street during her early years, perceived the welfare rights, civil rights, and Black Power movements as interrelated, and she participated in several different struggles during the 1960s. She became involved with the freedom movement while in high school at Manassas, at the encouragement of Rev. Harold Middlebrook. Along with other students, she participated in downtown pickets and sit-ins until the birth of her daughter in 1961. She soon became active again, not only in Memphis but also in Mississippi during Freedom Summer, 1964, and in Fayette County. After her son was born in 1966, she found herself with two handicapped children to support — her daughter had been born deaf, and her son in his early years suffered from severe allergies — with a monthly income of ninety-seven dollars from public assistance. As a public housing resident, she became involved with welfare rights after hearing a presentation by Willie Pearl Butler at LeMoyne Gardens. Welfare rights became a jumping-off point for her work organizing parents of children with disabilities to pressure the state to provide education for them, an effort she launched by announcing a meeting over WDIA. Thornton also became the first welfare recipient to attend Memphis State University, through President Nixon's work incentive program. An admirer of Dr. King, she also traveled to Marks, Mississippi, then the poorest town in the United States, to take part in the "Mule Train" that opened the Poor People's Campaign, two weeks after King's assassination.[54]

Especially after the assassination of Dr. King in 1968, the ideas of Black Power also influenced Juanita Thornton and various other women and men involved with antipoverty struggles. Her friend Janice Payne, for example, worked with welfare rights, BOP, and the Invaders, and successfully crusaded for a free lunch program in city schools. "They couldn't see that if you were on welfare you could have pride," she asserted. "They were putting men on the moon, but felt that paying a woman $97 a month was a lot of money."[55]

"I *Am* a Man" and the Memphis Sanitation Strike

The 1968 sanitation strike represented a turning point in this larger ferment over race, gender, and power.[56] Because the labor, civil rights, and antipoverty agitation preceding the strike has not previously been researched, the strike has been posited either as a wholly new phenomenon or a return to the militancy of the World War II era. By connecting the strike to other mid-1960s activism, we can see that it simultaneously *reflected* this surge in black working-class agitation and *reshaped* it by articulating black workers' concerns through highly public mass protest. The strike's challenge to racial paternalism and submissiveness, two sides of the "plantation mentality," resonated with other workers, while the "intangibles" addressed in EEOC complaints were engaged by the sanitation strike in terms of manhood and freedom. "I *Am* a Man" would also be adopted as a slogan by other struggles in Memphis and other cities, beginning with the strike by employees at the city's public hospital who became part of the sanitation workers' Local 1733 of the American Federation of State, County and Municipal Employees (AFSCME). By explicitly tying freedom to labor justice and racial equality, the strike underscored to a broad public that the goal of freedom remained an unrealized one.

As we have seen,[57] the sanitation workers, many of whom were World War II veterans still indignant about the racist employment conditions they faced when they returned home from the war, started organizing in 1959 and 1960—the same period in which black students launched the Memphis sit-in movement. A large number had migrated to the city from Fayette County, the heart of rural civil rights conflicts in west Tennessee, with smaller numbers coming from nearby rural counties and only a minority from Memphis.[58] Many of the men compared their long working hours to field labor and likened their supervisors to plantation bosses. "It was the same thing that you would put on farmhands—can-to-can," recalled Clinton Burrows. "That means get up as early as you can and leave when they tell you you can . . . sunup to sundown." Moreover, sanitation workers rejected racist references to them as "boys," since the labor they did, hoisting heavy fifty-five-gallon drums, sometimes filled with rainwater, onto their heads and carrying them from backyards to the trucks, clearly demonstrated their manhood. Robert Beasley insisted this heavy work was proof of the workers' adult strength: "We were men, not boys. . . . [I]f we were carrying fifty-five-gallon cans, we had to be men."[59]

Even seemingly straightforward issues such as wages bore disturbing gendered meanings that reinforced perceptions of the sanitation workers as dependents. Because average wages fell below the poverty line, many workers qualified for federal assistance to supplement their wages. Many also found themselves made into objects of charity by white housewives who gave them "handouts" of cast-off clothing. For the workers, wearing "handouts" publicly marked them as different. "You could tell a worker when you saw him in the streets because his hat was too big, his coat was too long, his shoes were too big . . . from handouts," Clinton Burrows declared. "We worked every day, [so] let us have the money and pick [our clothes] like other people do." His critique made problems of fair wages and dignity of consumer choice central to conceptions of manhood.[60]

Workers also detested aspects of their work that they felt made other people place them outside humanity, connecting them to garbage and filth. Robert Beasley recoiled at being "called 'walking buzzards' by the public." This term cast workers as vultures that preyed on garbage. "We felt we should be treated as human beings," Beasley declared, emphasizing that this meant "the right to be recognized by the City of Memphis." Taylor Rogers described garbage dripping over them: "We had to go into the back yard with the tubs and bring them out to the trucks," he recalled. "And tubs be on your head and on your shoulder. . . . And those tubs had holes in them, and that stuff would leak all over on you." Leaking garbage was not just a question of cleanliness but degradation.[61]

Other sanitation workers felt that leaking garbage and poverty-level wages tainted their household relations, in addition to their public images. Having to wash off dirt and maggots before crossing the threshold of their homes made them feel like they were polluting their households and fueled their claims to humanity, as well as masculinity. Leroy Bonner remembered his wife's horror at seeing maggots crawling on his body while he was bathing. These concerns, combined with their low wages and reliance on government assistance, contributed to a sense that their jobs undercut their status as fathers and husbands. Workers also lacked benefits, including workers' compensation, that would have aided their families.[62]

These concerns about servitude, dependency, and dehumanization — "intangibles" that intertwined labor problems with race and gender — spurred workers' organizing efforts. T. O. Jones and others again attempted to unionize in 1963, this time with assistance from Retail Clerks Local 1529. The city swiftly ended their walkout by firing thirty-three workers; ultimately seventeen were rehired. Jones and others remained off the job but continued to organize. In 1964, they established an independent workers association that affiliated with AFSCME, and chartered Local 1733, choosing that number in recognition of the 1963 firings. The sanitation workers also sought help from the NAACP in early 1965, complaining that workers had been fired for union organizing. In 1966, workers voted to strike, but they remained at their jobs after the city obtained a court injunction.[63]

As pressure mounted for a strike, in defiance of the city's threats to fire anyone who joined a walkout, sanitation workers worried about losing their jobs. Robert Beasley, who helped organize the union and rode the same truck as T. O. Jones until Jones was fired, believed that before 1968,

Memphis sanitation workers hoisting tubs of garbage.
(Photo from Sanitation Strike Collection, courtesy of Special Collections, University of Memphis)

a majority of workers were too anxious about losing their jobs to maintain a strike. He emphasized what Sally Turner describes as feeling "glued in and . . . afraid to step out of it," an aspect of the "plantation mentality": "Our people were really afraid to stand out there," Beasley asserted. "It took from 1959 to 1968 to get together." Before the strike, he recalled, the local held two meetings a week to build confidence. "Being men," to Beasley, Taylor Rogers, and others, meant breaking with what they perceived as submissiveness, ending a form of white domination that depended upon black compliance.[64]

In early 1968, two disturbing incidents led to a vote to strike despite the risks. In the first, black workers in the Sewers and Drains Division were sent home on January 30 without pay during a rainstorm while white truck drivers and supervisors remained and drew a full day's pay. An incident two days later was a more chilling reminder of the problems that troubled workers. Two men in sanitation (where employees worked regardless of rain) were crushed to death by a garbage compactor in which they had taken refuge during a rainstorm, after an electrical malfunction triggered the switch. They had no workmen's compensation or life insurance—a final reminder of their difficulties in providing for their families. When a meeting with the public works commissioner fell apart over issues of union recognition, workers voted to strike on Monday, February 12.[65]

The strike immediately took on unusual political significance by becoming a showdown between the workers and Mayor Henry Loeb that placed Memphis's historical legacy of racial paternalism at the center of the conflict. The second day of the strike, during a meeting with national AFSCME officials and T. O. Jones, Loeb demanded to know whom they represented, suggesting that he, not they, knew the workers' concerns. After hearing an account of this meeting, twelve to thirteen hundred men voted to march several miles from the Firestone union hall in north Memphis to city hall. According to AFSCME official William Lucy, Loeb declared to the crowd that he "had known the men and their fathers before them and he was always fair" and that "he would give the shirt off his back." At this, Lucy recalled, a worker called out, "Just give me a decent salary and I'll buy my own!" To Lucy, this incident exemplified Loeb's desire to reinforce a "master-servant mentality," but it also indicated workers' public rejection of it. That this confrontation took place in a public venue involving all the workers meant that stories about this meeting would help frame the strike.[66]

In late February, the strike drastically changed character after workers and their supporters were attacked by police. The violence followed two dramatic days of meetings. On February 22, hundreds of workers packed city hall for a meeting with city council members, hoping to reach an agreement that would bypass Loeb's refusal to grant union recognition and dues checkoff. Frustrated at the lack of progress, 700 workers, union leaders, and supporters launched a sit-in. Workers sang "We Shall Not Be Moved" and other freedom songs, ate sandwiches provided by women on the strike support committee, and waited for the city council's Public Works Committee and strike leaders to hammer out a proposal to bring to the full council the next day. They left jubilantly after hearing a plan for union recognition and a form of dues checkoff. The next day, February 23, they returned to find that the council majority had substituted its own resolution that ignored dues checkoff and left all final decisions to the mayor. Furious workers poured outside for a hastily organized march, only to encounter throngs of police officers. Strike leaders arranged for the march to proceed, but police cars began edging the crowd into the curb, until a woman marcher, Gladys Carpenter, cried out that one of the cars had run over her foot. Carpenter had intentionally walked on the outside, thinking her presence would help shield the marchers because police would not hurt a woman. Strikers surrounded and began rocking the car. The police seized the moment to spray mace at, club, and chase marchers, including black ministers, reporters, and several white human rights leaders.[67]

Overnight, the strike transformed into a mass movement involving thousands of black Memphians, as stories of this violent police response drove home the racial power relations bound up with the strike. For Rev. H. Ralph Jackson, being maced represented a shocking moment of recognition. The minister took to the airwaves of black radio station WDIA and in a voice filled with emotion declared that he had been maced because he was black, regardless of his social standing. Within twenty-four hours of the incident, 150 African American ministers and community leaders had organized COME (Citizens on the Move for Equality). This strike support movement ballooned, now encompassing nightly mass meetings, daily marches, and a downtown boycott, with Rev. James Lawson, a veteran of both the freedom movement and antipoverty organizing, chairing COME's strategy committee.[68]

For many middle-class black Memphians, including religious and business leaders, teachers and other professionals, the sanitation workers had always been ubiquitous symbols of racial servitude from whom they sharply distinguished themselves. At this point, however, the workers became the moral vanguard. Bettye Coe Donahue, a schoolteacher from the labor activist Coe family, believed that black middle-class Memphians suddenly saw the sanitation workers as emblematic of all African Americans. When Minerva Johnican, a school librarian, heard H. Ralph Jackson's expression of shock on WDIA on her car radio, it was a defining moment. Instead of going home, she drove to Clayborn Temple and joined the support committee.[69]

The strike also mobilized small student support movements on high school campuses, with participants attending mass meetings and even skipping school to join COME's marches. Some of these youth staged innovative demonstrations, with assistance from Rev. Harold Middlebrook, a young activist minister at Middle Baptist Church who had earlier sparked Juanita Thornton's interest in the freedom movement. For example, the students turned one march into a mock funeral procession and service at which they "buried justice" at city hall. College students at Owen, LeMoyne, Memphis State, and Southwestern also urged support for the strike, with BOP members playing a prominent role. The Invaders helped organize high school students, although they chafed at the religious nonviolence espoused by COME.[70]

Working-class women, however, remained at the heart of the strike support movement. Bill Lucy admitted that AFSCME leaders expected the wives to be a drag on the strike because they would be worried about feeding their families. "What we discovered was the wives were stronger or as strong as the men were," he asserted. "They weren't about to put pressure on them to return to work until this thing got settled." Women from the workers' neighborhoods, churches, and other networks became central to the group Concerned Citizens for the Sanitation Workers and their Families. "Well, the women, we were marching, honey," stated Bessie Rogers, the wife of sanitation worker Taylor Rogers, in an interview: "The women was marching and then they would be down at the union hall fixing the dinner, fixing the food and doing stuff like that. We just worked with our husbands." And Hazel McGhee recalled neighbors and local shopkeepers helping her family during her laundry strike and then during her husband's strike. According to Ida Leachman, members of Progressive Missionary Baptist Church, most of whom had never participated in a civil rights or labor rally before, now attended rallies and marches. The strike "was on the news and at church. Everywhere you went, that was the topic," she remembers.[71]

Black union members, from Firestone to the furniture workers, also figured among the strongest supporters of the strike. Naomi Jones, for example, as a member of Local 282, devoted time and resources to the strike, despite the risks incurred for her on her own job. At RCA, although the city's "racial harmony" had reportedly convinced company officials to choose Memphis, in 1968 a large portion of the employees in the workforce, which was two-thirds African American, and a majority female, had become ardent supporters of the sanitation strike. In late March, Virgil Grace, the African American president of International Union of Electrical, Radio and Machine Workers (IUE) Local 30 informed the IUE president that the Memphis strike "involves all the Sanitation Workers in this viciously Anti-Union City, so we have voted all our financial assistance to this strike because of the importance, as we see it, of making Memphis and the mid-South Union minded."[72]

"I *Am* a Man" became the strike's predominant slogan in the weeks that followed the city hall sit-in and police macing incident. Strikers originally carried signs reading "Dignity and Decency for Our Sanitation Workers," or "We Are Together Once and for All." According to Bill Lucy, "I *Am* a Man" was first used sometime in March, after he and a few community leaders brainstormed one night at Clayborn Temple, hoping to come up with a phrase to encapsulate workers' demands for respect and dignity. "I *Am* a Man," he stated, "jumped off the page." They first used it at a strike meeting, and it "caught hold." That the more specific origin of the term remains unclear, with different explanations presented by various people, only underscores the salience of this claim to manhood in this period.[73]

The slogan's emphasis on respect, assertiveness, and courage differed from the masculinist and hypersexual political rhetoric that was becoming associated with Black Power in this same period. "I *Am* a Man" galvanized both the strikers and their working-class supporters because it publicly articulated long-standing critiques of racial servitude, dependency, and dehumanization. Otha B. Strong (whose very name echoes the slogan) declared that "I *Am* a Man" struck a chord among workers at Memphis's public hospital because they "wanted more than the supervisor standing up over us treating you like you wasn't a human being."[74]

For some supporters, "I *Am* a Man" addressed the workers' dependency on government assistance. In one strike photograph, a young woman holds a handmade sign with rounded soul-style lettering that reads, "48% of the Garbage Collectors Need Welfare to Earn a Living Wage." Indeed, many women who were becoming involved in welfare rights struggles also marched with the sanitation workers because, as welfare activist Juanita Miller Thornton put it, "we were all in the same boat. The sanitation workers had nothing new on welfare recipients. We knew what it was like to fight for food stamps." Thornton attended marches and sang in the Freedom Choir during meetings held to raise money for the strike. These supporters posed black economic dependence as a problem created by local authorities, not a personal trait.[75]

Many female strike supporters felt the slogan underscored their assertiveness as women. Everlena Yarbrough, a union activist who began working at Trojan Luggage during the sanitation strike, recalled women adopting the slogan in her workplace. Black women far outnumbered white female and black male employees and were especially concerned with issues such as not being allowed time off to care for a sick child. After the strike, they began using "I *Am* a Man," Yarbrough remembered, to "galvanize" the male workers in their plant to "stand up . . . and take a part and do their share" to support workers. Even during the sanitation strike, some working-class women believed their own support efforts exceeded those of the strikers. Naomi Jones described how she and other furniture workers were "out there taking chances with our lives, and running to meetings and everything involved, with the street marches." By becoming active strike supporters, she and others risked losing their own jobs and put themselves in danger at demonstrations that involved encounters with the police. She "felt hurt because at the time I didn't feel that the sanitation workers were doing all that they could do."[76]

The strike and its slogan drew national and international attention as civil rights leaders Bayard Rustin, Roy Wilkins, and Dr. King came to Memphis. King, thrilled by the massive, exuberant crowd at Mason Temple on March 18, announced that the upcoming Poor People's Campaign would begin there. The national media, however, focused only on the issue of violence, after the massive march he led in Memphis ten days later, on March 28, ended in a police riot sparked by an episode of window smashing and looting by fired-up youth and disaffected Beale Streeters. Officers chased, clubbed, teargassed, and maced panicked participants trying to flee the area, resulting in the shooting death of teenager Larry Payne. In the chaotic days that followed, National Guardsmen patrolled city streets and President Johnson vowed to "not let violence take over this country." Mayor Loeb turned down Johnson's offer of federal support, while King, pilloried by the press, vowed to return to Memphis a week later to prove his ability to maintain nonviolence by leading another march. Before King could join this next march, an assassin's bullet struck him down as he stood joking with colleagues on the balcony of the Lorraine Motel on April 4.[77]

Ultimately, many workers believed, it was only the tragedy of King's assassination that settled the strike. "If Dr. King hadn't got killed, Henry Loeb would have never gave in," insists Taylor Rogers. "He was just that hard set on not recognizing the union." With riots erupting in Memphis and around the country as word spread, President Johnson canceled a planned trip to Hawaii for Vietnam talks, just days after announcing he would not run for reelection but would concentrate on ending the war. Local and national pressure, including Undersecretary of Labor James Reynolds's participation in negotiations, finally convinced Loeb to recognize the union and have the city collect union dues. On April 16, workers rose to their feet in a unanimous vote to accept the contract.[78]

A crowd of sanitation strike supporters gathering
in front of Clayborn Temple, March 28, 1968.
(© Ernest C. Withers, courtesy of Panopticon Gallery)

For supporters of the sanitation strike, learning about the assassination of Dr. King over the radio represented a moment that was at once
intensely personal and deeply shared, one of extreme emotional pain and
enormous challenge. Many recall having premonitions of the slaying.
Naomi Jones, who had attended King's speech at Mason Temple the night
before and shaken his hand, says she "just screamed." "I didn't know what
to do," she remembers. "I was afraid to go out on the street that night because they were burning. The store over here was burning, the store on
the corner was burning. It was like it was the end of the world." Eddie May
Garner felt similarly. She simply lay down on her bed. Minerva Johnican
walked out of her teachers' meeting and drove to Clayborn Temple, unwill-
ing to go home to face reality alone even after rioting erupted.[79]

At WLOK, a short walk from the Lorraine Motel, radio personnel struggled to respond, not only for themselves but as communicators to their vast

black listening audience. Some DJs had devoted themselves to the strike and knew King personally from his many visits to the city. Joan Golden, who had conversed with King about the violence of March 28, recalls that just hours before the assassination, Jesse Jackson, who was in town with King and SCLC, visited the station during the afternoon with a request from King to play "Keep on Pushing," the 1964 hit by the Impressions—a request that, in retrospect, took on profound meaning. She remembers a young newsman later in the day running into the station crying: "Martin Luther King has just been shot!" Rev. Bill Adkins, then a newsman at WLOK, ran over to the Lorraine Motel upon hearing the announcement on another station, found the surrounding streets already barricaded, and raced back to the station to confirm the news. Adkins, who felt an awesome responsibility, remembers telling the DJ on the air to stop his regular pop music show so they could play hymns and begin to tell people what happened. Meanwhile, Isaac Hayes and David Porter at Stax also sped from the studio to the Lorraine Motel after hearing the news when they emerged from a recording session, but they could not reach the site. "There were thousands of people in the streets. Everywhere," Porter remembers. "At that time everything stopped."[80]

These memories blend with accounts of King's apocalyptic "mountaintop speech" at Mason Temple the previous evening, which those who did not attend describe as vividly as those who did, an indication of the collective nature of the story's retelling. With thunder crashing and rain pouring down on the roof, they recall, King told his audience that he, like Moses, had seen the promised land. With a "peculiar look on his face," he told them that he might not get there but they would reach that land. King's listeners understood the promised land to be freedom, which meant both deliverance and salvation, both collective and personal. Freedom had not been attained, yet because of the self-transformation inspired by their movement, they had the ability to achieve it. The promised land in other periods of African American history had denoted the end of slavery, or the northern terminus of the Great Migration. In 1968, it meant a profound cultural and structural transformation of American society: the achievement of racial equality and labor justice, as well as a new humanity—a new manhood and womanhood.

The media's emphasis on violence in 1968—both the earlier violence that had prompted King's return to Memphis and the riots that erupted across the country following his death—obscured the richness of urban working-class African American agency and the complex meanings of freedom during the sanitation strike. The textured, gendered meanings of "I

Sanitation strikers and supporters march through downtown
Memphis between National Guardsmen and tanks, March 29, 1968,
the day after violence erupted during the march from Clayborn Temple.
(Sanitation Strike collection, Special Collections, University of Memphis)

Am a Man" were further blurred as media attention shifted to the upsurge
of black nationalism in the wake of King's assassination that placed the
language of black masculinity firmly within the arenas of hypersexual
male aggression and antiwhite violence. Subsequent scholarly accounts
that have focused specifically on the effect of King's death on the national
civil rights movement have, for different reasons, shifted attention away
from the meaning of this trauma for black Memphians.

An indication of its significance could be seen on April 8, when Memphis's largest march ever attracted some 40,000 participants, many from
out of town en route to King's funeral in Atlanta, but the preponderance
from Memphis itself. Art Gilliam, then a black reporter for the *Commercial
Appeal* who has since become owner of WLOK, recalls "miles and miles" of
marchers walking to city hall, led by Coretta Scott King and her children,
along with many other national movement leaders and well-known black

artists, from Harry Belafonte to James Brown. The mood of the march was one of such somber determination, he remembers, that it became clear to him and others that the civil rights movement would not just fade away. Indeed, many working-class black Memphians attended their first freedom march that day.[81]

African Americans in Memphis involved in the sanitation strike, and some of these newcomers, developed multilayered understandings of the "promised land" that dovetailed with their understandings of the strike as a struggle to overcome the "plantation mentality." Workers' challenge to the "plantation mentality," and the assertiveness denoted by "I *Am* a Man," struck out at fear and compliance. African Americans staked a claim to a human equality that included but was not synonymous with desegregation. They also attacked ideological beliefs that, by casting African Americans as dependents and inferiors, purported to justify humiliating racist practices. Working-class activists who resisted these markers of servitude identified with the politics of masculinity projected by the sanitation strike's slogan. "Being men," in the context of the strike, meant claiming freedom — freedom as both a goal and the ongoing process of achieving that goal.

Equating the slogan with freedom, however, risks obscuring the specific gendered concerns that women and men brought to their understandings of freedom. While men attacked racist practices and stereotypes that excluded them from recognition as independent wage earners and heads of household, black women rejected racist distinctions of black and white womanhood. Rather than fitting themselves into norms based on white bourgeois femininity, women claimed identities of themselves as equals, not subordinates, of black men.

Memphis, as the urban hub of the Mississippi Delta, was historically a matrix of regional and national developments in the cotton economy, in politics, and in popular culture. The sanitation strike and the urban rebellions around the country that followed King's assassination made Memphis key to the future direction of the nationwide freedom movement, which had increasingly become multiracial. Battling the plantation mentality, previously seen as a problem pertaining specifically to the two-way road between the urban and rural Deep South, now constituted the challenge that the movement would have to confront in the coming years.

Conclusion

Black Memphians participating in the sanitation strike support movement had their eyes trained on the present and future of American society and of their own lives, yet their understandings of freedom had emerged out of years of struggle with what many identified as the "plantation mentality." For urban black southerners in the mid-twentieth century, many of them migrants from the rural South, critiques of the "plantation mentality" resonated with meaning, given their earlier efforts to remove themselves geographically from the power relations of the plantation. Their use of the term imbued the idea of freedom with complex and historically specific meanings, which involved dismantling racist practices that influenced everyday life and rejecting racial identities that associated blackness with servitude and even inhumanity. The idea of the "plantation mentality," which surfaced as part of the black vernacular of the 1960s, offers new insights into nearly three decades of struggle between the Second World War and the sanitation strike, a crucial period in the history of the black freedom movement and American society. Grappling with that period today demands that we analyze both the actions and the thoughts of those who struggled on many fronts to claim a new manhood and womanhood and to change their society.

The freedom movement sparked by the 1968 sanitation strike did not conclude with Mayor Loeb's agreement with the union but inspired further struggles, both immediately and over the next decade. Motivated by the symbolism and momentum of the strike, and deeply moved by the fact that King had lost his life in Memphis, black Memphians in workplaces, public housing, high schools, and elsewhere launched protests to challenge racial injustice and demand equality. Whether they had taken to heart King's message about reaching the promised land or interpreted "I

Am a Man" as a call to demand respect, black Memphians mobilized following the strike and King's assassination.

This is not to say that such struggles resulted automatically from the tragedy of King's assassination in Memphis, or from the intense weeks of meetings and demonstrations on behalf of the sanitation workers that had preceded it. Quite the contrary. Many black Memphians describe the devastation they experienced in April 1968 and for months thereafter. Naomi Jones, a member of Local 282 of the furniture workers union who had been involved with the strike support movement, remembers that she "felt so let down for six or eight months after Martin Luther King died." Songwriter and performer Isaac Hayes, who grew up in Memphis and worked at Stax, describes himself as "filled with so much bitterness and anguish, till I couldn't deal with it." Hayes "couldn't write for about a year," he recalls.[1]

It is important to see, therefore, that the movements that ensued in the aftermath of the sanitation strike had already been under way before the sanitation strike but now gained new steam from workers' responses to the tragedy of King's death, and identification with the ideas conveyed by the strike. When public employees at John Gaston Hospital, for example, initiated their own strike almost immediately after the sanitation strike ended, they adopted "I *Am* a Man" as their own slogan and joined AFSCME Local 1733, the sanitation workers' local. Although the hospital had finally desegregated as a result of the 1964 Civil Rights Act, orderlies, nurses, and assistants continued to confront low wages, long hours, and humiliating treatment.[2] Organizing in manufacturing sweatshops and mass industries also intensified, as did the nascent welfare rights movement. For Local 282 of the furniture workers union, the strike would inspire numerous new organizing drives and usher in a new young leadership, with Willie Rudd, a militant young black Memphis worker, elected as president. The reinvigorated local made racial justice and community-based protest fundamental to organizing, as was especially the case during the 1980 strike against the Memphis Furniture Company, when workers finally won union representation after a protracted, difficult struggle. The dynamic, black-led labor organization also elected to key positions women like Ida Leachman, who was unable to get a factory job until 1969, when a plant where she had been unable to procure a job in the early 1960s finally desegregated.[3]

At RCA, where black workers had also supported the sanitation strike, King's assassination ignited so much rage that management temporarily suspended production. The language of freedom and opposition to the "plantation mentality" that framed the sanitation strike influenced the way RCA workers perceived their own struggle. "[T]he day of reckoning is at hand," wrote Virgil Grace, president of IUE Local 30, to RCA's personnel manager in June 1968. The local would not allow its members to be "raped of their dignity and pride," he declared. "The days of slavery and all it's [*sic*] attendant misery was abolished a century ago. We will not allow RCA to institute it all over again. RCA must realize that our foreman is not our Lord and Master and the Corporation does not own us body and soul." Grace threatened to ignore the contract's no-strike clause if "non-concern for the Grievance Procedure and mal-treatment of our members" did not cease. His highly charged gendered language of slavery and rape drew on biblical allusion to reject the idea that anyone but God could be one's master, and it reverberated with the sanitation workers' slogan, "I *Am* a Man." RCA workers threw their support behind workers at other plants as well, including Hunter Fan, where roughly 500 of the 1,300 employees were black women, hired as a result of the Civil Rights Act. They likewise had become determined to "stand up for what you want," in the words of Hunter Fan worker Earline Whitehead, a participant in a three-month-long strike in 1969 and many civil rights demonstrations.[4]

In addition to these burgeoning struggles in labor and welfare rights, Memphis students challenged the nature of their education. Working with the NAACP, high school students launched a massive protest movement in 1969 aimed at desegregating the public schools and winning black school board representation. Fifteen years after *Brown v. Board of Education*, only a token number of black students had been permitted to enter "white" schools. Desegregation in Memphis had become an urgent, daily issue for African American children and parents, since the overcrowding of "black" schools had reached appalling proportions in the 1960s, resulting in split shifts and the use of gyms, auditoriums, and other spaces as classrooms. The "Black Monday" movement, a weekly boycott of high schools on Mondays by thousands of students (to some parents' dismay), encompassed mass meetings and marches of as many as 15,000 participants, coordinated by the NAACP, especially executive secretary Maxine Smith, who was eventually elected to the school board.[5]

In a different vein, student protesters at LeMoyne-Owen College, who identified more with the ideas of Black Power than those of the NAACP, halted classes and flew a "flag of Black America" over campus buildings that they occupied and declared part of a "liberated zone" for several days. The students, led by members of a campus group called the Black United Front, presented grievances about the college administration's approach to black education, which they considered bourgeois and conformist to the expectations of white society. Demonstrators included members of

Black Power groups off campus and white students active with Students for a Democratic Society on other Memphis campuses, including Southwestern.[6] Despite their new orientation, black Memphis students continued to define their own agency in relation to the historical racial power relations in Memphis. A student writer for the LeMoyne *Inquirer* in May 1968 referred to this history in an article that lambasted recently approved racist policies, including one in which the board of education canceled proms and other social events to keep white and black students from dancing together. The writer denounced not only white officials but also black administrators who conceded to these policies. Referring to the Crump political machine's notorious tactics to win black votes, the article insisted that African Americans need to "show our white counterparts that we no longer accept [their] 'divided and unequal policies,' that we will no longer take a 'barbeque sandwich for a vote' for now, united we stand." The student rejected a past history in which African Americans relied on white paternalism to net meager material benefits, demanding black independent critical thought and racial equality.[7]

Participants in these movements drew upon concepts of freedom and black liberation (the term they used to mark affinity with anticolonial movements) that reflected decades of struggle with racial power relations that, for many African Americans, invoked cultural memories of slavery. Black Memphians at different points in the twentieth century contended that although slavery had been eradicated decades earlier, its impact on thought and behavior in everyday life persisted, even in the city. In the 1920s, black political commentator Lt. George Lee, who had earlier migrated to Memphis from Mississippi, observed that both the white man and the black man maintained "mental reservations" emanating from slavery that needed to be eradicated for different race relations to be achieved. The struggle for freedom involved demands for both the end of white supremacy and a changed political perspective among black leaders who emphasized cooperation over militancy. This struggle over black political perspectives became an urgent problem in the face of the Crump machine's "reign of terror" on the eve of the Second World War.

The complexity of achieving genuine freedom in the urban South anticipated the multifaceted struggles that erupted in Memphis during and after the Second World War, in the context of an intense outpouring of rhetoric about American democracy. Not only in politics per se but in workplaces, neighborhoods, and popular culture — all spheres that are frequently overlooked in histories of the black freedom movement — an array of conflicts brought to the fore contentious issues about African American identities, racial ideologies, and the meaning of freedom. Working-class people, many of them recent migrants from the rural plantation counties of west Tennessee, Arkansas, and Mississippi, seized on rhetoric about American democracy to challenge police violence and discriminatory employment practices that served as reminders of the plantation regime they sought to leave behind.

Concomitantly, heated debates about portrayals of African Americans in mass culture, prompted by the censorship of movies showing blacks outside of servant roles, made the racial ideologies underlying these conflicts over labor and police brutality even more explicit. In a critique of this attempt to control the racial imaginary of both black and white people, an article in the LeMoyne newspaper referred to Memphis as a place still in "slavery territory" when it came to "mental liberties." In contrast, the advent of black-oriented radio established a new public sphere that, despite the limitations of Jim Crow society, made it possible to push this racial imaginary in new directions.

Freedom involved the transformation of culture, consciousness, and politics — a process that was neither linear nor unitary but contradictory and multifaceted. Indeed, in the mid-1940s, during crises ranging from the Crump machine's cancellation of labor and civil rights leader A. Philip Randolph's scheduled mass meeting, to the mayor's refusal to permit the Freedom Train to visit the city, activists at LeMoyne and elsewhere denounced the conciliatory stance of current black community leaders, which they found humiliating and degrading. While berating those who sought racial harmony in exchange for "benefits" from the Crump machine, they presented themselves as "fighters for freedom." A. Philip Randolph, during a controversial return visit, succinctly articulated this challenge by declaring in a highly publicized speech that black Memphians did not want to be "well-kept slaves."

Even as public attention was riveted to the breakthroughs achieved in civil rights by the Supreme Court's 1954 decision in *Brown v. Board of Education*, struggles in multiple arenas of urban culture and creative expression persisted, shaped by the ongoing rural-urban relations that dominated Memphis and other southern cities. When black Memphis students suddenly began to sit in at public facilities demanding desegregation, their actions overlapped with a movement for voting rights by sharecroppers in neighboring Fayette and Haywood counties, heightened political activism in Memphis, the first efforts by the sanitation workers to organize a union, and the rise of Stax Records and soul music. "Making history," in the students' view, was not limited to winning the right to eat in restaurants alongside whites. It also meant collectively confronting and making sense of their own past experiences of the racial intimidation and humiliation they endured in everyday acts as simple as riding a bus. Through this process they were able to claim new self-identities based on their own agency as activists in the freedom movement. The crescendo of activism, especially among working-class black Memphians and young people, in the aftermath of the Civil Rights Act and Voting Rights Act underscores that the achievement of desegregation in most public facilities in the early 1960s neither concluded the movement nor resolved the problem of freedom.

The 1968 sanitation strike most fully and publicly articulated the complex understandings of freedom that had emerged among African Americans in Memphis during the civil rights era. Begun as a labor dispute over the right of municipal employees to organize a union, the strike quickly transformed into a mass movement led by African Americans on the lowest rung of the social ladder, who worked in jobs that were the most despised—and the most racially marked—in southern cities. The slogan "I *Am* a Man" resonated powerfully with black Memphians because they located in it profound issues with which they all had contended, albeit in different ways. Strikers and their supporters not only rejected their role in what they considered the master/slave relations of the city; they also renounced the internalization of those relations, whether by black elites seeking rapprochement with white officials or within themselves. In rejecting the "plantation mentality," they staked a claim to an equal humanity—to manhood and womanhood.

While all of these struggles over schooling, labor, welfare, and many other issues have persisted well beyond the 1960s, they too, like the conflicts discussed throughout this book, need to be seen in light of their historical context. Although the courts finally forced the city to desegregate its public school system by initiating a busing program in the early 1970s, for example, a movement of white parents to place their children in private institutions has made de facto segregation and inferior schools continuing facts of life for most youth in Memphis public schools. Moreover, many of the plants where black workers won important victories, including Memphis Furniture, have since shut down and, in some cases, moved out of the United States, a process anticipated by the closure of the RCA plant and its shifting of production overseas in 1970. As the economy has shifted, other manufacturing plants and distribution companies have moved to Memphis and elsewhere in the South to escape higher wage and union workforces. They are now employing multicultural workforces, including immigrants from Southeast Asia, Mexico, and Central America, along with African Americans and native-born whites, that may have more in common with the segregated workforces of the past than meets the eye. And Beale Street, now a major tourist attraction, has not been an epicenter of black Memphis since the surrounding neighborhood was razed during urban renewal in the 1970s.

What, then, does one make of the history of the civil rights era and the massive 1968 sanitation strike? The battle over the "plantation mentality" might seem to be over, but, interestingly the term is now used more, not less, than it was in the 1960s. Moreover, nearly all the African Americans interviewed in Memphis for this project were eager to tell their stories, no matter how painful they were to tell. Their desire to share their stories, therefore, has nothing to do with nostalgia; rather, it has to do with discerning the significance of this history for today, when many Memphians continue to face serious problems of poverty and powerlessness and when, just as importantly, struggles for racial justice continue, often in complex multiracial contexts.

We need new ways of understanding the history of the mid-twentieth-century black freedom movement. If we fail to analyze the thoughts and experiences of the people who made this history and motivated the upheavals of this crucial period, we risk reducing their goals to the specific civil rights won through federal court decisions and legislation. As a result, we also risk reducing their movement to a narrative that lacks relevance for today's very different political, cultural, and economic terrain. By grappling with the transformation of consciousness, culture, and politics that this battle against the "plantation mentality" inspired, on the other hand, we can discern the continuities and discontinuities between then and now, between history and the present.

Notes

Abbreviations

Beecher Papers
John Beecher Papers, Harry Ransom Humanities Research Center, University of Texas, Austin, Texas

Chandler Papers
Walter Chandler Papers, Memphis and Shelby County Room, Memphis Public Library and Information Center, Memphis, Tennessee

FEPC Records
Selected Documents from Records of the Committee on Fair Employment Practice, RG 228 of the National Archives (microfilm), Glen Rock, N.J.: Microfilming Corporation of America, 1970

FEPC-Region VII
Records of the Committee on Fair Employment Practice, RG 228.5.7, Regional Files, Region VII, Southeast Region, National Archives and Records Administration, East Point, Georgia

LMOC Archives
College Newspapers, Box 34, LeMoyne-Owen College Archives, Hollis F. Price Library, LeMoyne-Owen College, Memphis, Tennessee

MAP-South
Memphis Area Project—South Office

NAACP-LC
National Association for the Advancement of Colored People Papers, Manuscript Division, Library of Congress, Washington, D.C.

NAACP Papers
National Association for the Advancement of Colored People Papers (microfilm), Bethesda, Maryland: University Publications of America

NAACP Papers-FT
National Association for the Advancement of Colored People Papers (microfilm), part 15: Segregation and Discrimination: Complaints and Responses, 1940–55, series B: Administrative Files, Bethesda, Maryland: University Publications of America, specifically on Freedom Train

NARA
National Archives and Records Administration, College Park, Maryland

Orgill Papers
Edmund Orgill Papers, Special Collections, Ned. R. McWherter Library, University of Memphis, Memphis, Tennessee

Pleasants Papers

James Pleasants Jr. Papers, Memphis and Shelby County Room, Memphis
Public Library and Information Center, Memphis, Tennessee

RCA-IUE Records

RCA–International Union of Electrical Workers Records, Special Collections
and University Archives, Rutgers University Libraries, New Brunswick, New
Jersey

Smith Collection

Maxine Smith NAACP Collection, Memphis and Shelby County Room, Memphis
Public Library and Information Center, Memphis, Tennessee

Tobey Papers

Frank Tobey Papers, Memphis and Shelby County Room, Memphis Public
Library and Information Center, Memphis, Tennessee

UFWA Papers

United Furniture Workers of America Papers, Southern Labor Archives,
Special Collections Department, Pullen Library, Georgia State University,
Atlanta

WPA

Works Progress Administration

Introduction

1. This account by Sally Turner is based on interview by author.

2. Taylor Rogers and Bessie L. Rogers interview by author.

3. See also comments by Waldo E. Martin Jr. on black self-consciousness, in *No Coward Soldiers*, 8. Martin asserts that a "vital aspect of the black social imagination is its emphasis on self-definition, self-fashioning, or what Arjun Appadurai terms 'self-imagining.'" The Appadurai reference is to *Modernity at Large*, 7.

4. See discussion of consciousness, culture, and politics in Martin, *No Coward Soldiers*, especially the concise presentation of these concepts in the introduction, 1–9. See also Green, "Battling the Plantation Mentality," 1–21.

5. The text of King's speech can be found in Washington, ed., *Testament of Hope*, 279–86, along with other speeches and writings by King. See also Green, "Battling the Plantation Mentality," 353–412, which includes a fuller discussion of King's relation to labor and welfare rights in the mid-1960s than has been included in this book; and Honey, *Going Down Jericho Road*. Honey's work, which is being published concurrently with this book, presents an extensive discussion of King's relation to the sanitation strike and his ideas about labor and the black freedom movement.

6. The oral histories that I conducted in summer 1995, were done in conjunction with Duke University's Center for Documentary Studies project, Behind the Veil: Documenting African American Life in the Jim Crow South, directed by William Chafe, Raymond Gavins, and Robert Korstad. As part of the Behind the Veil project, transcripts and tapes of the Memphis interviews have been deposited both at Duke University's Special Collections and LeMoyne-Owen College's Hollis F. Price Library in Memphis.

7. Roosevelt's January 1941 State of the Union address, also known as the "Four Freedoms" speech, calls for "four essential human freedoms": freedom of speech, freedom of religion, freedom from want, and freedom from fear.

8. Quoted in Sigafoos, *Cotton Row to Beale Street*, 137. More generally, Sigafoos's book is a good source for information about Memphis's economic development.

9. On Beale Street's history, see Lee, *Beale Street*; and McKee and Chisenhall, *Beale Black and Blue*. See also David Goldfield's commentary on the rural-urban relations that shape southern cities, including Memphis, in *Region, Race, and Cities*, 37–68.

10. Pete Daniel (*Lost Revolutions*, 1) estimates that eleven million rural southerners left the land during the first two decades after World War II. For more on rural southerners' cultural impact in the city after the war, see especially Book II of Daniel's work.

11. Daniel Dean Carter to Thurgood Marshall, January 8, 1941, *NAACP Papers*, part 18, group II, 28:976–77.

12. Dailey, Gilmore, and Simon, *Jumpin' Jim Crow*, 3–4.

13. On southern politics after World War II, see especially Frederickson, *Dixiecrat Revolt*; and Bryant Simon, "Race Reactions: African American Organizing, Liberalism, and White Working-Class Politics in Postwar South Carolina," in Dailey, Gilmore, and Simon, eds., *Jumpin' Jim Crow*, 239–59.

14. Martin Luther King Jr., quoted in Beifuss, *At the River I Stand*, 194–95.

15. Ruby Hurley, Southeast Regional Office, Report from Field Trip, March 27, 1952, NAACP-LC, group II, box C186, folder: Memphis, Tennessee, 1951–55.

16. For an important philosophical discussion of this kind of nonlinear, contradictory development, see radical philosopher Raya Dunayevskaya's comment in reference to the African revolutions of the postwar era, that "the whole point seems to be to hold on to the principle of creativity, and the contradictory process by which creativity develops" (*Philosophy and Revolution*, 246).

17. Dittmer, *Local People*; Payne, *I've Got the Light of Freedom*.

18. Michael Honey's *Southern Labor and Black Civil Rights*, an examination of CIO organizing in World War II–era Memphis, argues that wartime CIO militancy provided a space in which black workers could simultaneously battle on two fronts, class struggle and racial justice, but that Cold War red-baiting of radical CIO unions and their leaders placed this confluence of economic and racial issues on hold until the 1968 sanitation strike. My research, however, reveals the continued importance of black workers' labor struggles in the intervening decades as working-class consciousness found expression in struggles in other spheres of community, culture, and civil rights. Recognizing that continuity, I argue, should help us to better understand the 1968 sanitation strike and the import of King's intervention, a topic Honey's new work, *Going Down Jericho Road*, also seeks to address.

19. Two works that also traverse these historiographical boundaries, albeit for different time periods, are Daniel, *Lost Revolutions*; and Hunter, *To 'Joy My Freedom*. Daniel's discussion of white southern migrants and Hunter's of working-class black women both examine intersections of politics, culture, and everyday life.

20. Kelley, *Race Rebels*, 9–10.

21. Rev. George A. Long, "Christ, Not Crump, Is My Boss," *Memphis Press-Scimitar*, April 3, 1944, 1; "Randolph Scores Attitude of Memphis Labor Leaders," *Memphis World*, April 4, 1944, 1.

22. On black masculinity and the "I Am a Man" slogan, see Estes, *I Am a Man!*, chap. 6; and on the slogan's meaning for recasting black manhood and black womanhood, see Green, "Race, Gender, and Labor in 1960s Memphis."

23. Lee, "These 'Colored' United States."

Chapter 1

1. This account is based on Susie Bryant interview by author. See also Clubb, ed., *Legacy of Achievers*, 123. On the 1870 Tennessee poll tax provision, see Cartwright, *Triumph of Jim Crow*, 223–27.

2. The "Dog" is famous from blues lore; the place "where the Southern crosses the Dog" is supposedly where Robert Johnson sold his soul to the Devil to become a blues musician. This crossroads is located in Moorhead, Mississippi, due west of Greenwood, Bryant's home before she migrated to Memphis.

3. On the Greenwood movement, see especially Payne, *I've Got the Light of Freedom*.

4. On migrants to Memphis in the 1920s, see Goings and Smith, "'Unhidden' Transcripts," 372–94.

5. "Memorandum on the Memphis Situation," December 30, 1940; Howard Lee to President Franklin D. Roosevelt, December 21, 1940; and "Gestapo Rules Memphis Says Crisis Magazine," May 2, 1941, all in *NAACP Papers*, part 18, group II, 1994, 28:940, 960, 1020; Bunche, *Political Status of the Negro*, 493–502.

6. Sigafoos, *Cotton Row to Beale Street*, 67, 72; Miller, *Memphis during the Progressive Era*, 45–47; Woodruff, *American Congo*, 8, 16–21. See also Woodruff's analysis of the region's "alluvial empire" in the context of world capitalist development.

7. Sigafoos, *Cotton Row to Beale Street*, 186, 191, 94, 143–44; Biles, *Memphis in the Great Depression*, 19, 53; Miller, *Memphis during the Progressive Era*, 52; Sigafoos, *Cotton Row to Beale Street*, 86, 136–37. Gerald M. Capers comments that "Memphis presented a strange paradox—a city modern in physical aspect but rural in background, rural in prejudice, and rural in habit," in *Biography of a River Town*, 206. See also Goldfield, *Region, Race, and Cities*, 37–68; and Cobb, *Selling of the South*.

8. Sigafoos, *Cotton Row to Beale Street*, 55–56, 60–63; WPA, "Housing Survey," 16–20; "Venereal Check of Servants Urged," January 8, 1937; and "One Servant in Two Has Syphilis," March 20, 1937, both in *Memphis Press-Scimitar*; Biles, *Memphis in the Great Depression*, 14–15; Goings and Smith, "'Unhidden' Transcripts," 372–94; Bunche, *Political Status of the Negro*, 56.

9. Melton, "Blacks in Memphis, Tennessee," 24–29; Michael Honey, *Southern Labor and Black Civil Rights*, 29–38; Lamon, *Black Tennesseans*, 133, 141. See also Nan Woodruff's discussion of planters' and lumbermen's use of vagrancy laws in the Delta, including the "Work or Fight" orders issued during World War I, in *American Congo*, 32–36, 59–61.

10. Lee, *Beale Street*, 62–64. See also Tera W. Hunter's analysis of Atlanta domestic servants and blues culture, in *To 'Joy My Freedom*, 168–86.

11. Biles, *Memphis in the Great Depression*, 17, 31–34; Tucker, *Memphis Since Crump*, 23–24; Miller, *Mr. Crump of Memphis*, 3–76. For the latest work on Crump see Dowdy, *Mayor Crump Don't Like It*.

12. Bunche, *Political Status of the Negro*, 73, 497; Biles, *Memphis in the Great Depression*, 40–42; Melton, "Blacks in Memphis, Tennessee," 36–38, 66–67; Miller, *Memphis during the Progressive Era*, 169–70; "Public Improvements Sponsored by City of Memphis for Colored Citizens, January 1, 1920–June 1, 1937," in Chandler Papers, box 6, folder: Race Relations, 1940. See Bunche's investigation of city expenditures on African Americans, *Political Status of the Negro*, 496. Only a tiny fraction of the municipal budget went to projects that benefited blacks.

13. The largest growers received huge AAA payments; in 1936, the British-owned Delta Pine and Land Company received $60,388. See "Johnston Tops AAA Payments," *Memphis Press-Scimitar*, May 22, 1937. Delta Pine manager Oscar Johnston helped write the federal legislation and advised growers at a 1933 meeting in Memphis on how they could bypass the requirement to share payments with tenants. See Biles, *Memphis in the Great Depression*, 72. On the AAA more generally, see Daniel, *Breaking the Land*, 91–109; and Wright, *Old South, New South*, 198–238.

14. "Calls Meeting on Farm Wages," May 21, 1937; "Farm Workers' 'Scale' Fixed," May 24, 1937; "Mexican Cotton Pickers Imported by Plantations," August 23, 1937; and "Idlers Forced to Pick Cotton," September 22, 1937, all in *Memphis Press-Scimitar*. See Lev Flournoy's "Cotton" series, January 2, 4, 5, and 6, 1937, and analysis of the Bankhead-Jones tenancy reform bill between January and April 1937, in *Memphis Press-Scimitar*. On the STFU, see Mitchell, *Mean Things Happening in This Land*; Grubbs, *Cry from the Cotton*; and Woodruff, *American Congo*, 169–81. On earlier black organizing in rural Arkansas, see Woodruff, *American Congo*, 74–109.

15. "Cotton Acreage Cut Will Be More Than 4,000,000," September 20, 1937; Jack Bryan, "Writer Says South's Use of Machinery is Turning 'Cropper into Laborers," September 15, 1937; "Cotton: Picking Machine Changes Picture," January 5, 1937; "A New Picker to Start Work," September 6, 1937; "Picker Machine's Reign Near, Says U.S. Report," October 25, 1937; and "For the First Time, Machines Probably Will Play a Part in Harvesting the South's 1938 Cotton Crop," October 25, 1937, all in *Memphis Press-Scimitar*; Cobb, *Most Southern Place on Earth*, 197; Wright, *Old South, New South*, 232–35. Wright states that between 1930 and 1940, Delta farmland cultivated by tenant farmers dropped from 81.9 to 58.2 percent (p. 233).

16. Naomi Jones interview by author.

17. Ibid.

18. Artherene Chalmers interview by author.

19. Ibid.

20. Bunche, *Political Status of the Negro*, 496; Melton, "Blacks in Memphis, Tennessee," 149; "Negro Domestics Finish 'Y' Course," March 9, 1937; Ada Gilkey, "'Commencement' Exercises Held for 50 Negro Girl Servant School Graduates," March 22, 1937; "Syphilis Test Important for Your Servant," March 18, 1937; and "One Servant in 2 Has Syphilis," March 20, 1937, all in *Memphis Press-Scimitar*.

21. "Negro Domestics Finish 'Y' Course," March 9, 1937; "One Servant in 2 Has Syphilis," March 20, 1937; Gilkey, "'Commencement' Exercises Held for 50

Negro Girl Servant School Graduates," March 22, 1937; LaVerne Swim, "If Cook Quits, Just Telephone for a New One," November 16, 1937; "Story Reverses City's Domestic Help Situation," December 31, 1937, all in *Memphis Press-Scimitar*. On the National Youth Administration, see Biles, *Memphis in the Great Depression*, 94.

22. Bunche, *Political Status of the Negro*, 501–2; Melton, "Blacks in Memphis, Tennessee," 155–56; Michael Honey, *Southern Labor and Black Civil Rights*, 101. On the carpenters' union and the NAACP, see Born, "Memphis Negro Workingmen," 104.

23. E. M. Norment, district supervisor, Memphis Public Employment Center, Tennessee State Employment Service, to Mayor Walter Chandler, September 30, 1941; and W. V. Allen, farm placement adviser, Bureau of Employment Security, Social Security Board to Police Chief Carroll Seabrook, September 29, 1941, both in Chandler Papers, box 2, folder: Tennessee State Employment Service, 1941; Clara E. Kitts, manager, United States Employment Service, Farm Division to Public Safety commissioner Joseph Boyle, October 11, 1945, Chandler Papers, box 22, folder: Public Safety, 1945.

24. Hal Holt Peel, district employment officer, WPA, Division of Employment to Honorable O. B. Ellis, county commissioner, February 15, 1940; Peel to Honorable Francis Andrews, county commissioner, February 24, 1940; Peel to S. T. Pease, Tennessee state administrator, WPA, April 8, 1941; and A. B. Clapp to Commissioner O. B. Ellis, all in Chandler Papers, box 2, folder: WPA — Division of Employment, Correspondence, 1940–41.

25. Hal Holt Peel to Honorable Clifford Davis, October 15, 1941, Chandler Papers, box 2, folder: WPA — Division of Employment, Correspondence, 1940–41.

26. "Tenant Union Linked to CIO," September 25, 1937; and "WPA Workers Not Forced to Gather Cotton," September 27, 1937, both in *Memphis Press-Scimitar*. Mayor Walter Chandler assured a Memphis lawyer/planter, "There are few negroes now on WPA who ever worked on a farm." The Farm Placement Division of the U.S. Employment Service was also "trying to send farm hands back to the farm." See W. C. Rodgers to Mayor Walter Chandler, March 31, 1941; and Chandler to Rodgers, April 3, 1941, both in Chandler Papers, box 3, folder: Correspondence — R — 1941.

27. On the NIRA in Memphis, see Biles, *Memphis in the Great Depression*, 73–74, 93–94; and Michael Honey, *Southern Labor and Black Civil Rights*, 25–26. For a comparative view of another southern city, see Korstad, *Civil Rights Unionism*, 127–30.

28. "Minor Disorders Flare at C.I.O. Girls' Strike," March 8, 1937; "200 Quit Work at Bruce Mill," March 9, 1937; and "Workers Back at Bruce Mill," March 10, 1937, all in *Memphis Press-Scimitar*. See also Michael Honey, *Southern Labor and Black Civil Rights*, 78–92.

29. "3-Hour Strike in Barrel Mill," March 11, 1937; "450 Furniture Workers Quit; Ask More Pay," March 12, 1937; "Negro Women Out on Strike," March 16, 1937; "Nut Shellers Go on Strike," March 16, 1937, "Dock Workers Go on Strike," July 10, 1937; "Free Negroes Held in Compress 'Strike,'" October 22, 1937; "Dock Workers Out on Strike," October 26, 1937; and "Longshoremen on Strike Here," December 2, 1937, all in *Memphis Press-Scimitar*.

30. "3-Hour Strike in Barrel Mill," March 11, 1937; "City O.K.'s Furniture Pickets;

Mayor Examines Wage Scales," March 12, 1937; and "450 Furniture Workers Out," March 12, 1937, all in *Memphis Press-Scimitar*.

31. Chickasaw workers joined the Coopers International Union in spring 1937, staging a strike in June in sympathy with striking workers at Chickasaw's Louisville plant. See *Memphis Press-Scimitar*, June 24, 1937.

32. For an extensive account of the 1939 waterfront strike and Watkins's own history, see Michael Honey, *Southern Labor and Black Civil Rights*, 1–6, 93–116.

33. Mayor Overton to E. H. Crump, August 13, 1937, cited in Michael Honey, *Southern Labor and Black Civil Rights*, 311. Biles (*Memphis in the Great Depression*, 86) concludes, "In effect, the New Deal was filtered through the Crump machine." For an example of competing white New Deal politics, see Simon, *Fabric of Defeat*.

34. See Thomas L. Stokes's series in the *Memphis Press-Scimitar*, January 7–22, 1937, and Benton J. Stong's articles January 22 and February 24, 1937, on towns that lured manufacturing plants to the South by offering low wages and a non-union climate, and passing bond issues that offered tax-free land or required employees to pay a portion of their wages for building costs. For a historical study, see Cobb, *Selling of the South*.

35. "Toward a Labor Policy," *Memphis Press-Scimitar*, April 1, 1937. See also "Whither Labor," *Memphis Press-Scimitar*, May 4, 1937. On his support for abolishing the state poll tax, see the *Memphis Press-Scimitar* editorial published on New Year's Day, 1941, "Talk Poll Tax Repeal!"

36. "Ford Worker Here Protests," June 2, 1937; "Ford Worker Ganged, Beaten Second Time," August 11, 1937; "Beaten Worker Stays in Bed," August 13, 1937; "Attempt Union at Ford Plant," September 7, 1937; "Auto Workers' Organizer Here to Form Union," September 8, 1937; and "City Outlaws CIO: 'We Won't Tolerate You,'" September 20, 1937, all in *Memphis Press-Scimitar*.

37. "The Mayor and the CIO," September 20, 1937; "Ministers 'Take Smack' at Mayor's CIO Attack," October 4, 1937; "Memphis Pastors Speak," October 5, 1937; and "Let's Have Good-Will in Memphis," October 6, 1937, all in *Memphis Press-Scimitar*. See also tensions within the Memphis Trades and Labor Council over their position on Overton's statement and the beatings, in "Labor Council Hits Beatings," September 24, 1937; "AFL Union Indorses Mayor's CIO Stand," October 8, 1937; and "Labor Council Refuses Moral Support to CIO," October 15, 1937, all in *Memphis Press-Scimitar*.

38. "2 CIO Auto Organizers Beaten on City Streets," September 22, 1937; "$1000 Reward for Help in Solving CIO Attacks," September 23, 1937; "CIO Organizer Gets New Help," September 25, 1937; "Smith Is Beaten Again, Gets 15 Gashes on Head," October 6, 1937; "Despairing of 'Satisfaction' at Police Hands, UAW Again Asks State, Federal Inquiry," October 6, 1937; "Federal Statute, Invoked in 'Bloody Harlan,' Applies in Memphis CIO Beatings," October 7, 1937; "Labor League Criticizes Overton in Requests for U.S. Probe of CIO Beatings," October 9, 1937; "CIO Director Wires Overton," October 12, 1937; Marshall McNeil, "Norman Smith is Coming Back," October 29, 1937; "Organizer Held in Jail 2 Hours," December 1, 1937; and "Civil Rights in Memphis," reprinted from *Richmond (Va.) Times-Dispatch*, December 10, 1937, all in *Memphis Press-Scimitar*.

39. Prentice Thomas to Thurgood Marshall, September 28 and October 31, 1937, quoted in Born, "Memphis Negro Workingmen," 105–6; "Tenant Union Linked to CIO," September 25, 1937, and "WPA Workers Not Forced to Gather Cotton," September 27, 1937, both in *Memphis Press-Scimitar*.

40. Biles, *Memphis in the Great Depression*, 94–96, 122; Melton, "Blacks in Memphis, Tennessee," 158–66.

41. Utillus R. Phillips to Frank P. Murphy, May 27, 1939, box C-367, NAACP-LC; E. L. Lung to Frank Murphy, May 21, 1939, quoted in Tucker, *Lieutenant Lee of Beale Street*, 125; "Officer Slays Negro Suspect," *Memphis Press-Scimitar*, March 30, 1937. Frantz's report is discussed in Bunche, *Political Status of the Negro*, 493–94. Months earlier, the *Memphis Press-Scimitar* reported that Clark chased and shot to death a man in the train station, believing he was an escaped killer, in "Fleeing Negro Trapped, Shot Down by Cops," *Memphis Press-Scimitar*, May 25, 1937.

42. "Charge Police Beat 2 Innocent Negroes," May 18, 1937; "Police Ignore Beating Story," May 19, 1937; "Stop Beatings, Mr. Mayor!" May 19, 1937; "Overton Won't Probe Beating," May 20, 1937; and "Yes, 'Sorry!'" May 20, 1937, all in *Memphis Press-Scimitar*.

43. Bunche, *Political Status of the Negro*, 499.

44. Tucker, *Lieutenant Lee of Beale Street*, 126; Biles, *Memphis in the Great Depression*, 104–5.

45. Thomas O. Fuller, quoted in Tucker, *Black Pastors and Leaders*, 58; Lee, *Beale Street*, 210–12; Lamon, *Black Tennesseans*, 24, 31–33; Melton, "Blacks in Memphis, Tennessee," 10–13. On black women's clubs in Memphis see Bond, "'Till Fair Aurora Rise'" and "'Every Duty Incumbent Upon Them.'"

46. Griggs, *Paths of Progress*, 46, 85. On his novels, see Moses, "Literary Garveyism," 203–16; and Thompson, "Sutton Elbert Griggs," 140–48. On his political shift, see Walker, *Metamorphosis of Sutton E. Griggs*. Tucker explains Griggs's shift as a response to financial losses with his early novels, in *Black Pastors and Leaders*, 71–86.

47. Griggs, quoted in Walker, *Metamorphosis of Sutton E. Griggs*, 63. These ideas are elaborated in Griggs, *Guide to Racial Greatness*.

48. Fuller, quoted in Cooper, "Five Black Educators," 298–99. Information on Fuller's early biography also from Cooper.

49. Fuller, *Bridging the Racial Chasms*, 20, 31; Thomas Fuller, "A Racial Situation in the South: A Message for the New Year," *Memphis Commercial Appeal*, December 31, 1922, 15.

50. Church and Church, *Robert R. Churches of Memphis*, 87–110; Melton, "Blacks in Memphis, Tennessee," 96. For more detail on these black business-civic leaders, see Tucker, *Lieutenant Lee of Beale Street*, chap. 3; and Melton, "Blacks in Memphis, Tennessee," chap. 2.

51. Church and Church, *Robert R. Churches of Memphis*, 67–72. According to Lamon, *Black Tennesseans*, 266, sharecroppers in Fayette County, a plantation area just east of Memphis, formed a short-lived NAACP chapter in 1918. Woodruff (*American Congo*, 65) notes that the Memphis NAACP in 1919 helped launch a local branch in the all-black town of Edmundson, Arkansas, where ninety-nine farmers comprised its membership.

52. Born, "Memphis Negro Workingmen," 96–107; Lamon, *Black Tennesseans*, 265–67; Melton, "Blacks in Memphis, Tennessee," 46–51, 74–76. Branch membership was 123 in 1923, earning the Memphis NAACP a place on the NAACP's national membership honor roll. See Melton, "Blacks in Memphis, Tennessee," 75.

53. Griggs, *Paths of Progress*, 11–12, 15, 20, 47; Bert Roddy, letter to Walter White, March 22, 1921, quoted in Melton, "Blacks in Memphis, Tennessee," 74; Born, "Memphis Negro Workingmen," 97. On migrants' self-organization see Grossman, *Land of Hope*.

54. Lee, *Beale Street*, 243–44, Lamon, *Black Tennesseans*, 42–44; Melton, "Blacks in Memphis, Tennessee," 97–99.

55. Lee, *Beale Street*, 244–49; Lamon, *Black Tennesseans*, 45–47; Melton, "Blacks in Memphis, Tennessee," 100–105; Tucker, *Lieutenant Lee of Beale Street*, 91–97. Overton quoted in Biles, *Memphis in the Great Depression*, 27.

56. Griggs, quoted in Lamon, *Black Tennesseans*, 46; Tucker, *Lieutenant Lee of Beale Street*, 63–64.

57. Lee, "These 'Colored' United States"; George W. Lee, letter to the editor, *Baltimore Afro-American*, June 8, 1929; Melton, "Blacks in Memphis, Tennessee," 89–90; Tucker, *Lieutenant Lee of Beale Street*, 66.

58. George W. Lee, letter to the editor, *Baltimore Afro-American*, June 8, 1929.

59. Lee, speech at Booker T. Washington High School graduation, 1932, quoted in Tucker, *Lieutenant Lee of Beale Street*, 97; Du Bois, "Talented Tenth," 33–75. For Woodson's views on the "talented tenth" see *Mis-Education of the Negro*, especially chap. 6. Woodson's book was not published until after Lee's speech, but Lee could have read it in Woodson's column in the *Negro World*, the Garveyite paper. Lee's view of whites controlling blacks by influencing their minds was likely inspired by Woodson's comments on this subject. See *Mis-Education of the Negro*, 84. Lee's mentor Robert Church was on the board of directors of Woodson's Association for the Study of Negro Life and History. See Tucker, *Lieutenant Lee of Beale Street*, 55. I thank Michael Flug at the Carter G. Woodson Library in Chicago for pointing out Woodson's writings in the *Negro World*.

60. Bunche (*Political Status of the Negro*, 494–95) bemoaned this loss of black businesses, especially the demise of "those glorious banks that radiated confidence in Negro business enterprise and gave credence to the slogan 'Buy Black.'"

61. Lee, "Political Upheaval in Memphis."

62. "Customers Searched at Negro Business," October 26, 1940; and "Searchings Continue at Negro Drug Store," October 27, 1940, both in *Memphis Commercial Appeal*; "Memorandum on the Memphis Situation," December 30, 1940, *NAACP Papers*, part 18, group II, 28:939–42; see also Church and Church, *Robert R. Churches of Memphis*, 180–84. See coverage of Willkie calling Jersey City mayor Frank Hague a "puny Hitler," in "Text of Wendell Willkie's Speech Made in Jersey City in Which He Attacks Hague" and "Willkie's Newark Text Hails Republican as the Party of Government by the People," *Memphis Commercial Appeal*, October 8, 1940.

63. "Boyle Says Martin Tried 'Big Racket,'" October 28, 1940; and "Boyle Tells Jenkins To Keep 'Hands Out,'" October 29, 1940, both in *Memphis Commercial Appeal*; *Elmer Atkinson and Willie Mae Atkinson v. Joseph Boyle et al.*, Declaration filed Octo-

ber 30, 1941, in the Circuit Court of Shelby County, Tennessee, Chandler Papers, box 6, folder: Public Safety-Police-1941. On Boyle's "clean-up" crusade, see Tucker, *Lieutenant Lee of Beale Street*, 127–31.

64. "Mayor Backs Boyle in Antidrug Crusade," November 1, 1940; "Boyle Issues Strong Rebuke to Group for Racial Charges; G-Men May Aid in Cleanup," December 5, 1940; "We'll Have No Race Trouble, Says Boyle," December 12, 1940; and "City Swings at a Beale Sign and Joe Louis Goes Down, Out," November 1, 1940, all in *Memphis Commercial Appeal*. On Crump's involvement, see, for example, letter about J. B. Martin, Mayor Chandler to E. H. Crump, November 27, 1940, Chandler Papers, box 6, folder: Public Safety-Police-1941.

65. Everett Amis, "Police Swoop Down on Beale, Other Sections, to Round Up 65 Knife-Carrying Negroes," November 14, 1940; "Knife-Toting Negroes Fined $3000 in Court," November 15, 1940; and "Police Drive Results Reflected in Court," November 19, 1940, all in *Memphis Commercial Appeal*; and Collins C. George to Thurgood Marshall, January 14, 1941, *NAACP Papers*, part 18, group II, 28:1011. Marshall quoted George's comments in a letter calling for an investigation by the U.S. attorney general. See Marshall to Honorable Robert H. Jackson, January 20, 1941, also in *NAACP Papers*, part 18, group II, 28:981.

66. Everett Amis, "Police Swoop Down on Beale, Other Sections, to Round Up 65 Knife-Carrying Negroes," November 14, 1940; "Knife-Toting Negroes Fined $3000 in Court," November 15, 1940; "Boyle's Crime Fight Is Showing Results," December 20, 1940; and "We'll Have No Race Trouble, Says Boyle," December 12, 1940, all in *Memphis Commercial Appeal*. On earlier concerns about cotton pickers, see "10,000 Cotton Pickers Needed for Harvest in This Section," October 4, 1940; and "5000 Cotton Pickers Needed by Planters," October 10, 1940," both in *Memphis Commercial Appeal*. Newspaper editorial quote from "Cotton Pickers Needed," October 11, 1940.

67. "Strike Here Closes Firestone Factory," December 5, 1940; "City, County Police to 'Restore Safety' at Firestone Plant," December 7, 1940; "Strike Is Settled at Firestone Plant," December 8, 1940; "Three Meetings Set for Rubber Workers," December 15, 1940; "Rubber Workers Vote Expected Next Week," December 16, 1940; and "Firestone Workers Choose A.F.L. Union," December 24, 1940, all in *Memphis Commercial Appeal*. On Dies, see "For Safety of All" and "The Guest Writer: Reds and Race Prejudice," December 12, 1940, both in *Memphis Commercial Appeal*. The same day the *Commercial Appeal* published a statement by Boyle, arguing that "foreign-born Communist agitators," along with black newspapers, had been stirring up the "young element of the negroes." See "We'll Have No Race Trouble, Says Boyle," *Memphis Commercial Appeal*, December 12, 1940. On Bass and the CIO drive, see Michael Honey, *Southern Labor and Black Civil Rights*, 155–65, 170–72.

68. NAACP Memorandum [n.d.]; Howard Lee to President Franklin Roosevelt, December 21, 1940; Edward Strong to President Franklin Roosevelt, December 28, 1940; Edward Strong to Walter White, January 3, 1941; Thurgood Marshall to Edward E. Strong, December 31, 1940; Edward E. Strong to Walter White, December 20, 1940; NAACP telegram to Attorney General Robert Jackson, [Dec. 1940], all in *NAACP Papers*, part 18, group II, 28:930–38, 960–69; and "What G-Man Did in Memphis Is Secret," January 7, 1941; John Moutoux and Clark Porteous, "U.S. Investiga-

tor Reports on Charges That Memphis Negroes Are Intimidated," January 8, 1941; and John Moutoux, "J-Man Reports on Memphis Negro Inquiry—Here's Result," January 9, 1941, all in *Memphis Press-Scimitar*.

69. "We Defend the Law," November 21, 1940; and "For Safety of All," December 12, 1940, both in *Memphis Commercial Appeal*; and "Salesman Arrested for Resisting Search," [n.d.], *Memphis Press-Scimitar*, included in *NAACP Papers*, part 18, group II, 28:949–50.

70. "Police Intimidation Charge Is Made Here," November 27, 1940; and "Boyle Issues Strong Rebuke to Group for Racial Charges; G-Men May Aid in Cleanup," December 5, 1940, both in *Memphis Commercial Appeal*; "Mass Meeting Is Planned by Racial Groups," January 28, 1941; "City Fathers to Confer with Interracial Group," January 30, 1941; and "Racial Commission and City Fathers in Harmony," January 31, 1941, all in *Memphis Press-Scimitar*.

71. Articles on the poll tax appeared in the *Memphis Press-Scimitar* daily between January 1 and January 25, 1941. Meeman's New Year's Day editorial, "Talk Poll Tax Repeal!" makes it clear that he perceived the newspaper as a combatant, not just an observer, in this fight.

72. Rev. J. H. Johnson to Mayor Walter Chandler, November 3, 1940; and Rev. W. C. Paine to Mayor Walter Chandler, November 3, 1940, both in Chandler Papers, box 6, folder: Race Relations, 1940.

73. Rev. J. H. Johnson to Mayor Walter Chandler, November 3, 1940; Rev. W. C. Paine to Mayor Walter Chandler, November 3, 1940; Rev. W. H. Winston to Mayor Walter Chandler, November 4, 1940; Rev. W. A. Johnson to Mayor Walter Chandler, November 4, 1940; and Rev. Arthur W. Womack to Mayor Walter Chandler, November 7, 1940, all in Chandler Papers, box 6, folder: Race Relations, 1940. The Golden Rule is a paraphrase of Matthew 7:12; "Therefore all things whatsoever ye would that men should do to you, do ye even so to them: for this is the law and the prophets" (King James Version).

74. Rev. Blair T. Hunt to Mayor Walter Chandler, November 4, 1940; and M. S. Stuart to Mayor Walter Chandler, November 1, 1940, both in Chandler Papers, box 6, folder: Race Relations, 1940. On the visit by Walker, Hunt, and Fuller, see "Memorandum Regarding Police Persecution of Dr. J. B. Martin of Memphis, Tennessee, Because of Political Activities in 1940 Presidential Election," *NAACP Papers*, part 18, group II, 28:936.

75. Yolande Hasson, "Negro Leader Warns against Listening to Fifth Columnists," *Memphis Commercial Appeal*, December 8, 1940; T. O. Fuller to Mayor Walter Chandler, Chandler Papers, box 8, folder: Housing Authority, 1941.

76. George W. Lee to Mayor Walter Chandler, November 10, 1940; Lee to E. H. Crump, November 19, 1940; Lee to Chandler, December 11, 1940; and Lt. George W. Lee, "Speech Introducing W. C. Handy at the Blues Bowl Game," December 6, 1940, all in Chandler Papers, box 6, folder: Public Improvements—Colored Citizens—1940. Although W. C. Handy is commonly hailed as "father of the blues," he did not invent blues music—no single individual could lay claim to that. Rather, Handy was one of the first to publish sheet music dedicated to the blues, beginning with "Memphis Blues" in 1912, and thereby helped launch it as an internationally

recognized genre. As a bandleader and entrepreneur, Handy not only arranged and published music, but in 1921 he also established Black Swan, one of the initial labels for black musical artists. See George, *Death of Rhythm and Blues*, 10.

77. Rev. George A. Long to Mayor Walter Chandler, November 4, 1940, Chandler Papers, box 6, folder: Race Relations, 1940; "Boyle Issues Strong Rebuke to Group for Racial Charges; G-Men May Aid In Cleanup," December 5, 1940; and "We'll Have No Race Trouble, Says Boyle," December 12, 1940, both in *Memphis Commercial Appeal*. Long letter to *Memphis Commercial Appeal*, quoted in "Memorandum on the Memphis Situation," *NAACP Papers*, part 18, group II, 28:941, 976–77. On Long's reference to an "unseen Judge," see 1 Corinthians 4:3–4: "But with me it is a very small thing that I should be judged of you, or of man's judgement: yea, I judge not mine own self. For I know nothing by myself; yet am I not hereby justified: be he that judgeth me is the Lord" (King James Version).

78. Marguerite E. Bicknell to Rev. James Robinson, October 26, 1940; Madison S. Jones Jr. to Daniel D. Carter, November 29, 1940; Daniel D. Carter to NAACP Board of Directors, November 25, 1940; and draft article on LeMoyne College Youth Council [Jan. 1941], all in group II, box E95, LeMoyne College folders, NAACP-LC.

79. Memphis NAACP Youth Council to Postal Inspector R. H. Tomlinson, November 26, 1940; Memphis NAACP Youth Council to Mayor Walter Chandler, November 26, 1940; Daniel D. Carter to Thurgood Marshall, January 8, 1941; and Milton N. Kemnitz to Collins George, January 27, 1941, all in *NAACP Papers*, part 18, group II, 28:947, 948, 974–75, 986.

80. See Cosgrove, "Zoot-Suit and Style Warfare," 77–91; and Kelley, *Race Rebels*, 161–82.

81. Daniel D. Carter to Thurgood Marshall, January 8, 1941; Collins George to Walter White, February 1, 1941; and Collins George to Madison Jones, [n.d.], all in *NAACP Papers*, part 18, group II, 28:974–75, 995–96, 1008.

82. NAACP memorandum, *NAACP Papers*, part 18, group II, 28:930–31.

83. "Boyle Says Druggist Gave Suit to Ex-Chief," November 31, 1940; and "Blues Bowl Blues for Three Negroes," December 11, 1940, both in *Memphis Commercial Appeal*; Collins C. George to Thurgood Marshall, January 14, 1941, *NAACP Papers*, part 18, group II, 28:1012.

84. Dave McConnell, "Reliefers Who Spurn Farms May Create Sizeable Class of Permanent Unemployables," *Memphis Commercial Appeal*, March 30, 1941.

Chapter 2

1. Altha Sims to President Franklin Roosevelt, July 9, 1942, reel 34, file: Complaints to Government Agencies, Office of Budget and Administration, Region VII, *FEPC Records*.

2. Altha Sims to Mayor Walter Chandler, September 1, 1942; and Chandler to Sims, September 2, 1942, both in Chandler Papers, box 11, folder: Correspondence S, 1942; FEPC Assistant Executive Secretary George M. Johnson to Altha Sims, reel 34, file: Complaints to Government Agencies, Office of Budget and Administration, Region VII, *FEPC Records*.

3. For nationally based analyses of how gender and sexuality figured into wartime

racial labor conflicts, see Boris, "'You Wouldn't Want One of 'Em Dancing with Your Wife,'" 77–108, and "'Right to Work Is the Right to Live!'" On black women workers during the war, see Korstad, *Civil Rights Unionism*. On black women in the World War II defense industry, see Lemke-Santangelo, *Abiding Courage*; Karen Anderson, "Last Hired, First Fired," 82–97; and Maureen Honey, *Bitter Fruit*.

4. Clarence W. Smith to War Manpower Administration director Paul V. McNutt, May 3, 1943, reel 25, file: Complaints Not against Particular Companies, Office of Budget and Administration, Region VII, *FEPC Records*.

5. "Randolph Scores Attitude of Memphis Labor Leaders," *Memphis World*, April 4, 1944; Rev. George A. Long, "Christ, Not Crump, Is My Boss," *Memphis Press-Scimitar*, April 3, 1944, 1.

6. War Manpower Commission Labor Market Development Report, August 15, 1943, Chandler Papers, box 14, folder: Labor—1943.

7. Field Report by John Beecher, [May 1942], reel 77, Office Files of John Beecher, file: Memphis, Tennessee, *FEPC Records*; Correspondence in box 13, folder: Housing Authority, 1943; box 5, folders: Fisher Body Company and Ford Plant; and Labor Market Report for Memphis, November 15 to December 15, 1942, box 8, folder: Labor, all in Chandler Papers; Michael Honey, *Southern Labor and Black Civil Rights*, 178; Sigafoos, *Cotton Row to Beale Street*, 207.

8. A 1942 USES survey found that 13.7 percent of white job applicants for defense jobs came from Arkansas or Mississippi. Sixteen percent of the 10,000 current employees of the four largest defense contractors in Memphis also came from Arkansas or Mississippi, in addition to those who came from west Tennessee. See United States Employment Service for Tennessee, "Preliminary Study of Memphis as an Interstate Labor Market Area," June 23, 1942, RG 183, box 357, folder: Memphis, NARA.

9. United States Employment Service for Tennessee, "Preliminary Study of Memphis"; Letter from Benjamin Bell to Paul McNutt, USES director, box 7, file: USES, 7-GR-60, 62, 82, 110, 113, FEPC-Region VII.

10. Michael Honey, *Southern Labor and Black Civil Rights*, 179–86 passim; "Appraisal of Wages in the Memphis, Tennessee, Plants of the Buckeye Cotton Oil Company," Bureau of Labor Statistics, U.S. Department of Labor, unpublished report to the Wage Investigator of the National War Labor Board, May 1, 1942, reel 76, Division of Field Operations, Office Files of Will Maslow, September 1943–January 1945, *FEPC Records*.

11. See Garfinkel, *When Negroes March*; and Reed, *Seedtime for the Modern Civil Rights Movement*.

12. War Manpower Commission, Labor Market Development Report for August 15, 1943, Chandler Papers, box 14, folder: Labor, 1943.

13. Ibid.; Evelyn Bates interview by author; Carter, "Local Labor Union," 44; Memphis Furniture, Mediation and Conciliation Service File 464-125, RG 280, NARA.

14. The OPM was created by Roosevelt in January 1941, partly to quell rising sentiments over discriminatory hiring procedures in the defense industry. The FEPC was initially administratively linked to the OPM. See Reed, *Seedtime for the Modern Civil Rights Movement*, 13, 21, 26. Beecher, an FEPC field examiner until the commit-

tee was reorganized in early 1943, was a white southern liberal and descendent of Harriet Beecher Stowe. Personal accounts of his FEPC experiences are in Beecher Papers.

15. Firestone's May 1942 workforce of 2,200 included 683 blacks, out of which 451 held jobs classified as unskilled; 181 worked in semiskilled service jobs such as tire cleaner or shipping and receiving, and only 51 worked in skilled positions as machine operators and mill men. See Field Report by John Beecher [May 1942] and Memo from Cy A. Record to Robert C. Weaver [May 1942], both in reel 77, Office Files of John Beecher, file: Memphis, Tennessee, in *FEPC Records*.

16. Field Report by John Beecher [May 1942] and Memo from Cy A. Record to Robert C. Weaver [May 1942], both in reel 77, Office Files of John Beecher, file: Memphis, Tennessee, in *FEPC Records*.

17. Field Report by John Beecher [May 1942] and Memo from Cy A. Record to Robert C. Weaver [May 1942], both in reel 77, Office Files of John Beecher, file: Memphis, Tennessee, in *FEPC Records*.

18. Field Report by John Beecher [May 1942] in reel 77, Office Files of John Beecher, file: Memphis, Tennessee, in *FEPC Records*. Eileen Boris discusses this trend of employers to explain their exclusion of black workers based on false assumptions about syphilis rates in "'You Wouldn't Want One of 'Em Dancing with Your Wife,'" 94.

19. Field Report by John Beecher [May 1942] and Memo from Cy A. Record to Robert C. Weaver [May 1942], both in reel 77, Office Files of John Beecher, file: Memphis, Tennessee, in *FEPC Records*. On the FEPC, see Reed, *Seedtime for the Modern Civil Rights Movement*.

20. Field Report by John Beecher [May 1942] and Memo from Cy A. Record to Robert C. Weaver [May 1942], both in reel 77, Office Files of John Beecher, file: Memphis, Tennessee, in *FEPC Records*; John Beecher to Virginia Beecher, May 21, 1942, Beecher Papers, box 14, folder: 1942, April–June. Black FEPC examiner John Hope II learned that he was closely monitored during his Memphis trips. See Reed, *Seedtime for the Modern Civil Rights Movement*, 226.

21. Report on Memphis, from Dr. Alva W. Taylor, [May 1944], Records of the Committee on Fair Employment Practice, RG 228, box 3, file: Buckeye Cotton Oil 7-BR-292, Regional Files, FEPC-Region VII; Memo from Cy A. Record to Robert C. Weaver [May 1942], reel 77, Office Files of John Beecher, file: Memphis, Tennessee, in *FEPC Records*; "1,541 Members Added to NAACP Branch," May 28, 1943, *Memphis World*; Melton, "Blacks in Memphis, Tennessee," 252–53.

22. Aubrey Clapp to Mayor Walter Chandler, June 18, 1943, Chandler Papers, box 17, folder: Welfare Department 1943.

23. Mediation and Conciliation Service Files 301-6897, 452-171, and 464-125, RG 280, NARA. As of October 1943, Memphis Furniture's workforce consisted of 220 men and 450 women.

24. Mayor Walter Chandler to Honorable Clifford Davis, November 13, 1943, box 15, folder: Labor-1944; and minutes, Committee for Economic Development, July 1, 1943, box 12, folder: Economic Development, Committee for, 1943, both in Chandler Papers.

25. Honorable Clifford Davis to Mayor Walter Chandler, December 1, 1943, Chandler Papers, box 15, folder: Labor-1944; Weekly Report memorandum from Witherspoon Dodge, FEPC Region VII Director to Will Maslow, FEPC Director of Field Operations, for the week ending July 27, 1945, regarding cases 7-BR-287, 2-BR-472, reel 52, Central Files, Office of Budget and Administration, Weekly Reports by Region, file: Region VII, Reports, 1945, *FEPC Records*. See also mention of this case in Michael Honey, *Southern Labor and Black Civil Rights*, 194.

26. Memorandum from A. Bruce Hunt, Director, Region VII, to Will Maslow, Director of Field Operations, June 21, 1944, reel 52, Central Files, Office of Budget and Administration, file: Weekly Reports By Region, Region VII, October 1943–June 1944; and Annual Report memorandum from John Hope II to John A. Davis, Director, file: Office Files of Eugene Davidson, FEPC Asst. Director, October 1941–April 1946, Division of Review & Analysis, both in *FEPC Records*; Benjamin F. Bell Jr. to Paul V. McNutt, July 28, 1943, RG 228, box 7, Closed Cases T–U, folder: USES, 7-GR-60, 61, 82, 110, 113, NARA. On newspaper advertisements by private employers, see, for example, National Fireworks's daily advertisements for "White Women" in July 1943, in both the *Memphis Commercial Appeal* and the *Memphis Press-Scimitar*.

27. George Townsel Sr. to Chairman of the FEPC, box 2, Active Cases S–Z, folder: USES, Memphis, TN 7-GR-639, FEPC-Region VII.

28. J. E. Walker, M. W. Bonner, M. S. Stuart to USES, September 5, 1942, reel 34, file: Complaints to Government Agencies, Office of Budget and Administration, Region VII, *FEPC Records*; and Benjamin F. Bell Jr. to Paul V. McNutt, July 28, 1943, RG 228, box 7, Closed Cases T–U, folder: USES, 7-GR-60, 61, 82, 110, 113, NARA.

29. Welfare director A. B. Clapp reported that a reputable source had informed him that there would be an "uprising among the negroes on Tuesday night of this week." See Honorable Clifford Davis to Mayor Walter Chandler, October 9, 1942; and A. B. Clapp to Chandler, October 3, 1942, both in Chandler Papers, box 9, folder: Negroes, 1942.

30. T. L. Ward, "White Man's View on Reputed Clubs to Create Race Trouble," *Memphis World*, June 29, 1945.

31. Ella Rose Dotson to President Roosevelt, January 7, 1943, RG 228, box 7, Closed Cases T–U, folder: USES 7-GR-1, 3, 4, 9, FEPC-Region VII.

32. Correspondence from and about Ella Dotson, January 1943–February 1944, RG 228, box 7, Closed Cases T–U, folder: USES 7-GR-1, 3, 4, 9, FEPC-Region VII.

33. Ella Rose Dotson to President Roosevelt, January 7, 1943, RG 228, box 7, Closed Cases T–U, folder: USES 7-GR-1, 3, 4, 9, FEPC-Region VII.

34. Correspondence from and about Ella Dotson, January 1943–February 1944, RG 228, box 7, Closed Cases T–U, folder: USES 7-GR-1, 3, 4, 9, FEPC-Region VII.

35. Susie Brister to President Roosevelt, July 2, 1942, reel 27, file: Complaints against a Particular Company, in Office of Budget and Administration, Region VII, *FEPC Records*.

36. Margaret Jackson to President Roosevelt, June 5, 1942, reel 27, file: Complaints against a Particular Company, in Office of Budget and Administration, Region VII, *FEPC Records*.

37. The 1938 Fair Labor Standards Act (FLSA)'s minimum wage and maximum hour requirements initially did not apply to laundry and cleaning establishments, regardless of their annual gross volumes. The FLSA initially also excluded agricultural and domestic workers, and restricted regulation of cotton compress and cottonseed processing workers' wages and hours to only fourteen weeks per year. A disproportionate number of black Memphis workers were thus excluded from FLSA provisions. See FLSA legislation and amendments and testimony by Dolly Lowther, Laundry Workers' Division of the Amalgamated Clothing Workers Unit, CIO, to the 1949 Senate Subcommittee on FLSA Amendments, in "'Among the Most Exploited': Fair Labor Standards Act and Laundry Workers," History Matters, <http://historymatters.gmu.edu/d/6262> (accessed February 12, 2006). Lowther declared, "Laundry workers have been among the most exploited of all groups of workers. Unprotected by the Fair Labor Standards Act, they have been afforded little protection by existing State legislation."

38. This account of Gertrude Carter and Katie Hall's struggle at Kennedy General Hospital between 1943 and 1944 is based on correspondence in the file on Kennedy General Hospital, Memphis, Tennessee, 7-GR-485–487, RG 228, box 1, Active Cases A–S, FEPC-Region VII.

39. "Laundry Workers Essential to War," July 9, 1943; and "Loeb's Laundry Workers Strike," August 21, 1945, both in *Memphis World*; D. K. Jones, Commissioner of Conciliation, Progress Report re Model Laundry, July 24, 1942, Mediation and Conciliation Service Files 209-3424, RG 280, NARA.

40. Hunter, *To 'Joy My Freedom*, 207–8; Jones, *Labor of Love*, 177–78, 209–10; Kessler-Harris, *Out to Work*, 112.

41. "Laundry Employees v. Employers," Little Rock, Arkansas, Docket No. 233, September 3, 1918, National War Labor Board, RG 2, NARA. Discussed in Green, "'Out of This Land of Sufring'"; and Haiken, "'Lord Helps Those Who Help Themselves.'"

42. Orleck, *Common Sense and a Little Fire*, 160–63. See also Jones, *Labor of Love*, 212; and Galenson, *CIO Challenge to the AFL*, 286–87.

43. "Laundry Workers Being Organized," July 2, 1943; "Laundry Workers Meet Wed. Night," July 6, 1943; "Kraus Employees on Strike, Backed by Laundry Union," July 23, 1943; "Second Week of Kraus' Strike," July 30, 1943; and "Loeb's Laundry Workers Strike," August 21, 1945, all in *Memphis World*; "206 Walk Out at Kraus Firm," July 21, 1943; and "Pickets on Job at Kraus Plant," July 26, 1943, both in *Memphis Press-Scimitar*; Mediation and Conciliation Service Files 209-3424 on Model Laundry and 199-7432 on Crescent Laundry, RG 280, NARA.

44. James Nimmo, President, Miami Laundry Workers Union to U.S. Department of Labor, November 18, 1942, reel 25, file: Miami Laundry Workers Union, Office of Budget and Administration, Complaints Not against Particular Companies, Region VII, *FEPC Records*.

45. "1,200 Laundry Workers Strike for Higher Pay," October 8, 1943; "Atlantans Told to Get Dirty Clothes," October 10, 1943; "Laundry Strike No Nearer Settlement," October 14, 1943; "Ministers Tell Strikers to Hold Out to the End," October 15, 1943; "Laundry Strike in Second Week," October 19, 1943; "Laundry Union Favors League

Strike Program," November 5, 1943; "Injunction Bars Laundry Pickets," November 10, 1943; "Laundries Fail to Open, Workers Fail to Appear," November 11, 1943; and "Ask for U.S. Aid in Laundry Strike," November 13, 1943, all in *Atlanta Daily World*.

46. "Loeb's Laundry Workers Strike," August 21, 1945; "Laundry Workers Being Organized," July 2, 1943; "Laundry Workers Meet Wed. Night," July 6, 1943; "Kraus Employees on Strike, Backed by Laundry Union," July 23, 1943; and "Second Week of Kraus' Strike," July 30, 1943, all in *Memphis World*; "206 Walk Out at Kraus Firm," July 21, 1943; and "Pickets on Job at Kraus Plant," July 26, 1943, both in *Memphis Press-Scimitar*.

47. Historian Tera W. Hunter discusses the washerwoman as both the archetypal domestic laborer and one who had more independence than cooks and maids. Once industrial entrepreneurs succeeded in moving laundry work into industrial settings, women laborers lost most of this autonomy. See *To 'Joy My Freedom*, 57, 207.

48. Memphis Negro Chamber of Commerce and Housewives League to White Rose Laundry Cleaners, October 5, 1942, Chandler Papers, box 9, folder: Negroes—1942. See also the discussion of this dispute in Melton, "Blacks in Memphis, Tennessee," 203–4.

49. Memphis Negro Chamber of Commerce and Housewives League to White Rose Laundry Cleaners, October 5, 1942; Mayor Walter Chandler to Walter Klyce and Arnold Klyce, October 6, 1942; and Walter Klyce and Arnold Klyce to Mayor Walter Chandler, October 14, 1942, all in Chandler Papers, box 9, folder: Negroes—1942.

50. "They Also Serve!" cartoon, *Memphis World*, August 6, 1943.

51. Roosevelt's Executive Order 8802 did not ban discrimination on the basis of sex or gender, yet as Eileen Boris has pointed out, racialized conceptions of gender became central to wartime struggles. See "'You Wouldn't Want One of 'Em Dancing with Your Wife.'"

52. The following account is based on the FEPC's extensive file on this case, May 5–October 9, 1945, reel 80, file: Veteran's Hospital, Memphis, Division of Field Operations—Active Cases, June 1943–April 1946, Region VII, *FEPC Records*.

53. Files on Henke Construction Company, Lee Construction Company, and Mayfair Construction Company, reel 27, Office of Budget and Administration, Complaints against a Particular Company; and Rev. George A. Bell to Dr. Robert Weaver, August 5, 1942, reel 34, Office of Budget and Administration, Complaints to Government Agencies, both in *FEPC Records*.

54. Files on Henke Construction Company, Lee Construction Company, and Mayfair Construction Company, reel 27, Office of Budget and Administration, Complaints against a Particular Company, *FEPC Records*.

55. James Smith to Paul McNutt, April 24, 1943, reel 25, file: Complaints Not against Particular Companies, Office of Budget and Administration, Region VII, *FEPC Records*. On FDR's decision to place the FEPC under WMC control in July 1942, see Reed, *Seedtime for the Modern Civil Rights Movement*, 74–75. See also Reed's lengthier discussion of Roosevelt's May 1943 Executive Order 9346 reestablishing and restructuring the committee (77–143 passim).

56. Correspondence and complaints in RG 228, box 4, Closed Cases D–J, folder: Fisher Memphis Aircraft (Division of GMC), 7-BR-109, 7-BR-130, 7-BR-287, FEPC-

Region VII. On Bell's role as executive secretary and the origins of the Memphis Urban League, see Nat D. Williams, "Focussing the News: An Urban League for Memphis," *Memphis World*, August 6, 1943.

57. Correspondence and complaints in RG 228, box 4, Closed Cases D–J, folder: Fisher Memphis Aircraft (Division of GMC), 7-BR-287, FEPC-Region VII.

58. Correspondence and complaints in RG 228, box 4, Closed Cases D–J, folder: Fisher Memphis Aircraft (Division of GMC), 7-BR-472, 7-BR-109, 7-BR-130, FEPC-Region VII.

59. Newspaper clipping, n.d., in reel 76, Tensions Files, file: Tennessee, Memphis, *FEPC Records*.

60. "Appraisal of Wages in the Memphis, Tennessee, Plants of the Buckeye Cotton Oil Company," Bureau of Labor Statistics, U.S. Department of Labor, unpublished report to the Wage Investigator of the National War Labor Board, May 1, 1942, reel 76, Division of Field Operations, Office Files of Will Maslow, September 1943–January 1945, *FEPC Records*. At its 1944 convention, UCAPAWA changed its name to the Food, Tobacco and Agricultural Workers Union (FTA). See Michael Honey, *Southern Workers and Black Civil Rights*, 201. Here, to avoid confusion I will use the UCAPAWA acronym.

61. "Appraisal of Wages in the Memphis, Tennessee, Plants of the Buckeye Cotton Oil Company," Bureau of Labor Statistics, U.S. Department of Labor, unpublished report to the Wage Investigator of the National War Labor Board, May 1, 1942, reel 76, Division of Field Operations, Office Files of Will Maslow, September 1943–January 1945, *FEPC Records*.

62. Mediators' Report, NWLB, June 18, 1942, Case No. 59, in Mediation and Conciliation Service File 196-8955, RG 280, NARA.

63. Ibid.

64. John Hope II to A. Bruce Hunt, [ca. April 27, 1944], RG 228, box 3, Closed Cases B–D, folder: Buckeye Cotton Oil, 7-BR-292, FEPC-Region VII. Quote on p. 6.

65. W. M. Whorton, Progress Report, December 9, 1943, Mediation and Conciliation Service File 301-3446, RG 280, NARA. For more on Copeland, see Michael Honey, *Southern Labor and Black Civil Rights*, 143–44, 210–12.

66. Reuel Stanfield, UCAPAWA Local 19 business agent, to A. Bruce Hunt, May 5, 1944; and Arbitration Decision in the Matter of the Buckeye Cotton Oil Company and UCAPAWA, May 28, 1943, both in RG 228, box 3, Closed Cases B–D, folder: Buckeye Cotton Oil, 7-BR-292, FEPC-Region VII.

67. Mediation and Conciliation Service File 300-6436, RG 280, NARA.

68. Mediation and Conciliation Service Files 442-620, 442-2182, RG 280, NARA. Five wildcat strikes, two averted strikes following votes to strike, and reported threats of strikes at both the Hollywood and Jackson Avenue plants are documented in the Mediation and Conciliation Service Files on Buckeye, RG 280, NARA. The Whorton quote is from U.S. Conciliation Service Progress Report, April 28, 1944, File 472-572, RG 280, NARA.

69. "Union Official Issues Appeal against Threatened Buckeye Wage Increase Strike Action," *Memphis World*, March 21, 1944; Mediation and Conciliation Service Files 442-620, 442-2182, RG 280, NARA; John Hope II to A. Bruce Hunt, [ca. April

27, 1944], RG 228, box 3, Closed Cases B–D, folder: Buckeye Cotton Oil, 7-BR-292, FEPC-Region VII.

70. "A. Philip Randolph Noted Labor Leader Speaks Here Sunday," November 5, 1943, 1; "A. Philip Randolph Speaks in Memphis November 7th," October 29, 1943, 1; and "Memphis Calls Off Randolph Mass Meet," November 9, 1943, 1, all in *Memphis World*; Harris, *Harder We Run*, 40–48, 72; Reed, *Seedtime for the Modern Civil Rights Movement*, 13–15; Garfinkel, *When Negroes March*, 63–77.

71. "Randolph Speaks at STFU Conclave — Mass Meeting Canceled," November 12, 1943; "Washington Hi Principal Answers Critics: Echoes of Canceled Meeting Contained in Principal's Letter to Friends and Press," November 23, 1943; "Randolph Scores Attitude of Memphis Labor Leaders," April 4, 1944; and "Crump Issues Comment," April 4, 1944, all in *Memphis World*; Blair Hunt to unspecified recipient, November 19, 1943, Chandler Papers, box 14, folder: Negroes; Tucker, *Lieutenant Lee of Beale Street*, 139–42. Various sources differ on the exact number of black leaders present and whether the meeting actually took place in a jail cell.

72. "Randolph Speaks at STFU Conclave — Mass Meeting Canceled," November 12, 1943, 1; "Randolph Sees March On D.C. for Next Spring: Says Fascism and Discrimination Are Increasing," November 12, 1943, 1; and "Opinion Divided on Projected Visit of Randolph to Memphis," March 14, 1944, 1, all in *Memphis World*; Layle Lane to Mayor Walter Chandler, November 19, 1943, and Reverend L. J. Sullivan to Mayor Walter Chandler, November 23, 1943, both in Chandler Papers, box 14, folder: Negroes; Jervis Anderson, *A. Philip Randolph*, 269–70.

73. "Randolph Speech Defended by Negro Labor Leader: Opinion Divided on Projected Visit of Randolph to Memphis," March 14, 1944, 1; "Randolph Ban Lifted Memphis Leaders Say," March 24, 1944, 1; "Randolph to Speak Friday Night at Beale Avenue Bapt. Church Labor Meet," March 28, 1944, 1; "Randolph Meeting to Be Held as Local Negro Saboteurs Are Named in Effort to Stop Rally," March 31, 1944, 1, all in *Memphis World*. An advertisement for the "Special Mass Meeting" lists as sponsors "the Pullman Car Porters, Memphis Division; the Teamsters Union, Local 667; the Longshorem[e]n, the United Textile Workers, the Laundry Workers, Local 263, the Freight Handlers, the Coopers Union, the Tobacco Workers and many others." See *Memphis World*, March 28, 1944, 1. The Lee comment is quoted in Melton, "Blacks in Memphis, Tennessee," 218.

74. "Randolph Scores Attitude of Memphis Labor Leaders," *Memphis World*, April 4, 1944.

75. A. Philip Randolph, "Freedom on Two Fronts: March on Washington Leader Sees Danger of Race Losing the Peace," in "Calling America to Victory," *Chicago Defender*, September 26, 1942.

76. A. Philip Randolph, "This Is a Crucial Year for the Darker Races," *Memphis World*, January 5, 1943; A. Philip Randolph, "A Reply to My Critics: Randolph Tells Philosophy Behind 'March' Movement," *Chicago Defender*, June 19, 1943.

77. "Crump Issues Comment," *Memphis World*, April 4, 1944.

78. Quoted in Jervis Anderson, *A. Philip Randolph*, 270.

79. "The Randolph Speech," *Memphis World*, April 4, 1944, 6. Even earlier, in response to Randolph's January 1943 column republished in the newspaper, a *Mem-*

phis World editorial had excoriated Randolph's support for Gandhism and civil disobedience. See "On Mr. Randolph's Proposal for Negro Action," *Memphis World*, January 22, 1944.

80. Rev. George A. Long, "Christ, Not Crump, Is My Boss," *Memphis Press-Scimitar*, April 3, 1944, 1.

81. "Rev. Long Welcomes CIO Local 19"; "Noted Speaker Lauds Roosevelt, Blames Local School Teachers"; and "Rev. Fisher Stirs Labor Meeting," all in *Memphis World*, October 20, 1944.

82. "Prof. Searcy's Passing Stuns Community," February 5, 1943; "Community Welfare League Selects Executive Secretary," May 25, 1943; and "Urban League Regional Director Makes a Study of Memphis Negro Status," January 21, 1944, all in *Memphis World*. See also Melton, "Blacks in Memphis, Tennessee," 214–18.

83. Benjamin F. Bell Jr., "Dixie Ways Rule Memphis; Skilled Jobs for White Only," *Chicago Defender*, January 22, 1944.

84. "Crump Wrath May Oust Urban League Leader in Memphis," *Chicago Defender*, January 29, 1944.

85. "Job Discrimination Charged against US Employment Service," August 24, 1943; "Urban League Head Is Back from Chicago Meet," October 8, 1943; "Janitor Frozen on Job Is Released," October 26, 1943; J. A. McDaniel, "League Secretary in Call for More Workers," May 1, 1945; and "Good Domestic Jobs Are Now Available," June 15, 1945, all in *Memphis World*; Witherspoon Dodge, Weekly Report, December 23, 1944, reel 52, Division of Field Operations, file: Weekly Reports, September 1943–May 1944, *FEPC Records*; Melton, "Blacks in Memphis, Tennessee," 215–18.

86. On the radio announcements, see Radio Announcement for WHBQ, June 30–July 7, 1944, Chandler Papers, box 15, folder: Negroes, 1944; on the streetcar placards, see Mayor Walter Chandler to John Arnold, Negro Junior Chamber of Commerce, and "car cards," July 15, 1943, Chandler Papers, box 14, folder: Negroes, 1943; on the Colored Methodist Center see "Workers Clinic to Open Here July 9th," *Memphis World*, June 29, 1945. See also Thelma N. Watson to Mayor Walter Chandler, January 9, 1946; and "Syllabus for the Working out of an Inter-Racial Commission on Domestic, Farm, and Unskilled Labor," n.d., Chandler Papers, box 25, folder: Negroes, 1946.

Chapter 3

1. Pseudonyms are used here to protect the privacy of these women and their families.

2. Except where noted, the following account of the police assaults and their immediate aftermath is based on sworn affidavits obtained by attorney Drury B. Crawley, at the request of the Memphis NAACP. See statements of the two young women and their mothers, August 15, 1945, *NAACP Papers*, part 8, series B, 1988, 25:00309–00310, 00312–00316, 00328–00333, 00334–00335, 00336–00338. The younger women's statements present painful, detailed accounts of their abduction and sexual assaults. Many details have been left out of the brief narrative presented here.

3. "Report from Memphis," n.d., *NAACP Papers*, part 8, series B, 25:00318.

4. This tactic of testing women for VD in order to undermine their charges of police misconduct had been used previously. In 1944, for example, Mayor Chandler suggested to Commissioner Boyle that a black woman protesting her arrest on a disorderly conduct charge might be subjected to quarantine if she tested positive for venereal disease. See Chandler to Boyle, Chandler Papers, box 15, folder: Public Safety, 1944.

5. "Judge Orders Two Ex-Cops Held on Assault Charges," *Memphis Press-Scimitar*, August 28, 1945.

6. "Press-Scimitar's Account of Police Attack Charges"; and "We Must Act on This!" both in *Memphis World*, August 14, 1945.

7. Myrdal, *American Dilemma*. On police race riot in Columbia, Tennessee, see O'Brien, *Color of the Law*. On other locales, see, for example, Kelley, "'Slanging Rocks'"; Thornton, *Dividing Lines*, 33–38; Fairclough, *Race and Democracy*, 106–34; and Bayor, *Race and the Shaping of Twentieth-Century Atlanta*, 20–21, 174–77.

8. On Montgomery, see Thornton, *Dividing Lines*, 34–35; and Burns, ed., *Daybreak of Freedom*, 8. On Panama City, see correspondence about the trial of James R. Dudley, April–November 1950, *NAACP Papers*, part 8, series B, Criminal Justice System, 1940–50, 24:00407–24:00415. See also Christina Greene's discussion of a 1952 sexual assault case in Durham that suggests the complicated gender and racial politics of protesting such incidents, in *Our Separate Ways*, 7–8; and documents concerning an east Texas case, *NAACP Papers*, part 8, series B, Criminal Justice System, 1940–50, 22:00576–22:00598. The NAACP's voluminous case files on police brutality include reports of incidents of violence against women; and its files on rape cases involve both defenses of black men accused of rape and incidents of white men assaulting black women. See *NAACP Papers*, part 8, series B, Criminal Justice System, 1940–50, files on Police Brutality and Rape.

9. Jill Nelson, in her introduction to *Police Brutality* (13), notes that "the sheer violence and horror" of certain police brutality cases has generated enough mass public outrage to bring about indictments and, in rare instances, convictions. This chapter analyzes the specific kinds of cases that sparked such responses in the immediate post–World War II period.

10. Montgomery protests against police brutality and demands for black police officers also won white support. See Thornton, *Dividing Lines*, 36–37. For more on this effort by southern moderates and the volatile, complex terrain of southern politics at the end of the war, see Frederickson, *Dixiecrat Revolt*, 47–52; and Simon, *Fabric of Defeat*.

11. Critical race theorist Kimberlé Williams Crenshaw warns that the "rape of black women . . . is usually cast as an assault on black manhood, demonstrating his inability to protect black women." In this case, concerns about black manhood became bound up with a conflict over the direction of black leadership. See Crenshaw, "Mapping the Margins," 370.

12. Elsa Barkley Brown analyzes the late-nineteenth-century process by which black men, in the face of racist images of them as bestial rapists, cast themselves

as community protectors, thereby emphasizing women's vulnerability. In this process, she argues, racial sexual violence against black women became sidelined as a "women's issue." See her "Negotiating and Transforming the Public Sphere," 48–50.

13. On rape and the transition from slavery to citizenship, see Wriggins, "Rape, Racism, and the Law"; and Rosen, "'Not that Sort of Women.'" Crenshaw ("Mapping the Margins," 369, 373) argues that while white women's sexual biographies entered into rape trials, black women themselves were considered naturally depraved, making it difficult for black women to secure convictions.

14. Kelley, "'Slangin' Rocks,'" 32. Payne, *I've Got the Light of Freedom*, 7–21, finds evidence of thirty-three lynchings in Mississippi from 1930 to 1950 but notes that this number represents a sharp decline over previous decades, due to a changing national political climate and the collapse of the cotton economy. Memphis newspapers reported on lynchings in the region in this period, but the last one in the city appears to have been the 1917 lynching of Ell Persons.

15. See Jackson, "'Stray Women.'"

16. Benjamin Bell complained about the regulation segregating black and white military personnel in the downtown and Beale Street areas, in "Dixie Ways Rule Memphis; Killed Jobs for White Only," *Chicago Defender*, January 22, 1944.

17. Memphis Housing Authority chairman J. A. Fowler reported in 1942 that out of 5,000 housing units constructed in 1940–41, only 50 were built for black residents. See Fowler to Congressman Clifford Davis, October 29, 1942, box 13, folder: Housing—LeMoyne Gardens, 1942–43; Fowler to Mayor Chandler, October 24, 1942, box 8, folder: Health Department, 1941; and Fowler to Chandler, June 27, 1945, box 15, folder: Housing Authority, 1945, all in Chandler Papers.

18. The 1940 WPA housing survey in Memphis had reported that 77 percent of the black population lived in substandard housing, as compared to 35 percent of the white population. The majority of blacks living in substandard housing lacked indoor plumbing. See WPA, "Housing Survey," 18–20; and J. A. Fowler to Mayor Walter Chandler, October 24, 1942, Chandler Papers, box 8, folder: Health Department, 1941.

19. P. L. Harden to Mayor Walter Chandler, October 8, 1942, Chandler Papers, box 9, folder: Negroes—1942.

20. Fairclough, *Race and Democracy*, 79, 109; Woodruff, *American Congo*, 219. See also Myrdal's comparison between policing in the urban South and that in the rural South, in *American Dilemma*, 535–40.

21. Lovie Mae Griffin interview by author.

22. "Mrs. Brown of Harlem, Victim of Brutality," *Memphis World*, March 19, 1943.

23. Sworn affidavits by Walter Frazier and Clifton Robinson, August 19, 1944; Brig. Gen. Royal Reynolds to Mayor Walter Chandler, August 19, 1944; Chandler to Reynolds, August 21, 1944; Chandler to Commissioner Joseph Boyle, August 21, 1944; and Chandler to Reynolds, August 28, 1944, all in Chandler Papers, box 15, folder: Public Safety, 1944. See also correspondence regarding the police killing of Jasper Miller in 1943 (January 6–January 15, 1943, Chandler Papers, box 15, folder: M Correspondence, 1943). After receiving a protest letter, the mayor instructed

Commissioner Joe Boyle to write a report stating that Miller had been drunk and was shot by the officer in self-defense.

24. Nat D. Williams, "State Patrolmen Beat Negro Soldier to Near Death at Grand Central," *Memphis World*, July 21, 1944, 1. For other reports of police brutality or killings, see "Police Officers Investigated for Beating Delivery Boy in Drug Fund," November 30, 1943; "Says Police Attacked Him with Blackjacks," June 29, 1945; "Police Kill Two in Weekend Tilts," July 6, 1945; and "Victim of Officer's Bullet Dies at John Gaston Hospital," August 7, 1945, all in *Memphis World*.

25. Lovie Mae Griffin interview by author.

26. In 1940, for example, U.S. Bedding Company plant manager Jacob Haaz complained to Mayor Chandler about police harassing his workers and demanded an investigation. See Jacob Haaz to Mayor Walter Chandler, March 27, 1940, Chandler Papers, box 6, folder: Public Safety—Police, 1940.

27. Benjamin F. Bell Jr., "Dixie Ways Rule Memphis; Skilled Jobs for White Only," *Chicago Defender*, January 22, 1944.

28. Tennessee had required segregation on streetcars since 1905, when the General Assembly passed a law that covered streetcar systems in all cities in the state. However, the state law left specific arrangements up to local control. See Lamon, *Black Tennesseans*, 20–36.

29. "Several Weman [*sic*] of City" to Chandler, September 20, 1942, box 9, folder: Negroes—1942; and Mayor Chandler to E. H. Crump, September 16, 1942, box 11, folder: Correspondence T 1942; both in Chandler Papers. See also other correspondence in "Negroes—1942" folder, box 9; and "Transportation—1940" folder, box 14, both in Chandler Papers. Several letters from middle-class white women expressed worry that proposed route changes would make it difficult for their maids to reach their houses.

30. Report on streetcar and bus lines, November 1943, Chandler Papers, box 17, folder: Transportation, 1942–43. For an analysis that likens buses to moving theaters for racial dramas, see Kelley, *Race Rebels*, 55–75.

31. Evelyn Bates interview by author.

32. Correspondence about the trial of James R. Dudley, April–November 1950, *NAACP Papers*, part 8, series B, Criminal Justice System, 1940–50, 24:00407–24:00415; Thornton, *Dividing Lines*, 34–35.

33. Brandt, *No Magic Bullet*, 146–47.

34. L. M. Graves, M.D., Superintendent of Health, to Mayor Walter Chandler, March 11, 1941; L. M. Graves to Walter Chandler, June 12, 1942; Walter Chandler to Clifford Davis, June 13, 1942; and Walter Chandler to Honorable Kenneth McKellar, June 13, 1942, all in Chandler Papers, box 8, folder: Health Department, 1941. By fiscal year 1942–43, the city Health Department projected a venereal disease control budget that would include $44,132 in federal funds. City officials, assisted by Senator McKellar and Representative Davis, lobbied Congress to maintain the fifteen million dollars currently allocated for VD control.

35. L. M. Graves, M.D., Superintendent of Health, to Mayor Walter Chandler, March 11, 1941, Chandler Papers, box 8, folder: Health Department, 1941.

36. "Disease Regulation Is Practiced on All," *Atlanta Daily World*, December 29,

1943, 1; Brandt, *No Magic Bullet*, 161–70; C. Arthur Bruce to Mayor Walter Chandler, July 11, 1942, Chandler Papers, box 8, folder: American Social Hygiene Association, 1941–42.

37. "War on Prostitution Called All-Out Here," *Memphis Commercial Appeal*, June 9, 1942. By way of comparison, see Jackson, "'Stray Women,'" in which Jackson analyzes how women migrating from countryside to city were stereotyped as transmitters of venereal disease in colonial Rhodesia (Zimbabwe). Neville Hoad suggested this comparison to me. In Memphis, both migrant women and African American women in general were so medicalized by public officials, but the former were construed as threatening on a transitory, not a permanent, basis.

38. "War on Prostitution Called All-Out Here," *Memphis Commercial Appeal*, June 9, 1942. Among the 102 white women arrested over a six-week period on various charges, including "soliciting males, vagrancy, being a suspicious person or loitering," 45 percent had syphilis. See "45 Per Cent Infected, Police Report Shows," ibid., December 17, 1942.

39. "Disease Regulation Is Practiced on All," *Atlanta Daily World*, December 29, 1943, 1.

40. Lt. Col. A. F. Brand, "Venereal Disease Control Officer Issues Statement Regarding Health Cards," *Memphis World*, June 22, 1945, 1.

41. Myrdal, *American Dilemma*, 1083–84. On the racist moral discourse of syphilophobia, see Brandt, *No Magic Bullet*, 157–58.

42. "VD Control Program at LeMoyne Gardens Thurs. Sailors to Show Films," *Memphis World*, August 28, 1945, 1. The Committee for Promotion of V.D. Control at LeMoyne Gardens was chaired by Lewis O. Swingler, *Memphis World* editor and local NAACP officer, and included many black social and civic organizations.

43. "Press-Scimitar's Account of Police Attack Charges," reprinted in *Memphis World*, August 14, 1945. On white moderates' efforts to promote good government and economic stability, see Frederickson, *Dixiecrat Revolt*, 47–51.

44. Edward Smith, "Writer Stresses Need to Consider State of the City for Negroes," August 10, 1945; and "Seek Funds to Help Prosecute Officers Accused of Assault," August 21, 1945, both in *Memphis World*.

45. "We Must Act On This!" *Memphis World*, August 14, 1945, 1.

46. "Plans for Prosecution of Rape Case Outlined by Many Civic Groups," August 21, 1945; and "Randolph Heard at Labor Conference," September 23, 1946, both in *Memphis World*.

47. Reverend A. J. Campbell to Thurgood Marshall, February 13, 1946, *NAACP Papers*, part 8, series B, 25:00366 and 25:00369.

48. Memphis NAACP membership grew from 400 in 1939, when Utillus Phillips, a railroad postal employee, took over the branch leadership, to 1,500 in 1943, 3,600 in 1946, and 4,000 in 1947, before plunging again in the late 1940s and remaining low until the mid-1950s. See Utillus Phillips to Ella Baker, May 13, 1946, box C185; Phillips to Walter White, July 28, 1943, box C185; Lucille Black to Officer and Delegates of Tennessee State Conference NAACP, August 24, 1950, box C187; and Phillips to Black, May 24, 1949, box C187, all in NAACP-LC, group II, series C. On the

branch's lack of programs during the war, see Melton, "Blacks in Memphis, Tennessee," 252.

49. "Plans for Prosecution of Rape Case Outlined by Many Civic Groups," *Memphis World*, August 21, 1945.

50. "Report from Memphis," 25:00318; and Charles S. Johnson to Roy Wilkins, August 15, 1945, 25:00327, both in *NAACP Papers*, part 8, series B. It is not clear whether this report was actually written by the *Memphis Press-Scimitar* reporter or by Mitchell.

51. "Report from Memphis," 25:00318; and Charles S. Johnson to Roy Wilkins, August 15, 1945, 25:00327, both in *NAACP Papers*, part 8, series B.

52. Roy Wilkins to Utillus R. Phillips, August 18, 1945, 25:00317; and Thurgood Marshall to Utillus Phillips, September 5 and 26, 1945, 25:00339–00340, 00342, both in *NAACP Papers*, part 8, series B; "Randolph Asks Investigation in Tenn. Case," *Memphis World*, August 31, 1945, 1.

53. In a more typical reaction, when angry citizens complained to Mayor Walter Chandler about the police shooting of Jasper Miller in January 1943, the mayor advised Public Safety Commissioner Joseph Boyle to report that he had "investigated promptly" and found that a police shooting was required for the "officer's necessary self-defense," since Miller was drunk. See Chandler to Mr. and Mrs. Hubert F. Fisher Jr., January 6, 1943; Chandler to Boyle, January 6, 1943; and Chandler to Mr. and Mrs. Fisher Jr., January 15, 1943, all in Chandler Papers, box 14, folder: M Correspondence, 1943.

54. In Tennessee, rape was legally defined as "the unlawful carnal knowledge of a woman, forcibly and against her will." Carnal knowledge was further defined as sexual penetration. Rape was punishable by death by electrocution or by life imprisonment. See *State of Tennessee v. J. W. Torrey and B. J. Lewis* (Criminal Court, Division I, Shelby County, Tennessee, 1946).

55. "Plans for Prosecution of Rape Case Outlined by Many Civic Groups," August 21, 1945, 2; and "Grand Jury Indicts Two Ex-Policemen," September 7, 1945, 1, both in *Memphis World*.

56. "Powerful Prosecution Fails to Move White Jury in Police, Negro Girls' Rape Trial," *Memphis World*, August 29, 1946, 1.

57. "Attitudes toward Negroes in Police Rape Case Balk Jury Selection — New Panel," *Memphis World*, November 9, 1945, 1; Robert Tillman to Memphis Branch NAACP, *NAACP Papers*, part 8, series B, 25:00354. Despite the Supreme Court's 1935 *Norris v. Alabama* decision, which set aside the lower court decision in a case involving one of the famed "Scottsboro boys" accused of raping two white women because it had been based on an all-white jury, most southern juries continued to be all white. On *Norris*, see Nieman, *Promises to Keep*, 135–36. In at least one federal court case in Memphis in the early 1940s, Judge Marion Boyd had recommended black male jurists, according to a letter from black American Legion official P. L. Harden to Mayor Walter Chandler, October 8, 1942, Chandler Papers, box 9, folder: Negroes — 1942.

58. "Two Girls Tell Their Stories to the Jurors, Then Point Accusing Fingers at

Two Ex-Cops," *Memphis Press-Scimitar*, January 23, 1946, 1; "Accused Policemen Declared Not Guilty," *Memphis Commercial Appeal*, January 25, 1946, 1; "Powerful Prosecution Fails to Move White Jury in Police, Negro Girls' Rape Trial," *Memphis World*, January 29, 1946, 1.

59. "Powerful Prosecution Fails to Move White Jury in Police, Negro Girls' Rape Trial," *Memphis World*, January 29, 1946, 1. For a discussion on how stereotypical ideas about illegitimacy sharply differed for white and black women, see Kunzel, "White Neurosis, Black Pathology," 304–31.

60. "Two Girls Tell Their Stories to the Jurors, Then Point Accusing Fingers at Two Ex-Cops," *Memphis Press-Scimitar*, January 23, 1946.

61. Various scholars have addressed the difficulties faced by black women who accuse white men of rape. Nell Irvin Painter argues in "Hill, Thomas, and the Use of Racial Stereotype" (p. 212), that because of the symbolic history of black womanhood, "black women have not been able to use our history of abuse as a corrective to stereotypes of rampant sexuality," despite a history of extreme vulnerability to sexual violence. See also Crenshaw, "Mapping the Margins," 369–73.

62. Robert Tillman to NAACP, *NAACP Papers*, part 8, series B, 25:00356.

63. See Jennifer Wriggins's analysis of the issues of chastity and race in rape cases ("Rape, Racism, and the Law," 120–21). Historically, she argues, black women were considered promiscuous and part of an "immoral race" in legal cases. At the same time, rape law historically precluded the determination of rape if the woman was proven to be unchaste. Thus, she states, "the association of Black women with unchastity meant not only that Black women could not be victims of statutory rape, but also that they could not be recognized as victims of forcible rape." See also Evelyn Brooks Higginbotham's discussion of pervasive white belief in black women's promiscuity and identification of them with syphilis, which combined to cast syphilis in the United States as a disease spread by black women. See "African-American Women's History," esp. 262–66.

64. "Accused Policemen Declared Not Guilty," *Memphis Commercial Appeal*, January 25, 1946, 1; "Powerful Prosecution Fails to Move White Jury in Police, Negro Girls' Rape Trial," *Memphis World*, January 29, 1946, 1.

65. Thurgood Marshall to Utillus R. Phillips, February 6, 1946, *NAACP Papers*, part 8, series B, 25:00366 and 25:00369.

66. Jeraldine Sanderlin interview by author. See also Higginbotham's discussion about limitations on black women's mobility in "African American Women's History."

67. Reverend A. J. Campbell to Thurgood Marshall, February 13, 1946; and Marian Wynn Perry to Rev. Campbell, March 9, 1946, both in *NAACP Papers*, part 8, series B, 25:00367–25:00369.

68. Donald Jones to Ella Baker, March 7, 1946; and Ella Baker to Donald Jones, March 14, 1946, both in NAACP-LC, group II, series C, box C185.

69. Donald Jones to Ella Baker, March 22, 1946, NAACP-LC, group II, series C, box C185; "Maurice Weaver, NAACP 'Columbia' Attorney, To Speak Here Sunday," March 26, 1946, 1; and "Memphians Get First-Hand Facts on Columbia Riot from NAACP Attorney," April 16, 1946, 1, both in *Memphis World*. On the Columbia riot,

see O'Brien, *Color of the Law*. In April 1946 the NAACP announced that the Memphis membership drive that spring had been the most successful ever, resulting in 3,000 memberships. See "Memphis NAACP Membership Drive Ends," *Memphis World*, April 26, 1946.

70. On efforts to revive the LeMoyne NAACP in early 1946, see *LeMoyne Democrat*, February 1, 1946, LMOC Archives.

71. "Speak Up!" *The Private Chatterer* II, January 31, 1946; and "Adieu," *LeMoyne Democrat*, September 13, 1946, both in LMOC Archives.

72. "Speak Up!" *The Private Chatterer* II, January 31, 1946; and "Adieu," *LeMoyne Democrat*, September 13, 1946, both in LMOC Archives.

73. "Jury Gives Death Verdict to 16-Year-Old Boy in Goss Case," *Memphis World*, March 1, 1946, 1.

74. "Fred Jackson's Parents Seek Funds to Save Youth from Chair Feb. 28," January 24, 1947; and "Fred Jackson Nears Doom — Governor Is Asked to Save Him," August 1, 1947, both in *Memphis World*.

75. Arthur Womack, "Is There Not Another Way," March 5, 1946; and "Negro Voters Join with Liberal Whites to Lift 'Iron Curtain' as Browning, Kefauver Win Posts," August 10, 1948, both in *Memphis World*.

76. "Willing Workers Club Aids Fred Jackson Fund," March 7, 1947; "Fund-Raising Mass Meet for Fred Jackson at Mason's Temple April 27," April 22, 1947; and "Fred Jackson Nears Doom — Governor Is Asked to Save Him," August 1, 1947, all in *Memphis World*.

77. "Testimony of Eyewitnesses Refute Police Denials of Beating Expectant Mother," *Memphis World*, August 8, 1947, 1.

78. Ibid.

79. Ibid.; "Public Responds to NAACP Appeal for Legal Funds," September 16, 1947; and "Adelaide Hudson's Case Will Be Tried Dec. 18th," December 16, 1947, 3, both in *Memphis World*; Hollis F. Price and D. V. Kyle to "Pastor," NAACP-LC, group II, series C, box C185, Memphis, Tenn., 1947–50; Utillus Phillips to Gloster B. Current, NAACP-LC, group II, series C, box C186, Memphis, Tenn., 1951–55; Marian Wynn Perry to Utillus R. Phillips, *NAACP Papers*, part 8, series B, 19:00952.

80. Harry Woodbury, "Use of Negro Police to Be Given Trial; Applications Sought," *Memphis Commercial Appeal*, September 10, 1948; "Speakers Voice Sentiment for Negro Police," *Memphis World*, September 26, 1947; "Atlanta Negro Police Question Referred to Council Committee," *Memphis World*, November 21, 1947.

81. Clippings in *NAACP Papers*, part 8, series B, 19:00007–00020, including "Eye Is Lost from Beating: 2 Policemen Are Jailed," *Memphis Press-Scimitar*, May 18, 1948; "Jury Sleeps On Fate of Two Ex-Policemen," *Memphis Commercial Appeal*, July 1, 1948; "Gerber Will Demand New Mayhem Trials for Two Policemen," *Memphis Commercial Appeal*, July 2, 1948; "Shocking Incident," *Memphis Commercial Appeal*, May 19, 1948; "Two Police Officers Accused Of Beating," *Memphis Commercial Appeal*, May 18, 1948; "Bryan Is Fined $51, Brewer Not Guilty," *Memphis Press-Scimitar*, July 1, 1948. See also "Memphis Police Sued for $20,000," June 29, 1948; "Police Officers on Trial for Brutalizing Negro," July 2, 1948; and "One Ex-Policeman Fined $50; Another Acquitted in Famed Police Brutality Case Here," July 2, 1948, all in *Memphis World*.

82. "Woman Victim of Police Beating Still Confined to Hospital with Charges," June 29, 1948, 1; and "Woman, Attacked by Police, Fined $78 in City Court," July 9, 1948, both in *Memphis World*.

83. Petitions in Pleasants Papers, box 6B, folder: Police Department, 1948; "Need for Negro Police, Hospital Voiced Topics Discussed by Chamber," July 23, 1948; and "Local Minister Urges Negro Police for Memphis as Curb on Unfair Treatment, Bias," July 13, 1948, both in *Memphis World*. On Atlanta, see Bayor, *Race and the Shaping of Twentieth-Century Atlanta*, 174–77. On Birmingham, see Kelley, "'Slangin' Rocks,'" 37.

84. "Negro Voters Join with Liberal Whites to Lift 'Iron Curtain' as Browning, Kefauver Win Posts," *Memphis World*, August 10, 1948.

85. "Militant AME Pastor Transferred to Georgia," *Memphis World*, November 19, 1948. Kyle lost his bid to defeat previously uncontested Congressman Clifford Davis.

86. See petitions and Pleasants's statement in Pleasants Papers, box 6B, folder: Police Department, 1948.

87. Note and newspaper fragment, July 23, 1948, Pleasants Papers, box 6B, folder: Police Department, 1948.

88. "Young Overseas Vet Shot to Death by Police Officers in His Yard — Binghampton Citizens Are Aroused," August 24, 1948; "Mayor's Office Gets Petition Seeking Race Police," September 7, 1948; "Donors to Mosby Fund," September 14, 1948; photograph and caption, September 21, 1948, all in *Memphis World*.

89. Henry Pilcher, for East Memphis Citizens Club, to Mayor James Pleasants Jr., August 25, 1948; and Petition from East Memphis Citizens Club to Mayor James Pleasants Jr., n.d., both in Pleasants Papers, box 6B, folder: Police Department, 1948. For more on this point regarding domestic violence, see Crenshaw, "Mapping the Margins," 362.

90. Petition from East Memphis Citizens Club to Mayor James Pleasants Jr., n.d., Pleasants Papers, box 6b, folder: Police Department, 1948.

91. Harry Woodbury, "Use of Negro Police to Be Given Trial; Applications Sought," *Memphis Commercial Appeal*, September 10, 1948; "Negro Police Makes Debut on Beale Street with Ready Arrest of Culprits," *Memphis World*, November 9, 1948; "Negro Officers Walking Their Beats," *Memphis Commercial Appeal*, November 6, 1948; Philip Ashford, "Beale Bolstered Black Policemen," *Memphis Commercial Appeal*, October 10, 1983.

92. Harry Woodbury, "Use of Negro Police to Be Given Trial; Applications Sought," *Memphis Commercial Appeal*, September 10, 1948; "Negro Police Makes Debut on Beale Street with Ready Arrest of Culprits," *Memphis World*, November 9, 1948; "Negro Officers Walking Their Beats," *Memphis Commercial Appeal*, November 6, 1948; Chris Conley, "Robinson, One of City's First Black Officers, Dies," *Memphis Commercial Appeal*, November 27, 1993. Matthew Thornton, in "Last of Negro Policemen Here Recalls Distant Days on Force," an interview with the *Memphis Commercial Appeal*, September 10, 1948, recalled his brief stint on the police force in 1919.

93. Nat D. Williams, "Down on Beale Ave.," *Memphis World*, November 9, 1948; Wendell Robinson and R. J. Turner, quoted in Philip Ashford, "Beale Bolstered Black Policemen," *Memphis Commercial Appeal*, October 10, 1983.

Chapter 4

1. Charles E. Lincoln, "Night Train to Memphis," February 14, 1946, *LeMoyne Democrat*, newspaper box 34, LMOC Archives.

2. These figures are from Bradsher, "Taking America's Heritage to the People," 241.

3. "Objectives and Plans," *The Beacon*, November 21, 1947, 1.

4. "Truman Doctrine," *Congressional Record*, March 12, 1947; Arsenault, *Freedom Riders*, esp. 33–55.

5. Three million U.S. workers struck in late 1945 and early 1946, disrupting all the basic industries and spurring general strikes in several cities. See Lichtenstein, Strasser, and Rosenzweig, eds., *Who Built America*, 531–34.

6. American Heritage Foundation pamphlet, "Conference at the White House for the Purpose of Organizing the American Heritage Program and Inaugurating the Freedom Train, May 22, 1947," Pleasants Papers, box 13, folder: Freedom Train.

7. Scholarship on the Freedom Train and early Cold War political culture includes Bradsher, "Taking America's Heritage to the People," 229–46; Kammen, "Public Sector and the Politics of Tradition," 571–81; Little, "Freedom Train," 35–68; Griffith, "Selling of America," 388–412; and Rodgers, *Contested Truths*, Epilogue. On Birmingham's Freedom Train conflict, see John White, "Civil Rights in Conflict," 121–41. Briefer discussions are in Michael Honey, *Southern Labor and Black Civil Rights*, 246, 249; Eskew, *But for Birmingham*, 73; and McCoy and Ruetten, *Quest and Response*, 74–75, 94.

8. The account of early planning for the Freedom Train in this paragraph is based largely on Bradsher, "Taking America's Heritage to the People"; and Little, "Freedom Train."

9. On the Advertising Council, see Griffith, "Selling of America." Little, in "Freedom Train," argues that the advertising and movie executives planned the project to construct a postwar consensus ideology linking American citizenship to a heritage of free enterprise, individualism, and the family.

10. Bradsher, "Taking America's Heritage to the People," 230–33; Little, "Freedom Train," 40–41; Griffith, "Selling of America," 396–99.

11. Truman, "Special Message to the Congress," 176–79; Bradsher, "Taking America's Heritage to the People," 231, 233. See Rodgers, *Contested Truths*, 214–18, for analysis of changing World War II and Cold War uses of "freedom" as a "keyword" of American political life.

12. American Heritage Foundation pamphlet, "Conference at the White House for the Purpose of Organizing the American Heritage Program and Inaugurating the Freedom Train," May 22, 1947, in Pleasants Papers, box 13, folder: Freedom Train.

13. Rodgers, *Contested Truths*, 214–18. See Dudziak's discussion of the Truman administration in *Cold War Civil Rights*, esp. chaps. 1, 3.

14. On Truman's Executive Order 9808 and June 1947 speech to the NAACP, see McCoy and Ruetten, *Quest and Response*, 49–53, 73–74; Gardner, *Harry Truman and Civil Rights*, 14–42 passim; Zangrando, *NAACP Crusade against Lynching*, 175–86 passim; and Berman, *Politics of Civil Rights*, 50–56, 61–65.

15. American Heritage Foundation pamphlet, "Conference at the White House for the Purpose of Organizing the American Heritage Program and Inaugurating the Freedom Train," May 22, 1947, in Pleasants Papers, box 13, folder: Freedom Train; Monaghan, *Heritage of Freedom*; Walter White to Winthrop Aldrich, September 20, 1947, *NAACP Papers*, part 15: Segregation and Discrimination: Complaints and Responses, 1940–55, series B: Administrative Files, 6:0218; Little, "Freedom Train," 55. After the May conference, White declared he was more concerned about "native totalitarianism" than "foreign ideologies," and Lester Granger, in a letter to Advertising Council director Thomas D'Arcy Brophy, warned that blacks would be disillusioned if segregation were permitted during the viewings. See *Chicago Defender* and White; both quoted in Little, "Freedom Train," 55; Granger quoted in Bradsher, "Taking America's Heritage to the People," 234.

16. News Release from the American Heritage Foundation, September 29, 1947, Pleasants Papers, box 13, folder: Freedom Train; Typed excerpt, "From the New York Times, Monday, Sept. 29, 1947, Page 17, Col. 5"; and "Memorandum from Mr. White To Mr. Wilkins," August 19, 1947," *NAACP Papers*-FT, 6:00216, 00507.

17. J. A. Rogers, "The Negro's Part in the Freedom Train," *Pittsburgh Courier*, November 1, 1947, reproduced in Little, "Freedom Train," 57; Editorial, *Chicago Defender*, September 20, 1947.

18. Hughes, "Freedom Train," 27. In his poem "Words Like Freedom," published the same year in *The Panther and the Lash*, Hughes says that the words "freedom" and "liberty" make him cry and concludes, "If you had known what I know / You would know why."

19. W. C. Handy to NAACP, October 3, 1947, *NAACP Papers*-FT, 6:00246. Robeson recorded a reading of Hughes's "Freedom Train" for the Southern Conference for Human Welfare, which then sold copies of the recording. See Bob Bialek to Roy Wilkins, December 9, 1947, *NAACP Papers*-FT, 6:00292. See Paul Robeson, performance of Langston Hughes's "Freedom Train" (Folk Era CD FE1447CD, 1998); and Ira Berlin, "Freedom Train," recorded by Bing Crosby and the Andrews Sisters, on Bing Crosby / Andrews Sisters: Their Complete Recordings Together (Universal Music & Vi CD 11503, 1996).

20. Freedom Train southern itinerary, n.d., *NAACP Papers*-FT, 6:0031. For examples of the AHF and Tom Clark's appeal to mayors to join other cities in welcoming the train, see J. Edward Shugrue to Memphis's mayor, September 5, 1947; and Tom C. Clark to S. Polk, October 20, 1947, both in Pleasants Papers, box 13, folder: Freedom Train.

21. President's Committee on Civil Rights, *To Secure These Rights*. On publicity for *To Secure These Rights*, see McCoy and Ruetten, *Quest and Response*, 92–94. Truman quoted in "Civil Rights Draft Hailed Nationally: Truman Hopes Special Report Will Be Human Freedom Charter 'In Our Time,'" *Memphis World*, November 4, 1947.

22. On the *Shelley v. Kraemer* brief, see McCoy and Ruetten, *Quest and Response*,

211–12; and Gardner, *Harry Truman and Civil Rights*, 173–78. See broader discussion of the Truman administration's use of amicus curiae briefs in Dudziak, *Cold War Civil Rights*, 90–102 passim.

23. Mayor Pleasants's November 23 radio address on the Freedom Train included the following statement: "Recently the Committee on Civil Rights made its report. This report advocated one school, one theater, one restaurant, one hospital, one public restroom, one hotel for both white and colored, to all of which both races would have equal access. This report advocated permitting any negro to live anywhere he pleased on any street. Do the people of Memphis and Shelby County want these things? I say most emphatically, NO! Such ideas go into the very teeth of our way of life." See typescript, Pleasants Papers, box 13, folder: Freedom Train.

24. "Freedom Train 'Derailed' by Race Segregation," *Memphis Press-Scimitar*, November 18, 1947; "Segregation Plan Bars Freedom Train Showing," *New York Times*, November 18, 1947, 1; statement by Mayor Pleasants Jr., November 18, 1947, Pleasants Papers, box 13, folder: Freedom Train.

25. My analysis of correspondence with the mayor's office about the Freedom Train in this and the next two paragraphs is based on over 400 letters, postcards, telegrams, annotated clippings, and telephone messages in five folders on the Freedom Train, November–December 1947, Pleasants Papers, box 12.

26. Oscar F. Bledsoe III to Frank Ahlgren, November 26, 1947; G. L. Seegers to Mayor Pleasants Jr., December 6, 1947; and Henry Hill to Mayor Pleasants Jr., November 18, 1947, all in Freedom Train correspondence, Pleasants Papers, box 12.

27. Mrs. L. N. Bergan and Mrs. Arthur N. Olson to Mayor Pleasants Jr., November 18, 1947, in Freedom Train correspondence, Pleasants Papers, box 12.

28. Jerome Barton to Mayor Pleasants Jr., November 18, 1947; and letter from Eighth Grade, Hubert, Arkansas, to Mayor Pleasants Jr., November 19, 1947, both in Freedom Train correspondence, Pleasants Papers, box 12. For examples of letters that contrast Pleasants's decision about Memphis to Hartfield's statement about Atlanta, see Anonymous, Stockton, California, to Mayor Pleasants Jr., November 24, 1947; and Lois McColloch, Milton, Massachusetts, to Mayor George Calhoun, Hattiesburg, Mississippi, carbon copies to Pleasants and Hartfield, January 15, 1948, both in Freedom Train correspondence, Pleasants Papers, box 12.

29. On Meeman's political role, see Hugh Davis Graham, *Crisis in Print*, 40–41; and Silver and Moeser, *Separate City*, 63–64, 67–68, 91, 94.

30. "Memphians Have Right to See Freedom Train," November 19, 1947; and "Freedom Train 'Derailed' by Race Segregation," November 18, 1947, both in *Memphis Press-Scimitar*.

31. Richard Wallace, "Freedom Train Getting Green Light in South: Except in Memphis—No Segregation in Richmond, Atlanta, New Orleans, Little Rock"; and "Memphians Have Right to See Freedom Train," both in *Memphis Press-Scimitar*, November 19, 1947. See daily coverage on the Freedom Train in the *Memphis Press-Scimitar*, November 18–December 18, 1947.

32. Richard Wallace, "Veterans Will Circulate Petitions for Train," November 21, 1947; Richard Wallace, "'Mayor Is Clouding the Freedom Train Issue,' Says AVC,"

November 23, 1947, 2; "2 More Memphis Groups Want Freedom Train," November 26, 1947, 1; and "Women Voters League Answers the Mayor," November 29, 1947, all in *Memphis Press-Scimitar*. See also Thelma Rust, President, League of Women Voters, to Mayor James Pleasants Jr., November 19, 1947; and Memphis Committee for Freedom Train to "Fellow Citizens," n.d., both in Pleasants Papers, box 12, unlabeled folder.

33. Hardy L. Fly Jr. to Mayor James Pleasants Jr., November 20, 1947, Pleasants Papers, box 12, unlabeled folder.

34. A group of white workers wrote about "big burley [*sic*] negroes" defiling their womenfolk on buses, while a more elite writer made derogatory comments about "full-fledged coal black Ethiopians," in "The 308" to Mayor James Pleasants Jr., November 19, 1947, and T. R. Montgomery to *Memphis Press-Scimitar*, November 20, 1947, respectively, both in Pleasants Papers, box 12, unlabeled folder.

35. R. H. French, Galashields Plantation, Jackson, Tennessee, to Millard Naill, n.d.; R. H. French to Mayor James Pleasants Jr., November 18, 1947; R. H. French statement, November 1947, all in Pleasants Papers, box 12, Freedom Train files. An attached note from mayoral assistant Marvin Pope reads, "I believe Mr. Crump would enjoy reading this. Looks like his Jackson friend has got something here."

36. Berniece Wiggins, "Let the Freedom Train Come, Say Two Church Leaders," November 22, 1947, 1; "VFW Post Wants Freedom Train Visit: 'No Race Issue,' 4 Ministers Say," November 25, 1947; and "Ministers Discuss Freedom Train: Are Divided," December 1, 1947, 2, all in *Memphis Press-Scimitar*; Reverend E. E. McNatt, Pastor, First Pentecostal Church of Memphis, to Mayor James Pleasants Jr., Pleasants Papers, box 12, unlabeled folder.

37. "Editor of Labor Review Attacks Train Action," *Memphis Press-Scimitar*, November 21, 1947.

38. Richard Wallace, "The City Administration's Attempts to Control Thought Denounced," *Memphis Press-Scimitar*, November 27, 1947.

39. Mayor James Pleasants Jr., Typescript of Radio Address, November 23, 1947, Pleasants Papers, box 13, folder: Freedom Train.

40. "Call Off Efforts to Bring Freedom Train to Memphis," November 23, 1947, 1; and Richard Wallace, "'Freedom Train Has Already Come to Memphis,' Says AVC, Answering Mayor," November 28, 1947, both in *Memphis Press-Scimitar*.

41. Richard Wallace, "The City Administration's Attempts to Control Thought Denounced," November 27, 1947; and "2 More Memphis Groups Want Freedom Train," November 26, 1947, both in *Memphis Press-Scimitar*.

42. "Citizens' Views on Freedom Train," *Memphis Press-Scimitar*, December 3, 1947. See also letter from Walter Hoffman, self-described as a "colored American who loves my country," who applauded the newspaper's efforts to bring the Freedom Train to Memphis, in "Let the Freedom Train Come, Say Two Church Leaders," *Memphis Press-Scimitar*, November 22, 1947.

43. Nat D. Williams, "Down on Beale Avenue," *Memphis World*, November 21, 1947, 6; Hughes, "The Negro Speaks of Rivers," 23.

44. "Memphis Mayor Takes to Air to Defend Segregation Policy in 'Freedom

Train' Ban Issue," November 25, 1947; "Checkin' on the Freedom Train," November 25, 1947; "The Freedom Train," November 25, 1947; and "States Rights at Any Cost" cartoon, December 9, 1947, all in *Memphis World*.

45. News release from AME Ministers' Council, n.d. [ca. November 28, 1947], Pleasants Papers, box 12, unlabeled folder; "Cancellation of Freedom Train Trip to City Scored by AME Ministers' Council," *Memphis World*, December 2, 1947, 1.

46. Annotated AME Ministers' Council news release and typed list of churches and notes, n.d. [ca. November 28, 1947], Pleasants Papers, box 12, unlabeled folder.

47. "$60,000 From Mr. Crump for Negro Blind—Negro Group Suggests Ways to Protect Fund from 'Fleecers,'" *Memphis World*, December 12, 1947, 1.

48. Freedom Train southern itinerary, n.d., *NAACP Papers*-FT, 6:00317–00325; "20,000 Roanoke Citizens Seeing Train Today," December 2, 1947; "Rain on the Train, and Damper on Eager Lad," December 6, 1947; and "Browning to Talk in N.O. and See Freedom Train," December 9, 1947, all in *Memphis Press-Scimitar*.

49. "Digest of Reports Covering Movement of 'Freedom Train' Through Certain Areas of the South," n.d., Pleasants Papers, box 12, Freedom Train Reports folder.

50. Correspondence and news reports on Montgomery Freedom Train visit, November 13–December 28, 1947, *NAACP Papers*-FT, 6:00456, 00458, 00462–00464, 00524, 00527, 00581; Digest of Reports, Pleasants Papers, box 12, Freedom Train Reports folder; Rosa L. Parks, "Local Freedom Train Comm. Snubs NAACP," *Memphis World*, December 16, 1947.

51. "NAACP Protest Freedom Train Jimcrow Reviewing Plan in B'ham," *Memphis World*, December 16, 1947; Correspondence and news reports on canceled Birmingham Freedom Train visit, December 1947, *NAACP Papers*-FT, 6:00468–00755; John White, "Civil Rights in Conflict," 121–41; Thornton, *Dividing Lines*, 229.

52. Ophelia Watson, "LeMoyne Student Gives Impression of Freedom Train," *Memphis World*, January 16, 1948; "Freedom Train Stops at Jackson; Skips Memphis," *Memphis World*, January 9, 1948; F.D., '50, "A Glance at Freedom," *LeMoyne Democrat*, n.d., in newspaper box 34, LMOC Archives; "Digest of Reports," Pleasants Papers, box 12, Freedom Train Reports folder.

53. "Not Yet, Freedom," *LeMoyne Democrat*, n.d. [ca. November 19, 1947], in LMOC Archives; Luther Ward, "Segregation Streamlined," *The Beacon*, March 5, 1948, in NAACP-LC, group II, box E95, folder: LeMoyne College.

54. Odessa Johnson, "I Am a Negro," *LeMoyne Democrat*, October 28, 1941, LMOC Archives.

55. "An American Pattern of Freedom and Justice in Black and White," May 30, 1947; Harry Lemmons, "The Luxury Of Democracy," October 18, 1946; and "Freedom's Day," September 20, 1946, all in *LeMoyne Democrat*, LMOC Archives.

56. "The College Chapter of the NAACP" and "Objectives and Plans," *The Beacon*, November 21, 1947, in NAACP-LC, box E95, folder: LeMoyne College.

57. "College Chapter to Celebrate 8th Anniversary," *The Beacon*, November 30, 1948, 1; and LeMoyne College Membership Reports for February and March, 1947, both in NAACP-LC, box E95, folder: LeMoyne College.

58. Charles E. Lincoln, "Night Train to Memphis," February 14, 1946; "NAACP

Drive On," March 22, 1946; and "There Are Things We *Can* Do," April 5, 1946, all in *LeMoyne Democrat*, LMOC Archives.

59. C. T. '50, "Charlie's Chats," *The Beacon*, April 23, 1948; and Bernard Cotton to Ruby Hurley, March 9, 1948, both in NAACP-LC, box E95, folder: LeMoyne College.

60. "Youth Council of NAACP Formed," *Memphis World*, December 2, 1947; "The College Chapter of the NAACP," *The Beacon*, November 21, 1947; and "Past Operations," *The Beacon*, May 27, 1948, both in NAACP-LC, box E95, folder: LeMoyne College; "NAACP News," *LeMoyne Democrat*, n.d. [ca. May 19, 1948], LMOC Archives.

61. William Gordon, "Plans for City-Wide Youth Rally in March Shaping Up," February 4, 1947; "Plans for City-Wide Youth Rally in March Gains Impetus," February 11, 1947; "Follow-Up Work Is Aim of Youth Rally Set for March 23rd," March 4, 1947; "City-Wide Youth Rally Gets Help from Many Groups," March 4, 1947; and "Youth Rally to Feature Dr. Paterson in Address at Mason's Temple," March 7, 1947, all in *Memphis World*; "Youth Rallies in Memphis," March 31, 1947; "There Are Things We *Can* Do," April 15, 1946; "Jesse Owen," March 31, 1947; and "Youth Program," n.d. [ca. April 23, 1948], all in *LeMoyne Democrat*, LMOC Archives.

62. A.V.C. Meets," October 31, 1946; "S.D.A. Supports Douglas for President," [n.d., ca. April 23, 1948]; "S.D.A. News," [n.d., ca. May 19, 1948]; "S.D.A. to Sponsor Dance" and "Report on the Berea Conference," both February 18, 1949; and "As I See It," March 31, 1947, all in *LeMoyne Democrat*, LMOC Archives. On University of Texas students' postwar emphasis on international peace, see Whittington, "From the Campus."

63. On these white reformers, see Tucker, *Memphis Since Crump*, 40–60. See also Streit, *Union Now*.

64. "Community Relations Group Improves Race Relations," *Memphis World*, June 8, 1948.

65. "Forum at Y.W.C.A.," n.d. [ca. February 21, 1948]; "Interracial Meeting to Be Held," n.d. [ca. April 23, 1948]; "Interracial Group to Meet," n.d. [ca. May 19, 1948]; "Hear Doctor Haridas T. Muzumdar," November 12, 1948; and "Indian Visitor on Campus," December 3, 1948, all in *LeMoyne Democrat*, LMOC Archives.

66. "Edmund Orgill Speaks," January 7, 1949; "Memphis Community Relations Committee," January 14, 1949; "Interracial Meeting: Dr. Everett Hughes Speaks," January 21, 1949; "Dr. Neil Bruce Speaks," March 4, 1949; "Another Inter-Racial Meeting," March 18, 1949; and "Interracial Meet," April 11, 1949, all in *LeMoyne Democrat*, LMOC Archives.

67. C. T. '50, "Charlie's Chats," *The Beacon*, April 23, 1948, NAACP-LC, box E95, folder: LeMoyne College.

68. Silver and Moeser (*Separate City*, 48–52) emphasize the significance of black participation in the 1948 elections, arguing that blacks began laying an "organizational basis for separate black activism" by establishing independent political organizations in the late 1940s and early 1950s. David M. Tucker (*Memphis Since Crump*, 40–60), on the other hand, places responsibility for the 1948 upset in the hands of "a small cluster of [white] liberals" who first united over the idea of federal unionism between the United States and Western Europe and went on to support Kefauver. Tucker argues that "White Memphians were more rebellious than black Mem-

phians" (58) but notes that in 1948, three majority-black precincts went to Kefauver and Browning. See also the detailed account of the black participation of the election in Melton, "Blacks in Memphis, Tennessee," 261–69.

69. Editorial, March 5, 1948, and "NAACP Poll," May 26, 1948, both in *LeMoyne Democrat*, LMOC Archives; "Mr. Truman Did Not Like Mr. Randolph's 'Kind of Talk,'" *The Crisis* (May 1948), reprinted in *The Beacon*, May 27, 1948, NAACP-LC, folder: LeMoyne. On Truman's executive order banning discrimination in the military, issued July 26, 1947, following the National Democratic Convention, see Dalfiume, *Desegregation of the U.S. Armed Forces*.

70. "Do We Want Segregation" and cartoon, *The Beacon*, March 29, 1948, NAACP-LC, folder: LeMoyne.

71. On Wallace's split with Truman, the formation of a third party, and Wallace's 1948 presidential bid, including his trips to the South and red-baiting by Cold War liberals, see Culver and Hyde, *American Dreamer*; White and Maze, *Henry A. Wallace*; and Kleinman, *World of Hope*.

72. "Politics in the Air," n.d. [ca. November 14, 1947]; and "Riot, No," n.d., [ca. November 19, 1947], both in *LeMoyne Democrat*, LMOC Archives.

73. Edward H. Crump quoted in Tucker, *Memphis Since Crump*, 57.

74. Edward H. Crump and Estes Kefauver quoted in Swados, *Standing Up for the People*, 36–38; and Melton, "Blacks in Memphis, Tennessee, 263–64.

75. Tennessee had not, historically, held an all-white primary, as had most other southern states, making it easier for African Americans to participate in this primary. The U.S. Supreme Court, in *Smith v. Allwright* (1944), pronounced the white primary illegal, but some southern states continued to bar most blacks from the all-important Democratic primaries.

76. Silver and Moeser, *Separate City*, 51; Melton, "Blacks in Memphis, Tennessee," 264; "Negroes Urged to Attend Voters' School July 28–29 at Vance Avenue YWCA," *Memphis World*, July 29, 1948.

77. Gorman, *Kefauver*, 55–58; Silver and Moeser, *Separate City*, 51; Melton, "Blacks in Memphis, Tennessee," 264.

78. Minerva Johnican interview by author.

79. While Crump-endorsed Judge Mitchell won 37,000 votes in Shelby County, Kefauver won over 27,000, as compared to the roughly 2,000 most opposition candidates had garnered in Shelby County previously. Incumbent senator Tom Stewart won only 2,640. Statewide, Mitchell's vote came nowhere near either Kefauver's or Stewart's, allowing Kefauver to edge out Stewart in the final tallies. See Swados, *Standing Up for the People*, 39; Gorman, *Kefauver*, 59; Tucker, *Memphis Since Crump*, 59; and "Negro Voters Join with Liberal Whites to Lift 'Iron Curtain' as Browning, Kefauver Win Posts," *Memphis World*, August 10, 1948, 1.

80. "Negro Voters Join with Liberal Whites to Lift 'Iron Curtain' as Browning, Kefauver Win Posts," *Memphis World*, August 10, 1948; "Crump Beaten in Election," *St. Louis Argus*, reprinted in *Memphis World*, August 17, 1948; "The People of Tennessee Take Back the Power," *Memphis Press-Scimitar*, reprinted in *Memphis World*, August 10, 1948.

81. "Browning-Kefauver Rally at Manassas School Thursday Night, Binghamp-

ton Monday," October 26, 1948, 2; "Negro Voters Join with Liberal Whites to Lift 'Iron Curtain' as Browning, Kefauver Win Posts," August 10, 1948, 1; and Dewitt T. Alcorn, "Says Kyle Was Not First Negro to Run for Congress from 10th Dist. Points to A. M. Wilkerson," November 30, 1948, all in *Memphis World*. See also Silver and Moeser, *Separate City*, 51–52; and Dwight Kyle, quoted in Tucker, *Lieutenant Lee of Beale Street*, 147. Kyle's transfer was announced at the AME Church's West Tennessee Annual Conference meeting in mid-November 1948. See "Militant AME Pastor Transferred to Georgia," *Memphis World*, November 19, 1948, 1.

82. "Organized Labor Promises Browing [*sic*], Kefauver Support during Rally at L. Temple," October 19, 1948, 1; "Browning-Kefauver Rally Brings out Voters from 11th, 14th, 25th Wards," October 22, 1948, 1; and "Browning-Kefauver Rally at Manassas School Thursday Night, Binghampton Monday," October 26, 1948, 2, all in *Memphis World*.

83. Henry Wallace, former Roosevelt cabinet member, vice president, and secretary of commerce, had been dismissed by Truman in 1946 after he questioned the president's hostility toward Russia. While campaigning, Wallace attempted to address integrated audiences throughout the South. The Memphis city administration permitted him to address an interracial crowd of several thousand in Bellevue Park on September 3. See "Henry A. Wallace to Address Mixed Audience Here Sept. 3," August 27, 1948, 1; "Thousands to Hear Henry Wallace Friday Sept. 3rd; Meeting at Bellevue Park," August 31, 1948, 1; Nat D. Williams, "Wallace Called 'Freedom Man' Following Address before 500 [*sic*] Memphians at Bellevue Park," September 7, 1948, 1, 3; and "Wallace Addresses Mixed Audience Here," September 7, 1948, 1, 6, all in *Memphis World*. See also Hamby, *Beyond the New Deal*, 29–143.

84. "Firestone Plant Worker Said Policemen Ran Him from Rally for Browning-Kefauver in Square" and "Negro Uncertainty About Court Square Settled by Police 'Chasing' at Rally," both in *Memphis World*, October 22, 1948, 1.

85. "Ministers Asked to Leave Court Square at Dewey-Acuff Political Rally; Refuse: 'We're Not Slaves," *Memphis World*, October 26, 1948, 1.

Chapter 5

1. *Lost Boundaries*, *The Beacon*, September 26, 1949, LMOC Archives. See also Velie, "You Can't See That Movie," 11. *Pinky* did eventually play in Memphis but was barred in other locales. See Cripps, *Making Movies Black*, 231, 239.

2. Nat D. Williams, "Down on Beale Ave.," *Memphis World*, November 23–26, 1948; Cantor, *Wheelin' on Beale*, 42–43. The first black-oriented radio program was Jack L. Cooper's "The All-Negro Hour," which debuted on Chicago's WSBC in 1929. See Mark Newman, *Entrepreneurs of Profit and Pride*, 55–92; and Barlow, *Voice Over*, 50–58.

3. On African American consumption and racial justice during and after the Second World War, see Cohen, *Consumers' Republic*, esp. 83–100, 166–91, 323–29. Cohen argues that a "demand of equality of access" rather than the desire for racial integration initially drove civil rights campaigns against racist policies in public facilities (174). I agree, but my emphasis here is on contestation over visual and sound representations themselves, which reflected ferment in other life zones such as

labor and politics, and contributed to the articulation of understandings of freedom during the late 1950s and 1960s.

4. On Hollywood "message movies" see Cripps, *Making Movies Black*. On network radio programs, see Savage, *Broadcasting Freedom*. On WERD and WEDR see Ward, *Radio and the Struggle for Civil Rights*, 160–68, 182–98.

5. Intersections of forms of popular culture can be seen in the 1940s *Memphis World*.

6. Rodie Veazy and Mary C. McNeal interviews by Paul Ortiz.

7. Imogene Watkins Wilson interview by Mausiki Scales; Naomi Jones interview by author. The number of theaters catering to African Americans is based on my survey of advertisements in the *Memphis World*, 1946–47. For total number of theaters see Shelton, "Movie Censorship in Memphis," 69.

8. Imogene Watkins Wilson interview by Mausiki Scales; George Holloway interview by Michael Honey, 6; Wade-Gayles, *Pushed Back to Strength*, 2–4.

9. "Negro Patrons Ejected from Malco Theater Following Bad Conduct of Youthful Hoodlums," *Memphis World*, September 22, 1944.

10. Wade-Gayles, *Pushed Back to Strength*, 2–4.

11. Daisy, New Daisy, and Palace Theater advertisements, *Memphis World*, 1946–47; Wade-Gayles, *Pushed Back to Strength*, 3. In oral histories, several black Memphians discussed Amateur Night, including Lanetha Jewel Branch in interview by Doris G. Dixon, and Eddie May Garner in interview by author. See also McKee and Chisenhall, *Beale Black and Blue*, 66–67.

12. Lanetha Jewel Branch interview by Doris G. Dixon, transcript, 4; Ace, Harlem, and Georgia Theater advertisements, *Memphis World*, 1946–47. On the plunging status of black independent films in the 1940s, see Cripps, *Making Movies Black*, 126–50.

13. Randall, *Censorship of the Movies*, 15–21; Carmen, *Movies, Censorship, and the Law*, 10–16. Randall notes that in 1921, thirty-seven state legislatures considered a total of almost one hundred censorship bills (p. 15). Chicago, with over 100 nickelodeons by 1907, created the first municipal motion picture censorship board that year, and Pennsylvania established the first state board in 1911 (pp. 11–12).

14. "Memphis Municipal Code, Article XIV, Public Amusements, Chapter 1: Censorship of Motion Pictures and Theatrical Performances," [1921], Chandler Papers, box 12, folder: Board of Censors, 1943. Carmen, *Movies, Censorship, and the Law*, 184, 206, cites 1950s studies that estimate the number of municipalities with censorship boards at anywhere from twenty to sixty.

15. "Beck Assails Censorships," *New York Times*, March 12, 1929; Velie, "You Can't See That Movie," 12, 66; Shelton, "Movie Censorship in Memphis," 15–23.

16. Shelton, "Movie Censorship in Memphis," 8–10.

17. *Memphis Commercial Appeal*, February 24, 1927, in Shelton, "Movie Censorship in Memphis," 14. Special thanks go to Brenna Kuhn, director of the Tapestry Dance Academy in Austin, Texas, for demonstrating the black bottom.

18. Shelton, "Movie Censorship in Memphis," 24–25; de Grazia and Newman, *Banned Films*, 185–86; Regester, "Black Films, White Censors," 159–60; Dupont, "'The Self in the Ring.'" In 1937, the *Memphis Press-Scimitar* announced a possible

southern tour by Schmeling, noting that he had become "very popular" in the South "because he toppled Joe Louis." See "Max Schmeling Will Stage Fistic Show in Memphis," January 19, 1937.

19. See Susan J. Douglas's discussion of radio announcers' blow-by-blow accounts of boxing matches and, in particular, her comments on Joe Louis fights, in *Listening In*, 205–9.

20. Amy Jones interview by Mausiki Scales, 38–39; Jarrett speech on panel "Black Journalism in the Chicago Renaissance," May 16, 1998, Vivian G. Harsh Research Collection of Afro-American History and Literature Archives, Chicago Public Library, Chicago. Jarrett also recalled watching newsreels of Louis fights from the balconies of segregated theaters. See Levine's discussion in *Black Culture and Black Consciousness*, 429–40, of Jack Johnson and Joe Louis as "black men operating victoriously on their own terms," thrilling audiences that included young Malcolm Little (Malcolm X) and Maya Angelou. These heroes "were not merely mechanisms of escape," he argues, but "paralleled and reflected" a new assertiveness among African Americans.

21. Melton, "Blacks in Memphis, Tennessee," 140; Shelton, "Movie Censorship in Memphis," 9. On *Birth of a Nation* and the NAACP, see Cripps, *Slow Fade to Black*, 41–69; and de Grazia and Newman, *Banned Films*, 3–6.

22. Lloyd T. Binford to Mayor James Pleasants Jr., October 7, 1947, in Pleasants Papers, box 13, folder: Memphis Board of Censors, 1947.

23. Cripps, *Making Movies Black*, 31, 52, 312 n. 52.

24. "Distorted Roles of Negro on Screen Must Go, Says White: Half Truths, Misconceptions Wrong, Says NAACP Secretary," *Memphis World*, October 22, 1943.

25. See Thomas Cripps's analysis of what he calls "conscience-liberalism" and the "Hollywood-OWI-NAACP axis" in *Making Movies Black*, esp. 26–34.

26. Commissioner Robert S. Fredericks, Department of Public Service to Mayor Walter Chandler, May 27, 1943; and advertisement for *Cabin in the Sky*, *Memphis Press-Scimitar*, May 26, 1943, both in Chandler Papers, box 12, folder: Board of Censors, 1943.

27. "Expresses Belief Race Riots Reacting against Negro-Starred Movie Trend: Box Office First Index of Feeling," *Memphis World*, July 30, 1943, 1.

28. "Memphis Municipal Code, Article XIV, Public Amusements, Chapter 1, Censorship of Motion Pictures and Theatrical Performances," [n.d.]; and Board of Censors Resolution, [n.d.], both in Chandler Papers, box 12, folder: Board of Censors, 1943. Neither the *Memphis Commercial Appeal*, the *Memphis Press-Scimitar*, nor the *Memphis World* provides evidence that this racially based censorship policy was voted on by the city commissioners, nor do the City Council Minute Books, which mention the board of censors only when new members were appointed. However, the typed resolution appears in the mayor's file on the board of censors, and language of the resolution became central to the board's decisions from 1943 until the late 1940s.

29. Nat D. Williams, "Focussing the News: 'Cabin in the Sky,'" *Memphis World*, June 4, 1943.

30. "Expresses Belief Race Riots Reacting against Negro-Starred Movie Trend," July 30, 1943; and "Creditable Negro Scenes Are Out in Southern Theatres Is Charge," July 21, 1944, both in *Memphis World*; Cripps, *Making Movies Black*, 85.

31. Movie advertisements in the *Memphis World*, 1946–49; Bogle, *Toms, Coons, Mulattoes, Mammies, and Bucks*, 132.

32. "Creditable Negro Scenes Are Out in Southern Theatres Is Charge," July 21, 1944; and "Another Film Is Censored in Memphis," June 29, 1945, both in *Memphis World*; Velie, "You Can't See That Movie," 66.

33. "Lena Horne Scene in 'Ziegfield's Follies' Censored," April 2, 1946; Velie, "You Can't See That Movie," 66; Lloyd T. Binford to Mayor Walter Chandler, February 12, 1946, Chandler Papers, box 24, folder: Memphis Board of Censors, 1945.

34. See hooks, "Oppositional Gaze," 247–64.

35. "World Famous Band Leader to Fill Dance Engagement on Beale St. Thursday, July 31," July 18, 1947; Nat Williams, "Down on Beale Ave.," July 29, 1947; and J. Richardson Jones, "Lena Horne Network Guest Friday Night," September 5, 1947, all in *Memphis World*; advertisements in *Memphis World*, January 4, 1946, June 7, 1946, July 18, 1947, July 25, 1947, August 1, 1947, August 8, 1947, August 15, 1947, September 5, 1947, September 26, 1947, October 24, 1947. See also *That's Black Entertainment* (1989), a documentary by Video Communications, Inc., on the independent "race movies," which includes footage from *Boogie Woogie Dream*.

36. "Creditable Negro Scenes Are Out in Southern Theatres Is Charge," July 21, 1944; and Don Deleighbur, "South Takes out Spite on Race by Censoring Films," July 28, 1944, both in *Memphis World*.

37. "500 Entertainers Ask Theatrical Industry to Treat Race Question with Understanding: Writers Urged to Stop Telling Lies in Scripts; Negro Artists Should Be Judged on Own Ability," June 2, 1944; and Harold Jovien, "Charge Radio Is Unfair to Negro," May 26, 1944, both in *Memphis World*. The black press applauded performers who rejected stereotypical roles. Tiny Bradshaw, an orchestra leader, for instance, received accolades after turning down a role in Disney's Uncle Remus movie, *Song of the South*, in which he would have to speak in dialect. See Leon Hardwick, "Tiny Bradshaw Turns Down Role in Uncle Remus Film," *Memphis World*, September 15, 1944.

38. On *The Southerner*, see Lloyd T. Binford, "The Southerner," September 20, 1945, in Chandler Papers, box 22, folder: Public Safety, 1945; and "Memphis Bans Film," July 26, 1945, and "Ban on 'Southerner' Lifted," August 22, 1945, both in *New York Times*.

39. Clipping from *Box Office*, October 6, 1945, in Chandler Papers, box 22, folder: Public Safety, 1945 (Comm. Joseph P. Boyle); Lloyd T. Binford, quoted in Shelton, "Movie Censorship in Memphis," 37; hooks, "Oppositional Gaze," 253–54.

40. Binford statement, in "'Brewster Millions' Is Barred in Memphis," *New York Times*, April 7, 1945. On Eddie Anderson's efforts to push the bounds of the servant role, see Leab, *From Sambo to Superspade*, 115–16.

41. Binford statement, in "'Brewster Millions' Is Barred in Memphis," *New York Times*, April 7, 1945; "Tennessee: Higher Criticism in Memphis," *Time*, August 13, 1945, 20–21; "Too Much Racial Equality, Movie Banned in Memphis," *Memphis World*, April 20, 1945; "Trillions for Brewster," *Commonweal*, May 11, 1945, 94–95; "'Strange Fruit' Author Hits Ban," *Memphis World*, April 24, 1945.

42. Lloyd T. Binford to Mayor Walter Chandler, [1945], in Chandler Papers, box

22, folder: Public Safety, 1945 (Comm. Joseph P. Boyle); "Shades of Blue Nosed and Blooded Boston! Record of the Memphis Censor Board," *The Private Chatterer*, August 31, 1945, in LMOC Archives.

43. "Memphis Woman on Coast Embarrassed by Movie Ban Here," *Memphis World*, April 27, 1945.

44. "Anti-Negro Film Irks GI's: Troops of Both Races Angered by Bad Cartoon," *Memphis World*, May 4, 1945; Cripps, *Making Movies Black*, 12–13.

45. "Marines Say Films Poisoning Native Islanders Toward Race: Protest Letter against Debasing Roles Is Mailed," *Memphis World*, June 8, 1945.

46. "Prof. B. T. Hunt Is Associate Movie Censor," *Memphis World*, June 1, 1945, 1; "All-Negro Movie Banned at Local Theater," *Memphis World*, July 27, 1945, 1. On attitudes toward women blues singers, see Carby, "Policing the Black Woman's Body."

47. S. I. Kahn, "Memphis Censor Goes on a Spree," *New York Times*, May 4, 1947. See also the voluminous files on the censorship of *Duel in the Sun* in David O. Selznick Collection, boxes 404, 596, 1038, 3368, 3369, Harry Ransom Humanities Research Center, University of Texas, Austin. On Memphis, see Harry Martin to David Selznick, April 22, 1947; and Selznick to Mr. Gillham, April 26, 1947, both in box 3368, folder 3368.16: Censorship, Apr.–June 1947; and S. L. Kahn, "Memphis Censor Goes on a Spree," *New York Times*, May 4, 1947. As noted in Kahn's article, Binford also banned three Jesse James films and two other westerns, *Destry Rides Again* and *When the Daltons Rode*, condemning them for their images of violence and crime.

48. Honorable John E. Rankin to Lloyd T. Binford, June 18, 1947, in Pleasants Papers; correspondence in David O. Selznick Collection, box 3368, folder 3368.10: *Duel in the Sun*—Criticism (Congressman Rankin), Harry Ransom Humanities Research Center, University of Texas, Austin. On Rankin, see Sullivan, *Days of Hope*, 116, 117, 218.

49. Letter to the *Commercial Appeal*, reprinted in "All Men, Regardless of Their Color Are Made by God, Binford Is Told," *Memphis World*, October 10, 1947; display advertisements for *Duel in the Sun*, in *Memphis World*, October 21, 24, 28, 1947; "'Duel in The Sun'—Barred in City, to Be Shown In West Memphis, Ark.," *Memphis World*, October 21, 1947.

50. On criticism by black commentators on the Vashti role and Vashti's similarity to Prissy in *Gone with the Wind*, see Cripps, *Making Movies Black*, 194–95.

51. Lloyd T. Binford quoted in "Films—Will Fight Memphis Censor," *New York Times*, September 20, 1947, 12. For background on *Curley* see Maltin and Bann, *Little Rascals*, 227–28.

52. Velie, "You Can't See that Movie," 12; Hal Roach quoted in Conrad Clark, "Memphis Ban on Film First Challenge to 'Freedom Train,'" *Memphis World*, September 26, 1947; and "Union Protests Film Ban," *New York Times*, October 6, 1947. See also correspondence on *Curley* censorship in Pleasants Papers, box 13, folder: Memphis Board of Censors, 1947.

53. "'Annie' to Miss Memphis: Negroes' Presence in Cast Held Issue as Show Cancels Stop," *New York Times*, September 29, 1947, 17; Harold Austin to Lloyd Binford, October 17, 1947; and Binford to Austin, October 30, 1947, both in Pleasants

Papers, box 6, folder: Board of Censors, 1948; "All Men, Regardless of Their Color Are Made by God, Binford Is Told," *Memphis World*, October 10, 1947.

54. *United Artists Corporation and Hal Roach Studios, Inc. v. Board of Censors of the City of Memphis, Tennessee and Lloyd T. Binford et al.*, Petition for Writ of Certiorari, n.d., Pleasants Papers, box 13, folder: Memphis Board of Censors, 1974; "Chancery Court Action Taken against Film Ban," *Memphis World*, October 10, 1947. "Film Censor Case Declined by Court," *New York Times*, May 9, 1950; Kupferman and O'Brien, "Motion Picture Censorship," 277–84.

55. Jane and Alan Otten, "Hour of Decision? Supreme Court Petitioned on Film Censorship," *New York Times*, October 15, 1950; Kupferman and O'Brien, "Motion Picture Censorship," 273–300. According to Kupferman and O'Brien, 286, it was rumored that the Supreme Court denied certiorari in the Atlanta *Lost Boundaries* case because the Court "did not feel it wanted to pass on another discrimination case at this time." On the *Mutual* to *Miracle* period (1915–52) see Randall, *Censorship of the Movies*, 9–32 passim.

56. *Lost Boundaries, The Beacon*, September 26, 1949, in newspaper box 34, LMOC Archives; Du Bois, *Souls of Black Folk*, 43–44.

57. Martha Jean Steinberg interview by Jacquie Gales Webb, in *Black Radio*, transcripts, 35–36.

58. Cantor, *Wheelin' on Beale*, 147, 107–9.

59. Brian Ward's *Radio and the Struggle for Civil Rights in the South* details how radio advanced civil rights across the South through the actions of station personnel, especially DJs. My analysis of WDIA in the late 1940s and 1950s explores black radio's subversive relation to white supremacy and Jim Crow in the years before the more organized events of the later freedom movement.

60. Douglas, *Listening In*, introduction, esp. 7–12. See also Darnell Hunt on black audiences' active responses to television newscasters, in *Screening the Los Angeles Riots*. Analyzing how black viewers responded to television reports on the 1992 Los Angeles riot, he discusses not only racial encoding of media reports but also the complex, social basis of audience reception based on the "intertextual memory of viewers" (33).

61. Radio scholars Michele Hilmes and Susan Douglas discuss listeners as an "imagined community," a term Benedict Anderson uses to conceptualize how readers of print media develop a shared sense of nationhood. Douglas analyzes how radio encourages listeners to imagine themselves bonded to both the station and each other, by showing how radio works in "informative," "dimensional," and "associational" ways. See Hilmes, *Radio Voices*, 11–14; Douglas, *Listening In*, 22–39 passim; and Anderson, *Imagined Communities*, 34–36.

62. In addition to copious commentary on the "Negro Market" in the late 1940s and 1950s, there have also been several historical analyses of this phenomenon. See, for example, Mark Newman, *Entrepreneurs of Profit and Pride*, 131–38; Kathy Newman, "Marketing Identities," 115–35; Barlow, *Voice Over*, 123–31; and Cohen, *Consumer's Republic*, 323–24.

63. Mark Newman, *Entrepreneurs of Profit and Pride*, 79–82; Douglas, *Listening In*, 223–24.

64. Cantor, *Wheelin' on Beale*, 13–24; Mark Newman, *Entrepreneurs of Profit and Pride*, 109–13; Barlow, *Voice Over*, 109–10.

65. Cantor, *Wheelin' on Beale*, 18–20; Mark Newman, *Entrepreneurs of Profit and Pride*, 110–12.

66. Mark Newman, *Entrepreneurs of Profit and Pride*, 93–103; MacDonald, *Don't Touch that Dial!*, 339; Lornell, *"Happy in the Service of the Lord,"* 116; Barlow, *Voice Over*, 98–99, 103–7. In 1948, the promotion manager of WMPS, an ABC affiliate, stated that 85,000,000 Americans were expected to listen to the upcoming Louis-Walcott fight and that two years earlier a national survey had found that the Louis-Conn fight had drawn "the largest audience ever tuned to a commercial broadcast." See Matty Brescia, "Louis-Walcott Fight to Be Aired over WMPS," *Memphis World*, June 18, 1948.

67. Cantor, *Wheelin' on Beale*, 22, 49–51; Barlow, *Voice Over*, 113.

68. "Police Drive on against Vulgar Jukebox Records," *Memphis World*, February 10, 1948, 1.

69. Nat D. Williams, "Down on Beale Ave.," *Memphis World*, November 26, 1948.

70. Eddie May Garner interview by author; Naomi Jones interview by author; Joan Lee Nelson interview by author; "Teen Town Singers New Program on Station WDIA," *Memphis World*, June 17, 1949; Cantor, *Wheelin' on Beale*, 66–68, 78–85, 92–96, 105, 126–27, 134.

71. Douglas, *Listening In*, esp. 225–33; quote on p. 230.

72. Educators Lanetha Jewel Branch and Bettye Coe Donahue, both of whom attended Booker T. Washington High School, remember Williams as a highly re-spected teacher. Donahue remembers him as "a very scholarly man . . . [who] had a lot of courage." However, as seen in other chapters, Williams also sometimes re-ceived criticism for his *Memphis World* columns from readers who felt he failed to take an oppositional stance toward the Crump machine. See Lanetha Jewel Branch interview by Doris G. Dixon and Bettye Coe Donahue interview by author.

73. Quote in Cantor, *Wheelin' on Beale*, 114–15; "Police Drive on against Vulgar Jukebox Records," *Memphis World*, February 10, 1948, 1.

74. Cantor, *Wheelin' on Beale*, 42–43.

75. Levine, *Black Culture and Black Consciousness*, 338, 344, 359.

76. Martha Jean Steinberg interview by Jacquie Gales Webb, in *Black Radio*, tran-scripts, 41.

77. Eddie O'Jay interview by Sonja Williams, 29.

78. Cantor, *Wheelin' on Beale*, 88–90; Barlow, *Voice Over*, 121–22, 148; Martha Jean Steinberg interview by Jacquie Gales Webb, in *Black Radio*, transcripts, 32. African American women's roles on radio have still received far too little analysis. For brief discussions that include material on WDIA, see Barlow, *Voice Over*, 121–23, 147–53; and Ward, *Radio and the Struggle for Civil Rights*, 88–92.

79. Joan Lee Nelson interview by author; Leah Brock, assistant field secretary, NAACP, to NAACP national office, [May 1950], NAACP-LC, group II, box C185, folder: Memphis, Tennessee, 1947–50.

80. Barlow, *Voice Over*, 122.

81. Martha Jean Steinberg interview by Jacquie Gales Webb, in *Black Radio*, tran-

scripts, 31–33; Cantor, *Wheelin' on Beale*, 91–92; Barlow, *Voice Over*, 122. Steinberg later became vice president and program director of WQBH, whose call letters stand for "Bring the Queen Back Home."

82. Martha Jean Steinberg interview by Jacquie Gales Webb, in *Black Radio*, transcripts, 36.

83. Ibid., 34; Hattie Leeper interview by Sonja Williams, 39–40, and Irene Johnson Ware and Novella Smith, quoted in Program 7, "A Woman's Touch," *Black Radio*, transcript, 8–9. Leeper quote in Barlow, *Voice Over*, 152.

84. Lewis O. Swingler, "Father of Maurice Hulbert Sr. Passes," *Memphis World*, May 24, 1946; Barlow, *Voice Over*, 116–18.

85. Maurice "Hot Rod" Hulbert Jr., quoted in Gilbert Williams, *Legendary Pioneers of Black Radio*, 107–8; Cantor, *Wheelin' on Beale*, 64–66; Barlow, *Voice Over*, 115–16. Hulbert's "high-octane pilot" routine that he developed at WDIA remained his trademark after he left WDIA and began working for a Baltimore station in 1951.

86. Lornell, *"Happy in the Service of the Lord,"* 115–19; Cantor, *Wheelin' on Beale*, 58–62.

87. Nat D. Williams, quoted in McKee and Chisenhall, *Beale Black and Blue*, 33–34; Cantor, *Wheelin' on Beale*, 129–30.

88. "Gatemouth Moore Is Ordained into Ministry Sunday at Cobb's Church," *Memphis World*, March 1, 1949; Cantor, *Wheelin' on Beale*, 70–74; Barlow, *Voice Over*, 119–20.

89. Cantor, *Wheelin' on Beale*, 98–105; Lornell, *"Happy in the Service of the Lord,"* 115, 121.

90. "Cousin" Eugene Walton interview by Christopher Lornell, 4; George Rooks interview by Christopher Lornell, 4.

91. Everlena Yarbrough interview by author; Joan Lee Nelson interview by author; Cantor, *Wheelin' on Beale*, 203–4.

92. Joan Lee Nelson interview by author. On black-appeal radio's role in forging the "soul consciousness" of the 1960s, see Mark Newman, *Entrepreneurs of Profit and Pride*, 129–66; and Ward, *Just My Soul Responding*, esp. 281–88.

93. Nat D. Williams, "Down On Beale Ave.," *Memphis World*, November 26, 1948. See also Cantor, *Wheelin' on Beale*, 64; and Barlow, *Voice Over*, 115–16.

94. Cantor, *Wheelin' on Beale*, 62. Although *Brown America Speaks* was the first black radio discussion show, Chicago's WSBV had initiated a ten-minute news program featuring Luther A. Townsley from the Associated Negro Press several years prior to this. See "Chicago Has First Negro Commentator," *Memphis World*, February 18, 1944. Brian Ward (*Radio and the Struggle for Civil Rights*, 184) notes that in 1941, Robert Durr in Birmingham claimed that his "Negro in the News" show on WSGN was "the only one of its kind in the world."

95. Cantor, *Wheelin' on Beale*, 62.

96. Ibid.

97. Ibid.; Naomi Jones interview by author; Joan Lee Nelson interview by author; Everlena Yarbrough interview by author.

98. Cantor, *Wheelin' on Beale*, 113, 197–200; Mark Newman, *Entrepreneurs of Profit and Pride*, 115.

99. "Memphis Furniture Workers on Strike," January 14, 1949; "Morale of Strikers at Memphis Furniture Co. Is Reported High," February 1, 1949; "Union Charges Unfair Tactics against Strikers at Memphis Furniture Company," March 4, 1949; "Two Women Arrested for Alleged Violence in Long Strike against Local Firm," June 7, 1949, all in *Memphis World*; Gene Day, Local 282, to Ernest March, UFWA, February 16, 1949, in box 21, folder 462, UFWA Papers; C.I.O. Regional Director W. A. Copeland to Honorable Watkins Overton, March 2, 1949, in Overton Papers, box 2, C.I.O. folder, Special Collections, McWherter Library, University of Memphis; Carter, "Local Labor Union," 53–61; Honey, *Southern Labor and Black Civil Rights*, 254.

100. Minerva Johnican interview by author; Everlena Yarbrough interview by author.

101. Cantor, *Wheelin' on Beale*, 202–16; Mark Newman, *Entrepreneurs of Profit and Pride*, 118–19.

102. Cantor, *Wheelin' on Beale*, 207; minutes of the Memphis NAACP Executive Board, June 7, 1960, June 26–August 9, 1960, Smith Collection. In 1946, Crump proposed a wing for "crippled negro children" at the "proposed negro hospital" near the existing public hospital. See Memorandum from Mayor Walter Chandler, July 7, 1946, box 25, folder: Proposed Negro Hospital 1942–45; and "City, County Prepare Crippled Negro Study," *Memphis Commercial Appeal* clipping, [ca. May 28, 1946], box 25, folder: Negroes, 1946, both in Chandler Papers.

103. Cantor, *Wheelin' on Beale*, 217.

104. Thomas interview by Kremer and Faudree; Cantor, *Wheelin' on Beale*, 94–95, 124, 174–76; "American Finishing Co. Employees Vote to Change from A.F. of L. to C.I.O. as Bargaining Agents," *Memphis World*, February 29, 1944, 1.

Chapter 6

1. "6 Employees Revolt over Bell Ringer," April 23, 1955; "All-Out Fight Looms in 'Patio 6' Case," April 30, 1955; "Seek Justice in 'Patio Six' Case, April 30, 1955"; and editorial on "Patio 6," May 7, 1955, all in *Tri-State Defender*.

2. "10,000 Defy Threats of Council: Hear U.S. Statesman C. C. Diggs," May 7, 1955; "Miss. 'KKK' Strikes; Top Minister Slain," May 14, 1955; L. Alex Wilson, "Plan Rally to Protest Lynching," May 21, 1955; and "We Weep for Mississippi," October 8, 1955, all in *Tri-State Defender*; "The New Fighting South: Militant Negroes Refuse to Leave Dixie or Be Silenced," *Ebony*, August 1955, 69–74; Ruby Hurley to Gloster Current, May 27, 1955, NAACP-LC, group II, box C225, folder: Southeast Regional Office: Reports, 1955.

3. Robert Talley, "Bridges' Name Enters Labor Investigation," October 19, 1951; and Talley, "Open Inquiry on Union Favored by Eastland," October 24, 1951, both in *Memphis Commercial Appeal*, both in Overton Papers, box 5, folder: Labor #2, Special Collections, McWherter Library, University of Memphis. On Eastland and the Dixiecrats, see Frederickson, *Dixiecrat Revolt*, 69–70, 135, 189, 232–33. Ruleville was also the home of Fannie Lou Hamer, a plantation laborer who became a famous civil rights activist in the 1960s. Eastland chaired the SISS and then the Senate Judiciary Committee.

4. Gene Day, UFWA International Representative to Ernest Marsh, UFWA Di-

rector of Organization, September 3, 1949, box 21, folder 462; "Letter of Protest to CIO Council, *Memphis Press-Scimitar*, n.d. [Oct. 1949], box 35, folder 844; and David Conner to Ernest Marsh, September 1, 1949, box 35, folder 844, all in UFWA Papers. On the NMU expulsions see Michael Honey, *Southern Labor and Black Civil Rights*, 272–74. See also Honey's detailed narrative of the Cold War anticommunist labor campaigns in Memphis on 245–77.

5. Melvina Rebecca McKinley interview by author; David Conner to Ernest Marsh, September 1, 1949, UFWA Papers, box 35, folder 844. See also Carter, "Local Labor Union," 57–58; and Michael Honey, *Southern Labor and Black Civil Rights*, 253–54.

6. Ernest Marsh to Rudolph Johnson, October 19, 1949, box 35, file 844; Gene Day to Ernie Marsh, October 29, 1949, box 21, folder 462; and Gene Day to Ernie Marsh, January 23, 1950, box 21, folder 462, all in UFWA Papers; Alzada Clark interview by author; Carter, "Local Labor Union," 58–63, 73–74.

7. Gene Day to Ernest Marsh, August 12, 1949, box 21, folder 462; and David Conner to Ernest Marsh, September 1, 1949, box 35, folder 844, both in UFWA Papers; Michael Honey, *Southern Labor and Black Civil Rights*, 264–71; Carter, "Local Labor Union," 61; Melton, "Blacks in Memphis, Tennessee," 349 n. 11.

8. Robert Talley, "Open Inquiry on Union Favored by Eastland," October 24, 1951; "Union Here Is Branded as Communist Outfit Seeking U.S. Overthrow," October 27, 1951; and "Red Activities Nearby Will Be Investigated," October 28, 1951, all in *Memphis Commercial Appeal*; Clark Porteous, "Memphians Named as High Reds," *Memphis Press-Scimitar*, October 26, 1951, both in Overton Papers, box 5, folder: Labor #2, Special Collections, McWherter Library, University of Memphis. See also account by Michael Honey, *Southern Labor and Black Civil Rights*, 267–72.

9. Robert Talley, "1100 Memphians' Names Demanded by Eastland for Red Union Inquiry," *Memphis Commercial Appeal*, October 26, 1951; and Clark Porteous, "Memphians Named as High Reds," *Memphis Press-Scimitar*, October 26, 1951, both in Overton Papers, box 5, folder: Labor #2, Special Collections, McWherter Library, University of Memphis.

10. Robert Talley, "1100 Memphians' Names Demanded by Eastland for Red Union Inquiry," *Memphis Commercial Appeal*, October 26, 1951, Overton Papers, box 5, folder: Labor #2, Special Collections, McWherter Library, University of Memphis.

11. Michael Honey, *Southern Labor and Black Civil Rights*, 271.

12. Ruby Hurley, Southeast Regional Office, Report from Field Trip, March 27, 1952, group II, box C186, folder: Memphis, Tennessee, 1951–55; Hurley to Gloster Current, August 5, 1953, group II, box C222, folder: 1953; and Hurley to Current, August 21, 1953, group II, box C224, folder: Reports — 1953–54, all in NAACP-LC. Membership in 1952 was 731; in 1960, the branch reported it had enrolled 5,200. See H. T. Lockard to Gloster Current, February 10, 1955, group II, box C185, folder: Memphis, Tennessee, 1951–55; Report from Workshop of Tennessee NAACP Branches, May 13, 1951, group II, box C221, folder: Southeast Regional Office, Correspondence 1951, January–June; and Lucille Black to Maxine Smith, May 19, 1960, group III, box C146, folder: Memphis, Tennessee, 1960, all in NAACP-LC; minutes of Memphis NAACP, July 24, 1960, Smith Collection.

13. Ruby Hurley, Southeast Regional Office, Report from Field Trip, March 27, 1952, NAACP-LC, group II, box C186, folder: Memphis, Tennessee, 1951–55.

14. Utillus Phillips to Leah Brock, February 7, 1950, NAACP-LC, group II, box C187, folder: Tennessee State Conference, 1948–1950. For membership statistics see H. T. Lockard to Gloster Current, February 10, 1955, group II, box C185, folder: Memphis, Tennessee, 1951–55; and Report from Workshop of Tennessee NAACP Branches, May 13, 1951, group II, box C221, folder: Southeast Regional Office, Correspondence 1951, January–June, both in NAACP-LC.

15. Hon. Russell Sugarmon interview by author; Allegra Turner interview by author; Melton, "Blacks in Memphis, Tennessee," 336.

16. "Rev. Malone New Head of NAACP," *Tri-State Defender*, January 16, 1954.

17. Allegra Turner interview by author; "Draft Boards Continue After Le-Moynites," *LeMoyne Democrat*, February 20, 1942, in LMOC Archives; H. T. Lockard to Gloster Current, March 23, 1955; and Lockard to Walter White, January 17, 1955, both in NAACP-LC, group II, box C185, folder: Memphis, Tennessee, 1951–55; and Hosea T. Lockard interview by author.

18. "NAACP Kicks off Drive April 4th," April 3, 1954; "'We'll Fight Bias to Finish Line' — Marshall," May 15, 1954; and "Round Table Discussion at Mound Bayou," May 22, 1954, all in *Tri-State Defender*.

19. Raymond F. Tisby, "To Be Free by '63, Marshall Urges," *Birmingham World*, May 11, 1954.

20. "Mississippi Civic Leader Urges Better Deal," December 1, 1951; "Dr. Howard Proposes a Delta Negro Council," December 15, 1951; and Daryl F. Grisham, "Launch Negro Delta Council: Leaders Meet at Cleveland, Miss. Dec. 28," December 22, 1951, all in *Tri-State Defender*. On the founding of the *Tri-State Defender* and its differences with the *Memphis World* see Imogene Watkins Wilson interview by Mausiki Scales.

21. George F. David, "Deep in the Delta," *Journal of Human Relations* 2 (Spring 1954): 72–75; "The New Fighting South: Militant Negroes Refuse to Leave Dixie or Be Silenced," *Ebony*, August 1955, 69–74; "Dr. T. R. M. Howard Speaks at Lane," *Memphis World*, April 2, 1946. For more on Henry, Moore, and Evers, see Payne, *I've Got the Light of Freedom*, 31–33, 37–38, 49, 58–89; and Dittmer, *Local People*, 32–33, 49.

22. Dr. T. R. M. Howard, Prospectus of the First Annual Meeting of the Mississippi Regional Council of Negro Leadership, May 2, 1952, William McBride Papers, Vivian G. Harsh Research Collection of Afro-American History and Literature, Chicago Public Library, Chicago.

23. Ibid.

24. "Expect 10,000 at Delta Regional Leadership Council Meet May 2nd," May 3, 1952; "'Vote for Lawmakers Who Defend Rights,'" May 10, 1952; "Highlights of Delta Council Voters Campaign," May 10, 1952; and "'Don't Get Mad . . . Get Smart,'" May 17, 1952, all in *Tri-State Defender*.

25. "Vigilantes for Segregation," September 18, 1954; "Miss. Leaders Plan Study of New Councils," September 25, 1954; "Mississippians Buck Pressure in School Row," October 2, 1954; "Mississippi Faces Economic War," October 9, 1954; L. Alex Wilson, "Leaders Map Campaign to Aid Victims of Race Credit 'Freeze' in Missis-

sippi," January 8, 1955; and "Meeting the Neo-Kluxism Challenge," March 5, 1955, all in *Tri-State Defender*; "Defer Integration Fight," *New York Times*, September 28, 1954. On the formation of the white Citizens' Councils see Dittmer, *Local People*, 45–46.

26. Hurley to Current, May 27, 1955, NAACP-LC, group II, box C225, folder: Southeast Regional Office — Reports, 1955; "The New Fighting South: Militant Negroes Refuse to Leave Dixie or Be Silenced," *Ebony*, August 1955, 69–70.

27. "The New Fighting South: Militant Negroes Refuse to Leave Dixie or Be Silenced," *Ebony*, August 1955, 69–74; "Donate $10,000 at Till Rally in Los Angeles," *Tri-State Defender*, October 22, 1955.

28. Untitled article, *New York Times*, December 22, 1955.

29. "Confab Rebukes, Humiliates Rev. Humes for 'Selling out in Mississippi,'" *Tri-State Defender*, September 17, 1955. For more on the Mississippi conflicts over school desegregation, see Dittmer, *Local People*, 41–59. The three deaths to which Borders referred were Lee's, Till's, and Lamar Smith's. Smith was a black farmer working on voter registration in Brookhaven who was shot dead in August 1955. On the Lamar Smith killing, see Payne, *I've Got the Light of Freedom*, 39.

30. "We Weep for Mississippi," October 8, 1955; and "Won't Be Deterred from Goal, Says Dr. Howard," May 28, 1955, both in *Tri-State Defender*.

31. *Gray et al. v. Board of Trustees of the University of Tennessee et al.*, 342 U.S. 517 (1952); and 97 F. Supp. 463 (1951), U.S. District Court for the Eastern District of Tennessee, Northern Division. See also *State of Missouri ex rel. Gaines v. Canada*, 305 U.S. 337 (1938); *Sipuel v. Board of Regents of the University of Oklahoma et al.*, 332 U.S. 631 (1948); *Sweatt v. Painter*, 339 U.S. 629 (1950); and *McLaurin v. Oklahoma State Regents*, 339 U.S. 637 (1950). The "rich traditions" quotation is taken from the Court's *Sweatt* decision.

32. "Try to Enter Memphis State: Refusal of President Is Ignored," June 5, 1954; "Gird to Push Memphis State Case: Will Go to High Court If Forced," June 12, 1954; "Let's Don't Confuse the Memphis State Issue," June 19, 1954; "Sectional Bias Now, Claims NAACP," September 11, 1954; "Approve Fund to End MSC Barrier," June 4, 1955; "Official to Answer on Admitting Five to MSC," June 18, 1955; "Lower Barriers for Grad Students to Memphis State," October 22, 1955; "Court of Appeals Puts 'Heat' on Judge Boyd in School Case," February 7, 1959; "Negro Students Expect to Enter MSU in Fall," July 11, 1959; and "Negro Students Won't Bow to Bias at MSU," September 19, 1959, all in *Tri-State Defender*.

33. "Won't Be Deterred from Goal, Says Dr. Howard," May 28, 1955; "Approve Fund to End MSC Barrier," June 4, 1955; [title missing], June 25, 1955 [note: the first page of article is missing from microfilm]; "See Success in NAACP's Fund Drive," July 9, 1955; "Atty. Flowers to Speak for NAACP Meet," July 23, 1955; "Universal Workers Give $115 to NAACP Drive," July 30, 1955; "Profit Group in Arkansas for Race Bias," February 19, 1955; and "New 'KKK' Unit Rears Its Head," April 2, 1955, all in *Tri-State Defender*; "Negro Club Council Upholds Court Edict," *Memphis Commercial Appeal*, July 4, 1954.

34. "12,000 Help to Swing Sen. Kefauver Victory," August 14, 1954; "First Move to By Pass Rule of High Court," December 18, 1954; "'Mum' About Biased Bill," Febru-

ary 12, 1955; "New Bill Hits Mixing Students," February 26, 1955; "Hot Potato for Gov. Clement," March 5, 1955; and "Governor Vetoes 2 Bills," March 26, 1955, all in *Tri-State Defender*; Biles, "Bittersweet Victory," 473. On the North Carolina legislation, see Chafe, *Civilities and Civil Rights*, 50; and Greene, *Our Separate Ways*, 71.

35. "Bill Seeks to Thwart Integration in Tenn.," *Tri-State Defender*, March 5, 1955.

36. "3 Leaders Rap Stainback Bill," *Tri-State Defender*, February 26, 1955.

37. "Negroes Plan Action in Dispute with MSR," *Memphis Commercial Appeal*, January 31, 1955; Silver and Moeser, *Separate City*, 133.

38. Evelyn Bates interview by author; Matthew Davis interview by author; "40th Ward Club Seeks Better Service in the Collection of Garbage," April 1, 1949; and "40th Ward Civic Club Not Satisfied with Garbage Collections from Homes," April 8, 1949, both in *Memphis World*; Matthew Davis and Mollie Alexander to Mayor Frank Tobey, July 28, 1954, Tobey Papers, box 22, folder: Civic Clubs, 1954.

39. Matthew Davis interview by author.

40. Alma Morris interview by author; Marie Fort interview by author; Lillie G. Kirklon interview by author; Betty J. Jones, "Civic Club Talent Show," in "Klondyke Tid-Bits" column, *Tri-State Defender*, December 5, 1953.

41. "Preliminary Statement," Mayor's Urban Rehabilitation Study Committee, Tobey Papers, box 19, Rehabilitation, folder: Slum Clearance, 1954; Cantor, *Wheelin' on Beale*, 20.

42. On racial struggles in northern cities over the location of postwar housing, see Hirsch, *Making the Second Ghetto*, and Sugrue, *Origins of the Urban Crisis*.

43. Biles, *Memphis in the Great Depression*, 95; Melton, "Blacks in Memphis, Tennessee," 336–37.

44. Vernon F. Gamble, East of Highland Improvement Club, to Mayor Watkins Overton, May 18, 1949, Overton Papers, box 2, folder: Civic Clubs #4, Memphis and Shelby County Room, Memphis Public Library and Information Center; "Mass Meeting Is Held over Negro Project," *Memphis Press-Scimitar*, January 30, 1950; Melton, "Blacks in Memphis, Tennessee," 337–39.

45. "Warned by Whites Not to Move In," April 18, 1953; "Masonic Leader, Family Now in Fordhurst Home," July 18, 1953; and "Deny Charge Made in Homes Row," July 25, 1953, all in *Tri-State Defender*.

46. "Whites Suggest Negroes Get Out," May 30, 1953; "'Won't Tolerate Bombings'—Mayor," July 4, 1953; "Pressure Realtor for Selling 'Gray Area' Homes," July 11, 1953; "Trouble Flares up Again over Olive St. Homes," August 29, 1953; "Seek Truce in 'Gray Area,'" September 5, 1953, all in *Tri-State Defender*; clippings in Negro Housing Problems folder, Tobey Papers, box 11.

47. Petition from African American organizations to Mayor Frank Tobey and the Memphis City Commission, [July 27, 1953]; and transcript of meeting between committee of African American leaders and Mayor Frank Tobey, August 12, 1953, both in Tobey Papers, box 14, Negro Housing Problems folder; NAACP press release, "Local Branch Protests Bombing," July 3, 1953, NAACP-LC, group II, box C186, folder: Memphis, Tennessee, 1951–55; "NAACP Hits Bombing, Seeks More Protection," *Tri-State Defender*, July 11, 1953; Dowdy, "'Something for the Colored People,'" 108–15.

48. "For the Record: It's Not 'Normal and Healthy,'" *Tri-State Defender*, July 18, 1953.

49. Melton, "Blacks in Memphis, Tennessee," 334–35.

50. "Negro Civic Leaders Present MSR Petition," January 24, 1954; and "Negroes Plan Action in Dispute with MSR," January 31, 1954, both in Tobey Papers, box 28, folder: Memphis Street Railway Newspaper Clips, 1954; "Plan Mass Meeting on Bus Boycott," January 2, 1954; "Mayor Plans Action on Trolley Incident," January 9, 1954; "Bus Operator Pulls Gun in Dispute," January 16, 1954; and "Showdown Begins on Bus Bias February 27," February 28, 1959, all in *Tri-State Defender*.

51. "Note Upsurge in Registration," May 31, 1952; and Andrew Winston, "Rally on June 20 to Get out Votes," June 21, 1952, both in *Tri-State Defender*; Lillie G. Kirklon interview by author; Matthew Davis interview by author; Melton, "Blacks in Memphis, Tennessee," 314–17. On the gender politics of voter registration in Atlanta in this period, see Nasstrom, "Down to Now," 113–44.

52. Andrew Winston, "Rally on June 20 to Get out Votes," *Tri-State Defender*, June 21, 1952.

53. Silver and Moeser, *Separate City*, 86–87; Melton, "Blacks in Memphis, Tennessee," 316–20; "National Baptist President to Address Voters Rally," *Tri-State Defender*, January 16, 1954, 1.

54. "Negro Club Council Upholds Court Edict," *Memphis Commercial Appeal*, July 4, 1954; "Refute 'Hint' Negroes Don't Seek End of School Barriers," *Tri-State Defender*, December 24, 1955. On Cold War implications of *Brown*, see Dudziak, *Cold War Civil Rights*.

55. "Orgill Lashes Rep. Sutton in TV Speech," July 24, 1954; "City Education Board Stands Pat on Bias," August 21, 1954; and "5 Schools to Expand under New Program," March 5, 1955, all in *Tri-State Defender*.

56. Melton, "Blacks in Memphis, Tennessee," 335. For more on the CRC, see Tucker, *Memphis Since Crump*, 62–78.

57. Matthew Davis interview by author; Lillie G. Kirklon interview by author; "National Baptist President to Address Voters Rally," January 16, 1954; "Orgill Lashes Rep. Sutton in TV Speech," July 24, 1954; and "12,000 Help to Swing Sen. Kefauver Victory," August 14, 1954, all in *Tri-State Defender*; Biles, "Bittersweet Victory," 472. See also Chafe, *Civilities and Civil Rights*, 42–70. White Memphis moderate elites responded similarly to those in Greensboro, initially expressing a grudging acceptance of *Brown* but soon retreating from this position and declaring allegiance to segregation.

58. "Thousands Mourn Loss of Mayor Frank Tobey," September 17, 1955; and "Now Is the Time," August 20, 1955, both in *Tri-State Defender*.

59. "Now Is the Time," August 20, 1955; "Voting Strength Is Now 40,774," July 30, 1955; "Mass Meeting Friday Spurs Campaign for More Voters," October 8, 1955; and "Veterans Voters Movement Starts Drive to Get 10,000 Registered," October 15, 1955, all in *Tri-State Defender*.

60. "The Memphis Political Scene"; "Hear Glowing Reports of Drive for Orgill"; and "Leader Lauds Overton Record and Platform," all in *Tri-State Defender*, November 11, 1955; "Voters Are Together" and "Pick Candidates for Campaign," both in

Tri-State Defender, October 22, 1955; "Weight of Record Vote Cast Helps Orgill; Rev. Love Bid Impressive," *Tri-State Defender*, November 19, 1955; Tucker, *Memphis Since Crump*, 76.

61. Silver and Moeser, *Separate City*, 88.

62. "Dr. Love Opens Campaign-Commission Plan Hit," September 10, 1955; "The Memphis Political Scene," November 5, 1955; "Voters Are Together," October 22, 1955; and "20,000 Negroes Behind Council's Effort to Meet with Armour and Stop Police Brutality," October 17, 1959, all in *Tri-State Defender*.

63. "The Memphis Political Scene," *Tri-State Defender*, November 5, 1955; "Loeb's Laundry Workers Strike," *Memphis World*, August 21, 1945.

64. "6 Employees Revolt over Bell Ringer," April 23, 1955; and "All-Out Fight Looms in 'Patio 6' Case," April 30, 1955, both in *Tri-State Defender*.

65. "6 Employees Revolt over Bell Ringer," April 23, 1955; "All-Out Fight Looms in 'Patio 6' Case," April 30, 1955; and "Seek Justice in 'Patio Six' Case," May 5, 1955, all in *Tri-State Defender*.

66. Carter, "Local Labor Union," 73–74.

67. Local 282 files, box 25, folder 581, and box 21, folder 464, UFWA Papers; Carter, "Local Labor Union," 63–68.

68. Gene Day to Ernest Marsh, September 20, October 22, 1949; Doyle Dorsey, Organizer's Reports, March 29, May 3, May 17, 1952; and R. G. Morrow, Memphis Furniture Manufacturing Co. to "our interested employees," November 25, 1953, all in box 21, folder 462, UFWA Papers; Edward L. Wertz, Organizer's Reports, February 19, June 18, 1955, box 25, folder 581, UFWA Papers. At least three plants closed, moved, or sold out in the early 1950s, including U.S. Bedding, a strong Local 282 shop. For Memphis Furniture election figures, see Carter, "Local Labor Union," 67. Despite Local 282's victory, the company refused to agree to dues checkoff, by which employees would have union dues deducted from their paychecks. The difficulty this refusal created for union security could be seen when the union lost another election at Memphis Furniture a year later.

69. Melvina Rebecca McKinley interview by author; and Eddie May Garner interview by author.

70. Alzada Clark interview by author.

71. Michael Honey, *Southern Labor and Black Civil Rights*, 271.

72. Doyle Dorsey, Organizer's Report, April 26, 1952, box 21, folder 464, UFWA Papers.

73. "Sues to End Park Bias," January 10, 1959; "Showdown Begins on Bus Bias February 27," February 28, 1959; "Evers Criticizes City's Position on Parks, Zoo," March 14, 1959; O. Z. Evers et al. to City Commissioners, August 13, 1958; and "Civic Club And NAACP in Hot Exchange," March 12, 1960, all in *Tri-State Defender*; O. Z. Evers et al. to Honorable Edmund Orgill, November 9, 1959; and Orgill to unnamed recipient, December 16, 1959, both in Orgill Papers, box 16, Negroes (1) folder.

74. Bettye Coe Donahue interview by author; Matthew Davis interview by author; Clarence Coe, in Michael Honey, *Black Workers Remember*, 150–53.

Chapter 7

1. Burleigh Hines, "5,000 Bury Uncle Toms at Rally," *Tri-State Defender*, August 8, 1959, 1.

2. "Memo to Negro Voters: An Editorial," July 25, 1959; "Vote Volunteers In!," August 22, 1959; and M. L. Reid, "Politicking: Say Job's Lost If Evers Runs," July 18, 1959, all in *Tri-State Defender*.

3. M. L. Reid, "Negroes Get No White Endorsers," *Tri-State Defender*, August 1, 1959; Hon. Russell Sugarmon interview by author. See J. Morgan Kousser's discussion about racial bloc voting in *Colorblind Injustice*, 147–63.

4. Russell Sugarmon, "Fight for Freedom"; Diamond, "Impact of the Negro Vote," 454–57; "Don't Crawl in Corner and Sulk," *Tri-State Defender*, August 29, 1959.

5. See Negroes (1) folder in Orgill Papers, box 16.

6. An entire file titled "Negroes" (2) in Orgill Papers, box 16, contains correspondence on the John Gaston controversy. On Orgill's 1957 statement see transcript in Orgill Papers, box 16, Negroes (1) folder; and Tucker, *Memphis Since Crump*, 85. On Orgill's statements during the gubernatorial race, see statement at Franklin, Tennessee, June 26, 1958; and "Mayor Orgill's Statement Regarding Segregation," n.d., Orgill Papers, box 16, Negroes (1) folder. On blacks' critique of Orgill, see "Just What Do You Mean, Mayor?," *Tri-State Defender*, May 30, 1959. See also Tucker, *Memphis Since Crump*, 82–86.

7. "Just What Do You Mean, Mayor?," *Tri-State Defender*, May 30, 1959; Tucker, *Memphis Since Crump*, 97; Kousser, *Colorblind Injustice*, 158. According to William Chafe (*Civilities and Civil Rights*, 42–70), white moderates in North Carolina also initially posited themselves as willing to comply with the mandate of the Supreme Court, but they then helped usher in pupil assignment legislation in an effort to get around the decision.

8. Lucius E. Burch Jr. to "Friend," October 30, 1958, Orgill Papers, box 16, Negroes (1) folder; Tucker, *Memphis Since Crump*, 119–21.

9. "Ex-DCC Bows, Kills Plank on Segregation," *Tri-State Defender*, September 19, 1959; Tucker, *Memphis Since Crump*, 100–101.

10. "Sues to End Park Bias," January 10, 1959; "Showdown Begins on Bus Bias February 27," February 28, 1959; "Evers Criticizes City's Position on Parks, Zoo," March 14, 1959; and O. Z. Evers et al. to City Commissioners, August 13, 1958, all in *Tri-State Defender*; O. Z. Evers et al. to Honorable Edmund Orgill, November 9, 1959; and Orgill to unnamed recipient, December 16, 1959, both in Orgill Papers, box 16, Negroes (1) folder; Allegra Turner interview by author.

11. Hon. Russell Sugarmon interview by author; Diamond, "Impact of the Negro Vote," 453–59; Kousser, *Colorblind Injustice*, 154.

12. Diamond, "Impact of the Negro Vote," 454–56; Hattie House, "Freedom Rally to Bring Top Men to Metropolitan Church for Talks," *Tri-State Defender*, June 27, 1959; Sugarmon, "Fight for Freedom."

13. "Drive on to End Cop Brutality," *Tri-State Defender*, September 19, 1959.

14. "Another Memphian Says He Was Beaten by Cops," September 26, 1959; and "20,000 Negroes Behind Council's Effort to Meet with Armour and Stop Police Brutality," October 17, 1959, both in *Tri-State Defender*; minutes of meeting of the Mem-

phis NAACP, October 25, 1959; and minutes of meeting of the Memphis NAACP Executive Board, November 3, 1959, Smith Collection.

15. "Klondyke Victim Says Cops Beat Him Again," *Tri-State Defender*, January 2, 1960. On other incidents within days of the Jones beating, see Chester Good, "Devout Church Family Says Cops Beat, Humiliated Them in Home," *Tri-State Defender*, December 19, 1959; and "Asks Help; Says Cops Beat Him," *Tri-State Defender*, January 9, 1960.

16. Joan Turner Beifuss's *At the River I Stand*, on which many later accounts rely for the strike's history, gives 1963 as the start date of sanitation workers' organizing efforts. See ibid., 32.

17. On the southwest Tennessee origins of many sanitation workers see Thomas Collins, "Unionization in a Secondary Market," 138.

18. "Evers, Farris Lock Horns on Union," February 6, 1960; and "Union Tells Negroes — 'Don't Cross Hotel Pickets,'" December 24, 1960, both in *Tri-State Defender*; Robert Worsham interview by author; Robert Beasley interview by Memphis Sanitation Strike Project; Taylor Rogers and Bessie L. Rogers interview by author; Joe C. Warren discussion with author.

19. "Evers, Farris Lock Horns on Union," February 6, 1960; "200 Sanitation Men Cheer Union Plans," March 19, 1960; "Sanitation Men Ready Petition," April 9, 1960; "Sanitation Men Ready to Strike," May 7, 1960; "Sanitation Strike Gets 2 Week Delay," May 15, 1960; and "Sanitation Workers Set to Strike," June 25, 1960, all in *Tri-State Defender*; Robert Beasley interview by Memphis Sanitation Strike Project; Taylor Rogers and Bessie L. Rogers interview by author.

20. "Evers, Farris Lock Horns on Union," February 6, 1960; and "200 Sanitation Men Cheer Union Plans," March 19, 1960, both in *Tri-State Defender*.

21. "200 Sanitation Men Cheer Union Plans," March 19, 1960; "Sanitation Men Ready Petition," April 9, 1960; "Sanitation Men Ready to Strike," May 7, 1960; "Sanitation Strike Gets 2 Week Delay," May 15, 1960; and "Sanitation Workers Set to Strike," June 25, 1960, all in *Tri-State Defender*. On federal and state policy regarding public employees, see Beifuss, *At the River I Stand*, 29.

22. "1st School Day Is 'Peaceful,'" September 26, 1959; and "Greyhound President Kills Segregation in Waiting Rooms of Bus Stations," October 3, 1959, both in *Tri-State Defender*; minutes of Memphis NAACP Executive Board meeting, November 3 and December 1, 1959; and minutes of branch meeting of Memphis NAACP, November 22, 1959, all in Minutes — Monthly Branch Meetings and Executive Committee Meetings, 1959, Smith Collection.

23. "Bar Negroes from Auto Show: City Is Blamed," January 16, 1960; "Negroes up in Arms over Auto Show Snub, Vow to Go Outside Memphis to Purchase Cars," January 23, 1960; "Protest Group Becomes Permanent," January 30, 1960; and "Dealer Apologizes but Letter from Auto Association Called 'Weak,'" February 20, 1960, all in *Tri-State Defender*.

24. "NAACP Youth Resolve to Extend Sit-Ins All over Southeast Area," *Tri-State Defender*, February 27, 1960.

25. On movements in Fayette and Haywood counties, see Hamburger, *Our Portion of Hell*; on Haywood, see Couto, *Ain't Gonna Let Nobody Turn Me Round*, 19–50.

26. "Background Information on Fayette County," leaflet, n.d.; and "A Call for Help," brochure, n.d., in Stuckey Papers, box 1, folder 1, 3, Chicago Historical Society, Chicago; Hamburger, *Our Portion of Hell*, 3–5; C. P. Boyd, quoted in Couto, *Ain't Gonna Let Nobody Turn Me Round*, 32–34; Current, "Which Way Out?," 133–35; "Resolutions Adopted by the 6th Annual Conference of Branches of the State of Tennessee NAACP," October 1952; and press release from Tennessee State Conference of NAACP Branches, November 27, 1952, both in NAACP-LC, group II, box C187, folder: Tennessee State Conference, 1951–55.

27. Tom Rice, in Couto, *Ain't Gonna Let Nobody Turn Me Around*, 32; Minnie Jameson, George Bates, and June Dowdy in Hamburger, *Our Portion of Hell*, 33, 66–73; Burleigh Hines, "Tells Background on Fayette Vote Fight," *Tri-State Defender*, December 5, 1959; Current, "Which Way Out?" Estes received death threats in March 1959 after a radio program in which he discussed his work with veterans in Memphis, but he vowed to continue. See "Leaders Back Atty. Estes in Vote Registration Campaign," *Tri-State Defender*, March 14, 1959.

28. "Man Who Escaped Mob Faces Murder," April 4, 1959; M. L. Reid, "Rev. Dodson Gets 20 Years; Seeks New Trial," April 11, 1959; "Fugitive Life Fine Compared to Penitentiary, Says CME Minister," April 11, 1959; and "Deny New Trial to Rev. Dodson," May 23, 1959, all in *Tri-State Defender*.

29. Square Mormon, quoted in Hamburger, *Our Portion of Hell*, 47; Hamburger, *Our Portion of Hell*, 4–5, 27; Current, "Which Way Out?," 135–36.

30. "Negroes in Fayette DID Try to Register," *Tri-State Defender*, February 13, 1960; Burleigh Hines, "Tells Background on Fayette Vote Fight," *Tri-State Defender*, December 5, 1959; "Voteless Negroes to Testify," *Pittsburgh Courier*, January 23, 1960; Hamburger, *Our Portion of Hell*, 3–31.

31. "Negroes in Fayette DID Try to Register," February 13, 1960; "Squeeze Tightens in Fayette County," May 7, 1960; "See Vote Referees in Haywood Area," May 21, 1960; "Kicked off Land for Registering," June 25, 1960; "Suit Filed for Rights in Haywood," July 9, 1960; "5,000 Tenn. Negroes in Protest March," September 24, 1960; and "Xmas Coming but Not to People of Fayette," week of December 10–16, 1960, all in *Tri-State Defender*; "Background Information on Fayette County," flyer, n.d., Stuckey Papers, box 1, folder 1, Chicago Historical Society, Chicago.

32. Minutes of Memphis NAACP Executive Board and branch meetings, June 1960–February 1961, Smith Collection; "Fayette Gets Help, More Coming," July 16, 1960; "Urge 'Don't Buy' from Oil Companies," July 16, 1960; "Seek Charter for NAACP in Fayette," July 30, 1960; and "M. Jackson to Sing at Ellis," December 24, 1960, all in *Tri-State Defender*.

33. "SCEF Asks End of Oil Boycott," June 25, 1960; "Urge 'Don't Buy' from Oil Companies," July 16, 1960; and "Help from Chicago for Fayette Co.," week of December 17–23, 1960, all in *Tri-State Defender*; correspondence on Fayette and Haywood counties, NAACP-LC, group III, box C146; correspondence on Emergency Relief Committee, Stuckey Papers, box 1, folders 1–3, Chicago Historical Society, Chicago.

34. Correspondence on Emergency Relief Committee, Stuckey Papers, box 1, folders 1–3, Chicago Historical Society, Chicago.

35. Operation Freedom brochure, Stuckey Papers, box 1, folder 3: Emergency Relief Committee for Fayette and Haywood Counties, Tenn., March–Dec. 1961, Chicago Historical Society, Chicago.

36. "The Boycott in Fayette County," July 2, 1960; and "Republic of Congo on Trial," July 16, 1960, both in *Tri-State Defender*.

37. On the importance of students' organizational experiences prior to the sit-in movement, see Morris, *Origins of the Civil Rights Movement*. With a different emphasis, Richard King discusses continuity and discontinuity in the freedom movement in *Civil Rights and the Idea of Freedom*, 3–11.

38. "Memphis Is Added to Negro Parade of Sitdowns," *Memphis Press-Scimitar*, March 19, 1960; "400 Attend Open House," *Tri-State Defender*, October 28, 1954, 1; "LeMoyne-Owen College — Welcome," <http://www.loc.edu/welcome/history.html> (accessed July 7, 2006).

39. Ernestine Hill Carpenter and Evander Ford interview by author; Johnnie Rodgers Turner interview by author; "All Library Branches Are Desegregated," *Magician*, October 1960, LMOC Archives.

40. "Sitdown Moves to Memphis Libraries," *Memphis Press-Scimitar*, March 19, 1960. On coverage of the sit-in in the black press, see, for example, articles and photos in *Tri-State Defender*, March 26, 1960, including L. F. Palmer Jr., editor, "Story from Inside Jail"; "Jail Fails to Stop 'Sit-Ins'"; and "Full Page of Pictures on Sit-Down Arrests."

41. Markham Stansbury, "Memphians Rally, Help Arrested in Sit-Downs," *Tri-State Defender*, March 26, 1960; "Memphis NAACP Pledges All-Out Support to 'Sitters,'" *Memphis Commercial Appeal*, March 20, 1960.

42. Markham Stansbury, "Memphians Rally, Help Arrested in Sit-Downs," *Tri-State Defender*, March 26, 1960; "Memphis NAACP Pledges All-Out Support to 'Sitters,'" *Memphis Commerical Appeal*, March 20, 1960.

43. Markham Stansbury, "Memphians Rally, Help Arrested in Sit-Downs," *Tri-State Defender*, March 26, 1960; Evander Ford interview (with Ernestine Hill Carpenter) by author.

44. Evander Ford interview (with Ernestine Hill Carpenter) by author; "Jail Fails to Stop 'Sit-Ins'"; and "Negroes at Fever Pitch, Vow All-Out Support of Students," both in *Tri-State Defender*, March 26, 1960; "Attorneys Appeal Fines of 'Sit-In' Students," *Magician*, April 1960, LMOC Archives.

45. Russell Sugarmon, testimony in U.S. Commission on Civil Rights, *Hearings before the United States Commission on Civil Rights*, 101.

46. Johnnie Rodgers Turner interview by author; Jay Hall, "Negro Meeting Votes Boycott," *Memphis Press-Scimitar*, March 22, 1960; minutes of Memphis NAACP meeting, March 27, 1960, Smith Collection.

47. Minutes of Memphis NAACP meeting, February 28, 1960, and minutes of Memphis NAACP Executive Board meetings, April 5 and July 5, 1960, Smith Collection. The NAACP had been banned or crippled in several southern states, including Alabama, the location of the southeast regional office. See Morris, *Origins of the Civil Rights Movement*, 30–39.

48. "9 Resume Sit-Ins," *Tri-State Defender*, May 21, 1960; "Students Request Service," *Magician*, May 1960, 11–12, LMOC Archives.

49. Elaine Lee Turner interview by author.

50. "Adults Join Pickets on Main Street," May 28, 1960; "May Picket St. Jude Benefit June 9," June 4, 1960; "Pickets Fell Tri-State Fair," June 18, 1960; "NAACP Attacks WDIA Revue Arrangements," June 25, 1960; "WDIA Family Fair Brings NAACP's Hot Resentment," August 13, 1960; Markham Stansbury, "Youth Meet Sharp Rebuffs after Bus Ride, Zoo Visit," August 13, 1960; Markham Stansbury, "Ministers with Those Arrested," August 27, 1960, all in *Tri-State Defender*.

51. Joseph S. Cotter Jr., "Is It Because I Am Black?" excerpted from James Weldon Johnson, ed., *The Book of American Negro Poetry* (New York, 1922), 186.

52. "Three More Lawsuits Now in the Works: More Sit-In Arrests Made," *Tri-State Defender*, April 9, 1960; minutes of the Memphis NAACP meeting, March 27, 1960, and minutes of the Memphis NAACP Executive Board, April 5, 1960, Smith Collection.

53. Elaine Lee Turner interview by author; minutes of the Memphis NAACP Executive Board, December 6, 1960, Smith Collection; "Nabrit Address[es] Student Movement Group," *Magician*, December 1960, LMOC Archives.

54. See correspondence and executive committee minutes in the Memphis Committee on Community Relations (MCCR) Papers, especially Vasco A. Smith Jr. to MCCR, April 2, 1967, box 1, folder 10, Special Collections, McWherter Library, University of Memphis.

55. Ernestine Hill Carpenter and Evander Ford interview by author; "5 Arrested at Pink Palace," *Memphis Press-Scimitar*, [March 1960].

56. Johnnie Rodgers Turner interview by author; Elaine Lee Turner interview by author. Johnnie Rodgers Turner was unable to get a job in the Memphis/Shelby County school system for several years due to her role in the movement. More recently she became executive secretary of the Memphis NAACP, replacing Maxine Smith after thirty-five years.

57. Elaine Lee Turner interview by author; Joan Lee Nelson interview by author.

58. On changing senses of pride, see Richard King, *Civil Rights and the Idea of Freedom*, 4–5.

59. Johnnie Rodgers Turner interview by author.

60. McKee and Chisenhall, *Beale Black and Blue*, 75–76.

61. "Why Students Picket Cotton Jubilee," May 14, 1960; and "From 'Darlings' to 'Goats,'" May 21, 1960, both in *Tri-State Defender*; minutes of Memphis NAACP, February 26, 1961; and press release from Maxine Smith, "Inter-Denominational Ministerial Alliance and N.A.A.C.P. Take Joint Stands against Cotton Makers' Jubilee," [April 1961], both in Smith Collection.

62. "Starlight Revue Blows Into Memphis July 1," June 18, 1960; and "Charity Show to Be Presented by WDIA," July 2, 1960, both in *Tri-State Defender*. Pepper and Ferguson sold WDIA to radio chain owner Egmont Sonderling in 1957, but Ferguson remained as executive vice president. See Cantor, *Wheelin' on Beale*, 108; and "NAACP Attacks WDIA Revue Arrangements," *Tri-State Defender*, June 25, 1960.

63. "NAACP Attacks WDIA Revue Arrangements," June 25, 1960; "Expect Pickets at WDIA Revue," July 2, 1960; Nat D. Williams, "Dark Shadows," July 2, 1960; and Burleigh Hines, "NAACP Fires Second Blast at WDIA; Pickets Ignored," July 9, 1960, all in *Tri-State Defender.*

64. Burleigh Hines, "NAACP Fires Second Blast at WDIA; Pickets Ignored," July 9, 1960; "WDIA Family Fair Brings NAACP's Hot Resentment," August 13, 1960; "WDIA Gives Up Fair Without Fight," August 20, 1960; and "Mixed Seating for WDIA Show," week of December 3–6, 1960, all in *Tri-State Defender.*

65. Bowman, *Soulsville, U.S.A.*, 14–18; Guralnick, *Sweet Soul Music*, 103–6; Cantor, *Wheelin' on Beale*, 66–68.

66. Guralnick, *Sweet Soul Music*, 107–12; Bowman, *Soulsville, U.S.A.*, 10–14, 36–40.

67. Robert Gordon makes this point in *It Came from Memphis*, 53. Laura Helper also offers an in-depth analysis of the impact of black musicians on white audiences at segregated dances and west Memphis clubs, in "Whole Lot of Shakin' Going On."

68. *WLOK Story.*

69. Al Bell interview by Joann Self.

70. *WLOK Story.*

71. "Larry Muhoberac and Onzie Horne Featuring Their Fine Orchestras," *Magician*, March 1961, 1, LMOC Archives.

72. "Memphis NAACP Pledges All-Out Support to 'Sitters,'" March 20, 1960; and "Negro Meeting Votes Boycott," March 22, 1960, both in *Memphis Press-Scimitar*; Markham Stansbury, "Memphians Rally, Help Arrested in Sit-Downs," *Tri-State Defender*, March 26, 1960.

73. "Students Hit Churches and Lunch Counters," August 27, 1960; and "Two Negroes, White Arrested at Church," September 3, 1960, both in *Tri-State Defender*; "Negro's Plea: Open Churches to All," *Memphis Press-Scimitar*, August 29, 1960; "3 Churches Reject Negro Worshipers," *Memphis Commercial Appeal*, August 29, 1960; minutes of the Memphis NAACP, August 28, 1960, Smith Collection.

74. Ernestine Hill Carpenter and Evander Ford interview by author. Based in Memphis, the Church of God in Christ emerged out of a religious movement in Los Angeles in the early twentieth century that was multiracial until whites formed separate churches in the late 1910s. On black Pentecostals, see Lincoln and Mamiya, *Black Church*, 76–91.

75. "14 Arrested at 'Public' Meet," *Tri-State Defender*, September 10, 1960.

76. "Judge Terms Negro Action 'A New Low,'" *Memphis Press-Scimitar*, September 1, 1960; "14 Arrested at 'Public' Meet," *Tri-State Defender*, September 10, 1960.

77. *State of Tennessee v. Evander Ford, Jr., et al.*, transcript, Access 69A1718, box 18, RG 21, NARA-Region VII.

78. Ibid., 124–25, 173, 177. On the rarity of pro-segregation ministers citing biblical passages to support their arguments, see Chappell, *Stone of Hope*, esp. 112–17. See also other works on religion and civil rights in the South, including Mark Newman, *Getting Right with God*; and Harvey, *Freedom's Coming*.

79. *State of Tennessee v. Evander Ford, Jr., et al.*, transcript, 157, 163, 166, 168, Access 69A1718, box 18, RG 21, NARA-Region VII.

80. Ernestine Hill Carpenter and Evander Ford interview by author; Johnnie Rodgers Turner interview.

81. Thurmond Lee Snyder, "The New Negro," *Magician*, March 1961, LMOC Archives. See also two poems by student Gloria J. Howard in the same issue, titled "Black Man" and "Today."

Chapter 8

1. Beifuss, *At the River I Stand*, 256–59; Fairclough, *To Redeem the Soul of America*, 371.

2. Martin Luther King Jr. address to striking sanitation workers, March 18, 1968, <www.aft.org/topics/civil-rights/mlk/memphis-speech.htm> (accessed October 30, 2005).

3. Eddie May Garner interview by author; Naomi Jones interview by author; "Dr. King to Speak at Mason Temple," *MAP-South Newsletter*, March 18, 1968, in MAP-South files.

4. Hazel McGhee interview by author.

5. Benjamin Muse, quoted in Silver and Moeser, *Separate City*, 97; Russell B. Sugarmon, quoted in "Rights Board Told of Surpluses and Shortages," *Memphis Press-Scimitar*, June 27, 1962. On the role of the daily press, see Biles, "Bittersweet Victory," 474–75. For a recent perspective, see James Dao, "40 Years Later, Civil Rights Makes Page One," *New York Times*, July 13, 2004, which suggests that a similar phenomenon took place in Lexington, Kentucky. For a view of Memphis's social climate before the sanitation strike that downplays the intensity of the sit-in movement, see Tucker, *Memphis Since Crump*, 152–72.

6. "29 Memphis Eating Spots Desegregate: Actions Taken by 10 Companies," *Memphis Press-Scimitar*, February 6, 1962; Clark Porteous, "700 at Meeting of Citizens' Council," *Memphis Press-Scimitar*, March 17, 1962. On MCCR, see Tucker, *Memphis Since Crump*, 120–22, 133–40.

7. Clark Porteous, "Rowan to Protest Memphis Incident," January 20, 1962; John Spence, "Negroes Win Appeal on Memphis School," March 23, 1962; and Paul Underwood, "Court Rules on Airport Facility," March 26, 1962, all in *Memphis Press-Scimitar*; "Goldberg Gives Integration Opinion," May 28, 1962; and "City Orders All Pools Closed as Parks Are Desegregated," May 31, 1963, both in *Memphis Commercial Appeal*. See also *Turner v. City of Memphis*, 369 U.S. 350 (1962); and *Watson v. Memphis*, 373 U.S. 526 (1963).

8. Kay Pittman, "Students Ask Rights Action," January 18, 1964; and "Six Pickets Return to Tea Room after Yesterday's Flare-up," May 7, 1964, both in *Memphis Press-Scimitar*; "Tea Room Pickets Await Discussion," *Memphis Commercial Appeal*, May 8, 1964; "From Presbyterian Church: Church's Men Guard Door in Person," *Tri-State Defender*, April 25, 1964; "Texas Presbyterians Attack Plans to Meet in Memphis," May 21, 1964; and "Presbyterians Set Showdown on Church's Racial Policies," June 16, 1964, both in *Memphis Commercial Appeal*.

9. William Thomas, "Civil Rights Does It for Democrats as Negro Bloc Buries GOP Hopes," November 4, 1964; and "Moment of History Lies Buried Beneath Ballot," November 8, 1964, both in *Memphis Commercial Appeal*; "Willis Sees Victory as 'Turning Point,'" *Memphis Press-Scimitar*, November 7, 1964.

10. On the Program of Progress and the 1967 election, see Tucker, *Memphis Since Crump*, chap. 6; and Kousser, *Colorblind Injustice*, 173–88.

11. George Grank to Freedom Committee members, November 27, 1964, Correspondence Notebooks Handwritten, 1964–72, Smith Collection, box 12; "Police Patrol Area, but All Is Peaceful," *Memphis Press-Scimitar*, September 10, 1963; Tucker, *Black Pastors and Leaders*, 128–29. Bettye Coe Donahue commented extensively on overcrowding at Hamilton High School, in interview by author. On school desegregation in Memphis, see Biles, "Bittersweet Victory," 470–83.

12. Complaint by Joe Ward, post office carrier, n.d. [April 24]; and Maxine Smith to U.S. Postmaster General John Gronouski, April 28, 1964, in Correspondence Notebooks Handwritten for March 17, 1964–May 8, 1964, Smith Collection, box 12. On LeMoyne, see "LeMoynites March; Price Sends Protest Letter to Commissioner Armour"; "The Clinton Jamerson Incident: A Case of Police Brutality"; and "Commissioner Lane Discusses Police Brutality with LeMoyne Students," all in *The Inquirer*, May 1967, LMOC Archives.

13. Quote from Annual Report, 1966, Memphis NAACP, in November 16, 1966–January 27, 1967 Notebook, Smith Collection, box 12. See also Maxine Smith to Robert McNamara and General Lewis B. Hershey, January 7, 1966, in November 29, 1965–January 7, 1966 Notebook; press release, "Memphis Branch NAACP Protests Discrimination in Selective Service Boards, n.d. [January 1966], in January 7, 1966–February 14, 1966 Notebook; Roscoe McWilliams to Governor Frank Clement, January 17, 1966, in January 7, 1966–February 14, 1966 Notebook; McWilliams to President Lyndon Johnson, March 1, 1966, in February 15–March 16, 1966 Notebook; press release, "President Johnson Asked to Help Rid Memphis Draft Boards of Racial Discrimination," March 4, 1966, in February 15–March 16, 1966 Notebook; Smith to Clement, n.d., and Smith to Hershey, n.d., in September 1, 1966–October 11, 1966 Notebook; and Smith to Johnson, January 25, 1968, in January 23, 1968–March 7, 1968 Notebook, all in Smith Collection, box 12; Fairclough, *To Redeem the Soul of America*, 334–35; and McKnight, *Last Crusade*, 47.

14. The march had originally been planned by James Meredith, the first black student to attend the University of Mississippi, but was taken up by King and SCLC, SNCC, and CORE after Meredith was shot. SNCC chairman Stokely Carmichael first used the phrase during an evening rally in Greenwood, Mississippi. See Sellers, *River of No Return*, 160–69.

15. Beifuss, *At the River I Stand*, 160–70; McKnight, *Last Crusade*, 44, 46; Juanita Miller Thornton interview by author. McKnight gives the figure of less than 100 based on his reading of FBI surveillance files. On masculinity and the Invaders, see also Estes, *I Am a Man!*, 141–43.

16. Van Deburg, *New Day in Babylon*, 204–16; Ward, *Just My Soul Responding*, chap. 9. Bo Diddley's "I'm a Man" (1955), re-recorded by Muddy Waters as "Mannish Boy," is a good example of a 1950s R & B hit that expressed resistance through hyper-

masculine sexuality. I thank Waldo Martin for suggesting that I compare the 1968 "I *Am* a Man" to Diddley's 1955 recording.

17. "Union Tells Negroes — 'Don't Cross Hotel Pickets,'" *Tri-State Defender*, December 24, 1960; Robert Worsham interview by author. At the 1962 Memphis hearings of the U.S. Commission on Civil Rights, Memphis Urban League executive secretary Rev. James McDaniel testified that discriminatory labor practices had led to 30,000 unemployed blacks in Memphis, and an additional 15,000–18,000 unemployed seasonal laborers in the Memphis area. See U.S. Commission on Civil Rights, *Hearings Before the U.S. Commission on Civil Rights*, 235–43.

18. Carter, "Local Labor Union," 236.

19. Eddie May Garner interview by author; Alzada Clark interview by author; Carter, "Impact of the Civil Rights Movement," 97, 101–4; Carter, "Local Labor Union," 74–88.

20. Black women's employment in the Memphis furniture industry grew from 3.3 percent during World War II to 22.7 percent in 1950 to 30.7 percent in 1970. See Carter, "Local Labor Union," 90.

21. The discussion of Sally Turner is drawn from interview by author.

22. Hazel McGhee's comments are from interview by author.

23. Naomi Jones interview by author; Report of Executive Secretary, July 5–September 5, 1967, in August 17–October 17, 1967 Notebook, Smith Collection, box 12.

24. Naomi Jones interview by author.

25. Ida Leachman telephone interview by author, June 14, 1999; Naomi Jones interview by author. On the themes of deliverance and salvation, see Marsh, *God's Long Summer*, 47.

26. U.S. Commission on Civil Rights, "Summary of the Civil Rights Act of 1964," *Civil Rights Digest*, August 1964, in Memphis Committee on Community Relations Papers, box 1, folder: MCCR Employment Committee, Special Collections, McWherter Library, University of Memphis. On Johnson, the Civil Rights Act, and foreign policy concerns see Dudziak, *Cold War Civil Rights*, 208–14.

27. Maxine Smith to EEOC commissioner Samuel Jackson, May 23, 1967, in May 23–June 19, 1967 Notebook, Smith Collection, box 12. These complaints are also discussed elsewhere in box 12, Correspondence Notebooks Handwritten.

28. Walter Brown complaint, [January 1965], and Maxine Smith to Veterans Administration, January 26, 1965, both in January 17–February 11, 1965 Notebook; Smith to Blake E. Turner, April 3, 1965, in March 27–April 30, 1965 Notebook; Smith to Herbert Hill, May 6, 1966, in April 26–June 6, 1966 Notebook; and Smith to Robert L. Carter, March 4, 1968, in January 23–March 7, 1968 Notebook, all in Smith Collection, box 12.

29. Complaint notes, [January 1965], January 17–February 11, 1965 Notebook; and Report of Executive Secretary, April 3–May 14, 1968, in April 26–May 15, 1968 Notebook, both in Smith Collection, box 12.

30. The term "intangibles" was important in the Supreme Court's school desegregation decisions leading up to and including *Brown v. Board of Education*. In the *Sweatt v. Painter* decision (1950), for example, the Court argued that the University of Texas Law School not only possessed superior facilities than the makeshift law

school it had established for black students but also "possesses to a far greater degree those qualities which are incapable of objective measurement but which make for greatness in a law school," such as the "reputation of the faculty . . . traditions and prestige." See *Sweatt v. Painter*, 339 U.S. 629 (1950), reprinted in Waldo E. Martin Jr., *Brown v. Board of Education: A Brief History with Documents* (Boston: Bedford/St. Martins, 1998), 116.

31. Smith to Veterans Administration, letters and notes in January 17–February 11, 1965 Notebook; Report of Executive Secretary, May 29–June 25, 1967, in June 19–August 17, 1967 Notebook; and Report of Executive Secretary, July 5–September 5, 1967, in August 17–October 17, 1967 Notebook, all in Smith Collection, box 12.

32. Smith to Samuel Jackson, EEOC commissioner, May 23, 1967, in May 23–June 19, 1967 Notebook; Smith to Alfred Feinberg, December 3, 1965, in November 29, 1965–January 7, 1966 Notebook; Smith to Herbert Hill, May 6, 1966, in April 26–June 6, 1966 Notebook; Smith to Hill, August 21, 1967, in August 17–October 17, 1967 Notebook; and Smith to Robert L. Carter, NAACP general counsel, March 4, 1968, in January 23–March 7, 1968 Notebook, all in Smith Collection, box 12.

33. "RCA Plant Will Employ Up to 8,000" and "Memphis Lands a Really Big One," December 21, 1965, both in *Memphis Press-Scimitar*; Charles Thornton, "City's Women Gave Memphis Edge for RCA," *Memphis Commercial Appeal*, December 22, 1965.

34. "Big RCA Plant May Draw Many Related Industries," *Memphis Press-Scimitar*, December 21, 1965; Charles Thornton, "City's Women Gave Memphis Edge for RCA," *Memphis Commercial Appeal*, December 22, 1965; Cowie, *Capital Moves*, 77, 78; Ciscel and Collins, "'On The Road to Taipei,'" 143–49; Collins and Ciscel, "Analysis of the RCA Television Assembly Plant," 3–7.

35. Charles Edmundson, "Women's Nimble Fingers Tickle RCA Executive Pink," January 17, 1966, *Memphis Commercial Appeal*; notes by Maxine Smith [Feb. 1966] and press release from Rev. S. B. Kyles, February 28, 1966, both in February 15–March 16, 1966 Notebook; Report of Executive Secretary, March 2–April 5, 1966, in March 17–April 25, 1966 Notebook; Report of Executive Secretary, January 5–February 7, 1967, Maxine Smith to Herbert Hill, February 13, 1967, and Report of Executive Secretary, February 8–March 7, 1967, all in January 27–March 9, 1967 Notebook, all in box 7, Smith Collection.

36. "RCA Plant Will Employ Up to 8,000" and "Memphis Lands a Really Big One," December 21, 1965; "Women Benefit Most from Plans," December 22, 1965; and Roy B. Hamilton, "RCA to Begin Memphis Production in May," January 11, 1966, all in *Memphis Press-Scimitar*; Charles Thornton, "City's Women Gave Memphis Edge for RCA," December 22, 1965; Charles Edmundson, "Third of Color TV Output Rolls from Indiana RCA Plant," January 16, 1966; and Edmundson, "Women's Nimble Fingers Tickle RCA Executive Pink," January 17, 1966, all in *Memphis Commercial Appeal*; Ciscel and Collins, "'On the Road to Taipei,'" 148.

37. "RCA Wastes No Time!," *Memphis Press-Scimitar*, June 16, 1966; "400 Sets Roll off at New RCA Plant," *Memphis Commercial Appeal*, June 16, 1966; Charles Edmundson, "RCA Workers Stage March over Union Representation," *Memphis Press-*

Scimitar, August 17, 1966; "IUE Is Chosen in RCA Voting," *Memphis Press-Scimitar*, December 17, 1966. On the IUE-IBEW dispute, see RCA-IUE Records, box 86.

38. "3 RCA Workers Arrested as Wildcat Strike Goes On," March 10, 1967; and Wayne Chastain, "RCA Strike Situation Unclear," March 11, 1967, both in *Memphis Press-Scimitar*.

39. Grace to G. J. Rooney, June 18, 1968; Grace to Jennings, June 24, 1968; Robert Vick to Jennings, November 18, 1968; D. H. Bartholomeu to IUE International President, November 18, 1968; and *IUE Local 730 News*, September 1969, all in RCA-IUE Records, group III. On responses to the sanitation strike, see Ciscel and Collins, "'On the Road to Taipei,'" 148; and Cowie, *Capital Moves*, 90.

40. Isserman and Kazin, *America Divided*, 107–12 (Johnson quote, 108); Orleck, *Storming Caesars Palace*, 86–88.

41. Maxine Smith to Memphis City Commission, December 15, 1964, and Samuel Kyles to [Memphis Board of Education], both in December 11, 1964–January 17, 1965 Notebook, Smith Collection, box 12.

42. Several recently published works on welfare, public housing, and civil rights detail this conflict over "maximum feasible participation" and discuss community empowerment in the War on Poverty. See Nadasen, *Welfare Warriors*, 63–70; Rhonda Williams, *Politics of Public Housing*, 159–64; Greene, *Our Separate Ways*, 109–10; and Orleck, *Storming Caesars Palace*, 109.

43. Reports of Executive Secretary and correspondence in Notebooks for August 1965–November 1965; Annual Report of Memphis Branch NAACP for 1965; and Jesse Turner to Sargent Shriver, OEO director, January 12, 1966, all in Smith Collection, box 12. Quote in Report of Executive Secretary, October 6–November 2, 1965. Information on Butler from Tarlease Matthews, "What Manner of Man — He Who Champions the Poor: A Look at Washington Butler Jr., *Memphis Citizen*, October 14, 1970, clipping in personal papers of Willie Pearl Butler.

44. Report by Elizabeth Jones on history of MAP-South and membership report in draft of minutes of general MAP-South membership meeting, April 20, 1967, Policy Committee minutes, 1966–68; and MAP-South Constitution and By-Laws, adopted December 1, 1965, both in MAP-South files.

45. Minutes, reports, and memoranda, January 5, 1967–April 20, 1967, MAP-South Policy Committee and Citizens' Association, MAP-South files.

46. "Myth of Welfare Chiselers," *MAP-South Newsletter*, October 17, 1967, in MAP-South files.

47. Willie Pearl Butler interview by author.

48. Ibid.; Edward L. Topp, "Mothers on Welfare Complain about New Jobs Plan," *Memphis Press-Scimitar*, May 28, 1968.

49. MAP-South Citizens' Association minutes, June 17, 1968, MAP-South files; Kay Pittman Black, "Welfare Mothers Protest," *Memphis Press-Scimitar*, November 29, 1968.

50. Juanita Miller Thornton interview by author; Willie Pearl Butler to NWRO, June 19, 1971, and report on MWRO, Bob Newell, n.d., both in personal papers of Willie Pearl Butler.

51. Kay Pittman Black, "Welfare Mothers Protest," *Memphis Press-Scimitar*, No-

vember 29, 1968; Kotz and Kotz, *Passion for Equality*, 181–217; Ann Wilson Harper interview by author.

52. Willie Pearl Butler interview by author.

53. Ann Wilson Harper interview by author.

54. Juanita Miller Thornton interview by author.

55. Ibid.

56. Because the strike has been discussed in depth in several historical accounts, this chapter presents only a brief outline of major developments. The fullest narratives are Beifuss, *At the River I Stand*, first published in 1985, and Honey, *Going Down Jericho Road*, published in 2007. See also Estes, *I Am a Man!*, 131–52; McKnight, *Last Crusade*; Michael Honey, "Martin Luther King, Jr.," 146–75; Garrow, *Bearing the Cross*, 575–624; Thomas W. Collins, "Unionization in a Secondary Labor Market," 135–41; and Green, "Battling the Plantation Mentality," chap. 6, 353–412, and "Race, Gender, and Labor in 1960s Memphis."

57. My dissertation, "Battling the Plantation Mentality" (1999), and subsequent article, "Race, Gender, and Labor in 1960s Memphis" (2004), presented the first analysis of the sanitation workers' 1959–60 organizing efforts, based on coverage of the 1960s meetings in the *Tri-State Defender* (see Green, "Battling the Plantation Mentality," 330, and "Race, Gender, and Labor in 1960s Memphis," 478–79). Until then, scholarly accounts of the sanitation strike, including Joan Turner Beifuss's work *At the River I Stand*, on which other accounts of the strike relied for their chronology, focused on 1962 or 1963 as the year when sanitation workers, led by T. O. Jones, launched their first organized efforts to unionize. See Beifuss, *At the River I Stand*, 32.

58. The best coverage of the early-1960 organizing meetings is in the *Tri-State Defender*, the black Memphis newspaper. Thomas Collins ("Unionization in a Secondary Labor Market," 136 and 136 n. 3) reported that of the 59 sanitation workers he interviewed, 35 came from Fayette County, 19 came from other rural counties, 5 came from Memphis, and 1 came from over 100 miles away. He attributed these findings about workers' places of origin to rural migrants' relative poverty—and thus the greater likelihood that they would need to take jobs as garbage workers—and their use of personal networks to locate jobs, however menial. On the chronology of the men's organizing, Collins notes that "a few employees had been carrying on organizing activities for ten years" prior to 1968, but states that the men "created an informal organization in 1962" (138).

59. Burrows, quoted in Cornell Christion, "Blood and Strife Bought Dignity for City Workers," *Memphis Commercial Appeal*, February 28, 1993; Robert Beasley interview by Memphis Sanitation Strike Project.

60. Clinton Burrows Sr. interview by Memphis Sanitation Strike Project.

61. Robert Beasley interview by Memphis Sanitation Strike Project; Taylor Rogers interview by Paul Ortiz.

62. Taylor Rogers interview by Paul Ortiz; Bonner, quoted in Cornell Christion, "Blood and Strife Bought Dignity for City Workers," *Memphis Commercial Appeal*, February 28, 1993.

63. Beifuss, *At the River I Stand*, 26–27; Report of Executive Secretary, March 3–

April 6, 1965, in March 27–April 30, 1965 Notebook, Smith Collection, box 12. Thank you to retired sanitation worker Joe Warren for this insight into the story behind the number 1733.

64. Robert Beasley interview by Memphis Sanitation Strike Project.

65. Ibid.; William Lucy interview by Memphis Sanitation Strike Project; Taylor Rogers and Bessie L. Rogers interview by author; Beifuss, *At the River I Stand*, 34–38.

66. William Lucy and Robert Beasley interviews by Memphis Sanitation Strike Project; Beifuss, *At the River I Stand*, 44–50.

67. William Lucy interview by Memphis Sanitation Strike Project; Beifuss, *At the River I Stand*, 93–121.

68. Minerva Johnican interview by author.

69. Bettye Coe Donahue and Minerva Johnican interviews by author.

70. Beifuss, *At the River I Stand*, 124–35; McKnight, *Last Crusade*, 44–51.

71. William Lucy interview by Memphis Sanitation Strike Project; Bessie L. Rogers during Taylor Rogers and Bessie L. Rogers interview by author; Hazel McGhee interview by author; Ida Leachman interview by author.

72. Naomi Jones interview by author; Virgil Grace to Paul Jennings, March 25, 1968, RCA-IUE Records, group III.

73. Ernest C. Withers photograph, in his *Pictures Tell the Story* (Norfolk: Chrysler Museum of Art, 2000), 81; William Lucy telephone interview by author. Robert Worsham, then a labor activist at the Chisca Hotel who assisted the sanitation workers, argues that the slogan originated with a 1962 poem he wrote titled "I Am a Man." Worsham asserts that community activist and key strike supporter Cornelia Crenshaw was familiar with the poem and suggested the slogan. See Worsham interview by author; and "'I Am a Man' Poem Part of Collection," *Memphis Commercial Appeal*, February 24, 1999. Estes (*I Am a Man!*, 209), based on comments by an ex-sanitation worker, attributes the slogan to Rev. Albert Hibbler.

74. Otha B. Strong Jones interview by author. On Black Power among low-income black women in Durham, see Greene, *Our Separate Ways*, 221; and Rhonda Williams, *Politics of Public Housing*, 187–91.

75. Photograph in *Memphis Press-Scimitar* Morgue Files, File 90012: Sanitation Department, Mississippi Valley Collection, Special Collections, McWherter Library, University of Memphis; Juanita Miller Thornton interview by author.

76. Hazel McGhee interview by author; Everlena Yarbrough interview by author; and Otha B. Strong Jones interview by author.

77. King, quoted in Beifuss, *At the River I Stand*, 256–59; "Aid Not Needed, Loeb Tells Johnson," *Memphis Press-Scimitar*, March 30, 1968.

78. Taylor Rogers interview by Paul Ortiz; "President Johnson Cancels His Trip to Hawaii," April 5, 1968; "Solution to Strike May Be Imminent," April 10, 1968; and "Sanitation Strike Settled; Workers to Return Tomorrow," April 16, 1968, all in *Memphis Press-Scimitar*.

79. Naomi Jones interview by author; Eddie May Garner interview by author; Minerva Johnican interview by author.

80. Joan Golden and Bill Adkins interviews included in *The WLOK Story*, dir. Joann Self; Guralnick, *Sweet Soul Music*, 354–55.

81. Art Gilliam interview by Joann Self; Beifuss, 442–48. Ann Wilson Harper was one of many who participated in her first march after King's death. See her interview by author.

Conclusion

1. Naomi Jones interview by author; Isaac Hayes quoted in Guralnick, *Sweet Soul Music*, 355.

2. Otha B. Strong Jones interview by author.

3. Leachman eventually became vice president of the historic Local 282, under Willie Rudd, and succeeded to the presidency after Rudd died. For her own account of her experiences, see Leachman, "Black Women and Labor Unions in the South," 385–94.

4. Virgil Grace to Paul Jennings, March 25, 1968; Grace to G. J. Rooney, June 18, 1968; Grace to Jennings, June 24, 1968; and *IUE Local 730 News*, September 1969, all in RCA-IUE Records, group III; Earline Whitehead interview by author. Grace's comments echo Paul's epistle to the Galatians, reminding them that Christ freed them from bondage and that God, not civil law, is master (Galatians 3:25, 5:1). See Cone, *Black Theology of Liberation*, 226; and Van Deburg, *New Day in Babylon*, 241.

5. Maxine Smith interview by author; Bettye Coe Donahue interview by author.

6. "Militants Seize LeMoyne Campus," *Memphis Press-Scimitar*, November 26, 1968. LeMoyne and Owen College had merged a few months earlier, becoming LeMoyne-Owen College. On protests at black colleges in 1967 and 1968 more generally, see Van Deburg, *New Day in Babylon*, 70–71.

7. "By Ourselves," *Inquirer of LeMoyne*, May 1968, LMOC Archives.

Bibliography

Archival Sources
Atlanta, Georgia
    Special Collections Department, Pullen Library, Georgia State University
        Southern Labor Archives
            United Furniture Workers of America Papers
Austin, Texas
    Harry Ransom Humanities Research Center, University of Texas
        John Beecher Papers
        David O. Selznick Collection
Bloomington, Indiana
    Smith Research Center
        Indiana University Archives of African American Music and Culture
Chicago, Illinois
    Chicago Historical Society
        Sterling Stuckey Papers
    Vivian G. Harsh Research Collection of Afro-American History and Literature,
        Chicago Public Library
        William McBride Papers
College Park, Maryland
    National Archives and Records Administration
        U.S. Department of Labor Records
            United States Conciliation Service, RG 280
            United States Employment Service for Tennessee, RG 183
        Records of the Committee on Fair Employment Practice, RG 228
East Point, Georgia
    National Archives and Records Administration, Region VII
        Records of the Committee on Fair Employment Practice, RG 228.5.7
        U.S. District Court Western District of Tennessee, Memphis Division, RG 21
Memphis, Tennessee
    Memphis Area Project — South, Office Files
    Memphis and Shelby County Room, Memphis Public Library and Information
        Center
        Walter Chandler Papers
        Clippings Files
        Everett R. Cook Oral History Collection
            Metropolitan Interfaith Association Project Collection
        William Ingram Papers

Henry Loeb III Papers
Watkins Overton Papers
James Pleasants Jr. Papers
Maxine Smith NAACP Collection
Frank Tobey Papers
Hollis F. Price Library, LeMoyne-Owen College
LeMoyne-Owen College Archives
Shelby County Archives
Criminal Court Records
Special Collections, Ned R. McWherter Library, University of Memphis
Lucius E. Burch Jr. Papers
Memphis Black Gospel Singers Oral History Collection
Memphis Committee on Community Relations Collection
Edmund Orgill Papers
Watkins Overton Papers
Russell Sugarmon Collection
New Brunswick, New Jersey
Special Collections and University Archives, Rutgers University Libraries
RCA–International Union of Electrical Workers Records
Washington, D.C.
Manuscripts Division, Library of Congress
National Association for the Advancement of Colored People Papers
Smithsonian Institution Archives
Radio Smithsonian, Smithsonian Productions

Court Cases

Gray et al. v. Board of Trustees of the University of Tennessee et al., 342 U.S. 517 (1952)
McLaurin v. Oklahoma State Regents, 339 U.S. 637 (1950)
Sipuel v. Board of Regents of the University of Oklahoma et al., 332 U.S. 631 (1948)
State of Missouri ex rel. Gaines v. Canada, 305 U.S. 337 (1938)
State of Tennessee v. Evander Ford, Jr., et al., U.S. District Court for the Western District of Tennessee, Western Division, Civil No. 5348 (1965)
Sweatt v. Painter, 339 U.S. 629 (1950)
Turner v. City of Memphis, 369 U.S. 350 (1962)
Watson v. Memphis, 373 U.S. 526 (1963)

Interviews

The following interviews were conducted as part of Behind the Veil: Documenting African American Life in the Jim Crow South, *sponsored by the Center for Documentary Studies, Duke University. Unless otherwise noted, they were conducted by the author in Memphis. Tape recordings and transcriptions are located in the* Behind the Veil: Documenting African American Life in the Jim Crow South *Collection, Special Collections, Perkins Library, Duke University, Durham, North Carolina, and Hollis F. Price Library, LeMoyne-Owen College, Memphis, Tennessee.*

Evelyn Bates, August 9, 1995

LeRoy Boyd, interview by Paul Ortiz, June 19–22, 1995, Memphis

Savy Bragg, August 16, 1995

Lanetha Jewel Branch, interview by Doris G. Dixon, June 16, 1995, Memphis

Susie Bryant, August 17, 1995

Willie Pearl Butler, August 19, 1995

Artherene Chalmers, August 15, 1995

John David Cooper, Barbara Lee Cooper, and Edgar Allen Hunt, interview by
    Paul Ortiz, June 29–July 7, 1995, Memphis

Marie Fort, August 15, 1995

Lovie Mae Griffin, August 15, 1995

George Holloway, interview by Michael Honey, March 23, 1990, Baltimore

Amy Jones, interview by Mausiki Scales, June 28, 1995, Memphis

Otha B. Strong Jones, August 8, 1995

Lillie G. Kirklon, August 18, 1995

Mary Lawson, August 6, 1995

Ida Leachman, August 10, 1995

Lenora Lewis, interview by Doris Dixon, June 14, 1995, Memphis

Hortense Mayweather, interview by Paul Ortiz, June 26, 1995, Memphis

Hazel McGhee, August 11, 1995

Melvina Rebecca McKinley, August 5, 1995

Mary C. McNeal, interview by Paul Ortiz, June 22, 1995, Memphis

Alma Morris, August 6, 1995

Taylor Rogers, interview by Paul Ortiz, June 19, 1995, Memphis

Harry Mae Simons, August 4, 1995

Maxine Smith, August 17, 1995

Allegra Turner, August 21, 1995

Elaine Lee Turner, August 22, 1995

Johnnie Rodgers Turner, August 10, 1995

Sally Turner, August 17, 1995

Rodie Veazy, interview by Paul Ortiz, June 16, 1995, Memphis

Dorothy G. Westbrook, August 14, 1995

Earline Whitehead, August 16, 1995

Imogene Watkins Wilson, interview by Mausiki Scales, July 5, 1995, Memphis

Unless otherwise noted, the following interviews were conducted by the author in
Memphis. Tape recordings are in possession of author.

Ernestine Hill Carpenter and Evander Ford, November 27, 1996

Alzada Clark, August 20, 1996

Matthew Davis, July 17, 1997

Bettye Coe Donahue, July 19, 1997

Eddie May Garner, July 22, 1997

Ann Wilson Harper, July 22, 1997

Minerva Johnican, July 21, 1997

Naomi Jones, July 18, 1997

Ida Leachman, telephone interviews, December 16, 1998, June 14, 1999,
    interview notes
Hosea T. Lockard, July 23, 1997
Jerome Long, telephone interview, November 3, 1998, interview notes
Lucius Albert Long, telephone interview, November 3, 1998, interview notes
William Lucy, telephone interview, April 18, 2001, interview notes
Joan Lee Nelson, July 16, 1997
Taylor Rogers and Bessie L. Rogers, November 9, 2000
Jeraldine Sanderlin, June 21, 2003
Hon. Russell Sugarmon, November 29, 1996, interview notes
Rufus Thomas, interview by Ray Ann Kremer and Pat Faudree, transcript,
    [August 1977], Memphis, Everett R. Cook Oral History Collection, Memphis
    and Shelby County Room, Memphis Public Library and Information Center,
    Memphis
Juanita Miller Thorton, June 6, 2001
Joe C. Warren, discussion with author, June 24, 2001, discussion notes
Robert Worsham, April 24, 2001
Everlena Yarbrough, July 17, 1997

The following interviews were conducted for Black Radio: Telling It Like It Was, *exec.
prod. Jacquie Gales Webb, Smithsonian Productions, 1996. Transcripts are located at
Smithsonian Institution Archives, Washington, D.C., and Indiana University Archives of
African American Music and Culture, Smith Research Center, Bloomington.*
Maurice Hulbert, interview by Jacquie Gales Webb, May 1995, Baltimore
Hattie Leeper, interview by Sonja Williams, April 22, 1995, Charlotte
Eddie O'Jay, interview by Sonja Williams, April 8, 1995
Martha Jean Steinberg, interview by Jacquie Gales Webb, June 13, 1995,
    Detroit

*The following interviews were conducted in Memphis by Christopher Lornell.
Transcripts or interview summaries are in Memphis Black Gospel Singers Oral
History Collection, Special Collections, Ned R. McWherter Library, University of
Memphis.*
Clara Anderson, April 18, 1982
Ford Nelson, June 2, 1982
George Rooks, November 27, 1982
"Cousin" Eugene Walton, February 5, 1983

*The following interviews were conducted by the Memphis Sanitation Strike Project in
Memphis. Transcripts are in Memphis Sanitation Strike Collection, Special Collections,
Ned R. McWherter Library, University of Memphis.*
Robert Beasley, July 10, 1991
Clinton Burrows Sr., May 14, 1991
William Lucy, May 30, 1991

The following interviews were conducted in Memphis by Joann Self, True Story Pictures, for The WLOK Story, *dir. Joann Self, Gilliam Foundation, 2002. Videocassettes located at True Story Pictures, Memphis.*

Al Bell, North Little Rock, Arkansas, April 1, 2002
Harold Ford Jr., April 2, 2002
Art Gilliam, March 8, 2002
Joan E. W. Golden, March 26, 2002
Hon. Benjamin Hooks, April 24, 2002
Rev. Samuel Kyles, March 12, 2002
Melvin Jones, February 15, 2002
Maxine Smith, April 9, 2002

Periodicals
Atlanta Daily World
Baltimore Afro-American
Birmingham World
Chicago Defender
Ebony
Memphis Commercial Appeal
Memphis Press-Scimitar
Memphis World
Negro World
New York Times
Pittsburgh Courier
Tri-State Defender

Published Microfilm Collections
National Association for the Advancement of Colored People Papers. Bethesda, Md.: University Publications of America, 1988. Microfilm.
Selected Documents from Records of the Committee on Fair Employment Practice, RG 228 of the National Archives. Glen Rock, N.J.: Microfilming Corporation of America, 1970. Microfilm.

Pamphlets and Reports
President's Committee on Civil Rights. *To Secure These Rights.* Washington D.C.: Government Printing Office, 1947.
Streit, Clarence K. *Union Now: The Proposal for Inter-Democracy Federal Union.* New York: Harper, 1940.
U.S. Commission on Civil Rights. *Hearings before the United States Commission on Civil Rights: Hearings Held in Memphis, Tennessee, June 25–26, 1962.* Washington, D.C.: Government Printing Office, 1963.
Works Progress Administration. "Housing Survey of the City of Memphis and Part of Shelby County, Tennessee." Memphis: Memphis Housing Authority, 1941.

Books

Anderson, Benedict. *Imagined Communities: Reflections on the Origin and Spread of Nationalism*, rev. ed. London: Verso, 1991.

Anderson, Jervis. *A. Philip Randolph: A Biographical Portrait*. New York: Harcourt Brace Jovanovich, Inc., 1972.

Anderson, Karen. *Wartime Women: Sex Roles, Family Relations, and the Status of Women During World War II*. Westport, Conn.: Greenwood Press, 1981.

Appadurai, Arjun. *Modernity at Large: Cultural Dimensions of Globalization*. Minneapolis: University of Minnesota Press, 1996.

Arsenault, Raymond. *Freedom Riders: 1961 and the Struggle for Racial Justice*. New York: Oxford University Press, 2006.

Barlow, William. *Voice Over: The Making of Black Radio*. Philadelphia: Temple University Press, 1999.

Barnouw, Erik. *A History of Broadcasting in the United States*. Vol. 2 of *The Golden Web*. New York: Oxford University Press, 1968.

Bayor, Ronald H. *Race and the Shaping of Twentieth-Century Atlanta*. Chapel Hill: University of North Carolina Press, 1996.

Beifuss, Joan Turner. *At the River I Stand: Memphis, the 1968 Strike, and Martin Luther King*. Brooklyn: Carlson Publishing Inc., 1985.

Berman, William C. *The Politics of Civil Rights in the Truman Administration*. Columbus: Ohio State University Press, 1970.

Biles, Roger. *Memphis in the Great Depression*. Knoxville: University of Tennessee Press, 1986.

Bogle, Donald. *Toms, Coons, Mulattoes, Mammies, and Bucks: An Interpretive History of Blacks in American Films*. New York: Viking Press, 1973.

Bond, Beverly G., and Janann Sherman. *Memphis in Black and White*. Charleston, S.C.: Arcadia Publishing, 2003.

Bowman, Rob. *Soulsville, U.S.A.: The Story of Stax Records*. New York: Schirmer Books, 1997.

Branch, Taylor. *Parting the Waters: America in the King Years, 1954–1963*. New York: Simon & Schuster, 1988.

Brandt, Allan M. *No Magic Bullet: A Social History of Venereal Disease in the United States Since 1880*. New York: Oxford University Press, 1987.

Broussard, Albert S. *Black San Francisco: The Struggle for Racial Equality in the West, 1900–1954*. Lawrence: University Press of Kansas, 1993.

Brownell, Blaine A. *The Urban Ethos in the South, 1920–1930*. Baton Rouge: Louisiana State University Press, 1975.

Bunche, Ralph J. *The Political Status of the Negro in the Age of FDR*. Edited and with an introduction by Dewey W. Grantham. Chicago: University of Chicago Press, 1973.

Burns, Stewart, ed. *Daybreak of Freedom: The Montgomery Bus Boycott*. Chapel Hill: University of North Carolina Press, 1997.

Cantor, Louis. *A Prologue to the Protest Movement: The Missouri Sharecropper Roadside Demonstration of 1939*. Durham, N.C.: Duke University Press, 1969.

———. *Wheelin' on Beale: How WDIA-Memphis Became the Nation's First All-Black Radio Station and Created the Sound that Changed America*. New York: Pharos Books, 1992.

Capers, Gerald M. *The Biography of a River Town: Its Heroic Age*. Chapel Hill: University of North Carolina Press, 1939.

Carmen, Ira H. *Movies, Censorship, and the Law*. Ann Arbor: University of Michigan Press, 1966.

Cartwright, Joseph H. *The Triumph of Jim Crow: Tennessee Race Relations in the 1880's*. Knoxville: University of Tennessee Press, 1976.

Chafe, William H. *Civilities and Civil Rights: Greensboro, North Carolina, and the Black Struggle for Freedom*. New York: Oxford University Press, 1980.

———. *The Unfinished Journey: American Since World War II*. New York: Oxford University Press, 1991.

Church, Annette E., and Roberta Church. *The Robert R. Churches of Memphis: A Father and Son Who Achieved in Spite of Race*. Ann Arbor: Edwards Brothers, 1974.

Chappell, David L. *A Stone of Hope: Prophetic Religion and the Death of Jim Crow*. Chapel Hill: University of North Carolina Press, 2004.

Clark-Lewis, Elizabeth. *Living In, Living Out: African American Domestics and the Great Migration*. Washington, D.C.: Smithsonian Institution Press, 1994; Kodansha International, 1996.

Clubb, Deborah M., ed. *A Legacy of Achievers: Women of Achievement, 1985–1994*. Memphis: Women of Achievement, Inc., 1994.

Cobb, James C. *The Most Southern Place on Earth: The Mississippi Delta and the Roots of Regional Identity*. New York: Oxford University Press, 1992.

———. *The Selling of the South: The Southern Crusade for Industrial Development, 1936–1990*, 2d ed. Urbana: University of Illinois Press, 1993.

Cohen, Lizabeth. *A Consumer's Republic: The Politics of Mass Consumption in Postwar America*. New York: Alfred A. Knopf, 2003.

Cohn, David L. *Where I Was Born and Raised*. Boston: Houghton Mifflin Co., 1948.

Cone, James H. *Black Theology and Black Power*, rev. ed. San Francisco: Harper and Row, 1989.

———. *For My People: Black Theology and the Black Church*. New York: Orbis Books, 1984.

Couto, Richard A. *Ain't Gonna Let Nobody Turn Me Round: The Pursuit of Racial Justice in the Rural South*. Philadelphia: Temple University Press, 1991.

Cowie, Jefferson. *Capital Moves: RCA's 70-Year Quest for Cheap Labor*. Ithaca: Cornell University Press, 1999.

Crawford, Vicki L., Jacqueline Anne Rouse, and Barbara Woods, eds. *Women in the Civil Rights Movement: Trailblazers and Torchbearers, 1941–1965*. Brooklyn: Carlson Publishing, 1990. Reprint, Bloomington: Indiana University Press, 1993.

Cripps, Thomas. *Making Movies Black: The Hollywood Message Movie from World War II to the Civil Rights Era*. New York: Oxford University Press, 1993.

———. *Slow Fade to Black: The Negro in American Film, 1900–1942*. New York: Oxford University Press, 1977.

Culver, John C., and John Hyde. *American Dreamer: The Life and Times of Henry A. Wallace*. New York: W. W. Norton, 2000.

Curry, Constance. *Silver Rights*. Chapel Hill, N.C.: Algonquin Books, 1995.

Dalfiume, Richard M. *Desegregation of the U.S. Armed Forces: Fighting on Two Fronts, 1939–1953*. Columbia: University of Missouri Press, 1969.

Daniel, Pete. *Breaking the Land: The Transformation of Cotton, Tobacco, and Rice Cultures Since 1880*. Urbana: University of Illinois Press, 1985.

———. *Lost Revolutions: The South in the 1950s*. Chapel Hill: University of North Carolina Press, 2000.

Dates, Jannette L., and William Barlow, eds. *Split Image: African Americans in the Mass Media*. Washington, D.C.: Howard University Press, 1990.

Davis, Allison, Burleigh B. Gardner, and Mary R. Gardner. *Deep South: A Social Anthropological Study of Caste and Class*. Chicago: University of Chicago Press, 1941. Reprint, Los Angeles: University of California Press, 1988.

Denby, Charles. *Indignant Heart: A Black Worker's Journal*, 2d ed. Detroit: Wayne State University Press, 1989.

De Grazia, Edward, and Roger K. Newman. *Banned Films: Movies, Censors and the First Amendment*. New York: R. R. Bowker Co., 1982.

Dictionary of Literary Biography. Detroit: Gale Research Company, 1986.

Dittmer, John. *Local People: The Struggle for Civil Rights in Mississippi*. Urbana: University of Illinois Press, 1995.

Douglas, Susan J. *Listening In: Radio and the American Imagination, from Amos 'n' Andy and Edward R. Murrow to Wolfman Jack and Howard Stern*. New York: Times Books, 1999.

Dollard, John. *Caste and Class in a Southern Town*. New Haven: Yale University Press, 1937. Reprint, Madison: University of Wisconsin Press, 1988.

Dowdy, G. Wayne. *Mayor Crump Don't Like It: Machine Politics in Memphis*. Jackson: University Press of Mississippi, 2006.

Du Bois, W. E. B. *The Souls of Black Folk*. 1903. Reprint, New York: New American Library, 1969.

Dudziak, Mary L. *Cold War Civil Rights: Race and the Image of Democracy*. Princeton, N.J.: Princeton University Press, 2000.

Dunayevskaya, Raya. *Philosophy and Revolution: From Hegel to Sartre, and from Marx to Mao*, 3d ed. New York: Columbia University Press, 1989.

Duster, Alfreda M., ed. *Crusade for Justice: The Autobiography of Ida B. Wells*. Chicago: University of Chicago Press, 1970.

Ely, Melvin Patrick. *The Adventures of Amos 'n' Andy: A Social History of an American Phenomenon*. New York: The Free Press, 1991.

Eskew, Glenn T. *But for Birmingham: The Local and National Movements in the Civil Rights Struggle*. Chapel Hill: University of North Carolina Press, 1997.

Estes, Steve. *I Am a Man!: Race, Manhood, and the Civil Rights Movement*. Chapel Hill: University of North Carolina Press, 2005.

Fairclough, Adam. *Race and Democracy: The Civil Rights Struggle in Louisiana, 1915–1972*. Athens: University of Georgia Press, 1995.

——. *To Redeem the Soul of America: The Southern Christian Leadership Conference and Martin Luther King, Jr.* Athens: University of Georgia Press, 1987.

Fanon, Frantz. *A Dying Colonialism*. New York: Grove Press, 1965.

Fite, Gilbert C. *Cotton Fields No More: Southern Agriculture, 1865–1980*. Lexington: University Press of Kentucky, 1984.

Forman, James. *The Making of Black Revolutionaries*. New York: Macmillan, 1972.

Frederickson, Kari. *The Dixiecrat Revolt and the End of the Solid South, 1932–1968*. Chapel Hill: University of North Carolina Press, 2001.

Fuller, Thomas O. *Bridging the Racial Chasms: A Brief Survey of Inter-Racial Attitudes and Relations*. Memphis: by the author, 1937.

Galenson, Walter. *The CIO Challenge to the AFL: A History of the American Labor Movement*. Cambridge: Harvard University Press, 1960.

Gardner, Michael R. *Harry Truman and Civil Rights: Moral Courage and Political Risks*. Carbondale: Southern Illinois University Press, 2002.

Garfinkel, Herbert. *When Negroes March: The March on Washington Movement in the Organizational Politics for FEPC*. Glencoe, Ill.: Free Press, 1959.

Garrow, David J. *Bearing the Cross: Martin Luther King, Jr., and the Southern Christian Leadership Conference*. New York: William Morrow, 1986.

George, Nelson. *The Death of Rhythm and Blues*. New York: Pantheon Books, 1988.

Gilroy, Paul. *"There Ain't No Black in the Union Jack": The Cultural Politics of Race and Nation*. Chicago: University of Chicago Press, 1987.

Goldfield, David R. *Black, White and Southern: Race Relations and Southern Culture, 1940 to the Present*. Baton Rouge: Louisiana State University Press, 1990.

——. *Cotton Fields and Skyscrapers: Southern City and Region, 1607–1980*. Baton Rouge: Louisiana State University Press, 1982.

——. *Region, Race, and Cities: Interpreting the Urban South*. Baton Rouge: Louisiana State University Press, 1997.

Gordon, Robert. *It Came from Memphis*. New York: Pocket Books, 1995.

Gorman, Joseph Bruce. *Kefauver: A Political Biography*. New York: Oxford University Press, 1971.

Graham, Allison. *Framing the South: Hollywood, Television, and Race during the Civil Rights Struggle*. Baltimore: Johns Hopkins University Press, 2001.

Graham, Hugh Davis. *Crisis in Print: Desegregation and the Press in Tennessee*. Nashville: Vanderbilt University Press, 1967.

Grant, Jacquelyn. *White Women's Christ and Black Women's Jesus: Feminist Christology and Womanist Response*. Atlanta: Scholars Press, 1989.

Grantham, Dewey W. *Southern Progressivism: The Reconciliation of Progress and Tradition*. Knoxville: University of Tennessee Press, 1983.

Greene, Christina. *Our Separate Ways: Women and the Black Freedom Movement in Durham, North Carolina*. Chapel Hill: University of North Carolina Press, 2005.

Griggs, Sutton E. *Guide to Racial Greatness; or, The Science of Collective Efficiency*. Memphis: National Public Welfare League, 1923.

——. *Light on Racial Issues*. Memphis: National Public Welfare League, 1921.

———. *Paths of Progress; or, Co-operation Between the Races*. Memphis: National Public Welfare League, 1925.

Grossman, James R. *Land of Hope: Chicago, Black Southerners, and the Great Migration*. Chicago: University of Chicago Press, 1989.

Grubbs, Donald H. *Cry from the Cotton: The Southern Tenant Farmers' Union and the New Deal*. Chapel Hill: University of North Carolina Press, 1971.

Guralnick, Peter. *Sweet Soul Music: Rhythm and Blues and the Southern Dream of Freedom*. 1986. Reprint, Boston: Little, Brown and Company, 1999.

Hamburger, Robert. *Our Portion of Hell: Fayette County, Tennessee: An Oral History of the Struggle for Civil Rights*. New York: Links Books, 1973.

Hamby, Alonzo L. *Beyond the New Deal: Harry S. Truman and American Liberalism*. New York: Columbia University Press, 1973.

———. *Man of the People: A Life of Harry S. Truman*. New York: Oxford University Press, 1995.

Harris, William H. *The Harder We Run: Black Workers since the Civil War*. New York: Oxford University Press, 1982.

Harvey, Paul. *Freedom's Coming: Religious Culture and the Shaping of the South from the Civil War through the Civil Rights Era*. Chapel Hill: University of North Carolina Press, 2005.

Higginbotham, Evelyn Brooks. *Righteous Discontent: The Women's Movement in the Black Baptist Church, 1880–1920*. Cambridge: Harvard University Press, 1993.

Hilmes, Michele. *Radio Voices: American Broadcasting, 1922–1952*. Minneapolis: University of Minnesota Press, 1997.

Hirsch, Arnold R. *Making of the Second Ghetto: Race and Housing in Chicago, 1940–1960*. Chicago: University of Chicago Press, 1998.

Honey, Maureen. *Bitter Fruit: African American Women in World War II*. Columbia: University of Missouri Press, 1999.

Honey, Michael K. *Black Workers Remember: An Oral History of Segregation, Unionism, and the Freedom Struggle*. Berkeley: University of California Press, 1999.

———. *Going Down Jericho Road: The Memphis Strike, Martin Luther King's Last Campaign*. New York: W. W. Norton & Co., 2007.

———. *Southern Labor and Black Civil Rights: Organizing Memphis Workers*. Urbana: University of Illinois Press, 1993.

Hughes, Langston. *The Panther and the Lash*. New York: Alfred A. Knopf, 1947.

Hunt, Darnell M. *Screening the Los Angeles Riots: Race, Seeing, and Resistance*. Cambridge: Cambridge University Press, 1997.

Hunter, Tera W. *To 'Joy My Freedom: Southern Black Women's Lives and Labors after the Civil War*. Cambridge: Harvard University Press, 1997.

Isserman, Maurice, and Michael Kazin. *America Divided: The Civil War of the 1960s*. New York: Oxford University Press, 2000.

Janiewski, Dolores E. *Sisterhood Denied: Race, Gender, and Class in a New South Community*. Philadelphia: Temple University Press, 1985.

Jones, Jacqueline. *Labor of Love, Labor of Sorrow: Black Women, Work, and the Family, from Slavery to the Present*. New York: Basic Books, 1985.

Kammen, Michael. *Mystic Chords of Memory: The Transformation of Tradition in American Culture*. New York: Alfred A. Knopf, 1991.

Kelley, Robin D. G. *Race Rebels: Culture, Politics, and the Black Working Class*. New York: Free Press, 1994.

Kessler-Harris, Alice. *Out to Work: A History of Wage-Earning Women in the United States*. New York: Oxford University Press, 1982.

King, Richard H. *Civil Rights and the Idea of Freedom*. Athens: University of Georgia Press, 1996.

Kleinman, Mark L. *A World of Hope, a World of Fear: Henry A. Wallace, Reinhold Niebuhr, and American Liberalism*. Columbus: Ohio State University Press, 2000.

Korstad, Robert Rodgers. *Civil Rights Unionism: Tobacco Workers and the Struggle for Democracy in the Mid-Twentieth-Century South*. Chapel Hill: University of North Carolina Press, 2003.

Kotz, Nick, and Mary Lynn Kotz. *A Passion for Equality: George A. Wiley and the Movement*. New York: W. W. Norton, 1977.

Kousser, Morgan. *Colorblind Injustice: Minority Voting Rights and the Undoing of the Second Reconstruction*. Chapel Hill: University of North Carolina Press, 1999.

Lamon, Lester C. *Black Tennesseans, 1900–1930*. Knoxville: University of Tennessee Press, 1977.

Lawson, Steven F. *Black Ballots: Voting Rights in the South, 1944–1969*. New York: Columbia University Press, 1976.

Leab, Daniel J. *From Sambo to Superspade: The Black Experience in Motion Pictures*. Boston: Houghton Mifflin, 1975.

Lee, George W. *Beale Street: Where the Blues Began*. New York: R. O. Ballou, 1934.

Lemke-Santangelo, Gretchen. *Abiding Courage: African American Migrant Women and the East Bay Community*. Chapel Hill: University of North Carolina Press, 1996.

Levine, Lawrence W. *Black Culture and Black Consciousness: Afro-American Folk Thought from Slavery to Freedom*. New York: Oxford University Press, 1977.

Lewis, Earl. *In Their Own Interests: Race, Class, and Power in Twentieth-Century Norfolk, Virginia*. Berkeley: University of California Press, 1991.

Lichtenstein, Nelson, Susan Strasser, and Roy Rosenzweig, eds. *Who Built America: Working People and the Nation's Economy, Politics, Culture, and Society*, Vol. 2, rev. ed. New York: Worth Publishers, 2000.

Lincoln, C. Eric, and Lawrence H. Mamiya. *The Black Church in the African American Experience*. Durham, N.C.: Duke University Press, 1990.

Link, William A. *The Paradox of Southern Progressivism, 1880–1930*. Chapel Hill: University of North Carolina Press, 1992.

Lipsitz, George. *"A Rainbow at Midnight": Labor and Culture in the 1940s*. Urbana: University of Illinois Press, 1994.

Logan, Rayford W., ed. *What the Negro Wants*. Chapel Hill: University of North Carolina Press, 1944.

Lornell, Kip. *"Happy in the Service of the Lord": Afro-American Gospel Quartets in Memphis*. Urbana: University of Illinois Press, 1988.

MacDonald, J. Fred. *Don't Touch that Dial! Radio Programming in American Life from 1920 to 1960*. Chicago: Nelson Hall, 1979.

Maltin, Leonard, and Richard W. Bann. *The Little Rascals: The Life and Times of Our Gang*. New York: Crown, 1992.

Marsh, Charles. *God's Long Summer: Stories of Faith and Civil Rights*. Princeton, N.J.: Princeton University Press, 1997.

Martin, Waldo E., Jr. *No Coward Soldiers: Black Cultural Politics and Postwar America*. Cambridge: Harvard University Press, 2005.

McCoy, Donald R., and Richard T. Ruetten. *Quest and Response: Minority Rights and the Truman Administration*. Lawrence: University Press of Kansas, 1973.

McKee, Margaret, and Fred Chisenhall. *Beale Black and Blue: Life and Music on Black America's Main Street*. Baton Rouge: Louisiana State University Press, 1981.

McKnight, Gerald. *The Last Crusade: Martin Luther King, Jr., the FBI, and the Poor People's Campaign*. Boulder: Westview Press, 1998.

McMillen, Neil R. *Dark Journey: Black Mississippians in the Age of Jim Crow*. Urbana: University of Illinois Press, 1989.

————, ed. *Remaking Dixie: The Impact of World War II on the American South*. Jackson: University Press of Mississippi, 1997.

Milkman, Ruth. *Gender at Work: The Dynamics of Job Segregation by Sex during World War II*. Urbana: University of Illinois Press, 1987.

Miller, William D. *Memphis during the Progressive Era, 1900–1917*. Memphis: Memphis State University Press, 1957.

————. *Mr. Crump of Memphis*. Baton Rouge: Louisiana State University Press, 1964.

Mills, Kay. *This Little Light of Mine: The Life of Fannie Lou Hamer*. New York: Plume Books, 1993.

Mitchell, H. L. *Mean Things Happening in This Land: The Life and Times of H. L. Mitchell, Co-Founder of the Southern Tenant Farmers' Union*. Montclair, N.J.: Allanheld, Osmun & Co. Publishers, 1979.

Monaghan, Frank. *Heritage of Freedom: The History and Significance of the Basic Documents of American Liberty*. Princeton, N.J.: Princeton University Press, 1947.

Morris, Aldon D. *Origins of the Civil Rights Movement: Black Communities Organizing for Change*. New York: Free Press, 1984.

Myrdal, Gunnar. *An American Dilemma: The Negro Problem and Modern Democracy*. New York: Harper and Row, 1944.

Nadasen, Premilla. *Welfare Warriors: The Welfare Rights Movement in the United States*. New York: Routledge, 2005.

Nelson, Jill. *Police Brutality: An Anthology*. New York: W. W. Norton, 2000.

Newman, Mark. *Entrepreneurs of Profit and Pride: From Black Appeal to Radio Soul*. New York: Praeger, 1988.

————. *Getting Right with God: Southern Baptists and Desegregation, 1945–95*. Tuscaloosa: University of Alabama Press, 2001.

Nieman, Donald G. *Promises to Keep: African-Americans and the Constitutional Order, 1776 to the Present*. New York: Oxford University Press, 1991.

O'Brien, Gail Williams. *The Color of the Law: Race, Violence, and Justice in the Post–World War II South*. Chapel Hill: University of North Carolina Press, 1999.

Orleck, Annelise. *Common Sense and a Little Fire: Women and Working-Class Politics in the United States, 1900–1965*. Chapel Hill: University of North Carolina Press, 1995.

———. *Storming Caesars Palace: How Black Mothers Fought Their Own War on Poverty*. Boston: Beacon Press, 2005.

Paris, Peter. *The Social Teaching of the Black Churches*. Philadelphia: Fortress Press, 1985.

Payne, Charles M. *I've Got the Light of Freedom: The Organizing Tradition and the Mississippi Freedom Struggle*. Berkeley: University of California Press, 1995.

Piven, Frances Fox, and Richard A. Cloward. *Poor People's Movements: Why They Succeed, How They Fail*. New York: Pantheon Books, 1977.

———. *Regulating the Poor: The Functions of Public Welfare*. New York: Pantheon Books, 1971.

Raboteau, Albert J. *A Fire in the Bones: Reflections on African-American Religious History*. Boston: Beacon Press, 1995.

Randall, Richard. *Censorship of the Movies: The Social and Political Control of a Mass Medium*. Madison: University of Wisconsin Press, 1968.

Redd, Lawrence N. *Rock in Rhythm and Blues: The Impact of Mass Media*. Lansing: Michigan State University, 1974.

Reed, Merl E. *Seedtime for the Modern Civil Rights Movement: The President's Committee on Fair Employment Practice, 1941–1946*. Baton Rouge: Louisiana State University Press, 1991.

Reverby, Susan M., ed. *Tuskegee's Truths: Rethinking the Tuskegee Syphilis Study*. Chapel Hill: University of North Carolina Press, 2000.

Robinson, Armstead L., and Patricia Sullivan. *New Directions in Civil Rights Studies*. Charlottesville: University Press of Virginia, 1991.

Robinson, Jo Ann Gibson. *The Montgomery Bus Boycott and the Women Who Started It: The Memoir of Jo Ann Gibson Robinson*. Edited with a foreword by David J. Garrow. Knoxville: University of Tennessee Press, 1987.

Rodgers, Daniel T. *Contested Truths: Keywords in American Politics Since Independence*. New York: Basic Books, 1987.

Rogers, Kim Lacy. *Righteous Lives: Narratives of the New Orleans Civil Rights Movement*. New York: New York University Press, 1993.

Rosswurm, Steve, ed. *The CIO's Left-Led Unions*. New Brunswick, N.J.: Rutgers University Press, 1992.

Ruiz, Vicki L. *Cannery Women, Cannery Lives: Mexican Women, Unionization, and the California Food Processing Industry, 1930–1950*. Albuquerque: University of New Mexico Press, 1987.

Savage, Barbara Dianne. *Broadcasting Freedom: Radio, War, and the Politics of Race, 1938–1948*. Chapel Hill: University of North Carolina Press, 1999.

Schulman, Bruce. *From Cotton Belt to Sunbelt: Federal Policy, Economic Development, and the Transformation of the South*. New York: Oxford University Press, 1991.

Sellers, Cleveland. *The River of No Return: The Autobiography of a Black Militant and the Life and Death of SNCC*. 1973. Reprint, Jackson: University Press of Mississippi, 1990.

Sigafoos, Robert A. *From Cotton Row to Beale Street: A Business History of Memphis*. Memphis: Memphis State University Press, 1979.

Silver, Christopher, and John V. Moeser. *The Separate City: Black Communities in the Urban South, 1940–1968*. Lexington: University Press of Kentucky, 1995.

Simon, Bryant. *A Fabric of Defeat: The Politics of South Carolina Millhands, 1910–1948*. Chapel Hill: University of North Carolina Press, 1998.

Smith, Suzanne E. *Dancing in the Street: Motown and the Cultural Politics of Detroit*. Cambridge: Harvard University Press, 1999.

Sugrue, Thomas J. *The Origins of the Urban Crisis: Race and Inequality in Postwar Detroit*. Princeton, N.J.: Princeton University Press, 1996.

Sullivan, Patricia. *Days of Hope: Race and Democracy in the New Deal Era*. Chapel Hill: University of North Carolina Press, 1996.

Swados, Harvey. *Standing Up for the People: The Life and Work of Estes Kefauver*. New York: E. P. Dutton & Co., 1972.

Thomas, Mary Martha. *Riveting and Rationing in Dixie: Alabama Women and the Second World War*. Tuscaloosa: University of Alabama Press, 1987.

Thomas, Richard W. *Life for Us Is What We Make It: Building Black Community in Detroit, 1915–1945*. Bloomington: Indiana University Press, 1992.

Thornton, J. Mills, III. *Dividing Lines: Municipal Politics and the Struggle for Civil Rights in Montgomery, Birmingham, and Selma*. Tuscaloosa: University of Alabama Press, 2002.

Tucker, David M. *Black Pastors and Leaders: Memphis, 1819–1972*. Memphis: Memphis State University Press, 1975.

———. *Lieutenant Lee of Beale Street*. Nashville: Vanderbilt University Press, 1971.

———. *Memphis Since Crump: Bossism, Blacks, and Civic Reformers, 1948–1968*. Knoxville: University of Tennessee Press, 1980.

Van Deburg, William L. *New Day in Babylon: The Black Power Movement and American Culture, 1965–1975*. Chicago: University of Chicago Press, 1992.

Von Eschen, Penny M. *Race Against Empire: Black Americans and Anticolonialism, 1937–1957*. Ithaca: Cornell University Press, 1997.

Wade-Gayles, Gloria. *Pushed Back to Strength: A Black Woman's Journey Home*. Boston: Beacon Press, 1993.

Wailoo, Keith. *Dying in the City of the Blues: Sickle Cell Anemia and the Politics of Race and Health*. Chapel Hill: University of North Carolina Press, 2001.

Walker, Randolph Meade. *The Metamorphosis of Sutton E. Griggs: The Transition from Black Radical to Conservative, 1913–1933*. Memphis: Walker Publishing, 1991.

Ward, Brian. *Just My Soul Responding: Rhythm and Blues, Black Consciousness, and Race Relations*. Berkeley: University of California Press, 1998.

———. *Radio and the Struggle for Civil Rights in the South*. Gainesville: University of Florida Press, 2004.

Washington, James M., ed. *A Testament of Hope: The Essential Writings and Speeches of Martin Luther King, Jr.* San Francisco: HarperCollins, 1986.

White, Graham, and John Maze. *Henry A. Wallace: His Search for a New World Order*. Chapel Hill: University of North Carolina Press, 1995.

Williams, Gilbert A. *Legendary Pioneers of Black Radio*. Westport, Conn.: Praeger, 1998.

Williams, Lee E., II. *Post-War Riots in America, 1919 and 1946*. Lewiston, N.Y.: Edwin Mellen Press, 1991.

Williams, Rhonda Y. *The Politics of Public Housing: Black Women's Struggles Against Urban Inequality*. New York: Oxford University Press, 2004.

Wilmore, Gayraud S. *Black Religion and Black Radicalism: An Interpretation of the Religious History of the Afro-American People*, 2d ed. Maryknoll, N.Y.: Orbis Books, 1983.

Withers, Ernest C. *Let Us March On! Selected Civil Rights Photographs of Ernest C. Withers, 1955–1968*. Boston: Massachusetts College of Art and Northeastern University, 1992.

Woodruff, Nan Elizabeth. *American Congo: The African American Freedom Struggle in the Delta*. Cambridge: Harvard University Press, 2003.

Woodson, Carter G. *The Mis-Education of the Negro*, 1933. Reprint, Trenton, N.J.: Africa World Press, 1990.

Wright, Gavin. *Old South, New South: Revolutions in the Southern Economy Since the Civil War*. New York: Basic Books, 1986.

Zangrando, Robert L. *The NAACP Crusade Against Lynching, 1909–1950*. Philadelphia: Temple University Press, 1980.

Articles

Anderson, Karen Tucker. "Last Hired, First Fired: Black Women Workers during World War II." *Journal of American History* 69 (June 1982): 82–97.

Becker, William H. "The Black Church: Manhood and Mission." In *African-American Religion: Interpretive Essays in History and Culture*, edited by Timothy E. Fulop and Albert J. Raboteau, 179–99. New York: Routledge, 1997.

Biles, Roger. "A Bittersweet Victory: Public School Desegregation in Memphis." *Journal of Negro Education* 55 (1986): 470–83.

Blight, David. "'For Something Beyond the Battlefield': Frederick Douglass and the Memory of the Civil War." *Journal of American History* 75 (March 1989): 1156–78.

Bond, Beverly Greene. "'Every Duty Incumbent Upon Them': African-American Women in Nineteenth-Century Memphis." *Tennessee Historical Quarterly* 59, no. 4 (2000): 254–73.

Boris, Eileen. "'The Right to Work Is the Right to Live!': Fair Employment and the Quest for Social Citizenship." In *Two Cultures of Rights: The Quest for Inclusion and Participation in Modern America and Germany*, edited by Manfred Berg and Martin H. Geyer, 121–42. Cambridge: Cambridge University Press and the German Historical Institute, 2002.

———. "'You Wouldn't Want One of 'Em Dancing with Your Wife': Racialized Bodies on the Job in World War II." *American Quarterly* 50 (March 1998): 77–108.

Born, Kate. "Memphis Negro Workingmen and the NAACP." *West Tennessee Historical Society Papers* 28 (1974): 96–107.

Bradsher, James Gregory. "Taking America's Heritage to the People: The Freedom Train Story." *Prologue* 17 (Winter 1985): 241.

Brown, Elsa Barkley. "Negotiating and Transforming the Public Sphere: African American Political Life in the Transition from Slavery to Freedom." In *Jumpin' Jim Crow: Southern Politics from Civil War to Civil Rights*, edited by Jane Dailey, Glenda Gilmore, and Bryant Simon, 28–66. Princeton, N.J.: Princeton University Press, 2000.

——. "To Catch the Vision of Freedom: Reconstructing Southern Black Women's Political History, 1865–1885." In *African American Women and the Vote, 1837–1965*, edited by Ann Gordon and Bettye Collier-Thomas, 66–99. Amherst, Mass.: University of Massachusetts Press, 1997.

Carby, Hazel V. "Policing the Black Woman's Body in an Urban Context." *Critical Inquiry* 18 (Summer 1992): 738–55.

Carter, Deborah Brown. "The Impact of the Civil Rights Movement on the Unionization of African-American Women: Local 282-Furniture Division-IUE, 1960–1988." In *Black Women in America*, edited by Kim Marie Vaz, 96–109. Thousand Oaks, Calif.: Sage Publications, 1995.

Ciscel, David, and Tom Collins. "'On the Road to Taipei': The Memphis Runaway Blues." *Southern Exposure* 4 (Spring 1976): 143–49.

Collins, Thomas W. "Unionization in a Secondary Labor Market." *Human Organization* 36 (Summer 1997): 135–41.

Collins, Tom, and David Ciscel. "An Analysis of the RCA Television Assembly Plant in Memphis, Tennessee: Why It Closed." *Mid-South Quarterly Business Review* 14 (April 1976): 3–7.

Cone, James H. "Black Theology as Liberation Theology." In *African American Religious Studies: An Interdisciplinary Anthology*, edited by Gayraud Wilmore, 177–207. Durham, N.C.: Duke University Press, 1989.

Cosgrove, Stuart. "The Zoot-Suit and Style Warfare." *History Workshop*, issue no. 18 (Autumn 1984): 39–50.

Cotter, Joseph S. "Is It Because I Am Black?" In *The Book of American Negro Poetry*, edited by James Welden Johnson, 186. New York: Harcourt, Brace and Co., 1922.

Crenshaw, Kimberlé Williams. "Mapping the Margins: Intersectionality, Identity Politics, and Violence Against Women of Color." In *Critical Race Theory: The Key Writings that Formed the Movement*, edited by Kimberlé Crenshaw et al., 357–83. New York: New Press, 1995.

Current, Gloster. "Which Way Out. . . ?" *Crisis* 68 (March 1961): 135–36.

Dailey, Jane, Glenda Gilmore, and Bryant Simon, eds. *Jumpin' Jim Crow: Southern Politics from Civil War to Civil Rights*. Princeton, N.J.: Princeton University Press, 2000.

Dalfiume, Richard. "The Forgotten Years of the Negro Revolution." In *The Negro in Depression and War: Prelude to Revolution, 1930–1945*, edited by Bernard Sternsher, 298–310. Chicago: Quadrangle Books, 1969.

Daniel, Pete. "Rhythm of the Land." *Agricultural History* 68 (Fall 1994): 1–22.

David, George F. "Deep in the Delta." *Journal of Human Relations* 2 (Spring 1954): 72–75.

Diamond, M. Jerome. "The Impact of the Negro Vote in Contemporary Tennessee Politics." *Tennessee Law Review* 34 (1966–1967): 454–57.

Dill, Bonnie Thornton. "The Dialectic of Black Womanhood." *Signs* 4 (Spring 1979): 543–55.

Dowdy, Wayne. "'Something for the Colored People': Memphis Mayor Frank Tobey and the East Olive Bombing." *West Tennessee Historical Society Papers* 51 (1997): 108–15.

Du Bois, W. E. Burghart. "The Talented Tenth." In *The Negro Problem: A Series of Articles by Representative Negroes of Today*, 33–75. New York: James Pott and Co., 1903.

Flug, Michael. "Organized Labor and the Civil Rights Movement of the 1960s: The Case of the Maryland Freedom Union." *Labor History* 31 (Summer 1990): 322–46.

Gaines, Jane M. "'These Boots Are Made for Walkin': Nancy Sinatra and the Goodyear Tire Sound-Alike." Chapter 4 in *Contested Culture: The Image, the Voice, and the Law*. Chapel Hill: University of North Carolina Press, 1991.

Goings, Kenneth W., and Gerald L. Smith. "'Unhidden' Transcripts: Memphis and African American Agency, 1862–1920." *Journal of Urban History* 21 (March 1995): 372–94.

Grant, Jacquelyn. "Black Women's Experience As a Source for Doing Theology, with Special Reference to Christology." In *African American Religious Studies: An Interdisciplinary Anthology*, edited by Gayraud Wilmore, 208–27. Durham, N.C.: Duke University Press, 1989.

Green, Laurie B. "Race, Gender, and Labor in 1960s Memphis: 'I *Am* a Man' and the Meaning of Freedom." *Journal of Urban History* 30 (March 2004): 465–89.

———. "The Rural-Urban Matrix in the 1950s South: Rethinking Racial Justice Struggles in Memphis." In *From the Grassroots to the Supreme Court:* Brown v. Board of Education *and American Democracy*, edited by Peter F. Lau, 270–99. Durham, N.C.: Duke University Press, 2004.

———. "'A Struggle of the Mind': Black Working-Class Women's Organizing in Memphis and the Mississippi Delta, 1960s–1990s." In *Frontline Feminisms: Women, War and Resistance*, paperback ed., edited by Marguerite Waller and Jennifer Rycenga, 399–418. New York: Routledge, 2001.

———. "'Where Would the Negro Women Apply for Work?': Gender, Race, and Labor in Wartime Memphis." *Labor: Studies in Working-Class History* 3, no. 2 (2006): 95–117.

Griffith, Robert. "Selling of America: The Advertising Council and American Politics, 1942–1960." *Business History Review* 57, no 3 (Autumn 1983): 388–412.

Haiken, Elizabeth. "'The Lord Helps Those Who Help Themselves': Black Laundresses in Little Rock, Arkansas, 1917–1921." *Arkansas Historical Quarterly* 49 (Spring 1990): 20–50.

Higginbotham, Evelyn Brooks. "African-American Women's History and the Meta-Language of Race." *Signs* 17 (Winter 1992): 251–74.

Hill, Herbert. "The Racial Practices of Organized Labor: The Contemporary Record." In *The Negro and the American Labor Movement*, edited by Julius Jacobson, 286–357. Garden City, N.Y.: Anchor Books, 1968.

Hine, Darlene Clark. "Rape and the Inner Lives of Black Women in the Middle

West: Preliminary Thoughts on the Culture of Dissemblance." In *Unequal Sisters: A Multicultural Reader in U.S. Women's History*, edited by Ellen Carol DuBois and Vicki L. Ruiz, 292–97. New York: Routledge, 1990.

Honey, Michael. "Martin Luther King, Jr., the Crisis of the Black Working Class, and the Memphis Sanitation Strike." *Southern Labor in Transition*, edited by Robert H. Zieger, 146–75. Knoxville: University of Tennessee Press, 1997.

hooks, bell. "The Oppositional Gaze: Black Female Spectators." In *Movies and Mass Culture*, edited by John Belton, 247–64. New Brunswick, N.J.: Rutgers University Press, 1996.

Hughes, Langston. "Freedom Train." *New Republic*, September 15, 1947, 27.

———. "The Negro Speaks of Rivers." In *The Collected Poems of Langston Hughes*, edited by Arnold Rampersad, 23. New York: Vintage Books, 1994.

Jackson, Lynette. "'Stray Women' and 'Girls on the Move': Gender, Space, and Disease in Colonial and Post-Colonial Zimbabwe." In *Sacred Spaces and Public Quarrels: African Culture and Economic Landscapes*, edited by Paul Tiyambe Zeleza and Ezekiel Kalipeni, 147–67. Trenton, N.J.: Africa World Press, Inc., 1999.

Kammen, Michael. "The Public Sector and the Politics of Tradition in Cold War America." Chapter 17 in *Mystic Chords of Memory: The Transformation of Traditions in American Culture*. New York: Alfred A. Knopf, 1991.

Kelley, Robin D. G. "'Slanging Rocks . . . Palestinian Style': Dispatches from the Occupied Zones of North America." In *Police Brutality: An Anthology*, edited by Jill Nelson, 21–59. New York: W. W. Norton, 2000.

King, William M. "The Reemerging Revolutionary Consciousness of the Reverend Dr. Martin Luther King, Jr., 1965–1968." *Journal of Negro History* 71 (Winter 1986): 1–22.

Korstad, Robert, and Nelson Lichtenstein. "Opportunities Found and Lost: Labor, Radicals, and the Early Civil Rights Movement." *Journal of American History* 75 (December 1988): 786–811.

Kunzel, Regina G. "White Neurosis, Black Pathology: Constructing Out-of-Wedlock Pregnancy in the Wartime and Postwar United States." In *Not June Cleaver: Women and Gender in Postwar America*, edited by Joanne Meyerowitz, 304–31. Philadelphia: Temple University Press, 1994.

Kupferman, Theodore R., and Philip J. O'Brien Jr. "Motion Picture Censorship: The Memphis Blues." *Cornell Law Quarterly* 36 (Winter 1951): 273–300.

Leachman, Ida. "Black Women and Labor Unions in the South: From the 1970s to the 1990s." In *Frontline Feminisms: Women, War and Resistance*, edited by Marguerite Waller and Jennifer Rycenga. New York: Routledge, 2001.

Lee, George W. "The Political Upheaval in Memphis." *The Messenger* 10 (February 1928): 30–31.

———. "These 'Colored' United States: Tennessee — The Last Stand of Justice in the Solid South." *The Messenger* 7 (July 1925): 252–53.

Little, Stuart J. "The Freedom Train: Citizenship and Postwar Political Culture 1946–1949." *American Studies* 34 (Spring 1993): 35–68.

Moses, Wilson J. "Literary Garveyism: The Novels of Reverend Sutton E. Griggs." *Phylon* 40 (Fall 1979): 203–16.

Nasstrom, Kathryn L. "Down to Now: Memory, Narrative, and Women's Leadership in the Civil Rights Movement in Atlanta, Georgia." *Gender & History* 11 (April 1999): 113–44.

Nelson, Bruce. "Organized Labor and the Struggle for Black Equality in Mobile during World War II." *Journal of American History* 80 (December 1993): 952–88.

Nelson-Cisneros, Victor B. "UCAPAWA Organizing Activities in Texas, 1935–50." *Aztlan* 9 (1978): 71–84.

Painter, Nell Irvin. "Hill, Thomas, and the Use of Racial Stereotypes." *Race-ing Justice, En-Gendering Power: Essays on Anita Hill, Clarence Thomas, and the Construction of Social Reality*, edited by Toni Morrison, 200–214. New York: Pantheon Books, 1992.

Payne, Elizabeth Anne. "'What Ain't Been Doing?': Historical Reflections on Women and the Arkansas Delta." In *The Arkansas Delta: Land of Paradox*, edited by Jeannie Whayne and Willard B. Gatewood, 128–49. Fayetteville: University of Arkansas Press, 1993.

Plank, David N. "Contrasting Patterns in Black School Politics: Atlanta and Memphis, 1865–1985." *Journal of Negro Education* 60 (1991): 203–18.

Regester, Charlene. "Black Films, White Censors: Oscar Micheaux Confronts Censorship in New York, Virginia, and Chicago." In *Movie Censorship and American Culture*, edited by Francis G. Couvares, 159–86. Washington, D.C.: Smithsonian Institution Press, 1996.

Rosen, Hannah, "'Not that Sort of Women': Race, Gender, and Sexual Violence during the Memphis Riot of 1866." In *Sex, Love, Race: Crossing Boundaries in North American History*, edited by Martha Hodes, 267–93. New York: New York University Press, 1999.

Thelen, David. "Memory and American History." *Journal of American History* 75 (March 1989): 1117–29.

Thompson, Betty E. Taylor. "Sutton Elbert Griggs." In *Afro-American Writers Before the Harlem Renaissance*, edited by Trudier Harris, 140–48. Vol. 50, *Dictionary of Literary Biography*. Detroit: Gale Research Company, 1986.

Truman, Harry S. "Special Message to the Congress on Greece and Turkey: The Truman Doctrine." *Public Papers of the Presidents of the United States, Harry S Truman, 1947*. Washington, D.C.: Government Printing Office, 1963.

Velie, Lester. "You Can't See That Movie: Censorship in Action." *Collier's*, May 6, 1950.

White, John. "Civil Rights in Conflict: The 'Birmingham Plan' and the Freedom Train, 1947." *Alabama Review* 52 (April 1999): 121–41.

White, Sarah. "Change in a Closed Little Town." *Southern Exposure* (1997): 44–46.

Woodruff, Nan Elizabeth. "Mississippi Delta Planters and Debates over Mechanization, Labor, and Civil Rights in the 1940s." *Journal of Southern History* 60 (May 1994): 263–84.

———. "Pick or Fight: The Emergency Farm Labor Program in the Arkansas and Mississippi Deltas during World War II." *Agricultural History* 64 (Spring 1990): 74–85.

Wriggins, Jennifer. "Rape, Racism, and the Law." *Harvard Women's Law Journal* 6 (1983): 103–41.

Dissertations, Unpublished Papers, and Theses

Bond, Beverly Greene. "'Till Fair Aurora Rise': African-American Women in Memphis, Tennessee, 1840–1915." Ph.D. diss., University of Memphis, 1996.

Brown, Millicent Ellison. "Civil Rights Activism in Charleston, South Carolina, 1940–1970." Ph.D. diss., Florida State University, 1997.

Carter, Deborah Brown. "The Local Labor Union as a Social Movement Organization: Local 282, Furniture Division-IUE, 1943–1988." Ph.D. diss., Vanderbilt University, 1988.

Cooper, Arnold. "Five Black Educators: Founders of Schools in the South, 1881–1915." Ph.D. diss., Iowa State University, 1983.

Dupont, Jill. "'The Self in the Ring, The Self in Society': Boxing and American Culture from Jack Johnson to Joe Louis." Ph.D. diss., University of Chicago, 2000.

Fairclough, Adam. "The Left, the Labor Movement, and the Transformation of the NAACP: Louisiana, 1936–45." Paper presented at the Annual Meeting of the American Historical Association, Chicago, January 6, 1995.

Fleming, Samuel H. Randolph, III. "Rural-Urban Migration of Blacks: Changing Social Organization in Memphis." Ph.D. diss., University of Virginia, 1974.

Flug, Michael. "Continuity and Discontinuity in Capitalist Production and Labor Struggles in the Deep South." Paper presented at the North American Labor History Conference, Detroit, Michigan, October 17–19, 1996.

Green, Laurie B. "Battling the Plantation Mentality: Consciousness, Culture, and the Politics of Race, Class, and Gender in Memphis, 1940–1968." Ph.D. diss., University of Chicago, 1999.

———. "'Out of This Land of Sufring': Black Womanhood, Consciousness, and the Great Migration, 1916–1930." Seminar Paper, University of Chicago, 1993.

Helper, Laura. "Whole Lot of Shakin' Going On: An Ethnography of Race Relations and Crossover Audiences for Rhythm & Blues and Rock & Roll in 1950s Memphis." Ph.D. diss., Rice University, 1997.

Jarrett, Vernon. Speech for panel, "Black Journalism in the Chicago Renaissance," May 16, 1998. Vivian G. Harsh Research Collection Archives, Chicago Public Library, Chicago. Videotaped recording.

Melton, Gloria Brown. "Blacks in Memphis, Tennessee, 1920–1955: A Historical Study." Ph.D. diss., Washington State University, 1982.

Nasstrom, Kathryn L. "Women, the Civil Rights Movement and the Politics of Historical Memory in Atlanta, 1946–1973." Ph.D. diss., University of North Carolina at Chapel Hill, 1993.

Newman, Kathy. "Marketing Identities: Broadcast Advertising and Consumer Activism in Post-War America." Ph.D. diss., Yale University, 1996.

Payne, Elizabeth Anne. "African American Activism in the Southern Tenant Farmers' Union." Paper presented at the Annual Meeting of the American Historical Association, Chicago, January 6, 1995.

Rise, Eric W. "The NAACP's Legal Strategy Against Police Brutality, 1920–1945." Paper presented at the Annual Meeting of the Law and Society Association, St. Louis, May 29–June 1, 1997.

Shelton, William E. "Movie Censorship in Memphis, 1920–1955." M.A. Thesis, Memphis State University, 1970.

Sugarmon, Russell. "Fight for Freedom: Civil Rights in Memphis." Speech presented at the Hooks Symposium on Social Change, University of Memphis, November 14, 2000.

White, Sarah. "Organizing the Mississippi Delta Catfish Industry: An Autobiographical Work-in-Progress." Paper presented at the North American Labor History Conference, Detroit, October 17–19, 1996.

Whittington, Erica L. "From the Campus to the Globe: Internationalism and American Postwar Student Activism, 1945–1960." Ph.D. diss. in progress, University of Texas at Austin, 2007.

Film and Radio Productions

Black Radio: Telling It Like It Was. Exec. prod. Jacquie Gales Webb. Smithsonian Productions, 1996.

The WLOK Story. Dir. Joann Self. 56 min. Gilliam Foundation, 2002.

Acknowledgments

As I call to mind the Memphians and non-Memphians who supported this project, I realize that my words here will no doubt fall short of the gratitude I feel, both to university scholars and to people whose life work lies far from the university.

I first wish to thank the women and men whose struggles, stories, and reflections became central to this project. Each interview became far more than a gathering of information, transforming instead into a challenging exchange about how to interpret historical memories. Indeed, these conversations became crucial to my decision to organize the book around the concept of the "plantation mentality" and the battles against it, in both thought and deed. I would particularly like to note the invaluable insights and encouragement of Ida Leachman, president of Local 282 of the furniture workers union and a descendant of Ida B. Wells, whose courageous writing against lynching in the 1890s resonated in the struggles of black Memphians during the twentieth-century black freedom movement.

The encouragement and engagement of many scholars have had a profound impact on this project since its inception. I am especially grateful to Thomas C. Holt for his challenging questions, thoughtful suggestions, and persistent support. His commitment to working out the problem of race and freedom, historically and in the present, has been inspirational. Michael Flug, director of the Vivian G. Harsh Research Collection for Afro-American History and Literature, at the Carter G. Woodson branch of the Chicago Public Library, has been extraordinarily helpful by urging me to think in new ways about the black freedom movement. I am similarly grateful to George Chauncey, who encouraged my work first at New York University, as a visiting professor, and then at the University of Chicago. Leora Auslander and Julie Saville also offered crucial insights during the completion of the dissertation.

In addition to Tom Holt and Julie Saville, several scholars of race, gender, class, and freedom in the postemancipation era have influenced my work. I especially thank several women scholars in that field who became close colleagues and friends, including Laura Edwards, Hannah Rosen, Nancy Bercaw, Cynthia Blair, and Gretchen Long. In the midst of my research I learned that Gretchen's great uncle was the courageous Rev. George A. Long who stood up to Boss Crump in the 1940s. I remain deeply appreciative of my thought-provoking discussions about the "plantation mentality" with each of these wonderful scholars and friends.

The women historians in my writing group at the University of Texas work in quite different fields, yet they made equally important contributions. For their sisterly support and intellectual insights during my final preparation of the manuscript, I am enormously grateful to Denise Spellberg, a scholar of Middle Eastern studies;

Kimberly Alidio, who focuses on Filipinos and American imperialism; and Elizabeth Bishop, whose scholarship spans the Middle East, Russia, and the United States.

I am similarly appreciative of discussions with anthropologist Laura Helper, whose exuberant intellectual engagement with this project since we met in Memphis, where she was working on her forthcoming book on race, ethnicity, and crossover music, has always been inspiring; with Tracy Sharpley-Whiting, a scholar of French and black feminist literature and theory; and with Jennifer Rycenga, a scholar of women's and religious studies.

The roots of this work go back to my graduate studies at New York University as an M.A. student, where I particularly benefited from the encouragement of Thomas Bender, the late Warren Dean, Carole Groneman, and Daniel Walkowitz, along with the Women's History Program faculty: Penelope Johnson, Molly Nolan, Susan Ware, and Marilyn Young; as well as the graduate students who met weekly at 8:00 A.M. over breakfast during my final year there. I especially thank Sarah Judson for our many hours of discussion of African American and women's history.

At the University of Chicago, I was fortunate to encounter a group of deeply thoughtful and engaged scholars. Along with those I have already mentioned, I would like to thank faculty members Kathleen Neils Conzen, Amy Dru Stanley, and Norma Field for their precious time, intellectual rigor, and crucial questions. I was also privileged to encounter and become friends with talented graduate students focusing on race and ethnicity, gender and sexuality, including Gabriela Arredondo, David Churchill, Kathleen Flake, Susan Gooding, Sharon Hayashi, Chad Heap, Theresa Mah, Miriam Paullac, Nayan Shah, Alexandra Stern, and Derek Vaillant. Many others at the university influenced my work, including members of the interdisciplinary Gender and Society Workshop, the Social History Workshop, and the Sawyer Seminar on Religion, Law, and Identity, sponsored by the Divinity School, and appreciate the comments I received on early drafts of material in this book.

In Memphis, numerous individuals enabled and enriched my research trips. Annie Rolack, a civil rights and labor activist offered me a place to stay and important conversations. Lynet Uttal and Dan Veroff, and their sons David, Eli, and Benjamin, also welcomed me as a houseguest, sometimes for weeks at a time. My late-night talks with Lynet, then on the University of Memphis faculty, helped me make sense of my research. Amit Sen, who works on Hegel, Fanon, and race in the University of Memphis philosophy department, also offered me a place to stay. Allison Graham, co-producer of the important film documentary *At the River I Stand*, on the sanitation strike, became a good friend and continues to stimulate my thinking about southern culture.

When I returned to Memphis in 2000–2001 as a Rockefeller Scholar at the University of Memphis's Center for Research on Women, program directors Barbara Ellen Smith and Kenneth Goings supported my project in many ways. Smith, Goings, and participants in the interdisciplinary faculty Race and Gender Salon, including Nancy Bercaw, Mary Beth Mader, Fred Knight, David Ciscel, Kimberly Nettles, and others, read an early draft of the final chapter of the book and contributed useful comments on the meanings of "I *Am* a Man." Several others in Memphis who have offered invaluable resources and insights include former national director of the NAACP Dr.

Benjamin Hooks; former Memphis NAACP executive secretary Maxine Smith; Le-Moyne professor Randolph Meade Walker; Center for Southern Folklore director Judy Peizer; and founder of True Story Pictures, Joann Self.

At the University of Texas at Austin, I have greatly benefited from my extraordinarily supportive colleagues, including many who helped this project come to completion: Kimberly Alidio, Judy Coffin, Toyin Falola, Alison Frazier, Aline Helg, Madeline Hsu, Mark Lawrence, Karl Miller, Gail Minault, Martha Newman, Robert Olwell, David Oshinsky, Denise Spellberg, Michael Stoff, Margherita Zanasi, and especially department chair Alan Tully, who has provided crucial assistance on several occasions. I am similarly grateful to Janet Davis, chair of American Studies, whose support has been invaluable; and to Gretchen Ritter, director of the Center for Women's and Gender Studies.

A number of graduate students contributed to this work, whether directly or indirectly. I would like to thank Verónica Martinez for her research assistance at the National Archives, and more generally the students in the graduate symposium, Critical Studies in the History of Women, Gender, and Sexuality, including Lissa Bolletino, Eric Busch, Leah Deane, Deirdre Doughty, Sandra Frink, Rebecca Montes, Michele Reid, and Erica Whittington.

During my final year of work on the book, I was a fellow in the University of Texas Humanities Institute, whose subject that year was "Remembering and Forgetting, Collecting and Discarding." I am deeply appreciative of suggestions I received from members of this group after they read drafts of portions of my manuscript, particularly those who have continued to meet regularly: Ellen Cunningham-Kruppa, Laura Furman, Pauline Strong, and Stacy Wolf.

Many other scholars influenced my work by commenting on drafts presented at professional conferences, in journals and in edited collections. For their thought-provoking questions and comments, which pushed me to see my research and writing from new vantage points, I would like to thank Beverly G. Bond, Eileen Boris, Elsa Barkley Brown, Patricia Cooper, Connie Curry, Gerald Gill, Darlene Clark Hine, Tracy K'Meyer, Kathy Nasstrom, Joe William Trotter, and Nan Elizabeth Woodruff. Christina Greene, Laura Helper, Hannah Rosen, and Rhonda Williams have all had an impact on my work through our participation on conference panels, as we shared early portions of our works-in-progress. I also benefited greatly from the symposium on the fiftieth anniversary of *Brown v. Board of Education*, organized by Peter Lau and the Center for Southern Studies at the University of South Carolina, where I presented an early draft of Chapter 6 and participated in a trip to Clarendon County to meet with original participants in the school desegregation litigation there, which eventually wound its way to the Supreme Court.

The innovative resourcefulness of archivists in many repositories enabled and enriched the research for this book. I am especially indebted to archivists and librarians at the Memphis and Shelby County Room of the Memphis Public Library; the Shelby County Archives; Special Collections at the University of Memphis; the Hollis Price Library at LeMoyne-Owen College; and the Vivian G. Harsh Research Collection of Afro-American History and Literature at the Carter G. Woodson branch of the Chicago Public Library. Several archivists engaged in extensive dialogue with me about my research; they include Ed Frank at the University of Memphis, John Dougan at the Shelby County Archives, Wayne Dowdy at the Memphis Public Library, and Michael Flug at the Harsh Collection. I am also grateful to those who offered access to papers and photographs outside of archives, including Joe Mullins and Autry Parker with the Memphis Area Project–South (MAP-South); Joann Self of True Story Pictures; and Willie Pearl Butler. I would also like to thank Lynn Phares, a good friend since we were graduate students in New York, for her research help at the National Archives.

Another major resource was the phenomenal collection of oral history tapes and transcripts that comprise the Behind the Veil: Documenting African American Life in the Jim Crow South Collection. The Behind the Veil Project, directed by William Chafe, Raymond Gavins, and Robert Korstad through the Center for Documentary Studies at Duke, provided funding for my summer 1995 interviews, now included in this collection. I am grateful to Leslie Brown and Annie Valk, field directors, and to Memphis interviewers Doris Dixon, Paul Ortiz, and Mausiki Scales.

This project would have been far more difficult without the financial help from several research grants and fellowships, including graduate fellowships at New York University and the University of Chicago. While completing my dissertation, I benefited from a Mellon Summer Research Grant, an Arthur Mann American History Graduate Award, a Markovitz Dissertation Fellowship, and a Sawyer Seminar Graduate Fellowship, all at the University of Chicago; an Albert J. Beveridge Grant from the American Historical Association; a Woodrow Wilson Dissertation Grant in Women's Studies; and a Louisville Institute dissertation fellowship. As I worked on my book manuscript, I was awarded a Rockefeller Humanities Postdoctoral Fellowship that allowed me to spend the year at the Center for Research on Women in Memphis. I also would like to thank the University of Texas for a Summer Research Award and Dean's Fellowship that supported research and writing as I completed the manuscript.

My relationship with the University of North Carolina Press extends back to the period when I was completing the dissertation, when Kate Torrey and David Perry discussed with me the potential of this project as a published work. Since he became senior editor at the Press, Chuck Grench has contributed enormously to this project. This is also true of Waldo Martin and Patricia Sullivan, editors of the John Hope Franklin Series, who have generously and consistently offered their support and feedback. I feel privileged to have had Jacquelyn Dowd Hall, Joe William Trotter, and Waldo Martin as manuscript readers; their suggestions helped make this a stronger work and I thank them warmly. I am also grateful to assistant editor Katy O'Brien, who brought knowledge — and calm — at important moments, and to manuscript editor Mary Caviness, who brought extraordinary perceptiveness to her work on the project.

Above all, perhaps, my family has been a wellspring of support during the most exciting and difficult times of my work on this project. My parents, Helaine and Jerry Green, introduced me to the civil rights movement in New Jersey and to the books in their living room by James Baldwin, Ralph Ellison, and Malcolm X, and years later helped in countless ways as I researched and wrote this book. My sisters, Andrea and

Claudia Green, have likewise been enthusiastic supporters as they watched this project take me from New Jersey to the South in pursuit of answers to the questions with which we grew up. My grandfather, Max Green, passed away before this book was completed but never failed to ask me about my research and to discuss my ideas. My grandmother Flossie Green, at age 100, had asked me to place her first on the list to receive a copy. Sadly, she died in February 2007 just before the book's publication, but her avid love of history and books, I hope, lives on here.

Finally, Jim Fabris's support throughout every stage of this work, from a mere flash in the pan to its completion, and through the move of our family to Memphis and then Austin, has been imaginative, incisive, and ceaseless. His engagement in hours of discussion about this project has helped make it possible and is reflected in myriad ways throughout the work. Our daughter, Sarafina Rose, remains my inspiration. Born shortly after this project was begun, she has grown up with it, offered to become my illustrator and, at age eight, started to write her own books. Whether or not they reach completion, I treasure her quest for knowledge and creative expression.

Index

Page numbers in italics refer to maps and photographs.

Broadway Rhythms (movie), 155
Bronze Venus (movie), 155
Brooks, J. B., *168*
Brophy, Thomas D'Arcy, 116, 324
    (n. 15)
Brotherhood of Sleeping Car Porters,
    73–74
Brown, Rev. A. D., 140
Brown, Annie, 36
Brown, Charles W., Jr., 158–59
Brown, Elsa Barkley, 315–16 (n. 12)
Brown, Gerry, *168*, 170–71
Brown, Ina, 135
Brown, James, 258, 287
Brown, Lorraine Guilford, 90–91
Browning, Gordon, 107, 137, 138, 140,
    199
Brown v. Board of Education, 120, 177–
    78, 183, 184, 185, 194–200, 206–8,
    214–15, 218, 219, 290, 292, 343
    (n. 57), 353 (n. 30)
Bruce, C. Arthur, 137
Bruce, Neil, 135
Bryant, Susie, 15–18, 23, 24
Buckeye Cotton Oil Company, 19, 69–
    73, 80, 187–88, 212, 312 (n. 68)
Buckman, Stanley, 219
Building trades unions, 25–26, 67–68
Bunche, Ralph, 18, 25, 33, 303 (n. 60)
Bunton, Henry, 216, 217
Burch, Lucius, 134, 137, 220, 239
Burrows, Clinton, 276–77
Burton, Charles, 72
Buses. *See* Public transportation
Businesses: black businesses, 7, 20, 35,
    37, 38–40, 43, 192–93; and Ku Klux
    Klan, 36; on Beale Street, 38–40,
    45–46; desegregation of Main Street
    in Memphis, 220, 232–33, 236–37,
    238, 239, 240–41, 254–55; Ralph
    Bunche on loss of black businesses,
    303 (n. 60)
Butler, Washington, Jr., 269
Butler, Willie Pearl (Ellis), 271–75

Cabin in the Sky (movie), 152–54
Calloway, Cab, 145, 152, 155–56
Campbell, Rev. A. J., 97, 102
Capers, Gerald M., 298 (n. 7)
Carmichael, Stokely, 352 (n. 14)
Carpenter, Ernestine Hill, 239–40, 249
Carpenter, Gladys, 280
Carpenter and Joiners Union, 29
Carter, Daniel, 9, 44
Carter, Deborah Brown, 258
Carter, Gertrude, 60–61, 65–67
Censorship: of movies generally, 9,
    145, 182, 292; Memphis Board of
    Censors, 142, 148; of movies after
    World War II, 142, 144, 159–63,
    334 (n. 47); of movies before World
    War II, 148–51; of dances, 149; self-
    censorship of movies, 149; Memphis
    municipal code on, 149, 153–55;
    of plays, 149, 161–62; of fight film,
    149–50; of movies during wartime,
    151–59; and racial restrictions,
    153–55, 332 (n. 28); of music, 166;
    municipal censorship boards, 331
    (nn. 13–14); state legislation on, 331
    (n. 13)
Chafe, William, 345 (n. 7)
Chalmers, Artherene, 24–25
Chandler, Walter: and Crump machine,
    33, 39; and Memphis Commission
    on Interracial Co-operation, 41;
    and black leadership, 42–44; and
    defense industry jobs, 47, 54, 55,
    68; and Eleanor Clubs, 58; and
    washerwoman image of laundry
    workers, 64; and A. Philip Randolph,
    75; and police violence and
    harassment, 89–90, 316–17 (n. 23),
    317 (n. 26), 319 (n. 53); and public
    transportation, 92; and juvenile
    delinquency conference, 133; and
    movie censorship, 153, 155; and
    testing for venereal diseases, 315
    (n. 4)
Chauffeurs Union, 62

Chicago Defender, 76, 77–78, 92, 118, 150, 192

Chickasaw Ordnance Works, 52, 53, 301 (n. 31)

Chickasaw Wood Products, 29

Christianity. *See* Churches

Church, Robert, Jr., 32–33, 35, 38, 43, 75, 303 (n. 59)

Church, Robert, Sr., 35, 37

Churches: music in, 7–8; and black freedom movement generally, 12–13, 18; and A. Philip Randolph, 12–13, 76–77; and mutual aid associations, 17; and labor unions, 31; and segregation, 33; and political participation, 36; and Crump machine, 42–43, 132, 190; and police violence, 97, 98, 102, 105, 107–8; and Freedom Train, 124, 126–27; and 1948 elections, 140; and religious programming on radio, 166, 174–76; and Patio 6 episode, 183, 211; and voter registration, 208; and student sit-ins, 234–35; and desegregation, 234–35, 237; "kneel-ins" and desegregation of white churches, 241–42, 247–49, 255; Assembly of God Church revival, 247–49; Church of God in Christ, 248, 350 (n. 74); and sanitation workers' strike, 280. *See also specific ministers*

Citizens' Association of Memphis and Shelby County (CA), 220

Citizens' Councils, 184, 185, 194–95, 198, 227

Citizens on the Move for Equality (COME), 280, 281

Civic clubs, 199–210, 212, 214–15, 220–21, 232

Civic Research Council (CRC), 207–8

Civil rights: and equal rights, 2; and freedom, 4; meaning of, 4; and sit-in movement, 6, 218, 220, 224, 226, 232–41, 249, 253, 254, 273, 275;

scholarship on, 11; and President Truman, 114, 117–18, 120–21, 134, 136, 137; and Freedom Train, 118; and 1948 election, 137–38; and labor unions, 139, 187, 210–14, 258–65; and Cold War, 184, 189–90; and "new militant" blacks in 1950s, 195, 196; and civic club activism, 199–210, 214–15; voter registration of sharecroppers, 218, 226–32; and Poor People's Campaign, 251; Memphis as crossroads for civil rights movement, 253; and Memphis march following King's death, 286–87; and equality of access, 330 (n. 3); and radio, 335 (n. 59). *See also* Black freedom movement; Desegregation; Freedom; King, Martin Luther, Jr.; Racial equality; Voting

Civil Rights Act (1964), 3, 250, 252, 253, 255, 256, 258, 262–66, 289, 293

Clapp, Aubrey B., 26, 54, 309 (n. 29)

Clark, Alzada, 187, 213

Clark, LeRoy, 187, 259

Clark, Tom C., 99, 116, 117, 120–21

Clement, Frank, 199, 255, 265

Coasters, 167, 181, 243

Cobb, Rev. Clarence, 174–75

Coblenz, William, 116

Coe, Clarence, 214

Coe, Lint, 214

Cohen, Lizabeth, 330–31 (n. 3)

Colbert, Claudette, 157

Cold War: and freedom, 6; and labor unions, 26, 30, 40, 184–89, 297 (n. 18); and Freedom Train, 112–17, 123, 140–41; and Truman Doctrine, 115, 117, 134, 159; and movie censorship, 159–63; and NAACP, 184, 189–90; and House Un-American Activities Committee, 185; and Senate Internal Security Subcommittee, 185, 188–89; and

Citizens' Councils, 194–95; and democracy, 194–95, 215. *See also* Anticommunism

Cole, Dick "Cane," 246

Coleman, Rev. E., Jr., 127

Coleman, F. D., 127

Colleges. *See* Higher education; *and specific colleges*

Collins, Thomas, 356 (n. 58)

Columbia, Tenn., race riot, 103, 107, 115, 132, 138

Commission on Interracial Co-operation (CIC), 41

Communism. *See* Anticommunism; Cold War

Community Welfare League, 25–26, 53–54, 56, 58, 77

Congress of Industrial Organizations (CIO), 18–19, 28, 30, 31, 40, 51, 54, 71, 124, 151, 178–79, 185–88

Congress of Racial Equality (CORE), 115, 231, 352 (n. 14)

Connors, Eugene "Bull," 129

Construction jobs. *See* Building trades unions

Cook, Fred, 246, 247

Cooks. *See* Domestic servants

Coopers International Union, 124, 301 (n. 31)

Copeland, William A. (Red), 71, 186, 187, 188

Coppedge, Mrs. Thomas, 25

Cotton, Bernard, 133

Cotton Carnival, 242

Cotton industry: and manufacturing, 7, 19–20, 49, *50*, 51, 52, 69–73, 78; strikes in, 22–23; Memphis blacks as seasonal cotton laborers, 26–27, *27*, 40, 46, 49, 51, 53, 79; and labor unions, 69–73; and Fair Labor Standards Act, 310 (n. 37)

Cotton Makers' Jubilee, 242–43, 250

Cox, Ida, 159

Crabtree, Charles, 74

Crawley, Drury B., 314 (n. 2)

Crenshaw, Kimberlé Williams, 315 (n. 11), 316 (n. 13)

Crime, 20, 36–37, 43, 103–4, 133–34, 227. *See also* Police violence and harassment; Sexual assault/abuse; Violence

Cropper, Steve, 245

Crouch, Paul, 188

Crowder, Earl, 186, 188

Crump, Edward Hull: as head of political machine, 6, 9, 21–22; death of, 9, 184, 207, 208; Rev. George Long on, 12–13, 77; and political candidates, 15, 36; Ralph Bunche on, 18; biographical information on, 21–22; and Lt. Lee, 43; and A. Philip Randolph, 74, 75, 76–78, 80, 99, 190; and public transportation, 92; and Freedom Train, 114; and Dixiecrats, 137; on Estes Kefauver, 137; on President Truman and civil rights, 137. *See also* Crump political machine

Crump political machine: blacks' relationship with, 5–6, 12–13, 18, 22, 36, 39, 41–45, 49, 53–54, 73–78, 96–99, 127, 132, 190, 292; and migration, 9; and police violence and harassment, 10, 18, 22, 32, 38–40, 44–46, 87, 96; and A. Philip Randolph, 12–13, 49, 51, 73–78, 80, 87, 152, 292, 313 (n. 79); and "reign of terror," 15, 18–19, 38–45, 53–54, 73–78; and voting, 15, 22; development of, 21–22; and racial harmony, 22, 75, 80; and labor unions, 30–31, 40, 54–55, 70; conflicts with, 30–33; white opposition to, 32, 41, 87, 96; and Ku Klux Klan, 36; U.S. Justice Department investigation of, 41; and churches, 42–43; and LeMoyne College chapter of NAACP, 44; and U.S. Employment Service, 55–59; and trial of white police as rapists,

99–101; and 1948 elections, 107, 111, 114, 136–41, 206, 328–29 (n. 68), 329 (n. 79); and Freedom Train, 112, 113, 114, 121, 124–25, 136–37, 138, 141, 292; paternalism of, 141; and censorship, 149–63; and radio, 166. *See also* Municipal politics

Curley (movie), 161, 162–63

Current, Gloster, 189

Dailey, Jane, 10

Dance, *45*, 149, 153, 173, 242. *See also* Music

Daniel, Pete, 297 (n. 10)

Davis, Bette, 151

Davis, Clifford, 26, 30, 54–55, 58, 68, 139, 317 (n. 34)

Davis, Matthew, 200–201, 221, 223

Davis, "Red," 186

Dawson, William L., 194

Day, Gene, 186, 187, 211

Deacons and Trustees Union, 97

Declaration of Independence, 114, 122, 124, 141

Dedicated Citizens Committee (DCC), 219, 220

Defense industry: and migration, 23, 46, 49, 51, 67, 307 (n. 8); and gender, 25, 47–48, 51–52, 58–59, 67–73; Roosevelt's ban on discrimination in, 47, 48, 51, 118, 311 (n. 51); newspaper advertisements for, 47, 56, 60; and black women, 47–48, 52, 54–55, 58–59, 64, *65*, 79–80; desegregation of, 49, 51; and race, 49, 51–53, 54, 58, 60, 79–80; statistics on, 50; and fair employment practice, 50–53; and white women, 51–53, 54, 58, 60, 67, 69; and black men, 52–53, 56, 67–73, 79, 80; and labor unions, 67–73; and whites, 67, 68, 69, 71–72; job classifications in, 68, 71, 72, 73, 76, 80; wages and wage discrimination

in, 69–72, 80; wildcat strikes in, 72–73; absentee records in, 89

De Mille, Cecil, 149

Democracy: Roosevelt on, 6, 79; and "Double V" campaign, 48, 49, 68, 151; World War II discourse on, 48, 59, 60, 291–92; and A. Philip Randolph on, 76; police violence as antidemocratic, 91, 108; and Freedom Train, 112–18, 123, 140–41; and Declaration of Independence, 114, 122, 124, 141; and racial equality, 132; movie censorship versus, 158–59; and threat of Citizens' Councils, 194–95; and Cold War rhetoric, 194–95, 207, 215; and equal opportunity, 207; and voter registration of sharecroppers, 231–32; and religious belief, 249. *See also* Freedom

Democratic Party, 41, 42, 107, 140, 228. *See also* Crump political machine; Dixiecrats

Desegregation: and sit-in movement, 6, 218, 220, 224, 226, 232–41, *236*, 249, 253, 254, 273, 275, 292; of defense industry, 49, 51; of military, 49, 51, 136; and Freedom Train, 112, 113, 114, 118, 120, 121, 123, 141, 324 (n. 15); of interstate public transportation, 115; of public schools, 120, 183, 184, 185, 191, 195–99, 207, 214–15, 218, 219, 255, 256, 290, 293; of higher education, 136, 196–97, 225, 352 (n. 14), 353–54 (n. 30); and NAACP, 185, 189–90, 193; and urban-rural relation, 191, 195–99, 214; opposition to court orders for school desegregation, 198–99, 219; and civic clubs, 206–7, 214; of public transportation, 213, 215, 219, 220, 225, 238, 239, 241; of recreational facilities, 213–14, 215, 219, 220, 221, 225, 239, 254, 255; and Firestone, 214; of libraries, 215,

Eggleston, Annie, 203
E. L. Bruce Company, 19, 28, 212
Eleanor Clubs, 58
Elections. *See* Voting; *and specific candidates*
Ellington, Duke, 152
Emergency Relief Committee (ERC), 231
Equal Employment Opportunity Commission (EEOC), 261, 263–64, 276
Equality. *See* Racial equality
Estes, James F., 191, 192, 197, 208, 227–28, 230, *236*
Evers, Medgar, 193
Evers, O. Z., 213–14, 217, 221, 224

Factories. *See* Manufacturing
Fair Employment Practice Committee (FEPC), 46, 47, 49, 51–55, 59, 61, 64–69, 71, 78, 79, 307 (n. 14), 308 (n. 20)
Fair Labor Standards Act (FLSA), 28, 60, 310 (n. 37)
Farber Brothers, 1–2, 259
Farming. *See* Sharecropping; Urban-rural relation
Farris, William, 224, 225
Fascism, 74–75, 76, 117, 122, 126, 127, 144, 151, 159
FBI, 30, 199
Fellini, Federico, 163
Ferguson, Bert, 165–66, 349 (n. 62)
Ferguson, J. L., 135
Films. *See* Movies
Firestone Tire and Rubber Company, 19–20, 40, 48, 50–52, 60, 93, 140, 200, 214, 224, 265, 308 (n. 15)
First Amendment, 163, 248
Fisher Aircraft, 52, 55, 59, 60, 68–69, 73, 80. *See also* Fisher Body Corporation
Fisher Body Corporation, 19, 28, 30, 50, 51. *See also* Fisher Aircraft
Fisk University, 98, 226, 233
Five Royales, 167, 181, 244
Florida, 56, 63, 86, 93, 124

Flowers, Eloise, 237
Flowers, Harold, 190, 198
Floyd, Eddie, 245
Food, Tobacco, and Agricultural Workers Union (FTA), 186, 187–88, 312 (n. 60). *See also* United Cannery, Agricultural, Packing and Allied Workers of America
Ford, Evander, 233, 234, 240, 247–48
Ford Motor Co., 28, 30, 31, 50, 51, 54, 265
Foreman, James, 231
Fort, Marie, 201, 221
"Four Freedoms," 6, 117, 132, 296–97 (n. 7)
Fourteenth Amendment, 44, 162, 197, 215, 248, 249, 250
Fowler, J. A., 89, 316 (n. 17)
Franklin, Aretha, 258
Frantz, Laurent, 32
Frazier, Walter, 91
Fredericks, Robert, 39, 153
Freedom: gendered language of, 2–3, 13, 14, 181, 252–53, 259, 261, 276, 282–83, 285–89, *286*, 290, 293, 357 (n. 73); and sanitation workers' strike, 2–3, 13, 14, 276, 285–89, 293; plantation mentality versus, 2–3, 288, 289–90; meanings of, for black southerners, 3–7, 9–10, 14, 231, 291–92; and Cold War, 6; and World War II, 6; and Roosevelt's "Four Freedoms" speech, 6, 117, 132, 296–97 (n. 7); ideological tensions among blacks on, 9–10; and agency, 11, 250; and black women, 13, 14, 252–53, 261, 282–83, 287; and rhetoric of democracy, 48, 59, 60, 291–92; and A. Philip Randolph on, 49, 75–76, 80, 96, 292; international perspectives on, 76, 77, 135, 231–32, 250; Rev. George Long on, 77; and Freedom Train, 112–21, 141; Truman on U.S. as leader of free world, 114; and Declaration of Independence, 114,

Gospel music, 145, 155, 165, 166, 167, 169, 174–76, *175*, 194, 243. *See also* Music

Grace, Virgil, 281–82, 289–90, 358 (n. 4)

Granger, Lester, 118, 324 (n. 15)

Gray v. University of Tennessee, 196–97

Green, William, 75

Greene, Christina, 315 (n. 8)

Greenwood, Miss., 16, 17

Griffin, Lovie Mae, 90, 91

Griffith, D. W., 150–51

Griggs, Rev. Sutton E., 33–37, 42

Guinozzo, John, 56, 58

Haaz, Jacob, 317 (n. 26)

Hale, E. W., 74

Hale, Frances, 272

Haley, Richard, 231

Hall, Katie, 60–61

Hamer, Fannie Lou, 338 (n. 3)

Handy, W. C., 43, 120, 305–6 (n. 76)

Harden, P. L., 89–90, 319 (n. 57)

Hardin, George, 233

Harding, Warren, 35

Hardwood industry, 7, 19, 28, 49, 51, 52, 259

Harper, Ann Wilson, 272–73, 274, 357–58 (n. 81)

Harris, Wynonie, 243

Hartsfield, William, 122

Hartwell Brothers, 29

Hattendorf, Albert, Jr., 60–61

Hayes, Isaac, 167, 245, 285, 289

Hayes, T. C. D., 138, 211

Hayes, T. H., 104

Hayes, Will, 148

Health care. *See* Hospitals

Hellman, Lillian, 151

Helper, Laura, 350 (n. 67)

Henry, Aaron, 193

Heyword, Sammy, 120

Hi-De-Ho (movie), 156

Higginbotham, Evelyn Brooks, 320 (n. 63)

Higher education: desegregation of, 136, 196–97, 225, 352 (n. 14), 353–54 (n. 30); and Black Power, 290–91. *See also* Education; *and specific colleges and universities*

Hilmes, Michele, 335 (n. 61)

Historical memory: and plantation mentality, 2–5, 252, 259, 260; of violence against black share-croppers, 16; of slavery, 115, 140, 291; of moviegoing, 145–48; of lynchings, 199, 227, 228–29, 273; of segregation, 240; of paternalism, 291

Hoffman, Walter, 326 (n. 42)

Holloway, George, 146, 236

Holloway, Mammie, 65–67

Holmes, James, 264

Honey, Michael, 297 (n. 18)

hooks, bell, 157

Hooks, Benjamin, *236*; as NAACP attorney, 191, 192; and Memphis State College desegregation lawsuit, 197; and restrictive housing covenants, 203; and public transportation boycott, 205; and voter registration, 206; and Patio 6 episode, 211; as political candidate in 1959 election, 216, 217; and Memphis and Shelby County Improvement Association, 225; and desegregation of churches, 249

Hoover, Herbert, 38

Hope, John, 61, 69, 71, 73, 78, 308 (n. 20)

Horne, Lena, 145, 152, 153, 155, 156

Horne, Onzie, 246

Hospitals: laundry workers in military hospitals, 60–61, 64–67; syphilis treatment clinics in, 93; separate black hospital, 179, 189, 190, 208; Joseph E. Walker on board of Gaston Hospital, 219; discrimination against black workers in, 263, 264; strikes by hospital workers, 276, 289; desegregation of, 289

Jones, Amy, 150
Jones, Ben F., 191, 203, 205, *236*
Jones, Booker T., 245
Jones, Donald, 102–3, 132
Jones, Ethel Bell, 82–83, 95, 96
Jones, Jennifer, 160
Jones, Lonnie, 140
Jones, Lucius, 72
Jones, Melvin, 246
Jones, Naomi, 23–24, 146, 167, 178, 261–62, 281, 283, 284, 289
Jones, Nebraska, 25–26
Jones, Robert F., 67–68
Jones, T. O., 277, 279, 356 (n. 57)
Jones, Waddell, 223
Jones, William Edwin, *238*
Jordan, Louis, 147
Jury service, 194, 225
Juvenile delinquency, 133–34

Kefauver, Estes, 107, 124, 137–38, 140, 206, 207, 329 (n. 79)
Kelley, Robin D. G., 11–12, 88, 316 (n. 14)
Keyes, Savannah, 183, 184
Kimberly-Clark, 50
King, B. B., 167, 175, *180*
King, Coretta Scott, 286
King, Martin Luther, Jr.: assassination of, 3, 6, 10, 252, 275, 283, 284–86, 288–89; speeches by, 4, 10, 216, 221, 251, 274, 284, 285; radio broadcast by, 178; at "Freedom Rally" for Volunteer Ticket (1959), 216, 221, 251; and voter registration of sharecroppers, 231; "Letter from a Birmingham Jail" by, 239; and Southern Christian Leadership Council, 246; on segregation of churches, 247; and Poor People's Campaign, 251, 283; and sanitation workers' strike, 251, 283; and general strike of black workers in Memphis, 251–52; violence following march by, in Memphis,

283; Memphis march following death of, 286–87; and desegregation of University of Mississippi, 352 (n. 14). *See also* Civil rights
King, Rev. Martin Luther, Sr., 106
King, Osie A., 69
King of Kings (movie), 149
Kirklon, Lillie, 201
Kitt, Eartha, 170
Kroger Baking, 264
Ku Klux Klan, 36, 137, 149, 227
Kyle, Rev. Dwight, 100, 107, 108, 127, 139

Labor. *See* Work and workers
Labor unions: and black women, 1–2, 12, 61–62, 186, 211–13, 259–62, 267, 281, 289, 290; violence against, 23, 30–31, 32, 40; for skilled trades workers, 25–26; and black men, 25–26, 28–31, 35, 40, 49, 51, 67–75, 185–88, 211–13, 297 (n. 18); anticommunism against, 26, 30, 40, 184–89, 297 (n. 18); and Wagner Act, 28, 30, 185; and biracial organizing, 28–30; and white women, 29, 260; police violence and harassment against, 30, 32, 54, 70, 186–87, 256, 279–80; and Crump machine, 30–31, 40, 54–55, 70; during World War II, 51; and defense industry, 67–73; and fascism, 74; and Freedom Train, 124; and Taft-Hartley Act, 137, 178, 185–86, 187; and civil rights in 1960s, 139, 187, 210–14, 258–65; radio coverage of, 178–79; and Patio 6 episode, 210–11; and workers' fear of reprisals, 211–12, 213, 277–78; and voter registration, 213; at RCA, 266–67, 289–90. *See also* Sanitation workers; Strikes; Work and workers; *and specific unions*
LaFollette Senate Committee on Civil Liberties, 31
Lamon, Lester C., 302 (n. 51)

155, 167, 177, 336 (n. 72); on Jackson murder case, 104, 107; on black policemen, 109; on Freedom Train, 126–30, 135; on 1948 elections, 138–39; on black-appeal radio, 143, 167, 177; on moviegoers, 147; on movie stereotypes, 152, 154; on Lena Horne, 155; on movie censorship, 156, 158, 160, 161; radio compared with, 177; compared with *Tri-State Defender*, 192; and student sit-in movement, 233

Meredith, James, 352 (n. 14)

The Messenger (black journal), 37, 74

Micheaux, Oscar, 147

Middlebrook, Rev. Harold, 270, 275, 281

Migration: and plantation mentality, 5, 16, 17–18; Great Migration to North, 7, 8–9, 34, 35–36; to southern cities, 8–9; and Crump machine, 9; reasons for, 16, 23, 193, 198; of agricultural workers during Depression, 16–17, 23–25; and defense industry, 23, 46, 49, 51, 67, 307 (n. 8); black women's decisions about, 24, 260; and police violence, 90; statistics on, 297 (n. 10). *See also* Urban-rural relation

Military: blacks in World War II, 45, 47, 60, 203; segregation of, 48, 89, 316 (n. 16); desegregation of, 49, 51, 136; hospitals for, 60–61, 64, 91; police violence against, 91; and antivice campaigns, 94; and venereal disease, 94, 95; draft for, 136, 257; blacks in Vietnam War, 257

Miller, Jasper, 316–17 (n. 23), 319 (n. 53)

Milligan, Annie Bell, 133

Ministers. *See* Churches; *and specific ministers*

The Miracle (movie), 163

Mississippi: voting in, 15; domestic servants in, 16, 25; civil rights activism in, 17; education in, 23–24, 198; segregation in, 24, 25, 146, 192; and black policemen, 109;

and Freedom Train, 121, 126; and movie censorship, 160; lynchings in, 178, 184, 195, 238, 273, 316 (n. 14); Regional Council of Negro Leadership in, 183–84, 191–95; murders of blacks in, 184, 195, 196, 341 (n. 29); Citizens' Councils in, 185, 194–95; NAACP in, 189; reasons for black migration from, 193; school desegregation in, 195–96, 207, 214; Poor People's Campaign in, 275; migrants from, and defense industry, 307 (n. 8); desegregation of higher education in, 352 (n. 14)

Mississippi Delta, *8. See also* Migration; Urban-rural relation

Mitchell, H. L., 22, 98

Mitchell, John, 137, 329 (n. 79)

Mitchell, Thelma, 61

Moeser, John V., 328 (n. 68)

Monroe, Willa, 167, *168*, 170, *171*, 172

Montgomery bus boycott, 128, 205

Moore, Amzie, 193

Moore, Dwight "Gatemouth," 174–75

Moore, Elmer, 233

Moore, Viola, 106

Moore, Willa, 170

Moreland, Mantan, 147

Morgan v. Virginia, 115

Mormon, Square, 228

Morris, Alma, 201, 221

Morrison, Mary, 33

Mosby, James, 107–8, 110, 139

Motley, Constance Baker, 225, 255

Movies: censorship of, 9, 142, 144, 145, 148–63, 182, 334 (n. 47); stereotypes of blacks in, 12, 143, 144, 150–51, 154, 156, 158, 161, 333 (n. 37); "passing" of African American characters in, 142, 163; and racial messages about cultural pluralism, 144; interracial movie scenes, 144, 160, 161; historical memory and racial geography of moviegoing, 145–48; musicals, 147,

152–56; self-censorship of, 148; fight film, 149–50; black independence or assertiveness in, 151, 292; and struggle to liberate minds, 151–59; deletions from, 155

Movie theaters: on Beale Street, 21, 147; segregation of, 143, 144, 146, 182; on Main Street, 146; in black neighborhoods, 147–48; desegregation of, 239, 255

Muhoberac, Larry, 246, 247

Municipal government employment, 214, 221. *See also* Sanitation workers

Municipal politics: and "reign of terror," 15, 18–19, 38–45, 53–54, 73–78; tensions over, in Jim Crow era, 33–38; and black political candidates, 206, 216–17, 221, 255–56; and local government organization, 209, 217, 256. *See also* Crump political machine

Murder. *See* Crime; Police violence and harassment; Violence

Murphy, Frank, 32

Music: on Beale Street, 7–8, 21, 144–45; all-girl orchestra from New York, 90–91; and Freedom Train, 120, 324 (n. 19); censorship of, 166; at Goodwill Revue, 179, 244; at Starlight Revue, 244. *See also* Blues music; Dance; Gospel music; Jazz music; Radio; Rhythm and blues; Soul music; Stax Records

Mutual Film Corp. v. Ohio, 148

Muzumdar, Haridas T., 135

Myers, O. E., 66

Myrdal, Gunnar, 86, 95

NAACP: LeMoyne College branch of, 9–10, 18, 40, 44, 98, 113, 142; Memphis branch of generally, 9–10, 32, 189, 191; and New Deal, 25; and labor unions, 31, 63, 178–79, 277; and police violence, 32, 44, 54, 90, 93, 97–103, 105, 107, 111, 190,

223, 256; membership statistics for Memphis branch of, 35, 54, 86, 98, 103, 111, 189, 235–36, 303 (n. 52), 318 (n. 48), 321 (n. 69); and northern migration, 36; and "reign of terror," 41; President Truman's address to, 117–18; and Freedom Train, 118, 128–29; high school organizing for, 133; and juvenile delinquency, 133–34; Youth Council of, 133–34, 243; and movies, 144, 150–52; and radio, 170; and segregation, 179, 189–90; anticommunism against, 184, 189–90; and desegregation, 185, 189–90, 192, 193, 197–98, 220–21, 225, 226, 232, 234–37, 255, 290; leadership of, in 1950s, 190–91, 237; and lynchings, 199; and housing conflicts, 204; and student sit-ins, 226, 234–37, 239; and voting rights, 229–31; nonpartisanship policy of, 237; and Cotton Makers' Jubilee, 242–43; and Starlight Revue, 243; and WLOK radio station, 246; and white churches, 247; Intercollegiate NAACP, 255; and draft boards, 257; and employment discrimination, 263, 266, 267, 269; and War on Poverty, 269; in Arkansas, 302 (n. 51); and farmers, 302 (n. 51)

Nabrit, Rev. James, 239

Nashville sit-ins, 226, 233

National Committee for People's Rights, 31, 32

National Federation for Constitutional Liberties, 41, 44

National Fireworks Company, 50, 52–53

National Industrial Recovery Act (NIRA), 27

National Labor Relations Act (Wagner Act), 27–28, 30, 185, 186, 225

National Labor Relations Board (NLRB), 28, 62, 187, 212

National Maritime Union (NMU), 51, 186

National Venereal Disease Control Act,
93
National War Labor Board (NWLB), 49,
55, 62, 70, 71, 72, 73
National Welfare Rights Organization
(NWRO), 272
National Youth Administration (NYA),
25
Neal, Olly, 239
Nelson, Ford, 23–24, 146, 167, 175, 176
Nelson, Jill, 315 (n. 9)
Nelson, Joan Lee, 167, 170, 176, 178,
240–41
New Deal, 22–23, 25–28, 30, 37, 299
(n. 13), 307–8 (n. 14). *See also*
Roosevelt, Franklin D.
Newell, Bob, 271
Newman, Mark, 165
Newspapers. *See specific newspapers*
Nicholas Brothers, 152
Nixon, E. D., 128
Nixon, Richard, 275
Non-Partisan Voters' League, 31, 206,
209–10
Norris v. Alabama, 319 (n. 57)
North Carolina, 198, 226, 232, 315
(n. 8), 345 (n. 7)
Northern migration. *See* Migration
Novins, Louis, 121, 122

Office of Economic Opportunity (OEO),
268–70
Office of Production Management
(OPM), 52, 53, 307–8 (n. 14)
Office of War Information (OWI), 64,
152
O'Jay, Eddie, 169–70
O'Keefe, Dennis, 157
Operation Freedom, 231
Orgill, Edmund, 134, 135, 137, 207, 208,
217, 218–20
Our Gang (movies), 161
Overton, Watkins, 27, 30–31, 36, 208
Owen, Chandler, 74
Owen, Rev. Samuel A., 211, 232, 270

Owen Junior College, 232–35, 247, 255,
257, 281
Owens, Harry, 71
Owens, Jesse, 133

Paine, Rowlett, 36
Paine, Rev. W. C., 42
Painter, Nell Irvin, 320 (n. 61)
Parker, Little Junior, 244
Parks. *See* Recreational facilities
Parks, Rosa L., 128
Paternalism: and police violence,
91–92; of Crump machine, 141; of
supervisors, 252–53; and laundry
workers, 260–61; and plantation
mentality, 276; and sanitation
workers' strike, 276, 278, 279, 287;
memory of, 291. *See also* Plantation
mentality
Patio 6 episode, 183, 184, 210–11
Patterson, Frederick, 133
Patton, H. F., 74
Payne, Charles, 11
Payne, Janice, 275
Payne, Larry, 283
Peck, Gregory, 160
Peel, Hal, 26
Pepper, Claude, 124
Pepper, John, 165–66, 349 (n. 62)
Perry, Marian Wynn, 102
Persons, Ell, 316 (n. 14)
Phillips, Charles, 31, 32
Phillips, Dewey, 245
Phillips, Utillus, 32, 99, 189–90, 318
(n. 48)
Pidgeon, Phil, 55
Pillow to Post (movie), 155
Pinky (movie), 142, 163, 330 (n. 1)
Pizer, Morris, 187
Plantation mentality: bucket and
dipper as symbols of, 1–2, 12, 259;
definition of, 2; and sharecropping,
2, 12; freedom versus, 2–3, 288,
289–90; and memory, 2–5, 252, 259;
working-class black challenges to

Prostitution, 39, 81, 88, 94, 318 (n. 38)

Public health: and stereotypes of blacks, 20, 53, 308 (n. 18); health cards for food service workers, 81, 83, 95; and blacks on public transportation, 92. *See also* Venereal diseases

Public libraries. *See* Libraries

Public transportation: segregation of, 25, 33, 92, 115, 151, 204, 317 (n. 28); harassment of blacks on, 46, 92, 204–5; and white women, 92, 317 (n. 29), 326 (n. 34); and black women, 93, 317 (n. 29); Montgomery bus boycott, 128, 205; boycott of, by blacks, 204–5; desegregation of, 213, 215, 220, 225, 238, 239, 241; and historical memories of segregation, 240

Quiller, Daisy, 178

R & B. *See* Rhythm and blues

Race: King on unity of Memphis, 10, 216; and movies, 12, 142–63; and "reign of terror," 15, 18–19, 38–45, 53–54, 73–78, 96; and job opportunities, 20, 52, 55, 56; and "racial harmony," 22, 49, 75, 80, 254–58, 281; and New Deal, 25–28; tensions over, in Jim Crow era, 33–38; and social engineering uplift theory, 34; Washington's ideology of racial cooperation, 34; Du Bois's "talented tenth," 37; Woodson on, 37; and wage differential, 52, 55; and mammy image, 64, 79, 183, 210; and antivice campaigns, 94–95; and postwar political leadership, 96–99; social scientists on, 135; "separate but equal" racial ideology, 136, 179, 189, 193–94, 197, 215; and radio, 142–45, 163–82; and mass culture, 144–45, 181–82; and "new militant" blacks in 1950s, 195, 196;

and "Uncle Toms," 216, 249; terms "boy" or "buddy" for black men, 223, 257, 276. *See also* African American women; Black freedom movement; Civil rights; Defense industry; Desegregation; Domestic servants; Labor unions; Laundry workers; Plantation mentality; Police violence and harassment; Racial equality; Segregation

Race riots: fear of, 67, 74, 144, 153–54; Crump on, 76–77; in Detroit, 89, 152, 153; in Columbia, Tenn., 103, 107, 115, 132, 138; after World War I, 115; "zoot suit" riot, 153; Watts riot (1965), 253; in Memphis, 283, 285. *See also* Violence

Racial equality: and civil rights, 2; Boyle's arguments against, 39; Roosevelt's ban on discrimination in defense industry, 47, 48, 51, 118, 311 (n. 51); and "Double V" campaign, 48, 49, 68, 151; and Declaration of Independence, 114, 122; and freedom, 132, 140, 262; as "human relations," 134–35; religiopolitical perspective of, 193, 247–49, 261–62; and democracy, 207. *See also* Black freedom movement; Civil rights; Civil Rights Act (1964); Freedom; Race

Radio: and urban-rural relation, 8, 9, 150, 164, 172, 173, 178; black-oriented radio, 9, 142–43, 145, 163–82, 218, 245–46, 292, 330 (n. 2); music on, 9, 145, 155, 165, 166, 169, 170–72, 174–76, 245–46, 253, 257–58; in rural areas, 9, 150, 164, 172, 173, 178; Truman's address to NAACP on, 117–18; on Freedom Train, 124–25, 325 (n. 23); and racial messages about cultural pluralism, 144; DJs on, 144–45, 163–74, *168*, *171*, 180–81, *180*, 206, 246; boxing matches on, 150, 166, 336 (n. 66);

stereotypes of blacks on, 156; and women DJs, 163–64, 169–73, *171*; advertising for, 165–66, 181; religious programming on, 166, 174–76; humor on, 169; homemaker and advice programs on, 169–71; community programming and politics on, 176–81, 275, 280, 337 (n. 94); charity events sponsored by, 179, *180*, 243–44; and segregated Starlight Revue, 179, 218, 243–44; and Goodwill Revue, 179, 244; and voter registration, 206; and Stax Records, 245–46; and WLOK, 245–46, 284–85; segregation of WLOK radio station, 246; on King's assassination, 284–85; and civil rights, 335 (n. 59)

Randall, Richard, 331 (n. 13)

Randolph, A. Philip: and Crump machine, 12–13, 49, 51, 73–78, 80, 87, 99, 152, 190, 292, 313 (n. 79); on freedom versus plantation mentality, 49, 75–76, 80, 96, 292; manhood of, 97; on police violence, 99; on draft and desegregation of military, 136

Rankin, John, 160

Rape. *See* Sexual assault/abuse

RCA, 265–67, *268*, 281, 289–90, 293

Record, Cy, 52, 53–54

Recreational facilities, 200, 204, *205*, 213–14, 215, 219, 221, 225, 239, 254, 255

Redding, Otis, 245, 258·

Regional Council of Negro Leadership (RCNL), 183–84, 191–95, 229

"Reign of terror." *See* Crump political machine

Religion. *See* Churches

Renoir, Jean, 156

Republican Party, 32–33, 35, 38, 46, 140

Restaurants: segregation of, 17; and Patio 6 episode, 183, 184, 210–11;

and student sit-in movement, 226; desegregation of, 226, 239, 254, 255

Restrooms, 186, 187, 261, 267

Retail, Wholesale, and Department Store Union, 189

Reynolds, James, 283

Rhodes College. *See* Southwestern College

Rhythm and blues, 145, 155, 165, 166, 169, 170–72, 175–76, 243, 244, 257–58. *See also* Music

Riots. *See* Race riots; Violence

Roach, Hal, 161

Roberts, William H., 271

Robeson, Paul, 120, 136, 324 (n. 19)

Robinson, Bill, 152

Robinson, Clifton, 91

Robinson, Wendell L., 109, *110*

Roddy, Bert, 35, 36 ⁻

Rogers, Bessie, 281

Rogers, J. A., 118

Rogers, Taylor, 2–3, 11, 14, 224, 278, 281, 283

Rooks, George, 176

Roosevelt, Eleanor, 58

Roosevelt, Franklin D.: and "Four Freedoms" speech, 6, 117, 132, 296–97 (n. 7); and labor unions, 30, 72–73; and blacks, 38, 58–60; and "reign of terror" in Memphis, 41; and ban on discrimination in defense industry, 47, 48, 51, 118, 311 (n. 51); on World War II issues, 76; on "Arsenal of Democracy," 79; and venereal disease control and treatment, 93; and May Act, 94; and War Advertising Council, 116; and fair employment practice, 263; and Office of Production Management, 317 (n. 14). *See also* New Deal

Rowan, Carl, 255

Rudd, Willie, 289, 358 (n. 3)

Rural-urban relation. *See* Urban-rural relation

Rustin, Bayard, 283

Sailor Takes a Wife (movie), 155
Sanderlin, Jeraldine, 102
Sanders, Laura, 178
Sanitation workers: strike of, 2–3, 6,
    10, 13, 14, 62, 179, 181, 210, 251–54,
    260, 275–76, 279–83, *284*, 293, 357
    (n. 73); "I Am a Man" slogan of strike
    of, 2–3, 13, 14, 181, 252–53, 259,
    261, 276, 282–83, 285–89, *286*, 290,
    293, 357 (n. 73); freedom and strike
    by, 2–3, 13, 14, 276, 285–89, 293;
    union organizing for, 214, 222–25,
    258, 276–78, 292, 346 (n. 16); racist
    employment conditions of, 224, 276;
    wages of, 224, 269, 276, 277; police
    brutality against, during strike, 256,
    279–80; wives of, as union activists,
    260, 261, 281; clothing as handouts
    for, 276–77; family status of, 277;
    public image of, 277, *278*; fear of,
    277–78; deaths of, in workplace
    accident, 279; and middle-class
    blacks, 280; supporters of strike by,
    280–84; end of strike by, 283, 288;
    places of origin of, 356 (n. 58)
Schmeling, Max, 149–50, 331–32 (n. 18)
Schools. *See* Education
Scott, J. Jay, 35
Scottsboro boys, 319 (n. 57)
Scruggs, Defense Attorney, 100, 101
Scruggs, Rev., 248
Seabrook, Carroll, 83, 96, 100
Searcy, L. J., 25, 54, 77
Segregation: of water fountains, 1,
    17, 24; of schools, 16, 22, 199, 207,
    253; of restaurants, 17; in Memphis
    compared with Mississippi, 24, 25,
    146; in Mississippi, 24, 25, 146, 192;
    of public transportation, 25, 33, 92,
    115, 151, 317 (n. 28); of housing,
    32, 89, 202; tensions over race and
    politics in Jim Crow era, 33–38; of
    military, 48, 89; of USES offices,
    56; A. Philip Randolph on, 76; and
    states' rights, 126; of movie theaters,

143, 144, 146, 182; and radio, 145,
    218, 243; of Starlight Revue, 179,
    218, 243–44; of restrooms, 186, 187,
    261; in Tennessee Constitution,
    199, 207; of recreational facilities,
    204, *205*, 213–14; of auto show, 225;
    of churches, 241–42, 247–49; and
    Cotton Makers' Jubilee, 242–43, 250;
    of WLOK radio station, 246. *See also*
    Desegregation
Selective Service. *See* Draft
Selznick, David O., 159–61
Senate Internal Security Subcommittee
    (SISS), 185, 188–89
Sensations of 1945 (movie), 155
"Separate but equal" racial ideology,
    136, 179, 189, 193–94, 197, 215
Sexual assault/abuse: by police, 9, 13,
    81–83, 86–88, 93, 96–103, 108–9,
    138; by slaveholders, 87; stereotype
    of black men as rapists of white
    women, 88, 315–16 (n. 12); trial of
    white police as rapists, 99–102, 110,
    111; of black women by white men,
    194; and black men as protectors of
    black women, 194, 315–16 (n. 12);
    legal definition of rape, 319 (n. 54)
Sexual harassment, 65–67, 79–80, 261
Sexual stereotypes: of black women,
    13, 88, 93, 99–101, 110, 111, 316
    (n. 13), 320 (n. 61), 320 (n. 63);
    and protection of white women in
    factories, 53; of black men as rapists
    of white women, 88, 315–16 (n. 12)
Sharecropping: and plantation
    mentality, 2, 12; collapse of,
    5, 8; violence against black
    sharecroppers, 16; migration
    of agricultural workers during
    Depression, 16–17, 23–25; and New
    Deal, 22–23; and mechanization
    of agriculture, 23; and "working
    out," 23; and gender, 24; women's
    responses to farm labor, 24, 46, 260;
    voting rights for sharecroppers,

218, 226–32, 250, 292; eviction of sharecroppers during voter registration movement, 229–30, *230*. *See also* Cotton industry; Urban-rural relation

Shelley v. Kraemer, 120, 122, 202

Sidewalk Clubs, 58

Silver, Christopher, 328 (n. 68)

Simmons, Tom, 124

Simon, Bryant, 10

Sims, Altha, 47, 48, 58, 59, 79

Sipuel, Ada Lois, 136

Sipuel v. Board of Regents of the University of Oklahoma, 136, 197

Sit-in movement, 6, 218, 220, 224, 226, 232–41, *236*, 249, 253, 254, 273, 275, 292

Skilled trades workers, 25–26

Slave mentality. *See* Plantation mentality

Smith, Clarence, 48, 80

Smith, Coby, 257

Smith, Edward, 96–97

Smith, Hazel Byrd, 87

Smith, James, 68

Smith, Lamar, 341 (n. 29)

Smith, Lillian, 157

Smith, Maxine, 235, 237, 243, 264, 349 (n. 56)

Smith, Norman, 30–31, 32

Smith, Novella, 172–73

Smith, Vasco, 239

Smith v. Allwright, 329 (n. 75)

Snyder, Thurmond Lee, 250

Sonderling, Egmont, 243, 349 (n. 62)

Song of the South (movie), 333 (n. 37)

Soul music, 176, 181, 218, 241–42, 245, 253, 257, 258, 292. *See also* Music

South Carolina, 90, 128

Southern Christian Leadership Council (SCLC), 226, 231, 246, 251, 257, 270, 285, 352 (n. 14)

Southern Conference for Human Welfare, 32, 41, 324 (n. 19)

The Southerner (movie), 156

Southern Negro Youth Congress, 32, 41

Southern Tenant Farmers Union (STFU), 22–23, 26–27, 31, 74, 77, 98

Southwestern College, 134–35, 255, 257, 281

Sprunt, Rev. David, 135

Stainback, Charles A., 198–200

Stanback, Elihue, 216–17

Stanfield, Reuel, 73

Starlight Revue, 179, 218, 243–44

State of Missouri ex rel. Gaines v. Canada, 197

Stax Records, 176, 218, 241, 244–46, 250, 271, 285, 292

Steelman, John, 54, 55

Steinberg, Luther, 171

Steinberg, Martha Jean "the Queen," 163–64, *168*, 169–73

Stereotypes: in movies, 12, 143, 144, 150–52, 154, 156, 158, 161, 333 (n. 37); of sexuality of blacks, 13, 53, 88, 93, 99–101, 110, 111, 316 (n. 13), 320 (n. 61), 320 (n. 63); and venereal disease, 20, 53, 308 (n. 18), 320 (n. 63); mammy image, 64, 79, 183, 210; of black men as rapists of white women, 88, 315–16 (n. 12); on radio, 156; of ignorant blacks, 199; of poor people, 271

Stewart, Jim, 244

Stewart, Tom, 107, 137, 138, 329 (n. 79)

Stokes, Thomas L., 301 (n. 34)

Stores. *See* Businesses

Stormy Weather (movie), 152–56

Streetcars. *See* Public transportation

Streit, Clarence, 134

Strikes: of garment workers, 18–19, 28; "mushroom strikes," 18–19, 28–29; of cotton pickers, 22–23; violence against strikers, 23, 186–87, 256, 279–80; in manufacturing plants, 28–29, 178–79, 186–87, 211, 213, 267, 289, 290, 301 (n. 31), 312 (n. 68); of laundry workers, 29, 62–63, 210, 260, 281; sit-down strikes,

30; in defense industry, 72–73; in 1945–46, 115, 323 (n. 5); radio coverage of, 178–79; at Memphis Furniture Manufacturing Company, 178–79, 186–87, 211, 213, 289; and strikebreakers, 186–87, 213; King's call for general strike in Memphis, 251–52; in 1960s, 259; RCA wildcat strike, 267; of hospital workers, 276, 289. *See also* Labor unions; Sanitation workers

Strong, Benton J., 301 (n. 34)

Strong, Otha B., 282

Stuart, Merah S., 35, 43, 56

Stuckey, Sterling, 231

Student "kneel-in," 241–42, 247–49

Student Non-Violent Coordinating Committee (SNCC), 257, 272, 352 (n. 14)

Students for a Democratic Society (SDS), 291

Students for Democratic Action, 134

Student sit-in movement, 6, 218, 224, 226, 232–41, *236*, 249, 253, 254, 273, 275, 292

Sugarmon, Russell, 191, 216, 217, 219, 221–23, 234–35, *236*, 254

Supreme Court, U.S.: and New Deal, 27; and Jackson case, 104; and desegregation of interstate public transportation, 115; and desegregation of education, 120, 136, 183, 196–97, 218, 292, 353 (n. 30), 353–54 (n. 30); and restrictive housing covenants, 120, 122, 202; and movie censorship, 148, 162–63, 335 (n. 55); and "separate but equal" doctrine, 197, 215; and desegregation of recreational facilities, 255; and desegregation of restaurants, 255; and Scottsboro boys case, 319 (n. 57); on white primary, 329 (n. 75). *See also specific legal cases*

Sutton, Pat, 207

Sweatt v. Painter, 197, 353–54 (n. 30)

Sweet, G. H., 66

Swingler, Lewis O., 54, 105, 318 (n. 42)

Syncopation (movie), 158

Syphilis. *See* Venereal diseases

Taft-Hartley Act, 137, 178, 185–86, 187

Taylor, Marie, 183, 211

Teamsters, 62, 224–25

Television, 165, 335 (n. 60)

Tenant farming. *See* Sharecropping; Urban-rural relation

Tennessee State Employment Service (TSES), 26

Tennessee Voters' Council, 221

Terrill, Bill, 246

Texas, 153

Thomas, Carla, 167, 181, 244

Thomas, Lorene, 181, 244

Thomas, Prentice, 31

Thomas, Robert "Honeyboy," *168*, 171

Thomas, Rufus, 167, 180–81, 201, 244

Thornton, Juanita Miller, 272, 275, 281, 282

Till, Emmett, 178, 184, 195, 238, 273, 341 (n. 29)

Tillman, Robert, 105, 124

Timber industry. *See* Hardwood industry

Tisdale, Charles, 132, 133, 135

Tobey, Frank, 203–4, 207–8

Toddy, Ted, 147

Torrey, J. W., 81–83, 99–101, 107, 109

To Secure These Rights, 120–21

Towles, Shepard, 229

Townsel, George, Sr., 56

Townsley, Luther A., 337 (n. 94)

Transportation. *See* Public transportation

Tri-State Defender: and radio, 177, 178; founding of, 177, 178, 192; on race relations, 184, 196, 204; compared with *Memphis World*, 192; on Regional Council of Negro Leadership, 192; on Citizens'

Councils, 194–95; on lynchings, 195; on school desegregation, 199; on housing conflicts, 204; on police brutality, 209; on "Freedom Rally" for Volunteer Ticket (1959), 216; on 1959 elections, 217; on Orgill, 219; on Dodson murder trial, 227; and student sit-in movement, 233; on Cotton Makers' Jubilee, 242; on Starlight Revue, 243

Truman, Harry: and civil rights, 114, 117–18, 120–21, 134, 136, 137; and Truman Doctrine, 115, 117, 134, 159; Crump on, 137; and Taft-Hartley Act, 185; and Wallace, 330 (n. 83)

Truman Doctrine, 115, 117, 134, 159

Tucker, David M., 328–29 (n. 68)

Turner, Big Joe, *180*

Turner, Elaine Lee, 237, 238–41, 349 (n. 56)

Turner, Jesse, 190–91, 221

Turner, Johnnie Rodgers, 235, 240, 241, 249

Turner, R. J., 109–10

Turner, Sally, 1–2, 3, 11, 12, 14, 259–60, 278

Turner v. City of Memphis, 255

Twigg, Louis Harold, 56

Uncle Tom's Cabin, 149

Unemployment, 257, 258, 353 (n. 17)

Unions. *See* Labor unions; *and specific unions*

United Auto Workers (UAW), 28, 30–31, 51, 55, 68–69

United Brotherhood of Carpenters and Joiners of America, 67

United Cannery, Agricultural, Packing and Allied Workers of America (UCAPAWA-CIO), 31, 51, 69, 70, 72–73, 77, 186, 312 (n. 60). *See also* Food, Tobacco, and Agricultural Workers Union

United Furniture Workers of America

(UFWA), 51, 54–55, 178, 186–87, 211–13, 258–59, 261, 289, 344 (n. 68)

United Laundry Workers, 62

United Packinghouse Workers of America, 187

United Rubber Workers, 40

U.S. Conciliation Service, 54–55, 62, 68, 71

U.S. Employment Service (USES), 26, 47, 49, 51, 55–59, 78, 79, 300 (n. 26), 307 (n. 8)

U.S. Justice Department, 31, 41, 94, 112, 115–16, 118, 228

Universal Military Training Act, 136

Universities. *See* Higher education; *and specific universities*

University of Mississippi, 352 (n. 14)

University of Oklahoma, 136, 197

University of Tennessee, 196–97

University of Texas, 197, 353–54 (n. 30)

Urban League, 25, 33, 138, 144, 178–79. *See also* Memphis Urban League

Urban-rural relation: and plantation mentality, 5, 17–18; and migration to southern cities, 8–9, 17–18; and radio, 9, 150, 164, 172, 173, 178; roots of Memphis in plantation economy, 19–22, 298 (n. 7); and segregation, 24, 25, 146, 198–99; and modern milieu of Memphis, 25; Memphis blacks as seasonal cotton laborers, 26–27, *27*, 40, 46, 49, 51, 53, 79; and mammy image, 64, 79, 183; and police violence, 90, 214–15; and Crump machine, 112; and Patio 6 episode, 183, 184; and Regional Council of Negro Leadership, 183–84, 191–95; and freedom, 184; and Citizens' Councils, 184, 185, 194–95; and NAACP, 189; and desegregation, 191, 195–99, 214; and labor unions, 214–15; and voting, 217–18, 226–32. *See also* Migration; Plantation mentality